SMUTS

THE SANGUINE YEARS

1870–1919

SMUTS

The Sanguine Years

1870-1919

BY

W. K. HANCOCK

CAMBRIDGE

AT THE UNIVERSITY PRESS

1962

PUBLISHED BY

THE SYNDICS OF THE CAMBRIDGE UNIVERSITY PRESS

Bentley House, 200 Euston Road, London, N.W. 1
American Branch: 32 East 57th Street, New York 22, N.Y.
West African Office: P.O. Box 33, Ibadan, Nigeria

©

CAMBRIDGE UNIVERSITY PRESS

1962

Printed in Great Britain at the University Press, Cambridge
(Brooke Crutchley, University Printer)

TO
Theaden

CONTENTS

Contents

PART IV. WAR AND PEACE, 1914–19

LIST OF ILLUSTRATIONS

PREFACE

In 1951 the Cambridge University Press invited me to write the biography of Field-Marshal Smuts, who had died the previous year. I accepted the invitation after satisfying myself that it had the support of Mr J. C. Smuts, the Field-Marshal's literary executor, and of the other members of the family.

At the same time I asked to be excused from being called 'the official biographer'. There have been other biographers before me, including Mr J. C. Smuts himself, and there will be others after me.

It is in another capacity—not that of biographer—that I have assumed an official position. I accepted responsibility for establishing the Smuts Archive and am academic adviser to the Trustees who control it. The immense riches of this great collection have been described in the Creighton Lecture for 1955 and will be exemplified in four volumes of *Selections*, covering the period 1887–1919, which are now in the press. I hope that in the not too distant future all the documents for this period will be accessible to scholars.

My references in this book (as distinct from the explanatory footnotes) are chiefly to the Smuts Archive. They are printed *seriatim* at the end of the book for the benefit of such students as may wish in future years to criticise my work and carry it further. As author, my first aim has been authenticity. Full and exact references to the primary sources are the means whereby an author enables his critics to test the accuracy of his facts and the integrity of his interpretations.

I have given no references to official documents beyond the 'open' period (which at present ends in 1910) nor have I quoted *verbatim* from such documents.

In quoting from documents which were written originally in Dutch or Afrikaans I have almost invariably used the translations made by my colleague, Dr Jean van der Poel. From time to time I have explained in a footnote that the original document is in another language; but I have not always thought this necessary: for example, the reader will gather from my text that all Botha's letters to Smuts, and all Smuts's letters to his wife from 1902 onwards, were written in Afrikaans.

xi

Preface

My descriptive nomenclature follows the usage of the times about which I have been writing. I am aware that the black people of present-day South Africa call themselves Africans; but in the period covered by this book they were called Natives. Similarly, during the same period Afrikaners were frequently called Africanders or Afrikanders. My use of these outmoded names will be ascribed, I hope, not to insensitiveness or disrespect, but (at worst) to pedantry: I have, for example, felt that it would be anachronistic of me to write 'African Policy' where contemporaries wrote 'Native Policy'.

I wish gratefully to acknowledge the encouragement and support which I have received from Mr J. C. Smuts, Mrs Bancroft Clark and other members of the Smuts family.

I am grateful to the institutions which have helped me: to the Smuts Archive, whose Trustees have treated me with great consideration; to the Nuffield Foundation, which has generously supported the Smuts Archive; to the Cambridge University Press, most helpful of publishing houses; to the Australian National University, which has given me constant support in the stress of recent years.

To the many individuals who have given me information or help of other kinds I express my thanks, particularly to Dr H. C. Brookfield (for the map facing p. 140), Mr Rodney Davenport, Miss M. Eyre, Mrs M. M. Gowing, Miss W. M. Greenshields, Mr Anthony Hamilton, Mrs P. Inman, Mr G. H. J. Kruger, Mrs J. Lynravn, Professor J. S. Marais, Mrs A. Mozley and Professor L. M. Thompson. In addition, I wish to thank the academic colleagues whose contributions I have acknowledged from time to time in footnotes.

I owe a special debt to three persons who gave me continuous and indispensable help while I was writing this book.

Mrs A. B. Gillett, of Street, Somerset, has made available to me nearly two thousand letters which Smuts wrote to her and her husband and to members of the Clark and Gillett families over a period extending almost to half a century. This beautifully ordered collection, together with other rich material, will pass ultimately to the Smuts Archive. For the use of it, and for the many illuminating discussions I have enjoyed with Mrs Gillett, I express my thanks.

In establishing the Smuts Archive I have had a colleague, Dr Jean van der Poel of the University of Cape Town. She has borne the brunt of the work and it is due to her alone that the highest standards of archival practice have been achieved. As an historian and a friend she has criticised my drafts, to my immense profit. My debt to her is great.

Greatest of all is my debt to my wife, who died the year before this book went to press. In 1951 she and I made the first rough inventory of the papers at Doornkloof, Smuts's home in the Transvaal. In the years that followed she gave me indispensable help in my researches together with encouragement which sustained and criticism which braced me. The week before she died she read my first four chapters. I had regarded them hitherto as the final draft; but after we had discussed them together I realised that I would have to revise them drastically. In revising the later chapters I have tried to achieve the standard which she set me and to deliver to my publishers a book worthy of being dedicated to her.

W. K. HANCOCK

AUSTRALIAN NATIONAL UNIVERSITY
CANBERRA

30 April 1961

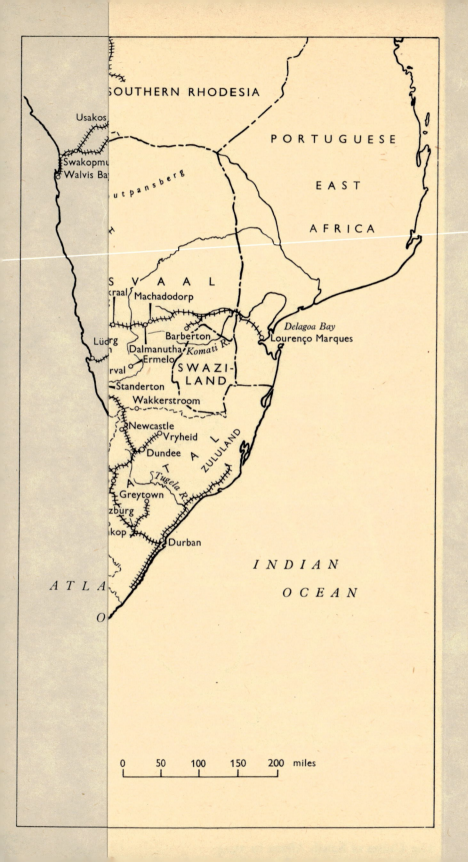

SOUTHERN RHODESIA

PORTUGUESE

EAST

AFRICA

Usakos

Swakopmu
Walvis Bay

utpansberg

VAAL

kraal
Machadodorp

Lüdrg

Barberton
Dalmanutha
Komati R.
Delagoa Bay
Lourenço Marques

Ermelo

SWAZI-
LAND

rval

Standerton

Wakkerstroom

Newcastle
Vryheid

Dundee

A
T
A
L
ZULULAND

A

Tugela R.

Greytown

zburg

kop

Durban

INDIAN

OCEAN

ATLA

O

| 0 | 50 | 100 | 150 | 200 | miles |

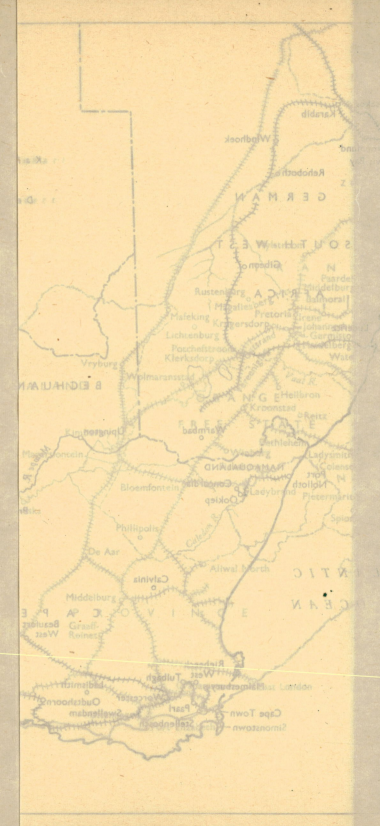

The Union of South Africa in 1914

PART I

FROM BOY TO MAN

CHAPTER I

'THE HILLS OF MY BEGINNINGS'

JAN CHRISTIAAN SMUTS* was born in 1870, on a day deemed propitious in that generation of loyal Cape Colonists, 24 May, Queen Victoria's birthday. Thirty years later the day was carrying an extra load of symbolism, for it had become in the meantime Empire Day; but Smuts, a Boer soldier in the field against Queen Victoria and her Empire, may well have thought that his birthday could have fallen more appropriately. His favourite political anniversary in that period of his life was 16 December, Dingaan's Day— a preference which continued in later years to gain ground among his fellow Boers after he himself had outgrown it.†

Throughout his life he was proud to call himself a Boer, even when the name was growing out of fashion. He could trace back his descent through seven generations of the direct male line to Michiel Cornelis Smuts, who came from Middelburg to Cape Town as a colonist some time before 1692. Within these seven generations he could enumerate in the male and female lines 105 ancestors, whose European origins he classified as follows:

Hollandsch	85
Fransch	18
Duitsch	2
	105

He did not take these calculations over-seriously; but he did all the same take pleasure in the very Dutch colour and shape of his family tree, in the brave company of Smutses, van Aardes, van der Byls, de Kocks, Eenmals and the rest who had pulled up their roots in Middelburg, Rotterdam, Utrecht and Leyden to send them deep down into the soil of South Africa; Hollanders by ancestry, Boers by transplantation.[1]

Literally, Boer means farmer, and the boy Jan Christiaan was born into a farming family which four generations back had taken

---

* On the spelling of his second name—Christiaan, with two a's—I have followed the entry in the Baptismal Register.

† During the Anglo-Boer War, he used to make Dingaan's Day (now called the Day of the Covenant) the occasion of fiery addresses to his commando.

up land about sixty miles north-east of Cape Town in the Swartland, the best wheat-growing district of Cape Colony.[2] At the beginning of the eighteenth century the Swartland had been wild country on the outer fringe of the advancing frontier, a land where trekking Boers hunted the wild animals and collected Hottentot cattle by barter or robbery and moved around with their flocks and herds; but by the end of the century it was becoming a settled community of substantial, hard-working farmers who lived decently in their solid, comfortable houses, enjoyed the regular ministrations of their Church, went shopping sometimes in the villages that were springing up to serve the countryside and took pains for the upbringing of their children. This for two centuries and more was the regular rhythm of Boer society, repeating itself in one district after another from south to north and west to east: sprawl prepared the way for growth; the trekkers moved ever further out in their quest for plentiful and cheap land; the settlers sent down their roots *behind* the moving frontier; the land-improvers followed the land-takers.[3]

After the Smuts family had been settled in the Swartland for thirty odd years they took transfer of the substantial and valuable farm named Ongegund, which lies three miles from the village of Riebeeck West in a beautiful valley where the vineyards and the wheatlands mingle with each other.[4] For six generations thereafter—until 1946, when the farm passed most regrettably into the possession of a cement company—Ongegund remained Smuts property: not by any means their only property, for they multiplied and ramified until at the present day the whole Swartland seems to be full of them and their farms; but Ongegund was the family hearth. The name was oddly sardonic—in English it means Begrudged—but they gave it a matter-of-fact nickname, Boplaas, the Upper Farm.

It lies 600 feet high on the broad shelf below the massive crag of Riebeeck Kasteel, looking eastwards across a wide, fertile valley to the saw-tooth range of the Vogelvlei which runs 3000 feet high north and south from horizon to horizon. In summer the valley is golden with wheat and green with orchards and vineyards and tawny with the dry grass; across the valley the mountain peaks seem close and cool in the morning shadow; at noon they are drenched in shimmering heat; in the evening their jagged line becomes a purple silhouette facing the western glow. Within this immensity of sun-drenched space the farmhouse and its outbuildings stand four-square, a Boer *opstal* enclosed within rectangular stone walls, a small corner of African soil taken by men for their own use and comfort, intimate and reassuring. About the middle of last century a new house was built within the enclosure; but the old house where the boy Jan Christiaan was born on 24 May 1870 still stands beneath its sheltering trees. The massive walls are blocks of stone cemented by clay and faced on the inside with unbaked brick. The roof is held up by solid wooden beams; the square, leaded windows are shuttered; the doors are solid and well hung; the wide planks of the yellow-wood floor are laid close and true; all the masonry and carpentry of the house is as honest as its eighteenth-century design. One imagines that the furniture was in character; but the only article of household equipment that still remains is a long wooden spade which the housewife used for pushing her dough loaves into the immense baking-oven. That operation, no doubt, fascinated her small son.*

In 1870 the master and mistress of the old house were Jacobus Abraham Smuts and his wife Catharina Petronella, or Cato, as she was always called in the inner circle of relations and friends.† Their portraits, which still hang in the family sitting-room at Klipfontein (a farm about a dozen miles from Ongegund, due very soon to appear in this narrative) show two sturdy, plump, kindly people of comfortable middle age, both of them so very Dutch-looking in feature and build that they might well have appeared, despite their Victorian decorum of expression and dress, in any family picture of eighteenth-century Leyden or Middelburg. In 1870 they would have been some twenty years younger than they appear in these photographs, and in the intervening time they had no doubt put on extra flesh and dignity; but in character and disposition they both remained constant throughout the years. The husband was a hard-working, intelligent farmer, whose main purpose it was to improve his land, to keep his family in decency and comfort and to give the children a good start in life. He was a pillar of his Church and took a leading part in the social and political life of the neighbourhood, which eventually elected him to represent it in the colonial parliament

---

* The wooden spade may have disappeared since these lines were written (1957) and the house itself may disappear when the cement company extends its excavations in that direction.

† They were married in 1866 and probably lived on in the old house (Smuts's grandparents moving to the 'new' house) until Jacobus Abraham was able to start farming on his own at Klipfontein.

at Cape Town. There he was content without any speechifying to vote in steady support of Jan Hofmeyr's Afrikander Bond. Yet in private company he was a lively talker, ready to tell a visiting English journalist what was what in South African politics[5] and rather too ready to spread dangerous news or express rash views in the hearing of persons who might intend him no good—so much so, that British Military Intelligence during the Anglo-Boer War made quite a large collection of the sayings of 'Mr Smuts, M.L.A.'* His character, even as reflected in the reports of spies, was endearing. He was the kind of man who builds within his own home a little world of confidence, joy, affection and practical common sense.

His wife was equally practical within her sphere. Many years after her death a biographer of her famous son pictured him running about in rags and tatters during his childhood—a libel which scandalised the schoolmaster's widow of Riebeeck West, who cherished the memory of 'Tante Cato' as a model housewife and mother. 'Everything in her home bore witness to good order and cleanliness. The little boys were dressed in clean blouses of white or blue with dark pantaloons and home-made hide shoes (*velskoene*). They helped their father with the farming, and because their skin was so white their mother made them put on their sunbonnets to shelter them from the heat of the sun. No, Jan Smuts and his little brothers and sisters never grew up in rags and tatters [het nie in *flenters, tatters* groot geword nie].' In addition to her Martha-like virtues, Cato Smuts possessed Mary's gifts of devotion and contemplation, besides some worldly graces, unusual among the Boer women of her time, which she owed to her father's zeal for education. He belonged to the de Vries family, of mixed Dutch and French descent, which had sent down roots in and around the little town of Worcester. He kept a shop in Worcester and there is a tradition in the family that one of his assistants robbed the till; but he could not have suffered over much either in his peace of mind or fortune, for he practised carpentry as a hobby throughout his life and spent considerable sums of money on the education of his children. He maintained his eldest son Boudewyn for six years in the Theological Faculty at Utrecht and he sent Cato first to the village school at Worcester and later to Miss Syfret's school in Cape Town, where she acquired accomplishments such as the pianoforte and French. When Boudewyn returned

* See below, pp. 143–4.

to South Africa he went as predikant to Riebeeck West, taking his sister with him to keep house. It was in this way that she had met her husband. The simple countryfolk were astonished and perhaps a little alarmed to see so fine and learned a lady—'so fyn so goed geleerd soos sy was'—coming to live among them on a Swartland farm; but she soon proved herself as a farmer's wife the equal of her most capable neighbours, without ever losing her own individual depth and delicacy of perception. Half a century after her death the fragrance of her memory was still lingering in the Swartland. Her children, and their children after them, remembered her with feelings of gratitude and love, almost of reverence.[6]

Her son Jan Christiaan loved throughout his life to revisit the country of his upbringing and to recapture the feelings of trust, joy and wonder which had enriched his childhood. On a winter day in his fifty-first year he wrote: 'This is Monday morning before breakfast. Saturday and Sunday I went to spend with my youngest brother on the farm Klipfontein where I grew up....I took a walk by myself over the farm, humming my monotonous tune to myself to the accompaniment of a gentle rain most of the time, and I felt uplifted once more. Those hills of my beginnings always have a great effect on me.' On another winter day seventeen years later he wrote: 'Yesterday I saw the vast line of blue Winterhoek mountains stretched out before Klipfontein with a beauty of colour and line and a majesty which made it even more to me than in the days of youthful romance in the far past. I could not think of anything more lovely in my long experience of scenery. And I blessed my good fortune in having been privileged to grow up in such surroundings and with home associations which remain an unforgettable memory. The beauty of home life was fully matched by the beauty of the world around me. If anything has gone wrong since I cannot blame it on my associations of home and nature.'[7]

Klipfontein, the farm to which he referred in these letters, could not stand comparison with Ongegund in the age and beauty of its buildings; but it possessed a wide outlook of comparable splendour. The family shifted house for practical reasons. At Ongegund, Jacobus Abraham was under the direction of his father. He wanted a farm all his own. If he had belonged to a poor family, he might have gone trekking—although that was ceasing to be a habit of Swartland people as the nineteenth century wore on—to free or

7

near-free land on the outer pastoral fringes of society; but well-to-do Boers almost never trekked. They preferred to use their capital and skill in improving the land, so that the same area would maintain more people; or in acquiring additional land near-by; or (as usually happened) in practising some combination of these methods—always with the purpose of remaining, if it could be managed, among friends and relations in the same familiar neighbourhood. The shift of the Smuts family to Klipfontein was precisely thirteen miles, which hardly took them into a new neighbourhood. To be sure, Moorrees-burg was their nearest shopping place henceforward; but they still drove every second Sunday to the Church in Riebeeck West and they sent their eldest boy to Mr Stoffberg's school in the same little town.*

Jan, their second son, was not yet six years old when the family moved to Klipfontein; far too young, his parents thought, for any formal education, if, indeed, he would ever need it; for it was the custom of the country for only the eldest son to be 'geleerd', that is, to be educated beyond the three R's so that he might enter one of the professions. Cato Smuts herself took the children through a little book called *Step by Step*, which gave them the rudiments of English grammar. She had a well-filled bookcase of her own and was, one imagines, very pleased when her son Jan read *Robinson Crusoe* from cover to cover before he could properly understand English. Apart from this achievement, a long time went by before Jan gave any sign of catching the reading disease. School was still six or seven years ahead of him when he began his explorations of Klipfontein, of the world of nature in which Klipfontein was set, and of himself as a part of that world. These explorations, one supposes, were in their beginnings spontaneous and unselfconscious; it was only in retro-spect that he recognised them for what they were—an early awakening of the feelings and faculties that were shaping him as a person and would one day shape his thought about the atom, the cell, mind, personality, the whole universe. On his father's farm he began to grow not only in body but in spirit—the word has grown old-fashioned, but it became common usage with him—long before he started learning things out of books.

The farm labourers, then as now, were coloured people, but there

* Moorreesburg had no permanent Church until 1879 and was not proclaimed a township until 1882.

was an intimacy then which is rare now between *baas* and *volk*; at harvest-time master, mistress and their whole family excepting the little children worked hard and happily in house or shed or field alongside the coloured families; on Sundays, when the parents and perhaps the elder children drove off to Church, the boys and girls who were left behind played wild games with the children of the *volk*. The boy Jan went wandering around the farm (it became a favourite recollection of his later years) with old Adam, a Hottentot servant who loved his master's children and loved teaching them the exciting little things of country life: where to dig for edible roots, where to look for tortoises, how to take shelter under a 'skerm' when it was raining and keep warm in front of a roaring fire. Taught by old Adam, the boy gained the confidence to go wandering by himself, a small speck in an immense landscape. Sometimes he lifted his eyes to the distant mountains, sometimes he gazed with intense concentration at the fascinating small things—lizards, tortoises, pebbles, grasses, flowers. His father began to think that he was mooning around too aimlessly and that it was time for him, like every other Boer son, to undertake some regular work on the farm. So he put him in charge of the *klein goed*—the pigs, ducks, fowls and other small animals of the farmyard. This did not suit the boy at all; he wanted to be out on the veld, and he allowed the pigs and poultry to stray from the farmyard until his father told him to go out and look after the *beeste*, the free-roaming cattle.[8]

It was the custom of Boer fathers to allot to their sons a share in the natural increase of the flocks and herds under their care. Thus it came about that the *beeste* of Klipfontein helped later on to maintain Jan Smuts at Stellenbosch and Cambridge. In the meantime, they gave him an early lesson in the meaning of property. He learnt that it is a good thing to own land, because 'land does not run away', as wealth of some other kinds is apt to do. This lesson was destined to stand him in good stead during his early middle age, when he was earning a good income and using his savings to buy farms. Throughout the rest of his life, these farms remained his shield against financial worry and his guarantee of freedom to live, think and act by the standard of his own will and judgment.

His boyhood made him a hard-headed farmer's son, an authentic Boer; but that was not its chief significance. On his father's farm he began to feel those perceptions of the natural world and those intimations of his own self which afterwards took shape in his thought, speech and writing. 'A torrent of joy' seemed to flow into him as he looked across the wide valley to the high mountains; a thrill of delight ran through him at the sight and sound and touch of the familiar near-by things. He shouted to the beasts and birds, talked to the little creatures in the crevices of the rocks, played with the pebbles and 'made love to the plants'. He felt himself akin to these natural things, as if he and they belonged to the same family. Yet sometimes a different mood swept over him and he felt himself to be Jan Smuts, a separate and lonely being, who was using words which the pebbles and plants did not understand, who was no longer talking to the creatures but talking to himself about them. All this was as yet no more than feeling, for the boy was still too young for conscious thought; but it was vivid and intense feeling, a joyous acceptance of the 'I and Thou' in which religion and art have their beginning; a primitive questioning of the 'I and It' which is the root of scientific thought.[9]

It was religious teaching that first offered him an explanation of his experiences. Had he been left without teaching, he might well have become an animist, discovering in every rock and tree a spirit akin to his own; or a pantheist, believing that God is everything and that everything is God: indeed, he was prone throughout his whole life to lapse into the pantheistic heresy. But from the time that he became old enough to drive with his parents in their Cape cart to the Sunday congregations at Riebeeck West, he heard from the pulpit of his uncle Boudewyn a simpler doctrine. Although some dispute existed within the Dutch Reformed Church of that time (and indeed of a much later time) between the literal and the liberal interpreters of Scripture, it scarcely ruffled the quiet Swartland.* The predikant of Riebeeck West inclined if anything to the liberal side, but the predikant's nephew received as literal and sufficient truth the whole Bible story, from Genesis to Revelation, of God, nature and man. Perhaps he absorbed, along with the story, some mental habits which Calvinist teaching tends to encourage: the habit, for example, of posing the most tremendous problems and of seeking the most sweeping solutions.

However, so long as he remained a boy, his religious life was all simple faith and piety. Early in the 1870's, when Dr Andrew Murray

* See below, p. 21.

undertook a mission of religious revival throughout the length and breadth of Cape Colony, 'Riebeeck West too shared in the blessing. A number of the school children gave their hearts to the Lord— among them Jan Smuts confessed that he had received the Lord Jesus as his Saviour. A little prayer meeting at *The Ark*. How can the dear children pour out their hearts to the Lord, in their childish speech? They just *talked* with the dear Jesus. Jan, too, and yet he prayed differently from the other children, more like a big boy— perhaps because he had so large a vocabulary.'[10]

The Ark was the house in which Mrs Stoffberg, the schoolmaster's wife in Riebeeck West, looked after the boarders at her husband's school. Jan Smuts did not go there until he was twelve, perhaps because he was delicate[11] and his parents wished to watch over him at home, perhaps because they thought it quite enough for the eldest boy to become *geleerd*. Be this as it may, Jan's elder brother, Michiel, died in 1882 and Jan immediately took his place at school. He was put into the lowest class. A week or two later the master went round the school examining the boys class by class. '"Come now, tell me, who can recite for me the Counties of England?" Up went Jan's hand and he recited them all without a single mistake. "Now Jan, come with me"—and he was put into a higher class.' Mr Stoffberg used to say that Jan Smuts was one of the most brilliant pupils he had ever taught and the hardest-working boy he had ever met. After three brief years at school the boy took the ninth place in the Colony's elementary examination; in the following year he took the second place (the winning boy had had seven years at school) in the *School Higher* examination. A few weeks before this examination he had become seriously ill and the doctor had ordered him to bed for a complete rest, with an absolute ban on books. The headmaster's wife has given a lively account of his attempts to beat the ban. 'We made up a bed for him in our own private little sitting-room. He would rest there under the Lord's blessing until he got well again. "But where is Hennie, our three-year-old boy?" "Oh, he is with Jan in the sitting-room." "Ah, Jan old boy, see how uncomfortably you are lying—I'm going to make your bed fresh and smooth for you." "Ah no, I'm lying beautifully comfortable."—But then it came out that little Hennie had had to fetch books for him out of the bookcase in the corner of the room! And there under his bedclothes was a heap of books.'

Such passionate addiction to reading might have been (as it has been so often among the up-and-coming youth of many countries) a measure of the boy's ambition to clear the examination hurdles along the track of his worldly advancement. Various people have told stories about his determination to make a great career for himself: among them D. F. Malan, his junior by three years at school and college and in later years his most dangerous political antagonist. In Riebeeck West Malan used to attend a Sunday School class in which Jan Smuts instructed the younger boys in Holy Scripture, garnished, it would appear, by secular knowledge; for he was talking one day about King Arthur's knights and explained that a knight was called *Sir* and that the Queen could still make a man *Sir* by touching him on the shoulder with her sword: 'When I grow up she will make me Sir Jan.'[12] In the dreams of boyhood, such a prospect may perhaps have dazzled Jan Smuts—but never Daniel Malan, that slow, persistent plodder; their schoolmaster used to say in later years that Smuts was like a Maxim gun and Malan like a Long Tom. In ambition (as distinct from its objects) there was probably little to choose between Malan and Smuts, and in the achievement of ambition many people would give the first prize to Malan. Be this as it may, it was not ambition but sheer joy of reading which incited Jan Smuts to raid the headmaster's library. The books that Mrs Stoffberg fished out from under his bedclothes had nothing whatever to do with his approaching examination. At Riebeeck West, as later at Stellenbosch and Cambridge, he read avidly *outside* the curriculum.

Whenever he returned on holiday to Klipfontein he brought with him a pile of books. His younger brother used to recall in later years the days when Jan was beginning Greek and used to bury himself hour after hour in the New Testament; for it was a great advantage, he explained, to study the Scriptures in the original tongue and a serious loss to him not to have Hebrew for studying the Old Testament. Yet he never became the complete bookworm. As soon as he was back on the farm he wanted to know everything that had been happening during his absence—how the farm-workers and their families had been getting on, how the crops were thriving, what had become of this horse or that bullock. He was eager to take his full share of the farm work, including heavy work like scything, for which his hands had grown too soft; but his father thought it better to send him out on horseback with messages to the farmers of the district about business affairs or the social and political concerns of the Swartlanders. Thus he became familiar with his own countryside over a widening range and grew to be at ease with the country people.

He also discovered during his schooldays a particular and perennial spring of happiness which can, perhaps, be best described in words which a kindred spirit had written in Germany three centuries earlier: 'I have determined, as long as God gives me life, to ascend one or more mountains every year when the plants are at their best —partly to study them, partly for exercise of body and mind....I say then that he is no lover of nature who does not esteem high mountains very worthy of profound contemplation. It is no wonder that men have made them the home of gods, of Pan and the nymphs. ...I have a passionate desire to visit them.'[13] From boyhood to old age Smuts felt the same love of mountains and the same delight in climbing them. Throughout his life he expressed these feelings frequently in letters to his close friends, and occasionally in public discourses. After the First World War he used often to upbraid himself for missing the chance of climbing Kilimanjaro when he was campaigning in East Africa. He felt vicarious triumph a generation later when his son Japie climbed it. Meanwhile, he himself had climbed scores of mountains in Cape Province. On the eve of his last illness, his mind went back to his very first ascent. He was still a small boy in Mr Stoffberg's school when he felt one day the impulse to climb the steep crag of Riebeeck Kasteel. On the summit he had a strange, intense experience; he did not describe it explicitly, but seemingly it had a mystic tinge.[14]

For all his thinking and dreaming he remained very much a Boer, the level-headed son of a practical and prosperous Swartlander. From the summit of Riebeeck Kasteel he would have seen, sixty miles away in the blue distance, the jagged peaks above Stellenbosch and the solid square mass of Table Mountain. Beneath those fascinating shapes lay the beckoning world of study and opportunity. On 12 June 1886, when he was just sixteen years old, he addressed a letter to 'Mr C. Murray, Professor, Stellenbosch'.

Dear Sir,

Allow me the honour of your reading and answering these few lines.... I intend coming to Stellenbosch in July next, and, having heard that you take an exceptionally great interest in the youth, I trust you will favour

13

me by keeping your eye upon me and helping me with your kindly advice. Moreover, as I shall be a perfect stranger there, and, as you know, such a place, where a large puerile element exists, affords fair scope for moral, and what is more important, religious temptation, which, if yielded to will eclipse alike the expectations of my parents and the intentions of myself, a real friend will prove a lasting blessing for me. For of what use will a mind, enlarged and refined in all possible ways, be to me, if my religion be a deserted pilot and morality a wreck?

To avoid temptation and to make the proper use of my precious time, I purposely refuse entering a public boarding department, as that of Mr de Kock, but shall board privately (most likely at Mr N. Ackermann's) which will, in addition, accord with my retired and reserved nature...

...Would the boy never come to the questions he wanted to ask? All of a sudden he fired them off, five of them in rapid succession— about entrance requirements, examinations, the dates of term, fees, textbooks. It was a startling change in thought and style from the pious to the practical.

CHAPTER 2

STELLENBOSCH

THE school at Riebeeck West did not take its pupils all the way to university entrance and Jan Smuts had still a year's work ahead of him in Stellenbosch before he could be enrolled as a matriculated student of Victoria College and the University of the Cape of Good Hope.* The examination lists of 1887 placed him in the first class of the higher matriculation examination. When he returned home on vacation, he puzzled the schoolmaster's wife at Riebeeck West by announcing his success in a manner which she found alarmingly offhand. 'In my heart the question arose, "What! Has Jan changed at Stellenbosch? What has happened to the boy? How comes it that he does not say, the dear Lord helped me so wonderfully in my examination that I was able to answer every question?"'

The anxious lady need not have troubled her peace of mind with misgivings about the boy's spiritual condition. Throughout his first year at Stellenbosch he had lived a life altogether exemplary both in diligence and piety. In the seclusion of Mr Ackermann's boarding-house he had worked prodigiously at his Latin and Greek, mathematics, science and English literature, and had written besides an essay on Labour, a metrical paraphrase of Isaiah xxv and a number of poems invoking Love, the Immortal Mind of Man, and God, 'the Steersman Great of Nature's ways'. He had taken no part in the sports and games of 'the puerile element' but had exercised himself in long solitary walks among the mountains. On Sundays he had attended Church twice a day and had conducted a Bible class for Coloured boys. On weekdays he had attended prayer meetings assiduously. He was, by common consent, *baie godsdienstig*—indeed, so consistently pious that he was in danger of becoming a prig. It was high time for him to fall in love.

All of a sudden, just after his seventeenth birthday, he discovered an irresistible compulsion to go visiting every evening at the house of Mr and Mrs Krige, a few doors away in Dorp Street. They had a

---

* The University was purely an examining body, serving in this capacity Victoria College, Stellenbosch, and the South African College in Cape Town.

small farm and a large family, which was divided by a broad gap of years into a first batch of five nearly grown-up boys and girls and a second batch of four little children. When the little ones heard Jan's voice in the evening they used to call out to him to come to their room and tell them a story before they went to sleep. His favourite story was about a calf that lost its mother and went looking for her in the dark until it found a large warm creature and snuggled up against her and went happily to sleep; but when it woke up in the morning it saw that the large warm creature was a lioness. Screams from the children, and Jan stopped his story until they asked him what happened next? In a slow sing-song voice he replied, 'The calf looked at the lioness and the lioness looked at the calf. The calf looked at the lioness and the lioness looked at the calf. The calf looked...'. He said it slower and slower until the children fell asleep and he was free to steal away from them on tiptoe and look for their elder sister and ask her to come walking with him.

Sybella Margaretha, or Isie, as everybody called her, was the second child in the first batch of Kriges. She was six months younger than Jan Smuts and a girl of such unusual character that many people thought her eccentric. She was pretty and charming, a very small person bursting with immense energy, mental as well as physical. She was capable and willing in the work of the family and a perfect elder sister to the younger children; but she had the temerity to aim at a higher education for herself. Her elder brother thought it absurd of her to want to go to College: girls *didn't*. But 'one Wednesday' she just went and the professors did not seem to think it at all strange. She and Jan used to walk to College in the mornings together and walk home again together in the evenings. After a few days the story went round among the students that they were engaged.[1]

Isie played the piano well and had a sweet voice. In the evenings she and Jan used often to sing together. German lieder became their favourites, for she had fallen in love with German literature and was bent on making him a Goethe lover. He in turn set out to make her a Shelley worshipper. 'Prometheus Unbound will be an agreeable companion in your quiet hours; it proved to be such to me.... People think Shelley was an atheist; but I have never read a poet who re-echoes so deeply the spirit of the Bible and who infuses such an ethereal spirit into me. His poetry is Love, Loveliness and

16

Thought....' But he relished just as much, he said, the poetry that she had written for him, and supposed that she would relish his poetry nearly as much! He enclosed some verses in a letter that he sent her for her seventeenth birthday. It was his first letter to her and it revealed a turmoil of love, joy, perplexity, doubt and faith more exhilarating by far than his rapturous discovery of Shelley.

Riebeek West
x. xii. '87

Dearest Isie,

When you receive this, it will be the 22 Dec. Need I express congratulations? Need I tell you what sympathy I feel for you on this your 17th birth-day? No, you know I have more than mere words can express. Some wishes I have expressed in verse,—some aspirations which I know accord with your own. May I add one more? It is that we may be faithful to each other, that our mutual love may be pure and unselfish, that in whatever relation and circumstances we may be, it may grow from more to more, and if possible, never be dissolved; that we may be bound together in Soul and Spirit by a holy and a true love.

People generally have but few chosen friends; so you needn't be surprised when I tell you I have only two on earth, you being one of them: and you are the only one to whom I feel myself drawn by every tie of sentiment and nature. You are the only one in whose society I feel alone, by myself, as if there is no second one, as if we two are one. I do not know whether my character and my ways accord in any way with your tastes and sympathies (I may hope they do) yet this I know,—and I not only know it, but I experience it inwardly as a part of my existence—that I sympathise with you, that I *love* you as my own Soul, (to use the phrase in which Jonathan's love for David is described).

Is this the issue of mere chance? Is it chance that we lived for such a long time only a few paces from each other without getting acquainted, and that we suddenly met some time ago and that we felt a mutual liking? No, this is certainly not chance. It is our Heavenly Master who has brought this about, that we may help each other onward on the path of Holiness and Love, and that in loving each other we may learn to love him more intensely. Whatever the whispering tongue of the world may allege, let our love never be romantic or sentimental, but the deep love of Truth, which Sticketh Closer than a brother, and is only purified, never dissolved, by adversity. You remember that I told you the morning after you had sent me those lines I was quite upset at reading them. Had I no reason to be upset and unseated by such a stanza as this:

> 'Oft I've tried to be a Christian,
> But I *cannot, cannot* be,
> So no hope to live in heaven
> Through Eternity I see.'

Now from the very first time that I began to know you I saw a christian in you, and I still maintain that you are one; so you can understand how I felt when I read that stanza. Isie! you *are* a christian, are you not?...

Anxiously he pleaded with her, wrestled with her demon of doubt, quoted the Scriptures, expounded the promise of Eternal Life and affirmed at last on her behalf his assurance of salvation.

You *are* a christian.

The rest of his letter was about Shelley, plans for the holidays (he advised her not to study too much) and explanations of the verses he had sent her. 'Their composition', he wrote, 'has decisively convinced me that I am no poet.'

Nevertheless, he continued his paraphrasing of Isaiah and similar poetic exercises which culminated two years later in twenty Spenserian stanzas addressed 'To I.M.K. on her Nineteenth Birthday'. Their theme was—

> thy soul-struggle to be free,
> What time the horizon dark and darker grew,
> And gloom o'erspread the heavens, and thick dew
> Fell bitter cold, and winds and storms closed round
> Of killing doubts and questionings not a few:
> Gloom and unrest within, wild storms around
> Banished the Light divine, and Music's heavenly sound.

Her soul, he told her, was a Shrine radiant with Divine Light, whither he had come to worship

> That Presence, which in darkness as in light
> Is felt as Love, embracing in its Wing
> The seen and unseen All.

He had seen the Shrine grow dark in the time of her spiritual conflict, but he had remained a faithful worshipper there, until at last—

> the Presence which ne'er
> Had left thee streamed through thee everywhere
> With starlike radiance.

Had he been too impetuous a year or two back when he declared himself to be no poet? Metaphor and imagery came to him naturally, even in a language that was not his mother tongue. He had a gift for rhythm and his Spenserian stanzas expressed musically, at times felicitously, a vivid personal experience. But he was never content merely to affirm an experience; he always wanted to explain it. This passion for explanation committed him before long to science, philosophy—and prose. Still, if he gave up trying to write poetry, he never gave up reading it. Throughout his life he kept turning to his favourite poets—to Shelley, Shakespeare, Goethe, Whitman, Emily Brontë—for revelations of truth which he could not find in science. As he grew older, Shelley ceased to hold a place in his thinking, but never in his remembrance. Fifty years later he read *Prometheus Unbound* again and recalled the freedom he had found in it when he was growing to manhood. 'I with my Calvinistic upbringing must have imbibed my brighter view of the world from Shelley in my College days. The innate goodness of man, the perfectibility of human nature, the evil in the world which is due to rotten and corrupt institutions—the sudden catastrophic collapse of Evil at the appointed hour, and the triumph of Good and Beauty in the world! It was a nobler, more poetic rendering than the catastrophic revolution of K. Marx, and resembled more the "Second Coming" of the Christians.'[2]

Optimism was a plant which rooted itself easily and grew sturdily in the soil and climate of Cape Colony, three-quarters of a century ago. At the risk of slowing up the biographical story, it is necessary to explore the prevailing ideas—educational, theological, political— of that far-off, blessed time.[3]

Victoria College, Stellenbosch, stamped its enduring imprint upon the mind of Smuts. The small teaching body, hardly more than half a dozen men, covered a wide curriculum; but the students also were few and carefully sifted for quality. Teachers and students were able in consequence to enjoy close individual contact with each other and —despite an essay that Smuts wrote in 1889, denouncing the hurry of modern life[4]—they were able to work in an atmosphere of leisure.

Whenever he had occasion in later life to visit Scotland, Smuts liked to tell his audiences that he owed his education to Scotsmen. Of the six professors at Victoria College in his time, three had come from Edinburgh University—Rev. Thomas Walker (English Literature and Logic), A. Macdonald (Classics) and W. Thomson (Mathematics and Physics). The last-named was a man of genuine academic distinction and all three appear to have been hard-working, intelligent men, moderate in their theological and political views and possessed of genuine public spirit. Walker, besides, had made a scholarly study of the Dutch language and literature and was, it may be assumed, an ally of Professor Mansvelt (Modern Languages), a

Hollander whose ambition it was to simplify Dutch and win for it complete equality with English in the public and educational life of Cape Colony.* While Smuts was still a student, Mansvelt went north to put his theories into practice as President Kruger's Minister of Education. His departure, one assumes, caused little inconvenience to Smuts, who had no interest in linguistic studies for their own sake but merely as aids in his explorations of literature, science and philosophy. On the scientific side, he learnt much from Professor Marloth, one of the great men of South African botany. In philosophy he had less luck; but the deficiencies of his own professor were compensated in large measure by a friendship which he made with J. I. Marais, a Professor in the Theological Faculty, an Afrikaner of Huguenot stock and a man of true scholarship, saintliness and humanity. As will appear in the next chapter, Marais came to his rescue a year or two later at an awkward crisis of his career.

Smuts was growing up in a cultural environment whose complexities were illustrated by the languages he had successively to master. In his home, and among the white and coloured people of the Swartland, he spoke the *taal*. The language of his Church was Dutch. At school and college his language of study was English.

His roots were in the *taal* and in the soil of his father's farm; but it was in the Dutch prayers and sermons of his Church that he first discovered coherent answers to the questions he was beginning to ask about the world of nature and the situation of man. The Church, besides, was close, far closer than the State of those days, to the traditional life of his people. Throughout his later years of political struggle, he had always to reckon with the Church as a powerful and often as a hostile force. It contributed a great deal to the making of his career and in the end to its unmaking.

The *Nederduits Gereformeerde Kerk* (N.G. Kerk) had in the Company's time been subordinate to the Classis Amsterdam, and even when British occupation of the Cape cut its formal tie with Holland, it still continued in large measure to follow both the constitutional and the doctrinal fortunes and fashions of the parent Church. The Calvinists of Holland, traditionally so jealous of their ecclesiastical and provincial freedoms, submitted in 1816 to a 'pale Arminianism' in the constitutional sphere—a unitary scheme of government where-

* This, be it noted, involved a fight on two fronts: against the pretensions both of English and the *taal* (Afrikaans). See below, p. 23.

by a National Synod legislated under supervision of the State. In 1824 the Church Assembly in Cape Town accepted a similar subordination to their British Caesar. Despite some subsequent relaxations, this subordination produced during the nineteenth century important historical consequences: in particular, it made almost inevitable the erection of an independent Calvinist Church (or Churches) in the northern Republics,* and it opened the road of appeal in cases of ecclesiastical discipline to the secular courts of Cape Colony. At a time when traditional Calvinist doctrines were formulated imprecisely and were moreover under strong liberal attack, the Church found itself thereby deprived of full power to define and defend its own order of belief.

The liberal movement in the Cape Church had its roots not in England nor even in Scotland but in Holland, where the hard intellectual creed of the sixteenth and seventeenth centuries had begun to grow soft under the influences of English latitudinarianism, German pietism and French rationalism. Throughout the first three-quarters of the nineteenth century, liberal theologians were making the running in the Dutch universities of Leyden, Groningen and Utrecht. It was in these three universities that ministers of the Cape Church received their education, until the Stellenbosch Kweekschool (founded in 1859) began at last to provide the means of theological training at home. Before this, from about the 1830's onwards, there had been a steady flow of liberal thought into the Cape ministry. The Afrikaner historian Hanekom (who writes as a severe critic of liberalism) has enumerated the doctrines of dubious orthodoxy that might have been heard from N.G. Kerk pulpits round about 1870: that the Bible was not exclusively the word of God and that it had no authority in matters of science: that God operated not by miracles but through natural laws: that Christ was man's exemplar rather than his redeemer: that the doctrines of predestination and original sin, along with a great deal else that was the very core of Calvinism, must be rejected. Hanekom has listed by name and place twenty-six

* The Cape Church had on the whole cold-shouldered the Voortrekkers, and this no doubt was a direct cause of the formation of the *Nederduitsch Hervormde Kerk* in the Transvaal and its separation from the N.G. Kerk in 1853; but there were in addition legal doubts (confirmed by a decision of 1862) whether the jurisdiction of the N.G. Kerk was not confined within the frontiers of the Colony. A later schism, which led to the establishment in the north of the sternly Calvinistic *Gereformeerde Kerk* ('the Doppers') arose chiefly from differences about the singing of hymns (*gesange*) which were not in the Bible, and about similar questions of worship.

ministers of the N.G. Kerk who held views of this stamp. Among them was the Rev. Boudewyn de Vries of Riebeeck West.[5]

Towards the last quarter of the nineteenth century the orthodox Calvinists, both in Holland and at the Cape, began to prepare their counter-offensive against the liberals. Its gradual but remorseless pressure in South Africa is dramatised in the career of Johannes du Plessis, a contemporary and friend of Smuts at Stellenbosch, a saintly man and a distinguished scholar, who was destined to face arraignment for heresy, to fight his accusers year after year in synod and court and, finally, in 1932, to suffer dismissal from his chair in the Stellenbosch seminary.[6] Neither Smuts nor du Plessis could ever have imagined during their student years that the tide would ever run so fiercely against liberal thought. Even then it may have begun quietly to turn; but they would never have noticed it, because the surface waters remained so still. The late 1880's and early 1890's were a period in which ardent young Christians at Stellenbosch could move confidently into the exciting new world of science, history and philosophy. In a time and place which offered such wide room for the free growth of young minds, they felt no call to rebel.

In politics also the late 1880's and early 1890's were years of good augury, in which the wind seemed set fair and the tide running strong towards unity, freedom, nationhood and all the other blessings to which an ardent young South African might aspire on his country's behalf. In retrospect, these years may appear merely a brief interlude in three decades of stress and storm: diamonds at Kimberley in the year of Smuts's birth and their embittering sequel of frontier disputes: native wars in the Transkei and Basutoland, in Natal and the Transvaal during the years of his upbringing on the farm: Carnarvon's federation campaign, Shepstone's annexation of the Transvaal, and its sequel at Majuba during his first year at school: gold on the Rand during his last year at school—and from there the hard straight line of arrogance and aggression which a patriot historian might draw (Smuts himself drew it in October 1899) from the Rand to the Jameson Raid and from the Raid to the Boer War. When Smuts looked back from 1899, it all seemed to hang together so tragically and so inevitably.* Nevertheless, it had all seemed quite different in 1889, when he was looking forward.

* See below, pp. 108–10, for an account of his propagandist tract, *A Century of Wrong.*

How clear the future appeared at that time may be shown by examining the political leadership that was offered to the Afrikaner people at Cape Colony. They were called upon to choose between two men of opposite character and two opposite ideals and programmes. In 1875 the eloquent but erratic predikant at Paarl, the Rev. Stephanus Jacobus du Toit, founded a political and propagandist society called *Di Genootskap van regte Afrikaners*. This society spread its news and views through *Di Patriot*, a newspaper edited by du Toit's brother. 'If any Afrikander asks us what our purpose is', *Di Patriot* declared in its first number, 'our answer is: TO STAND FOR OUR LANGUAGE OUR NATION AND OUR COUNTRY.'[7] This manifesto might well have included a pledge to defend orthodox Calvinism, for the Rev. S. J. du Toit exemplified the common root of the ecclesiastical, nationalist and linguistic struggles of Afrikanerdom, and continued to wage bitter war against moderate theologians of the Boudewyn de Vries stamp long after he had crossed from the nationalist camp into the camp of Cecil Rhodes. In the 1870's and 1880's, no friend or enemy of du Toit would have believed him capable of such a desertion, for his political preaching in those years was hotly anti-British and his political goal was a United States of South Africa under a republican flag, marching forward in the brotherhood of the *taal*.*

Du Toit needed a political party to fight for his programme and in July 1879 he founded the 'Afrikander Bond'. Its progress was slow until the Transvaal War of Independence made its programme popular not only throughout Cape Colony but in the northern republics. At this juncture du Toit, always a restless spirit, made the mistake of flitting north to take the post of Superintendent of Education in the Transvaal. Back in Cape Colony remained J. H. Hofmeyr, a politician as deeply rooted and steady as du Toit was mercurial and flighty. Hofmeyr had been organising the farmers of the Western Province and disliked the competition of du Toit's

---

* *Di Patriot*, except for retaining as its motto the fifth commandment in High Dutch, was written in the *taal*. The *Genootskap* furthered its linguistic propaganda by publishing the first Afrikaans grammar (1876) and school reader (1878). It should be noted that the interweaving of the ecclesiastical, nationalist and linguistic strands came gradually and remained for a long time provisional and potential: with du Toit personally the interweaving was not apparent until about 1882, and there followed, as has been seen, his eccentric combination of strict Calvinist orthodoxy and partisanship for Rhodes. In his republican days he had never committed himself to the Vierkleur as the flag of the United Afrikaner state: consequently I have written 'a (not "the") republican flag'.

organisation. By steady persistence he engineered a union between his own *Boeren Beschermings Vereeniging* (Farmers' Protection Union) and the Afrikander Bond. Thereafter, he set to work with the most striking success to transform the purposes, programmes and tactics of the Bond. By the middle 1880's he had made it by far the strongest party in the Colony and had made its representatives in parliament the arbiters of political power. He could, had he so wished, have made himself prime minister.

Hofmeyr was a contrast to du Toit in everything, in temperament, theology, outlook upon the past, aspiration for the future, political ideal and political method. He was never the man to rush his fences and his favourite motto was *wacht een bietje*: wait a little. In his religious life he remained a lifelong member of the *Kaapse Kerk*, but avoided such extreme dogmas as were inconsistent with the proven scientific knowledge of his age or its humane aspirations. In his political life he was so unusually steady and clear-headed that the thread of his purpose can be traced without any break from his first speech in 1875 to his last speech in 1907.[8]

His first political task was to arouse and organise his own *Boeren* and to rectify the inequalities imposed upon them by English-speaking officialdom. The ratio of Boers to British in Cape Colony was 2 to 1 (across the Orange river it was 10 to 1), but English had been the language of the Courts since 1827, the language of the Assembly since 1852 and the medium of instruction in the higher classes of government schools since 1865. Hofmeyr used the voting power of the Afrikander Bond to attack these inequalities. Du Toit might have done the same. Where, then, lay the political contrast between the two men?

The contrast might have been deduced in large measure from their different usage of the word Afrikander (or Africander).* Quite often (for example, in making or modifying the constitution of the Afrikander Bond) the meaning of the word became a matter for political discussion and even for majority vote, so that it would have been ingenuous to expect from any individual complete consistency of usage from one occasion to another. Nevertheless, du Toit did persistently incline towards an exclusive and Hofmeyr towards an inclusive interpretation of the word. Du Toit regarded the Afri-kander as a man who spoke neither English nor yet Dutch but the

---

* The established modern usage is Afrikaner; but as I have to quote a good deal from Hofmeyr and others I have thought it best to stick to their contemporary usage.

taal, and upon this foundation of linguistic exclusiveness he built a structure of political exclusiveness: Afrikanders were a people apart: they were apart of course from the Bantu and Coloured people (that needed no argument), but apart also both from their Dutch ancestors and their British fellow citizens. All these propositions were repugnant to Hofmeyr. To begin with, he rejected the linguistic presupposition; he loved his Dutch Bible, and his prescription for bridging the gap between the written and the spoken word of his people was not to reject, but to simplify the Dutch language. He had the same feeling about Dutch history and would no more have expelled it from the culture of his people than he would have expelled Shakespeare and the Bill of Rights from the culture of English-speaking South Africans; on the contrary, he believed that to be European merely in blood was not enough and that the European *cultural* inheritance of *both* communities was needed for South African citizenship. 'I am a better man', he once said, '—I go further, I am a better Africander—because as well as Dutch I also know English.'[9] Believing this, he had to discover some other test than the linguistic one for defining an Africander. 'My definition of the word Africander', he declared on 28 March 1898, 'is as wide as that originally contained in the constitution of the Bond, but removed, if I am not mistaken, by the influence of a gentleman who now ranks high in the favour of our Progressive friends.' (This was an allusion to du Toit's defection into Rhodes's camp.) 'My definition embraces everyone who, having settled in this country, wants to stay here to help to promote our common interests....'[10]

The word Africander, thus defined, became a programme. Hofmeyr summarised it thus: 'firstly, equal rights for the English and Dutch Africander; secondly, the close linking together of the Dutch and English Africander'.[11] 'Linking', 'reconciliation', 'cooperation' were favourite words of his. He appealed to the example of Switzerland, where the diverse linguistic cultures of the Germans, French and Italians had found fulfilment within a common citizenship. He appealed to the example of Canada, where English and French Canadians had discovered their common destiny in the Dominion and were working side by side within a bi-lingual party. He would have wished to make his own Afrikander Bond such a party; but since the majority of English-speakers held aloof from it, he offered them cooperation across party lines.

Cooperation to what ends? In a time of rapid change and intermittent crisis the answer was bound in some measure to vary with
circumstances; but on the three central issues—Native policy, national
union and imperial relations—Hofmeyr preached consistent doctrine.

In his Native policy he asserted a principle but applied it with
caution. He repudiated the *voortrekker* dogma of racial inequality and
upheld the 'colour-blind' franchise of the Cape; yet he also believed
(as indeed the majority of politicians in Great Britain still believed)
that the right to vote was conditional on the possession of specific
capacities. In Hofmeyr's judgment, only a small minority of South
African Natives had as yet acquired these capacities. Consequently,
his policy safeguarded the voting predominance of European South
Africans in the present and for a long time to come. All the same, it
left the door open for the sharing of power in some distant future,
and offered in the here and now political rights to the handful of
Bantu, and the much larger number of Coloured people, who were
rising towards the European standard of prosperity and education.
What still remained uncertain was whether Hofmeyr possessed the
resolution, or indeed the power (for a politician must satisfy his
constituents) to stick to his principles when these began appreciably
to dilute the political predominance of white people.*

In his national policy Hofmeyr advocated a gradualist approach
towards the goal of South African union. He had been at first a
supporter of the federation proposals of 1877 but had seen them
come to grief because Lord Carnarvon and Sir Theophilus Shepstone
rushed their fences. Subsequently, he recognised and resisted a
similar impatience and arrogance in du Toit's propaganda for a
republican, Afrikaans-speaking South Africa 'stretching from the
Cape to the Zambesi'. Partisan zeal and narrow nationalism,
whether of the British or the Boer brand, were not in his opinion the

* The qualification for the franchise fixed in 1852 (property, including communal
property, to the value of £25) was extremely low, and threatened a swamping of the
electorate by 'raw' Bantu, particularly after the incorporation of the Transkei. On two
occasions, 1887 and 1892, Hofmeyr played a part in the precautions that were taken,
quite consistently with the theory of those times, against this danger. A law of 1887 laid
it down that land held in tribal, communal tenure did not constitute the economic qualification for the franchise. A law of 1892 raised the economic qualification and, for the
first time, introduced an elementary educational qualification. Hofmeyr's personal
preference would have been to achieve the same objective by the more positive method of
granting multiple votes to certain types of electors—a device that became familiar in the
programmes of moderate liberals in eastern and southern Africa in the mid-twentieth
century.

road to union, nor would union be worth having if one section of South Africans forced it upon the other; 'reconciliation and rapprochement', he declared, 'is the foundation of my hopes'.[12] He did not expect to see these hopes realised except by patient striving, and in the meantime he thought it dangerous to drive towards union by the straight political road. His policy in the late 1880's was to approach union by the indirect path of an agreement on customs and railway policy. The Orange Free State was willing at that time to follow this path with him; but not the Transvaal.

Hofmeyr's views about the imperial connection found expression in his proposal to the Colonial Conference of 1887 that all self-governing territories of the Empire should impose upon themselves a customs levy of 5 per cent as a contribution to their common defence. He could have offered no more striking demonstration of his faith in the creative reconciliation of *imperium et libertas*. This faith was rooted in his experience of self-government in Cape Colony, whereby his people were achieving *within* the Empire a more substantial freedom than they would be likely to achieve outside it. Could not a united South Africa achieve freedom and nationhood within the same shelter? A century hence, perhaps, South Africans might realise du Toit's dream of republican independence outside the Empire, but here and now they would find it more prudent to follow the Canadian example of national freedom within the family of the Crown. Thus Hofmeyr calculated; but his allegiance had deeper roots than calculation. In March 1898, when his traditional loyalties were under intolerable strain, he declared: 'Mr Chairman, I was born under Her Majesty's Government and I am content to remain under it.'[13]

This was the world of ideas and affections within which Smuts grew up. To this world he was destined to return, after the bitter exile that was to be forced upon him soon after the close of his student years.

Let us now return with him to Stellenbosch and observe the response that he was making to the promptings of his own nature, to the teaching of his Scottish professors and to the political gospel of Jan Hofmeyr. We left him composing Spenserian stanzas 'To I.M.K. on her Nineteenth Birthday'. Their theme was her spiritual struggle to discover her true self in unity with 'the seen and unseen All'. In that phrase he expressed an intuition or idea which remained his companion to the end of his life. He might have pursued the idea further through the medium of verse composition, if only he had been patient enough to devote months and years of his life to linguistic and metrical experiment. But that was contrary to his temperament. He could never have made himself a poet because he would never have allowed himself time enough for the meticulous polishing of language. He valued content above form, seized the images and phrases that came first into his head (it is astonishing that they were so often vivid) and maintained continuous hot pursuit of new facts and ideas. The notebooks that survive from Stellenbosch reveal an unusual range of mental activity: Latin and Greek vocabularies (the German ones do not survive): the *Eclogues* of Virgil and the *Ajax* of Sophocles: optical physics: electrical problems: inorganic chemistry and metallurgy: geology: organic chemistry leading into agriculture. In 1890 and 1891 he acted as College laboratory assistant in botany while pursuing courses of study in literature and philosophy, mathematics and the natural sciences. In 1892 he obtained a 'divided degree' with first-class honours both in Arts and Science.

In this insatiable quest for new knowledge he never allowed his mind to sprawl. All his adventures of ideas were contained within one adventure, one insistent question which forced itself upon him in all his separate studies. The question found expression in a long essay called *Homo Sum*, which he wrote and published just after his nineteenth birthday. The essay began as an historical review of slavery but ended as a speculative inquiry into *Eenheid*, Unity: whether its highest embodiment was to be found in impersonal Law or in Personality? Although he was well aware of the pantheistic snare in which he might entangle himself, he answered without hesitation: 'Not Law, but the Person is the highest reality.'[14] In *Homo Sum*, as in the verses addressed to Isie Krige, we see foreshadowed his philosophy of holism.

We see it foreshadowed even more sharply in a powerful study of *South African Customs Union*, which he wrote when he was twenty years old. It was a long essay of sixty-one closely written foolscap pages which he entered in 1890 for the J. B. Ebden prize. Although his work was 'highly commended', he did not win the prize. Perhaps the examiners thought that he took too long in coming to the point. Whether he knew it or not, his expanding interests and ambitions were driving him forward from poetry, through philosophy into politics; but he could not bear to leave the philosophy behind him.

Before getting his teeth into the political and economic problems of the customs union he wrote page after page about the philosophy of history, physics and politics, evolution and ethics. In these higher flights of fancy his style suggests that one of his Scottish professors had introduced him to Carlyle: or was it the rhythm and rhetoric of the innumerable Calvinist sermons which he had listened to that found an echo in his parables and similes, his rhetorical questions and hortatory imperatives, his imaginary dialogues between Truth and Error? His prose grew overheated; but it never collapsed into absurdity. There was fitness of a kind in the ardent language which expressed such ardour of thought and feeling. He had discovered direction, if not purpose, throughout the entire evolutionary universe of matter and mind. He tried to convey his vision in the language of chemistry: the law of the conservation of energy, he declared, is at work not only in the chemical but also in the moral world: in consequence, great nations do not pass away—all that happens 'is only a rearrangement of spiritual forces'. A *rearrangement*, not merely a repetition; for spiritual forces, like chemical ones, are more than the sum of their parts, and each new structure marks a new stage along the ascending path of evolution. This thought is holistic; but the twenty-year-old student had not yet discovered his key word. So he borrowed a familiar phrase—the principle of association—to convey the idea that he was groping after. 'Association is the fundamental fact of our mental consciousness...' (he appealed to psychology). 'Association is the first law of nature...' (he appealed to physics). 'Association (in the form of Love) is the fundamental law of our spiritual nature, or of Religion.'

This philosophical cosmology (if that is the right expression for it) became a permanent part of his outlook and found expression many times in his later, more systematic writings, as well as in hundreds of letters to intimate friends written throughout his life. What concerns us now is the relation which he discovered between its spatial and temporal immensities and the small, time-restricted problems of his political essay. In his view, the relation was so obvious that it scarcely called for proof: the principle of association meant for South Africa the coming together of Boer and Briton within each separate territory and the coming together of the four territories within the emergent South African nation. 'No policy in any Colony or State is sound', he declared, 'which does not recognise, and frame its measures as

29

much as possible in accordance with, the fact that South Africa is one, that consisting as it does of separate parts, it yet forms one commercial and moral unity. This is the corner stone of South African politics.' In the practical application of this principle he came down from his philosophical clouds to Jan Hofmeyr's solid earth. No more high-falutin' theories or rhetorical flourishes: in terse, effective prose he unravelled the complexities of past politics and expounded his own sober plan for a railways and customs union.

All the same, he knew that nations are not made by administrative arrangements alone. He discussed the ideological and emotional implications of South African nationhood in a later essay which he called 'The Conditions of Future South African Literature'.[15] A true national literature, he declared, did not as yet exist, nor could it exist until a true South African nation had come to birth. What were the hindrances? Language was not a hindrance, for it had proved no barrier to social unity in the old-established settlements of Dutch, French and English people, which had long since taken the same South African stamp. The barrier, in his view, was a different one; it was the division of habit and outlook between the old settlers, both Boer and British, and the latter-day populations of the diamond and gold fields. He sympathised with the conservative patriots of the Transvaal who feared that their old, pious ways would be swamped in the new flood; but he tried to make them see that South Africa needed these hustling European immigrants. 'Where two or three are gathered together there is something more: there is the working of that eternal Force, that inscrutable Dynamic, which is propelling humanity towards its exalted destiny.' There spoke again the ardent young philosopher; but also the hard-headed political realist, who saw no safety for European civilisation in South Africa except through true unity between all sections of a rapidly growing European population. They must all stand together, he said, because '. . . the race struggle is destined to assume a magnitude on the African continent such as the world has never seen and the imagination shrinks from con-templating; and in that appalling struggle for existence the unity of the white camp. . . will not be the least necessary condition—we will not say of obtaining victory but of warding off (the ultra pessimists say of postponing) annihilation'.

This passage on the Native question—*the* South African question, he called it—struck a more urgent note than any to be found in

Hofmeyr's speeches and writings. In the concluding pages of his essay, Smuts shed his evolutionary optimism and discovered history to be 'a *via dolorosa*, a path of sorrow'. But how, precisely, did he envisage 'the tragic element' in the history of his own people? In an enigmatical passage he suggested that it was not the browning of the blood that he feared but 'the browning of the heart and head'.

In his four years at Stellenbosch (including the pre-matriculation year) Smuts had covered a lot of ground. After his first year he had begun to cast off some of his shyness and even to find himself at ease with 'the puerile element'. He joined the militia, contributed essays to the College magazine and became a leader of the debating society —to which, in 1889, he introduced a promising new recruit from Riebeeck West, his former pupil in the Sunday school, D. F. Malan. In 1890, when the College received a visit from Cecil Rhodes and some of his political colleagues, he made on behalf of the student body a speech which the greatest parliamentary orator in South Africa still remembered with admiration more than twenty years later.[16]

His fellow students felt that he was destined for great things. One day, when a group of them were talking about their future careers, a youth called Carel van Zyl demanded their serious attention and prophesied that there was not a post in the British Empire that Smuts might not win if God Almighty spared him.[17] The young men were on their way to the examination room, which was the vestibule of opportunity for all of them. Smuts passed through that vestibule into Christ's College, Cambridge.

In the examinations of 1891 he took his double first and was awarded the Ebden scholarship to Cambridge. The runner-up was Robert (later Sir Robert) Kotzé, a student of the South Africa College in Cape Town who had in front of him a distinguished career in engineering. Kotzé used to say in his old age that Smuts 'outwitted him' at the examinations by offering Science and Arts together and thereby piling up additional marks. He felt no malice; on the contrary, he had taken up philosophy after his retirement and had turned to Smuts for criticism and encouragement. Still, he did seem to believe that Smuts owed his scholarship to his phenomenal memory, rather than to any true understanding that he had of the principles of science.

There can be no doubt that Smuts, as an expert examination

hurdler, owed a great deal to his memory. According to a tradition which there is no reason to doubt, he had not known that Greek would be required of him at his matriculation examination; but as soon as he heard the news he shut himself up in his room to master it in the remaining week and passed at the head of the list. Other clever boys, perhaps, might have done the same; the unusual thing with Smuts was that he retained his Greek after it had served his utilitarian purpose; he absorbed it as nourishment into the tissues of his mind, so that he was able even in his middle sixties to rediscover the Greek Testament and make it his daily companion until his last illness and death. It was the same with his botanical studies. For three decades or more he seemed quite forgetful of them: so much so, that he told a friend in the mid-1920's—'I cannot imagine how we have gone on all these years without Botany'. When she said that she was using Asa Grey's *Structural Botany*, he exclaimed: 'Why, I always use it, and it is the book from which I learnt my little botany in the 'eighties! It is of course quite out of date, but still very useful for nomenclature.'[18] His teacher in the 1880's, Professor Marloth, used to take him rambling on Saturday afternoons in search of botanical specimens. Thirty years later, when Smuts was a world-famous political figure, teacher and pupil resumed their rambles.

Smuts was fortunate in having an unusual memory, but he never used it mechanically, as a vulgar careerist would have done; he used it creatively, to strengthen and enrich his understanding. The last word on his performance as a student at Stellenbosch may be left with one of his examiners, a scholarly and humane philosopher, Monsignor Kolbe: 'Many years ago, when I was examining in Philosophy, a very thoughtful set of papers was sent in by a student of Stellenbosch.... Other students in various years sent in papers equally good, one at least much better... but their philosophical education seems to have ended there. They reproduced the thoughts of others,... but they did not *think*. Jan Smuts started with a handicap. ...But the germs of thought were there.'[19]

The germs of many things were there. What had been planted at Stellenbosch promised to grow well at Cambridge. And yet Smuts was strangely innocent in the ways of the world when he set out on his first voyage. It was typical of his trusting optimism that he sailed north into the European winter with the underwear that he wore to keep him cool in the South African summer.

CHAPTER 3

CAMBRIDGE

THE 1890's saw the beginnings at Cambridge of a golden period, which has been recalled in some of its aspects (although not, perhaps, the most important ones) by many nostalgic memoirists of the mid-twentieth century. When Smuts came up to Cambridge in 1891, A. N. Whitehead was a young don and Bertrand Russell an undergraduate in his second year; G. E. Moore came up the following year and remained to spread lucidity and light amongst the bright intelligences which flitted, ten years or so later, from Cambridge to Bloomsbury. Bliss was it then to be alive, for all these gifted young men. But not for Smuts.

It always pleased Smuts to remember anniversaries, even if their associations were macabre. On 23 September 1930, he recalled that he had narrowly escaped assassination on the same day of the same month in 1915, and that on the same date in 1891 he had set sail from Cape Town in 'a horrible little ship' where he became at once 'horribly sick'.[1] Seasickness was an affliction that he was destined to endure many times, until the progress of invention offered him the release and pleasure of air travel. Seasickness, all the same, was not the heaviest affliction of his first voyage. Homesickness was far worse. He carried that malady with him to England and remained 'utterly desolate' throughout the whole of his first year at Cambridge.[2]

In his lodgings at 13 Victoria Street he lived a lonely life. There was, of course, no chance at all that young aristocrats of birth and intellect, such as Bertrand Russell, would ever meet him or ever wish to meet anybody of his type; Russell was quite certain, even in his first term, that he knew every one of his Cambridge contemporaries who could possibly be thought worth knowing.[3] Such self-sufficiency of class, upbringing and mental habit would have been too formidable a barrier for Smuts to penetrate, even if his temperament had permitted him to make the attempt, or if the opportunity had come his way.

What seems surprising at first sight is his neglect to make the best of such opportunities as did come his way. For example, his fellow lodger at 13 Victoria Street* was a serious and friendly young man called John Gregg, who became in later life Archbishop of Armagh. Gregg invited him in the first week or two to come for a walk and recalled in his old age that Smuts opened the conversation by giving his views on a text from St Paul, 'Sin revived and I died'; but Smuts never proposed a second walk and Gregg got the impression that he wanted to be left to himself. In the same year at Christ's there was a warm-hearted medical student called Auden, who became in later life Chief Medical Officer at Birmingham and the father of a famous poet; but Smuts never returned the invitations to breakfast which he received once or twice from Auden and their acquaintance never ripened. Early in his first term Smuts received and accepted invitations to join the debating society and to write for the College magazine; but he never followed up the chances of friendship which these activities put in his way. It was not that there was anything in his appearance, manner or speech that need have made him feel awkward in the company of young Englishmen. Gregg thought that he spoke correct English with a slightly foreign accent and was surprised to discover 'that this spare, flaxen and slightly curly-haired, blue-eyed youth was of Boer origin'. Auden took note not only of his accent, his spare build and the blond, rather irregular moustache that he wore for a term or two, but of his unusual mental powers. If Smuts had also possessed physical powers, or the training and inclination to exercise them in games, he would, like the majority of his South African contemporaries at Cambridge, have got to know plenty of young Englishmen on the playing-fields and in the changing-rooms. But he took his exercise in long country walks as he had done at Stellenbosch, with the difference that he found in the flat, alien countryside of Cambridge no views to admire, no plants to collect and no friends to walk with. He walked very fast, alone with his own thoughts.

He had come up to Cambridge at the age of twenty-one, three years

* In 1952 Canon C. E. Raven, formerly Master of Christ's College and Vice-Chancellor of the University during the late 1940's, when Smuts was Chancellor, wrote very kindly on my behalf to the surviving Christ's men (approximately ten) who had been contemporaries of Smuts sixty years earlier. Many of the replies were illuminating. It is perhaps regrettable that their combined evidence makes it hard to believe that the rooms in College which a pious tradition ascribes to Smuts were ever occupied by him: 13 (later changed to 12a) Victoria Street was almost certainly his address throughout his stay in Cambridge.

or so older than his English fellow-undergraduates, and possibly he felt the same disdain for 'the puerile element' as he had felt when he first went to Stellenbosch. Certainly, he was not attracted by English habits of verbal play and he was repelled by the laxity of sexual morals which he observed among some of the young Englishmen. Frivolity and laxity, however, were not characteristics of Auden or Gregg. First and foremost, it was an unlucky accident which prevented Smuts from getting to know young men of their stamp. He simply could not afford to return their hospitality. He had to spend the whole of his first winter shivering in the cold and damp of Cambridge because he could not afford to buy himself woollen underwear.[4] Owing to a bank failure, his Ebden scholarship was worth only £100 a year instead of the customary £200. By selling the animals that had accrued to him on his father's farm he had been able to pay his sea passage and to put some money into the bank, but there still remained a dreadful gap between his resources and his bare needs as an undergraduate. During his first year at Christ's he won a College scholarship, but its money value was pitifully small. He began to feel that he would be entering the battle of life under a crippling burden of debt, and bitterness started to gnaw at him. In his second year at Cambridge he addressed to the Trustees of the Ebden Scholarship a letter of protest so harsh in tone that the Registrar of the University invited him in his own interest to withdraw it. A month or two later he drafted a letter of complaint against Christ's College, alleging that it had encouraged him to expect an increase of £50 in his scholarship and had then broken its promise (as he took it to be) with the result that he had missed the chance of securing a good scholarship in another College and now felt himself constrained to seek enrolment as a non-Collegiate student.[5]

He drafted this letter in a scribbling book and then scored it through. Perhaps it was a feeling for his own dignity which held him back from sending it; perhaps it was compunction for his tutors, who knew by now that the highest academic prizes were within his reach and were encouraging him to strive for them. But he had another reason for scoring through his draft. He was being sustained, both financially and morally, by a friend at Stellenbosch, Professor J. I. Marais of the Theological College.

The letters that Smuts wrote to Marais have not survived; but from Marais's letters to Smuts a clear picture emerges of a relationship that did credit both to the older and to the younger man. Smuts, it appeared, discovered the full hopelessness of his financial position at the end of his first term and appealed to Marais for help. Marais wrote back straight away thanking the young man for showing such confidence in him and enclosing a cheque for £50. At the same time he made the gesture of proving himself a sound business man by getting Smuts to take out a life insurance policy for the first £50 and all subsequent loans: they amounted in the end to £250, plus the premiums on the insurance policy, which Marais took it upon himself to pay. A sound business man indeed! If Smuts had died, the loans would have been covered by the insurance policy; but as long as he lived his integrity was the only cover. Marais took this for granted and kept reminding Smuts to write whenever he needed more money; Cambridge was an expensive place; he must not allow himself to be stinted. Six months or so after Smuts's return to South Africa Marais submitted a complete statement of account and suggested that Smuts should pay interest at 5 % until he could clear the debt. Smuts acknowledged the debt with interest at 6 %.[6]

In their letters to each other Smuts and Marais found much to discuss besides money matters. The middle-aged theologian could not refrain from preaching just a little; but he did it so gently that Smuts (who anyway had his own strong bent towards preaching) could not possibly feel himself the victim of unfair moral pressure. It did him no harm, for example, to have to defend his choice of law as his examination subject. No doubt he had chosen it because he wanted to get on in the world, to make money, to get married and have a family, to make his entry into politics. Marais did not deny that law possessed these practical advantages or that it might open up for Smuts 'a vast career of usefulness' in Parliament or on the Bench; but from the philosophical point of view he considered it 'utterly useless' and from the moral point of view no better than 'classified humbug'. This taunt stung Smuts into beginning work on a treatise or book entitled, *The Nature and Function of Law in the History of Human Society*—starting with Jewish nationalism, which always fascinated him, and proceeding from the law of Moses to St Paul, in whom he discovered not only a theory of law but a philosophy of history, 'a fundamental canon of human development', as he called it. He never completed this treatise; but he did produce for the College magazine an essay entitled *Law, A Liberal Study*, in which he cited the accusation, 'classified humbug' and then set out by systematic reasoning to refute it. 'Along the channel of Law', he declared, 'are flowing the most permanent currents of human thought and activity': flowing from the primitive Family to the modern State, from the 'independence' to the 'interdependence' of states and finally to 'that consummation which Cicero foresaw, in which there would be but one Law for all humanity.' Smuts believed that this long journey of Law towards the unity of mankind was also a journey towards individual freedom. 'The Person', he exclaimed, 'is recognised more and more; the rights of Personality become more and more inviolable.'

One has the feeling that Smuts had Marais very often in his mind as he arranged the pattern of his conduct and of his reading and as he put pen to paper. It would have saddened his old friend had he turned his back on the religion of his upbringing, and nothing pleased Marais more than to hear by a roundabout source that Smuts belonged to a little band of South Africans who were regular worshippers at the Presbyterian Church in Cambridge. It would have infuriated Marais if Smuts had shown any inclination to de-nationalise himself. 'An anglicised Afrikaner', he wrote, 'is as disgusting a creature as an anglicised Scotchman. Take Andrew Lang with his English drawl, his hatred of the Covenanters, his libellous attacks on John Knox. What a poor silly creature—Carlyle would say. You understand me. Anglophobia is a curse from which may God deliver us, but Anglomania is an evil equally great. I detest the ultra Afrikander Bond-men; I equally detest the angli-cised Afrikander, whose mental state is by no means an enviable one. I pray that God may make you a large-hearted, liberal-minded, God-fearing, country-loving lawyer.' Perhaps it was in response to this ardent prayer that Smuts took out of his drawer for final revision his patriotic essay on 'The Conditions of Future South African Literature'.*

Marais was a man of wide reading, to whom an eager student could pour out his enthusiasm for Sophocles and Plato, Schiller and Goethe: great spirits indeed, the old man said, 'and yet what is even Plato or Sophocles as compared to Paul?' It was a text from St Paul, it will be remembered, that Smuts discussed with John Gregg on the

* See p. 30 above.

first and only walk that they took together; it was in St Paul that he had discovered in his treatise on Law 'a fundamental canon of human development'; sixty years later, it was to St Paul, not to Plato, that he returned when he felt the need to strengthen the foundations of his faith during the war against Hitler. As to his philosophy: it would be going too far to say that Marais incited Smuts to continue the explorations which he had begun at Stellenbosch; but he certainly encouraged him to continue them. If only he could begin his own studies again, he exclaimed, he would choose Physical Science in the broadest sense, because nothing deepened the mind so much as a study of Nature, and there were many roads which led from Nature to Nature's God....As one looks through Smuts's notebooks of the Cambridge years, one has the feeling that he had less than half of his mind upon his examination subjects and more than half of it on 'Nature'. He might well have been a philosopher who had got wind of the research which J. J. Thomson was pursuing at the Cavendish, or a biologist who had been stimulated to philosophical reflection by an impulse, coming along some indirect track, from James Ward or A. N. Whitehead.

Between September 1892 and January 1893 he wrote a closely packed essay of thirty-six pages *On the Application of Some Physical Concepts to Biological Phenomena.* He graded the classes of phenomena susceptible of scientific study in an ascending hierarchy: at its base the Material or the Energical (two aspects of the same thing), then upwards to the Biological, the Psychical, the Ethical. Each class in the series, he said, showed an increase in the number and the complexity of its conditions, and he asked—'Cannot we, in trying to penetrate into the secrets of the higher, more complex forms of development, make use of the information gained in our study of the lower?' His answer was Yes: both the information gained in physical science and the method employed in gaining it can be of use in the more complex inquiries. So he started with the concept of Force in physics and carried it from the inorganic world into the organic; if he had stuck to his original plan he would have carried it still further, for he had written down the word *Mind,* and then crossed it out.

It would be foolish to take too seriously the unpublished essay of a twenty-two-year-old candidate for the Law Tripos; but it may be interesting to quote from it some sentences dealing with two concepts —continuous creation and the life force—which were not yet familiar to the reading public. 'And as Energy constitutes a permanent part of the Universe', wrote Smuts, 'we may say that the creation of the worlds is still proceeding as of old, and will proceed so long as matter will remain an indestructible source of possibilities, and there will be force to regulate the struggle into existence of those possibilities.' This was the last sentence in the section of his essay that dealt with inorganic phenomena. He headed the next section 'Force-Life', and argued his way, through a criticism of current definitions of Life, to the following conclusion: 'It is evident that Life corresponds exactly to the conception of Force which we have tried to make clear. Life is not energy; it is not development; it is not motion; it is not an equilibrium of motions or a harmony; it is a Force. Life is a regulative principle, latent in the material substratum, which rises into activity whenever, and continues to act as long as, certain parts of matter have certain relations to one another or form certain collocations. Life is not the totality or the aggregate of the constitutive particles, nor the aggregate of the relations of those material particles. It is something more, something over and above all that.'

How in the world did this young law student hit upon ideas such as these? A good many years were to pass before they were put into general circulation by the well-known books of Henri Bergson, Lloyd Morgan and Samuel Alexander.[7]* It might perhaps be worth while for some historian of science to inquire whether these ideas had found their way into the scientific and philosophical periodicals of the early 1890's; but even if they had, Smuts could hardly have been a reader of this specialist literature. Perhaps they were 'in the air'. But then, as we have seen, the germs of them were sprouting in his head before he left Stellenbosch. Could it possibly be that he had put himself by his own unaided efforts on to the main highroad of neo-Darwinian thought?

Certainly, he got no help from the official teachers of philosophy at Cambridge. He secured an introduction to Professor James Ward and asked permission to attend his lectures; but Ward would not run the risk of admitting a dilettante philosopher from the Law School. Nearly thirty years later, Ward wrote to Smuts in considerable perturbation because somebody had told him that Smuts had said unkind things about his book, *The Realm of Ends*. Smuts was able with a good conscience to send him a comforting answer. It is odd

* See below, pp. 49–50, 302–4.

to think of the Cambridge professor seeking reassurance from the pupil he had turned away.[8]

Continuous creation and the life force were ideas which carried Smuts a long way from the book of Genesis; but they did not carry him far away in sympathy or mutual understanding from Professor J. I. Marais. Admittedly, he was moving towards an intellectual position in which, if he had been a theologian of the Dutch Reformed Church, he would sooner or later have found himself, like his friend du Plessis, on trial for heresy;* Marais, however, was not much interested in heresy and recognised in Smuts the continuing Christian impulse, *anima naturaliter Christiana*. Indeed, the really interesting thing about Smuts in his Cambridge years was not his rejection of narrow theological dogma (for that was a commonplace of the time), but his rejection of narrow scientific dogma. His contemporary at Cambridge, Bertrand Russell, was content during those same years to think of the world as 'a heap of shot'[9]—a picture hardly more relevant than the stories of Genesis to the scientific age that was then opening. Russell, besides, was a mathematician and philosopher uninterested as yet in social questions; whereas Smuts was trying to enlarge the Darwinian perspective so that it might include, at the one end, inanimate nature, and at the other the human person with his ethical and political strivings. A profound difference between the two men, both then and later, was Russell's indifference to synthesis and Smuts's passionate pursuit of it. Russell, no less than Smuts, was a determined moralist; but he never felt the need for a system of thought which would embrace both his description of nature and his evaluation of good and evil; he was content to leave these two activities of the mind in separate compartments. Smuts hated separate compartments. Whatever he wrote about the philosophy of nature had to be coherent, implicitly if not explicitly, with his philosophy of conduct and of religion.

Still, he realised that there were other ways of apprehending and expressing truth than the method of science. He left among his Cambridge papers not only the essay on physical concepts in their application to biology, but another essay on *Christ in History*, and some draft chapters of a more ambitious treatise to be entitled *The Cosmic Religion*. In the latter, he took as his text 'I am come to fulfil, not to destroy', and described the decay of religious belief as 'a

* See p. 22 above.

calamity'. It was a calamity, he declared, which could not be repaired by repudiating science, that most majestic activity of the human intellect; but it might be repaired by a deeper philosophic understanding both of religion and of science. For science, like religion, had its crudities; within its narrow specialisms it was too cock-a-hoop, too much in love with its 'parts and particles', too much out of love with synthesis. For the rubbing out of the hard little contours around the man-made specialisms Smuts looked both to philosophy and to literature. 'It is to certain great literary artists', he wrote, 'who occupied themselves with the study and contemplation of wholes instead of parts and fractions, that this century is indebted for such practical wisdom and counsel as it has received.' He went on to quote Walt Whitman, a literary artist not at all in favour with the young Englishmen of Cambridge, but already his chosen companion for the attempt that he had in mind to carry further the 'study and contemplation of wholes'.

All this was in the midst of his hard grind at the law and in the midst of his loneliness. Still, the loneliness began to be mitigated during his second year at Cambridge. A South African contemporary of his, N. J. ('Klaasie') de Wet, his close friend throughout the next half a century or more and a future Chief Justice of the Union, recalled in his old age that there had been a young woman—he could not remember her name—to whom Smuts had written many letters and with whom he had gone walking among the hills—he could not remember where: perhaps the Lake District? The clue was tantalisingly vague, yet good enough to lend special interest to an Ethel Brown who appeared once or twice among Smuts's correspondents during his middle and later years. Yes: he had written many letters to her when he was an undergraduate at Cambridge and would have been glad, forty years later, to have the letters returned; but she evaded his requests. By that time she had become a shadowy, perhaps an eccentric old lady. In 1917, when she had written to welcome him on his arrival in England at the crisis of the First World War, it had been a clear, unselfconscious image of herself which her letters reflected—the image of a simple patriotic Englishwoman whom life was treating harshly, but without damage to her natural sweetness of disposition. She would have liked Smuts to come to see her for the sake of old times: those happy times when her company had been healing medicine for the tense and lonely young student.[10]

In 1892 or 1893 Smuts had gone to Derbyshire one vacation in flight from the flat landscape of Cambridgeshire. He had found deep content in long rambles amongst the Derbyshire hills, alien though they were in their contours and colours from the stark and vivid mountains of his own Swartland. He had found, too, an agreeable walking companion, a girl of his own age called Ethel Brown, who lived with her widowed mother and her sister Gertie at 'The Orchard', Belper. Her social and intellectual background was as remote as could be imagined from that of the confident and sophisticated young Englishmen of Cambridge, but not so very remote in its simplicity, decorum and kindliness from the society in which Smuts had grown up. She lacked the mental training to follow the trend of his arguments about philosophy, science and politics but was ready to listen to him for ever as he talked and talked about everything that he had in his head. She encouraged him to believe that he would some day make a great reputation for himself: that was quite easy, he used to answer; the real difficulty was to keep the reputation after one had made it! He might, perhaps, have found her insipid if she had been all the time the admiring listener; but Derbyshire was her beloved world and she was the guide in their long walks from hilltop to hilltop and valley to valley. Perhaps she was pretty? He found her at any rate a charming and sympathetic friend and when he returned to Cambridge he wrote to her frequently and at length; but not love-letters; a young man so serious of purpose could never permit himself to be in love with two girls at the same time. Did she ever venture to call him Jan? When she wrote to him again after more than twenty years' silence, she began her letter, 'Dear Mr Smuts'.

It was not at 13 Victoria Street, Cambridge, but at 'The Orchard', Belper, Derbyshire, that Smuts first felt himself to be at home in England. And when he returned to Cambridge he brought back with him some of the rest and peace which he had found in Derbyshire. He was no longer so fierce a recluse as he had been during his first year, although, even now, it was not among the young Englishmen that he found his companions. The same South African friend who in his old age vaguely recalled the existence of Miss Ethel Brown had a more distinct recollection of Smuts going for walks with two

42

'Afghan princes'—an unlikely picture, so it seemed, until Aftab Ahmad Khan and his brother Sultan Mohammad appeared in the correspondence of Smuts's middle years: certainly they were not Afghan princes, but Indian Moslems of good birth who walked and talked with Smuts at Cambridge and subsequently achieved distinction in the service of their country.[11] Another man who used to go walking with him was Richard Maclaurin, a New Zealander 'who just preceded Rutherford at Cambridge and just missed equal distinction': Maclaurin became in his middle age Director of the Massachusetts Institute of Technology.[12] Among the letters that Smuts wrote and received in later life there is mention of one or two other men who used to walk with him 'along the Roman road by the Gogs'. And then there was the South African group, F. S. Malan, N. J. de Wet, L. Krause and the rest who remained his friends throughout the strenuous years ahead. These were the men who used to join him on Sunday evenings in attending the Presbyterian service and taking supper afterwards in the manse; they would have liked also to have had his company at their weekday gaieties and did once persuade him to join them at cards; but he handled his pack as if he were reading a book. They also persuaded him one Boat Race Day to join them on the cheap railway excursion to London; somehow or other they lost him between Liverpool Street and Putney; but he was there on the platform to greet them in the evening after enjoying every minute of his day—in the Library of the Middle Temple.

He ceased to be lonely but he still remained terribly serious: this, perhaps, was the main barrier separating him from the young Englishmen at Cambridge. It was not a barrier separating him from the dons. In the letters that he exchanged with his law tutors there is evidence of mutual respect and liking; elsewhere there remains clear record, direct or indirect, of two friendships which played a significant part in his life. He became intimate with E. W. Hobson, a Senior Wrangler, Fellow of Christ's and Sadlerian Professor of Pure Mathematics; in all likelihood it was this intimacy which paved the way for his later friendship with J. A. Hobson, the professor's brother, who went to South Africa on the eve of the Boer War as correspondent of the *Manchester Guardian*.[13] The Hobsons, like the Hobhouses—another English family which was destined to influence his life—were radicals in the tradition of John Bright, and perhaps there is historical importance in the fact that it was their vision of

England's destiny, not the vision of Rosebery or Chamberlain, which became imprinted on the mind of Smuts while he was still an undergraduate at Cambridge. As will appear later, the name of John Bright recurred like a refrain in his political thinking.*

His closest friend among the dons was H. J. Wolstenholme, another radical, who had set out to become a Congregational minister but had succumbed to doubts and settled himself on the fringes of academic society in Cambridge, where he made a modest living by teaching German. Wolstenholme was a member of the Combination Room at Christ's but appeared there infrequently, for he was a valetudinarian and semi-recluse who preferred to stay alone with his books in his small house off the Huntingdon Road, reading widely in philosophy, sociology and economics, and thinking at times of the important work which he knew in his heart he lacked the strength to write. It was surely a godsend to him that Smuts sought his company. Their friendship lasted from 1892 until his death in 1917, and it probably gave him the only opportunity that ever came his way of rendering steady service to a fellow human being. The relationship between this strangely assorted pair was charming and just a little comical: Smuts so full of enthusiasm, drive and the itch for system-building: Wolstenholme so tired, so timid, so submissive to his own sad conception of a planless, purposeless, morally indifferent universe, yet not at all submissive to the iniquities of governments and men, for he was a lapsed Christian who retained his Christian conscience.[14]

Too large a dose of this middle-aged pessimism and scepticism would have quenched the ardour of most young men but Smuts was unquenchable; if there was any danger at all in his incessant disputations with Wolstenholme it was that they might distract him too much from his legal studies. He had it in mind to attempt both parts of the Law Tripos in one and the same year—an unprecedented and hazardous attempt which would normally have justified, and indeed demanded, the exclusion of all studies extraneous to the curriculum. Smuts, however, spent his last long vacation before the Tripos as if his testing-time were still two or three years distant. His intellectual history during the vacation is recorded in a small black notebook that he labelled CHIPS. It contained, among many other things, the plan of a novel about a promising young man who succumbed to a

* See below, pp. 106, 147, 198, 204.

temptation which, no doubt, assailed Smuts himself often enough. 'A Cape Youth, clever, high-minded, bent upon the effectualisation of his personality, comes to Europe.' The opening sentence of a success story? On the contrary! The high-minded youth goes out one evening with a loose woman. From that moment 'the radiant colours of promise' darken to shadow, to storm, to catastrophe— 'Cf. Oedipus Rex, Walt Whitman'. The story gathers pace as a melodrama of sin, suffering, remorse, suicide. There but for the grace of God, he may have said, goes J. C. Smuts.

The idea of God (Wolstenholme notwithstanding[15]) was continually in the mind of Smuts that summer. The idea of science was also in his mind and he was trying to discover whether, and if so how, the two ideas could be reconciled in his thought with each other. 'God is at the beginning', he wrote, 'God is at the end, but is He always between these limits?' Other aphorisms and notes in CHIPS show him persistently in search of a philosophy which would reconcile the universe of scientific mechanism with the universe of value and purpose. Nothing would ever shake his acceptance of evolution: nothing would ever shake his experience of personality. Could he, perhaps, build a bridge between the two ideas of evolution and personality by studying the life of one representative person? The notes in CHIPS reveal him already at work on Walt Whitman.

Mercifully, they reveal him also at work on his law-books: not that this need ever have been in doubt, for throughout his life he pursued poetry, philosophy, botany, archaeology and all his other interests during the time available to him *after* he had taken the measure of his day's work. He was able to do this because he worked immensely faster than other people and because he found recreation, not in the things that are fritterers of time, but in reading, thinking, writing, exploring. Walt Whitman and the rest were his recreation during the long vacation of 1893; he recorded his strict work in the long lists of law-books that he wrote down and in the legal problems that he set himself: for example—'Exam. of all the cases in which a vendor passes to vendee more than the former has'. From 6 July to 8 October he kept a graph recording his hours of work each day. He expressed dissatisfaction on discovering that the average over the whole period worked out only at 7·8 hours. He made up his mind to push the figure up: 'If I work from October 9 to December 9 at 11 per day', he wrote, 'average from July 6–Dec. 9 = 9.'

No doubt he maintained the same cracking pace right up to his Tripos next summer, for although Wolstenholme thought him 'slight and frail',[16] he had plenty of stamina. There is evidence in his letters before and after the examination that he finished the race in good health and heart. Of all the evidences of his success—his double First, his prizes, the congratulations of his tutors—the one most worth quoting is a letter that he received from the greatest academic lawyer produced by the English universities within the past century and more. 'Dear Mr Smuts,' the letter began, 'will this do? I have seldom written a testimonial with a better will. . . .' The writer went on to tell Smuts that he had it in him to achieve a task which no German could tackle and no Englishman was likely to tackle—he had it in him to become the great Romanist, the Ihering of English law. 'I am going to ask you [he concluded] to accept a copy of Bracton's Note Book which will come to you from the Press in memory of Yours very truly, F. W. MAITLAND.'[17]

To remain in Cambridge, to enjoy the comforts and cultivation of a Combination Room, to achieve eminence in the academic study of law—these were the prospects which now opened out before Smuts. They did not allure him. He was committed in heart and mind both to the world of philosophy and to the world of South African politics.

CHAPTER 4

THE WAY HOME

By three years of hard work Smuts had earned an extra year which he might, had he wished, have made an easy one. He had been the first man ever to take both parts of the Law Tripos in one year and had been placed not only first but 'brilliantly first' in the examinations. He had won the George Long Prize in Roman Law and Jurisprudence, an unusual achievement, because the prize was never awarded except to candidates of the highest distinction and in most years was not awarded at all. On the recommendation of his examiners, Maitland and Bond, he was granted an extra year of the Ebden scholarship and an extra sum of money to make good its depreciated value. Six months later, in December 1894, he passed the Honours Examination of the Inns of Court, again first in his year and with two prizes, each of £50. At long last he had escaped the curse of poverty.

And yet he still denied himself relaxation. After the Law Tripos, he had allowed himself a month in Bismarck's Strassbourg but had spent his time there reading English conveyancing and German philosophy.[1] From Strassbourg he went to London to read for the bar in the chambers of John Roskill, 1 Paper Buildings, Middle Temple. It appears from some telegrams and letters exchanged in later years between Roskill and Smuts that they got on well together; but no contemporary record remains of their relationship or, indeed, of any other aspect of Smuts's life in London, except his work. Probably his life was all work, barring the hard exercise that he took walking round and round Kensington Gardens or some other open space. Nothing that he said or wrote in later years contains any suggestion of his ever going to a play or a concert, or visiting the National Gallery, or wandering through London with his eyes open to its historical splendour or architectural beauty or human oddity.

In the Middle Temple he read his law-books. In the British Museum he read philosophy and every bit of published print that he could find by or about Walt Whitman. In his lodgings at night

47

he worked on a book of his own, *Walt Whitman: A Study in the Evolution of Personality*.[2]

What was it in Whitman that appealed to him? Half a century later he read Fausset's book and wrote to a friend: 'Fausset has a great deal of fresh material about Whitman which I did not have in 1894, although I then read everything there was in the British Museum....Whitman did a great service to me in making me appreciate the Natural Man and freeing me from much theological or conventional preconceptions due to my very early pious up-bringing. It was a sort of liberation, as St Paul was liberated from the Law and its damnations by his Damascus vision. Sin ceased to dominate my view of life, and this was a great release as I was inclined to be severely puritanical in all things.'[3] He went on to admit that he had discovered in after years and from deeper thought that there was more in the old view of things than Whitman understood. Still, there can be no doubt that he always placed Whitman alongside Shelley and Goethe in the front rank of the great Liberators of his youth.

The deeper he delved into Whitman in those months of 1894 and 1895 the deeper his conviction grew that Whitman and he were kindred spirits. He discovered affinities of ancestry and upbringing: Whitman had had Dutch blood in his veins as well as English—a mixture of sober strains conducive to democratic realism and 'devotion to the common and even commonplace'—but Whitman's mother, like his own mother, was not at all commonplace; she was a woman of rare spiritual sensitivity, who lived her life in the 'inner light' of Quaker experience. (Could Smuts have foreseen the time when he himself, like Whitman in his later years, would share this experience, or something akin to it?) Whitman, like himself, was deeply influenced in his early childhood by the splendour of his natural surroundings—alas, not the mountains; but in their stead the ocean: Smuts imagined Whitman growing up on the shores of Long Island like Heraclitus on the shores of Asia Minor, picturing the universe as incessant flux and discovering his own significance within the flux, 'a point in the Biodynamic Immensity'.

Whitman, besides, was a man of the present age, a 'new' man, about whom there would be many new things to say. Smuts had the natural ambition of the young author to make a big literary hit. And yet the merits that he claimed for his book were not so much literary as philosophical. He explained in his first chapter that he would have been just as ready to write about Goethe as about Whitman. For it was not the particular man that mattered to him so much as Man in general: not this or that person, but Personality.

He still remained, and would remain throughout his life, in hot pursuit of the paradox that had puzzled him in his boyhood, when he felt himself joyously akin to all the natural things on his father's farm but felt himself also to be a separate, lonely being, Jan Smuts, a person. As a student at Stellenbosch he had grown to understand nature as a process, which human intelligence was summarising in a series of laws; yet neither the process nor the laws, he declared, were the whole of reality; the most real thing in the universe was the person. As a student at Cambridge he had written a paper anticipating by a decade or more the philosophy of emergent evolution, picturing the universe as a developing continuum of atom, cell, mind, personality—a continuum stretching from the particle of the physicists to the soul of Plato and St Paul. Surely the soul was a more complicated, more astonishing thing than the particle? Surely the person was a proper object of study? But by what method?

In his book on Whitman he set out to demonstrate a method. Scientists, he said (and here he was going beyond the argument of his Cambridge essay), had been too readily satisfied with the study of origins and of the simpler phenomena in the evolutionary chain: or, if they did sometimes consider the more complex phenomena, they were prone to explain the complex in terms of the simple, 'to explain, for instance, human morality and progress by reference to the principles which seem to dominate the animal world'. Psychologists, on the other hand, appeared to be victims of an opposite fallacy, for they wrote about mind as if it were a superior and separate entity, as if minds did not belong to persons and persons to the natural world.

In the mid-1890's, when the analytical school of psychology was still predominant, this reproach was well merited. The psychologists of that time paid little attention to the subconscious part of personality, which Smuts thought immensely important, and split the conscious part into fragmentary activities: cognition, conation, volition, etc. Analysis of this kind, said Smuts, will by itself get us nowhere: we need synthesis also. To know a person we must know the whole of him and know him as a whole. He wrote his book about Whitman to prove that the thing could be done.[4]

His attempt was a brave one; but, writing as he did only three years after Whitman's death, he did not possess many of the materials which later on would be thought essential for a biographical study. Nor did he possess the sophistication of a later time; for all his sympathy, he remained an innocent young man who could not understand—for example—the homosexual impulse in Whitman. Despite these and other impediments, he wrote a powerful book. Had it been published when it was written, it would have advanced the study of Whitman. Unpublished, it advances the study of Smuts.

In the young Whitman he discovered a 'cosmic catholicity', a faculty of 'acceptivity' so deeply rooted in the emotional life that it enabled him 'to take both sides at the same time', to absorb each separate sensation, to receive each separate idea, although these sensations and ideas contained in their totality contradictions which the conscious intellect would have rejected. In the maturing Whitman he discovered his own zeal for synthesis, his own passionate craving to apprehend and comprehend this puzzling totality as an ordered and harmonious Whole. 'I will not make poems in reference to particulars, but I will make poems, songs, thoughts with reference to ensemble.' That quotation was from the period which Smuts named 'period of naturalism'. In Whitman's maturer phase, which he named 'period of spiritualism' (perhaps the label did not appear so incongruous then as it does now) he recognised, or believed that he recognised, a deepening apprehension of *ensemble*, a philosophic vision of 'the ultimate harmony of all things'—of Nature; and of Man as belonging to the natural world, but transcending it in his endeavour to understand its laws and to conduct his life within them and beyond them; of Man in quest of Deity.

> Nature and Man shall be disjoined and diffused no more
> The true Son of God shall absolutely fuse them.

The design of a later book which Smuts had already in his head was implicit in some sentences that he wrote about Whitman's *ensemble* and his own *Idea of the Whole*. Here, he said, was 'One of the Ideas just referred to that have the force and value of real entities. It has perhaps not yet exercised any great historical influence in the shaping of thought and belief; but I venture to think that it will become one of the mightiest intellectual and spiritual forces of the future.' He felt so confident, when he wrote this sentence, that the world of thought would soon be acclaiming his first book and waiting impatiently for the second. Instead, he spent his last weeks in London hawking his *Whitman* from one unresponsive publisher to the next. Longmans wrote politely about it; Chapman and Hall, advised by George Meredith, wrote with warmth; but no English firm of that time would accept the commercial risk of a book on Walt Whitman—a man 'so little considered in this country'.[5]

By June 1895 Smuts was back in Cape Town with the manuscript of his unwanted book in his luggage. He still had faith in it and was not yet ready to give up all hope of seeing it in print. In early September he offered it to the *Nineteenth Century* for publication as a series of articles: if the editor would accept only the last two chapters, he said, he would be greatly obliged. It was a long shot and it did not come off. So at last he admitted his defeat in the great world of letters and switched his energies upon the task immediately ahead, to make a reputation for himself in the little world of Cape Colony: more urgent still, to make a livelihood and to get married.

During his four years of absence life had gone hard with Isie Krige. She had wanted to study medicine, an unheard-of thing for a young girl in that place and time: anyway, her parents had many other children to bring up and could not afford to keep her so long at college. So she went away to teach in a little country school at the wage of £5 a month and found herself so poor, 'dat as ek onverwags 'n sikspens gekry het was dit vir my 'n groot ding'. This was the picture she retained fifty years later of her teaching years—it would have been a wonderful stroke of luck for her if even an extra sixpence had come her way.

But of course everything would come right now that Jan was home again. And Jan himself was just as sure that the briefs and fees would come in quickly so that he and Isie could get married. Meanwhile he kept himself afloat by writing articles for the newspapers. In an article that he dashed off within a few weeks of his return he discussed the recent session of the Cape Assembly with as much confidence as if he had been present from the very beginning to report its proceedings.

The political scene did not seem to him very different from what it had been at the time of his departure from Cape Town four years ago. Cecil Rhodes was still at the summit, premier of Cape Colony by support of the Afrikander Bond and master of Rhodesia-to-be by his own financial and personal power. In both capacities he had met a few difficulties; but he had come through them triumphantly. There had been a period during 1892 and the first part of 1893 when the financial prospects of the Chartered Company appeared uncertain; but victory over Lobengula's impis restored the confidence of investors. There had been some embarrassment in April 1893 when John X. Merriman and two of his political friends withdrew from the Cape government; but Rhodes reshuffled his ministry and won the elections of 1894. The great man of the Afrikander Bond, J. H. Hofmeyr, resigned his seat in parliament for reasons of health; but he retained his hold over the Bond and the Bond retained its faith in Rhodes.

On this rock of solidarity between Cape Dutch and Cape English the future destinies of Cape Colony and the whole of South Africa, as Smuts envisaged them, appeared secure. The ties of interest and sentiment joining Rhodes and the Afrikander Bond seemed so strong that Smuts took their permanence for granted. The Bond was predominantly a farmers' party with a zeal for the free importation of everything except competitive foodstuffs; Rhodes offered it moderate agricultural protection and the prospect (if he could make good his plan of a railways and customs union) of an expanding market on the Rand goldfields. As regards Native policy, there existed within the Bond some diversity of opinion but a blessed unconcern with doctrine: on the political side, nobody wanted either a wrangle about first principles or a multiplication of voters in the newly annexed and densely populated districts east of the Kei river: on the economic side, everybody wanted a brimming labour market in the neighbourhood of his own farm, just as Rhodes wanted it in Kimberley. The franchise act of 1892 quietly settled the political question, without any disturbance of the Cape's 'colour blind' tradition, by raising the property qualification for the vote and imposing a rudimentary educational qualification. The Glen Grey Act of 1894, among its other provisions, stimulated the labour supply by imposing a tax on all non-landholding Native males who did not go out to work for three months in the year.

Hofmeyr's ambition to achieve equality between the Dutch and English languages was completely acceptable to Rhodes, a lifelong zealot (theoretically, if not always in practice) for the solidarity of the Teutonic peoples; in 1892 he helped Hofmeyr to bring Dutch nearer to equality with English in the schools of Cape Colony. He and Hofmeyr were just as much at one with each other in their advocacy of 'colonialism', which meant at that time the very opposite of what it came to mean half a century later: not imperial domination but 'elimination of the imperial factor', not the subordination but the vigorous assertion of local and national interests.

To Rhodes and Hofmeyr alike the local interest of the Cape signified the national interest of South Africa in the making. That is why Hofmeyr tolerated, and in the end approved, Rhodes's enterprises of economic and territorial expansion in the north. The time had been when he had doubted the wisdom of policies which showed every appearance of stealing a march upon the northern Boers and hemming them in; at any time, he would have been ready to work with them in an equal partnership for the common good of South Africa. But there was no agreed definition of the common good. Ever since the goldmines of the Rand had brought wealth and power to the Transvaal, its leaders had seemed set upon playing their own separate hand; if ever they thought at all about a united South Africa, it was a South Africa made in their own image, a domination of the old ways over the new ways, of Boers over all the rest: the very opposite of the South Africa upon which Hofmeyr had set his heart. So it seemed to him. It also seemed to him that new ideas and new leadership were bound sooner or later to prevail in the Transvaal, and that everything would come right with time and patience. He did not know that Rhodes was at the end of his patience.

In comparison with Hofmeyr, Smuts of course knew practically nothing either about Rhodes or any of the other important persons whose plans or plots were shaping the history of his country. He knew nothing about the retiring High Commissioner, Sir Henry Loch, who had submitted twelve months earlier to a disapproving Colonial Secretary proposals for a rising in Johannesburg, to be supported by a military incursion from the Bechuanaland Protectorate. He knew nothing about the new High Commissioner, Sir Hercules Robinson, returning to a South Africa well acquainted with him and well disposed towards him. He knew nothing about the new Colonial Secretary, Joseph Chamberlain, who took office in the very month of his own return to Cape Town. He knew nothing about President Kruger and his ministers nor about Charles Leonard, Lionel Phillips and the other leaders of the Uitlanders. He had never been north of the Vaal river, nor even the Orange river.

That omission, anyway, could be repaired. Towards the end of October he published in *De Volksbode* the account of a recent visit he had made to the Transvaal, at the very time when Kruger, by closing the fords over the Vaal river, had transformed a war of railway rates into an acute political crisis.[6] As a true Cape Colonist and (he believed) a patriotic South African, Smuts took a hotly partisan view of that crisis; but as a philosophic student of politics he wrote sympathetically about the dilemma of the Transvaalers: there they were, a small and simple pastoral people, deeply attached to their old way of life and suddenly foisted with a new, super-modern industry and an immense, unwanted concourse of urban immigrants. They were, however, not at all averse from 'milking' the new industry and the new immigrants. And they had been stupid enough to call in a crowd of Hollanders who were now running the country on the principle of *divide et impera*. It would have been far better, Smuts suggested, to have called in civilised Cape Colonists, experienced in the more difficult but more rewarding arts of reconciliation and cooperation.

All this was good Hofmeyr doctrine, perhaps with some extra emphasis of his own at the end. It seemed to him dangerous that the South African Republic should be putting Hollanders in the key positions. In an essay that he wrote about this time he restated the theme of his undergraduate papers on South African nationality, with some variations suggested by the new conditions. The emergent South African nation, he said, was battling against three hindrances: first, the English tendency, the reluctance of English-speaking South Africans to send their roots down deep into South African soil: secondly, the Afrikander tendency, the desire of the Franco-Dutch section of the white population to keep itself apart from the rest or even to impose its own will upon the rest: thirdly, the Hollander tendency, that recent poisonous excrescence north of the Vaal which was spreading division and embitterment throughout South Africa.[7]

Smuts had examined Paul Kruger's claim to South African leadership and had rejected it. Towards the end of October 1895 a great opportunity came his way of proclaiming himself a follower of the alternative claimant, Cecil Rhodes. Enemies had challenged the Colossus in his own stronghold of Kimberley. They were, in their way, formidable enemies—Olive Schreiner, who commanded a large reading public throughout the English-speaking world, and her husband Samuel Cronwright, a prickly and pertinacious radical. The Cronwright-Schreiners had written a paper on the political situation of South Africa, in which they attacked Rhodes for misleading or seducing the Afrikander Bond and making it the instrument of his capitalist plots in the north. They called upon all South Africans, irrespective of race or colour, to join forces against Rhodes. Cronwright delivered this paper as an address to the Literary Society of Kimberley; subsequently, he and his wife published it as a pamphlet under their joint authorship.

Back in Cape Town, Smuts had by this time made himself well acquainted with the leaders of the Bond. They appreciated both his ability and his ardent support of the party line, and decided that he was the very man to send to Kimberley to deal with the Cronwright-Schreiners. So on 29 October he found himself on the platform of the Kimberley Town Hall, speaking to an audience which the town newspaper next day called large, representative and enthusiastic. Cronwright, however, said that the hall was only half full and the speech a failure.[8]

Smuts, probably, had written it out just like one of his essays and had tried to loosen and liven it up when he saw he was speaking over the heads of Kimberley's miners, clerks and shopkeepers. The speech as reported is long, wordy and more commonplace in its imagery than was customary with him. Still, it possessed clarity of design and purpose. Smuts saw South Africa face to face with two fundamental problems: first, consolidation of the white race; secondly, white policy towards the other races.

The need to fuse or consolidate the 'two Teutonic peoples' of South Africa seemed to him self-evident. 'At the southern corner of a vast continent, peopled by over 100,000,000 barbarians, about half a million whites have taken up a position, with a view not only to working out their own destiny, but also of using that position as a basis for lifting up and opening up that vast dead-weight of immemorial barbarism and animal savagery to the light and blessing of ordered civilisation. Unless the white race closes its ranks in this country, its position will soon become untenable in the face of that

55

overwhelming majority of prolific barbarism.' Material forces, he said, could not by themselves draw the two white peoples together; the sentiment of nationality must work with them. That sentiment had found its first powerful expression in the Afrikander Bond and had reached a higher stage in the Bond's partnership with Rhodes. Suppose that the new capitalistic society of Kimberley had come into conflict with an entrenched and unyielding Afrikanderdom? This was not an imaginary danger: Kimberley might even now be suffering the troubles of Johannesburg; the white community of Cape Colony, like that of the Transvaal, might even now be rent and divided, save for the leadership of Rhodes and the Bond. The same leadership had saved them from another great danger. Suppose that a foreign Power—to be precise, Germany, which was already established in South-west Africa—wanted to take a hand in South African affairs? Suppose, simultaneously, a northward expansion of the South African Republic into Central Africa? The rivalries of the great European Powers would then be sucked and drawn into the very heart of South Africa. There could be no greater danger than this to the unity of the white peoples. From this danger Rhodes had delivered them by his northward march. It was the march of South African nationhood.

Smuts defended the policy of Rhodes on every front. He held up to ridicule the charges of corruption brought against him and defended his policy of moderate agricultural protection. But his main concern, once he had answered the advocates of 'The Little Cape Policy', was to defend the Native policy of Rhodes. For some parts of that policy Kimberley was already enthusiastic; towards other parts it was, to say the least, lukewarm. Kimberley, taking always for granted the sacred custom of '£1 a day for the white man and £1 a week for the black', was ready for the Glen Grey Act or anything else that would teach the Natives 'the dignity of labour'. Kimberley knew already that the democratic aspirations of the Cronwright-Schreiners were moonshine. But Smuts was not content to leave it at that; he insisted that the white people of South Africa had duties to perform as well as rights to assert and interests to defend. 'I for one', he said, 'consider the position of the white race in South Africa one of the gravest responsibility and difficulty. They must be the guardians of their own safety and development; at the same time they are the trustees for the coloured races. The situation is unique.' Because the situation was unique, it could not be treated by an appeal to abstract principle, least of all the democratic principle. That principle, said Smuts, had never yet been applied without qualification: not even in England, which still retained the House of Lords and stopped short of universal suffrage: not even in New Zealand, which had established a differential franchise for the Maoris. Only in the United States was the democratic principle enthroned, but its enthronement there was a pretence; the law conceded democratic equality but physical force took it away.

> I mention these facts [he said] simply to remind you that the question of the application of advanced political principles to any people, or part of a people, is not an abstract, but a very practical question, to be decided on the facts of each individual case. . . . Now the mistake that has been made in the past is to assume that the full and entire democratic formula applied to our South African racial conditions. Mr Saul Solomon and others looked upon the abstract political or religious formula of universal equality as a safe rule of practical politics. I am afraid they were wrong. Their theory would have been inapplicable to civilised Europe; *a fortiori*, it was inapplicable to barbarous Africa. And I think one of the most conspicuous advances we have made in Cape politics during the last decade or more consists precisely in recognising that they were wrong. . . . that we have come down from the Utopian cloudland of abstract theory; and that now for the first time we are in a position to consider our great racial problem on its merits.

In Native policy, Smuts proclaimed himself an empiricist. The contending dogmas of equality and of inequality, of unity and of separateness were equally repugnant to him. He took his stand not upon dogma but upon the situation which had been created by history and the needs which arose from this situation, so far as he could interpret them. The white people of South Africa held political power; let them exercise it in a spirit of responsibility and prudence. If they abused their power by oppressing the Natives, they would arouse feelings of resentment dangerous to themselves. If they allowed the Natives to sink into degradation, that degradation would infect their own civilisation. As in his student days, it was the 'browning' of the white man's character, not merely of his skin, that Smuts feared. It seemed to him perverse to deny that the majority of the black people here and now were raw, barbarous, uncivilised— whichever word he used, his meaning was clear enough: people in that stage of development must receive differential treatment under the law of the land. But an appreciable number of the black people were getting beyond that stage of development: this was a process which the law ought to recognise and, with all appropriate caution, to encourage.

Smuts saw this undogmatic, practical approach exemplified in the recent Franchise Act and the Glen Grey Act. Under the leadership of Mr Rhodes, Native policy, like everything else in South Africa, was taking the right direction. He ended his speech with a panegyric on Rhodes.

The speech made him widely known as a rising young politician. Among the messages of congratulation which he received was a letter from the Attorney-General, W. P. Schreiner, Olive's brother, who welcomed with especial warmth his exposure of the 'mischievous fallacy' that abstract democratic principles were applicable to the complex racial situation of South Africa.[9] Olive Schreiner took the opposite view, not only on Native policy and other particular arguments, but upon the major premiss underlying the whole speech, namely, the trustworthiness of Rhodes. She had been unable to attend the meeting, but her husband was in the hall, approving the honesty of the speaker but rejecting his arguments: 'He is very earnest and sincere, but he *doesn't know Rhodes*!' That was the comment he made to his wife when he got home from the meeting. Evidently they talked to each other a good deal about Smuts during the next two months. On the last day of the year, when news came through of the Jameson Raid, he exclaimed— 'What will Smuts say now!!!'[10]

Smuts did not know what to say or what to think. The ground had seemed so firm under his feet; but now he felt himself to be in the quicksands. He did not know where to look for a path. From the short-term political point of view, his bewilderment did not much matter; after all, he had no inside information and no political responsibility; he was merely an aspiring young man who had wanted to enter politics and had answered the wrong cue. Whether he knew it or not, he would have to wait two years or more before receiving a second call and nothing that he said or did in the meantime would make much difference to the course of South African politics. All the same, his personal convictions were destined in long term to play a large part in the history of his country and even in short term he had some influence as a political journalist. Consequently, there is historical as well as biographical interest in following his attempts to get things clear within his own mind.

To begin with, he had to define his attitude towards Rhodes. He was reluctant at first to join the hue and cry against him. Rhodes, he wrote, *appeared* to be guilty; but appearances were sometimes deceptive. Surely it would be prudent to wait a little? Some people were inciting the Afrikander Bond to declare immediate war upon Rhodes: but the Bond would do better to maintain a watchful neutrality until the facts became clear.[11] How long Smuts was able to hold his own judgment in suspense is uncertain; perhaps only a few days, for on 14 January he appeared with John X. Merriman on an anti-Rhodes platform at Philadelphia, near Malmesbury. He could no longer doubt that Rhodes had betrayed his trust and had thereby destroyed the whole fabric of policy which he, Smuts, had expounded so confidently a few months back at Kimberley. But what was the alternative? He could see no alternative that satisfied his reason; but his emotions told him that Jingoism was incorrigible, that 'blood is thicker than water', that Afrikaners must rally to each other across the frontiers to defend their language, their tradition and their destiny as a free people.[12]

Smuts could never give his loyalty by halves; he must always give it fully, or not at all. He could no longer give it to Rhodes. But no more could he bring himself to vilify Rhodes. In July 1896, when the local committee of inquiry had established beyond doubt that Rhodes had betrayed his trust as prime minister of Cape Colony, Smuts wrote, not in anger, but in lament for fallen greatness.[13] That was still his mood a year later when he recalled the devotion of his people to Rhodes up to the Jameson Raid. 'The Dutch set aside all considerations of blood and nationality and loved him and trusted him and served him because they believed that *he* was the man to carry out that great Idea of an internally sovereign and united S. Africa in which the white race would be supreme—which has been the cry of our forefathers even as it is our cry today. Here at last our Moses had appeared—and it made no difference that he was an Egyptian in blood.' This was not merely vivid historical description but a cry from the heart. Smuts, surely, was writing not only about his people's feelings but his own when he added these poignant words: 'It was hero worship pure and simple.'[14]

Smuts at first could see no person, no cause, worthy of the loyalty which Rhodes had thrown away; but his feelings told him that he was more likely to find them in the Transvaal than in Cape Colony. About this time he became intimate with Olive Schreiner, who was contributing to the *Fortnightly Review* a series of articles under the heading, 'Stray Thoughts on South Africa'. They expressed with power her passionate but contradictory intuitions: anti-capitalist, pro-Boer, pro-Native, anti-Whitehall—she believed that she could be all of these contradictory things at the same time. Smuts reviewed her articles as they came out, agreeing with her in some things, disagreeing with her in others. She wrote to thank him and to argue with him. It would be a great pleasure, she said, if she could meet him; they could have a political fight![15] They met and made friends. From this time onwards it became her habit to bombard him (until in later years she switched the bombardment to his wife) with long sprawling letters of passionate intensity. The moral and emotional heat which she turned upon him was an incitement, almost always, towards extremist action.

Smuts himself had a passionate heart but he also had a cool head. In his attempt to take systematic stock of the causes and consequences of the Jameson Raid, he had felt the need, first of all, to define his attitude towards Rhodes. After that, he felt himself compelled to define his attitude towards the British government. There is no evidence in his papers that he suspected Chamberlain of having been privy to the Rhodes–Jameson plot; at any rate, he made no attempt to probe the problem in detail. What interested him far more was the general trend and purpose of British policy under Chamberlain's direction. Between February and July 1897, when the parliamentary committee at Westminster was investigating the Raid, he kept asking himself what its purpose was? To clear Rhodes? To arraign the Transvaal? To break the Chartered Company? But it was not, he said, either Rhodes or the Transvaal or the Chartered Company that was on trial. It was British policy that was on trial. The trend of policy throughout the British Empire, it used to be said, was from force to consent. There now seemed to be signs of a reverse trend. If it were really so, the British government and people had better start counting the cost. They might find it as high as the cost of the American Revolution, or higher.

The immediate threat of force, he believed, was directed against the Transvaal. Whether the threat was intended seriously or not could easily be tested: the acceptance or rejection of arbitration on the matters in dispute would give the answer. In giving evidence before the British committee of inquiry, W. P. Schreiner had called for arbitration; but Chamberlain had appeared to rule it out, on the ground that it was inconsistent with the rights of Great Britain as the Paramount Power in South Africa. Smuts let himself go on that. As a lawyer, he could understand the concepts of suzerainty, protection or confederation; but paramountcy, he declared, was 'unknown to the vocabulary of jurisprudence and was simply invented by journalists for the slipshod purposes of their craft'.

The South African Republic was an independent State, even if it was a little one and weak in military power. Smuts took his stand upon this fundamental principle and would be ready, if need be, to fight for it. He did not yet know whether or not it would come to a fight, for he recognised both the legal complexities arising from the Convention of London, which defined the relations between Great Britain and the Republic, and the social and political complexities arising from the activities of the go-ahead Uitlanders amidst the slow-moving Boer population. He thought that it would be possible, given patience and good will, to unravel these complexities; but he was beginning to doubt whether patience and good will were virtues which 'the vigorous Colonial Secretary' possessed. One thing he felt sure about: that the British were far weaker, the Boers far stronger than Chamberlain realised. Schreiner, in giving evidence in London, had affirmed the loyalty of Cape Colony to the British connection, and he was right up to a point; but the sentiment of loyalty was not so deep as the sentiment of kinship. The loyalty of the Cape Dutch was conditional; it depended on the conviction that Great Britain stood for justice and fair play; if this conviction were destroyed, the loyalty would be destroyed with it. Rhodes had already shaken it. Did Chamberlain want to break it? Was he ready to risk war against the united Afrikaner people, and against all the British South Africans who would join their Afrikaner brothers if it should come to a fight for national freedom? It sickened Smuts to think of having such a war forced upon South Africa. Give the South Africans the chance of setting their own house in order! 'We are weary of the past; we are weary of our own errors and the errors of Downing Street, old, new and newer; and our prayer now is that we may be left alone to redeem ourselves.'[16] Smuts failed to find a publisher for this powerful article—if, indeed, he had even tried to find one. Perhaps he had written it with the main purpose of clearing his own head.

He was no longer in close touch with any of the politicians. In September or October of 1896 the news had got round that he was proposing to leave Cape Town. 'Are you going to the Transvaal?', Professor Marais wrote to him. 'I had so wished that you would stay among us. We need leaders. But who can interfere if your calling is there and not here? God be merciful to our poor country. I mourn for it. We have no leaders of *character*....God knows that I have sometimes hoped that you were the man chosen by God.'[17] But Smuts no longer believed that leadership in South Africa was a prerogative of the Cape. Politics in the Cape had run into a dead end: after Cecil Rhodes, Sir Gordon Sprigg—he took no joy in pursuing that small game. The political stage seemed cluttered up with inept elderly actors. There seemed no room on it for an ardent young man like himself: or even if there were room, he could see no part that he would find worth playing. Despite everything that he had said about Paul Kruger's Republic, he hoped that it would offer him better opportunities than Cape Colony had done.

He was thinking not merely, perhaps not mainly, of political opportunities but of the chance to get married. His friend Berthault van der Riet had had the luck to get appointed to a chair at Stellenbosch, and in March 1897 Smuts had submitted his own name for a lectureship at the South Africa College. He desperately wanted it, and said on his own behalf all the flattering things that his tutors and examiners had said about him; but the electoral committee chose a lawyer of early middle age who had seen service on the Bench.[18] One cannot help speculating about the difference it would have made to the history of South Africa (and of some other countries) if Smuts had settled down at the age of twenty-five in quiet academic groves. Instead, he ranged hungrily through Cape Town, living on his pickings as a tutor and a journalist. The College gave him a little examining. His articles for the *Telegraph* brought him in about £10 a week, by far the greater part of his journalistic earnings. He had not paid back the money that he owed to Professor Marais. Isie Krige was still fending for herself in the country on her wage of £5 a month.

In retrospect, his years in Cambridge and London seemed to him golden in comparison with the year that he had endured in Cape Town. Before his departure on 20 January, 1897, he checked with Marais the total of his debt and found it to be £323. 3s. Before twelve months had elapsed, he had reduced this total almost by half. It was a wonderful new experience for him to find himself, almost as soon as he had settled in Johannesburg, capable of earning a decent living at the Bar.

At the end of April 1897 he appeared unannounced at the house of Mr and Mrs Krige in Stellenbosch and said that he wanted to get married to Isie the next day because the day after he would have to leave for the Transvaal again. It was not quite so sudden as it might have seemed, for although there had never been any formal engagement between Jan and Isie he had 'served for her' for ten years. They were married by Professor Marais, 'the man who was so good to us': so Mrs Smuts used to recall his memory in her old age. They made their home on Hospital Hill in Johannesburg, in a house which was pulled down many years later to make way for a new building in which the United Party, the political organisation which served Smuts, had its headquarters for some years.

They were happy. He was working hard and doing well at the Bar but did not allow his whole life to be engulfed in work. They began to read French together. He bought a piano and music for her to play. They used to sing Schubert's songs together, particularly his favourite cycle *Die Schöne Müllerin*. They had sadness to share with each other as well as joy. In 1898 twins were born to them but died within a few weeks. Soon after that they set up house in Pretoria, following Smuts's appointment in June as State Attorney. In April 1899 a healthy son was born to them. They called him Koosie, short for Jacobus: so he was christened in accordance with the Boer custom of naming a boy after his paternal grandfather.

Fourteen months later, news of the death of his little son came to Smuts in the Magaliesburg, where he was fighting the British.

PART II

WAR AND PEACE, 1898–1905

CHAPTER 5

COMMITMENT

AT the beginning of June 1898 Smuts took office under President Kruger as State Attorney of the South African Republic. He was not a burgher of the Republic, he had had no parliamentary or governmental experience and he was only twenty-eight years old—according to the law of the Republic, two years too young for ministerial office. For all these reasons, his appointment might have been thought surprising; yet nobody expressed surprise. On the contrary, there had been much discussion in the newspapers during the last two weeks of May of his chances of being appointed State Secretary, the minister responsible under the President for conducting the foreign policy of the Republic.

It is obvious that he must have made a reputation for himself during his short period of residence, only eighteen months, in Johannesburg. Of course, Johannesburg was a small community, hardly more than 50,000 white people, with the English and Afrikaans speakers roughly half and half in number, although the former had a much larger proportion of adult males. Among the little group of professional men everybody must have become intimately acquainted with everybody else. Smuts had joined the society of law teachers and was fond of telling his pupils that they were not merely technicians or money grubbers but members of 'a consecrated priesthood, working in a worthy manner for the attainment of the highest ideals of humanity'.[1] If some of his colleagues in that raw town thought him too idealistic, they had to admit that he had prodigious learning and was the equal of anybody in arguing a case. Except for one scurrilous journalist, nobody had ever questioned his integrity.[2] The *Volkstem* described him as 'a young man of strong character and well-balanced mind and with strong opinions regarding the rights of the people'. The *Standard* admitted that he was rather young to join the government; but youth, as Pitt had said, was a fault that would be cured with age. The *Star*, an organ of the Uitlanders, insisted that he was too young even if he were as brilliant as Pitt; but it agreed that he was 'an able lawyer of good repute and conscientious'. Finally, it is worth while quoting an opinion of him given nine months later by his most redoubtable political enemy. 'I am inclined to think him high minded', wrote Milner, 'as he is certainly able, but whether he has real staying power and real political insight I have no idea.' Milner was destined to be given more proof than he had ever bargained for of the staying power, and more proof of the political insight than he would ever have thought possible.[3]

Smuts had been introduced by his friend Hans Malan, first to Piet Grobler, Kruger's nephew and secretary, and through him to the President himself. For a time there had been a real chance of his being made State Secretary; but in the end his youth barred him from this more important office and it was given to F. W. Reitz, ex-President of the Orange Free State, with the expectation that Smuts's turn might come later on. 'Reitz is weak', Malan telegraphed from Pretoria, 'and will not persevere long and then your turn. Are you satisfied?'[4]

Smuts was exhilarated, as well he might be, at getting such a chance; and so was his wife. She rehearsed him for the part he would have to play when he took the oath of office and agreed that his critics were right; he *did* look far too young, with his slight figure and his flaxen hair and his clear, glowing complexion which was always ready (such a nuisance it was to him, even after he had grown middle-aged) to flush like a girl's. Looking him up and down, she decided that he would have to dress in something more imposing than his trim brown suit, so when the great day came he set off for Pretoria in a cut-away coat, black trousers with a stripe, a stiff white shirt and a grey top-hat. However, she decided before long that he would never need the top-hat again, so she fixed handles to it and used it as a sewing-basket. She soon felt herself quite at home with the old President, although at the beginning she had not known quite what to make of his ponderous humour. 'Whatever were you doing to marry such an ugly woman?', he exclaimed to Smuts when he brought her along to be presented. But then he turned to Isie and exclaimed 'And whatever were *you* doing to marry such an ugly man?' So that was all right.*

* 'Wat het jou makeer om met so 'n lelike vrou te trou?'—and the equivalent to Smuts: this is how Mrs Smuts told the story sixty-three years later. The swearing-in ceremony took place on 8 June, not in the Volksraad, but in the house of the President, who was ill at that time.

1. The young State Attorney

The old President was charmed by the vitality and good looks of the young couple and he soon realised that his new State Attorney was also a man of formidable power and drive. In the memoirs which he dictated in his exile he described him as a man of 'iron will', destined, if he were spared, to play a great role in the history of South Africa.[5] It might have been expected that the intellectual gap between the brilliant young lawyer and the old Boer, who read no book except the Bible and preached to the simple congregations of the Dopper Church, would have been too wide to bridge; but it was bridged by the plain virtues of loyalty and courage which moulded both men on the heroic scale and by the deep personal affection which united them. Their relations, Smuts used to say, were 'like those of father and son'.*

It is necessary to consider briefly the state of the nation at the time when Smuts took office. To begin with, something should be said about two controversies of mainly domestic concern upon which he held strong views. The first was the habit of appointing Dutchmen to high office in the Republic; as has been seen, Smuts had bitterly attacked this 'Hollander tendency' soon after his return from England, and his own appointment, with that of Reitz, in succession to the Hollanders Coster and Leyds, may be regarded as a victory for the argument that home-grown patriots ought to hold the key positions.† The second controversy was a shattering row between the Chief Justice, Sir J. G. Kotzé, and the President and Volksraad.

In January 1897, giving judgment in the case of *Brown* v. *Leyds N.O.*, the High Court had claimed such drastic powers of judicial review ('the testing right') as to cast doubts upon the validity of most of the laws hitherto in force in the Republic.[6] The root of the trouble was the slipshod character of the constitution, which in origin had been a political compromise between the warring factions rather than a coherent legal document. In the Orange Free State, things had been better arranged; the well-constructed constitution of 1854 had never given any trouble and nobody had seriously questioned the right of the Court of Appeal (established in 1874) to interpret its provisions. The constitution of the South African

* See p. 189 below.
† Leyds's appointment as Minister Extraordinary in Europe cannot, however, be regarded as a demotion.

Republic, on the other hand, was so full of theoretical obscurities and practical contradictions that it had never been taken very seriously. In particular, the Volksraad had from the very beginning ignored the distinction laid down in the constitution between *wetten* (laws) and *besluiten* (resolutions). The former were supposed to be the vehicle of all important legislation and only became effective after they had been published for three months; the latter, which became effective immediately they were carried by a simple majority, were not supposed to be true legislation. In practice, the Volksraad from the very beginning had enacted nearly all its legislation, including amendments to the constitution itself, by means of *besluiten*. No doubt this was constitutionally unfortunate; but suddenly to invalidate the past practice of four decades would have had the most shattering political consequences. As the State Attorney explained to the Volksraad, 'bad laws are no good, that is unanswerable, but worse than bad laws is legal uncertainty, not to know what laws one has'. The judgment given in *Brown* v. *Leyds* made *ius incertum* a universal condition of the Transvaal. It cast doubt, for example, upon the Gold Law, the Liquor Law and the constitution itself.[7]

Moreover, it could reasonably be suspected that the Chief Justice was moved by motives not merely of constitutional propriety or legal pedantry but of political calculation. He was not only a judge but a politician, who in 1892 had stood for the presidency against Kruger. In all previous cases of this kind he had taken the opposite line from the one that he took now. He was an Anglophile who chose a time of dangerous crisis to make himself the hero of the Uitlanders. No wonder that Kruger and the Volksraad decided to treat the judgment in *Brown* v. *Leyds* as an attack on the safety of the Republic. The Republic defended itself in Law 1 of 1897, by which the Volksraad denied the competence of the Courts to exercise the testing-power and empowered the President to question the judges on this issue and dismiss them if their answers were unsatisfactory.

A great outcry thereupon arose in the English-speaking press that the government was attacking the independence of the judiciary and the liberties of the subject. Kotzé had the support of his colleagues of the High Court and the majority of the Johannesburg bar. However, the President and Volksraad had the support of some prominent legal personalities, including Ewald Esselen, a senior advocate of the Transvaal, and Sir Henry de Villiers, Chief Justice of Cape Colony, who was invited to the Transvaal as mediator. He arranged a compromise, by which the judges undertook not to exercise the testing-right, on the understanding that the President would 'as soon as practicable submit a draft...whereby the Grondwet will be placed on a sure basis...after the example...contained in the Constitution of the Orange Free State'. The President appointed a commission to make recommendations about this 'firm basis', but it was slow in getting on with its work and Kotzé lost patience. In February 1898 he wrote to the President withdrawing his pledge not to exercise the testing-right. The President immediately dismissed him in terms of Article 4 of Law 1 of 1897. This time, however, Kotzé had failed to carry with him his colleagues on the Bench. To the intense annoyance of Sir Alfred Milner, who would have liked to make his dismissal the occasion of a big row with the Transvaal, he failed even to win the approval of the legal advisers to the Colonial Office and of Joseph Chamberlain.[8]

The part which Smuts played in this affair has been greatly over-emphasised. His biographers, almost without exception, have represented him as an Athanasius among the lawyers, standing alone in support of the President; but it was not so. Some very high legal opinion believed Kotzé to have given a bad decision in *Brown* v. *Leyds*. Later, when his dismissal brought under discussion the broad question of the independence of the judiciary, the legal profession of the Transvaal passed a resolution in his support; but even then there were prominent lawyers who took the contrary view.

Among them was Smuts. On 31 December 1897, when the crisis was working up to its second climax, he wrote to Jan Hofmeyr: 'I expect a serious constitutional struggle in this republic over Kotzé's decision in the case of *Brown* v. *Leyds, N.O.* According to the decision (in conflict with two of his most important previous decisions) the constitution of 1889 is invalid, the Immigration and Press Laws and many others are invalid. The judges no doubt think that the time has come "to strike a blow for power, England looking on",[9] but this decision grieves me very much, both as jurist and politician.'[10] This letter reveals clearly enough where Smuts stood; but he published no statement over his own signature.[11] Still, we may agree broadly with his biographers that he came out strongly, in discussion if not in print, on the side of the executive, and that his strong advocacy came to the notice of President Kruger.

Something must now be said about the state of Anglo-Boer relations at the time when Smuts took office. But emphasis must first of all be laid upon the impropriety, indeed the impossibility of cramming full-scale political and diplomatic history into a single chapter even of a long biography. The writer of a political and diplomatic monograph must be concerned always with *all* the personalities and *all* the forces which shaped the developing situation; but the writer of a biography is concerned principally with the reflection of that situation in the thought, emotion and action of one man. It would show a profound misconception of the biographer's task to try to tell all over again in this chapter the whole story of Uitlander grievances, of Boer resentments and fears, of the incessant diplomatic wrangle between Great Britain and the South African Republic from the Jameson Raid right up to the outbreak of the Anglo-Boer War.[12] Admittedly, when Smuts himself comes into the centre of the diplomatic story, as he does increasingly from December 1898, it will become necessary to look more closely at the situation; but even then the emphasis must fall mainly upon what *he* thought and did, not upon the situation itself and its development in response to the thought and action of all the people who were involved in it.

Meanwhile, it must be remembered that Smuts, up to the time of his taking office, knew nothing more about the situation than he could glean by reading published print and listening to what people said. This was enough to convince him that Anglo-Boer relations had reached a stage of dangerous tension. The partnership of Boer and Briton which Hofmeyr had stood for and which he himself had preached with all the fervour of youth was now completely in ruins. The sequel to the Jameson Raid was a war of 'races' (that was the word which everybody used) conducted by clamorous and incessant propaganda. On the British side, the propaganda was directed by the South African League, which had been founded soon after the Raid in the eastern districts of the Cape and had then spread rapidly through the whole of Cape Colony, Natal and the Uitlander districts of the Transvaal. In the Cape, the League's hero was Cecil Rhodes and its instrument the Progressive party. W. P. Schreiner, John X. Merriman, and some other English-speaking Cape Colonials had the strength of character to stand out against it; but for their pains they were treated as lapsed Britons or eccentrics, if not worse. By and large, the Boer sheep and the British goats of Cape Colony were being swept into different kraals.

In the Transvaal, the League was an instrument of political warfare against President Kruger's government. The objectives and tactics of this warfare, however, were different from those of the National Union before the Raid. The National Union had been quite ready to contemplate a transfer of power to the Uitlanders within an independent republic under its own flag; but the League asserted, in the first article of its constitution for the 'province' of the Transvaal, its 'unalterable resolve to support the supremacy of Great Britain in South Africa'. The guiding purpose of its incessant propaganda was British intervention, with the ultimate aim of bringing the Transvaal, along with all the other territories of South Africa, under the British flag. This aim found logical expression in the tactics which the League adopted; it addressed its resolutions and petitions, not to the government of the Republic, but to the Queen.[13]

For the League (as indeed for the Republic and the whole of South Africa) the crucial question was whether or not the British government was willing to support this vociferous racial propaganda. In London, the propaganda was taken up, diffused and amplified by the South African Association. But how did the British government regard it and what instructions about the League did it propose to give to its representatives in South Africa? In December 1896 Conyngham Greene arrived in Pretoria as the new British Agent; he took an early opportunity of advising the League not to be provocative and he remained for some time unwilling to receive petitions from it. In May 1897 the new High Commissioner, Sir Alfred Milner, landed in Cape Town, seemingly in full accord with his chief, Joseph Chamberlain, on the need for patience and restraint. The Raid, Chamberlain had impressed upon him, had put the British government into a false position. War with the Transvaal, unless it came as the result of flagrant aggression by the Boers, would make trouble in Cape Colony and be unpopular with the British people. Time was on the British side and meanwhile it would be prudent to play a waiting game.[14]

For nine months or thereabouts Milner showed exemplary restraint; but it went against the grain of his temperament and convictions. What those convictions were, not only in 1897 but to the end of his life, can best be expressed in a Credo or political testament which he wrote in his old age.

Credo. Key to my position.
I am a Nationalist and not a cosmopolitan....I am a British (indeed primarily an English) Nationalist. If I am also an Imperialist, it is because the destiny of the English race, owing to its insular position and long supremacy at sea, has been to strike roots in different parts of the world. I am an Imperialist and not a Little Englander because I am a British Race Patriot....The British State must follow the race, must comprehend it, wherever it settles in appreciable numbers as an independent community. If the swarms constantly being thrown off by the parent hive are lost to the State, the State is irreparably weakened. We cannot afford to part with so much of our best blood. We have already parted with much of it, to form the millions of another separate but fortunately friendly State. We cannot suffer a repetition of the process.[15]

Normally, it would be unsound in historical method to quote an old man's summing-up of his faith as evidence of his opinions thirty years earlier; but as one reads what Milner wrote, week after week, and year after year, in his official despatches and his private letters, one comes irresistibly to the conclusion that he might quite as well have composed his Credo at any time during his seven years' service in South Africa.[16]

Milner's advent gave the South African League its heaven-sent leader; but nearly a year went by before people in South Africa had evidence of this. In his private correspondence, Milner soon began to make slighting references to the men who were trying to heal the breach between Britons and Boers, men like Hofmeyr, de Villiers and Merriman, all of whom have gained stature in historical retrospect as loyal subjects of the Queen and great South African patriots. In his public pronouncements, Milner remained conciliatory up to March 1898, when he made a speech at Graaf Reinet with the deliberate intention, as he put it, of bringing about 'a separation of the sheep from the goats in this sub-continent'. If Her Majesty's loyal subjects in Cape Colony, he told his Afrikaner audience, really wished to serve the cause of peace, then let them bring pressure to bear on the party which was disturbing it, that is to say, on the South African Republic. For if there was any danger of war (which he did not admit) it came, not from the aggressiveness of the British government, but from the 'unprogressiveness, I will not say the retrogressiveness, of the Government of the Transvaal'.[17]

74

In these early months of 1898 Milner was coming towards the end of his patience and was trying to make his masters in London see that time was *not* on the British side. For the past year, Chamberlain had been following the tactics of pushing hard to assert British rights against the South African Republic, but within the strict limits defined by the articles of the London Convention of 1884: for example, by Article IV, which gave the British government control of the Republic's treaty-making activities, and by Article XIV, which established liberty of entrance, travel and residence for all persons except Natives. Recently, the Volksraad had passed an immigration law which the British government regarded as a contravention of Article XIV; this caused a direct collision, ending in May 1897 with a complete climb-down by the President and Volksraad, after the British had sent a naval squadron to Delagoa Bay. But no victory was ever final in this nagging controversy. While giving way on the immigration law, the President had suggested international arbitration on matters in dispute under the Convention, and this led Chamberlain in December to reaffirm the Queen's suzerainty, which, he said, made arbitration inappropriate. To be sure, there was no mention of suzerainty in the London Convention; but it had been affirmed three years earlier in the preamble to the Pretoria Convention. Chamberlain's citation of this preamble opened the way to an endless theoretical argument. The Boers might say that the Pretoria Convention had been superseded by the London Convention. If that were so, the British might retort, the Republic had no legal basis; for it was in the Pretoria Convention that the British government had recognised its existence. No! the Boers might answer, they derived their statehood not from a British grant, but from the original sovereignty of their own people. Thus the argument could, and in fact did, continue interminably. Smuts, as has been seen earlier, had already cut into it as a free lance and he cut into it again later on in his official capacity.*

Amidst these disputes the Republic continued to build up its armaments, while the British government made spasmodic gestures of force. And all the time the newspaper argument grew more shrill. As might have been expected, the Boers thought it a bad time for changing their leadership. In February 1898 they re-elected President Kruger by a great majority. The dismissal of Chief Justice

* See p. 61 above and p. 102 below.

Kotzé followed almost at once. It was the cumulative effect of these and similar events which made Milner conclude that time was no longer on the British side.

Milner saw little profit in scoring points of theory against Kruger's government or in denouncing its breaches or evasions of the London Convention. In February he told Greene that he was doing as little as possible of 'this useless protesting, complaining, reminding business': still, he was willing to do as much as was necessary, 'not with any immediate hope of results—but with a view to the great day of reckoning'. He wanted to get the British case against the Boers on to a firmer foundation than 'that miserable old instrument', the London Convention. Greene agreed: Convention or no Convention, he said, there was no means of settling the intolerable situation except by 'an ultimate appeal to Caesar, that is, the British Government'. Unfortunately for Milner and Greene, Caesar, as embodied in the person of Mr Chamberlain, was not yet ready to accept such an appeal, despite the heavy pressure put upon him by Milner. On 23 February Milner posted a long despatch enumerating British grievances and a still longer letter arguing the case for drastic action. He said that there was no way out of the political troubles of South Africa except reform in the Transvaal or war. The prospects of reform, he added, were at present worse than ever. Looking at the question from a purely South African point of view (for it was not his business to consider the Imperial outlook as a whole) he would be inclined 'to work up to a crisis'. As to the method of doing so, he saw no sense in making a fuss about trifles: better by far to maintain inflexible pressure for the redress of substantial grievances and the assertion of 'strong popular points', whether or no they were covered by the Convention.

Chamberlain, however, was not yet ready to go beyond the Convention. He sent a terse telegram to Milner insisting that the principal object of Her Majesty's government in South Africa at present was peace. Thereupon Milner sent a warning to Greene: 'We must keep up our wicket but not attempt to force the game.' All the same, he continued to remind his masters in London that it was not the trumpery treaties or suzerainty that mattered, but 'the big facts, all of them internal Transvaal questions, with which *in theory* we have nothing to do'. This argument finally prevailed in London. In a letter of 28 June, which in effect closed this animated correspondence, Lord Selborne assured Milner that Mr Chamberlain and he fully agreed with him in principle. The only disagreement between them was about the time factor. Lord Selborne still believed that time was on the British side and that the aim of a united South Africa 'under the aegis of the Union Jack' might be achieved without war. Milner felt convinced that Chamberlain and Selborne were completely wrong in their judgment of the time factor; but he realised that 'the great day of reckoning' would have to be postponed for the time being. He told Greene that the thing to do was 'steadily, uncontentiously, to make them realise the facts. They will draw the conclusion for themselves sooner or later.'[18] Meanwhile, there ensued a period of relative quiet from June, the month in which Smuts took office as State Attorney, until nearly the end of 1898.

Smuts would have been foolish had he not realised that the Anglo-Boer tension might lead to war; but he would have been going beyond the evidence that was available to him had he looked upon war as inevitable. His labours throughout the next twelve or more months can be regarded as a sustained effort to remove the causes of war, in so far as they had roots in the policy and administration of the Transvaal.

He knew only too well the difficulties of the situation in which his government and people found themselves. A simple and slow-moving country folk had seen suddenly arise in their midst a super-modern capitalist industry and a strident urban conglomeration of alien immigrants. In his student essays, Smuts had exhorted the Boers to welcome this 'new dynamic'; but he had understood, even then, their natural desire to defend their old way of life and to remain the masters in their own house. In 1890 this desire had found expression in legislation which raised the franchise qualification from five to fourteen years' residence, with naturalisation and an age limit of forty years. To be sure, provision was made at the same time for the beginnings of local government on the Rand, while the immigrant population was given the opportunity of voicing its needs and wishes (not of determining policy) in a 'Second Volksraad'; but these concessions, Smuts realised, did not meet the main grievances. We may infer from what he said and did later on that it was genuine conviction, as well as the crack of Milner's whip, which set him moving along the path of electoral reform.

He was also aware that the immigrant population had some genuine economic grievances. It had been the policy of the government to foster industrial development by granting concessions—for the construction of railways, the manufacture of dynamite and many other enterprises. As in other countries and in earlier times, this policy had failed to work according to plan; the concessions had sometimes become an article of sale, and even when they had not, their monopolistic structure had laid additional costs upon the basic industry, gold mining. A committee of investigation appointed by the Volksraad in 1895 had produced in the following year some drastic proposals for reform; but the government showed little inclination to act upon them. Meanwhile, the opposition was growing more vociferous, particularly against the dynamite monopoly.

All these complaints and some additional ones (for example, the complaints against the Dutch-medium educational system established by Mansvelt, who had been an instructor of Smuts's youth at Stellenbosch) arose in the field of high policy. As will soon appear, Smuts allowed very little time to go by before he began to invade this field; but his office gave him no automatic entry to it. He was a member neither of the Executive Council nor of the Volksraad, but attended these bodies only when he was summoned. The specific duties laid upon him by his office were not political, but legal and administrative. Even so, they had important political implications. The Uitlanders and their supporters in South Africa and Britain were always denouncing the Republic for the inefficiency and corruption of its legal and administrative system. To what extent this denunciation had firm ground in fact has never been sufficiently examined; but it lacked nothing in reiteration and vituperation. So far as in him lay, Smuts was determined to refute it, not by words but by deeds.

The State Attorney's records amount to many hundreds of volumes, consisting chiefly of copies of letters despatched, and of letters, reports and other documents received. All the copies of letters despatched (except those to the British Agent, which were typed) were written by hand on flimsy paper in ink which frequently smeared and faded. This intractable but important collection of historical material has never been systematically examined.[19]

It would appear that Smuts made up his mind almost at the start that he possessed too small a staff for the efficient performance of the duties laid upon him. He started work on 8 June 1898, and before

July was out he had secured the appointment of an assistant State Attorney (L. J. Jacobsz) and additional headquarters staff: at peak it amounted to sixteen, a small enough number, considering the various and far-reaching tasks which the State Attorney was expected to perform. On the criminal side, no trial was possible without his action, for it fell to him to decide whether or not to institute a prosecution; he was also responsible for the execution of sentences and for the control of the police, with the exception (which Smuts resented) of the detective branch. On the civil side, he was expected to appear in court, by deputy if not personally, in all cases to which the government was a party. We soon find Smuts complaining that he was losing touch with the Courts because of the other calls made upon his time. To begin with, the Volksraad was in session and soon made up its mind that it wanted his advice at *all* its meetings, not merely occasional ones, as the terms of his appointment had suggested. The Executive Council also requested his attendance constantly. This suited his book, for he was temperamentally attracted to the centres of power; but it cut deeply into the time which he needed to get through his office work. He was legal adviser, not only to the Volksraad and the Executive Council, but to all the departments of government. The records show him reading, criticising and amending all draft contracts and concessions, with the fixed determination to let no new monopolies get by. They show him giving learned and trenchant advice to the Commandant-General, the head of the Mining Office and the Superintendents of Education and of Native Affairs. This advice, which in theory was purely legal, trenched continually upon important matters of policy and administration. For example, we find Smuts engaged upon a persistent campaign to secure satisfactory standards in the appointment of civil servants and in recruitment to the professions. He interested himself in the qualifications of attorneys' clerks and launched a blistering attack upon the quacks who infested Johannesburg. No detail was too trivial for his attention. Yet he never allowed himself to become submerged in detail. He made himself the driving force of the commission appointed to collect and arrange the statutory law of the Republic. Hitherto, the *wetten* and *besluiten* had been scattered about all over the place; but they were now systematically arranged and indexed in the edition of *Locale Wetten* which remains to this day the indispensable tool both of lawyers and of historians.

It was also part of Smuts's duty, or he made it so, to draft new legislation. Later in this chapter he will be seen hard at work upon the franchise bill, which took the central place in the disputes that led to the Anglo-Boer War. In the early months of his appointment the bill that took most of his attention was a bill against *ontucht*, immorality. That was systematic. Smuts was out to conquer the crime wave. It was a tall order, what with the get-rich-quick mentality of the goldfields, the shifting white and black populations with their high preponderance of males, the difficulties of policing the Gold Law and the Liquor Law and—most infuriating of all—the unreliability of some senior officials of the police force. It was in a spirit of cold determination that Smuts attacked his tremendous task. An Englishman who became in later years his close friend has described as follows the intimidating reception which he gave to people who interrupted his work: 'Smuts received me coldly, if not with mistrust. The lean, unsmiling visage, the piercing blue-grey eyes, the quick impatient speech, the frigid bearing of the new State Attorney—all were disconcerting. This was no man to suffer fools gladly or at all.'[20]

Indeed, he had no time to spare for fools, when the knaves were taking so much of it. In Johannesburg, the prostitutes on the streets were making themselves such a nuisance that a public meeting of citizens on 28 September made a formal protest to the government.[21] Smuts asked for extra police but discovered almost immediately that the police officer in charge of the *ontucht* section was himself in league with the prostitutes and brothel keepers. Smuts dismissed the man and gave orders for his immediate prosecution.

In his attack upon illicit gold buying, Smuts uncovered a similar spoor. In the Johannesburg press it had been openly alleged that senior officers of the police had been lining their own pockets in this traffic. Smuts took these allegations seriously and hired a man called Jacobs to shadow the chief detective, Ferguson. From Jacobs and from other persons, some of whom had rather spotty reputations, a good deal of evidence came in against Ferguson. The evidence still remains unsifted by historians in the State Attorney's papers, but Smuts sifted it and thought himself justified in demanding Ferguson's dismissal. The demand was acceded to, though not without some opposition in the Volksraad. Thereupon Smuts went further and proposed that the detective force, which had been hitherto an independent branch of the civil service, should be put under his own direct control. The Volksraad gave its blessing to this proposal, but there must have been some hitch, for it was not until June of next year, after the detective branch had made some bad trouble for him, that he got control of it.[22]*

It is impossible to give any further account of the battle which Smuts fought against the law-breakers, such as the counterfeiters of money and the illicit liquor sellers. There can be no doubt that he gained credit by his reforming zeal both for himself and his government. In February 1899 John X. Merriman encouraged him to continue 'the good fight...putting down the criminal population'; in August, a newspaper hostile to the republican government admitted that he had done 'all that an honest and patriotic man could do to impart a little honesty and purity into a corrupt administration'.[23] Smuts would have denied this sweeping implication of corruption; at the same time, he would have pleaded to be given time enough to finish his job of cleaning up the bad spots.

The people who most noisily attacked the abuses of republican rule showed no interest in the efforts which Smuts was making to remove them. Their interest was in discovering or manufacturing sensational grievances as ammunition for their attack upon the Republic. In December 1898 they let loose a furious agitation against the administration of justice, which meant in effect against Smuts himself, seeing that he was the minister responsible for justice. The occasion of their campaign was a street brawl between two Uitlanders, Edgar and Foster—a commonplace event which would not have merited the hundreds of thousands of printed words subsequently spent upon it, had it not involved in its aftermath the conduct of the police, the courts, the leaders of the South African League, the agents of the British government, and, last but not least, the State Attorney.

What follows will be the briefest possible summary of the State Attorney's files on the Edgar case and its aftermath. No attempt will be made to pronounce upon the rights and wrongs of the case or to explain what other people thought, said and did about it: it will be sufficient to record what Smuts thought, said and did. On the morning of 20 December he had on his desk reports of the violent events of the night before; of the fight in the street between Edgar

* See below, p. 94.

and Foster, resulting in dangerous injuries to the latter, and of the death of Edgar in his own house, it was said, while resisting arrest. Smuts set in motion the machinery of the law which led to the trial for culpable homicide of Jones, the constable who had shot Edgar. The Uitlander champions said that he should have been tried for murder and they objected to the bail of £200 that had been granted to him. Moreover, Mr Justice Kock, in delivering judgment of acquittal, uttered some *obiter dicta* of encouragement to the police which were furiously attacked in the English-speaking press. Smuts called for the records of the Jones case, and after examining them carefully gave orders for the retrial of Jones. Meanwhile, the leaders of the South African League in Johannesburg had been making preparations for a monster protest meeting in the open air (which was against the law) and had forwarded a petition to the British vice-consul.

Smuts believed that his order for the retrial of Jones had removed all justification for the protest meeting. Moreover, he had received an assurance from the acting British Agent that he would do his best to have the meeting called off. Nevertheless, it took place in the open air on 24 December. Smuts thereupon instructed the Public Prosecutor in Johannesburg to send him evidence which he could use against its leaders and against the British vice-consul, whom he suspected of being in league with them. He was fighting his battle on various fronts. On 28 December he gave orders that Jones should on no account be let out on bail. On 1 January 1899, he began to collect evidence to prove that the death of Foster, which had just occurred in the Johannesburg hospital, was due to the wounds inflicted upon him by Edgar. On 5 January he gave orders for the arrest of Thomas Dodd and Clement Webb, two high officials of the South African League and leaders of the previous week's protest meeting, on a charge of contravening the Public Meetings Act.

The arrest of these two men raised another storm and led to a second protest meeting in Johannesburg on 14 January. This time the leaders took pains to keep within the law by holding the meeting in an enclosed space (a circus building called the Amphitheatre), but Smuts foresaw trouble and appealed to some leading burghers to use their influence in keeping good order on the Boer side. Nevertheless, the meeting was broken up, allegedly by instigation of an official on the staff of the Public Prosecutor. There followed a new torrent of agitation which was fomented and co-ordinated by a specially formed Edgar Committee. The acquittal of Jones, when his case came up for retrial in February, made no difference.

It was bad luck for Milner that he had been in England when the storm blew up, and that the newly appointed Commander-in-Chief, Sir William Butler, was Acting High Commissioner during his absence. To Butler it seemed quite obvious that the South African League and the Johannesburg rabble, not the State Attorney and the Boers, were the real disturbers of the peace. To Milner's intense chagrin, he refused to accept the Uitlanders' petition and he gave his opinion of their conduct in a series of emphatic reports to Joseph Chamberlain. The government of Cape Colony also put the blame upon the Uitlanders and their backers. All this made it very difficult to use the Edgar case for working up to a crisis.

Nevertheless, this trivial and vulgar episode has real historical importance. It was the first 'appeal to Caesar'. Sir William Butler stopped it from getting through; but Milner would see to it that the next one got through. Henceforward, he and Conyngham Greene maintained the closest possible relations with the South African League and used it as an instrument of Imperial policy.

The episode has also great biographical importance. Smuts had found himself for the first time face to face with a malevolent and determined attempt to wreck his work for peace, order and good government. He had given clear proof of his capacity and will to fight relentlessly and skilfully if he were forced into a corner. Still, he wanted to avoid the fight if it were humanly possible. With this purpose in mind he now began to take his place as a principal, in the end as *the* principal representative of the Republic in its negotiations with the Imperial power.

On 23 December 1898, when the agitation about Edgar was rising to its first crest of frenzy, Smuts held a meeting with Fraser, the acting British Agent, about the alleged ill-treatment of Cape Coloured residents in the Transvaal and some other matters of current controversy. When the two men had got through their official business in the presence of a witness, Fraser stayed behind and spoke with brutal frankness about the state of Anglo-Boer relations. The note which Smuts made of Fraser's statement is important enough to quote at some length:

He said that the British Government had now sat still for two years because her own officials had put her in a false position in the Jameson Raid. The time had now however come for her to take action. I asked him what he meant. He said that Gladstone had made a great mistake in giving the country back after Majuba before having defeated the Boers. The Boers throughout South Africa had a vague aspiration for a great republic throughout South Africa and that Gladstone had by his action encouraged this aspiration in them. The British Government knew of this but had always remained sitting still, but in his opinion the time had now come to make an end of this 'by striking a blow'.[24] When he left London he was instructed that England would be satisfied if the South African Republic should become a richer Orange Free State; but that was not the intention of the South African Republic, to play a humble role. She would have nothing to do with the paramount influence of England but had always tried to play a role among the nations and had with a view to that always coquetted with the European powers. In his opinion the time had come to make an end of all this by showing the Boers that England is master in South Africa. I asked him what would give occasion for this. He said that England was very dissatisfied about the maladministration and especially about ill-treatment of her subjects which was worse here than elsewhere. On this point England would take action. He knew well that England would not go fighting about abstract subjects, such as suzerainty, which are not understood by the English people and then only in the street. She would fight about things that everyone could understand....

Fraser then enumerated some of the abuses which gave England the right to intervene. He admitted that there had been some improvement since the appointment of Reitz and Smuts but asserted that 'there was still enough to complain of'. Smuts saw a connection between his tirade and the rumours in the newspapers that England was strengthening her forces in South Africa and preparing 'to make serious representations to this Government'.[25]

From the New Year of 1899, Smuts was widely recognised throughout South Africa as the leading personality, after the President, of the Transvaal government. Plentiful but contradictory advice and exhortation came to him from his friends and admirers. Be heroic! cried Olive Schreiner. She invoked the memory of Doornkop, where the Jameson Raiders had been defeated; to be sure, it had been a trivial scuffle from the military point of view, but to her it was the greatest battle of the nineteenth century, the first victory of free men over 'the capitalist horde'. 'God's soldiers sometimes fight on larger battle-fields than they dream of. To me the Transvaal is now engaged in leading in a very small way in that vast battle which will during the twentieth century be fought out—probably most

bitterly and successfully in America and Germany—between en-
gorged capitalists and the citizens of different races. It is this that
makes our little struggle here something almost sacred, and of world-
wide importance.'[26] From John X. Merriman, the most colourful
personality in the government that had been formed last October in
Cape Colony by Olive Schreiner's brother, cooler counsels came.
Merriman approved the reforming drive which Smuts was making
in the Transvaal and believed that it should be extended into the
political field, by giving the Uitlanders fair representation in the
Volksraad. At the same time, he maintained passionately that
Imperial interference would not help this work, but spoil it. 'Let us
begin', he cried, 'to settle South African affairs in South Africa—
not in newspapers six thousand miles away.'[27] It was reasonableness
and realism, not heroism, that Merriman asked of Smuts.

In the disposition of Smuts there were chords which vibrated to
both these appeals. Did he belong to the peace party or the war
party in Kruger's government? That question assumes a clear-cut
division of forces which probably did not exist; but it was raised by
various people at various times in 1899 and historians have not as
yet given a clear answer to it. From the letters and memoranda that
Smuts wrote between January and October it would have been
possible to select an anthology of patriotism fervent enough to
satisfy Olive Schreiner. But he wrote a great deal more in the
Merriman strain. One has the feeling that his explosions of patriotic
defiance were the expression, not of his hopes, but of his disillusionment—if they want war, let them have it! To understand what he
was working for during those nine months it is better not to peer
myopically at particular sentences in his letters but to stand some
distance away from the moving picture of his intense activity and
try to distinguish its successive phases. We see him in March trying
to reach an understanding with the Johannesburg capitalists. He
failed. We see him in June and July trying to reach an understanding
with Milner. He failed. We see him in August making his last
desperate bid for peace with Conyngham Greene. He failed. Then,
but not till then, did he commit himself, passionately and irretrievably, to war with the British.

It must once again be repeated that no attempt will be made in
this chapter to unravel the causes of the war or to follow step by step
the negotiations which preceded it. Other people have told this

story at length from their different points of view; our concern is with Smuts and his point of view. We saw him last in late December, engaged in a talk of shattering frankness with Fraser, the acting British Agent in the Transvaal. Fraser gave him plain warning that the Imperial power was at the end of its patience and intended to secure its paramount position for all time by 'striking a blow' here and now. But supposing the Boers could evade that blow by a timely tactical retreat? The idea began to take shape in Smuts's mind of approaching the great capitalists and reaching an agreement with them which would take away the pretexts for local agitation and Imperial intervention. On 13 March he wrote to Merriman, 'Very serious efforts are now being made to bring about a reconciliation between the Mining Industry and the powers that be—I hope not in vain.'[28]* Three weeks later he wrote again in sombre mood. The talks with the capitalists had reached breaking-point and a new offensive of the National League and the Imperial power might be expected to follow their failure. Still, the government had demonstrated its willingness to seek reform and reconciliation, and perhaps it might find encouragement and support in that *zamenwerking* of all the South African governments which Merriman had at heart. 'I hope that the policy of conciliation which the President has lately declared will help to strengthen your hands. Our opponents especially abroad are getting furious to see that after all the apple is not yet so rotten as they thought. Now however is the time for us to draw together more closely, for only the fear of a general crisis will prevent our enemies from precipitating a particular one with us.' Merriman wrote an encouraging reply but he also urged Smuts to press ahead with the work of removing just causes of complaint and, consequently, of intervention. That was the policy which Smuts proposed to follow; but the doubt was forming in his mind whether it would be effective. Did Milner and the South African League really want to see a reformed Republic? Or were they aiming at its overthrow?[29]

The capitalist negotiations had been a disillusioning experience. From the hundreds of pages of official and unofficial print in which they have been described the following generalisations may be distilled. First, Smuts had been too optimistic in his dream of

* Steyn was also in favour of trying to conciliate the mineowners, particularly in regard to the dynamite monopoly, and advised Kruger in this sense.

making them purely a local affair, which would demonstrate the capacity of Boers and Uitlanders to settle their differences constructively without interference from outside. From the beginning, the capitalist negotiators, above all Percy Fitzpatrick, had been in constant touch with the leaders of the South African League in Johannesburg and the representatives of the British government in Pretoria, Cape Town and London. It would appear that there was no desire among these people for the negotiations to succeed. Had such a desire existed, the capitalist counter-proposals at the end of March would have become the basis for further discussion, instead of being published as a manifesto. The negotiations, in Milner's view, were a welcome sign that the Boers knew themselves to be 'in a tight place'; they could be used to push them into a still tighter place, to provide the leverage for the extra pressure that he meant to put upon them, although he thought it too soon 'to break the crockery'. This was also the view of Fitzpatrick. He had never taken the negotiations seriously, but had jeered at them as 'a plant' or 'a spoof'. The interesting thing is that Milner, Fitzpatrick and Conyngham Greene were all agreed in giving Smuts credit for sincerity. They had doubts about his associates, Reitz and Leyds; but Smuts, they said, was 'quite genuine'. Milner, in particular, had no doubt at all that Smuts had 'made up his mind that mere promises and sham concessions are no good any longer and that it is policy to give something substantial'.[30]

What Smuts thought and felt about his first experience of high political negotiation is revealed in a letter he wrote on 30 April to Leyds, the Republic's Minister Extraordinary in Europe, who had returned briefly to Pretoria to report on his mission and had taken a hand in the negotiations. Smuts began his letter with some expressions of affectionate deference towards the older man, a master fifteen years ahead of him 'in experience and ripeness of judgment', from whom he had much to learn. Then he gave vent to the feelings of disillusionment, anger and defiance which had been surging within him.

As regards the present situation I can only say that our earnest attempt to facilitate a lasting reconciliation has been a disastrous failure. Conditions here are today worse than they have been for 15 years—thanks to our attempts. Yes, the general position here today is so obscure and puzzling that I at least cannot decipher it. The press campaign in the *Star*, the new

87

Transvaal Leader and other capitalist organs, is more violent than ever; nightly meetings are held on the W.W.Rand, where Cornwall miners, who send all their earnings 'home' every week and have no other thought than to go back 'home' as soon as possible, shout for the franchise night after night with violent threats.

A few days ago George Albu* was with me and with great emotion he asked me whether I knew that we were facing a war, a war in which it would be decided whether England would retain her position among the Great Powers and whether the S.A.R. would go down altogether. 'By God', he said, 'great powers like France quake when England frowns, and when war does break out you may be sure that you will be utterly extinguished.' ...I think, however, that England will not be so stupid as to risk the arena without good formal cause, and that the unrest which is being artificially stoked up is meant to make us lose our heads and so make a wrong move. This artificially stimulated unrest is England's answer to our policy of reconciliation! If we had sat still, then England would also have remained sitting, in the firm expectation that the apple would soon be ripe enough to drop into her lap. To her amazement she saw that the old tree can still put forth very vigorous foliage....Added to that is the great victory of the Bond in the recently fought elections....It is natural that Chamberlain cannot but with envious eyes watch the growth of a current so dangerous to him and his policy, a current, moreover, which, according to English opinion, has its source in the S.A.R.

I had a talk yesterday about the situation with Sir Henry de Villiers, who is at present here on a visit. He thought the Government would entirely wreck the game of Rhodes and Chamberlain by fixing the franchise at 5 years. In my opinion, however, the franchise has nothing to do with the situation and even if we did what he suggested, England would still seek and find a cause for hostilities in other points of dispute. If hostilities break out, England will need an army of at least 150,000† in South Africa, and that would provide the opportunity for France and Russia to attack her elsewhere and revenge Fashoda. I think also that something may be done with the Centre in the Reichstag.[31]

It was a bellicose end to a bitter letter. Smuts had begun to reckon the chances of war; but only because he believed that England was bent on war. Or did he believe it? When one looks carefully at his letter to Leyds, one sees that it contains two conflicting appraisals of England's intentions: she would never be so stupid as to risk war 'without good formal cause': she would never, no matter how accommodating the Boers might be, allow herself to be cheated of the war she was bent upon. Smuts oscillated between these two

* One of the mining magnates.
† As it turned out, they needed nearly half a million. Contrast Milner's optimistic forecasts (see pp. 93, 96 below).

appraisals of British intentions; but it was the first that he took as his working hypothesis for the next four or five months. From April to August, he did everything that lay in his power to remove the causes of war.

About this time his son Koosie was born.* He had joy in his home but it would have been strange had he still been in the mood to sing *Die Schöne Müllerin* in the evenings with his wife. The burden of work, worry and fear that he had to carry was growing too heavy.

He had been right when he told Leyds that their attempt to reach agreement with the capitalists had made matters far worse. One result had been to put the franchise into the centre of dispute, which was precisely what Milner wanted. Smuts had thought that it had been a big step forward to persuade Kruger to treat the franchise as negotiable; but all that had been achieved so far was to reveal the immense gap between the negotiators. The President had offered (and not without some 'ifs and ands') a vote to naturalised immigrants after nine years' residence, in place of the existing fourteen years. But the capitalists, in their final statement on 27 March, had endorsed Uitlander demands for a return to the pre-1890 position: that is to say, franchise after five years' residence.

Meanwhile, public agitation on the Rand was reaching a new crest. Here the initiative lay not with the Chamber of Mines, which was imperfectly representative of Uitlander opinion and far from solid on the main political issues, but with the South African League, which had wide support among professional, business and working men. To counter the government's prohibition of open-air meetings, and the difficulties which it put in their way of securing a large hall, these people organised numerous small meetings all over the Rand. It was their immediate intention to collect signatures for a monster petition to the Queen, and by 27 March, the day the capitalist negotiations broke down, the figure had already topped 21,000. The leaders then decided to send the petition in immediately. Its terms and tone were uncompromising. After a vehement recital of the grievances of the British subjects in the Transvaal, it besought 'Your Most Gracious Majesty to extend your Majesty's protection to your Majesty's loyal subjects resident in this State...and to direct your Majesty's Government in South Africa to take measures which will secure the speedy reform of the abuses complained of, and to obtain

* Koosie (or Kosie) is diminutive of Koos which is short for Jacobus.

substantial guarantees from the Government of this State for recognition of their rights as British subjects'. Here was 'the appeal to Caesar'.

Milner had given his promise in advance that he would receive this appeal and forward it to the British government. He did so the very next day. On 10 May Chamberlain informed him that the petition had been studied by the Cabinet and in principle accepted. Henceforward, the British government was committed up to the hilt to intervention. Meanwhile, Milner had been composing a series of despatches which were intended for publication in support of the interventionist case. In the most famous of these despatches, that of 4 April, he painted a picture of 'thousands of British subjects kept permanently in the position of helots', called upon Great Britain to give proof of her intention not to be ousted from her position in South Africa, and declared: 'The case for intervention is overwhelming.'[32]

This correspondence was not published until after the Bloemfontein Conference. Smuts, therefore, had no precise knowledge of the case which Milner was building up against his people and government. Still, he knew well enough that a major political offensive was being prepared. What plans did he have for countering it? As he had made clear in his letter to Leyds, he hoped that the British could be made to count the cost to themselves of pressing their demands to the point of war. He hoped that they would count both the military and political cost—the size of the armies they would need, the risks of foreign intervention, the dangers of colonial revolt. This last factor, however, depended on the state of feeling in Cape Colony and upon the views of the Cape government. Smuts was not quite sure what moral to draw from the April elections, which had shown a big swing towards the Bond and Schreiner's government. From one point of view, they seemed to him to have made the position worse, for they had driven the British to speed up and sharpen their attack against the Republic, in the hope of forestalling the Afrikaner rally in its support. From another point of view, the elections appeared a boon: they gave the Cape government the authority to uphold the principle that South African affairs must be settled first and foremost by South Africans, and to press upon the High Commissioner counsels of moderation and peace.

Smuts had miscalculated. The High Commissioner's authority

weighed heavier in the balance with Schreiner and his colleagues than Afrikaner pleading. They accepted Milner's argument that the removal of Uitlander grievances was the royal road to peace. On 6 May Schreiner wrote to Smuts: 'Do endeavour, my dear brother in the cause of Peace, to secure reasonable concessions. If you have done that it will be an immense service to South Africa. Imagine the joy with which Rhodes, Garrett & Co. would welcome the fact, if the President and Raad should be stung into an attitude of refusing to do what is reasonable—and do not allow them that satisfaction.'[33] From Jan Hofmeyr, still the great architect and manager of the Afrikaner Bond, staccato telegrams came to Smuts: '...state of affairs most serious. This is time for pouring oil on stormy waters and not on fire. Do not delay.'...'I can only repeat situation is serious and time precious.'[34]

Although he admitted that 'the best minds' agreed with Hofmeyr about the urgency of the danger, Smuts himself was less alarmist. He simply could not see what cause for war the British could find. He told Hofmeyr on 10 May:

'The President thinks, so far as I can gauge his feeling, that war is unavoidable or will soon become so—not because there is any cause but because the enemy is brazen enough not to wait for a cause. But that is exactly my difficulty. If the enemy were asked in what respect the position today is worse than it was a year or two ago he would have to admit that things are a thousand times better here than they have been for a long time. How then, could he justify an unmotivated or weakly motivated war on the republics—not only before the public opinion of the world, but especially of South Africa? If England should venture'—Smuts began to sound his trumpet note of defiance—'if England should venture into the ring with Afrikanerdom without a formally good excuse, her cause in South Africa would be finished. And then the sooner the better; as we for our part are quite prepared to meet her. Our people throughout South Africa must be baptised with the baptism of blood and fire before they can be admitted among the other great peoples of the world. Of the outcome I have no doubt. Either we shall be exterminated or we shall fight our way out; and when I think of the great fighting qualities that our people possess, I cannot see why we should be exterminated. So, even if the worst happens, I am quite calm and await the future with confidence.'

Then he harked back to the question of British motive. Every Englishman and capitalist admitted that the position in the Republic was much improved. In view of this, what possible motive could Great Britain have in letting loose a war? Looking for an answer, he recalled the indiscreet revelations which Fraser had given him of the British state of mind. If the British were now in so great a hurry, the reason must be their dismay at the recent elections in the Cape: they must be feeling that now or never was the time to strike. Smuts added that he had just seen Sir Henry de Villiers, who seemed to expect a great deal of Milner—'but of him as of Bartle Frere one may ask: *which* Milner do you mean? Steyn has asked our President if he is ready to come to Bloemfontein to meet Milner; we have answered "yes". The future is on the knees of the gods.'[35]

This letter, implicitly if not explicitly, called upon Hofmeyr and his friends to put pressure in the cause of peace, not merely upon the Republic but also upon Milner. They lacked the strength to do that. Hofmeyr hastened to disabuse Smuts of his dangerous illusions: he was wrong to assume a connection between the Bond's electoral victories and the intensification of British pressure: he was wrong to imagine that the Cape Afrikaners 'will rush en masse to arms if hostilities break out'.[36] Schreiner begged Smuts not to exaggerate the influence of 'our poor political party' and pleaded with him to show patience and conciliation, tact and temper: above all, to secure from the President concessions far greater than any that he had announced so far. As a return for these concessions, Schreiner held out the hope (it could be no more than a hope) of British recognition of 'the big principle, for which I would think much indeed might be yielded, of arbitration in Convention matters'.[37]

By this time, the High Commissioner and the President were making ready to meet each other in Bloemfontein. The Conference had been arranged, with the cooperation of President Steyn, through the good offices of 'the Cape friends'. It was the only contribution they had been able to make so far to the cause of peace. Did it possess any substance? Schreiner had wanted to go with Milner to Bloemfontein but Milner would not hear of it. The only practical help which Schreiner had given to Smuts was the advice to trade large concessions for a mere hope. On the eve of the Bloemfontein Conference, everybody except Milner seemed to be talking about concessions. Even Olive Schreiner, for once, was in the conceding mood. She asked Smuts whether she might not help the cause of peace by going to Bloemfontein to plead with Milner and she suggested that the President might dramatise his concessions by announcing them on the anniversary of Gladstone's birthday: this, she thought, would help 'to convince England...that we are not to be coerced, but that we are not unmindful of any sympathy and justice which she has shown or can show us'.[38]

England's mood, however, so far as Milner represented it, was not at all Gladstonian. Milner was delighted to learn that 'the funk' among Afrikaners—Hofmeyr's Afrikaners at any rate—was 'something terrific'. He hoped that Kruger's Afrikaners might be in almost as big a funk. It was 20 to 1, he told Selborne, 'that absolute down-right determination plus a large temporary increase of force' would ensure a climb-down. 'And...if it didn't, and there was a fight, it would be better to fight now than 5 or 10 years hence, when the Transvaal, unless the Uitlanders can be taken in, in considerable numbers, will be stronger and more hostile than ever. Bold words these, you will say....' Yes, they were almost as bold as the words which Fraser had spoken so indiscreetly to Smuts, and very similar in their mood and meaning. Milner was going to Bloemfontein not for agreement but for victory: if things went smoothly (which he did not expect), victory at the Conference; if not, victory after it. On 10 May he told Greene that he did not expect results at the Conference but that he was 'mugging up' his case. On 22 May he told Chamberlain in outline what his case would be: five years' retrospective franchise with at least seven members for the Rand: if the Boers would not agree to that, 'Municipal Government for the whole Rand as an alternative, with wide powers, including control of police': if they rejected that also, there would be no point in discussing anything else. On 24 May, a bare week before the Conference, he told Selborne that he was not hopeful of results and that the question had got to a stage when its *military aspect* was becoming of supreme importance. He discussed that at length, emphasizing the need for the speedy and effective reinforcement of British forces. If it did come to a tussle, the next few months would be 'better for us' than later in the year. However, he still thought 'that if we are perfectly determined we shall win without a fight or with a mere apology for one'.[39]

What would Schreiner have thought about these letters if he had been able to see them? Would he still have urged upon Smuts the virtues of 'tact and temper', 'infinite patience and conciliation'?[40] What would Smuts have thought about the letters? Would he still have seen any point in going to Bloemfontein? He had by now nearly completed his first year of service under President Kruger. He had won almost universal respect for his achievements of legal and administrative reform. He had demonstrated, even to suspicious or hostile parties such as Fitzpatrick, Greene and Milner, the sincerity of his will to achieve political reform. Unfortunately, he had been condemned throughout the past six months to pursue the reformer's path amidst a noisy crowd of hostile demonstrators. The Imperial government had now come out openly in support of this crowd and was encouraging its leaders 'to keep pegging away'. What was the reformer to do in face of such violent pressure? If he gave up his attempt to achieve reform, he would appear to justify the hostile agitation; if he persisted in it, his friends might well reproach him for yielding to threats and his enemies might conclude that they had him on the run. At the age of twenty-eight, with no previous experience of parliament and government, Smuts had found himself exposed to a war of nerves which at that time was almost unprecedented, although half a century later it would have ceased to be a novelty. In retrospect, it seems literally true that Smuts was never given the chance to make a choice between the good and the bad; he could only make up his mind as to which course of policy open to him in the given circumstances was the least bad. Amidst the turmoil in which he was condemned to work and plan it is surprising that he made so few mistakes; he did make one mistake a fortnight before the Bloemfontein Conference, when he showed himself too credulous and impulsive about a bogus 'army plot';* but he quickly retrieved it. We may conclude that he was right, on the evidence before him, to go to the Bloemfontein Conference in the mood of intermingling doubt and hope which he revealed in a letter to his wife on the morrow of the opening session.

Last night there was a large soirée at President Steyn's where I also was present for an hour; but you can of course understand that my thoughts were on the conference and the subjects discussed there. Yesterday afternoon we had a long session; everything goes peacefully and in a good spirit. Milner is as sweet as honey but there is something in his very intelligent eyes that tells me that he is a very dangerous man. Although it is for us a great humiliation to confer with H.M. representative about our own affairs it is and remains my earnest wish that all may come right.

---

* The detective branch had reported it but it proved to have no basis. Smuts made this fiasco the occasion of getting the branch transferred at last to his own control (see p. 81 above).

The present situation of tension is having a bad effect on the spirit of our people and hinders the progress of the country. The position in the O.F.S. is also very strained because people feel that things are very urgent for us and our poor little people.[41]

In the blue-books, in Headlam's selected *Milner Papers*, in the biographies, the memoirs and the histories, many hundreds of thousands of words have been printed about the Bloemfontein Conference. Here there is no more space for it than a single paragraph. Let this paragraph be written, then, from Milner's point of view. He submitted to President Kruger his proposals for a five years' retrospective franchise and stuck to them. In his opinion, they were a fair compromise between the conflicting claims. They had been endorsed in principle by authoritative and independent persons such as Chief Justice de Villiers. They must be treated as the irreducible minimum. It was quite irrelevant for Kruger to exclaim, with the tears coursing down his cheeks, 'It's our country that you want'. All that he wanted (so Milner protested) was a reasonable, not a dominant share of political power for the Uitlanders. By accepting his moderate proposals, Kruger would strengthen, not weaken the independence he was always harping upon; for the existence of a rational franchise would remove the main causes of British intervention. Milner would have nothing to do with the 'Kaffir bargain' (it was his phrase, not Kruger's) which the Boers were trying to strike. First let the franchise be fairly settled: it would then be time to see whether agreements could be made about arbitration and the other peripheral matters which Kruger wanted to bring into the discussion. By his clarity of mind and strength of will, Milner kept the discussion firmly in focus upon the franchise, until he forced Kruger to produce franchise proposals of his own. To Milner's advisers in the Cape, these proposals appeared 'practical, reasonable and a considerable step in the right direction'; but Milner saw at once that they were full of tricks and traps. Milner was demanding a vote after five years' residence, with simple and straightforward terms of admission; Kruger was offering a vote after seven years' residence, with so many qualifications, complications and intricacies of procedure that very few Uitlanders would ever qualify for it. Still, might not it be possible to simplify and clarify the Boer draft and by patient discussion to achieve a fair compromise between the British and Boer points of view? Chamberlain sent a telegram to Milner advising him to practice patience with the Boers, a people 'devoted to prolonged bargaining'. But the very idea of bargaining, in any form, was abhorrent to Milner. Before Chamberlain's telegram reached him he had made up his mind that the Conference was a failure, just as he had expected it to be. Six days of inconclusive argument had been quite enough for him. On the afternoon of Monday, 5 June, he declared: 'This Conference is absolutely at an end, and there is no obligation on either side arising out of it.'

What was to follow? Eight days after the end at Bloemfontein, Milner, although his hand could 'hardly hold a pen', wrote a long letter to Chamberlain revealing his innermost thoughts. Their kernel was as follows:

As regards the general situation, British S. Africans are more absolutely *united and in better heart* than they have been for 20 years. Their confidence in *you* is profound and they support me with really touching heartiness. The Dutch are wavering. O.F.S. has thrown in its lot with the Transvaal but...not very heartily. They will fight but in a lukewarm sort of way. In the Transvaal itself there will be much shirking, and in fact, though I think the beginnings of a war would be *very unpleasant* owing to our scattered outposts and the fact that the thinly peopled *centre* of the country is quite Dutch, I do not think the result doubtful, or the ultimate difficulty, when once we had cleared the Augean Stable, at all serious. *Thousands* of people would at once swarm into the Transvaal, and the balance of political power which even now would be clearly ours in S. Africa as a whole under a system of equal rights, would be rapidly and decisively turned against the Boer for ever. On the whole I must say I hope that now we have gone so far we shall see it through.[42]

So it was to be war[43]—unless Kruger could be pushed to the point of surrender without fighting. That was worth trying, and until it had been tried an ultimatum would be premature. This advice, which Milner gave on 9 June, was very welcome to Chamberlain, who had difficulties with his colleagues and was anxious about public opinion. Care had to be taken not to start a war before the British public was ready to back it up.

Milner was more immediately concerned with the opinions and plans of his ministers in Cape Town. Although Schreiner had pronounced the Boer proposals at Bloemfontein to be 'a considerable step in the right direction', he admitted under cross-examination that further steps needed to be taken. Thereupon, Milner told him that he had better address his advice to the government of the South African Republic rather than to Her Majesty's government.[44]

The Boers now found themselves under heavy pressure from all sides—public pressure from the Uitlanders, who now presented a new petition, and from the British government, which issued a Blue Book containing, amongst other things, some of the hard-hitting despatches of recent months; private pressure from 'the Cape friends', who for the next eight weeks never stopped urging them to produce a settlement of the franchise which would satisfy the claims of justice, of expediency, and (it was to be hoped) of Milner. It was Smuts who bore the brunt of the pressure. It was he, not Reitz (already wilting under the strain), whom the President had chosen to go with him to Bloemfontein as his chief adviser. In all probability, it was he who had drafted the President's counter-proposals on the franchise. It now fell to him to draft a franchise bill for presentation to the Volksraad.* This exposed him to an almost daily bombardment of advice from Cape Town. Hofmeyr opened the bombardment the day after Milner had closed the conference and he continued it almost without a break until late June.[45] His purpose was to impress upon Smuts the urgent need of forestalling British action by speedy and far-reaching reforms. But Smuts, in the bitter aftermath of Bloemfontein, saw things differently. On 10 June he telegraphed to Hofmeyr: 'We are setting our course. All eyes are now fixed on the Afrikaner Bond. Will the ties of brotherhood become closer or weaker? Afrikanerdom has never been at a more critical point than now.' Two days later he telegraphed: 'My fervent prayer is that England may see that Afrikaners are standing together as one man. That alone can bring her to a realisation....After a few years all will be well.'

On 13 June, the very day that Milner was revealing to Chamberlain his innermost thoughts about the approaching war and the need to 'see it through', Smuts revealed to Hofmeyr his innermost thoughts about the struggle for peace. In a long and carefully argued letter, he pleaded for a clear but circumspect affirmation of Afrikaner solidarity. He asked for three specific demonstrations of colonial

---

* The draft was submitted to the Volksraad in the second week of June and was to be further considered by it when it reassembled, after an adjournment to test feeling in the constituencies, early in July. This procedure opened the possibility of improving the draft law by amendments.

support: first, a resolution approving in principle the Transvaal's franchise proposals but suggesting that they might be modified in detail: secondly, an expression of opinion that the situation 'can quite properly be resolved in a peaceful way': thirdly, a resolution supporting arbitration in disputes arising from the London Convention. 'Surely', he pleaded, 'there can be no objection to this, as you would not be following us blindly: at the same time you have a perfect right to pass a strong resolution in favour of peace and peaceful remedies, for the Cape Colony has as direct an interest in peace as the South African Republic itself.' He knew that such a resolution would be unwelcome to Milner, whom he now recognised as 'a very dangerous person', more dangerous, even, than Rhodes; but he begged his friends in Cape Town not to be too frightened of treading on Milner's toes. Peace was more important than the High Commissioner's susceptibilities. For the sake of peace, the Republic was ready to go still further along the road of concession; but it was necessary at the same time to make England realise the risks she would run if she went to war. 'England will never go to war when she knows what the true opinion of the Colonial Afrikaner is, and all that the republics demand of you is that this opinion should be expressed in a cautious way.... A little time is all we need; has not our policy already undergone a great change in the last six months?'[46] Five days later he wrote in the same vein to Merriman. The situation, he said, was very puzzling.

I had thought that of late both our administration and legislation as affecting the Uitlanders had been rapidly improving—and all at once I find that 'the case for intervention' has become overwhelming! I should say that the case for intervention is today weaker than it has been ever before.

But it has become perfectly plain to me that we have to do with a second Sir Bartle Frere.... I pray you therefore by all the aims you have fought for as a true South African to be exceedingly careful, to forestall the tactics of the enemy and, in time, to take such steps as will render perfectly clear to the Home Government and to the English people that there is no case for forcible intervention in South Africa, and that those who urge such an insensate course are enemies of South Africa.

Our people are gradually realising that they are becoming a great state and that with their rapidly developing importance come more onerous duties of careful administration and statesmanlike legislation. But then there must be no despatches with threats of intervention. I have great hope that within a few years all just causes of complaint will have disappeared altogether and it fills me with a savage indignation to think that the work of those who are spending their substance and lifeblood for South Africa is to be undone in a moment by academic nobodies who fancy themselves great imperial statesmen.[47]

To explode like that made him feel better. He became again the cool-headed statesman. The very next day he telegraphed to thank Hofmeyr for the suggestions he had been sending in about the draft franchise bill. 'Some of your points may still be carried out. I have already worked day and night and still have good hopes.'[48] He took it in good part when Merriman reproved him for getting excited and commended to him the motto, *reculer pour mieux sauter*; when his friend F. S. Malan pleaded with him, 'Old chap, do do your best to get the proposed changes through'; when Schreiner exhorted him to keep very calm, to move forward and 'do right though the Devil jeers'.[49] He was now looking forward to the visit, arranged for the end of June, of Abraham Fischer of the Free State, who was acting as an intermediary between Cape Town and Pretoria. Unfortunately, that visit coincided with new threats—publicity for Milner's helot despatch, the movement (it happened to be accidental) of artillery to Kimberley, vociferous agitation by the South African League, a pledge by Chamberlain at Birmingham 'to see the business through'. It is scarcely to be wondered at that nothing much came of the talks with Fischer. However, in the first week of July, Hofmeyr himself came north and found Smuts to be in general agreement with him about the amendments which were needed to liberalise the draft franchise bill. Threats or no threats, Smuts was making it his business to achieve a big instalment of political reform and had come to realise that the Cape friends could give him useful leverage against the Boer die-hards. On 15 July he telegraphed to Hofmeyr: 'I begin to be more hopeful about the situation. Spirit here is not bad.' On the 16th he telegraphed: 'Have in the last few days worked with all my powers to get article 4 fixed at 7 years. There is a chance of success. Do send a strong telegram at once to strengthen my hands.'

The amended bill was due to be passed by the Volksraad within a few days and Hofmeyr sent in more last-minute suggestions than Smuts could cope with. He telegraphed on 18 July: 'I regret that your suggestion can not be fulfilled as law will be passed today or tomorrow. I regret very much that you find the administrative provisions too complicated. In my opinion they are reasonable and will work well. The seven years retrospective has been passed. If your public is not now satisfied we can not help it. We have honestly done our duty and may leave our cause in the hands of providence.'[50]

Indeed, the amended bill which the Volksraad approved on 18 July contained the essential improvements which the Cape friends had urged upon Smuts, and it received their 'hearty congratulations'.[51] It established the seven years' retrospective franchise with a substantial allocation of seats to the Rand. It met one of Milner's main demands by making provision for British subjects seeking naturalisation and citizenship in the Republic to retain their old political status until they were fully qualified for their new one. Moreover, the manner of getting the reforms through had been conciliatory. Following Milner's closure of the Bloemfontein Conference, there was no obligation upon the President's government to keep the representatives of Great Britain informed about their plans of reform; but the Cape friends had pleaded with Smuts to restore 'the conference spirit' (an essence which it would have been difficult to define) and Smuts had responded by sending copies of his drafts to the British Agent. He now received his reward. *The Times*, inspired by Joseph Chamberlain himself, announced that the crisis was over.

For Milner this was a dreadful announcement. He had been sure all along that the reforms were 'plainly intended not to satisfy but to disarm us'.[52] He had told Chamberlain only three days ago that no scheme which the Transvaalers adopted of their own accord would be 'calculated to carry out the object we have in view'. He had proposed that their government be told that 'no franchise measure will be accepted as satisfactory unless its provisions are agreed upon between the two governments and guaranteed by compact between them. This is the only chance of obtaining decent measure, and if they kick at our demands we shall have a principle to contend for and not mere details.'[53] Yet here was *The Times*, with Chamberlain's direct approval, telling the world that the British government was satisfied with the franchise law and that the crisis was over!

Milner set to work to repair the blunder. He telegraphed to Chamberlain to report his misgivings and the 'consternation' which *The Times* announcement had created 'among the British Party here'. He telegraphed instructions to Greene to inform 'our friends' (the Uitlander leaders) that the British government, although it had felt obliged for tactical reasons to admit that a large advance had been made, did not intend 'to climb down'.[54] He set to work to get London into line again. In a telegram of 26 July he defined 'the real issue'—not the details of the franchise bill, but the 'practical assertion of British Supremacy'.[55] Next day, Lord Selborne was able to send him reassuring news. The worst was over. British policy was back again 'on the old right tack'. The Cabinet was 'all right'.[56]

Lord Selborne meant by this that the British government had fallen into step again with its High Commissioner. It really was quite easy. When one examined the franchise bill, its imperfections became obvious. Smuts had felt obliged to issue an explanatory memorandum to accompany it—a glaring confession, as Chief Justice de Villiers pointed out, of bad drafting. (The wonder is that Smuts had been able, amidst all the fierce pressures that had been put upon him, to get his reform bill drafted at all.) Milner found plenty of points to make against it. The familiar game began again. Hofmeyr telegraphed to warn Smuts that 'we are not yet out of the wood'. Smuts set to work to satisfy Hofmeyr that he was still striving for reform and for peace. He issued instructions to officials which cleared up the administrative obscurities which Hofmeyr had complained of in the franchise reforms and he announced the appointment of two strong commissions, one to delimit the new constituencies, the other to report on the dynamite monopoly.[57]

All to no purpose. Milner had got the British government back 'on the old right tack' and on 27 July the Boers found themselves faced with a new demand. The new franchise bill must be submitted to a joint inquiry by representatives of the two governments: following the report of this joint inquiry, another conference between the President and the High Commissioner might discuss arbitration and other outstanding matters. Chamberlain put these proposals forward 'in the most friendly terms'; but it was agreed between him and Milner that their rejection would be followed by a stern demand for a final settlement: in effect, an ultimatum.[58]

Smuts began to feel that he was cornered. To accept this new demand would be an ignominious admission that the Republic had surrendered its legislative sovereignty; to reject it would mean war. From the friends in Cape Town came the strongest pressure to accept it. In Pretoria there was hesitation, perhaps division, certainly procrastination. In response to an anxious inquiry from Cape Town, Smuts telegraphed on 12 August: 'Answer still being earnestly considered. We realise profoundly the meaning and consequences of it.'[59] That very day, the State Secretary was instructed to notify the British government that its invitation to set up the joint inquiry could not be accepted; but he was also instructed to hold back this notification. It was not delivered until 1 September. In the interval, Smuts tried and failed in his last bid for peace.

He had sought and had received permission to make a direct approach to Greene, the British Agent, with radical proposals for a comprehensive settlement. Two days later, he initialled the report which Greene made of their provisional agreement. Its main gist was as follows. Provided the British would withdraw their demand for the joint inquiry, the Boers would send a note proposing new franchise concessions. These concessions were listed *seriatim*. The agreed summary then continued: 'In putting forward these proposals, the Government of the S.A.R. will assume that H.M. Government will agree that their present intervention shall not form a precedent, etc. Further that H.M. Government will not further insist on assertion of Suzerainty, the controversy on this subject being tacitly allowed to drop. Lastly arbitration, from which foreign element is excluded, to be conceded as soon as franchise scheme has become law.' In a second telegram to Milner, Greene gave further details of his talk with Smuts. Before he received Milner's telegram reproving him for his 'irregular methods', Greene had thought that he had done a good day's work for his country. He believed the Boers to be 'horribly frightened' and had no doubts about the 'huge surrender' which they had made. Chamberlain felt the same. If the proposals were genuine, he telegraphed to Milner, they constituted 'an immense concession and even a considerable advance on your Bloemfontein proposals'.[60]

And yet they came to nothing. This time, it took Milner only a few days to get British policy back again 'on the old right tack'. It may well be that Smuts gave him some help. On the Boer side, some tactical mistakes were made: in particular, it would have been better not to offer any 'explanations' of the formal proposals which President Kruger made on 19 August. The note containing these 'explanations' was dated 21 August and signed by Reitz. We cannot doubt that Smuts played a big part in drafting it, nor can we doubt that in doing so he gave the enemies of his country some useful ammunition for their propagandist war. But this mistake, and any others that Smuts may have made, did not affect the main issue. It is perfectly plain from the Milner–Chamberlain correspondence that no alternatives were left to the South African Republic except total capitulation or total war. Milner was moving in to the kill.

We may leave to the diplomatic historians the tangled story of the last weeks of cold war diplomacy. Our concern is with the mind and mood of Smuts. We have seen him clinging tenaciously to the hope that peace might still be saved. We have seen his desperate attempts to save it. But now, in the anti-climax of his agreement with Greene, he threw his hope away. When, precisely, he discovered its hollowness it is impossible to say. Perhaps he finally saw the light (for he had a deep disdain for vulgarity) when Chamberlain entertained his constituents at Birmingham on 26 August with the spectacle of Mr Kruger dribbling out reforms like water from a squeezed sponge. It had to be settled once and for all, declared Chamberlain, which was the Paramount Power in South Africa. 'The sands', he cried, 'are running out.' Smuts felt the same. His pride could stand no more.

His biographer cannot but regret that he does not know more about the personal relations of Smuts with his friends and enemies throughout this agonising time. In confrontation with Milner, a clear picture of him emerges. Historical research will doubtless reveal new facts about his relations with the Executive Council, with the Volksraad and with 'the old burghers'. It would appear that his intrusion into the sphere of Reitz did not provoke that intelligent but easy-going colleague to jealousy; in the critical weeks of July, Reitz was away with his family at the seaside and in the August crisis he left it to Smuts to attempt the last forlorn hope. Smuts, it is quite certain, was the chief minister under President Kruger. But no contemporary record remains of his day-to-day relations with the President. When one thinks of it, one is astonished that the conservative old man should have allowed himself to be pushed or persuaded into advancing so far along the road of political innovation. He felt in his bones that his young State Attorney was far too sanguine. In May, Smuts himself had reported the President to be convinced already that war was inevitable, or would soon become so.* In

* See p. 91 above.

103

August, Steyn reported him to be deeply sceptical about his State Attorney's last bid for peace.[61] And yet he gave him his head. Such tolerance and trust cannot be explained merely by his respect for Smuts's brains; there were also strong bonds of loyalty and love uniting the two men. We shall see later how these bonds held firm in the years of adversity.*

We may be sure that Smuts received unfaltering support from his wife throughout the agonising suspense of 1899. This has to be inferred from later evidence, not least from her heroic constancy in the years immediately ahead. During the crisis of 1899, he was seldom away from her and no letter that may have passed between them has survived, except the one he wrote to her from Bloemfontein. In the third week of August, she received a letter from Olive Schreiner, which concluded: 'I have a feeling that whether we fight or don't things will come right; only we mustn't give up *too* much, there are worse things than fighting even.'[62]

Isie Smuts would have endorsed that sentence. No doubt she quoted it to her husband.

At the beginning of September he fell ill and she nursed him at home. She brought him pen and paper and he set to work on an eighteen-page memorandum for his government. It was a document of terrific power which began as an appraisal of the political situation and continued as a plan for the impending war:

The relations between the South African Republic and England become day by day more strained; if at Bloemfontein last June there still was hope of a peaceful, and, for both parties, honourable solution, the last few months have taught that that hope is idle, that the enemy is quite determined that this country will either be conquered or be reduced by diplomatic means virtually to the position of a British colony.... All approaches from our side have been arrogantly rejected...humanly speaking a war between the republics and England is certain; and it is in view of that fact that I wish to present the following suggestions to the Government for very serious consideration.

Now followed his war plan. Its critical examination must be postponed to the next chapter; but a rapid enumeration of its main headings will reveal the mood that he was now in. He called upon the government to launch a sudden whirlwind of assault and simultaneously to prepare for a long war; to fall on the British in Natal and destroy them before they built up their forces; to drive

* See pp. 188–90 below.

through to Durban and Cape Town; to hold the coast and coastal ranges against the seaborne counterstroke; to enforce upon the Afrikaner people a total mobilisation of manpower and wealth; to stir up revolt in India and the other mutinous lands of the Empire; to incite the Empire's foreign enemies in Europe and America; to pull down the whole crazy structure of the British Empire; to build an Afrikaner Republic that would inherit British power from Cape Town to the Zambesi.[63]

One pauses to take breath. The man who wrote so furiously in his sick-room was twenty-nine years old. One recalls the essays of his student years, with their visions of brotherhood between Boer and Briton. One recalls his innocence when he returned from Cambridge and the speech that he had made at Kimberley, only four years ago. What had happened to him during those four years? The answer has been given in the preceding narrative. Surely it can be used as fair comment upon British policy at that time.

In the midst of his fury Smuts still remembered that there was another England besides that of Chamberlain and Milner. Four weeks later, when the day of decision was very near, he revealed his mind and mood to a young engineer called Guy Enock, a member of the Society of Friends, who felt himself one morning called after prayer 'as one who sincerely believes in the message of Jesus Christ delivered from God' to write to President Kruger. Enock respected the President and his advisers; he believed that Smuts especially had toiled honestly and patiently for agreement and peace; he believed that the real aggression was on the British side. It was his dream to shame and confound the war-makers by a gesture of Quaker meekness which President Kruger would endorse. So he drafted a cablegram to his Quaker friends in London announcing that he had seen the President and found him ready to continue negotiations for a friendly settlement—ready, in the first instance, to 'make a further offer' of the terms of 19 August. His next step was to seek an interview with President Kruger in order to secure his endorsement of the message. Making an appointment proved a long and difficult business; but on 2 October he met Reitz and Grobler, aroused their interest, and secured an appointment in the President's office at 4 p.m. the next day. At the appointed time he found the President engaged, but Reitz and Grobler received him and encouraged him until '...Smuts came in and upset the whole position by appealing to the worst feelings of the other two men—"Are we to eat dirt before these people?" he asked. "Are we going on our hands and knees before them?" and so on. He influenced the others so much that they veered round a great deal, and Reitz commenced a tirade against the British Government, the Uitlanders, the Jameson Raid, and everything British....'

At this moment a burst of cheering arose from the street and the three Boers went to the window to watch a commando ride by. As the rear files clattered away Smuts swung round on Enock—'"You see what is going on, Mr Enock, yet you still think there is good to be gained by your cabling." With as much outward calm as I could command I replied: "Do you believe, Mr Smuts, that all this in any way indicates that God wishes for war upon earth, or that He has gone back on the declaration Christ made?" He was silent....' But he wrecked the peace plan. Or so the earnest peacemaker believed. When he was admitted at last to Kruger's presence he received a kind welcome and felt that he was making headway with his pleading until Smuts came in and swayed them against the plan by his taunts and innuendos.

In the end they pared his cable down between them and twisted it into the very opposite of Quaker meekness, into a demand served upon Great Britain to withdraw her troops from the borders and order her troopships back to their home ports. Smuts must have known that this twisted and mutilated telegram, if ever the Quakers in London forwarded it to Lord Salisbury (it seems they did), would stiffen rather than weaken the British will to war. Perhaps he had in his head already the irrevocable words of his country's defiance.* Yet suddenly there arose within him the memory and vision of a different England, of a great and magnanimous nation with whom his own small people might have lived in peace. He turned to Enock and said—'If there were only another John Bright'.[64]

* The tone of the Boer ultimatum is so similar to that of Smuts's memorandum of 4 September as to suggest that the drafting was in large measure his.

CHAPTER 6

A PLAN AND ITS COLLAPSE

THERE is a story, probably true, of a botanical expedition that Smuts made sometime during the 1920's with a university team from Durban, to which was attached a distinguished woman botanist newly arrived from the United States. When the American lady asked the Professor to name a grass that was new to her, he answered, 'I don't know—but ask the General over there'. Nobody had told her who the General was, and he astonished her not only by his prompt identification of the grass but by his vivid exposition of its distribution and ecological background.

'How is it', she exclaimed, 'that I am learning all this not from the Professor but from you, a *General*?' 'But, my dear lady, I'm only a General in my spare time.'

It was a jest, but something more. Before he died, war had engulfed a full thirteen years of his life; yet he always looked upon war as an interruption of life's proper business. Still, if wars had to be fought, he wanted to be at the centre of them, where he could see their whole pattern and help to shape it. Merely to command his own forces was never enough for him. Despite his ardour in the field, grand strategy was his true bent.

Yet one might read many histories of the Anglo-Boer War without discovering that the Boers possessed any grand strategy at all. The British official history, for example, divides the war into two main periods: first, the period of field operations, with its opening phase of defeat from October to the New Year and its following phase of victorious advance culminating in June 1900 in the capture of Pretoria: secondly, the two-year period of guerrilla fighting, which again is divided into a pre-blockhouse and a post-blockhouse phase. These divisions and subdivisions are determined almost entirely by the exposition of British plans and their execution; a bias which is perhaps forgivable, seeing that British military documentation was voluminous, whereas the Boer governments and high command produced but a small and diminishing quantity of paper, of which only disjointed fragments fell into British possession. The British official historians studied these fragments carefully and at times with insight, yet in their own despite they wrote a story of British action and Boer reaction, of British organisation and Boer disorganisation, of British planning (even when it was mistaken) and Boer plan-lessness.[1]

If Smuts had ever completed and published the book about the war that he began to write when the fighting was over[2] he would have given currency to some very different interpretations; for his whole story—even of petty manœuvre, privation and spasmodic action—is illuminated by the concept of strategical objectives and tactical means. Nor was it merely in retrospect that he discovered rational planning on his own side of the hill; from the outbreak of war, and indeed before the outbreak, his mind was furiously at work upon grand strategy. In the last six hectic weeks before the shooting started on 11 October he produced a plan of political warfare, a plan of economic mobilisation and a plan of military operations.

Governing all three was his conception of the British Empire as a ramshackle structure, dominating 'great countries largely inhabited by antagonistic peoples (Cape Colony, India, Egypt, etc.) without any adequate military organisation designed to keep the peace in case of disturbance or attack. The dominion that the British empire exercises over the many tribes and peoples within its jurisdiction rests more upon prestige and moral intimidation than upon true military strength....'[3] Defeat in the field would shake this hollow prestige. So too would subversion among discontented subjects, which Smuts was willing to organise himself, starting with India. So too would the pressure of foreign powers; of the French, still enraged by Fashoda; of the Russians, Great Britain's natural enemies in Asia; of the Germans and Americans, her rivals for world trade.

The first task of political warfare was to inflame the minds of all these peoples, starting with the Afrikaner people, against the mon-strous evil of British aggression. Smuts shouldered the task himself. During the last weeks of peace he called in a lawyer friend, J. de Villiers Roos, to chase up quotations from Theal and Froude; he dictated to other helpers disjointed fragments of rhetorical narrative; he fused these bits and pieces into a sustained and passionate indictment of British policy throughout the past hundred years. He called his tract *A Century of Wrong*.[4] It was a version of history whose over-simplifications would have shocked him, even a few weeks back, while he was still searching in good faith for a response of good faith from the British side; a version of history whose distortions were revealed to him not so many years later, after he had visited England again and found 'another John Bright' in Campbell-Bannerman. He was destined thereafter, throughout the long years of his struggle for reconciliation between Boers and Britons, to recognise the poison at work within the rhetoric that he had made his weapon in September 1899. But at that time he did not see it as rhetoric, he saw it as stark truth. The revelation according to Sir Alfred Milner had illuminated with its harsh glare all the dark places of his country's history.

Brother Africanders!

Once more the day has dawned in our blood-written history when we are compelled to take up arms and renew the struggle for liberty and existence, and to entrust our national cause to that Providence which has led our people by miracles through South Africa. The struggle which has now lasted almost a century, which began with the forcing of a foreign ruler upon the Dutch population of the Cape of Good Hope, is rapidly nearing its end; we have reached the last act in the great drama, fraught with such tremendous issues for the whole of South Africa; we have arrived at that point at which it must be decided whether all the sacrifices which our fathers and ourselves have laid upon the altar of liberty have been in vain, whether all the blood of our people by which, as it were, every part of South Africa is consecrated has been shed in vain; or whether, by God's grace, the copestone shall now be placed upon the building that our forefathers began with so much suffering and sorrow. The hour has come when it will be decided whether, by vindicating her liberty, South Africa shall enter upon a new and grander period of her history, or whether our people shall cease to exist, shall be extirpated in the struggle for that liberty which it has always valued above all earthly treasures, and South Africa shall in future be governed by soulless goldkings acting in the name and under the protection of an unjust and hated government 7000 miles away....

An historical treatment will also bring us nearer to that naked truth which shall yet decide between us and our enemy before the bar of impartial history. The questions of these last days which have terminated in the prospect of war have their origin back in the history of our past; by the light of that history alone it is possible to test and judge the motives of the present, and by this means attain to the truth to which our people appeal as its final justification in the approaching struggle. That history will prove conclusively that the allegation of humanity, civilisation and equal rights, upon which the British Government bases its actions, is nothing but a cloak for that hypocritical spirit of annexation and piracy which has always characterised her actions in all her relations with our people.

He packed the 'naked truth', as he then saw it, into a propagandist tract of approximately 30,000 words, in which he wrote down all the familiar outrages from Slachtersnek to the Jameson Raid and painted the familiar contrast between 'the aristocratic descendants of the proudest and toughest nations of Europe' and the oppressor government which speaks now for the missionaries and now for the capitalists but all the time speaks insults and lies—the persecutor government, the robber government, 'the violator of all treaties'. It was powerful invective, with some cogent legal and political argument in the penultimate pages and a passionate peroration:

Africanders, I ask you to act as Leonidas with his 300 at Thermopylae in the face of the vast hordes of Xerxes, and to ignore men like Milner, Rhodes and Chamberlain, and even the British Empire, and to commit your cause to the God of your fathers and the Justice which sometimes acts tardily, but never sleeps or forgets....

Even as in 1880 'we lay our whole case with full confidence before the world. Whether we conquer or whether we die: Freedom shall rise in South Africa as the sun arises from the morning clouds, as Freedom rose in the United States of North America. Then shall it be from Zambesi to Simon's Bay: AFRICA FOR THE AFRICANDER.'

South Africa is not the only country where politicians have rewritten national history as a rhetorical overture to war: for example, Italian politicians in quite considerable numbers were doing very much the same thing on the eve of 1848. Alas, their *quarantottate* did not advance the national struggle, except perhaps by teaching a few leaders that rhetoric unsupported by discipline is both futile and ridiculous. This lesson, at any rate, the Smuts of 1899 had already learnt for himself.

If his political warfare was more than half rhetoric, his economic planning demanded a discipline that was in advance by some decades of European practice and theory. He envisaged a long struggle, which his small nation could not possibly sustain except by an immense shift of resources from the ordinary activities of peace to the extraordinary purposes of war. The allied Republics must put into the field the maximum number of fighting men, both burghers of their own and volunteers from Cape Colony. They must supply

these men with the munitions of war. They must make these munitions for themselves, because the enemy would bar their entry by
sea; consequently, they must assemble in urgent haste the requisite
machinery, materials, floor-space and manpower. They must build
their new industries in the shortest possible time. Yet they dare not
too much denude the old industries. For example, gold: the government might economise labour and materials by concentrating them
in the most efficient mines; but it must sustain and if possible increase
the output of gold, both to support the currency at home and to
finance such overseas imports as could circumvent the blockade.
Above all, agriculture: despite the suction of manpower into the
armed forces and war factories, sufficient labour must be retained
on the farms to feed the soldiers, the workers, and the entire civilian
population.

It has been convenient to use the jargon of a later time to describe
the plan of war economy that Smuts put forward; the jargon reveals
his thought in its modernity; he was planning as the British government began to plan many years later when it settled down to the job
of defeating Hitler. In 1899, of course, Smuts used a simpler
language—'*All possible efforts must be made to continue agriculture as in
peace time.*' '*The Treasury must not be allowed to become empty...*'—with
a terse paragraph of detailed recommendations to support each
staccato proposition.

His plan of military operations had the same terse realism but a
different time-length. The war of his economic planning was the long
war that would have to be fought after the British Empire had rallied
for counter-attack; the war of his military planning was the short
campaign the Boer generals must win here and now. '*The republics
must get the better of the English troops from the start.*' The South African
Boer, he argued, was the best soldier in the world: but for the past
fifty years he had not suffered defeat, and if he were to suffer it now
his fighting spirit might collapse. 'The great question then is: in
what way we shall be able to get the upper hand from the start. My
humble answer is: *by taking the offensive, and doing it before the British
force now in South Africa is markedly strengthened.*'

The best military writers, he continued, have proved the advantage
of the offensive. It raises the moral courage of the attackers and
demoralises the enemy; it gives the attackers freedom to choose the
place and time of battle; it enables them to fight in the enemy's

country and live on his supplies. 'Seldom in the history of the world have these advantages applied in such a remarkable fashion as in the present situation in South Africa where an English army of at most 15,000 men (8500 in Natal, 3500 in Cape Colony and about 3000 volunteers in Bechuanaland and Rhodesia) is opposed to a force of about 25,000 Transvaalers and 15,000 Free Staters without any possibility of getting any reinforcements within four or five weeks.'

A speedy and complete victory in Natal was to be had for the taking and its effects throughout the ramshackle Empire would be immense. 'The capture of Natal by a Boer force together with the cutting of the railway line between the Cape Colony and Rhodesia will cause an immediate shaking of the British Empire in very important parts of it; the British Government would under these circumstances not be able to dream of weakening her forces in India, Egypt or elsewhere. Quite possibly it will be necessary in such a case to strengthen her troops in these countries.'

And then there were the foreign rivals of England, who would take advantage of a defeat inflicted upon her but would possibly 'remain sitting still' if she defeated the Boers. 'Thus all considerations not only of a military but also of a political nature indicate the great desirability of the South African Republic taking the offensive against England while her forces in South Africa are still weak and can be defeated without great difficulty.'[5]

To carry through the Smuts plan a commander was required as fierce and sharp and resolute as Smuts himself. Instead, there was old General Joubert, who had risen to supreme command without ever fighting any wars except petty tribal ones and who was content to dodder defensively in the hilly borderland of Natal. General Buller's blunders and the superb shooting of the Boer commanders presented him with golden opportunities which he frittered away in the siege of Ladysmith, while Cronjé's commandos on the western front were sitting down with equal ineptitude around Kimberley and Mafeking, and all the time the enemy's transports were making port at Durban and Cape Town. The younger Boer commanders— Botha, de la Rey, de Wet and the others who achieved power when it was too late—must have fumed as Smuts did as they saw their leaders throwing away the chance of a quick drive through to Durban and an insurrection in the Colony to threaten Cape Town.

December may have seemed 'black' in London but for the Boers it was a fleeting gleam. Smuts knew by then that his plan was a wreck.

What had he been doing throughout those four frustrating months? The documentary evidence is sparse: his private papers contain no trace at all of his activities; his *Memoirs of the Boer War* do not begin until the fall of Pretoria in June 1900; his appearances in the State Attorney's records are spasmodic. For that there is a sufficient reason. He had taken the first chance of rushing off to the front. Young Roderick Jones of Reuter's saw him arrive at a Natal railway-station in command of a supply train from Pretoria with a Long Tom from one of the forts. 'I found him, in a slouch hat and a khaki waterproof, moodily pacing up and down. Grave and preoccupied, he clearly cherished no illusions about the magnitude of the task confronting the united Republics.'[6] He must have found it depressing on Joubert's sluggish front; but he found it still more depressing when he was back in Pretoria shuffling papers. The *Staats Procureur*'s files record little work which he would have thought worth while doing in wartime and they reveal him making repeated attempts to get back to Natal. 'You know that I can be of assistance to you', he wrote on 13 November to one of the generals. His importunity prevailed, and for many weeks to come he was an absentee State Attorney. There is a particular tang to one sentence in the last letter that he wrote to his office from the camp outside Ladysmith: 'What truth is there in the rumour that Churchill has escaped but has been caught again?'[7]

Apart from that sentence, there is little that is worth quoting from the official files. They do not mirror the military collapse. In the New Year of 1900 Roberts and Kitchener arrived with forces large enough for an advance northwards in great sweeps of encirclement. In February the lumbering Cronjé allowed himself to be rounded up at Paardeberg. Buller relieved Ladysmith, Roberts took Bloemfontein. Although he waited there too long, he was ready by May to press forward to Pretoria, as he thought, to the final kill.

The only letter that Smuts can have written with any satisfaction in that depressing time is one that he sent on 2 April to Louis Botha,[8] naming him as Joubert's successor in Natal (but not yet as Commandant General of the Boer forces) and encouraging him to 'continue on the road of Colenso and Spion Kop'. For the following weeks and months there survive in his papers only a few fragments of rhetoric, burning words of defiance and appeal. There is, for example, the copy of a circular which he telegraphed to all the landrosts; it is undated, but the context makes it clear that the enemy's occupation of the Orange Free State was already extensive and his attack on the Transvaal imminent. Meanwhile, the Boer commandos were melting away. Smuts ordered the landrosts in each district to set up committees of influential and earnest men 'to go from farm to farm to rustle out the burghers to commando'. He gave them full authority to punish skulkers and malingerers. By exhortations and threats he tried to rekindle the flame of militant patriotism. What was at stake, he declared, was not merely the nation's independence but its very existence. If the British had their will they would destroy the people and perhaps transport fathers and sons to fight their battles overseas, as they were now doing with the Irish. In the districts they had occupied the farms had been laid waste and now they were being offered to the Australians, Canadians and anglicised Afrikaners who had deserted to their side. If these things were happening to the Free Staters, what would happen to the Transvaalers, against whom the enemy was being driven by every possible incentive of hate and revenge? Let the Transvaalers stand up and fight like men! 'The sacred cause of freedom for which we fight is God's cause and he will not fail or desert us; in our greatest need he will give help and deliverance, as long as we do our duty and do not frustrate his work by our neglect and tardiness.'

Throughout his life (for example, throughout the six long years of his battle with Hitler) Smuts always kept returning to this idea: that God, in working out his purposes, calls upon men to work with him. But in May 1900 the Boers, except for a faithful few, failed to answer the call. Botha was fighting back in the east, de Wet and de la Rey were harassing the enemy's lines of supply, but the western commandos were melting away as the burghers slipped back quietly to their families and farms. Only a remnant of brave men rallied on Pretoria. They believed their government to be waiting for them there with the plan of a great battle to fight and win under the protection of the forts. 'They did not know', Smuts wrote later,[9] 'that in the inner circle...it had already been decided to abandon Pretoria without a serious resistance and that the hope of those who saw furthest and thought deepest in the Boer cause was not in the fortified town but on the illimitable veld.'

At the end of May, President Kruger, Reitz and some of the senior officials slipped out of Pretoria by night to establish the seat of government eastwards along the line to Delagoa Bay, leaving Smuts behind them to salvage the Republic's hoard of gold and its reserve of munitions. With only 'such authority as the law confers on the State Attorney in ordinary peaceful times' and in competition with a peace-and-order committee of timorous citizens—the 'surrender committee', he called it—Smuts policed the city as best he could; but he failed to save the food stores from pillage, so that when the hungry Boer forces reached Pretoria 'they scarcely found anything to eat and thousands passed with sad hearts and empty stomachs through the ungrateful capital'. It was the climax of their disillusionment. 'The resolution of the Government not to defend Pretoria now began to be bruited about and had the most discouraging effect. If Pretoria was not worth fighting for, what was? So argued the tired burghers, and too many of them clinched their argument by straightway going home in the districts or surrendering to the British forces near Pretoria.'

Could the leaders continue the war without soldiers? On the evening of Friday, 1 June, a conference of officers decided to put before the President the arguments for ending the war at Pretoria. 'I shall never forget', wrote Smuts, 'the bitter humiliation and despondency of that awful moment when the stoutest hearts and strongest wills in the Transvaal army were, albeit but for a moment, to sink beneath the tide of our misfortunes. What all felt so keenly was that the fight had gone out of the Boers, that the heroes who had stood like a stone wall on the Tugela and the Modder river...had lost heart and hope, had gone home and forsaken their officers....It was not Lord Roberts' army that they feared; it was the utter collapse of the Boer rank and file which staggered these great officers. And it staggered the iron-willed old President also, for his reply was that he would consult President Steyn.' Steyn answered by declaring in so many words that the Transvaalers were cowards. To bring ruin on the Free State and the rebels of Cape Colony and then to whimper about peace as soon as the war spread to their own territory was disgraceful. Whether or not the Transvaalers made peace, his own people would fight on to the bitter end. 'His answer meant two years more of war, the utter destruction of both Republics, losses in life and treasure compared with which the appalling losses of the preceding eight months were to dwindle into utter insignificance. Aye, but it meant also that every Boer that was to survive that death struggle, every child to be born in South Africa was to have a prouder self-respect and a more erect carriage before the nations of the world....'

Meanwhile, the rout continued. Throughout Saturday and Sunday the retreating commandos kept pouring into Pretoria and disappearing 'as in some quagmire'. On Monday, 4 June, Lord Roberts advanced his main force to within sight of Pretoria's forts and sent General French on a sweep northwards and eastwards to cut off the city from the rear. But the British forces did not move fast enough. They left Smuts time enough to cut short his negotiation with the National Bank about the government's gold reserve, to take it by a show of force and get it safely out of the doomed city. (The main sum he sent to Middelburg by train under a police guard; he took with him, when he rode out of Pretoria, for the payment of salaries, £25,000, which he sent on to the government next day by train from a small station.) 'It has ever after been some consolation to me', he wrote a few years later, 'that this paltry sum of less than half a million in gold and coins which I succeeded in removing through shot and shell from Pretoria on that eventful occasion held its own for two years against something like 200 million sterling from the British Treasury. Nay more, after having nobly done its work during the war and as the lawyers say "usu consumptus" it continued thereafter to spook in the minds of great British statesmen and to conjure up visions of millions hidden away on the veld or secretly despatched to Europe to supply the sinews of war in the future national campaign of the Boers.'

On that Monday night Smuts finished his work in Pretoria. He said farewell to his wife and his little son. The last trains were steaming out of Pretoria laden with munitions and British prisoners of war as he rode away.

His wife too had completed her own particular tasks of salvage before the enemy soldiers arrived next day to search her house. There were the secret telegrams to her husband that had come to the house from the government's temporary headquarters down the eastern railway line; she rolled them up and stuffed them into a pair of those large hollow curtain rods that used to be a feature of Victorian house furnishing; half a century later they still remained very well preserved in that queer shape.[10] There was her own private gold reserve, two hundred sovereigns that her husband had left her before he rode away; she sewed them into a money belt and when she saw the soldiers coming she dropped the belt into the boiling water of the kitchen copper. There were the letters her husband had written to her since their student days together; these certainly she must keep from prying British eyes; so she cut them all up into little pieces (all except his first letter, the most precious of them all) and then, whether with the idea of some day joining the pieces together again, or in one of her characteristic moods of interwoven tenderness, impishness and practical common sense, she stuffed the pieces into a cushion. But when she and her husband returned to their home after the war the cushion was not to be found.

She was ready for the soldiers that June morning of 1900. Then and for many years to come she was implacable in her hostility to the uniform they wore and the country they served. Nevertheless, they were men who had been living for many months past on tinned meat and hard biscuit and she gave them bread still warm from her oven.

CHAPTER 7

ATTACK

IN retrospect it seemed to Smuts that his people during those early
June days were on the very brink of a collapse both physical and
moral. The leaders, after their brief wavering, had recovered faith,
but the rank and file were sinking ever deeper into despair and
demoralisation.

To one who did not actually see in what pitiable state of mind they
were it would be impossible to imagine how the brave men who went to
the war with such high hopes and determined resolutions could ever have
become so demoralised; and yet they had gone through a terrible process
of disillusionment.

They had expected so much of their high officers who had acquired
reputations for prowess and craft in the kaffir wars, and they had found
out that in many senses these so-called kaffir Generals had lost the war
for them. They had had implicit faith in their own military instincts and
organisation, and had found that this organisation was the most loose,
unmilitary and inefficient imaginable, that it led to the slaughter of the
brave, the skulking with impunity by those who felt so inclined, the cancer
of leave of absence, and the certain failure of almost all movements which
required cooperation between different commanders. They had found
the Commandant General and the big War Councils powerless to punish
high officers who had committed the most criminal blunders and who
continued in their commands only to commit more fatal blunders still.
They had lost faith in their organisation, they had lost faith in most of
their officers, and—what was ugliest—they had lost faith in themselves.

Smuts believed that Lord Roberts might have finished the war
then and there if he had sent French on a southerly sweep instead
of a northerly one, to cut the Delagoa railway behind the demoralised
commandos, or else had called up Buller at speed from Natal to
catch them in the rear while he was pressing his own frontal attack.
Instead, he wasted a precious week at Pretoria in the vain hope of
inveigling Botha into negotiations for surrender. That week was just
time enough for Botha to rally 6000 men on a wide but strong front
athwart Donkerhoek in the Magaliesberg range, and by some
miracle of leadership to convince these men that they possessed at
long last a commander who knew his business: 'At the darkest a

light began to shine once more, the wells of faith in themselves, in their cause, in their sacred right began to flow once more....And so it came to pass that when the British attack opened early the morning of the 11th June, the Boers were determined once more to stand as men stand only for the greatest of all causes.'

They stood for two days and then they withdrew, leaving the way open for a British advance down the railway-line to their President's headquarters and to the Portuguese frontier beyond. In September the President slipped across the frontier and took ship from Delagoa Bay for Europe. British forces occupied Komatipoort, the last railway-station on South African soil. The war should now have been over, according to British ideas. According to Boer ideas, the war was beginning afresh. The battle of Donkerhoek, Smuts said, was a defeat for the Boers—'but with an inspiriting effect which could scarcely have been improved by a real victory'.[1]* At Donkerhoek, the rank and file recaptured their fighting spirit and self-confidence; the commanders captured time for preparing the unorthodox, macabre, heroic counter-stroke of the Boer people. Smuts called Donkerhoek the last defensive battle of the war.

It might seem paradoxical to talk about a Boer offensive when the commandos were scattering in flight; but *vlucht volmoed*, flight in full courage, belonged to the tactics of aggression. For a month or two past de Wet had been practising these tactics in the Orange Free State. Early in 1900, when the Boers were massing their forces to defend fixed positions, they had found themselves helpless before the encircling movements of an enemy who outmatched them heavily both in numbers and equipment; but by scattering into small groups they gained the power to threaten at innumerable points the enemy's overstretched lines of communication.[2] By the middle of 1900 the Boer leaders in the Transvaal were ready to translate this brilliant demonstration of de Wet's into a calculated plan of warfare. Their first move after Donkerhoek was to scatter, Botha to the east, de la Rey to the west, with their sub-commanders dispersed over the countryside. Their second move was to rebuild the commandos by bringing back the men who had taken the oath of neutrality or had simply slipped away to their own farms.

---

* Donkerhoek is a *poort* or gorge in the Magaliesberg north-east of Pretoria; behind this *poort* is a secondary rand or plateau called Diamond Hill. The Boers named the battle from the *poort*, the British from the plateau.

Inadvertently, Lord Roberts aided them by the policy of farm burning which he proclaimed in August and September of 1900. A case could be made for these proclamations. The Boers no longer seemed to possess any proper base; 'their new base was the farmstead and all pertaining thereto; private property had become indistinguishable from the magazines, stores and depots of an army in the field'.[3] In strict military logic such things, wherever they may be located, are a proper object of attack. Yet military logic is not necessarily identical either with humane or prudential reasoning; by laying waste the land and destroying the homes Lord Roberts both committed his country to 'methods of barbarism' and made himself a recruiting agent for the reviving commandos. Botha, de la Rey and the new breed of zealous officers whom they were raising made good use of the ruined and embittered men who came to them from the burnt homes. Before September was out the Transvaal, newly annexed as a colony of the Empire, was lost to British control except for the towns and railways and the flying columns that were scurrying hither and thither after commandos that seemed to be springing up everywhere.

The tactics of the Boer counter-stroke were intelligent and effective; but were they governed by a rational strategic objective? Was there any purpose at all in continuing the war beyond the determination of a small people to defy overbearing power and to achieve the glories of national martyrdom? This thought was in the mind of Smuts when he wrote, some years after the war—

It is a question whether in purely human interest the Boer war does not transcend all the great struggles of the past; such as for instance the Persian Invasion of Greece or the Eighty Years War in the Netherlands. For the Greeks and the Hollanders fought for success and achieved victory, while the Boers, who certainly faced greater odds than they did, were destined to fail in that struggle.... The shadow of failure broods over the heroic struggle of the Boers and communicates to it an atmosphere of tragic gloom which is to a large extent absent from the other great struggles referred to. The Boer war is a story of disaster, but of a disaster which did not unnerve or paralyse the defeated but spurred them to even greater efforts in which, in spite of their weakness and ill-success, they sometimes seemed to rend the very fetters of their fate. It was a Titanic struggle fought, if one may say so, by pygmies, and constitutes a record of dauntless battling against invincible fate.... Surely, if their cause was just—as I have no doubt it was—then their history is entitled to rank among the most fascinating annals of national martyrdom; and if perchance they were wrong, then...[4]

Smuts never finished his sentence, nor the preface to his book, nor the book itself. The tragical retrospect of national defeat lost its poignant fascination for him as he saw opening up ahead the prospect of national resurrection and reconciliation in the Union of South Africa which was the goal of his political striving.

Indeed, his sanguine disposition did not readily harbour the image of defeat, either in retrospect or prospect. Throughout the hectic months that followed the fall of Pretoria he had kept before him the image of victory; not a miraculous victory, the product of some lucky stroke of fortune, but a calculable victory, to be achieved by the rational adaptation of military means to political ends. He was an avid reader of such newspapers as he could seize, and his reading of them convinced him that Great Britain's 'splendid isolation' was becoming distinctly uncomfortable. There appeared to be some possibility of foreign intervention, provided the Boers held out long enough. There appeared also to be some prospect of British war weariness, leading to a reversal of policy like the one that had followed Majuba. Smuts, it must be remembered, had been in close touch during the previous year with a number of pro-Boer, anti-capitalist liberals. J. A. Hobson in particular had encouraged him to believe that the British people would not be greatly in love with 'a mine-owner's war'. The mine-owners themselves, in Smuts's view, were not patriots but profit-seekers. Was it likely that they would still think the war worth fighting if it destroyed their profits at the root? In April and May, when the British army was approaching Johannesburg, the Boer leaders had taken a harsh line with firebrand advocates of sabotage; but by October they were planning a sudden raid upon the Rand with the object of blowing up the mines.[5]*

Smuts no doubt deceived himself if he ever seriously imagined that sabotage on the Rand 'would detach the financial wing' of the jingo–capitalist alliance; indeed, the picture he painted of that alliance was something of a caricature. But his picture of the situation in his own Cape Colony was closer to the truth. There was a strong bond of sympathy between the Boers of the Cape and those of the Republics. The Cape seemed potentially a rich recruiting ground for the republican commandos. It was also a British Colony enjoying extensive rights of self-government; British forces, therefore,

* In April, Judge A. F. Kock had planned to blow up the mines and Botha had had him arrested.

could not possibly lay waste its fields and pastures or destroy its farms. The arguments of supply, of tactics and of grand strategy were in harmony with each other: was it then too late to revert to the original plan which Smuts had launched in September 1899, of fighting the war on Colonial territory?

At a conference between the leaders of the Orange Free State and the Transvaal, held at Cyferfontein in the Magaliesberg in October 1900, it was decided (1) to concentrate forces for an attack on the Rand mines; (2) to invade Cape Colony. The opportunity for mounting the first operation never presented itself; but Smuts never wavered in his determination to carry through the second. '...We did not proceed aimlessly', he reflected subsequently, 'in the prosecution of the war...we had a great plan which promised success.'

It would be going beyond the evidence to suggest that the adoption of this plan was wholly due to Smuts; nevertheless, he was in a position to make his advocacy of it effective, for he attended the Cyferfontein conference in a double capacity, both as State Attorney of the South African Republic and as a kind of political commissar attached to General de la Rey. His commission to administer the western districts of the Transvaal, jointly with de la Rey, had been officially published on 17 July.[6] Its terms were sweeping, because, as Smuts explained later, 'I took care...that the Executive Council should pass a formal resolution constituting de la Rey and myself what really amounted to a separate Government for the Western Districts of the Transvaal. This I thought necessary as it would be practically impossible to refer to the Government or wait for the formal ratification by the Government of acts and measures which might brook no delay.'[7] Among these acts and measures were punishment of traitors, purging the districts of British sympathisers and establishing everywhere local administrations zealous for the war effort. All commissar's work! Yet within a week or two Smuts was by turns chief-of-staff to de la Rey, a fighting general at the head of his own commando, and on occasion still *Staats Procureur*— whenever reassumption of that dignity appeared to promise some advantage to the cause.

In the main, fighting was his business henceforward,* and he learned the business quickly in de la Rey's school amidst the folds

---

* For himself, not physical fighting. Throughout the war he carried a riding crop and a revolver, which he never once fired (information from the late Mrs Smuts).

and gorges of the Magaliesberg. His feeling for the country and his devotion to de la Rey were both intense. Of the Magaliesberg he wrote:

It is impossible to contemplate this bleak and uninviting and apparently insignificant mountain range, the silent and grim spectator of so much in the history of Southern Africa, without melancholy emotion.

Rising like a bastion on the lower slopes of the highveld, it looks on the south at the smiling grassy plains and uplands of the highveld and on the north at the endless dreary prospect of the lowveld bush. And with the same cold callous look which it wears today it has regarded the beautiful valleys north and south along its slopes occupied and cultivated by successive races of men. It saw the nation of the Magatese grow up here in comparative peace....It saw the Magatese power broken and annihilated by the Zulu armies under Moselekatze....It saw in turn the Zulu power smashed in 1837 by the emigrant Boers. It saw the country all around converted into one of the most beautiful and fertile parts of South Africa and Boer and Magatese enjoying the fruits of peace in a land of plenty for more than 60 years....It saw the youthful Boer nation, instinct with all the virile promise of the future, clutched by one of those old-world monsters called Empires which one hopes will one day become as extinct as the cognate mastodon. It watched with cold cynicism the progress and close of this dreadful struggle....

The Magaliesberg rises from the highveld north-east of Pretoria and sweeps westwards to the north of the goldfields until it merges in the plains beyond Rustenburg, 100 miles or more away in the western Transvaal. Its numerous *poorts* and *neks* offered many alternative paths of flight and foray to the commandos of de la Rey, which were battling for mastery of the Moot, the fertile valley along the southerly slopes of the range. 'The Moot', wrote Smuts, 'is the Shenandoah valley of the Transvaal and de la Rey is its Stonewall Jackson.' One of the weapons that de la Rey used with great effect against the British was flight—'sheer headlong flight deliberately practised as an act of war'—to draw the enemy columns after him in hot pursuit and then swing round to attack the flank of one of them as it straggled or to assail a supply depot or camp that had been left short of men. These were risky tactics, for it was the aim of the British columns to throw a cordon around the Boers, and sometimes they missed success only by a hair's breadth. If the roles had been reversed, Smuts thought, not a British soldier would have escaped. It was not, he believed, the superior mobility of the Boers which saved them—for at this stage of the war the mounted columns of the enemy could move as fast as the commandos—but their superior resolution. The British were not timorous; but they were self-distrustful. More than once they held the commandos in a trap but failed to spring it through hesitancy at the critical moment. 'Indeed, I came to count on the nervous shyness of the enemy at this critical moment in a great movement or action—on this aversion to the last embrace with the Boers—as a fixed factor, and often in the subsequent course of the war, when to me our game seemed to be up, and the choice remained between capture or annihilation, I counted and not in vain on this nervous paralysis for our salvation.'

It was not only the technique of the game that Smuts learned from de la Rey but also the spirit of the game and above all the confidence to play it audaciously. He remained with his beloved master and leader until December 1900. Their campaign had prospered; but they had not as yet passed the supreme test of war, victory in a pitched battle. Their Mauser ammunition was running low and they had it in mind to capture British Lee Enfields. They also had it in mind to capture Christmas dinners for their men. On 12 December they attacked the camp of General Clements at Nooitgedacht and took it by storm. On 16 December, Dingaan's Day, they gathered their men to a solemn service of commemoration and dedication. A few days later they separated.[8]

The campaign in the Magaliesberg was ending, not for military reasons but because the devastated countryside could no longer support the Boer forces. Smuts's last shot in the campaign was an act of political warfare, a letter to President Steyn, intended for print, passionately denouncing farm burning and the other horrors.[9] Throughout the war, many of his letters and despatches were written with deliberate propagandist intent: so much so, that he felt it prudent, later on, to mark *Niet voor publicatie* those that he did *not* want to get into published print. There were committees in Amsterdam and Paris which printed and circulated his passionate propaganda.

There was nobody on either side who waged such furious political warfare as Smuts did. But the life of physical action had gripped him and by December 1900 it had become his vehement determination to command his own men in the field. He submitted a plan that de la Rey was pleased to approve: namely that he should take over control in the westerly districts of the Transvaal around Potchefstroom, where the affairs of the Republic were at a low ebb.[10] The commandos, instead of fighting the enemy, had been bickering with each other; many burghers who should have been in the field were skulking at home; the civil administrations were riddled with defeatists and traitors. As commissar, Smuts found plenty of work to do in cleaning up this mess;[11] as general, he found good guerilla country in the Gatsrand, a rough plateau or range that runs north-east from the neighbourhood of Potchefstroom towards the Witwatersrand. 'I have of late been busy', he wrote on 23 January to his friend N. J. ('Klaasie') de Wet, 'clearing the stables of Augeas in this area, and you will understand that I have worked myself almost to death. Now, however, things are in order and I hope to be able to meet the enemy soon.'[12] He met them a week later at Moddersfontein and proved himself a worthy pupil of de la Rey. He stormed the British camp, beat off a counter-attack launched by General Cunningham with 2500 men, inflicted heavy casualties on the enemy and took over 200 prisoners, besides equipping his commandos with Lee Enfield rifles and large stores of ammunition and provisions. The British forces, he reported to Botha, had been wholly driven from the Gatsrand; the Boer commandos, so recently a rabble, had fought splendidly. It was a notable sign of God's guidance.[13]

Yet to Smuts it was merely a sideshow. His mind was fixed upon the grand strategical plan approved in October last at Cyferfontein. No sooner had he arrived in the Gatsrand than he was plaguing his superiors for permission to lead an expedition to the Cape. On Christmas Day he wrote to de la Rey giving the gleanings of his newspaper reading. A great Afrikaner gathering at Worcester in Cape Colony had passed resolutions demanding independence for the Republics and the recall of Lord Milner. There were other signs to show that opinion in the Cape was 'ripe for greater things'. In England the will to war was weakening; in the Republics the Boers held the initiative. The time had come for a great effort to drive the enemy south of the Orange river. But—'if there is no chance of this and we are not able to clear the republics, then I do not see why we should not rather go and fight in the Colonies and give our country a rest from the enemy. It is indeed always better to carry on war in the territory of the enemy....I hope that you will consider this plan and will write about it to the Commandant General.'[14]

Smuts wrote himself to Botha vehemently urging the great plan. He wrote with equal vehemence to General de Wet, who already had it in mind to infiltrate Cape Colony with Free State commandos. But Smuts was aiming at something much bigger—'a general revolution and declaration of independence in Cape Colony...the beginning not only of the real independence of the Republics, but of the deliverance of the whole of South Africa and the Union of our people into a great nation from Table Bay to the Equator'.[15] De Wet was all in favour of bigness and asked for two commandos to be sent from the Transvaal. Smuts thereupon proposed to Botha that General Beyers and he should both be sent. Unfortunately, in trying to get his scheme through with a rush he got it all tangled up. To begin with, neither his immediate commanding officer, de la Rey, nor the Commandant General himself felt that Smuts could be spared. De la Rey gave flattering personal reasons for not letting him go; Botha thought it would be improper for the State Attorney of the Republic to leave his own territory. But the State Attorney's office was closed down, protested Smuts; all his time was taken up by his duties as commissioner and field general in the western districts; he was State Attorney only in name.

And yet, only a few days later, he was insisting upon the dignity of his office. A dreadful misunderstanding had occurred. Botha had read one of his letters hastily and concluded that he was volunteering to invade Cape Colony under the command of General Beyers. That might, he thought, be quite a good idea. But it was quite impossible, protested Smuts. To inflict such subordination upon the State Attorney of the Republic would be a shocking impropriety!

Smuts and Beyers had fought together with de la Rey at Nooitgedacht; but between them there was a temperamental incompatibility. Smuts considered Beyers 'an able officer and a man of character' but could not stomach 'the wonderful combination of prayer and pillage practised by his forces'.[16] Admittedly, he might have found hard things to say against anybody who was thrust between him and the independent command in Cape Colony for which he craved: anybody, that is to say, except his hero and friend, Oom Koos de la Rey. In a flash of insight he saw how to cut through the tangle into which he had got himself. 'If you went to the Colony', he wrote to de la Rey on 16 February, 'I should most willingly be under your instructions as an officer; but every right-thinking person would admit that I have not deserved to be placed under General Beyers.' To serve under de la Rey! That would be the best solution both for himself, for Beyers and for the cause. But supposing de la Rey felt unable to go? The very next day Smuts wrote again: 'After I had written the previous letter, I have thought for almost the whole of last night what the best solution would be and what would best advance our cause. More and more I come to the conviction that you yourself must go to the Cape Colony....Let Beyers then go separately or also be placed under your orders....If however you do not want to go yourself then I that think it will be best to put me in command of the western burghers who go to the Colony, as I have explained in my previous letter. In any case I have not enough confidence in the policy of General Beyers to put myself under him.' His importunity won the day. Nothing more was said about putting him under Beyers or, indeed, of sending Beyers to the Cape in any capacity. It was agreed that Smuts should go ahead of de la Rey to get things started. Meanwhile, he began to receive letters addressed to him as 'Supreme Commander of the Republican Forces in Cape Colony'.

These decisions were taken in February; but it was not until the night of 4 September that Smuts and his commando splashed through a ford of the Orange river into Cape Colony. To explain this frustrating delay it is necessary to review briefly the general war situation.

Early in 1901, just when Smuts was winning his local successes in the Gatsrand and imagining them to be the pattern of the future, things began to go badly for the Boers. To begin with, General de Wet made a premature and disastrous incursion into the Cape. He sent ahead of him two over-cautious commanders, Hertzog and Kritzinger, and failed to support them quickly enough, with the result that his own commando, when it did set out, ran into a concentration of British force. De Wet himself was lucky to escape back across the Orange with the loss of nearly all his commando.[17] Admittedly, that was only a tactical defeat and soon there were tactical successes to be reckoned on the other side of the account. Far more serious was the new strategy which the enemy was now pursuing. Kitchener had succeeded Roberts at the beginning of the year and began at once to build blockhouses throughout the countryside. Here was an answer far more effective than farm burning to the Boer tactics of flight and foray.

By late February, Kitchener had so tightened his grip as to feel justified in approaching Botha with a view to peace talks. After consulting his government, Botha accepted the invitation[18] and the meeting took place at Middelburg. It is hard to know for certain what was in the minds of the two men. The reports which they made to their governments, as published in the British blue-books, were so different in their emphasis that they might almost have been discussing different conferences. Their arguments and their motives are differently interpreted by their biographers, and by the biographers of Steyn and Milner. We can be certain that Milner was annoyed with Kitchener for initiating the talks; his aim was total victory and unconditional surrender, whereas Kitchener would have been ready for compromise. Whether, if Milner had not brought him to heel, he would have offered a compromise far-reaching enough to satisfy Botha, can never be known with complete certainty. To the biographer of Smuts, the question has importance because of its connection with the views which Smuts held in 1917 and 1918 on the issues of war and peace. In those years he was the consistent advocate of limited war aims. If the Germans had been willing to admit limited defeat, he would have favoured a negotiated peace. The idea of prolonging unnecessarily the suffering of Europe was abhorrent to him. The implication is that he believed that the suffering and ruin of his own country had been prolonged unnecessarily in 1901 by British insistence upon the knock-out blow. In retrospect, Botha and Kitchener agreed that this was so. They had a talk in June 1911 in London, where Botha was attending the Imperial Conference. In a letter of 15 June 1911, Botha told Smuts that Kitchener 'now says that if England had listened to him and to me at the Middelburg negotiations, we would have saved England some £100,000,000 and thousands of lives, and everywhere people come and ask me and I confirm'. Milner's reputation, he emphasised, was on the downgrade.[19]

Be this as it may, the terms which Kitchener offered at Middelburg proved unacceptable. He would have liked to offer an amnesty for the Colonial rebels; but Milner would not tolerate such a compromise. Botha, for his part, would not compromise on the issue of independence.

Yet Botha felt himself compelled in early May to summon a

conference of senior military and civil officers to discuss the near-desperate military situation. Their decision was to seek Kitchener's permission to send an envoy (they had Smuts in mind) for consultation in Europe with President Kruger and the 'Deputation' of the two Republics. When Kitchener refused permission, they drafted proposals for an armistice and forwarded them to President Steyn. But to Steyn it seemed disgraceful even to think of suing for peace. 'Stand fast man!', he wrote to Smuts, 'Trust in God, there lies our strength.'[20] He proposed a conference of the leaders of the two republics. In preparation for it, Smuts was instructed to write to the President and the Deputation setting out the stark facts of the situation and seeking such guidance as leaders in exile could give. The exiled leaders left the final decision to their comrades in South Africa; but they made it quite clear that peace talks would, in their view, be premature so long as hope remained of European intervention and a rising in Cape Colony. They also insisted that neither Republic should adopt a course of action which its ally did not approve.[21]

The issue was finally decided in a Council of War of the allied leaders held at Waterval on 20 June 1901. They resolved: 'That no peace shall be made, and no peace proposals entertained which do not ensure our independence, and our existence as a nation, or which do not satisfactorily provide for the case of our Colonial brethren.'

If any chance at all survived of making good this brave resolution, it was in Cape Colony. And if any man was destined to lead the forlorn hope—destined by his birth and upbringing, his political and military experience, his passionate and persistent advocacy of the plan—it was Smuts. He saw ahead of him an exciting new chapter of action.

But his wife saw ahead of her the same familiar chapter of loneliness, sorrow and waiting. From the June evening of 1900, when her husband rode away, until June of the following year, she had received not a single letter from him. He wrote; but the letters did not come through. He sent her messages when he could, usually through doctors in the English ambulance; but only one of the messages came through.[22] Whenever she sent him a letter or a message she dared hardly hope that it would reach him. She telegraphed to him in the third month of their separation when their little boy died after a sudden illness; but the telegram never reached him. She had to bear in loneliness her own and her husband's sorrow. On the evening following her bereavement she was joined by Ella de Wet, the wife of N. J. de Wet, a close friend of her husband's since their years together at Cambridge. That was a great comfort to her, and so was the company of her eleven-year-old sister Queenie, who had been with her since before the outbreak of war. She was shifted with her two companions by Lord Kitchener's orders from Pretoria to Pieter-maritzburg and lodged in a small house, despite her attempts to get herself shut up in a camp like an ordinary Boer woman. She filled her days with housework and in making scarves and similar comforts for the women in the camps or for family friends; there are many letters from Olive Schreiner thanking her for such small gifts. Sometimes she saw news of her husband in the English papers—the kind of news that military men are wont to release about an enemy whom they look upon as a brigand. Rumours reached her from time to time of his being pursued, wounded, perhaps killed.

But at last she received a letter written in his own hand from Standerton on 2 June 1901. He and the other Boer leaders were waiting there, with Lord Kitchener's permission, for the letter from the Deputation in Europe which would decide whether or not they would enter into negotiations for an armistice and peace. He had Kitchener's assurance that his letter to his wife would be delivered. 'My dearest Isie,' he wrote, 'A few weeks ago I left my commandos in the western districts in order to consult with the Government which was at the time near Ermelo. There I heard for the first time from Klaas de Wet that you had been sent to Maritzburg for some reason or other and that Ella de Wet had accompanied you into exile. Klaas however told me that Lord Kitchener had consented to Ella's going to the Cape Colony to join her people and probably you are quite alone by this time. As I am staying here for a few days, I intend writing to Lord K to obtain leave for you likewise to go to your or my people in the Cape C.' He told her that important political business had brought him to Standerton and he described in a few sentences his work in the western districts.

I hope soon to return to my work with renewed energy—unless certain developments should take place. I warn you not to be influenced by anything you may see in the papers about my being ill or wounded or dead. Should I be seriously wounded or killed, you will be officially informed of the fact. So don't worry yourself with groundless fears. I have never been in better health or spirits in my life. Military life agrees wonderfully with me.

From time to time stray items of news about you have reached me. Of Kosie's death in August I heard for the first time near the end of last year; of mother's death I heard last March. How deeply I have felt these losses —especially the first, I need not tell you. But more than all I have felt for you in all your sore trials and disappointments. I can fathom the depth of agony which you must have endured especially since I left Pretoria just a year ago. But I have been cheered by the certainty that your heroic spirit would bear up against all misfortune and that in adversity no less than in prosperity you would be approved as a worthy daughter of your little people. Our future is very dark—God alone knows how dark. Perhaps it is the fate of our little race to be sacrificed on the altar of the world's Ideals; perhaps we are destined to be the martyr race. ...In any case there is nothing worse awaiting us than death....

He wrote to her about honour, destiny, truth, justice. He quoted Goethe. And then he told her about his thoughts of her and of their little son. He ended—'Tell all my friends with whom you correspond, especially Olive Schreiner, that I am well both in spirit and body and hope yet to give a good account of myself! Do not expect a letter from me again. Farewell.' His wife replied to this letter on 11 June. 'I have read it and reread it so often that I know almost the whole by heart and now I shall be able to live on those loving words for the many weary weeks to come...and Oh, Boetie,* how I did yearn for one word of comfort from my husband when our last little treasure was taken from us and I knelt by his death bed alone. How utterly alone I have felt ever since he left....But I won't grieve you by talking thus, for am I not a Boer woman and can I not bear what has been laid on my shoulders as well and as bravely as the rest?' She wrote to him about her life since he had left her, returning again to the sickness and death of their little son and her grief for him, until she recollected a second time that she was a Boer woman and that her lot was no harder than that of others. And might not God perhaps return her husband to her?

There are so many, many things I would like to tell you and ask you but I'm afraid to do so now—Don't worry about me, Boetie; I am quite well and my spirit is still strong as ever....I am satisfied that my husband is doing his duty bravely and fulfilling the difficult work allotted to him as

* An affectionate diminutive (from *broer*, brother) which might be translated 'partner' or 'chum'.

a worthy son of our little race—Heaven grant I may do a daughter's duty as well! Take care of yourself, Boetie, and remember that your wifie* is with you in thought and prayer wherever you are, by day and by night, and her spirit is ever hovering around you to cheer you in danger and watch over you when the bullets fly around, or when you rest your weary limbs after a hard day's work—O that I might be beside you in very deed and share every danger with you!

They wrote these letters to each other in English, contrary to their practice from the end of the war until the end of their lives of writing to each other and to their children in Afrikaans. Perhaps they thought during the war that by writing in English they would expedite their letters through the British censorship? (And perhaps they taught the censors something about the Boer character?)

While the pause continued, the British permitted them to meet for a day in Standerton. She was ill and had to spend the day lying down. Smuts made application to Lord Kitchener for her to be transferred to Stellenbosch, where her own family would care for her. The application was refused.

---

* A literal translation of *vroutjie*: the Dutch diminutive is tender not vulgar.

CHAPTER 8

THE INVASION OF CAPE COLONY

On the morning of 2 August 1901 Smuts paraded his men at Koppieskraaldrift on the Vaal river. The meeting opened with prayers led by the Rev. Kriel, and then Smuts spoke. The enemy, he said, was resolved upon the extermination of the whole Afrikaner race; no branch of the race could survive by itself; either they would all go under together or they would survive as a United South Africa. That was why he was leading them to Cape Colony. Terrible privations awaited them on this expedition and many of them would never see their native country again. Their tombs would become a hallowing memory for the generations to come. But this war was not only a struggle for the Afrikaner people; it was a struggle for Right, for God.—If they failed, God would fail too. A man's life was a small thing in itself, but it became noble and great when it served the cause of Truth and Justice. He who loved his life more than the Right was unworthy to be a man or a burgher. The flag of the great Republic would yet float from the Equator to Simonsbay; happy the man who helped to hasten that day and accursed the man who aided the foreign oppressor. He and his commando would never retrace their steps; they would come back by train or else find their graves in Cape Colony. If any man among them shrank from the dangers ahead let him say so now and depart to his own place.

It was a brave speech. But perhaps too high flown? To suggest that 340 Transvaalers facing south across the Vaal river could tilt the balance of the war and of South African destiny was rather absurd? Some flourishes of rhetoric may be permitted to the leader of a forlorn hope; but if they are quite unrelated to the military realities of the time and place they will appear ridiculous in historical retrospect.

To the retrospective judgment of British official historians the words and deeds of Smuts did not appear ridiculous. They gave him credit for a true appreciation of the strategic possibilities and a realistic attempt to exploit them. 'To a commander in the field', wrote Sir Frederick Maurice, 'a more constant anxiety than an open foe is a wavering ally....When, in addition, so doubtful a friend dwells upon the chief lines of communication, the difficulty of dealing with him is doubled; for, even should he himself be too weak or timorous to strike, he may have a welcome for others bolder than himself....Such was the position of a large portion of Cape Colony throughout the war in South Africa.'[1]

According to this view, the shortcomings of the Cape expedition were not of conception but of weight and timing: too little and too late. Smuts, the passionate advocate from 1899 onwards of carrying the war into enemy territory, was not to blame for that. Nor was he at fault in believing that his little force even at this late hour might still achieve great things. From the wreckage of earlier forays into the Colony there remained behind in the mountains of the east and centre and in the arid plains of the west nine or ten little commandos. To the British they seemed merely a nuisance, so long as each spent its energies in fending for its separate self; but they would become a real danger under a bold and clear-sighted leader capable of giving them discipline and direction such as Smuts had given to the commandos of the Gatsrand. A unified Boer force in the north and west of the Colony would be a magnet for Colonial rebels and a rallying point for new expeditions from the Republics; unless it were scotched, its growing strength might endanger Cape Town itself.[2]

High British officials did not at the time envisage a threat so serious as that; but they did fear an indefinite prolongation of the war, with its attendant dangers of incitement to foreign intervention and of war weariness both in the Colonies and at home. Hely-Hutchinson, the Governor of Cape Colony, reported that 50 per cent of the white population was 'more or less' pro-Boer and that the greater part of the Colony was 'in a half suppressed state of secret rebellion' which the advent of Smuts and his Transvaalers might very well transmute into 'a war of revolution against British rule'.[3] Milner, on his return in late August from London, with plans for reconstructing the Republics and suspending self-government at the Cape, confessed himself to be deeply anxious not on military but on political grounds: the writ of British rule did not run beyond the towns and railways, no prospect was in sight of a return to normal life, the civilian population was profoundly depressed, the soldiers might be tempted into rash action which would exacerbate present discontents and disorders.[4] 'The invasion of the Colony is serious—

very serious,' he wrote to a friend a few months later, 'but it is not quite so bad as it is painted in some quarters.' He did not doubt that the situation basically remained under British control; but he feared that it might slip out of control unless he raised 'a perfect pandemonium of noise to waken the seven sleepers (5 Ministers, the General and the Republic) that makes seven, you see'.[5]

Against this background it is easy to understand the feverish attempts that the British forces made from July onwards to clean up the commandos on the borders of the Free State and the Colony and to corner Smuts and his Transvaalers when they came across the Vaal. Early in the month one of these columns overran the military and political headquarters of President Steyn and captured almost everybody there except Steyn himself. On 20 July their military Intelligence gave warning that Smuts was ready to set out. The flying columns were alerted and sometimes six or seven of them at once were on his trail as he felt and fought his way across the rivers into the tangled borderland where the Free State and the Colony and Basutoland touch each other and then southwards from range to range deep into Cape Colony. To the British official historian, as he studied the maps and movements a few years later, it seemed almost miraculous that Smuts should have made good his escape. 'Yet it was not to be called escape. If the Boer leader had shown his heels, it was not to avoid a superior opponent but rather to invade his enemy's own territory. Throughout the campaign in South Africa there was scarcely a more striking feat of perseverance, daring and good fortune than Smuts' ride of 300 miles, through one British army after another from the Gatsrand up to and over the banks of the Orange.'[6]

The invasion of Cape Colony may be studied in detail in the records of the British War Office. The Boer records are by comparison sparse; but throughout the first three and a half months of hectic action (August to mid-November) Smuts kept a diary. (He kept it to begin with on the backs of unused railway forms and later in a pocket notebook that he had captured.) After the war, while his memories still remained fresh, he expanded some of these terse entries into descriptive notes for the book that he had in mind; no doubt Deneys Reitz made use of them many years later when he was writing *Commando*. The only retrospective survey of the epic march that Smuts himself completed is contained in a despatch that he sent to President Kruger towards the end of 1901, after he had fought his way through the mountains into the wide sparse country westwards of the Cape–Witwatersrand railway. This despatch, since he intended it for print and political warfare, might well have contained some exaggerations of the Boer exploits; such, at any rate, was the expectation of the British officials who put a translation of it one morning on Mr Chamberlain's desk, with the advice that he might spare himself the trouble of reading it. But Chamberlain did read it and wrote a Minute ordering an investigation of its accuracy. 'Smuts says he killed and wounded 73 Lancers and captured 50 with the loss of only 1 killed and 5 wounded on his own side. Pretty discreditable to the Lancers *if true*. See also p. 9 summarising the exploits of his 200 heroes.' The Intelligence section of the War Office, after receiving this rather nasty comment, produced a tabular comparison in two parallel columns of the figures given respectively by Smuts and by the British commanders for five separate engagements. Their conclusion was as follows: 'The above are the principal incidents in Smuts' report and with the exception of the action on 3rd October are singularly accurate.' In reporting to the Colonial Office their figures and findings, the War Office felt constrained to confess 'that the British cavalry never distinguished themselves against Smuts as he did against the Lancers'.[7] Evidently, Smuts was an accurate recorder.

His expedition was not merely the rattling adventure story that Deneys Reitz and others have told with such spirit but a systematic and thoughtful military operation. It falls naturally into four phases: first, the 300-mile trek from the Gatsrand through the Orange Free State (from 1 August to 3 September): secondly, the southward ride (another 200-odd miles) and the grim struggle in the Eastern Province of the Cape (September–October): thirdly, the trek of 300–400 miles from east to west (October–November): and lastly, the campaign in the Western Province (November 1901–April 1902). This last phase was meant to be the harvest-time of all the earlier struggle and toil but it led instead to the Peace of Vereeniging.

A few extracts from the diaries and notebooks will reveal what Smuts thought and felt when he and his men were in the thick of the struggle.

Aug. 4. Arrived at Rechter's farm between Rhenoster and Valsch rivier. Address on Lament. 3.27. Heard that eleven Eng. columns are-concentrating just before me; probably their destination is Cape C. Yesterday on Koot Krause's farm found a sheep kraal, filled with sheep and then blown up with dynamite, most only mangled. On Claassen's farm flocks were put in pens and set grass on fire so that poor animals were roasted alive.

Aug. 7. Last night at Zandspruit. Dams everywhere full of rotting animals; water undrinkable. Veld covered with slaughtered herds of sheep and goats, cattle and horses. The horror passes description. But the saddest sight of all is the large numbers of little lambs, staggering from hunger and thirst round the corpses of their dead or mangled mothers. ...Surely such outrages on man and nature must move to a certain doom. English are probably in Bulfontein, still pursuing one of my small parties in front of them.

13 Aug. Reconnoitred Drift on Modder River at Brits' farm personally.

There are numerous references in the diary to his going ahead of his men to scout, and in the longer notes that he wrote later he developed this theme. One of the main advantages that his forces had over the British, he believed, was their better scouting, a superiority that was due in large measure to the general making it his own job, a thing that British generals never thought of doing. Other entries in the diary that he expanded later on record the sermons that he preached. Was any British general his own preacher?

He also recorded and underlined his occasional strokes of luck in getting hold of books worth reading.

18 Aug. Still at Touwfontein; address on Habakkuk I. Found here Xenophon's Anabasis and works of D. Erasmus in Latin.

In his retrospective notes he wrote:

In the war after the fall of Pretoria I read through Überweg's History of Philosophy (found at Parys). Much of Kant's Kritik (found at Leliefontein) and quite a number of theological and critical disquisitions. On the whole we were much hampered by want of literature, many of the boers highly educated, and one of the pleasures of capturing an English convoy was the number of English books found among the officers' kit. In case like ours where there was so much continual disappointment and mental suffering quite apart from the physical privations, books and all healthy forms of mental pabulum were great desideratums.

Not that he could have had any time for reading during those hectic weeks of August and September. His diary records incessant marching with many narrow escapes from tight corners. It also records his meeting in the last week of August with the Free State leader Kritzinger, to whom he transferred 100 of his men, on Kritzinger's undertaking (which was never made good) to follow him into Cape Colony. So his march became from that time onward the Trek of the Two Hundred.

Before daybreak on 4 September he went scouting ahead, found an unguarded ford over the Orange river, led his men through it into Cape Colony, ran into trouble with some hostile Basutos and found some English newspapers which announced that it was 'now impossible for the Boers to come through the river'.

Sep. 7. Great misfortune in Moordenaarspoort. I went to reconnoitre an English force with Captain [Adendorff] and Corporal Adendorff* and Jan Neethling. In the gorge we were [fired at] by the enemy and our horses shot dead. I alone escaped in miraculous fashion. As enemy was only 20 to 30 yards from us, all three are probably dead.

It was at Moordenaarspoort that he lost his Xenophon and Erasmus. The British reported him wounded, perhaps killed, and the news reached his wife in Pietermaritzburg. It was well that he had warned her not to believe unconfirmed reports of his death.

During the following days and weeks he must have been close to death many times.

Sep. 10. Allemanspoort; enemy is beaten back; four lagers try to surround me.

Sep. 11. Enemy continue to close me in; I retire to Labuschagne's pass.

Sep. 12. Last night I marched over Gardner's footpath along Jakhals-kop to Stafelberg through two English lagers half an hour apart. Towards midday enemy forces overtook me and a battle took place on Stafelberg in which one burgher (de la Rey) was killed and enemy was beaten back with heavy loss. Their loss about 50 to 60. At dark I marched over Dordrecht railway line and . . . .

Sep. 13. About 8 a.m. over East London railway line to Putterskraal. I have now not slept for three nights and have continued to march forward. Men and animals exhausted. Camp at Schoeman's farm on Smith's river.

To the British military historian, Smuts's crossing of the railways in appalling weather and in the face of overwhelming odds was 'one of those sudden miracles of judgment and endurance' which characterised his leadership.[8] To Smuts himself, these days and nights of mid-September appeared in retrospect the time of heaviest strain. But better times were ahead.

* The two Adendorffs were brothers and Neethling was Smuts's adjutant.

Sep. 16. March over Hondenek to Fanie Venter's farm, where plentiful green fodder. Terrible weather continues.

Sep. 17. March from there to Elandsrivierpoort, where I come up against enemy camp of from 200 to 300 men (17th Lancers). At once give order to attack; camp is taken within an hour; hand maxim and Armstrong 12½ are captured. Enemy losses great; my losses one dead (Tyner) six wounded (Cohen, Lombaard, etc.). Much ammunition and rifles captured, 250 mules and horses, canon destroyed. Fallen, Lord Vivian, Captain Sandeman, Lieutenants Nowitt, Sheridan etc.

Smuts's report of this engagement, as we have seen, aroused Joseph Chamberlain's sceptical curiosity. The story that Deneys Reitz told of it many years later is perhaps the most vivid battle-piece of *Commando*.

The diary from mid-September to mid-October remains full of action but the tension gradually slackens. One entry, an often-told adventure story of the trek, records an accident that remained vivid in everybody's memory.

Sep. 30. Enemy arrives; I beat him back and march further into the Zuurberg. About 70 burghers poisoned with me through eating Hottentots bread.

This stuff was a fruit or vegetable growing in clusters rather like a bunch of five or six pineapples. The Hottentots used to dry the stuff before cooking it but Smuts and his men flung it straight on to their fire and ate it in a moist mash. They were all horribly ill. A sentry reported English forces approaching. *Loop skiet hulle, loop skiet hulle,* groaned Smuts—Go and shoot them, go and shoot them. Fortunately, the English rode away after firing a few shots.*

On 21 October Smuts recorded a tragic event. News reached him that day that the enemy had executed one of his men, Jack Baxter, whom they had captured a week earlier in British uniform. It was perhaps inevitable that they should proclaim it a capital crime of war for the Boers to fight in khaki, for they had lost precious lives by mistaking enemies for friends and thought that the Boers were practising deliberate treachery. But the Boers had not as yet heard of Kitchener's proclamation against their wearing khaki. Moreover, as Smuts reported to President Kruger, 'they were wearing these

---

* This account, rather more laconic than the story told in *Commando* and the biographies, was given to the author in April 1954 by P. S. (Tottie) Krige, Smuts's brother-in-law and his military secretary at that time. (His parents had nicknamed him Tottie (from Hottentot) when he was a baby because his hair was very dark. Later it turned fair.)

clothes not for spying purposes, but simply because they would otherwise have been compelled to go naked'.

It became easier for them to supply their needs of clothing and everything else when they reached the more open country and the friendlier population of the Western Province. On 13 October General van Deventer crossed the main railway-line and Smuts arrived a little later with the main force.

So this heroic band [he reported to his President] arrived in this district after much trouble and danger....The feeling of my burghers is strong, although they have, perhaps, suffered much more heavily than any other commando in this war, and they look forward hopefully to the future. They are convinced that no force of the enemy, however strong, will be able to check their progress until 'Right triumphs over Might'!...The general situation in Cape Colony is very promising, but about this I send you a separate Report.

The tone of this separate report[9]—which Smuts marked 'Not for Publication'—was not quite so exuberant. Smuts admitted that the progress achieved up to date in Cape Colony fell short in some respects of expectations. Recruitment had been disappointing among the Cape people, not because they lacked zeal for the cause but because the British had taken their horses away. Reinforcements had not been forthcoming as promised from the Free State; on the contrary, Kritzinger had lingered north of the Orange and had let his forces scatter into small commandos which the British rounded up one by one. The commandos that survived south of the Orange were ineffective because they lacked co-ordination and leadership. In consequence of all this, Smuts thought it premature to carry out the policy agreed upon at Waterval of establishing a 'third party' in Cape Colony—that is to say, of proclaiming an independent State with belligerent forces of its own. Nor did he think that the advent of de la Rey would by itself make any great difference; the time was past when 'a great name' could achieve miracles. De la Rey with strong forces to back him would be a different matter. Smuts asked for 1000 more Transvaalers here and now and he hoped that de la Rey would follow with many more. In the meantime, he took to himself the powers of Commander-in-Chief in Cape Colony.[10]

Within four or five weeks he had carried through a drastic re-organisation of the Boer forces. He fused the scattered commandos into four coherent groups or divisions under 'fighting generals'

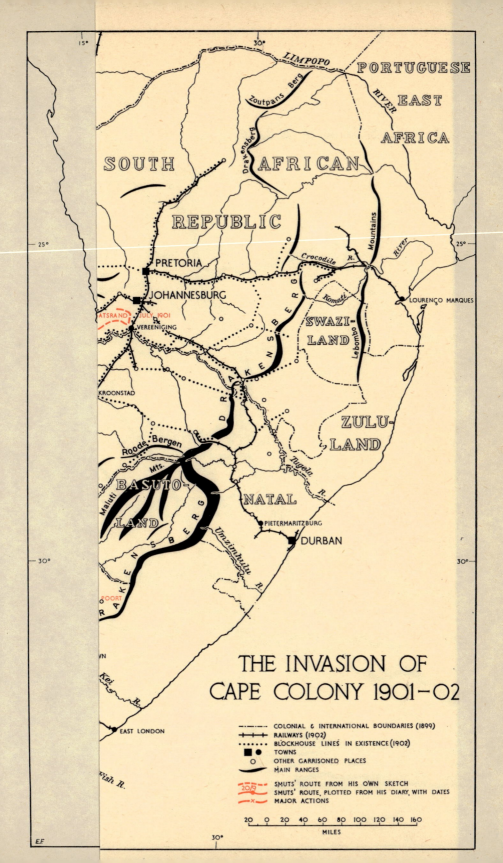

THE INVASION OF
CAPE COLONY 1901–02

COLONIAL & INTERNATIONAL BOUNDARIES (1899)
RAILWAYS (1902)
BLOCKHOUSE LINES IN EXISTENCE (1902)
TOWNS
OTHER GARRISONED PLACES
MAIN RANGES

SMUTS' ROUTE FROM HIS OWN SKETCH
SMUTS' ROUTE, PLOTTED FROM HIS DIARY, WITH DATES
MAJOR ACTIONS

20 0 20 40 60 80 100 120 140 160
MILES

responsible directly to himself: one division, under Malan, eastwards across the railway-line; a second, under Maritz, north-westwards towards the German frontier (across which he established effective communication with the Boer Deputation in Europe);[11] a third, under van Deventer, southwards towards Worcester; a fourth, under Lategan, northwards along the Orange. Thus he imposed a coherent pattern upon 'the whole'.

He imposed discipline and order upon each part. Every commando, under its commandant and field cornets, must be divided henceforward into 'corporalships' of twelve men who would saddle and ride and off-saddle together. Every burgher who should absent himself without leave or lie idle on a farm would be punished henceforward with pack-saddle—or with the lash, if he repeated the offence. A field cornet might impose pack-saddle. A council of commandants and field cornets might order the lash. A military council of three officers and two burghers might impose sentence of death for treason or espionage. Within this wide range of crime, punishment and procedure, Smuts distinguished many and various gradations. Amidst them all his purpose was simple and clear: to enforce discipline and soldierly conduct in camp and on the march, in battle with the enemy and in transactions with civilians. There must be no scrambling for booty in battle or after battle; the officers would divide the booty fairly among the commando. There must be no taking of strong drink, except by permission of an officer. On pain of pack-saddle there must be no shooting except at the enemy. There must be no breaking and entering into houses. There must be no ill-treatment of civilians, be they white, coloured, or even 'British disposed persons'. There must be no ill-treating of prisoners. There must be no beating up or murdering of spies—white or coloured, it made no difference; every spy must be brought for trial before a properly constituted court.[12]

A spy-story that has become legendary in the saga of this campaign needs revision. Early in February a mean creature named Colyn offered himself as a recruit to Commandant Bouwer's commando, betrayed his comrades for English gold and brought some of them to their deaths. The Boers caught Colyn and brought him before Smuts. The wretched creature wept and howled and begged for his life but he deserved death and he suffered it. . . . So far this often-told story is true. But Deneys Reitz and other writers have over-dramatised the part that Smuts played in it. They have put into his mouth some implacable words, 'Vat hom weg en skiet hom dood'—Take him away and shoot him. If Smuts did say something like this, he said it not as a man presuming to inflict death upon a fellow man by his own arbitrary will, but as the president of a duly constituted military court. The records of the court were written out at length in a school exercise book which is preserved among Smuts's papers. They include depositions under oath of the witnesses and of the prisoner, all duly signed and countersigned, and sentence of the court delivered in due form by its president. The procedure was scrupulously correct and the verdict was just.[13]

In the documents of the early months of 1902 there is no sign that Smuts foresaw military and political defeat for his side. At the beginning of January he issued a proclamation to the inhabitants of the districts of Cape Colony under his occupation, an immense triangle of territory with its base on the Orange and its apex pointing south towards Cape Town. He forbade the inhabitants to obey British laws and in particular to bring provisions into the scattered townships which the enemy still controlled.[14] Later in the month he wrote to de la Rey a long letter full of fight and hope, reporting his reorganisation of republican forces in Cape Colony and its good effects both present and prospective.[15] He admitted that things were moving more slowly in Cape Colony than he had expected, but they were moving in the right direction and if reinforcements were sent from the Transvaal he looked forward to victory within twelve months. He professed himself greatly encouraged by the political news coming to him by the line of communication that he had established through German South-West Africa. The English people were getting sick of the war and prominent persons were urging their government to come to terms with the Boers; the foreign peoples were becoming ever more embittered against the English because of the terrible conditions in the refugee camps. Smuts quoted the figures given in British official reports of the death-roll among women and children. 'This fearful state of things has undoubtedly touched the conscience of the English Public, as the papers are full of bitter complaints from influential supporters of the Salisbury Policy. Perhaps God's will is that through our ill-treated women and children a decisive end should be made to this war.'

Smuts had a pen ever ready to assist God's will and the Boer cause. In a terrific burst of energy he produced at speed the longest and most powerful propagandist tract that he had written since *A Century of Wrong*. This tract began as an historical excursus emphasising the recovery of his people after the fall of Pretoria and their brilliant prospects in October 1901, the month of his invasion of Cape Colony; it continued as a tirade against the barbarities and illegalities practised by the British against the resurgent Boers—their systematic lying, their barbarous methods of devastation, their cruelty to women and children, their employment of Natives as soldiers, their savage proclamations of confiscation, banishment and execution. No wonder that Smuts was making his name known among the British not only as a determined and skilful soldier but as an implacable political enemy. By a strange coincidence, his vitriolic pamphlet was published by a committee of pro-Boers in Paris on the very eve of his journey to Vereeniging.[16]

As he explained in his despatch of 26 January to de la Rey, his military plan was to hold the western and northern districts of Cape Colony and from that base to strike south and east. Striking south would bring him into the hills and valleys of his boyhood and among his own people. They were expecting him. Early in January he let his brother-in-law, Tottie Krige, go south with one or two friends to greet the families in the Swartland and at Stellenbosch. Travelling on foot and in the dark they spent four nights on the journey. It would not take the commandos so long as that when they rode in! But Smuts had fallen into a sombre mood and told his brother Koos, in a letter which Tottie carried, that he had had many fortunate escapes but could not expect his good luck to last much longer. 'And now, dearest brother, farewell; I have hardly any hope of ever seeing you in this life again. I only trust that you will do your best to help Isie.'[17] But Smuts's family, and in particular his father, were not at all in sombre mood. 'Mr Smuts, M.L.A.', as the British secret agents always called him, had lost his wife the previous March but was planning a second marriage and was full of exuberant talk about everything under the sun, including the heroic deeds and the vast plans of his soldier son who would soon come riding south, maybe all the way to Cape Town but anyway as far as Malmesbury. The British would never succeed in keeping him out; they had ruined the country but there were still plenty of cattle and horses for the commandos and when they rode in every able-bodied man in the district would join them. As for himself—'Of course,' he says, 'the British have been trying to get me into gaol for more than 12 months now, but if I have to go in there, I might as well have the satisfaction to know that I have done something for our cause on that account'.[18]

Alas, the great occasion of getting himself into a British prison never came the way of Mr Smuts, M.L.A. The great day never dawned that would have seen his soldier son riding into Malmesbury at the head of the Boer commandos. This master-stroke of war might have been possible two years, perhaps even one year earlier; but now the grand design of strategy was crumbling away because weight of power was lacking to make it good. Up in the north, Botha and de la Rey were finding themselves too hard pressed to spare the reinforcements for which Smuts pleaded. Down in the south, General French was multiplying the blockhouses and the troops that barred the approaches to Cape Town. For the time being, Smuts retained his freedom to roam at will over thousands of square miles of empty country. But to what purpose?

His strategic vision could discover in the arid northern districts of Cape Colony no effective means of damaging British power; but his fighting spirit discovered a means of damaging their pride. Amidst the sandy wastes of Namaqualand there were deposits of copper and a little cluster of mining towns, O'okiep, Springbok and Concordia, which were supplied by a railway-line from Port Nolloth. Early in April Smuts surrounded these miserable settlements. He captured Springbok at a rush and collected a heap of dynamite that the mining company had stored there. Then he went scouting with a patrol around Concordia. He found the place very well fortified (*verschanst*) and decided that it would be costly to storm. So he sent a message to the officer in command demanding the surrender of the town—otherwise he would blow it all up.[19] The officer was a coward and he surrendered. 'The surrender of Concordia', reported Kitchener's Director of Military Intelligence, 'strikes me as being the most disgraceful affair of the war. The Town Guard was 100 strong, and on being summoned to surrender did so without firing a shot, on condition that the Mine Property (Namaqua Copper) should not be injured. Smuts got 130 rifles and heaps of dynamite.'[20]

He then advanced with his men and his dynamite upon O'okiep and served the same summons there—surrender or I'll blow you all

11. At O'okiep, April 1902

1. Field Cornet C. Brink   2. Commandant B. D. Bouwer   3. Field Cornet A. G. Boshoff   4. General J. L. van Deventer   5. B. D. Bouwer Senior   6. General J. C. Smuts   7. Field Cornet W. Kotzé   8. Corporal H. Vermaas   9. General S. G. Maritz   10. Field Cornet J. van Brummelen   11. Commandant S. Schoeman   12. J. Brink   13. Field Cornet A. Standers   14. Field Cornet J. van den Berg   15. Field Cornet P. F. Visser   16. C. T. Möller   17. Marquis Robert de Kersauson   18. Field Cornet B. Coetzee.

up. But Colonel Skelton, the officer in command, was a man of spirit. Politely but firmly he told Smuts he could go to the devil. So Smuts sent a force westwards to destroy the bridges on the railway-line to Port Nolloth while he surrounded O'okiep with his main body and attacked its outposts one by one. Meanwhile the commanding officer in Port Nolloth was sending panicky telegrams to Cape Town, although really he had nothing to worry about, because H.M.S. *Barracuta* was steaming north from the Cape and the troops that were following were more than enough to scatter Smuts's small force. Colonel Skelton and Smuts had both of them a truer understanding of their little affair. One gets an impression from the documents that they also understood each other: Smuts offered Skelton a truce so that he could get the women and children out of the firing line; Skelton took a day to think the offer over and then told Smuts that he believed his non-combatants would be safer in the town than out on the open veld.

It is pleasant to recall at the close of this horrible war a few happenings which do just a little suggest 'the gentleman's war' of romantic legend. And it is pleasant to record this little campaign, a characteristic last act of cheeky aggression which concluded the republican career of General J. C. Smuts. The British relieved O'okiep in the first week of May. Smuts by then was already travelling under British safe-conduct to Botha's headquarters and to his place at the peace conference.

CHAPTER 9

THE BITTER END

IT is only by flashes that a picture can be seen of Smuts as others saw him at this time. The war for him was a forcing-house of growth and change both in his inner life and his outward appearance. There survives among the papers of the British Military Intelligence a photograph of him as he was before the war, a young man trimly clad in a dark suit with stiff shirt and collar and black tie, clean shaven, lips firm but flexible, firm chin, eyes set well apart and looking straight ahead with intense concentration—an ardent spirit in a body rather too frail.[1] Wolstenholme, his best friend among the Cambridge dons, had been afraid that the hardships of campaigning might wreck 'the pale stripling' whom he remembered, but was 'relieved and rejoiced' to receive after the war the photograph of a powerful, broad-shouldered man deeply stamped with all the marks of experience, keenness and determination. As Smuts confessed to his wife, the bitter years of campaigning had been in some senses a happy time for him. They had at any rate brought him to the maturity of his powers, both physical and mental.[2]

An Intelligence notice circulated by the British towards the close of the war described him as follows: 'Smuts, Jan: General or Hooft Commandant in command of about 600 Transvaalers; about 30 years of age: about 6 ft: slender built, dark hair, brown eyes, dark brown moustache and French cut beard; slight burr in speech; well liked in commando; has pet name of "Oom Jannie"; former State Attorney of S.A. Republic.'[3] This verbal portraiture had some good touches but one wonders how anybody could have made such a howler about the colour of those most unusual pale blue eyes? One wonders, too, whether his men really made quite so free with his 'pet name'? To Tottie Krige, Deneys Reitz and a few others within the small circle of kinship or family intimacy he certainly was Oom Jannie; but in the diaries that some of his men kept he is almost always The General: The General's orders are these; The General has told us that. One diarist, on a solemn occasion, recorded an address delivered to the commando by 'The Honourable General Smuts'.[4]

Still, one would hardly expect to find faultless accuracy of detail in an Intelligence notice; the historical value of the document lies rather in its general tone and point of view. If it can be taken as a fair sample, there was nothing disrespectful or unfriendly in the language that British military persons used in describing Smuts; they did not, for example, describe him as a brigand—though Chamberlain, to Smuts's bitter resentment, denounced Boer 'brigand-age' during the last phase of the war. By and large, the civilian leaders showed more hostility towards the Boers than the military leaders did. Smuts, the smart young colonial spoilt by too much education, the Cambridge man gone wrong, was a particular object of their distrust and dislike. Whenever his name occurs in official papers of the Colonial Office or the Foreign Office, the implication is that he is the dangerous, crafty, implacable enemy of everything British. This view of him (and of his wife) persisted after the war; it is to be found, for example, in the confidential notes that were composed from time to time for the benefit of important British personages visiting South Africa. And it has been perpetuated in various historical writings of later years, for example in Armstrong's biography *Grey Steel*, where Smuts's bitter, cunning, implacable enmity towards the British is projected backwards to the Bloemfontein Conference and even to his first arrival in the Transvaal.

Such over-dramatisation misses the complications of his character and of the debate that took place within his mind between conflicting ideas and affections. There survive among his papers six or seven letters of an English private soldier, Johnnie Butterworth, a homesick boy who read the Bible, played the harmonium in chapel, sang hymns, quoted poetry, gazed at the stars on clear dark nights and got his thoughts into a tangle as he brooded over his duties as a patriot and the evil he was doing by fighting on the side of Chamber-lain, Rhodes and the great capitalists. I am doing my duty, he told his sister; and yet the Boers believe that *they* are in the right. 'It does come home to one, lass, at a time like this, the need for more John Brights and Cobdens, *Peace* men.'[5] This was just what Smuts had said to Arthur Guy Enock that October day when the commandos were marching by to the frontier. If only there were another John Bright....

Not that he troubled himself with fruitless yearnings or regrets when once the decision had been taken. From that time onward he was a fully committed man, ready and eager for any exploit or stratagem, within the rules of war, that would give victory to his side. The British were fully justified, on the evidence of the propaganda that he got into print, in writing him down as a relentless enemy. Their justification would have been even more clear had they been able to read his secret papers, beginning with the plan of war that he composed in September 1899, or to hear the speeches that he made to his men on Dingaan's day and other great occasions. And yet from time to time he struck a note very different from his usual rhetorical blare of nationalistic self-assertiveness. In a little masterpiece of patriotic writing he recorded a talk which he had had in April 1901 with a courageous Boer woman, who was able in her greatness of soul to show understanding and pity even for a traitor.* In an essay upon Boer patriotism he affirmed his passionate love for the soil of South Africa, 'the unbuilt country coming virgin from the hands of God'.⁶ His patriotism, at the deepest levels of feeling, was a patriotism more of place than of race; the city-dwellers who spoke English, he declared, could never love South Africa with the same understanding and self-surrender as belonged by birth and up-bringing to the country-dwelling Boers. The argument might appear intolerant and hectoring, yet it opened a new prospect of hope: for could not the two warring peoples find reconciliation in a different struggle—not to dominate each other, but to outmatch each other in loyalty and service to their common country?

This thought found expression in a long political tract which he wrote in January 1902 and addressed as an open letter to W. T. Stead, with the intention (so he told Abraham Fischer, a member of the Deputation in Holland) of appealing to the conscience of the English people. The tract began, in the manner of all his propagandist writing at that time, with denunciations of the British and all their works in peace and war, their impatience and cupidity, their contempt for the rights of small nations, their breaches of the rules of war, their outrages against humanity and even against animals. Against such abuses of power, he declared, his people would fight to the bitter end. But suppose ruin was waiting at the bitter end for both peoples? Smuts brought the black men of South Africa into his picture. 'The war between the white races will run its course and pass away and may, if followed by a statesmanlike settlement, one

* *Een Boeren Vrouw*: English version, *A Talk with a Boer Woman* (unpublished).

day only be remembered as a great thunderstorm, which purified the atmosphere of the sub-continent. But the native question will never pass away; it will become more difficult as time goes on, and the day may come when the evils and horrors of this war will appear as nothing in comparison with its after effects produced on the native mind.' He was pleading now for a return to the policies of 'evolution and cooperation' which, he argued, would have obliterated within ten years every ground of contention between the two white peoples had not British impatience flung the opportunity away. He was pleading—as he was to plead in later life many times—for an agreed, not a dictated peace, from which would arise a new South African nationality and a new Imperial order, if Empire still remained the right name for the free and fraternal association which he envisaged.

For South Africa, the name which he had in mind was Commonwealth. The question at issue between the British Empire and the Boer Republics, he declared, was a moral question. Let the British government 'openly and manfully confess that they have been wrong and with a single eye try to undo that wrong'. Let them first of all recognise the independence of the Republics. Here was the true road to a rational peace and to the reconciliation and union of the warring peoples. 'On this basis, and in a generous spirit of forgive and forget, let us try to found a stable Commonwealth in South Africa, in which Boer and Briton will both be proud to be partners; let it be clearly understood that England shall meddle as little with the internal concerns of this Commonwealth as with those of Canada or Australasia, and the best solution of the South African problem under existing circumstances will have been made, and a new Commonwealth of untold possibilities will have been launched on a joyous and prosperous career.' But if England 'hardens her heart', he continued, 'then the ghost of the murdered Boer people will haunt the British Empire to its grave; then across the centuries the terrible curse of Isaiah will blast the British Empire: Woe to thee that spoilest....' Smuts spelled out Isaiah's curse at length.[7]

It is plain from his covering letter to Abraham Fischer that he was beginning to doubt whether his people would be able 'to bear the burden much longer'. Their sufferings were indescribable. He meant the sufferings of the people, not of the men on commando. 'The worse the suffering, the better they fight; the boers surely have never fought as of late. On that score I have no fear for the future, but one must keep the whole situation in mind.' Smuts professed himself ready, should the opportunity offer, 'for a reasonable settlement on the basis of our independence'. He had not recognised, even yet, the stark fact that a reasonable settlement and Afrikaner independence were, in the British view, incompatibles.

Sometime during the early months of 1900—precisely when, it is impossible to say—he brought himself to admit that his little nation was not going to defeat the British Empire. Never before in any of his commitments, private or public, had he contemplated failure, and this first taste of it was bitter. A change becomes apparent in the tone of the quotations that he wrote down in his notebook: on one page Carlyle on Justice, a stanza from Byron's Isles of Greece or some similar affirmation of patriotism and defiance: on the next page lines like these from Thomas à Kempis: 'I have received the Cross, I have received it from Thy hand; I will bear it, and bear it till death, as Thou hast laid it upon me.'

This was his mood as he made his way to Vereeniging. In a farewell message to his soldiers at Concordia, dated 24 April 1902, he declared: 'God grant that this war, which has already demanded from us so much sacrifice, may be ended honourably and justly. Should the conditions, in respect of the two Republics and the interests of the Colonists, prove unacceptable, I feel assured that we shall renew the struggle with new courage and zeal. Officers and burghers can be sure of this—that we shall do our best for the permanent good of Land and People....Continue in your duty with all your energies and without too much thinking about peace.'

The official record on the Boer side of the discussions that led to the Peace of Vereeniging was kept in the Dutch language and subsequently published by the secretaries of the two Republics, Rev. J. D. Kestell of the Free State and the Transvaaler, D. E. van Velden. There is a translation of the record by van Velden which deserves to rank among the classics of political debate in English print.[8] Like the soldiers of Cromwell's army who met at Putney in 1648 to determine the future of the English nation, these Boer soldiers opened their meetings with prayer and felt themselves to be in the presence of God. In the vivid imagery of their country upbringing and their Calvinist belief they expressed the agony which each man felt in his soul as he struggled to declare and to do what his conscience told him was right. Their testimony, and their pleading one with another, had a poignancy not to be found in the debates of Cromwell's soldiers, who had met together after victory to build a new Jerusalem on English soil; whereas the Boer soldiers were meeting in face of defeat, with no immediate hope for their people beyond sheer survival.

Their struggle was a tragic drama in five acts: the first at Klerksdorp, where the leaders of the two republics met from 9 to 11 April: the second at Pretoria, where they held conference with Kitchener from 12 to 17 April: the third at Vereeniging, where representatives of the people—thirty burghers from each Republic—debated the issues of peace and war from 15 to 17 May: the fourth at Pretoria, where a commission negotiated from 9 to 28 May with Kitchener and Milner (and indirectly with the British government): the fifth and last act again at Vereeniging where the burghers met on 29 May for the last agonising debates which culminated in the signature of peace on 31 May.

The prologue to this drama was a long-drawn-out correspondence, first between the British government and the Netherlands government, which on 25 January had offered its good offices for peace negotiations; and secondly, between Lord Kitchener and Acting-President Schalk Burger of the South African Republic. The salient facts of this correspondence were, in the first place, Great Britain's refusal to accept foreign mediation or to permit any communication at all between the Boer leaders in South Africa and their Deputation in Europe; secondly, the acceptance by Schalk Burger, subject to President Steyn's agreement, of the British offer to receive proposals of peace from the Boer leaders within South Africa. It took a considerable time to discover the whereabouts of Steyn, but on 28 March he wrote to Schalk Burger accepting the proposal for a meeting between their two governments. They met at Klerksdorp— six Transvaalers and five Free Staters, with their secretaries—on 9 April. And there the drama opened.

The discussion soon revealed a deep cleavage of emotion and thought between the Free Staters and the Transvaalers. 'President Steyn said that, as far as he was concerned, there was only one condition upon which he could make peace, and that was: Independence....If the enemy did not wish the Republics to remain independent, the struggle must continue....Rather than make terms with the British he would submit unconditionally to them for ever.'

It is worth pausing for a moment to reflect upon these two words, so ominous for the coming century of conflict, 'unconditional surrender'. Extremes meet extremes, and Milner was at one with Steyn in loathing the idea of any middle term between total victory and total defeat. Milner found it alarming to think that Kitchener would have the steering of the peace talks in their opening phase; Kitchener, he knew, was sick of a war which brought him no credit and might cheat him of his coveted command in India; Kitchener could not be trusted to keep his talks with the Boers within the strictly military sphere. Milner hated the prospect of the war ending with a written document containing conditions and pledges that would restrict the freedom of British action. And that, *mutatis mutandis*, was precisely what Steyn hated: if the Boers could not defeat the British, then let them be beaten to the ground, rather than give pledges which would hamper them when the day came, as it surely would, for them to rise again and break the shackles of the British Empire.

A treaty recognising Boer independence or no treaty at all; indefinite prolongation of the war or unconditional surrender: these alternatives, put by Steyn, were too stark to win acceptance. Successive speakers shuffled between them, with suggestions for 'encumbered independence' or similar compromises, until on the third day Botha, in a speech just as forthright as Steyn's, affirmed a totally different doctrine of national and individual duty. 'How must this war end? Must they wait until everyone had been captured? or should they, for the sake of the people, take another course? His Government, his officers and he himself could say: "Let the enemy carry out their proclamations concerning us. We have nothing more to lose. We have fought for nothing else than our country, and wish to have that back or nothing else. Banish us, banish the Government" But then, what about the People? The People could not be banished. Was there now not still a chance to save something for the People?' In other words, republican independence was not an absolute. There might be higher claims.

For the present, these deep cleavages of conviction could be covered over. Everybody agreed with Hertzog that the two governments could not by their own decision 'meddle with the independence'; if that issue arose, they would have to put it to representatives of the people.[9] But perhaps the issue need not arise. On 11 April they decided to seek a personal meeting with Kitchener and to present him with proposals for peace which combined a repudiation of British sovereignty with a recognition of British hegemony.

Proceeding from the basis that they do not recognise the annexation, the two Governments are prepared to conclude peace by conceding the following matters:
   1. The concluding of a perpetual Treaty of friendship and peace...
[three main heads were listed].
   2. Dismantling of all State Forts.
   3. Arbitration in all future differences....
   4. Equal education rights for both the English and Dutch languages.
   5. Mutual amnesty.

If the security of British interests and the recognition of British paramountcy in South Africa had been the aim of the British government, these proposals would have satisfied it. But its aim was nothing less than sovereign dominion. When Kitchener received the Boer leaders next day in Pretoria, he expressed astonishment at their preamble.[10] 'Must I understand from what you say', he exclaimed, 'that you wish to retain your Independence?' The Boers thought that his astonishment was feigned; but possibly it was genuine, seeing that independence was excluded, in the British view, not merely by the proclamations of annexation but by the official correspondence which the Boers themselves had accepted as the starting-point of the negotiations. Kitchener refused to transmit their proposals to London until they had allowed him to strike out the brave opening words which repudiated British annexation, and until he had secured their agreement to some new words which opened the way to proposals of a very different kind. '...But if these terms are not satisfactory, they desire to know what terms the British Government would give them in order to secure the end they all desire.'

The reply from London reached Kitchener next day (13 April) and made it clear beyond all doubt that independence and a negotiated peace were incompatibles. His Majesty's government, like the Boer leaders, ardently desired peace—'But they have already stated in the clearest terms, and must repeat, that they cannot entertain any proposals which are based on the continued Independence of the former Republics which have been formally annexed to the British Crown. It would be well for you and Milner to interview Boer Representatives and explain this. You should encourage them to put forward fresh proposals, excluding Independence, which we shall be glad to receive.'

Now was the time for the Boer leaders to break off the negotiations if they were determined at all costs to stick by independence. Instead, they kept the negotiations alive by asking leave to send an envoy for consultation with the Deputation in Europe. They also asked leave to summon a representative gathering of their people in South Africa, and for this purpose they requested an armistice. Meanwhile, they sought to elicit a statement of the terms that His Majesty's government would grant 'subsequent to a relinquishment of Independence'. These various requests took them a long way down the slippery slope of surrender.

The British reply brought them no comfort; it was an offer to accept 'a general surrender' on the terms that Kitchener had offered a year previously at Middelburg, 'with such modifications in details as may be mutually agreed upon'. Here was a second opportunity for the Boer governments to break off negotiations. Instead, they agreed to accept the facilities offered by Kitchener (short of the armistice they had requested) for bringing to Vereeniging a representative gathering of their people, which would have before it both the Middelburg proposals and the record of the recent discussions. Independence, it appeared, if not as yet admitted to be expendable, was admitted to be a matter for debate.[11]

The admission was made while Smuts was still fighting his little war in far-away Namaqualand. The two opening acts of the drama, at Klerksdorp and Pretoria, had determined the drama's theme and possibly its climax; but Smuts had played no part in them at all. In all probability he did not even know until the last week of April that negotiations for peace were taking place. The fact needs emphasising, for it has been customary to ascribe to Smuts a decisive, if not *the* decisive part in the negotiations. In the later stages his influence was certainly considerable, but the chief praise or blame (both words have been used, but it would be better to say, the chief responsibility) belongs to the representatives of the two Republics who were in the business from start to finish.

Smuts was summoned to Vereeniging, not as an elected representative of the people but as legal adviser to the government of the

South African Republic. On 24 April he boarded a British ship at Port Nolloth for Simonstown and from there he travelled north in a British train, arriving among his old comrades with rather more time in hand for informal discussion than Deneys Reitz has suggested in his lively account of the journey.[12] The only incident of any importance along the way was the meeting that he had with Kitchener at Kroonstad on 4 May.

According to the notes that Smuts wrote down in his little brown notebook[13] Kitchener gave a fair report of the negotiations up to date and a blunt statement of his own views—which were not in every case the views of his colleague Milner or of the British government.

1. Natives to be disarmed and no franchise until after self-government.
2. Surrender with honour; retention of weapons under permits; as regards horses burghers will be treated with 'generosity'.
3. No chance of immediate self-government, no chance whatever.
4. K. strongly disapproves unconditional surrender as this will indicate that Boers wish to rise again and then prisoners will not return without delay. English government prefers unconditional surrender but K. as friend of the Boers strongly against it. . . .
8. If we go on fighting no prisoner of war will ever come back unless he take up arms against us as proof of loyalty.

Smuts did not show himself unduly impressed by Kitchener (we have the testimony of Deneys Reitz on that), but he must have realised during the interview that the alternatives he would have to face at Vereeniging were stark. Nor is it likely that he heard anything during the following days from Botha, Schalk Burger, F. W. Reitz and his other Transvaal friends that would make the impending decision appear any easier.

A letter that he wrote to his wife on 12 May shows that he was still uncommitted, but moving in his thought towards Botha rather than towards Steyn.

What the upshot of the present negotiations will be I cannot say; I only hope that it won't be another twelve months before I see you again. Klaas de Wet is remarkably fortunate in seeing Ella so often,* but then our cases are very different, and I and my work are regarded with much bitterness and hatred. Nothing will however deter me from doing my duty, for I do not regard the favour either of my friends or my enemies but shall ever strive to do my duty, to retain my own self-respect and sense of personal

* See p. 130 above.

rectitude and—last not least—the goodwill and respect of her who is the last thing left me in this life. A man may lose his possessions, even his home and country, but he may yet remain a citizen of that larger and higher kingdom whose limits are the conscience and aspirations of humanity.

He told her about his reading during the past twelve months and his endeavours to attain 'the higher Stoicism'. 'I am writing coldly and frigidly, but you know me, my Mia; you know how warmly I feel and how much I long that we shall be tranquil in soul even amid the severest losses that life can bring. Who knows what is still in store for us—what losses, what disappointments, what renunciations —but there are treasures, treasures of the soul, of love and truth and endeavour which no man can ever rob us of. ...' His letter appeared to be turning into a stoic homily; but he ended it as a love-letter.[14]

When the third act of the drama opened at Vereeniging three days later Smuts found himself in the morning playing a lawyer's and in the afternoon a soldier's part. At the outset, the Assembly of the People had to decide whether their members were bound by the instructions of the commandos that had elected them (some commandos had imposed 'mandates' ruling out the surrender of independence) or whether each man was free to reach his decision according to his own conscience and his judgment of the situation. Steyn favoured the first opinion, Botha the second. The two lawyers, Hertzog and Smuts, settled the question in Botha's favour. The debate proceeded with a speech by Schalk Burger explaining the circumstances under which the Assembly had been called and entreating its members to act in a spirit of unity and make their decision with the head rather than the heart. The chairman, General Beyers, then called upon the military leaders to report upon the situation within their several districts. Smuts, when his turn came, gave a clear account of conditions in the Cape Colony. There were 3000 men under arms there, he said; but they were hampered by lack of horses, forage and reinforcements. 'These conditions', he declared, 'have led me to the conclusion that there will be no general rising in the Cape Colony, and that the continuance of the war will depend more upon the Republics than upon the Cape Colony.'

The Transvaalers, with one or two exceptions, gave evidence against continuing the war, not merely for military reasons but because its continuance would inflict irreparable ruin upon the people. 'Our people do not deserve to be annihilated', declared

Schalk Burger. 'Let us do what we can to save our people,' pleaded Botha, 'even if we must lose our independence.' But the Free Staters, almost to a man, declared their independence sacrosanct. 'I have nothing to do with facts', exclaimed General de Wet. 'The entire war is a matter of faith.' He called upon the burghers to renew their covenant with God.

On the second afternoon the outline of a compromise took shape in a proposal by F. W. Reitz: that the Republics, while standing firm on the basis of their sovereign independence in domestic affairs, should offer to accept the status of a British protectorate, to surrender the conduct of foreign relations, to sign a treaty of defence and to cede the Witwatersrand and Swaziland. Hertzog and Smuts were instructed to draft proposals in this sense. Meanwhile, although the debate continued with unabated passion, it swung definitely against the Free Staters when de la Rey, who hitherto had supported them, fell into line behind Botha. On the third day, 17 May, the Assembly empowered the two governments to conclude peace on the basis of Reitz's proposals, as embodied in the Hertzog–Smuts draft. It also appointed Botha, de la Rey, Smuts, de Wet and Hertzog as a commission with powers to negotiate at large with the British (in the event of their rejecting the latest Boer proposals) with the proviso that any document which they agreed upon must be submitted to the Assembly for ratification.

It was not a promising brief, but Smuts made the best of it. On 19 May, when the commission met Kitchener and Milner at Pretoria, he made himself the main advocate of the three salient Boer proposals: surrender of independence in foreign relations; retention of self-government under British supervision; cession of territory. He even tried to persuade his sceptical antagonists that political ambiguity was a positive virtue.

General Smuts: As history teaches us, it has happened before that questions were solved by compromises. And this draft proposal is as near as we can come to colonial government.

Lord Kitchener: Do you accept the annexations?

General Smuts: Not formally, but I do not understand that this proposal would be in conflict with the annexation proclamations.

Lord Kitchener: I fear that my mind is not clear enough to understand this. There will have to be two Governments in one State. And how do you propose that the government should be carried on?

General Smuts: A fuller explanation would have to be given to the word *supervision*; and I thought this was exactly the point which could be further discussed, and on which we could negotiate.

Lord Milner: I shall certainly not depart from a clear basis to accept a vague basis.

Lord Kitchener: I feel convinced that your proposal could never be carried out in the practical government of the country.

The argument continued throughout the morning but it led nowhere. During the adjournment, the commission discussed the situation and 'sent General Smuts to talk over a few matters with Kitchener and Milner'. We may assume, from the course the proceedings took in the full conference that afternoon, that the exchange of views between Smuts and the two Englishmen was sternly realistic. They must have made it clear to him once and for all that the British government would insist upon the Boers laying down their arms and admitting themselves to be British subjects. Smuts must have demanded a clear statement about the treatment that the Boers could count upon if they laid down their arms. In his little brown notebook there is a list, unfortunately undated, of points which he believed to be agreed: amnesty for all deeds of war, comprehensive financial aid, the reunion of families, the disarmament of Natives, economic rehabilitation of the Boer families and farms. Following this list comes a most astonishing entry: 'Within two years self-government as in the Cape Colony will be granted with franchise as in the Cape Colony and constituencies more or less on the basis of voters. The boundaries of both republics will not be altered until federation for South Africa is introduced....' Responsible self-government within two years! That flattering prospect, certainly, was not painted by Milner. The biographers both of Kitchener and of Smuts have told a story about Kitchener drawing Smuts aside and encouraging him to look forward to the victory of the Liberals in Britain and the consequential grant of self-government to the Boers. The words which have just been quoted suggest that the story is true: indeed, that Kitchener's prophecies were more fantastically rash than has hitherto been suggested.

It may be doubted whether Kitchener gained any additional prestige or popularity with Smuts by going behind the back of his colleague. It may also be doubted whether Smuts considered his forecasts of the course of British politics to be any more competent than those that he could make for himself without Kitchener's aid.

Be this as it may, the conference set itself to work, on the afternoon of 19 May, upon more immediate business. Milner produced a document which affirmed the surrender of the Boers and their acceptance of British allegiance: to this, he said, a schedule could be added, varying the terms which had been offered fourteen months earlier at Middelburg. After a good deal of argument, a committee representing both sides was appointed to draft the schedule. Its members were Milner, Sir Richard Solomon (his Attorney-General in Cape Colony), Hertzog and Smuts.

From this time on the articles of the peace settlement began to take shape. Kestell in his book pays a tribute to the achievements of Hertzog and Smuts on the drafting committee: above all, he says, they insisted 'that the Governments of both States, if a treaty of peace were made, should sign it as the Governments respectively of the South African Republic and of the Orange Free State, and this virtually forced the British Government to treat the "annexations" of the two Republics as non-existent...'.[15] That point, no doubt, had importance for psychological reasons; but the emerging document contained also a substantial gain for the Boers which Kestell did not record. Under the Middelburg proposals of March 1901 the question of a Native franchise in the ex-Republics was not to be considered until they were granted representative institutions. In Milner's original draft of May 1902 the decision was postponed still further by writing 'self-government' in place of 'representative institutions'. However, the draft seemed also to prejudge the decision in the Natives' favour. The actual words were: 'The Franchise will not be given to Natives until after the Introduction of Self-Government.' The implication was clear that it *would* be given to them then. If the article had remained unaltered, the principle of votes for Natives would have been written into the treaty. Smuts made one or two shots at tinkering with the article but in the end he rewrote it completely: 'The question of granting the Franchise to Natives will not be decided until after the introduction of self-government.' This form of words left it completely open whether or not the Natives would ever be given any voting rights at all. When Kitchener, Milner and the British government accepted the new article they threw away their country's case on what has remained from that day to this the most crucial issue of South African politics. Surrender was not all on the Boer side.

Milner, of course, achieved—but for how long?—the political and cultural domination of Britons over Boers which was the essential object of his policy. Immediate and complete military surrender, recognition by the Boers of King Edward VII as their lawful sovereign, recognition of English as the official language of their country and as predominant in their schools, military government to be followed (although self-government would be granted some day) by Crown Colony government: these were the main terms which the Boer commission took back on 27 May for presentation to the Assembly of the People. The commission was told that no amendment of these terms would be tolerated and that the Boers must answer Yes or No before midnight on 31 May.

Smuts, meanwhile, had received news that his wife was seriously ill. On 26 May he wrote to her: 'As we lose in worldly possessions, in political status and in the outward accompaniments of wealth and power and influence, we shall be thrown back all the more powerfully upon ourselves and each other. Hand in hand and soul in soul we shall go through life, and no noise of the outside world shall penetrate into our little sovereign kingdom of the soul. So wait and suffer patiently for a short while yet.'[16]

On 29 May the Assembly of the People met again under the shadow of the British ultimatum. After all the debating and all the drafting of the past seven weeks the question they had to answer remained essentially the same as the question that Steyn and Botha, from their different standpoints, had put at the very outset: whether their highest duty was to the Boer Republics or the Boer people. Really, there was nothing new to be said, although some speakers achieved grandeur in saying what they had said before—or in unsaying it. At last, on the afternoon of 31 May, a motion which Smuts and Hertzog had drafted was put to the vote. It recited the reasons why the Republics could not continue the war; it deplored the refusal of the British government to recognise their independence; it recommended acceptance of the British terms. Of the sixty Boers assembled at Vereeniging, all but six—three Transvaalers and three Free Staters—voted for the motion. The terms of peace (or of surrender) were signed that night, just within the time limit stipulated by the British.

The document which closed the Anglo-Boer War is usually called the Treaty of Vereeniging; but it was signed at Pretoria, and its

III. A page from the penny notebook, May 1902

claims to be called a treaty are disputable. It was given no official title and its preamble said merely that the signatories 'agree on the following articles'. Milner called them terms of surrender. Kitchener called them terms of peace. Botha called them a treaty. It was chiefly to please Botha that the British began, later on, to call them the Treaty of Vereeniging.[17]

There was room for dispute, not merely about the general description of the document, but about the obligations which it imposed. Six years later, Milner was denouncing as a 'Great Betrayal' the timing and the terms of self-government in the Transvaal. Twelve years later, some of the men who had voted for accepting the British terms were in arms against the King.

They had signed under protest. The motion of protest—but also of acceptance—had been drafted by Hertzog and Smuts. Let us return to Vereeniging and try to enter the mind of Smuts during the last critical days. The high moment of drama had been reached on the morning of the second day, when the announcement was made that Steyn, who had been for months past close to the edge of physical collapse, had freed his neck at last from the hateful collar by resigning his office as President of the Free State. Smuts spoke late that afternoon. He knew precisely what he was going to say.[18] Of all the entries that he made at that time in his small brown notebook, none is more illuminating than the famous passage which he quoted from Lincoln's Second Inaugural. It was the purpose of his speech to persuade his comrades in war that the time had come 'to bind up the nation's wounds'.

He began quietly with an affirmation of his personal responsibility as a member of the government that had entered into the war with England, and with a definition of the Assembly's responsibility. They represented the people, not merely the army; the decision they had to make was not merely military but political.

Now, if we consider the matter from a military standpoint, if we consider it only as a military matter, then I must admit that we can still go on with the struggle. We are still an unvanquished military force. We have still 18,000 men in the field, veterans, with whom you can do almost any work. We can thus push our cause, from a military point of view, still further. But we are not here as an army, but as a people; we have not only a military question, but also a national matter to deal with. No one here represents his own commando only. Everyone here represents the

Afrikaner people (*die Afrikaansche Volk*) and not only that portion which is still in the field, but those who are already buried and those who will live after we are gone. We represent, not only ourselves, but also the thousands who are dead, and have made the last sacrifice for their people, the prisoners of war scattered all over the world, and the men and women who are dying by thousands in the Concentration Camps of the enemy; we represent the blood and tears of an entire nation. . . .

. . .Hitherto we have not continued the struggle aimlessly. We did not fight merely to be shot at. We commenced the struggle, and continued it to this moment, because we wished to maintain our independence, and were prepared to sacrifice everything for it. But we may not sacrifice the Afrikaaner people for that independence.

He recalled his correspondence with President Kruger a year before and the advice the President had given to keep on fighting in the hope of European intervention and a general rising in Cape Colony. They had done their best in Cape Colony and now they knew that they could not expect a general rising there. Europe had offered sympathy, and would continue to offer sympathy—nothing more— 'until the last Boer hero lies in his last resting place, till the last Boer woman has gone to her grave with a broken heart'. While they continued fighting, the objective for which they were fighting—their independence—moved further and further away; but the destruction of their people came nearer and nearer. And now the enemy offered terms of peace with a promise of amnesty for their colonial brothers —'I fear that the day will come when we shall no more be able to rescue the so-called rebels, and then they will have just cause to reproach us that we have sacrificed their interests also for our already hopeless cause'. That was the last argument of his speech. In one short sentence of shattering simplicity he stated the conclusion: 'Broeders, wij hebben besloten tot het bittere einde te staan; laten wij als mannen erkennen dat het einde voor ons is gekomen—gekomen in bitterder vorm dan wij ooit hadden gedacht.' ('Brothers, we resolved to stand to the bitter end; let us admit like men that the end has come for us—has come in a more bitter form than we had ever thought possible.')

Indeed, the end had come irretrievably for the Boer republics. But Smuts refused to believe that it had come for the Boer people and for South Africa. Dark though the future was, he cried, they must not give up their courage and hope and trust in God. No one would ever convince him that the unparalleled sacrifice which the Afrikaner people had laid upon the altar of freedom was all to no purpose. 'The war of freedom of South Africa has been fought, not only for the Boers, but for the entire people of South Africa. The result of that struggle we leave in God's hands. Perhaps it is His will to lead the people of South Africa through defeat and humiliation, yea, even through the valley of the shadow of death, to a better future and a brighter day.'

When the treaty had been signed Smuts had still to perform his last duty as a Boer general. The instructions that he drew up for the orderly disbandment of his forces in Namaqualand comprise the last entry but one in the surrender notebook.[19] The story of that sad ceremony is told in a diary kept by one of his men. The commando knew nothing about the war beyond their own victories and imagined that it was the British who were suing for peace; but on the evening of 14 June their general returned from Vereeniging and told them that their comrades in the north had surrendered their arms and that they must now do the same and become henceforward obedient subjects of their new government. On 16 June the general paraded them in face of a British column drawn up to receive their weapons. Many of the men had tears in their eyes as they laid their rifles down. Then the commando made its last ride together to a place where 'the Colonial brothers' were taken from the ranks and put into a separate camp. The Transvaalers then rode south to a tented camp where they stayed eight days 'well and free as air' and received visits from the neighbouring families who brought them fruit and wine and tobacco and wonderful cakes and tarts that the girls had baked with their own hands. 'They...praised our heroic spirit and heroic deeds and thanked us for what we had done in coming to the Cape Colony to help them shake off the English yoke. And then we went away and after 8 more days came safe and sound to our dear fatherland.'

For this young soldier there was some happiness at the journey's end; but in letters that Smuts received for many years to come from burghers of his commando many stories may be read of broken lives.

CHAPTER 10

STRANGE DEFEAT

At Vereeniging and for many weeks afterwards Smuts was suffering constant anxiety about his wife's state of health. Her weight was down to seven stone; she had pains in her back and other symptoms of an illness difficult to diagnose; she could not find out from her doctors whether or no they proposed to operate on her; she could not foresee when she would be well enough to leave Pietermaritzburg and join her husband. Another woman might have begged her husband to come to her; but she took it for granted, as he did, that he must first fulfil every duty laid upon him as a former minister and general of the South African Republic.

He wrote to her on the morning of 1 June: 'The tragedy is over. The curtain falls over the Boers as British subjects and the plucky little republics are no more. Peace was signed last night at Pretoria. ...So we shall start afresh, working along the lines opened by the new conditions. I accept my fate—that is the only manly course left.' He told her that he would be setting out next morning for Cape Colony to perform the act of surrender and to secure as best he could fair treatment for the men of his commando, particularly the colonial rebels. He asked her to write to him c/o General Sir John French and not to forget that he had 'reverted to plain J. C. Smuts'. Finally, he spoke of the new duties and opportunities awaiting plain J. C. Smuts and his wife in the immediate future: 'Let us do our best to bind up the old wounds, to forgive and forget, and to make the future happier than the past has been.'[1]

His absence in Cape Colony lasted a month. After the commando had been disbanded, he rode south with Tottie Krige to the farm Klipfontein, the home of his boyhood, where he met and approved his father's new wife, a girl who had been in the same class with him at school. Next evening he and Tottie were with the Krige family in Stellenbosch, amidst memories of past happiness which he found almost unbearably poignant. 'Ah Lappie, everything here in Stellenbosch reminds me so much of you, of the happy days of the golden past before we knew worry and care, pain and humiliation, when

IV. Smuts and Tottie Krige

our souls burgeoned like two branches from one stem—that it is too painful for me to be here without you.' Lappie means Little Rag, and was a pet name that he had given to Isie Krige when they were students together in Stellenbosch. It was better for him to recall the lighter moods of those golden years than to dwell with too much intensity upon the grief of their passing. He continued his letter on the note of affectionate teasing which she so well remembered, intermingled with family gossip, news of their house at Pretoria and a few words at the close of reassurance and endearment.[2]

In Cape Town he held some discussions with T. L. Graham, a former friend of his who was now Attorney-General and acting Prime Minister of Cape Colony.[3] Graham gave assurances of fair treatment for the colonial rebels which convinced him that he was free at last to go north to Pretoria and from there to Pietermaritzburg.

His visit to Pietermaritzburg was necessarily short, but long enough to satisfy him that his wife would be well enough to join him within five or six weeks. He knew that he would be hard put to it within that time to make everything ready for her. The Imperial Yeomanry had taken over their home during the war. Smuts told his wife that they had left it in better shape than he had expected; he did not tell her that they had wrecked his law library. He admitted that there was some wall-papering to do (but Ella de Wet had made a start with that) and some furniture to buy (but he was having very good luck in the sales). Their garden, he confessed, was in a sad state of neglect; but a cousin of hers was pruning the trees and he himself was hard at work alongside a Native boy, preparing the vegetable beds and planting the seeds and seedlings. 'Everything will be right for your Honour's arrival....I hope the mealies, peas and potatoes will have grown well when your Honour returns.'

He sent her no news that was not cheerful. 'My health', he wrote, 'is first class, etc. etc., so you can take it that everything is first class with me.' He told her about his activities in getting passes, permits and jobs for returned burghers, about the legal work that was coming his way, about the kindness of Jimmie Roos, their solicitor and friend, in helping him to get their affairs straight. Roos had his law manuscripts safe and was guarding her nest-egg of £500. 'So no threat of starvation.'[4]

Isie Smuts had another comforter, Olive Schreiner, who wrote to her every week and sometimes twice a week. The letters, however, were almost too solicitous in their affection, and their effect may have well been to aggravate rather than to alleviate her sorrow and anxiety. For Olive Schreiner was ill and overstrained. She had been separated from her husband for over a year and was living in one room without a single soul for company. She and her husband were looking forward to setting up house again in a little tumbledown cottage, but she was afraid of the physical work awaiting her there, because the Native boys in her part of Cape Colony were boycotting her as a pro-Boer. Indeed, she was far too weak to cope with washing, scrubbing and cooking. She was suffering, besides, all the agonies of the frustrated artist. 'If only one could write one would feel that there was still some reason for one's going on living.'

In mid-August, when Isie returned to her husband, Olive Schreiner wrote to wish them joy and to announce her intention of visiting them soon. The visit took place in September, but its happiness was marred by misadventures: on the journey to Pretoria she fell so ill that she had to leave the train at Johannesburg and spend some days in bed there; on the return journey she was bullied and insulted on Pretoria station by 'obscene little officials' and jingo workmen. They overcharged her shamefully on her luggage and pocketed the receipt; they snatched her travel permit, waved it in the air and told her that it was only a piece of dirty paper and that she would never get away from the Transvaal. The station-master came to her rescue but as soon as his back was turned her tormentors surrounded her again. 'Even after I was sitting in my carriage, just before the train left, a filthy little foreman came in and shook his fist at me and jeered at me and told me I would never be allowed to leave the Transvaal.'[5]

When Smuts received her letter he went immediately to the railway-station to recover the excess charges which the clerks had made her pay on her luggage. This was but one of the battles that he fought during the early months of the conquest against the petty malice of petty conquerors. As will appear later he also fought some bigger battles against bigger men. And so the reputation that he had gained during the war of implacable hostility to everything British still clung to him. At the very time when his private correspondence was full of a passionate longing to end the senseless feud between Briton and Boer, British Intelligence notes contained passages such as the following about him and his wife: 'Smuts—the clever man of the

v. The parents with their first daughter, Santa, January 1904

whole Dutch combination and, as is well known, fought us hard in the Western province during the war. Pleasant, plausible and cunning. Educated at Cambridge. His wife a dreamy, untidy woman with a large knowledge of Greek. Lost some children during the war and it preys on her mind. Hates the English and everything connected with them.'

A young Englishwoman from a Quaker home in Somerset visited the Smuts household a year or two later and formed a very different impression of it. It was a funny household, she admitted, and not the most comfortable in its domestic arrangements, but the people were delightful. She had an entrancing talk about horses with Deneys Reitz, a gifted young man, son of the former State Secretary, whom General and Mrs Smuts had persuaded to come back from his voluntary exile in Madagascar and who lived with them for four years almost like an eldest son. She found the General as sympathetic in temperament as he was formidable in mental power. He did not use his great intellect to squash 'an inferior person', although he was not above using it to tease her. She felt that she had never made a friend so invigorating and responsive and altogether satisfactory. She found Mrs Smuts much occupied with her two babies; 'but she was very kind to me—as indeed they all were'.[6]

The two babies were both girls, born in 1903 and 1904. During the next ten years four more children were born, two boys and two girls.* The home in which the children grew up was probably a good deal livelier than the home of their father's childhood in the Swartland, but it was just as stable and sheltering.

Like the good strategist that he was, Smuts set purposefully to work after the Anglo-Boer War to get his private affairs into good order. The task was, to begin with, financial; for he would have thought it incompatible both with his dignity and his freedom to live perforce a precarious and anxious life in his own home. So he sought

---

* This is a convenient place for recording the birth of the Smuts children.

Twins { Koosie, born 5 March 1898, died 31 March 1898.
{ Jossie, born 5 March 1898, died 2 April 1898.

Jacobus Abraham (Koosie), born 16 April 1899, died 14 August 1900.
Susannah Johanna (Santa), born 14 August 1903.
Catherina Petronella (Cato), born 3 December 1904.
Jacob Daniel (Japie), born 17 July 1906, died 10 October 1948.
Sibylla Margaretha (Sylma), born 27 July 1908.
Jan Christian (Jannie), born 15 August 1912.
Louis Annie de la Rey (Louis), born 1 November 1914.

and won success at the bar. Plentiful briefs came his way, some of them very lucrative; in one big case he made well over £1000.[7] He saved what he could and invested the proceeds in land. Within the six years that followed the Peace of Vereeniging he bought half a dozen farms; ten years later he possessed nearly a dozen of them, aggregating over 50,000 acres.[8] 'Land', he always remembered, 'does not run away' and so long as he possessed a sufficiency of it he need never worry whether or no he was running an overdraft at the bank. The farms that he bought during the five years of his exclusion from public office became the foundation of his freedom to seize the great opportunities destined in later life to come his way.

Yet land meant far more to him than a financial asset; his boyhood love of it grew stronger as he grew older and discovered in Nature not only an emotional but an intellectual joy. He would always have preferred to live on a farm rather than in a suburb; but he had to wait until 1908 before he found the perfect farm within easy distance of his work in Pretoria. Meanwhile, he and his family lived happily in the comfortable house in Sunnyside which he had taken when he became President Kruger's State Attorney. The house was full of the noise and play of young children—a perennial delight to Smuts from his youth to his old age, provided he could shut himself away from the children when he wanted to work. There were plenty of visitors, particularly old comrades of the war, Louis Botha, Schalk Burger, Koos de la Rey, and many others. Smuts and Botha were near neighbours in Sunnyside; they seldom had need to write to each other because they could so easily talk with each other. Their geographical neighbourhood became symbolical of the close under-standing and friendship uniting each with the other.

In building or rebuilding the foundations of his life Smuts felt need of philosophy in the original meaning of that word—the love of wisdom, the search for fundamental truth. Even during the war he had carried philosophical books in his kit and had struggled as best he could to follow the guiding lines of thought which he had dis-covered during his student days and expounded in *Walt Whitman*. In the little notebook which records his thought and action during the agony of Vereeniging—his estimates of Boer forces still in the field, the notes of his talks with Kitchener, the headings of his great speech in the Assembly of the People—the last entry is the note of a new book on Personality. But how could he know whether the book was worth reading? His mental isolation had been absolute during the war; the mitigations of it which Pretoria could offer him in peace-time were trivial. In working his passage back to the world of learning he needed the sympathy and criticism of an understanding friend.

Within a few months of his return to Pretoria he received a letter from H. J. Wolstenholme, the lonely don with whom he had read Goethe and discussed philosophy during his undergraduate years at Cambridge. Wolstenholme had suffered distress because a letter which he had written to Smuts on the eve of the Boer War had been returned to him from the dead-letter office; he was afraid that Smuts might believe his silence to have been intentional, 'either through indifference, or on political grounds'. Such a belief, if Smuts had ever entertained it, could not have survived his reading of this new letter, in which his friend touched with tactful sympathy on the loss of his little son and the sufferings of his wife during 'the most iniquitous war in modern English history', and expounded from a stoutly liberal point of view the trends of thought and the probable course of policy in Great Britain. It was the longest letter that Wolstenholme had written for years, his modest but eager bid for a renewal of the friendship that mattered most in his life. Smuts responded at once with two letters in successive mails.

Thus began a correspondence—half a dozen or more long letters on each side every year—which lasted until Wolstenholme's death in 1917. It is a great misfortune that Smuts's letters have been lost (it would seem irrevocably);[9] but Wolstenholme's replies were so comprehensive and careful that a clear image of Smuts's mind is visible in them, as if in a mirror. The central theme of the corres-pondence was determined by a question which Wolstenholme asked on 9 January 1903: 'Can I be of any use to you in procuring English books?' To Smuts it was a heaven-sent offer; he had a craving for books, the one personal indulgence on which he was ready through-out his life to spend money extravagantly. But never indiscriminately: he depended on Wolstenholme to guide him through the jungle of newly published writing; in return he gave clear guidance about the classes of writing—mainly, but not exclusively, philosophical and political—which he wanted Wolstenholme to examine and if need be to purchase on his behalf.[10] The letters exchanged between the two friends were apt to begin in the vein of critical bibliography and to continue in ardent pursuit of ideas—ardent at least, on Smuts's side, for Wolstenholme kept telling him that he was far too reckless. He told him, for example, that the study of personality (with or without a big P) required a combination of psychological analysis and keen metaphysical criticism of hypotheses very different from the headlong frontal attack which he seemed to have in mind. 'Has the leap from the "psychic ego" of psychology as a science, to the Ego (of God or man) as a consistently conceivable, tangible and metaphysically impregnable reality, ever yet been successfully made?' All 'leaps' were repugnant to Wolstenholme. He implored his friend to abjure the method of Kant and Schopenhauer, with their *a priori* speculations, and to follow instead the method of Lotze, Ward, Taylor and similar modern writers, who grounded their thought upon experience, patiently studied facts and criticised with unsleeping vigilance the abstractions, hypotheses, categories, principles, or whatever instruments they might be using to elucidate and frame their knowledge. 'And if the results seem meagre and poor, compared with our yearnings, we should remember that we *must* be limited by what *is*, by what is *for us* as we can know it; no Titanic rebelliousness, no Faustian longing to penetrate the veil, can avail us or even be regarded as rational.'

Wolstenholme could see no sense in 'The Idea of the Whole' which Smuts was so ardently pursuing: it was a delusion, which ascribed to the cosmic process a purposefulness, perhaps even a morality, that had no existence except in individual minds; it was a will-o'-the-wisp, which credulous people mistook for a person and named God. Wolstenholme declared his 'utter repulsion to the very idea of a personal God'—or to any other idea, religious or philosophical, which purported to explain the universe as a system of unity, reason and purpose. All the same, he never sloughed off his non-conformist upbringing and expected men and nations to act as if objective standards existed of reason and morality.[11]

He told Smuts that his philosophic quest was bound to end in failure and urged him instead to write history and practise politics— two down-to-earth activities that went very well together. Smuts, however, remained convinced that philosophy and politics went together even better. He continued to pursue philosophy in his own way. But how could he practise politics in a British Crown Colony? He might propose; but Lord Milner disposed.

In defiance of professional opinion (for example, of the advice which Sir William Butler gave when he was commander-in-chief) Milner had looked forward to a quick and easy conquest of the Boers. On the eve of the Bloemfontein Conference he had said that the Boers might give way without fighting; but, if not, it would be 'a mere apology' for a fight. He had admitted a few weeks later that the war might be very unpleasant in the opening phase; but after that he foresaw no serious difficulty; the Augean stables would soon be cleared and then the British immigrants would come swarming in, to swing the balance of political power against the Boers, rapidly, decisively and for ever.*

Milner's military calculations had been proved wrong. His political calculations were now to be tested by events. He held in his hand the entire power for which Kruger and Rhodes had contended; yet not quite so firmly as he would have wished. In the former Boer republics his rule was as near absolute as the Crown Colony system permitted, for within the first few weeks of peace he got rid of military government (as the terms of peace permitted and as he had always intended) and thereafter he wielded supreme executive and legislative power, with lieutenant-governors to assist him in Pretoria and Bloemfontein. In the old British Colonies, however, he had to reckon with elected parliaments and responsible governments—not that they caused him much worry in Natal; but in Cape Colony their existence both irked and alarmed him. 'There is no doubt whatever in my mind' (he wrote as the war was ending), 'that the Dutch will try, for a time at least, to recover by politics what they have lost in arms, and that the Cape Colony will be their base of operations.'[12] This fear drove him into persistent efforts to get the constitution of Cape Colony suspended: he failed, but did not suffer any troublesome consequences, for the Cape rebels had forfeited their right to vote and the elections of 1904 gave power to the Progressive party of Dr Jameson, the raider turned politician. All in all, Milner could count on possessing a secure enough base in each of the four colonies. He enjoyed, besides, unusual personal authority throughout South Africa and the opportunities of leadership which belonged to his office as High Commissioner. He was able to bring

* See pp. 74, 96 above. Milner's military estimates remained erroneous to the very end of the war; later in 1901 he estimated that there were not more than 6000 Boers in the field—less than one-third of the actual total.

the northern railways under a single administration, to establish, temporarily at least, a South African Customs Union embracing all the territories south of the Zambesi, and to carry through the first comprehensive examination of Native policy.

If the powers concentrated in his person were unprecedented, so too were the labours expected of him. The whole land north of the Orange river was laid waste and its people scattered; most of the mines were still closed down and the urban industries undermanned; the ports and railways, already overstrained, were now called upon to meet the triple demands of military evacuation, civilian repatriation and economic restoration. There were 150,000 civilians, men, women and children, and 33,000 prisoners of war, including 24,000 in camps overseas, to be returned to their homes. This task he completed to all intents and purposes within nine months; but the achievement was bound to remain precarious unless it could be supported by further measures. The linked sequence of policy, as Milner envisaged it, was: repatriation, resettlement, economic development.

In the Treaty of Vereeniging the British government had engaged itself to provide £3,000,000 for resettlement; but its assessment of the task proved to be both imprecise and optimistic. What kind of claims would be admitted? For compensation only, or for the real costs of resettlement? How would the claims be assessed? And what categories of claimants would be recognised—bitter-enders only, or hands-uppers, national scouts, British subjects, Natives? An attempt was made to interpret the obligation restrictively; but it aroused great bitterness among the Boers, and the British found themselves compelled in the end to make provision for claimants of all kinds, at three times the cost that they had reckoned on originally. Lord Milner had to get the best value he could from this money during a period of protracted drought, and in the early years of 'the rural exodus' which the collapse of the trek economy was causing and would have caused even if there had been no war. Despite all this, Milner and his assistants performed most efficiently their task of rural rehabilitation, not merely as an emergency operation, but with far-sighted planning which inaugurated in South Africa a new era of scientific agriculture.

Land settlement was of particular importance for social and political reasons; but in economic policy the gold mining industry held the central position. In Milner's view, 'the overspill' from the Witwatersrand must irrigate the whole South African economy. Unfortunately, the British government had in its head a discrepant idea: the mining community, which had been involved so deeply in the origins of the war and was a main beneficiary of British victory, ought in equity to bear a substantial share of the cost. When Chamberlain arrived in Johannesburg in December 1899 he had it in mind to impose upon the Transvaal a war debt of £72,000,000. On this issue, Milner found himself for once in agreement both with the mining magnates, who thought Chamberlain's demand financially excessive, and with the Boers, who thought it politically intolerable—taxation without representation. The war debt was scaled down to £30,000,000 and subsequently was wiped out altogether. This was sound economic policy, for overseas capital would be better employed in building the economic future than in liquidating the political past. Milner secured a loan of £35,000,000 for reconstructing and expanding the transport system and other basic services of the economy.

To service public borrowing, to attract private capital, to pay for the flow of imports which an expanding economy would require and to promote rapid development in all sectors, it was requisite above all to get the mines working again at top speed. This, however, could not be done unless prompt measures were taken to overcome the shortage of unskilled labour which afflicted the industry after the war. Economists have explained the shortage by emphasising the obstinacy of the mine-owners, supported by white trade unionists, in trying to buy unskilled labour below the market price. Milner put pressure upon this joint monopoly to raise Native wages; but the increase was too little and too late to meet his urgent time-table.* So he took the short cut of Chinese labour. By February 1904 he had cleared all the administrative and constitutional hurdles and within the next twelve months over 20,000 Chinese labourers were brought into the mines. The economic consequences of their advent fulfilled Milner's expectations; the political consequences were disastrous, both to him and to his supporters in Great Britain. Their time was now nearing its end.

Milner always regarded his three years of reconstruction in South

* The wages of Native mineworkers were: in 1899, 60s.; in October 1900, 30s.; in January 1903, 45s. per month.

Africa as the great creative period of his life. Indeed, his administrative achievement was immense: amidst the ruins of war he built the foundations of an efficient South African State. That, however, was the smaller part of his purposes. Efficiency had small significance for him except in service of a cause. In defining the cause, he used the traditional symbols of Crown and Empire, but his thought was forward-looking and adventurous. 'It is not', he declared, 'the domination of Great Britain over the other parts of the Empire that is in my mind when I call myself an Imperialist. . . . I am prepared to see the Federal Council of the Empire sitting at Ottawa, in Sydney, in South Africa—sitting anywhere—if in the great future we can only all hold together.'[13] When he wrote these sentences, the word 'Imperialist' was already falling into evil repute and the paper plans for a Federal Council were being torn to pieces by Sir Wilfrid Laurier and other Dominion nationalists. But the word and the paper plans did not much matter: what mattered was the vision of a family of nations living together in freedom and brotherhood within the circle of the Crown.

Milner's vision was spacious; but it contained one fatal flaw. His family of nations, when one looked at it more closely, became a consortium directed by 'the British race'. As we have seen, he liked to call himself a British Race Patriot.* In this conception of his mission is contained the clue to all his striving in South Africa from the time of his arrival in 1898 until his departure in 1905. In two sentences that he wrote in December 1900 (but he might have written them at any time) he revealed with frank crudity his innermost purpose. 'If, ten years hence, there are three men of British race to two of Dutch, the country will be safe and prosperous. If there are three of Dutch to two of British we shall have perpetual difficulty. . . .'[14]

In the light of this purpose, all Milner's policies—economic, educational, constitutional—became charged with a new, and to the Boers a sinister, meaning. Economic development became the means of promoting an inflow of settlers to establish British numerical preponderance over the Boers. Educational development became the means of winning Boer children from their mother-tongue and filling their heads with British ideas about the past and future of their nation. Constitutional development—but, of course, it must wait

* See p. 74 above.

(despite the half-promise given at Vereeniging) until Lord Milner had sufficiently swamped and denationalised the Afrikaner people.

That was how Milner's policy appeared to Smuts and the other Boer leaders. That, by and large, was its reality, as revealed in Milner's personal letters and official despatches, and in the reports of his political subordinates, immigration and land settlement officers and directors of education. It was a policy with a long history both in Europe and in the overseas dependencies of European countries: consciously or unconsciously, the Germans had pursued it in Bohemia and the British in Ireland: on South African soil, the Dutch had practised it with spectacular success in their dealings with the French Huguenots. But times were changing. Unfortunately for Milner, the policy was falling out of fashion. It had become easier, during the nineteenth century, to resurrect nations and even to invent them than to overlay or absorb them. Metternich was not the only European statesman who found himself condemned to prop up the 'mouldering edifice' of an Imperial power, gnawed at and eaten away by the unforgetting, unforgiving nations which it harboured.

The British Empire (the case of Ireland notwithstanding) had handled this explosive stuff of nationalism with exceptional dexterity. The classic example was Canada, where English-speaking and French-speaking Canadians had learnt the art of maintaining their separate cultural nationalities within the framework of a political nationality common to them both. Intelligent South Africans in each of the European linguistic groups—men like Merriman, Hofmeyr and Smuts himself—were well aware of the Canadian achievement and anxious to emulate it; but Milner's mind was three generations back with Lord Durham, with his contempt for the 'petty' nationality of French Canada and his conviction that British racial predominance was the indispensable guarantee of British political institutions.

Lord Durham's great report had been marred (as his own son-in-law, Lord Elgin, discovered ten years later) by a confusion of constitutional and 'racial' doctrine; yet from the practical point of view Durham's mistake was more easily defensible than Milner's repetition of it sixty or seventy years later. Durham may well have thought that he had a chance of creating his British predominance by uniting the two colonies of Upper and Lower Canada. Milner, on the other hand, knew that he had to depend for *his* British pre-dominance upon the operation of demographic, economic and social forces. These forces he could not command and did not understand. As things turned out, these forces operated, more often than not, in a direction quite contrary to his anticipation.

From the time of his arrival in South Africa almost until the time of his departure, Milner knew little about the facts of the demo-graphic situation. It was not until 1904 that he secured reasonably accurate census returns from the four colonies.* They revealed roughly a fifty-fifty balance between Britons and Boers, with a marked preponderance of unmarried males among the former and of women and children among the latter. Given the comparative figures of age and sex, it was safe to predict an eventual Boer pre-dominance over the British. The only thing that could upset this prediction (unless the Boers grew reluctant to breed) would be a massive British immigration. Milner hoped for it and planned for it, but it did not happen. He set particular store upon diluting the Boer predominance in rural areas; but his land settlement boards, for all their efforts, established no more than 1200–1300 British farmers on the soil of the Transvaal and Orange Free State. He anticipated a spontaneous British influx into the cities and industrial areas of South Africa, and believed for a short time that it was happening; but the gains of 1902 were wiped out by the losses of 1903 and 1904. It was plain to Smuts, when he studied the census returns of 1904, that Milner's immigration policy, so far, was failing.[15]

Immigration was not, however, the only means at Milner's disposal in his struggle to make South Africa securely British (as he understood that word). He set almost as much store upon education. Certainly, to win over Boer children and young people to the English language and English ways of thought—if he could do it—would have the same effect as an influx of English-speaking immigrants upon the political destiny of South Africa. Long before the war

---

* The following generalisations depend not on information directly supplied in the Census (which did not differentiate Europeans by any criteria of cultural nationality), but upon the following assumptions:

(1) that members of the four Dutch churches (49·32% of the European population) may conveniently be called Boers or Afrikaners;

(2) that the English-speaking section of the white population was predominantly urban.

Prior to 1904, it is necessary to go back to 1891 for censuses in Natal and the Cape and to 1890 in the S.A.R.

ended, Milner had a clear picture in his head of the ends and means of educational policy.

Next to the composition of the population [he wrote in December 1900], the thing which matters most is its education....In the new Colonies the case will be easier to deal with,* provided we make English *the language of all higher education.* Dutch should only be used to teach English, and English to teach everything else....Language is important, but the tone and spirit of the teaching conveyed in it is even more important. Not half enough attention has been paid to school reading books. To get these right would be the greatest political achievement conceivable. I attach especial importance to school *history books.* A good world-history would be worth anything....[16]

An educational policy such as this may prove to be a two-edged weapon: should the balance of political power ever be upset, the weapon may be seized and used by the opposing side. Milner, however, failed to envisage so remote a possibility. A most unusual opportunity was presented to him, not so much by his own planning and plotting as by circumstances. He himself bore no responsibility for the farm-burning policy, nor for the attempt to mitigate its rigour by putting women and children into camps; it was the soldiers who did these things—but they did them so badly that the administration of the camps was taken away from them by the British government and given to Milner. Thus he found himself responsible for the survival and well-being of well over 100,000 women and children. To a man of his capacity and idealism it was not enough to institute good sanitation in the camps and to conquer the epidemics; he felt impelled to make provision, not only for the physical, but also for the mental well-being of the people under his charge. Above all, he felt an obligation to educate the children. The educators whom he sought were men and women of good professional quality and he took it for granted that he must look for them in Britain and in British settlements overseas. Thus it came about that the education of the Boer children, in the camps to begin with and subsequently throughout the two Crown Colonies, was entrusted to an English-speaking inspectorate and teaching body under the direction of a high-minded and efficient official, Mr E. B. Sargent. Before very long it became quite common, so Mr Sargent reported, for Boer

* Easier, that is, than in the Cape, where responsible government was a barrier to an anglicising educational policy.

children to talk to each other in English and to 'join in round games to the accompaniment of well-known old English rhymes and songs'.[17]

It might have been better for Milner if his educational drive had been less purposeful and its direction less obvious. During the latter years of the nineteenth century the use of English had been spreading by a quiet and natural process; the first movement for Afrikaans (which anyway was aimed as much against Dutch as against English) was petering out; the most probable outcome of the linguistic competition appeared to be a comfortable co-existence, with English gradually assuming the ascendancy. The Jameson Raid and the Anglo-Boer War changed all that. The Boers became fiercely jealous of their linguistic identity as a people. True, it took them some time to achieve an agreed linguistic programme: some of them wished to bring Nederlands, the language of worship and public record, into closer neighbourhood with daily speech; others wished to transform the *taal* into a literary language. The latter purpose began to be achieved after the war when Totius, Celliers and other writers of Afrikaans expressed the suffering and grief of their people in lyric poetry of intense poignancy.

> Dis'n graf in die gras
> Dis'n vallende traan
> Dis al.

Words such as these touched the heart. Nevertheless, both heart and head could still find good reasons for favouring a reformed Nederlands: for preferring (as Smuts did) the conservative dignity of *Ons Land* to the radical zeal of *Die Volkstem*.[18]

These differences of emotional and intellectual response to the language question contained some seeds of political discord; but in the period now under review the Boer front remained solid against Milner's cultural offensive. Whether or no Afrikaans was destined in the future to supplant Dutch, it needed the shelter of Dutch while it was building its strength. The Treaty of Vereeniging had left this shelter a flimsy thing: its only positive stipulations on the language question permitted the teaching of Dutch in schools, 'where the parents of children desire it', and its use in the courts of law, 'when necessary for the more effectual administration of justice'.[19] In consequence, Milner felt himself free to insist upon the use of English as the sole official language and the sole medium of instruction in the schools.

The Boers fought back. Led by their Church, they denounced the centralising, secularising and denationalising machine which Milner had set up. In opposition to this machine they established their own 'Christian National Education' (Christelike Nasionale Onderwys: C.N.O.). In the Transvaal, the C.N.O. schools outlasted the Milner regime; in the Free State, they were constrained at last by their poverty to accept amalgamation with the government schools on terms of compromise. It did not much matter. By now (March 1905) Milner was on the eve of retirement and his whole system was under direct political attack both in South Africa and Britain.

From the beginning, Smuts had been the brains of the Boer attack. A little later on we shall try to assess his strategy and follow the development of his tactics from the end of the war up to and beyond the retirement of Milner. But first let us explore his mood. A legend has grown up that he relapsed under Milner's rule into embitterment, ennui and despair. Phrases suggestive of such a mood occur in a letter that he wrote on 24 February 1904 to Miss Emily Hobhouse—the famous letter which she, without waiting to ask his leave, sent to *The Times*. This letter, however, is only one of a long and varied series; throughout 1904 he and Miss Hobhouse were writing to each other almost by every mail. This correspondence, and the friendship out of which it grew, will repay exploration.

When the war ended, Smuts and Miss Hobhouse were both in deep disfavour with the British authorities. In September 1902 Chamberlain took pains to draw a distinction between two prominent Smutses of Pretoria—the virtuous Registrar of Deeds, Mr J. Smuts (known to Milner's young men as 'the other Mr Smuts') and the vicious ex-State Attorney, the 'altogether inadmissible' Mr J. C. Smuts.[20] About the same time, a gentleman who was being introduced to Emily Hobhouse asked her—

> Are you *the* Miss Hobhouse?
> Well, I rather thought that I was *that* Miss Hobhouse.[21]

Her family belonged to the gentry of Somerset and she grew up in her father's Cornish vicarage, dedicated to parochial good works. In 1895 her father died and she found herself in her middle thirties free to seek larger outlets for her reforming zeal. She went to America and fought an heroic but exhausting battle against the degradation and corruption of a mining community in Minnesota. Back in London a year or two later, she absorbed from her uncle, Lord Hobhouse, liberal views about Anglo-Boer relations, and when the war broke out she became secretary of the women's branch of the South African Conciliation Committee, which disseminated news and views supplied principally by the liberal Afrikaners of Cape Colony. When news came through of the farm burnings and concentration camps she formed the South African Women and Children's Distress Fund, and in December 1900 she set out for South Africa to make her own investigation of conditions in the camps. 'Be prudent, be calm', Leonard Courtney advised her. 'Oh well,' she answered, 'we've tried prudence and we've tried caution. Perhaps a little imprudence may do better.'

In South Africa she was well received by Lord Milner, who was shocked at the army's inefficiency in managing the camps—as well he might be, for well over 20,000 deaths occurred in them during the war and at the time of Miss Hobhouse's visit the death-rate was approaching its peak of 343 per thousand. She completed her investigation within four months and at the end of May returned to Britain to fight the battle of the Boer women and children. She was a wonderful fighter—not merely a tireless organiser of public meetings and press campaigns, but an aristocrat who knew her way around the great world and dealt as an equal with the political leaders of the nation. Her master-stroke was to win Campbell-Bannerman to her side. On the morning of 14 June 1901 she talked to him for two hours about the camps; the same evening he made his famous speech about 'methods of barbarism'.

The army took its revenge. In October, when she returned to Cape Town, she was forcibly put back on board ship and deported to England. Next month, however, the management of the camps was transferred to the Colonial Office, that is to say, to Lord Milner. Early in 1902 a Commission of Ladies, sent out from England to investigate conditions in the camps, was able to report high standards of food, fuel, water-supply, sanitation and general management. By the end of the war the death-rate was down to twenty per thousand. The principle credit for this transformation belongs to Emily Hobhouse. It was her investigation and agitation which aroused the British people and drove the government into taking action.[22]

Eleven years later, the government of the Union of South Africa invited Emily Hobhouse to Bloemfontein to unveil the monument to the women and children who had died in the camps. She was too ill to get further than Beaufort West and her speech had to be read for her. It contained words which she alone of her nation had the right to use. 'As your tribute to the dead, bury unforgiveness and bitterness at the foot of this monument for ever.' In 1926 she died, and her ashes were taken to South Africa to be buried at the foot of the monument. Speaking in Afrikaans, Smuts recalled her mission of mercy and healing. 'We stood alone in the world, a small people ranged against the mightiest Empire on earth. And then one small hand, the hand of a woman, was stretched out to us. At that darkest hour, when our race almost seemed doomed to extinction, she appeared as an angel, as a heaven-sent messenger. Strangest of all, she was an Englishwoman.' Speaking now in English, Smuts told how this woman had changed the whole meaning of the South African war and made herself 'the great symbol of reconciliation between the closely kin peoples who should never have been enemies'. Her life was proof, he said, that patriotism is not enough: that a wider loyalty is requisite for the redemption of mankind. He quoted Marcus Aurelius—'The poet has said: Dear City of Cecrops, and shall we not say, Dear City of God?'[23]

To cite in this chapter a speech which Smuts did not deliver until twenty-one years after Milner's departure from South Africa is not quite so anachronistic as may appear; for Smuts, it will be remembered, was reading Stoic philosophy as the war was ending and finding guidance in it both for his personal life and his political thought. Moreover, he was rediscovering 'the desire and pursuit of the Whole' which had possessed him throughout his student years. Surely its political counterpart was the brotherhood, not the strife of peoples?

Emily Hobhouse was a passionate, indeed a militant evangelist of the gospel of human brotherhood. She and Smuts were in some respects temperamental opposites; he, for all his visions and dreams, remained always the political realist, the practitioner of the art of the possible; whereas she, for all her practical capacity and experience, remained incorrigibly the perfectionist, impatient of compromise and prone to impulsive, even to reckless action. These contrasts of temperament were destined as they grew older to separate them intellectually, but never to impair their friendship.

The things that divided them never became so important as the things that united them: mutual respect for each other's ability and integrity, a common standard of values, above all, an unshakeable personal loyalty.

They met for the first time in July 1903. She had recently arrived from England with some charitable funds and a plan for cooperative ox-teams to help poor farmers—a good cause, but not nearly so exciting as a political fight. She smelt a political fight at Heidelberg, where the Transvaal Boers were holding their first organised meeting since the war to protest against the abuses of Crown Colony rule, particularly the iniquitous capitalist plot to import Chinese labour. Emily Hobhouse flung herself into the fray and quickly picked upon Smuts as her chief ally. Or did he pick upon her? After the Heidelberg conference, their friendship grew rapidly. She became intimate with the Smuts family, invented her own pet names for the children and became the first member of her nation to gain admittance across the barriers of pride which Mrs Smuts had built against the conquering English. Her presence in the home at Sunnyside was living proof of the faith which Smuts had never wholly surrendered, even in the darkest years, that there was another England besides Chamberlain's and Milner's, the England of John Bright. He and Miss Hobhouse became fellow workers for its resurrection. They discussed with each other not only her charitable enterprises in South Africa, but the political campaign which she proposed to launch in England. Towards the end of her stay in South Africa she paid him a final visit at Gordon's Bay, where he was taking a seaside holiday with his wife and children. She set sail at the end of the year with the knowledge that she could depend upon him to keep her well supplied with propaganda, and from the first week of her return to England she wrote to him by every mail with news of the pamphlets, public meetings, private interviews and all the other activities of her liberal pressure-group. Go on protesting hot, she told him, and go on sending me lots of ammunition.[24]

Consequently, the letters that he wrote to her were not altogether private: not that he intended her to publish them, but he did intend her to quote them to her friends and otherwise make use of them to help the good cause. In one and the same letter he would be writing to her intimately, as friend to friend, and then addressing her all of a sudden as if she were a public meeting—a page or two of blazing rhetoric, the kind of stuff she could put into her next pamphlet. He never told her explicitly what his tactics were; possibly he never told himself, but wrote at speed in alternating moods of spontaneity and calculation.

It was a time of emotional stress and mental excitement, the crisis-time of Milner's Chinese policy. Milner had launched the policy at the Bloemfontein Customs Conference in March 1903, and then left it to the mining magnates to make propaganda, while Sir Arthur Lawley's Labour Commission was collecting facts. Towards the end of 1903 the commission reported a deficiency of 129,000 unskilled workers in the mines. This gave Milner his cue. In January 1904 he secured leave from the Secretary of State to introduce an ordinance legalising the importation of Chinese indentured labour; in February he passed the ordinance through his nominated Legislative Council. Nothing now could prevent the Chinese from coming unless the ordinance were disallowed at the last minute by the British government.

What Smuts wrote for propaganda during this crisis was emotionally akin to his private feelings—abhorrence of Chinese indentured labour; fear that it would prove to be, like its counterpart in Natal, not a temporary but a permanent complication of the racial tangle; humiliation at the thought of his people's impotence to withstand or even to deflect Lord Milner's purpose. What most infuriated him was the imputation that the Boers were consenting parties to Milner's 'Chinese cure', or at any rate passively acquiescent in it. On 21 February he burst into a violent tirade against this misrepresentation of their feelings.

That a large proportion of the Boers are apathetic is no doubt true, but these are the people who have lost all hope and heart.... Naturally to such people (and in my bitterness I sometimes think they are right) the importation of Chinese is but an incident, an item in the main account which is being rapidly run up to a gigantic amount. But surely *such* apathy ought to give Lord Milner even greater pangs than the fiercest opposition. For beneath this apathy there burns in the Boer mind a fierce indignation against this sacrilege of Chinese importation—this spoliation of the heritage for which the generations of the people have sacrificed their all. Often when I think of what is happening now all over South Africa my mind stands still—for the folly, the criminality of it all is simply inconceivable. ...I sometimes ask myself whether South Africa will ever rise again; whether English statesmen will ever *dare* to be liberal and generous in

South Africa. They however ought to know what is best for the British Empire. An awakening will come some day; but I am afraid it may come too late to save either South Africa or the British Empire.

Eighty per cent of the gold mines, he exclaimed, were bogus and fit only to be closed down; there was labour enough for the *genuine* needs of the industry! But the mine-owners and foreign administrators looked upon South Africa as a black man's country, 'good enough to make money or a name in, but not good enough to be born in or to die in'. As for Lord Milner, his heart was thumping with unholy joy because his jingo friends had won the election in Cape Colony.

For he has dreamed a dream of a British South Africa—loyal with broken English and happy with a broken heart—and he sees the dream is coming true. But will it not yet be with this South Africa as it is today with the British population on the Rand? Today they are imploringly stretching forth their hands to the Boers to save them from the consequences of their evil work in the past. But the Boers, like Rachel's children, are not. Similarly, I see the day coming when 'British' South Africa will appeal to the 'Dutch' to save them from the consequences of their insane policy of today. And I fear—I sometimes fear, with an agony bitterer than death—that the 'Dutch' will no more be there to save them or South Africa.[25]

It was a wild letter. And that wild woman, Emily Hobhouse, sent it straight away to the editor of *The Times,* with a few cuts which did not attenuate but if anything emphasised its exaggerations. When news came to Smuts of what she had done he cabled to her at once to say that she must get his consent before publishing any more of his letters; three more of them were already on the way and he was afraid that they would give the government a good enough excuse for deporting him; for they were full of furious rhetoric about England's new Assiento Treaty, about Lord Milner's 'brutal *vae victis* policy', his shameless manipulation of bogus councils, his 'criminal trifling' with dangerous situations, his insufferable autocracy—Smuts compared him with the Bey of Tunis and would have thought him destined to be Emperor of Heligoland, if only the British had not ceded that wretched island to the Germans! He consoled himself by envisaging the retribution which Milner was piling up for his country. 'As sure as I write here, there is a God that will judge; now is our dark hour and agony of bloody sweat. But I can already hear the distant tramp of Nemesis, and unless the conscience of England is roused now and she undoes the foul deed of shame, there will be many dry eyes when *her* hour comes, as come it will.'

These extraordinary letters[26] were not of one piece; intermingled with their mood of passionate rebellion was another mood of cynical despair. What was the use of fighting? What was justice but the right of the stronger? What could a conquered people do? 'Truly to be weak is to be miserable. To see your fate coming, coming, coming, and to be unable to offer any effective opposition; to be so weak as to be only capable of feeling self-pity, even self-contempt—is the direst punishment which could be inflicted on a human being.' For himself he saw nothing worth doing except to read philosophy and to plant and water his orange trees.

You know it is really curious how differently people are constituted: I could spend all my days in peace and quiet and would far prefer that state of existence: whereas you seem made for battle, for the excitement which accompanies great endeavours and achievements. And sometimes when I think over the past and my own now vanished and subdued pugnacity, I wonder whether after all it would not be best for the Africander people to quit the lists, to resign the arena to their English opponents and in peacefulness and quiet to find that consolation to which they are now justly entitled after a century of fruitless strife.... Suppose you were an Africander and had our traditions behind you and you had to undergo what we have had: I doubt whether you would have any heart left for the hopeless old struggles. But belonging as you do to a conquering, a victorious race....

The last imputation infuriated Emily Hobhouse—a warrior who never throughout her life could bear to fight on the stronger side. She protested that she was only half Anglo-Saxon; the other half of her was 'Celt pushed away by the conquerors into the remote Cornish hills', where her family had ever since been living aloof and apart from the conquering English. 'You think it bad to be an Afrikander at this moment—believe me it is *far* worse to be an English person. Your defeat may be bad but is material; *ours* is moral. Your country is in its youth and will overcome all difficulties —ours is, we greatly fear, undergoing decadence—at any rate for the time—if not permanently.' She would not tolerate his postures of renunciation and quietism, his philosophising and gardening and similar gestures of escape. In a long breathless sentence of badly punctuated protest she asked him what was the good of remaining an unsoiled flower however delicate and beautiful if only in a desert where it could achieve no useful purpose, perhaps it was better, though suffering loss of bloom and beauty in the doing to make oneself of use in one's short day. She upbraided him and reasoned with him.

Perhaps nature intended you for a philosopher rather than a fighter, but circumstances made you that—and you braced yourself to fight and now both physically and mentally you are suffering from the reaction and long naturally enough for the peace of a quiet life. I am, however, confident that if you transplanted yourself to some ideal spot far from Pretoria and from all worries you would soon be restless to return to the scene of action. The consciousness of power, the sense of justice and the impossibility of composure when one *knows* things are going wrong, would not allow you to rest in rural peace....Holding the position you do, there is no escape for you, I feel sure of that. Perhaps you hardly realise that you are the *only* Afrikander unless we except Olive Schreiner (whose sphere after all is the purely imaginative one) who has the power of expressing on paper the sentiments, moral and political, of your people. For the most part the Afrikander people are still dumb, only able to express themselves in deeds, and one longs for one of them to speak and make England and the world know what they think and feel. I *know* what they are and think and feel, having imbibed it amongst them, but I cannot except *here* and *there* hand on my knowledge. It lies with you to do this and to be the tongue for your people. In the whole continent I have not seen or met another who can do it. It was because all who read it recognised this, that I published your letter which went right to the *hearts* of the country and unknown before, made you at once a figure in the South African scene.[27]

The secret was out—she had published his letter with the deliberate intention of thrusting greatness upon him. He took it well. Certainly, it made him squirm to see in print his 'scarcely excusable' calumnies of the mining industry and similar exaggerations; but he told her that he was sitting tight and preparing himself for the battle that he would soon have to fight for dear life, now that he had unwittingly crossed the Rubicon. She thought it adorable of him to write without '*one word of scolding*' and confessed that she felt all the more scolded; she told him that she would never forgive herself if she had done him a real injury—but if she had forced him across the Rubicon, so much the better, and if Milner were rash enough to deport him, the effect would be splendid! 'It would be a nice holiday for you in which you could come to Engd. and work wonders. I wish he would do it but he is too canny for that.'[28]

In this spirited correspondence one mood chased another from letter to letter and from sentence to sentence within the same letter. On Smuts's side, moods of revolt, despair, and submission found expression in the early months of 1904; but Emily Hobhouse knew him well enough not to take everything that he wrote *au pied de la lettre*. When he told her that he was of a mind to give up politics altogether and devote himself to philosophy, she reminded him that he had committed himself irretrievably to politics by decisions that he had taken in the past; that he had made his choice already between the contemplative and the active life. But had he? From youth to old age it remained his ambition to live both lives together. There were times—for example, the 1920's—when his great strength seemed able to support the double strain; but there were other times when he felt himself torn in two between his commitment to politics and his zeal for philosophy. Throughout his life he wrote scores, if not hundreds of letters lamenting his enslavement to the political treadmill and the frustration of his philosophic quest; sometimes he indulged himself with dreams of escape; but his friends always told him that there was no escape—or, if they did not tell him so, he told himself. It was always a sure sign, when he talked about 'quitting the lists', that he was already hotly engaged in them.

Throughout the early months of 1904, for all his talk of planting oranges and reading Kant, he was in the thick of the fight. What was more, he felt no doubt at all of winning it. We must still postpone a little longer the story of the moves which he and his friends were making in South Africa; but this is a convenient place for showing how closely he had his eyes fixed upon the movement of political opinion in Britain. In March 1904 he wrote an exuberant letter to Emily Hobhouse, prophesying the imminent downfall of the Conservative government and the return of the Liberals to power by a great majority. What he was not so sure about, he said, was the use the Liberals would make of their power when they won it: if they granted self-government immediately, everything would yet be well; if not, there would be trouble. 'Mind you, I do not advocate generosity or magnanimity but simply good, sound policy. An army of occupation won't keep the Boers down; honest real *bona fide* self-government will satisfy them and make them really contented. But are the liberals educated up to this point? That is what I want to know from you. England is at the parting of the ways; it will be too late to meet the Boers when she is in difficulty. Let the Liberal party choose to do the right thing and the just thing, and all will yet be well.'[29]

In April he gave an enthusiastic account of a political conference which Botha had presided over at Fordsburg. 'The Anti-Chinese resolution was passed unanimously—no one even venturing to say a word against the resolution. So much for Milner's valuation of Boer opinion. We refused to say anything about responsible or representative government, as we are not certain of what we are going to get while Lord Milner has to settle the terms of the grant. We prefer to wait and have a gift from our friends than having it from—well, those who are not exactly our friends.'[30] Evidently he had got wind of the scheme of representative (not responsible) government which Milner and the Colonial Secretary were concocting—the abortive Lyttelton constitution. It was published in August and Smuts lost no time in telling Emily Hobhouse precisely what he thought of it. 'We are viewing with the gravest concern the grant of "representation" to us. I have drafted a strong memorandum to Lord Milner which is now being circulated for approval among our leaders. So long as we are distrusted we don't want anything, and if we are not distrusted why retard self-government? God save us from our present friends and rulers—and He will.'[31]

On that confident note let us leave for a time the correspondence of Smuts with Emily Hobhouse. It interleaves psychologically, if not chronologically, with another correspondence which he had begun a year earlier, but which came to a full stop in 1904. Early in 1903 he had begun writing to Holland in the hope of arranging the return of President Kruger to his own country. His opening letter was resonant with the rhythms of the Dutch Bible, which came into his head spontaneously whenever he sat down to write to his old leader. 'Verily God's hand is heavy on our people. Sometimes it seems to me that we have prepared a heritage for the stranger and shall not ourselves possess it. But then again we feel encouraged by the beautiful promise which will remain when heaven and earth have passed away.' When he contemplated the condition of the Afrikaner people, he said, his heart contracted with fear and pity. He wrote about the severe drought which was afflicting the land. And then he let the old man know how much it would mean to his people to have him back among them. Would he be willing to come?[32]

He received in reply a message of comfort and strength, with directions for his reading of the Bible and long quotations from the Book of Joel, chapters 2 and 3, and from Psalm 25, in the Dutch metrical rendering. The President exhorted him not to waver from his faith in the promises of the Lord. 'The Lord chastiseth hard, but it is not punishment: it is only to temper his people....The Lord knoweth his appointed time and at that time he will come to lead and comfort his people.' In his imagination, the old man saw once again the parched veld, thirsty for the autumn rains which were so slow in coming. But perhaps they would have come at last and 'the great and terrible drought' would be broken by the time his letter reached Pretoria? So he rambled on; but without answering the question which Smuts had put to him.[33]

Smuts, meanwhile, was in touch with the President's secretary, Hermanus (Manie) Bredell. On 28 June he told Bredell that he had telegraphed two months ago urging the old baas (master) to come back and live in Cape Colony. He had received no answer; but—

From your letter I can see very well what is going on in the mind of the old baas and therefore, I shall now try another tack. Oom Frikkie* is going to Europe next August and I hope we shall have everything in black and white to get the old baas home....We long very much for you all and trust that our wish to see you all back will soon be fulfilled. It must be bitterly hard for the old baas and all of you to be separated so long from people and kindred. But all will be well. God makes good his word and in due time all the promises will be fulfilled. The people of the Transvaal are expectant—waiting on God; and I know we shall not be disappointed. It will be a glad day when we can welcome our old and most respected President in our midst.[34]

Botha and Smuts went together to interview Milner and seek his permission for the President's return. Milner replied that it was not in his power to give permission; it was for the Colonial Office to decide. They then asked him if he would advise the Colonial Office to grant the application when it was made. His reply was non-committal; but Smuts had the feeling that he was well disposed, and he advised Bredell to approach the Colonial Office 'through our old friend Leonard Courtney'.[35]

And then, in mid-July, news came that the old President had died.

I knew him so well [wrote Smuts to Emily Hobhouse], and the relations between us were so much like those of father and son that I could not but

* Oom Frikkie (F. C. Eloff) was Kruger's son-in-law.

be deeply affected by this more than national loss. He typified the Boer character both in its brighter and darker aspects and was no doubt the greatest man—both morally and intellectually—whom the Boer race has so far produced. In his iron will and tenacity, his 'never say die' attitude towards fate, his mystic faith in another world, he represented what is best in all of us. The race that produced such a man *can* never go down, and with God's help it never will.[36]

Some time went by before the Dutch government (Emily Hobhouse wished that it had been the British) provided the ship which brought the President's body back for burial in his own country. On the railway journey from the Cape to the Transvaal the engine-driver had orders to stop the train wherever a light was shown: 'and so all through the night they stopped whenever the farmers had driven in little parties up to the line to bring their wreaths; so in his death the old man seemed as easy of access to all the plainest people as he had been in his life'.[37]

His burial in Pretoria on Dingaan's day, 16 December 1904, became a symbol of the resurrection of the Boer people.

To construct the chronicle of a man's moods before that of his deeds is an unusual and perhaps a confusing procedure. Its faults must now be corrected, so far as possible, by telling the story of Smuts's political activity from Vereeniging onwards.

The most that he had been able to do in the early months of peace was to help individual Boers to rebuild their private lives, as he was rebuilding his own. Politics began to enter when he discovered, or believed that he discovered, obstruction at the hands of authority. Why was the Cape government so slow in releasing the colonial rebels? He suspected a breach of the understanding that he had reached with Graham and wrote a letter of furious protest.[38] Why were the Transvaal authorities preventing ministers of the Dutch churches from returning to their parishes? He compiled a list of names and demanded an interview with Lord Milner.[39] In these and other brushes with the conquerors he defended the rights of his people with all the pertinacity of a lawyer-politician, at one and the same time appealing to the strict terms of the Treaty and endeavouring (so Milner thought) to stretch them.

His activities in the early months of peace were not much in the public view. The spokesmen of the Boers in the eyes of the world were the three generals, Botha, de la Rey and de Wet, who toured Europe in the autumn of 1902 in an endeavour to raise funds for the relief of distress among their people. Their mission was not very successful financially; but it succeeded in annoying Chamberlain, who invited them to an interview on 11 November and told them that it was not necessary for them to go around Europe begging, as though the British government would do nothing for them. He also told them that he had recently had it in mind to constitute legislative councils in the two Crown Colonies; but now, thanks to their imprudence, he felt obliged to postpone the plan: all the same, he proposed to make an early visit to South Africa to inform himself at first hand about conditions there. The Boer generals listened politely to this petulant harangue and told Mr Chamberlain they were very glad that he would be coming to visit them in South Africa.[40]

Botha had kept in touch with Smuts by letter while he was away in Europe and as soon as he was back in Pretoria he and Smuts set to work together in preparation for Chamberlain's visit. Here was the beginning of a political partnership which lasted until Botha's death seventeen years later and was reinforced, amidst all the stresses of that creative and harrowing time, by bonds of mutual trust, loyalty and love such as have seldom, if ever, united two political leaders. Unfortunately, few documentary traces remain of this unique personal and political friendship. Botha's papers, including almost all the letters which he received from Smuts, have been lost, perhaps irretrievably. The letters which Smuts received from Botha survive in his papers, but they are few in number, for the sufficient reason that the two men were seldom apart from each other for more than a few weeks, until Smuts was called away on military and political service during the First World War. Even then, the letters which he received from Botha dealt chiefly with day-to-day political affairs, intermingled with personal and family news. Not that Botha and he were indifferent to the deeper political and human problems; on the contrary, they were so much of one mind upon them that they never felt the need (as Smuts and Merriman felt it) consciously and purposefully to formulate and probe them. At any rate, not in writing. Talking suited them better. We have to envisage them continuously engaged upon a common task and taking its measure, not by writing to each other, but by talking with each other.

Political action, however, depends largely upon the written word.

In the Botha–Smuts partnership, it was Smuts who did most of the writing. Probably, we shall not go far wrong if we envisage a procedure rather like the following: a talk between the two friends; a draft prepared by Smuts; further talk and then a finished document under Botha's signature, followed perhaps by the signatures of Smuts and such other persons as might be concerned in the business. To an historian depending solely upon these documents and observing the decisive part which Smuts almost invariably played in preparing them, it would naturally appear that Botha was dancing to Smuts's tune. But this was not so. The truth was, that Smuts was good at composing political documents and Botha was bad at it. Botha had linguistic difficulties: for many years to come he remained apologetic even for his spoken English and never wrote it except under extreme compulsion. When he did put pen to paper he wrote a sprawling, ungainly, badly punctuated prose of his own, half-way between Nederlands and Afrikaans. Yet he had first-rate political brains and a strong will. In his letters which survive in the Smuts Archive two simple words frequently recur, *Ek wil*: my decision is this; I want you to do that.

When all this has been said, it still remains worth noting that there is probably not a single memorandum or letter of any political importance to which Botha put his signature during the period of Lord Milner's rule, which did not originate in a draft by Smuts. For example, it was Smuts who drafted the documents which opened and closed, on the Boer side, the episode of Chamberlain's visit to the Transvaal. The opening document was a letter, signed by the most prominent Boer leaders, stating the requisites of 'reconciliation', which Chamberlain had announced to be the purpose of his mission: in effect, it was a statement of Boer grievances and demands, both within and without the terms of the Treaty. The closing document was a letter to L. T. Hobhouse, and through him to the English press, which Smuts drafted for Botha's sole signature. This letter suggests that Chamberlain's visit to the Transvaal produced acrimony rather than healing.

We saw him only once in a joint body as a public deputation. For the rest he saw none of us and preferred to gather his information and advice from quarters about which the less I say the better. At the public meeting he adopted a line of reply which could not but be considered insulting and which was so considered by everybody present. When we prayed for amnesty he pointed out how we had sjambokked and shot *our* rebels; when we asked for equal rights for Dutch and English, he asked us whether that was in our Charter—the conditions of surrender at Vereeniging; when we asked that in view of the impoverishment and devastation of the country no war debt be laid on the country until the population had been given self-government and the people's voice could be heard thereon, he did not even deign to reply to us. His great taunt was our ingratitude and non-recognition of the fact that the government was spending 15 millions sterling on the restoration of the country to its pre-war condition. Everybody then and since has been wondering and asking where and how and on whom this vast sum of money has been spent, for there is certainly no public evidence of it, except perhaps in the Blue Books which are sent to the Colonial office for home consumption.[41]

If any further evidence is needed of Smuts's feelings towards Chamberlain, it may be added that at the meeting referred to in this letter he refused to transact his part of the business in English but did it through an interpreter.

Certainly, Chamberlain's visit was a poor preparation for the invitation to join the new legislative council which Milner issued on 30 January 1903 to Botha, de la Rey and Smuts. As usual, it was Smuts who drafted the consequential documents for signature by his two friends and himself. The first of them was a most skilful letter to Lord Milner, arguing that the country's immediate need was not a nominated legislature but a rest from politics and a clear recognition of the government's unfettered responsibility: nevertheless, if Lord Milner wished to proceed with his scheme, the signatories would welcome an opportunity of discussing it with him. Milner rose to this fly and replied, first of all by telegram, fixing a date for their meeting, and then by letter, arguing the case for his legislative council and doing his utmost to inveigle them into it. They, in the meantime, had consulted the Boer leaders in the districts about the dilemma facing them: whether to enter a sham legislature in which they would be only three among thirty, or else to stand aside and see their places filled by Boers who would be subservient to the government. Their final decision (though surely it had been in their minds from the beginning) was to wait until they could take a real and substantial share of responsibility, and in the meantime to let Lord Milner's government take the whole praise and blame of its deeds and misdeeds.[42]

Events proved them right. It became clear towards the middle of the year that Milner was pushing ahead with his plans for importing Chinese labour. The Boer leaders discovered more effective means of fighting back than by voting against the government in a minority of three to twenty-seven. Their liberal friends in England, if properly briefed, could be trusted to raise an outcry against 'Chinese slavery': in the letter to L. T. Hobhouse which has just been quoted (it was not sent until 13 June) they gave the signal for a furious campaign of propaganda throughout Britain and the British Empire. This letter also announced a new and important move which they were making in the Transvaal. At the time of Chamberlain's visit, Botha had given an undertaking not to start any political association without first consulting the High Commissioner. He now notified him (again it was Smuts who composed the letter) that circumstances had changed since then.

Since then an enlarged Legislative Council has been created which will have to deal shortly with important public measures without having any mandate from the people of the country; the question of labour for the mines, of the status of coloured people, of popular education and many other questions of vital importance for this country have been raised. These questions are being discussed almost daily by the press which speaks and can speak only for a certain section of the population. Under these circumstances my friends and myself would be failing in our duty if we did not speak out and give the burgher population of the country an opportunity for expressing their opinions on some of the most important public questions of the day. We therefore propose to hold some meetings at the more important centres during this and the following months.... [43]

They held their first meeting on 2 July 1903 at Heidelberg and passed three resolutions for transmission to Lord Milner and through him to the Imperial government. The first resolution denounced the capitalist plot to import Asiatic labour; the second demanded equality of Dutch with English and local control of education; the third denounced the imposition of a debt upon the Transvaal without the consent of any legislative body—a constitutional enormity such as had never been known in the British Empire since the loss of the American colonies.

These three resolutions were hard-hitting in style and argument— the first fusillade in the fight for self-government. We have already noted the appearance at Heidelberg of that pertinacious fusilier, Emily Hobhouse, and the arrangement that she made with Smuts for getting ammunition sent to her in England. Before she returned home, she had plenty of opportunities for seeing him in action in his own country. In September he drafted a document for Botha to present to Sir Arthur Lawley's Labour Commission, arguing with great cogency that the labour shortage was a short-term problem, for which less dangerous remedies could be found than 'the Chinese cure'. Thereafter, he fought an obstinate rearguard action against every new thrust of the Chinese policy; he went with Botha to interview Milner and reaffirm the unshakeable opposition of the Boers; he drafted letters of protest against the government's misrepresentation of their feelings; he collected signatures for their last appeal to the Secretary of State. Perhaps he never quite believed that he and his friends would be able to stop Milner from bringing in the Chinese, but he now had in view a larger campaign and a larger victory. As we have seen from his letters to Emily Hobhouse, he began early in 1904 to aim at nothing less than the total overthrow of the Milner regime.

To achieve this, two things were necessary: a victory of the Liberals in Great Britain and the formation of a popular front in South Africa. Smuts began to fear that the Liberal victory might be delayed by the Russo-Japanese War and other international complications, but he did not greatly mind; the prolongation of Milner's rule, he told Emily Hobhouse, might prove to be a blessing in disguise, because it was such an irritant to all classes. Indeed, it was not only the Boers who found it irksome; some of the ex-Uitlanders had begun to feel almost from the day the fighting stopped that they could run the country without the help of their erstwhile champion. By 1904 demands for the traditional rights of Englishmen were taking visible political shape. Before the year was out two organised parties of English-speaking Transvaalers had come into existence, the Transvaal Progressive Association and the Transvaal Responsible Government Association—the 'Retrogressives' and the 'Irresponsibles', as they called each other. The leaders of the former were all closely connected with the mining industry; the leaders of the latter belonged chiefly to the professional and commercial classes. Smuts envisaged an alliance between the 'Irresponsibles' and the Boers against the great capitalists and the jingoes.

However, the Boers had first of all to organise themselves, before starting to look for allies. They had made a beginning at their conference at Heidelberg in July 1903. In April 1904 they held a conference at Fordsburg (a suburb of Johannesburg), followed next month by a 'convention' of 160 delegates at Pretoria. Botha, the steersman of both these gatherings, thought it prudent to maintain complete silence upon the constitutional question until an effective political party had taken shape. The Pretoria convention appointed a committee of seven to draw up a scheme of permanent organisation. The work of this committee (in particular, the work of Botha and Smuts) came to fruition on 28 January 1905, when the party called Het Volk was inaugurated at a rousing meeting in the Empress Theatre at Pretoria.

Meanwhile, Milner and Lyttelton (Chamberlain's successor as Colonial Secretary) had come independently to the conclusion that it would be wise to forestall the advent of the Liberals to power and their probable grant of responsible government to the Transvaal by establishing straight away a representative system under Milner's guidance. This Lyttelton Constitution, as it was called, came formally into existence by letters patent on 31 March 1905; but it never came effectively into operation. Within a few weeks of its proclamation it became only too plain that not only Het Volk, but also the Responsible Government Association, would refuse to operate it.

What Het Volk objected to was not only its denial to the legislature of control over the executive, but also its system of electoral representation. Two formulas or slogans were in competition with each other. The Progressives cried 'One vote one Value'; Het Volk cried 'Representation by Population'. The first formula, if it were embodied in the voting system, would favour the town-dwelling, English-speaking section of the population, which contained an abnormally large proportion of adult males; but the second formula would redress the balance in favour of the country-dwelling Boer section, with its far higher proportion of women and children. By and large (there is no space to give the details) the Lyttelton Constitution favoured the first formula, one vote one value.

For this and for other reasons Het Volk thought it essential to prevent the Lyttelton Constitution from coming into effect. The surest way of achieving this aim was to make a deal with the Responsible Government Association. After some months of hard bargaining, the deal was announced on 14 April.[44] It embodied concessions from Het Volk such as were never demanded from Orangia Unie, the party which Steyn and Hertzog formed in the Free State later in the year. The electoral system was left open for decision at a future date; the educational programme recognised the equality of Dutch and English in theory completely but in practice incompletely. Still, these were shortcomings which might be corrected later on. On some matters of importance, such as 'the principle of a franchise and representation for white men only', the two parties were in whole-hearted agreement. Above all, they were in agreement in their demand for full responsible government. This agreement sounded the death-knell of Milner's system. His retirement had already been announced and he sailed for England before the month was out.

As happened so often with Smuts, these large political events had a personal accompaniment. During the second half of 1904 Emily Hobhouse had been seeking his advice about her plans for the future. The inheritance of a small legacy had given her the opportunity of making provision for her old age—but where? In England or in South Africa? She told him that she could no longer go on living this dual life with her body in one country and her mind in the other; she must cut herself free from one or the other—but which?

Smuts was glad that it was now his turn to play 'the ridiculous role of comforter'. He had discovered more and more, he said, that

the world is not exactly made after our pattern and that things do not usually come out in the way we choose—and somehow the world's and nature's way is fundamentally no worse than what we would have chosen. We learn more and more what our Dutch word expresses so aptly—to 'berusten', to 'rest' in the world-order, to attain the attainable and to pay silent homage to the unattainable.

Now about your piece of ground. . . . You know in old age (which to you will come as to all) we turn back to our youth and relive the beginnings of our life. . . . I think you will be happier in that England of yours than you will be here. . . . Place me in old age among the hills and kopjes where as a little kid I looked after the sheep and the cattle and let me lie where I was raised from Mother Nature. Think of these points of view and reflect before you make up your mind finally.[45]

But Emily Hobhouse had made up her mind to come to South Africa. Whether or no it would be for all her life she perhaps left open; but she brought her household furniture with her. She had conceived the idea of helping Boer women to help themselves by teaching them to spin, dye and weave the wool that was grown on their own farms, and she had recruited an assistant, Margaret Clark, the daughter of a Quaker family of Street in Somerset and the

197

granddaughter of John Bright. Remembering how Smuts was wont to invoke that name as the symbol of a better England, she wrote: 'I feel sure that it will add to your interest in my scheme when I tell you that the lady who is going to help me to carry it out is a grand-daughter of John Bright and like yourself studied at Cambridge and says that she often heard of you there.'[46]

The two ladies sailed for South Africa at the end of January 1905. Their company on board the *Kronprinz* included the Steyn family, General Botha's daughter Helen and Dr D. F. Malan, Smuts's junior at school and college and in later years his most formidable political enemy. Dr Malan gave them lessons in Afrikaans.

Their arrival proved to be a significant event in Smuts's life, even more significant, perhaps, than the departure three months later of his old enemy, Milner, whom he now looked upon as a defeated man. In victory, he had an unusual way with his enemies.

Will you allow me [he wrote to Milner] to wish you 'Bon Voyage' now that you are leaving South Africa for ever? I am afraid you have not liked us; but I cherish the hope that, as our memories grow mellower and the nobler features of our respective ideals become clearer, we shall more and more appreciate the contribution of each to the formation of that happier South Africa which is surely coming, and judge more kindly of each other. At any rate it is a consolation to think what is noble in our work will grow to larger issues than we foresaw, and that even our mistakes will be covered up ultimately, not only in a merciful oblivion, but also in that unconscious forgiveness which seems to me to be an inherent feature of all historical life. History writes the word 'Reconciliation' over all her quarrels....[47]

It is difficult to believe that Milner can ever in his whole life have received a letter which he found more astonishing. Today, in the retrospect of six decades of conflict, the last quoted sentence remains no less astonishing than it seemed to Milner. It belongs to the sanguine years.

Smuts knew that the verdict of the Anglo-Boer War was in process of being reversed. Power was swinging to his side. How did he propose to use it? What, for that matter, was 'his side'? On the eve of Vereeniging he had written into his notebook Abraham Lincoln's words about binding up the nation's wounds; but if he had quoted these words in the Assembly of the People almost all his hearers would have thought that he had in mind the wounded *Afrikaansche*

Volk, whose sufferings he had so vividly depicted. It was only in the closing sentences of his speech that he revealed the larger vision of South African nationhood which was growing within him. The war of freedom, he declared, had been fought for 'the entire people of South Africa'.

He meant, specifically, that it had been fought for Britons as well as for Boers. He had said the same thing a few months earlier in his open letter to W. T. Stead and he said it a few months later in a letter to T. L. Graham, the Attorney-General of Cape Colony:

I was fighting [he declared] for a United South Africa in which there would be the greatest possible freedom, but from which the disturbing influence of Downing Street would have been finally eliminated. I was not fighting for 'Dutch' supremacy or predominance over English Afrikanders. ... Let us try so to arrange our politics, our administration and our legislation that a compact South African nationality may be built up with the best elements of both parts of the colonial population, so that when eventually we become politically independent (as we necessarily must in course of time and who knows how soon) we shall no longer be at our old battle of the Kilkenny cats but shall be united within and present a united front to the outside world. Then this war which we have gone through will remain for *all* South Africa as a memory and heritage of glory and not as a nightmare.[48]

Here was the governing and guiding purpose of his political struggle. It was a purpose which many of his old comrades in the military struggle did not share and could not understand. But Botha shared and understood it.

Once again, we cannot but regret that the documents do not exist which would enable us to see Botha and Smuts at work together in bringing their central purpose to the point of definition in theory and practical policy. In compensation, we possess a lively and revealing correspondence between Smuts and John X. Merriman. In their letters to each other the two men showed no awareness of the gap of twenty-nine years which separated them in age, except that Smuts could never bring himself, even when Merriman's was the descending and his the ascending star, to forsake the form of address due to seniority; to Merriman's 'My dear Smuts' he always replied, 'Dear Mr Merriman'. Indeed, there was almost a filial quality in his feeling for the older man. There were many occasions which he could recall with gratitude and affection—their first meeting at Stellenbosch, when Merriman heard him speak in the students' debating society and encouraged him to dream of greatness:

the anti-climax of his return from Cambridge, when Merriman supported his hurt pride by admitting him as an equal into the circle of discussion in his home, 'Schoongezicht': the agonising months of 1899, when Merriman put steady but never unfair pressure on him to persist in the struggle for peace.

Merriman was more profoundly English in his use of language and habit of thought than any other statesman of that time and place; but in his loyalties he was irrevocably South African. He had spent his early childhood in the village (as it was then) of Street in Somerset, a place that was destined later on to become very close to Smuts; but his adult life became an inseparable part of the history of constitutional freedom in Cape Colony. In politics he was a Liberal hewn out of the Whig block, a colonial Mr Gladstone, zealous for financial rectitude, the liberties of the subject and the rules of parliamentary debate; the unrelenting enemy both of demagogic passion and of autocratic arrogance. He believed that the people of Cape Colony, and for that matter of South Africa, were just as competent as the British people were to manage their own affairs, provided they could overcome the intrusions of Imperial power and their own internal divisions. His ideal was a united South Africa, solidly grounded on the common citizenship of Briton and Boer, with room—but, in the beginning, cautiously circumscribed room—for participants from the other South African peoples. In short, he was the English-speaking counterpart of Jan Hofmeyr.

It was characteristic of Merriman that he should postpone renewing his correspondence with Smuts, which the war had interrupted, until he had occasion in May 1903 to seek practical aid on a question of individual liberty. Its intricacies need not concern us; but Smuts wrote back at the end of the month with the news that he had disentangled them and with a request for practical advice: should he and his friends 'growl a bit', as some English Liberals were inciting them to do, or should they continue for a while to maintain their quiet demeanour? Smuts believed that the latter course would be the wiser and Merriman agreed with him completely.

Our friends to whom you allude in England are excellent good fellows, but they do not live on the spot, and have not to bear in their own persons the effect of a policy of recalcitrant irritation....Apparently they cannot understand, that we are sincere in our wishes for a fusion of races nor do they seem to grasp the fundamental point that the question at issue is between Capitalist rule and the creation of a state on the model of Canada and Australia. Feeling all this very strongly I have discountenanced the formation of any South African Committee in our supposed interests, in England, as in the face of our protests against Imperial Leagues and similar bodies and their continued interference in our internal affairs, such a body would utterly destroy the arguments we use for a free control of our own affairs. As long as one body of Colonists in South Africa—I do not care which it is—continues to look across the water for aid in our own political questions, so long there will be a continuance of strife and confusion. In saying this I fear that I must add that my advice was most unpalatable to those good people who think, perhaps justly enough from their point of view, that the political odium they have faced during the late struggle has given them a sort of prescriptive right to benevolent interference on our behalf.

For all their faults Merriman thought the Liberals better than 'the Tory plutocracy'. Anyway, he believed it impossible that England would consent for long 'to govern communities of white men without representative institutions'. The proper policy for Smuts and his friends was summed up in 'the old O.F.S. motto *Geduld en Moed*' (Patience and Courage). He advised Smuts to lay particular stress on *geduld* and to employ his enforced leisure from political life in studying the history of British colonial policy in its bearing upon the problems which must soon come up for discussion and settlement. He appended a list of books—the Durham Report, the Life and Letters of Lord Elgin, and so on—which he had found useful.[49]

Within the next six months Merriman found reason to think again about the merits of *geduld*. In December 1903 he made a strong speech against Chinese labour and visited Smuts at Gordon's Bay for some joint planning of their counter-attack. Early next year he had the mortification of losing the Cape elections to Dr Jameson's Progressive party and of suffering defeat in his own constituency. 'I assure you', wrote Smuts, 'that we up here who have followed your brilliant work in Parliament as leader of the South Africans feel this as a personal blow. If I could be of any assistance to you, I would do my best to see you in without delay. If no other remedy suggests itself I shall try to prevail on my father to withdraw in your favour.... We are rapidly going to a great political crisis and I want *you* to lead the battle in Parliament, as you alone could do it.'

Smuts failed to persuade his father to give up his seat but Merriman got himself returned to Parliament after a hard fight in Victoria West. *Geduld* was no longer the watchword, for him any more than for Smuts. Emily Hobhouse had exploded her bomb in London. Merriman thought that she had played Smuts a scurvy trick by publishing his letter and quoted some advice that old Lord Rosmead had once given him: 'Always write as if you knew your letter would appear in a Bluebook.' What Merriman was himself writing at that time about Dr Jameson would have scorched the pages of any 'Bluebook'. 'Now we have the arch disturber of the peace as our Prime Minister there might be some excuse if he were chosen for any special ability but he is as incompetent in political knowledge as he is in courage or military leadership and one cannot but feel that he is chosen, not in spite of, but on account of his past career as a means of irritation to all right-thinking men.' But after all, 'that most incompetent creature' was merely the figurehead of 'Hoggenheimer & Co.', the plutocrats who were trying 'to set up an oligarchy and to control the fortunes of the whole of South Africa'.[50]

The Hoggenheimer symbol would be an enticing theme for historical research. It pictured the uncultured cosmopolitan capitalist waxing fat on Witwatersrand gold at the expense of honest South African patriots. A brilliant cartoonist, D. C. Boonzaier, was producing very pretty Hoggenheimers by 1908 and may have been their original creator. The creature first appears in the Smuts Papers in a letter from Merriman dated 4 June 1904; he reappears in a letter from Outhwaite, a radical Australian journalist, dated 27 March 1905;[51] thereafter he becomes a frequent and, indeed, a welcome visitant. One feels quite sorry to lose him after 1907, when Smuts took responsibility under Botha for the good government of his country, and quickly learnt that the resources of the Rand were the indispensable foundation of South African economic life, and that men like Farrar and Fitzpatrick bore no close resemblance to Hoggenheimer and Co.

All the same, the Smuts–Merriman assault upon the big capitalists, despite its lamentable demagogic lapses, was sound not merely in tactics but in principle. For it was the Chamber of Mines which financed and controlled the Progressive party, and it was the Progressive party which whipped up jingoistic and 'racialist' emotions among the English-speaking community. That chain of dependence needed to be broken, if ever the South Africans were to achieve the reality of self-government and the opportunity of union. In a letter to Merriman of 30 May 1904, just after the Fordsburg conference,

Smuts stated the problem in terms which were at the same time severely realistic and sincerely idealistic.

As you will have seen in the papers we had a very representative Congress here last week, and a resolution was passed in favour of an organisation on broad national lines. Our anxiety is to avoid racial issues and to have such a platform that every fair-minded Englishman can take his place on it beside the Boer. Could you suggest some programme of principles? Some time ago you referred to the desirability of substituting for the Bond a broader organisation which would not have to contend with the same rooted prejudices. Well, we wish to follow up your suggestion and make an experiment of such a policy here. If it succeeds the organisation, or at least its principles, could spread over the whole of South Africa. I shall be most grateful if you could assist now with some suggestions. We must now try to lay the common foundation for the policies of the future when Federation would have consolidated the popular party in South Africa just as it has consolidated the labour party in Australia; and I am sincerely anxious that that foundation shall be a durable one in all respects.

Don't you think as soon as the Liberals get into power we ought to make a move in the direction of Federation? That would perhaps take us out of the narrow rut into which we have been getting and supply a larger and ampler ideal for South African patriotism. You know with the Boers 'United S.A.' has always been a deeply-felt political aspiration and it might profitably be substituted for the Imperialism which imports Chinese, a foreign bureaucracy and a foreign standing army.[52]

In this exposition of principles and plans there was only one element missing to make it a complete statement of the political faith for which Smuts stood from that time until his death forty-six years later. Merriman supplied both the missing element and the prophetic word.

I was very glad to hear from you [he wrote on 4 June] and to know that amid all the cares of a busy life you are looking forward. Only you will forgive me for saying, there is one expression in your otherwise admirable letter which jars upon me, and that is when you speak of 'foreign' troops. I know or think I know what you mean, and what the expression would mean in the mouth of an Australian or Canadian, but in your position you cannot be too careful, and as your correspondence may be and probably is subject to espionage, such a phrase may be twisted out of your true meaning and be used some day to your disadvantage. We must look forward to the time when British troops will be the troops of the British Commonwealth of which South Africa as well as Australia, New Zealand and Canada will form an integral part with all the rights of a free self-governing community.[53]

The British Commonwealth—Merriman was not the only man who was experimenting with that name; but it was the destiny of

Smuts to get it accepted as the proper description of the third British Empire. When he launched the new name upon the world in his famous speech of 17 May 1917, one wonders whether he remembered Merriman?

Between the two men a complete accord was reached during 1904 on every important issue except one. Merriman applauded his friend's determination to take up as soon as possible the question of Federation or Union (his own preference was for the latter); but he gave notice that a national constitution, whatever form it might take, would be dangerously inadequate if it failed to express a united national will on the Native question. 'The crux of any union in S. Africa will be native policy and I fear that recent events may set up the sort of division that there used to be between the North and South in America, which indeed still operates. Natal seems hopelessly Asiatic and the Transvaal drifting that way. Would it be possible to get over the Native difficulty by a very much higher franchise for the union legislature—reversing in fact the German example?'[54] Two years later, with self-government well on the way and with union already in sight, Merriman and Smuts thrashed this question out in pertinacious argument. But in 1904 they let it drop for the time being. By tacit agreement, they decided to concentrate their energies on the reconciliation of Briton with Boer and the achievement of self-government.

After the great letters which they had exchanged in mid-1904, the two men allowed a long time to go by without writing further to each other. Merriman gave as his excuse the repugnance that he felt for having his letters pawed over and peered at by the spies and censors of the Transvaal. But really, he and Smuts were already so much in harmony with each other in the work that they were doing that they felt no need to write. From time to time they were able to see each other. In November 1905, after an exhilarating meeting in Pretoria, Merriman declared that Botha and Smuts were a reincarnation of Washington and Hamilton.[55]

Next month the Liberals achieved office in the United Kingdom and Smuts set sail for England. Appropriately, one of his fellow passengers was Margaret Clark, the granddaughter of John Bright, who had been helping Miss Hobhouse with her Home Industries. Smuts was still in quest of that other England and was counting upon its political resurrection.

PART III

STATE-BUILDING, 1906–14

CHAPTER II

SELF-GOVERNMENT

SMUTS took with him to England for distribution among members of the new government a document entitled *Memo. of Points in reference to the Transvaal Constitution*.[1] It was persuasive, forceful and short. In language closely attuned to the mood of British liberalism Smuts went straight to his main point.

What South Africa needs above all things after the storms and upheavals of the past is tranquillity. But that can only be secured by the removal of all just grounds of discontent and the unreserved application of Liberal principles to the government of the new Colonies, by showing a statesman-like trust in the people of the land, of whatever race, and granting them a fair and equitable constitution under which they can work out their own salvation.

There may be some danger in trusting the people too soon, but there may be much greater danger in trusting them too late.

Let it be understood once for all, he continued, that the Boers and their leaders accepted accomplished facts and had no wish to challenge the annexation of their country to the British Crown: let it be understood that they were ready and anxious to work the institutions of self-government in a spirit of equal partnership with their fellow South Africans of British descent. It was not linguistic and cultural diversity but the over-mighty power of the capitalists which constituted the crucial South African problem.

It cannot be too strongly insisted that the great practical issue in Transvaal politics, before which the racial issue has receded, is the distribution of political power as between the mine-owners and the permanent population of the land, English as well as Dutch. The struggle by the mine-owners for political domination which began before the war, but has been enormously accentuated since the war, is obliterating all other issues and is today, and will long continue to be, the dominant factor in Transvaal, perhaps in South African politics: English and Dutch alike, who are jealous of the political ascendancy of the mine-owners, will combine (as they already do) on a defensive basis for the protection of the general interests and the liberties of the people; English and Dutch alike, who are dependent on the mines, will, for the present, at any rate, go with the mine-owners. The racial issue which the mine-owners are doing their best to raise is a false issue, and is only intended to excite English suspicions against the Boers and to divert attention from the unreasonable and somewhat discredited pretensions of the mine-owners.

In two trenchant paragraphs Smuts had cut his way to the heart of his argument. There were two practical propositions that he wanted to prove, at any rate to the satisfaction of the Liberals: first, that the time for self-government was now; secondly, that self-government required a different electoral base from the one laid down in the Lyttelton Constitution.

The first proposition, it might have been thought, needed no proving, seeing that Campbell-Bannerman had publicly committed himself more than twelve months earlier to an immediate grant of self-government. Still, might not his party think him too rash? When Smuts presented his memorandum, less than four years had gone by since the Boers had been in arms against the British Empire. Was it conceivable that they could become in so short a time loyal subjects of the Crown? Would it not be better to postpone self-government, as Milner advised, until there was an English-speaking majority in the Transvaal? Might it not even be prudent to choose for prime minister somebody less impulsive than Campbell-Bannerman? In December 1905 a move was afoot for promoting him to the House of Lords. Although it came to nothing, a strong wing of the party, including Asquith, Grey and Haldane, remained very receptive to Milnerite arguments. These people might very well persuade their colleagues to go slow with self-government.

Or they might persuade them that continuity of policy had its virtues and that it would be prudent to erect the superstructure of self-government upon the Lyttelton foundations. Smuts believed this to be the more probable menace and set out to scotch it. His people, he declared, would never accept self-government upon such terms.

While the Boers think that Responsible Government will be the proper and natural remedy for many of the ills under which the new Colonies are at present suffering and that the time has come when the grant of responsible institutions might fairly and safely be ventured, they wish it to be clearly understood that Responsible Government granted on the basis of the present constitution will only make matters worse and...will simply substitute the mine-owners for the Colonial Office in the government of the Transvaal; and the Boers would rather have an indefinite period of

Crown Colony administration than see the Transvaal permanently put under the government of the financial magnates. With a fair constitution adjusted on a population basis, Responsible government will bring tranquillity to the land; on the basis of the present constitution it will simply add a new and most potent source of discord and agitation.

Smuts devoted more than half of his memorandum to developing this argument in detail. Let us briefly report him. His starting-point was the Lyttelton Constitution with its provisions for an economic qualification for voters and equal constituencies on the voters' basis. The economic qualification was low (£100 occupational, or £100 per annum wage), but the Boer community was poor and many thousands of *bywoners* and other Boers would fail to qualify for the voters' roll. In protest against their exclusion Smuts affirmed the 'true democratic principle' (which, to be sure, had never been applied in republican days in favour of the Uitlanders) of adult male suffrage for the white population. In protest against equal consti-tuencies on the voters' basis he demanded a rearrangement which would give larger representation to the country constituencies, which were predominantly Afrikaans-speaking. Admittedly, they con-tained fewer adult males; but they were more richly endowed with women and children who, Smuts declared, were 'an asset infinitely more important than all the gold and diamond mines in the country'.

Representation by population versus one vote one value: Smuts imported into his memorandum this battle of slogans. But he took particular pains to avoid the imputation of immoderate partisanship. In the rearrangement of electoral boundaries which he proposed he made provision for two- or three-member constituencies which, he said, would improve the electoral opportunities of minorities. It was his contention, supported by detailed calculations in an appendix to the memorandum, that the English-speaking element of the popu-lation would still possess under his scheme a majority in the Assembly: at least, they would do so if the voters organised themselves according to their languages. It was, of course, his main contention that they would not do so.

Time and time again Smuts reiterated his main thesis: the issue was not one of Boers against Britons, but 'of the liberties of the people as against the encroachment of the money power'. This was a thesis which the Liberals, fresh from their campaign against 'Chinese slavery', could scarcely challenge. Besides, Smuts took pains to eschew the exaggerations which he and Merriman had painted with so much delight; his memorandum did not contain the image of Hoggenheimer but rather that of a great industry, which, once its excessive pretensions had been curbed, could justly claim support for its real interests. Moderation was his keynote.

From time to time he permitted himself to strike a higher note. He did so, for example, in his references to his Boer comrades south of the Vaal. 'Whatever our mistakes in the Transvaal before the war, it is generally admitted that the administration of the Orange Free State was the simplest, most efficient and satisfactory in South Africa. The Orange Free State, in a spirit of chivalrous attachment to its legal obligations towards the Transvaal, sacrificed its all in the war. And it is our sincere wish that to the Orange River Colony may be given the freest and best constitution in all South Africa, as its people is in every way worthy of and ripe for it.' The keynote of this passage was magnanimity—a virtue, he had told Emily Hobhouse, which he was not asking the Liberals to practise: all he was expecting of them was good, sound policy. Still, in the document that he was now presenting to them, it was hard to draw a distinction between these two virtues; the magnanimous policy was also the prudent policy, and would produce political results in which the contending and contentious policies of the past would find redemption, reconciliation and fulfilment. At the beginning of his memorandum he had invoked the example of Canada; towards its close he envisaged 'the federation or unification' of South Africa within the next few years.

His memorandum did not contain a single sentence or word that might jar Liberal susceptibilities. Its persuasiveness to the Liberal mind was flawless. But when Smuts reached London on 6 January 1906 he found no Liberals at hand to be persuaded. The ministers and the other parliamentary candidates were away in the constituencies, fighting the elections.

Smuts usually was impatient of forced inaction; but for once he was content to rest a while and even to loiter. He had brought with him to London the mood of benign relaxation which had come over him while he was at sea, enjoying the first complete rest that he had given himself for many years. In the long, playful letters that he wrote from the ship to his wife and his two little daughters, he made fun of the seasickness which afflicted him on the rough waters of the

Cape and the Bay of Biscay. His sufferings in these stormy latitudes were a small price to pay for two glorious weeks of calm sea and blue sky, the delights of leisurely reading and the company of Miss Clark. She was well known in the family at Sunnyside both as the friend and helper of Emily Hobhouse and as a welcome visitor in her own right; but Smuts now got to know her as a woman of independent thought and deep feeling, a spirit wholly in tune with his own. They were akin not only in their political convictions (at Newnham she had stood up for the Boers in defiance of flag-wagging dons and undergraduates) but also in their aesthetic, philosophical and religious impulses. She was a Friend, a Quaker, probably the first of that Society whom Smuts had ever got to know well. He and she enjoyed the same kinds of reading and talk and shared a semi-mystical feeling for natural beauty—a feeling that was saved from sentimentality by their healthy gusto for out-of-doors life and by the scientific curiosity which in later years made ardent botanisers of them both. On their voyage to England in January 1906 they could not possibly have envisaged the strong and intricate web of friendship which was destined to unite them and their families in the years to come; but perhaps they felt a foreshadowing of it one golden day when their ship lay at the coaling-pier of Las Palmas and they went up to the mountain village of Monti, in company with a dull German, whom they would most willingly have lost. 'It was one of the most pleasant and beautiful days that I have had in my life. Winter—but still so warm that one saw flowers everywhere. Deep ravines full of banana plantations, with vineyards and orange orchards between and everywhere pretty little white houses—and the road climbed up along these ravines until we were almost on top of the high mountains. The birds sang, the people were gay and cheerful and nicely dressed as it was a feast day; everything was lovely and the day will long remain in my memory as a very pleasant remembrance of an unpleasant voyage.' An *unpleasant* voyage? But he was writing to his wife and family just after his landing, in rueful memory of the storms that blew and the seasickness that plagued him all the way from Las Palmas to Dover.[2]

Still, he had a happy landing at Dover pier, where Mrs Clark was waiting to greet her daughter and extended the greeting to him —an event of good augury, he might well have thought: all these years he had retained in his mind the image of John Bright's England

and now he was being welcomed by John Bright's daughter. She found him 'quite young, very simple and friendly'. They travelled together to London 'in great comfort 2nd Class and much attended by porters'. Before they separated, she extracted a promise from him to visit her family in their Somerset home.[3]

Meanwhile, he was free to rediscover old friends in London and to make new ones. John Hobson was not due to return from America until the following week; but L. T. Hobhouse, Emily's brother, the philosopher of liberalism and one of its journalists, introduced him to the Courtneys and other friendly families. Here he was in the thick of the political bustle; but after a day or two he bought a ticket to Cambridge, where he spent the evening and most of the next day with Wolstenholme. To the lonely don, the memory of that day was 'a very pleasant one of life and of such hope as it is given to mortals to entertain'. Wolstenholme at sixty was older than his years and out of love with life; but it delighted him to find in his friend so lively a current of energy and faith, to find him 'so well and vigorous, so cheerful and full of interests'.[4] Indeed, Smuts was livelier by far than he had been in his undergraduate years and ready for new experience. In the old days he had shunned the theatre (in Riebeeck West they might have thought it sinful), but when Margaret Clark came up from the country he took her to see *A Midsummer Night's Dream*. A day or two later, on Friday, 12 January, she took him back with her to her people in Street.

Both sides of the family, the Clarks and the Brights, had been Quakers for many generations. On both sides there was a tradition of sober, self-respecting industry; they had been farmers, tanners, shopkeepers, shoemakers and cotton manufacturers of a middling position in life. The Brights, perhaps, had the wider intellectual interests, but the Clarks were not so far behind; one of them had contrived an ingenious combination of classical culture and mechanical dexterity—a machine for making Latin verses, which can be seen to this day in the shoemaking factory at Street. On both sides of the family there was a tradition of civic responsibility and a lively interest in education, temperance, the rights of women and other radical causes. These public virtues were deeply rooted in personal religion, 'the inner light' of Quaker experience. Here was the England that Smuts had been looking for, at one and the same time simple and subtle, familiar and strange, peaceful and exciting: readings from the Bible in the morning and at night, just as if he were in his father's home at Riebeeck West; readings from Gilbert Murray's latest translation of Euripides; talk of the little world around them and of the great world beyond, of poetry and politics—and the election results coming through.

On Saturday morning they heard the first news, a great Liberal victory at Ipswich. In the afternoon, they went driving to Glastonbury Abbey and Wells Cathedral. What happened next day is best told by Mrs Clark: 'Jan. 14, Sunday. I received from Leonard,* as we were going to Meeting, a telegram giving the great news from Manchester, Rochdale, Oldham. "No Conservatives left in Manchester." Our guest watched our excitement and joy with interest. Meeting a time of thankfulness. Our guest spoke a few touching words of gratitude to English friends—very curious—and I think acceptable to most—alluding to passing thro' the valley of shadows, and to the effort to do the best thing so far as one could know the best.'

On Monday he caught the morning train for London. The victorious Liberals were thronging back, but the ministers were not yet settled into their work and he had to wait a week or more before getting to grips with his task. He spent the time pleasantly enough in talk with John Hobson, now back from America, and with other friends old and new, including Margaret Clark and her sister Alice, both of whom had work which took them a good deal to London. But the strain of waiting was beginning to tell on him. In the last week of January, when the ministers were ready at last to receive him, his mood rose and fell between one interview and the next. 'I am getting a little weary and melancholy amid these surroundings', he wrote to Margaret Clark on 1 February. 'Do not be surprised if I run away next Saturday. I really do not know what more I can do here. Most of the Ministers I have seen. Kindest of all were C.B. and John Morley. The latter felt very deeply what I told him (and as I left he said, "I wish I could say what it is in my heart to say to you". Keep this to yourself). I feel certain that the Government mean well, but whether we shall get justice is another matter.'[5]

He felt no confidence in the two ministers who shared responsibility for Colonial affairs, Lord Elgin, the Secretary of State, and Winston Churchill, the Parliamentary Under-Secretary. The latter wrote to

* Her nephew from Rochdale.

him that he would read his memorandum with attention and that he looked forward to a settlement 'fair to both parties in South Africa'. He concluded by wishing Smuts a pleasant journey home.[6] It was a friendly letter, but dispiriting to Smuts in its suggestion of an Olympian decision made over his head and of a ragged compromise between his own arguments and those of the mine-owners. The old phrases about submission to Fate and bearing the Cross reappeared in his letters, alongside confident affirmations of 'striving for the best' and 'building Jerusalem'.[7]

He was poised in doubt between alternating visions of his country's destiny, alternating plans for the years ahead and even for the days ahead. He realised in the end that it was impossible for him to leave England with everything still hanging in suspense between faith and doubt. He must seek a second meeting, a real encounter this time, with Campbell-Bannerman. In the meantime, Street was the best place for him. How he spent his last weekend there is told in Mrs Clark's diary.

Feb. 2   Alice went to town. . . .
Feb. 3   She returned by last train, bringing also Mr Smuts.
Feb. 4, Sunday   M. took Mr Smuts a long walk in place of morning Meeting. T. and Esther to dinner.* In the afternoon we had a walk in the Windmill direction. Then went to tea at John's. . .where we sat and talked till supper time when we came back. . .after reading.† We sat up talking. . . .
Feb. 5   Our attractive friend left us at 10.30 much to general regret.

Indeed, they had taken him into their hearts and he had fallen in love with them all, young and old. Their affection and trust were a world apart from the aristocratic embrace commonly extended to Colonial politicians in London. Their quiet little village charmed him, their countryside was the legendary land of Alfred and Arthur and Joseph of Arimathaea. In that land and with those people he felt himself to be at peace with England.

Whether or no the peace would be sealed depended on his second meeting with Campbell-Bannerman, which had been fixed for the evening of Wednesday, 7 February. The story of that meeting has been told by many people, but never more vividly than by Smuts himself, in a few pages which he wrote forty-two years later for the

---

* T. is for Thompson, Christian name of S. T. Clothier, husband of Esther, the Clarks' eldest daughter.
† The evening Bible-reading.

magazine of Campbell-Bannerman's old school.[8] He recalled how an evening paper had described him as the most dangerous man then walking the streets of London, the man who had come over to upset the Boer War settlement—a bad prophecy, he reflected, in the light of later events, yet it might have proved a good shot if his mission had turned out a failure. Who could have foreseen in 1906 that eleven years later he would again be walking the streets of London, but this time as a member of the British War Cabinet, helping in the conduct of the First World War?

The man who wrought the miracle was Sir Henry Campbell-Bannerman, to all appearances an ordinary man, almost commonplace to the superficial view, but a real man, shrewd and worldly-wise, but rooted in a great faith which inspired a great action. I discussed my mission with many members of the Cabinet—perhaps the most brilliant Government Britain had had for a long time—and with men among them like Asquith, Edward Grey, Lloyd George, John Morley, and last but not least, Winston Churchill. Campbell-Bannerman looked the least distinguished in that galaxy of talent. But what a wise man, what statesmanship in insight and faith, and what sure grip on the future! My mission failed with the rest, as it was humanly speaking bound to fail. What an audacious, what an unprecedented request mine was—practically for the restoration of the country to the Boers five years after they had been beaten to the ground in one of the hardest and most lengthy struggles in British warfare. But with Campbell-Bannerman my mission did not fail. I put a simple case before him that night in 10 Downing Street. It was in substance: *Do you want friends or enemies? You can have the Boers for friends, and they have proved what quality their friendship may mean. I pledge the friendship of my colleagues and myself if you wish it. You can choose to make them enemies, and possibly have another Ireland on your hands. If you do believe in liberty, it is also their faith and their religion.* I used no set arguments, but simply spoke to him as man to man, and appealed only to the human aspect, which I felt would weigh deeply with him. He was a cautious Scot, and said nothing to me, but yet I left that room that night a happy man. My intuition told me that the thing had been done.

Smuts always looked upon his meeting with Campbell-Bannerman that night as the crisis, the creative encounter of his political life. The older he grew, the more vivid grew his vision of it, until it illuminated the whole of his experience. This was the natural outcome of his intellectual and temperamental disposition, for although he was a system-builder, in politics as in philosophy, he could never tolerate disembodied systems; he could never feel that an idea was fully alive within his mind until he had translated it into a relationship of *I and Thou*. Wolstenholme had reproached him for writing about Personality with a capital P, but it was always *the person* that he was looking for. His philosophical quest led him in his undergraduate days to Goethe and Walt Whitman; his religious Odyssey led him back at last to St Paul and Jesus. It was the same with his political life; it was woven into one piece on the loom of personal loyalty—to 'Onze Jan' Hofmeyr, to Paul Kruger, to Koos de la Rey, to Louis Botha, to Henry Campbell-Bannerman. In his memory, Botha and Campbell-Bannerman became linked together with the greatest of political virtues, magnanimity.

...Botha was a man of like stature to Campbell-Bannerman. Greatness of soul met greatness of soul, and a page was added to the story of human statesmanship, of unfading glory and inspiration to after ages. Seven years later Campbell-Bannerman had passed away, but Botha was once more a commander-in-chief in the field, this time, however, in common cause with Britain and over forces in which Dutch and British were comrades.

The contagion of magnanimity had spread from the leaders to their peoples. Nor does the story end there....The story may never end. To great deeds wrought by the human soul there is no end.[9]

'The contagion of magnanimity'—when Smuts wrote these words he was an old man, almost worn out, and anxiously aware of those opposite contagions which were spreading among his own people and throughout the world. In moments of doubt and depression he found reassurance in the portrait of Campbell-Bannerman, which hung on the wall behind his desk in the study at Doornkloof.* Magnanimity had been achieved once, at any rate, in the dealings of man with man and nation with nation.

These recollections and reflections of his old age did not enlarge or distort the significance which he had given nearly half a century earlier to his encounter with Campbell-Bannerman. His feelings at that time were expressed in a phrase which kept recurring in his talk with Margaret Clark: Campbell-Bannerman, he told her, was 'The Rock'.[10] It was true. At the famous Cabinet meeting on the following morning, 8 February 1906, Campbell-Bannerman over-

---

* It was an engraved portrait which originally had hung in a place of honour in the house of William Clark at Street. After he and his wife died in the late 1920's, Smuts asked for it and had it sent to Doornkloof. Mrs Smuts once told the present writer that when King George VI saw it there in 1947 he remarked that South Africa owed more to Campbell-Bannerman than to anybody else in Britain.

came the doubts and hesitations of his colleagues and committed his country to a policy of trust towards the Boers.[11]

It took some time to work the policy out in detail. The British government did not at a single stroke introduce responsible government. Nor did it accept, then or later, all the electoral arrangements which Smuts had argued for in his memorandum. That would have been more than he was demanding. His proposal was that the Lyttelton Constitution should be withdrawn and an impartial commission appointed to study the facts on the spot and recommend an equitable system of representation. This was the course of action which the Cabinet decided to follow.

Two days after the Cabinet meeting of 8 February Smuts set sail for home in the knowledge that he had succeeded in his mission. A contingent from Street was on the platform at Waterloo to see him on to the boat train. In saying goodbye, Mrs Clark expressed anxiety at the presence of a dangerous looking man who claimed his acquaintance, a South African with a wide-brimmed hat and the air of a brigand. This was a matter for teasing and laughing at a parting which might otherwise have been too serious. Smuts felt—as he certainly had not felt in 1894—that it hurt him to say farewell to England.[12]

On the ship he found no congenial company, but he had with him a parcel of books from Alice and Margaret Clark—Gilbert Murray's translations of the *Electra* and the *Trojan Women*, and Browning's *Balaustion's Adventure* (to keep him still in love with Euripides), the *Journal of John Woolman* (to keep him in love with the Friends), Housman's *Shropshire Lad*, Lowes Dickinson's *The Idea of the Good*. He endured his usual torments of seasickness and then settled himself to reading. He also began to write, and by the time he reached Cape Town had completed seventy closely packed pages of his *Memoirs of the Boer War*. When he told Margaret Clark about these chapters she asked him to send them over for her to read. No, he replied, he would need to carry the story further and get it into proper shape before it would be worth reading.[13] But he never had time to get it into proper shape.

When Smuts faced Campbell-Bannerman and asked him to show 'a statesmanlike trust in the people of the land, of whatever race', he was not thinking about the peoples of non-European race who lived in the land. Nor was he thinking about them a year later, when he told W. T. Stead that a wonderful opportunity had come at last 'to work away from racialism—the dead centre of South African politics, from which no movement or escape seemed possible before'.[14]

Around 1900 the word 'racialism' had a different connotation from the one that it acquired later. In the propaganda of the South African League before the Boer War, Kruger's policies were dubbed racialist because they asserted Boer supremacy over the British; in the propaganda of the *Afrikaner Volk*, Milner's policies were dubbed racialist because they asserted British supremacy over the Boers. On both sides, it was a case of the pot calling the kettle black. From the Jameson Raid onwards, Hofmeyr's doctrine of fraternal collaboration between Boer and Briton was submerged year by year ever more deeply under the flood of nationalism, or 'racialism', which was swirling into each section of the European population. After the collapse of his last effort for peace in August 1899 Smuts allowed himself to be swept away by the flood. Two and a half years later, he surveyed the ruin which it had inflicted upon his country and made up his mind that it must never happen again.

In the last days of his campaign in Cape Colony he copied into his notebook Abraham Lincoln's words about binding up the wounds of war. He wrote to his wife in the same spirit. He recaptured his earlier vision of reconciliation between Boer and Briton and made it manifest at the conclusion of his great speech at Vereeniging. From that time to his meeting with Campbell-Bannerman he made clear in scores of letters to his friends his abhorrence of 'racialist' policies, both those that Milner was practising against the Boers, and those that the Boers, so Milner said, would practise against the British, if ever they were given the chance.

But what about 'racialism' in its other meaning—the attitude of Europeans, both British and Boers, towards the non-European peoples of South Africa? Long ago, in his student days, Smuts had recognised the Native question as '*The* South African question'.* Unfortunately, it was a question to which he could find no clear answer, either in his undergraduate writings or in the speeches that he was making and the letters that he was writing a dozen years later. He admitted that it was the crucial question in long term; but

* See p. 30 above.

he insisted that the question of Boer and Briton was the crucial question in short term. Consequently, his memorandum of January 1906 had made only one mention of the Native population of the Transvaal: in the country constituencies which contained many Natives, so he had argued, there ought to be some weighting of the *white man*'s vote. On the question of a vote for non-whites his memorandum was completely silent.

For this omission he was taken to task by John X. Merriman. Immediately on his return to South Africa, Smuts had sent Merriman a copy of the memorandum, thereby starting a correspondence that came as close to the bone of South African realities as anything that any two statesmen of that country have ever written to each other. Replying to Smuts on 4 March 1906 Merriman let fly with all his guns. He had found himself in complete agreement with most of the memorandum, and particularly with its attack on the money power; but he could not swallow its franchise proposals.

What struck me at once in reading your admirable remarks on liberal principles was—that they were open to the same objection in kind to [*sic*] the American declaration of Independence—viz. that you ignore ¾ of the population because they are coloured.* I know what a very delicate subject this is and believe me I touch on it with great reluctance. I am sorry to see that since I got your memorandum the matter has been brought up in the House of Commons and some very—in my opinion—injudicious speeches made on it. Nothing can do more harm to all of us, to those who like myself incline to a liberal policy and to those who wish to adhere to the written agreement of Vereeniging in spirit as well as in letter. I can see an infinity of trouble in this native question however carefully we handle it. I gather that the policy of Milner and of those on whom his mantle has

---

* Whereas in the two Republics it had been a basic law to give the franchise to every adult Boer and to deny it to every non-white, in Natal there had been the pretence, but not the practice, of a colour-blind franchise. Of 23,686 registered voters in Natal in 1909, 99·1 % were whites: there were 150 Asian, 50 Coloured and 6 Native voters.

The Cape franchise has been explained above (pp. 26 and 57). In 1909 of 142,367 voters, 85·2 % were Whites, 10·1 % Coloured and 4·7 % African (see *The Unification of South Africa*, by L. M. Thompson (Clarendon Press, 1959), pp. 109–12).

The population figures, according to the 1904 census, were:

	Cape Colony	Natal	Transvaal	Orange river Colony	Total	Percentage
Europeans	579,741	97,109	297,277	142,679	1,116,805	21·58
Native	1,424,787	904,041	937,127	225,101	3,491,056	67·45
Coloured	395,034	6,686	24,226	19,282	445,228	8·60
Asiatic	10,242	100,918	11,321	253	122,734	2·37
	2,409,804	1,108,754	1,269,951	387,315	5,175,823	

fallen is to unite the two white races in opposition to the black. From their point of view this is Machiavellian in its astuteness. Now taking myself as an example of those who are not negrophilists but at the same time believers in our native policy [i.e. the Cape's policy]. I do not like the natives at all and I wish that we had no black man in South Africa. But there they are, our lot is cast with them by an overruling providence and the only question is how to shape our course so as to maintain the supremacy of our race and at the same time do our duty.

In this situation, said Merriman, two courses of policy were open: first, the Cape policy—'our' policy—of giving a vote to all persons of any colour who achieved the educational and economic standards established by the franchise laws: secondly, the policy followed by the two Republics and Natal of denying the franchise to all Natives. Merriman admitted that the Cape policy had its dangers—the fear that Coloured and Native voters might some day swamp the white voters by their numbers; and, meanwhile, the temptation to truckle to the enfranchised minority for their votes. However, he thought the first danger remote and the second one unimportant. Contrari-wise, he believed that the dangers arising from the policy of total disfranchisement were immediate, cumulative and extreme.

What promise of permanence does *this* plan give? What hope for the future does it hold out? These people are numerous and increasing both in wealth and numbers. Education they will get if not through us then by some much more objectionable means. They are the workers and history tells us that the future is to the workers. And above all we have the saddest of all spectacles the 'poor white', that appalling problem which must cause the deepest anxiety to anyone who loves South Africa, or who wishes to see it flourish. People who in many cases sink below the level of the clean living native. Does such a state of affairs offer any prospect of permanence? Is it not rather building on a volcano, the suppressed force of which must some day burst forth in a destroying flood, as history warns us it has always done?

Our policy you may say is unpleasant, it is derogatory to the pride of the European—but so is the poor white. But it is a safety valve and though it makes some noise and a nasty smell it is the most reasonable guarantee against an explosion. I write this, I know to my own detriment, ... but I could not do my duty if I did not tell you what I thought on this subject, which is bound to be in the future as it has been in the past the source of most infinite trouble. The worst of which is that it affords a pretext for the fussy interference of busy bodies on both sides of the water. Really as a practical matter it does not seem to me that it affects you so very much. If you had our franchise with the educational test I wonder how many coloured names would appear on the register. I doubt if there would be a hundred....

But there would be thousands of white names missing from the register!
'Give every man who qualifies a vote', argued Merriman, 'but set
the qualification reasonably high.' Such a procedure would en-
franchise a few 'rich blacks' and disfranchise many 'poor whites'.*
Any other procedure seemed to Merriman 'false doctrine'.

But alas for his determination! His forthright letter ended with an
apologetic postscript, in which he confessed that everything he had
written about the Native question was 'merely a pious opinion' and
from the practical point of view 'impossible'.[15] Smuts might have
seized upon this postscript as an excuse for evading Merriman's
challenge; he might have confined his reply to the statement of one
brutal fact: that any Transvaal politician, British or Boer, who was
rash enough to make proposals for enfranchising Natives and dis-
franchising Whites would thereby commit political suicide. To say
this would have meant a brusque end to the discussion; but Smuts
kept it alive.

With much that you say [he wrote on 13 March] I most cordially agree.
In principle I am entirely at one with you on the native question. I
sympathize profoundly with the native races of South Africa whose land
it was long before we came here to force a policy of dispossession on them.
And it ought to be the policy of all parties to do justice to the natives and
to take all wise and prudent measures for their civilisation and improvement. But I don't believe in politics for them. Perhaps at bottom I do not
believe in politics at all as a means for the attainment of the highest ends;
but certainly so far as the natives are concerned politics will to my mind
only have an unsettling influence. I would therefore not give them the
franchise, which in any case would not affect more than a negligible
number of them at present. When I consider the political future of the
natives in S.A. I must say that I look into shadows and darkness; and then
I feel inclined to shift the intolerable burden of solving that sphinx problem
to the ampler shoulders and stronger brains of the future. Sufficient unto
the day, etc. My feeling is that strong forces are at work which will
transform the Africander attitude to the natives....

On manhood suffrage I frankly disagree with your old-world Toryism.
The poor white is corruptible, but my experience is that the rich white is
even more so. And the way to raise up the poor white is not to ostracise
him politically. So let us agree to differ.

There were other issues, Smuts suggested, on which he and
Merriman were in complete agreement and could act together here

---

* According to Smuts, 10,000 were disfranchised under the economic qualifications
(which, as has been seen, were low) of the Lyttelton Constitution.

and now. The Constitutional Commission was on its way to the Transvaal and he wanted Merriman to give evidence before it. The decision taken in the Transvaal would profoundly affect the future of Cape Colony and of all South Africa. The goal to aim at was federation or union; for if Hoggenheimer had to deal not only with the crippled population of the Transvaal but with the people of South Africa, there would be some chance of keeping him in his place.[16]

Smuts wanted Merriman to agree that the things which united them were more important than the things which divided them: in other words, that votes for Natives were a question of secondary importance. But Merriman would not yield without a struggle.

From what you say about the natives [he wrote on 18 March], I gather that you take the view of those good men the missionaries who have done, with much good, an incredible amount of harm in South Africa, viz. keep the native as a child; give him all the moral pocket handkerchiefs and flannel petticoats he requires with a birch rod when he is naughty provided *we* manufacture them. This is pleasant as long as it lasts but unfortunately the children grow up, or some-one ill-treats them and then there is always a demand for the interferences of those good ignorant hysterical people in England like Stead and Byles, which is the *fons et origo* of all our evils in South Africa.

God forbid I should advocate a general political enfranchisement of the native barbarian. All I think is required for *our* safety is that we shall not deny him the franchise on account of colour. We can then snap our fingers at Exeter Hall and Downing St., and experience teaches me that there is no surer bulwark for all the legitimate rights of any class or colour than representation in Parliament. The only alternative is physical force and the volcano.

It was a powerful argument; but Merriman weakened its force, as he had done before, by admitting it to be 'mainly academic'—which meant that he would not let it become a matter of political contention between Smuts and himself. He agreed with Smuts that the Afrikaner attitude to the Native question was improving; the greatest enemies of the Natives, in his view, were 'the newcomers who dread them as rivals and the capitalists who wish to exploit them as machines'. He wondered whether capitalist plotting had played any part in the recent disorders among the Zulus of Natal? Switching to other themes, he reaffirmed his opposition to white manhood suffrage and twitted Smuts on the doubts that he had expressed—unbefitting 'an ardent young liberal'—on the value of politics 'as a means for attaining the highest ends'. After all this, he ended his letter on the note of agreement: union, he said, was the goal, and the way to reach it was by calling a convention or congress. This was what the Americans and the Australians had done when they forged their political nationhood.[17]

All in all, Smuts might well have thought that the debate had gone well for him and that there was no longer anything to be gained by keeping it alive. However, he wanted to demonstrate that he was a committed man, and in the last week of March he sent Merriman the report of a hard-hitting speech that he had delivered on the 23rd, reaffirming everything that he had said privately about the mine-owners, Chinese labour, the franchise and Native policy. In this speech he attacked Lord Milner for saying that the Boers, for all their talk about Chinese slavery, wanted to establish 'Kaffir slavery': on the contrary, Het Volk would stand by the Natives on any question of right and justice: they did not wish to have political rights given to the Natives, but they would resist any curtailment of existing Native rights.[18]

This set Merriman off again.

The tone of your remarks is excellent on Native matters but you will forgive me for saying that a benevolent paternal policy will never take the place of political status. *Mutato nomine* that is Milnerism—who professed to wish to treat the Dutch as we propose to treat the natives. In that case the *reductio ad absurdum* was manifest because it was easy to show that man for man the Dutch are as good as the English. In the native case we are fettered by the notion which all of us entertain that the native is a 'schepsel'.* But he is a human being though an undeveloped one and my contention is that the only *safe* way of management is to give him a chance to acquire political rights if he shows himself fit to exercise them—however unpleasant this necessity may be and that it is unpleasant I do not deny. Therefore I confess I dread what you call manhood suffrage. In my humble opinion this is a country for a high franchise, and for a property qualification. I am a Whig, you are a radical as far as regards white men at any rate.

Between white men and Natives in the South African hierarchy lay two communities, the Indians and the Cape Coloured, whose problems were commonly treated separately. The Indian problem was destined to remain with Smuts for the rest of his political life, producing as its by-product a close personal tie between him and Gandhi. With the leader of the Coloured people, Dr Abdurahman,

* 'Schepsel' signifies a creature as distinct from a human being.

he was already establishing a friendly relationship. Strangely enough, this was displeasing to Merriman. 'May I without offence advise you to be cautious with Dr Abdurahman. He is himself a pathetic figure with European culture and the fatal bar of colour but the men whom he represents never appeal to me much.... If I was to choose I would rather disfranchise the Coloured man than the Kaffir but of course there are good Coloured men that are perfectly fitted to enjoy political rights.'

For the rest of his letter Merriman addressed himself to the situation in Natal, where a panic-stricken government was putting down the last tribal revolt on South African soil by methods which were as clumsy and callous as was the policy that had provoked the uprising. Merriman wanted to know what Smuts thought about the constitutional consequences of martial law in Natal, and he asked him once again whether the mining magnates had had any hand in the troubles.[19]

During the next month or two Natal took the first place in the Smuts–Merriman correspondence. Both men were horrified by 'the savagery', the 'horrible iniquity' of the repression that was being perpetrated in Zululand, but each pointed the moral that best suited his political argument. The ineptitude of the Natal government was threatening to provoke 'Imperial interference', which both men regarded as an intolerable evil, to be warded off (said Merriman) by a colour-blind franchise, or (said Smuts) by a union of the four colonies, which would bring the Natalians under discipline. They agreed that it was sheer effrontery to continue putting all the blame for the failures of Native policy upon the Boers, and to ascribe all its successes to the British.[20]

Meanwhile, Merriman was shifting his emphasis from the political to the economic aspects of Native policy. He was impressed by the increasing overlap of social condition between Natives who were rising and Boers who were sinking in the social scale. The remedy, it seemed to him, was 'a white Rand'. 'I am glad to see', he wrote on 11 April, 'that you keep hammering on the Chinese.... May I say, that I think you insist too much on native labour as a substitute? What we really want is that the mines should be worked mainly at any rate by white labour. Think what a community of 100,000 white workers would mean to South Africa. If I had my way I would keep the natives out of the mines as they keep the Chinese out in California and as they keep the negroes out of the mills in the Southern States. Let the blacks till the soil hew wood and draw water and let white men do work that is done by white men all over the world.'[21] Smuts replied that the problem was not so simple as all that. At this very time he was keeping a close watch upon an experiment with white labour that was being tried out by Colonel Creswell, a mine-manager and politician who became later on leader of the Labour party. He was keeping in close touch with Lionel Curtis, one of Milner's young men who had stayed on in the Transvaal and was now proposing a radical investigation of the poor white problem and a resolute educational campaign. These measures had his support, but he did not accept Merriman's restrictionist economics. Indeed, he must have thought it odd that so great an enemy of the political colour-bar should now proclaim himself a champion of the economic colour-bar.[22]

The great debate on Native policy between Smuts and Merriman had illuminated the main issues but settled none of them. It would have been hard to say which of the two men was the victor. If the debate had been looked upon as a struggle of wills, the award would have gone to Smuts, for Merriman kept shifting his ground while Smuts stood firm. If it had been regarded as a dispute in logic, the award would have gone to Merriman—in so far as he had confined himself to the franchise. On that issue he had an immediate answer to an immediate question, a policy for the here and now; whereas Smuts felt himself lost in 'shadows and darkness' and had no policy beyond trusting to 'the stronger brains of the future'. Smuts never gave an answer to Merriman's argument about the safety valve. Nor did he give any answer to some dispassionate comment which came to him from his wise old friend in Cambridge. 'The native question', wrote Wolstenholme, 'is I know a very thorny one, but I cannot help regretting that you do not see your way to the cautious and gradual granting of the franchise to such of the natives as in education, etc. show themselves capable of exercising it. No class of subjects with any degree of intelligence and ambition to raise its standard of living, and to enjoy its rightful share in civilisation, has ever obtained justice from a ruling class, over whom they have no control by a share in the representation; and no such class will ever be content to remain in such subjection.'[23]

Seen in the perspective of the half century ahead, no document of the year 1906 appears more important than the letters which Smuts and Merriman wrote that March and April to each other about the black man's vote. But Smuts had his gaze fixed upon the near horizon. He was looking forward to the arrival of the West Ridgeway Commission, whose main task it would be to report upon the white man's vote.

Sir J. West Ridgeway and his colleagues were appointed towards the end of March and finished their work before the end of June. Smuts began by thinking them to be 'well meaning but weak kneed'; before long, however, he discovered them to be 'good right minded people of the cautious type' who wanted to do the right thing. Their method of work was not to take formal evidence but to seek the opinions of representative leaders and to win their support for an agreed settlement, which must also, of course, be acceptable to the British Liberal party, including its 'imperialist' wing. This procedure pointed to a compromise, for which Smuts might have been thought unready, in view of his forthright advocacy of representation by population; but in his negotiations with the commission he showed himself quite ready for give and take. He was having 'some quiet fun', he told Margaret Clark, in watching the surprise of the commissioners as they discovered that the magnates of the Rand were outrageous in their demands, whereas the Boers by comparison were moderate and reasonable people. Indeed, Het Volk had decided by late May or early June to recognise the principle of 'one vote one value' in exchange for manhood suffrage and some other arrangements (for example, acceptance of the census figures of 1904) which would reduce the voting power of the over-mighty Rand in relation to that of the country districts.[24]

When that old Whig Merriman heard how the settlement was taking shape he was appalled by its doctrinal enormities—a political colour-bar cheek by jowl with 'the whole batch of ridiculous democratic shibboleths': one man one vote, one vote one value, no second chamber (he was misinformed about that), single-member constituencies, no adequate weighting of the country vote, the periodical and mathematical redistribution of seats.

You make no provision for a second chamber [he wrote on 26 June], nor for a referendum nor for any of the safeguards that are supposed to hedge round the antics of democracy. I confess the prospect as far as you are concerned is pretty hopeless. You accept a faulty basis and then proceed to build illogical conclusions thereon. How can you without blushing talk of manhood suffrage and exclude of design ⅔rds of the population—God forbid you should dream of including them on that basis—but then what becomes of your shibboleth? South Africa is and I hope will remain a society on an aristocratic basis. You wish to pretend that it is a democracy which in your case will inevitably turn into a plutocracy of the most odious kind dominated by strangers and run in their interests. You might not, it is true, have got all you wanted on the other lines, but at any rate you would have been logical and have had the respect of your enemies, but when the yeoman poses as a democrat he does not cut a very admirable figure.

This was Merriman's last outburst for that year. In early August, he was confessing that the constitution was not so bad after all: in November, he was backing Het Volk to beat Hoggenheimer: in December, he was planning the break through to Union—but not too fast, he told Smuts; they must not let Lord Selborne and his clever young men stage-manage them but must wait until they themselves could control the nation's march from their seats of power in Pretoria, Bloemfontein and Cape Town. By now he was thoroughly infected with his friend's sanguine spirit. Doctrinal differences were one thing, a good political fight was another. In the approaching fight he and Smuts were sworn allies.[25]

While the constitutional commission was at work Smuts was in correspondence with another eminent citizen of Cape Colony, Sir Henry de Villiers, the Chief Justice, whose steady judgment was perhaps more useful to him (though not nearly so enlivening) as Merriman's ups and downs. De Villiers felt confident from the start that the West Ridgeway commission would produce an acceptable and workable settlement.[26] And so it did. On 31 July the British government embodied its main findings in a statement of policy which won almost unanimous support among Liberals. Letters patent inaugurating the new constitution were issued on 6 December.

For Smuts, the two and a half months from then to polling day (20 February 1907) were the climax to a terrific burst of work. On his return from England the previous February he had flung himself into his law work, into pertinacious letter-writing to dozens of people in two countries, into public speaking up and down the country. From April to June he had borne the main burden on his party's behalf of the critical discussions with the West Ridgeway Commission. When that work was over he became 'a political vagrant' once again, stumping the country in a series of whirlwind tours. Back in Pretoria, he poured his overflowing energy into the party machine; he drafted a declaration of principles and a programme of action, he composed innumerable manifestos, he shared all the decisions of the head committee in such important matters as the choice of candidates and the electoral pact with 'the Responsibles'.

These people had decided in July or August to give themselves a new name—the National party. Smuts had been thinking that a new name might be a good thing for his own party. Why not call it the South Africa party?[27] But this would have been a bad psychological mistake, besides being quite unnecessary. The label *Het Volk* did not, as he had once feared, alarm the party's English-speaking supporters. In his own constituency of North Pretoria voters of the two language groups were fairly evenly balanced. He felt confident that they would return him by a big majority.

For some time past his confidence had been steadily growing. In early August, he had prophesied a Progressive victory in the present election, but a victory for his own party 'tomorrow or the day after. *Morgen is nog een dag.*' By the end of the same month, he was counting on a victory for Het Volk and their allies, and the formation of a coalition government under Sir Richard Solomon, the leader of the National party. As the elections drew near he became convinced that Het Volk had greatly underestimated its own strength and was helping its rather weak allies to win seats which it could easily have won for itself.[28]

The event proved him right. When the election results came out Het Volk stood head of the list with an absolute majority over all other parties:

Het Volk	37
National party	6
Labour party	3
Transvaal Progressive party	21
Independents	2

There was no question now of a serving under Sir Richard Solomon, who had been beaten in a dramatic fight with Sir Percy Fitzpatrick, the most popular of the Progressive leaders. The leadership, obviously, must come from Het Volk. Smuts told Merriman that he himself might have been prime minister but that he had refused to take precedence over Botha.

Botha's government was sworn in on 4 March. The same evening Smuts wrote to Merriman: 'My mind went back to Vereeniging—

separated from the present by only six brief years.... For six years we worked away from the chasm which divided South Africa and in which its peoples had been almost engulfed—and here is the result. I do not know whether the new government will succeed or fail—but this I know, that the people of S. Africa have advanced at an astonishing rate for the last six years, that they are really ripe for great things, and that failure will be due either to weakness of leaders or to cursed fate, but not to the people. They have done their duty. It now remains for us to try to do ours.'[29]

CHAPTER 12

CONCILIATION

'I am exceedingly anxious', Smuts wrote to Merriman, '*not* to have a pure Het Volk Ministry. On our policy of racial peace we carried many English constituencies with us, and I think we should continue that policy night and day.' Botha certainly continued it when he formed his government, for out of six ministerial posts he offered two to the Nationalists (formerly the 'Responsibles') although they held a bare six seats in the Assembly, and only four to Het Volk, although it held thirty-seven seats. In form it was a coalition government; but in fact it was close to the Canadian model of parliamentary politics, in which representatives of the two linguistic groups worked together within the same party and cabinet. Indeed, the Nationalists were destined very soon to accept fusion with Botha's party; in the meantime, it occurred to nobody to speak of the Botha–Hull government. Many people, however, spoke of the Botha–Smuts government.[1]*

In reviewing the aims and achievements of this government the biographer of Smuts faces two difficulties: first, the familiar one, that the Botha–Smuts relationship is so little documented on Botha's side: secondly, a new one, that a vast bulk of official documentation begins to overlay and confuse the record of the things permanently significant in the thought and life of Smuts. The first difficulty contains the danger of a serious falsification of history, a blurring of the truth that Botha was prime minister not only in name but in fact and that the responsibility for policy fell in the last resort upon him; the second difficulty contains the danger of an over-emphasis upon history at the expense of biography.

Smuts continued to be the draftsman of the partnership, as he had been throughout the past five years. He became, in addition, its chief parliamentary spokesman. For he, unlike Botha, was thoroughly

* The government was: Louis Botha, Prime Minister and Minister of Agriculture; J. C. Smuts, Colonial Secretary and (very soon) Minister of Education; Jacob de Villiers, Attorney-General and Minister of Mines; H. C. Hull, Treasurer; J. F. B. Rissik, Minister of Lands and Native Affairs; E. P. Solomon, Minister of Public Works. Sir Richard Solomon was appointed Agent General in London.

VI. Ou Baas and Klein Baas off to work

bilingual. He spoke the mother-tongue with his wife and children and many of his old friends; but it was his habit to think in English when he found himself at grips with a problem of philosophy or politics. Botha, on the other hand, always did his thinking in the mother-tongue, translating his thought, when needs must, into English which for some time to come remained unreliable. This put him at a disadvantage in a country where English had been for many years the language of industry and commerce and, since the annexation, of administration. In parliament, both languages were permitted but in practice English was often essential. Botha spoke it no more than he had to. This meant that Smuts had to do much of the parliamentary speaking which in normal circumstances would have fallen to the prime minister.

Indeed, if words had been counted, Smuts's score would have compared quite well with that of all the other ministers added together. There was hardly a motion or a bill of any importance on which he did not speak at length. When he was responsible for piloting the bill, it was his habit to take pencil notes of the criticisms offered during the debate; these he would discuss with his departmental advisers; he would then make further notes and get into typescript all the material that he needed for his speech in reply.[2] Even with a moderate legislative programme, the burden of this work would have been heavy; but the programme was formidable—thirty-seven bills in the session of 1907 and thirty-eight in the session of 1908. It was an immense parliamentary load that Smuts was carrying, on top of his departmental work and the preparations that he soon had in hand for South African Union.

It follows from all this that the printed official sources for the biography of Smuts become voluminous from 1907 onwards. The biographer must cope with their brute mass as best he may. He must, to begin with, make a clear distinction in his own mind between political biography and political history. The Arms and Ammunition Bill, the Townships' Bill, the Field Cornets' Bill and many other legislative chores of the session of 1907 may be important for the historian of the first Transvaal parliament; but they are not important for the biographer of Smuts. A man's life is not to be confused with all the odd jobs that he does from week to week and month to month; what gives it significance is the continuing purpose which guides and governs his thoughts, words and deeds. This does not necessarily mean that the little things in his daily life have no importance; they become important when they illuminate the guiding themes.

The central theme of the Botha–Smuts policy was contained in a word which seemed shining when it was first used but before long became distinctly tarnished, at any rate in the eyes of some people. The word was 'conciliation'. From the Afrikaner point of view it had a good history, for it had been much in use during the war among the British opponents of jingoism. Emily Hobhouse herself had been secretary to the South Africa Conciliation Committee, with its mission of healing. And yet ten years later she was telling Smuts that she hated the word conciliation and was sorry that Botha had ever adopted it, 'the more so as it seems to have worked out as always conciliatory to the other side'.[3]

'Reconciliation', the word which Smuts had used in his letter of farewell to Milner, would not have lent itself so easily to this reproach, for its overtones were more robust. It connoted an active will on both sides to bury past feuds and to create in their place a brotherhood of the two peoples. We have seen Smuts passionately and persistently affirming this idea, not only in the time of defeat and humiliation but in the following time of confident attack. He felt that the Europeans of South Africa were at the crisis of their fate. Behind them lay 'the chasm' of civil war. They might fall into it again if they looked backwards. Their only hope was to look forwards, to accept accomplished facts and mould them into a new pattern of unity and nationhood. To do this they must learn to forbear with each other. But that was easier said than done. 'Let us forgive and forget', he had written to his wife from Vereeniging. She found it a hard precept. So did many another true Afrikaner. 'Some people', President Steyn once said, 'seem to forget so easily.' Surely, to remember the past was an obligation of piety? And yet, remembrance could so easily prolong the embitterment. When Smuts was invited to ceremonies commemorating the fallen heroes, he felt himself torn in two: on the one hand, there was the act of piety to be performed; on the other hand, as he once told Emily Hobhouse, there was 'an aspect of my experience which as a rule I keep under seven seals'.[4] *He* might succeed in keeping under seven seals his grief for the death of his little son; but for most of the bereaved parents of his people such strength of will was more than could be looked for.

All the more reason, therefore, to press forward resolutely and quickly towards a new goal. In the memorandum which he had taken with him to England, Smuts had prophesied the advent of South African unity 'within a few years'. Actually, less than two years went by between the inauguration of self-government in the Transvaal and the meeting of the National Convention. Such rapid success would have been impossible—indeed, success might never have been achieved at all—had not Botha and Smuts pursued their policy of conciliation.

This policy did not spring merely from their subjective idealism. It was also an objective necessity arising from the distribution of voting power in the Transvaal. The European population was roughly half and half Afrikaans- and English-speaking; but the majority of adult males, and consequently of voters, was on the English-speaking side. In his own constituency, Smuts had no chance of winning and keeping his seat unless he could persuade a good proportion of the English-speakers to vote for him. That, by and large, despite Afrikaner dominance on the *platteland*, was the situation of Het Volk. Orangia Unie, the sister-party in the Free State, was in a completely different situation, for the English-speaking element was barely 10 per cent of the total population between the Vaal and Orange rivers.

Botha and Smuts were thus doubly committed, as Steyn and Hertzog never were, to the task of building a bridge of mutual trust between Boers and Britons. This could not be done unless confidence and trust were established also between the Transvaal and Great Britain. In his attack upon Campbell-Bannerman's policy, Balfour had declared that there was nothing to prevent the Transvaal from 'making every preparation, constitutionally, quietly, without interference, for a new war'. This was a fantastic and dangerous misreading of the intentions of Botha and Smuts. It needed to be disproved.

Consequently, Botha was right when he made it his first duty as prime minister to attend the Colonial Conference of 1907. In South Africa there were mixed feelings about his journey; some people thought it a triumph, but others thought it a trap. 'Some wag has said', wrote Smuts, 'that the British people paid 250 million in cash and thousands in lives in order to make him Prime Minister, and surely he ought to go and show them what value they have received for that little outlay.' Merriman, on the other hand, thought that the British wanted to get him to London 'to bird-lime him there for their Imperial circus'. When news came through of the great reception that London was giving him, Merriman exclaimed, 'Woe unto you when your enemies all conspire to praise you'. It particularly infuriated him to read of Botha and Jameson chumming up with each other. He hated 'the gush and guzzling' of the Imperial metropolis and was afraid that Botha might be seduced into surrendering the real interests of his country. Yet, when it was all over, he confessed that his fears had been groundless.[5]

Indeed, the conference of 1907 produced results which were clean contrary to those that Merriman had feared. In spirit it was far closer to the Commonwealth club of 1926 than to the Colonial circus of 1887. One of the things that it did was to remove the Colonial label from the self-governing communities overseas; henceforward they were to be called Dominions. This was the opening move in the long campaign for equality of status—a move which was made by the British government without any strings attached to it; for in 1907 it was the Australians, not the British, who were calling for a joint secretariat to co-ordinate policy throughout the Empire. Laurier, the Canadian prime minister, rejected this proposal as a threat to the autonomy of the Dominions. Botha supported Laurier. All in all, Botha was able to bring back with him convincing proofs that self-government within the Empire was not a sham, but a living reality, capable of expansion to complete nationhood. He also brought back with him remission of the war-debt which the mining industry had accepted under pressure from Joseph Chamberlain, together with the promise of a £5 million loan to finance a new Land Bank and some other useful ventures.

Even Steyn was reassured. He felt, all the same, that Botha and Smuts were inclined 'to lay on the loyalty butter too thick'. For example, there was the affair of the Cullinan diamond, a precious stone of 3025 carats which was valued at £$\frac{1}{4}$ million, although it was far too big to be saleable. On 10 August 1907 Botha gave notice of a motion to offer it to King Edward VII, his heirs and successors, 'as an expression of the sentiment of loyalty and affection on the part of the people of the Transvaal towards His Majesty's person and throne'. Paradoxically, the leaders of the Progressive party opposed the motion (not without some mutiny among the rank and file) while Het Volk solidly supported it.

On our side [declared Smuts] there is nothing behind this. I know it will be said again that this is another instance of slimness (laughter) but, Sir, this is not a case of slimness. This is a profound sentiment that we have here. We say that great things have been done for this country, and great things have been done to retrieve the irreparable wrongs of the past. His Majesty's government has given us millions and millions to help us to restore the damages of the war. They have absolved us from the thirty million war debt which the hon. members opposite were willing to pay, and they are even now helping us with a five million loan.[6]

He went on to speak of the gift as a symbol of racial reconciliation, a proof of the people's determination to raise themselves 'from the rut of the past' to a higher level of statesmanship. He won a notable debating victory over his inept opponents. One wonders, all the same, whether the victory was worth while. The discomfiture of Sir George Farrar was only a trivial and ephemeral incident; but the suspicions of President Steyn contained the seeds of schism.

The origin and growth of those suspicions will be reviewed a little later on. Meanwhile, the salient policies of the Botha–Smuts government must be considered in their immediate context of economics and politics in the Transvaal. The government had come to power at the very bottom of a severe economic depression. There could be no recovery from the depression without an expansion of mining on the low-grade reefs. This, in turn, could not take place without an assured and expanding supply of labour. But Het Volk had won self-government and subsequently the elections, largely on the strength of its opposition to Chinese labour, which was the mine-owner's sovereign remedy for the labour shortage. On this policy there could be no going back. To be sure, the government might have been willing in some degree to slow down its operation if no substitutes had been found for the Chinese labourers before the expiry of their indentures; but substitutes were in fact found, partly by an increased flow of African labour from Mozambique and elsewhere, partly by the speeding up of mechanisation.[7] These increases were achieved in large measure by the mine managements themselves, but the managements might have been laggard had not they been convinced of two things; first, that the government meant business in its plans for sending away the Chinese: secondly, that it was prepared, in everything else, to listen sympathetically to the requests of the mining industry.

By one means and another, a sufficient margin was established of profits over costs to produce a great expansion on the Rand and a fructifying 'overspill' throughout the country. Not that Botha and Smuts would have employed this Milnerite expression, nor followed the one-way track of economic reasoning which it connoted; the mining industry, they would have said, was not only a giver but also a receiver of benefits, the most conspicuous beneficiary of a wise public policy which was restoring confidence at home and attracting financial support both from the British government and from private investors overseas. Amongst the other beneficiaries of public policy, Botha would have signalled out the farming community, which was encouraged at this time by a strong up-swing of prices to make the most of the Land Bank and the other facilities which he, as Minister of Agriculture, was providing for it.

Economic recovery, stemming no doubt from diverse origins, was well under way before the end of 1908 in agriculture, mining, commerce—indeed, throughout the whole economy of the Transvaal. Contrariwise, in the coastal colonies, particularly in the Cape, which was afflicted at this time by a collapse of the diamond market, recovery was still lagging, if indeed it had ever begun. These contrasts of economic fortune, accentuated by a revenue system which rested primarily on customs duties and railway rates, were reflected in the public finances; the Transvaal was enjoying surpluses while the coastal colonies were enduring deficits. From a financial point of view, Transvaalers might well have argued that it would pay them better to make a merger with their Portuguese neighbours, who supplied them with many of their mine labourers and offered them the most profitable railway and port facilities, rather than to tie themselves to the other British colonies.* Should they decide, largely for political reasons,

* Distribution of Transvaal trade (percentages):

	1903	1904	1905	1907	1908
Lourenço Marques	30·9	43·0	51·5	58·0	63·5
Durban	44·0	40·8	36·5	29·0	24·0
Cape ports	25·1	16·2	12·0	13·0	12·5

Length of line over which railway rates were payable to the Transvaal:

	Miles	Per cent proportion within Transvaal
Port Elizabeth	49	6·8
East London	49	7·3
Durban	178	36·4
Delagoa Bay	341	82·5

These geographical facts, together with the facts of the labour market, had found expression in the much discussed *modus vivendi* made under the Milner regime between the Transvaal and Portuguese East Africa.

to pursue a federation or union of British South Africa, they would find themselves able to bargain from a position of strength.

The Transvaal owed its strength not only to the facts of its economic geography but also to the policy of its government. The missing component, hitherto, had been political confidence, and it would have remained missing had not the business community been persuaded that the era of civil dissension was at last closed. But was it really closed, or was it being diverted into new channels? There was a price to pay for the *rapprochement* between the government and the great capitalists. Its very rapidity was hard for some people to understand and accept. Smuts soon discovered Hoggenheimer to be a fictitious animal. Within a month of taking office, he told Merriman that he had received a deputation from the Chamber of Mines and had discovered in their reasoning 'a sound substratum of fact'. Within twelve months, if not sooner, he had established frank and cordial relations with Lionel Phillips, who was perhaps the brightest intelligence in the Chamber of Mines. But the growth of his intimacy with Phillips was accompanied by the decline of his intimacy with Cresswell, one of the old 'Responsibles', who was destined very soon to become the leader of the emerging Labour party. Cresswell, like Merriman and Lionel Curtis, was the advocate of an all-white Rand. Smuts himself was willing to try out the experiment of a government mine, employing white workers only: this may have pleased Cresswell but it did not please Merriman, who hated socialistic quackeries of the Australian stamp and believed that the best way of getting the white unemployed to work was to treat them rough. The mine-owners, at this time, were treating them very rough, cutting their wages and breaking their strikes. What line would the government take? In the big strike of 1907, it brought Imperial troops into the Rand to support the police. Smuts declared that it was merely holding the ring; but the strikers accused it of taking sides with the capitalist bosses against the workers—by which they meant the white workers.[8]

All this was ominous for the relations in a not very distant future between Smuts and the trade unionists of British origin. Looking further ahead, the wage-cutting and strike-breaking of 1907 accelerated, if it did not initiate the entry of Afrikaners into the mines, in substitution for the more demanding British miners. No doubt this substitution was on a small scale to begin with; but its steady continuance in the years to come was destined to produce large political consequences unfavourable to Smuts and his party.

It must have been difficult to strike a balance between the contending forces, not only in the industrial sphere but also in other spheres of policy. The manning of the civil service is a case in point. The civil service, it was generally agreed, was overgrown, and plans for reducing it were under study even before Het Volk took office. It was, moreover, overwhelmingly English-speaking and overdue for an Afrikaner infusion. Yet the problem of timing was a tricky one. If the government moved too slow, it would offend its Afrikaner following; if it moved too fast, it would lower standards in the civil service and destroy confidence in its impartiality. It is not to be wondered at that the government ran into criticism from both sides. It appointed a new chief of police, who began posting Afrikaner policemen to the country districts. Lord Selborne himself protested against that: local popularity, he told Smuts, was not a proper criterion for appointing policemen; or, it if was, it should be applied impartially, not only on the *platteland*, but on the Rand.[9] Other complaints were made by retrenched civil servants who believed that they had been treated unfairly. These complaints were taken up in the English-speaking press of the Transvaal and repeated by the conservative newspapers in London. There was not much substance in them. On one occasion, the civil service commissioner himself complained that the normal procedures had been waived in a case of promotion; but this was not a case of 'racial partisanship'; the promoted official was English-speaking and a relative of Mr Moor, the premier of Natal! By and large, the government observed the rules. Botha and Smuts believed that to make self-government a success, and to make it the stepping-stone to Union, they required a non-political civil service with high standards of efficiency and integrity. But what about accessibility and intelligibility? How could English-speaking officials, with the best will in the world, deal sympathetically and competently with people, especially with country people, whose language they could not understand? As viewed from the Free State, the Het Volk government was far too tender towards the alien bureaucracy which it had inherited from Lord Milner.[10]

It was also far too tender, according to the Free State politicians, towards Milner's school teachers, inspectors and educational administrators. And yet Smuts had good reason for rating their services high. As Minister of Education, he had the support of Dr J. E. Adamson, an Englishman of philosophic insight who had been Director of Education during the Milner regime and now worked loyally under his new master. The Smuts Education Act of 1907 was testimony to their creative partnership as minister and civil servant. Drafted at speed within the first month or two of the new government, it established an educational code far more thorough and comprehensive than any that had existed hitherto in South Africa—for example, it laid the foundations of a school system for the Natives, who had never before been so much as mentioned in the educational legislation of any of the four colonies. The act, nevertheless, was destined to be judged (both at the time of its introduction and in historical retrospect ever since then) not primarily by educational, but by political criteria. Educational policy was then, and remains today, explosive stuff. 'It has stirred almost more feeling', declared Smuts, 'than any other question.' These words would have been true half a century later.[11]

In his speech on the second reading, Smuts affirmed the following principles: the educational system must be unitary—which assumed that there was no longer any justification for the C.N.O. (formerly opposition) schools; it must recognise the equality of the English and Dutch languages; it must be established upon Christian foundations; it must be free and compulsory at the primary level; it must combine central direction and oversight with local initiative. These were the principles which Het Volk had been fighting for against the centralising, secularising and anglicising policy of the Milner regime, and Smuts maintained that his act embodied them. There were one or two members of Het Volk, such as A. D. W. Wolmarans and C. F. Beyers, who believed that he should have carried the fight further; but the party as a whole was solid in his support. It was not until the following year that the act came under dangerous fire—and then not in the Transvaal, but the Free State.

Controversy fastened upon the clauses which purported to embody language equality. All the other clauses came as near to perfection as circumstances permitted. The combination of a central Directorate, a central advisory board and local committees possessing a strong elective element represented the best achievable compromise between the two principles of governmental responsibility and local initiative. On the religious issue, provision for prayers every morning and two and a half hours of Bible-reading every week satisfied most, if not all of the ministers.[12] But on the language issue the act fell short of full equality. It stipulated that the mother-tongue should be the medium of instruction in all subjects up to the third standard, but after that it retained English as the medium in all subjects except two. Moreover, it made the study of the English language obligatory for all children but left the study of the Dutch language optional. Consequently, the act did not disturb the linguistic isolationism of English-speaking Transvaalers nor shake their calm assumption that English would remain for all time the dominant language of business, culture and even of politics.

South of the Vaal, such an assumption appeared intolerable. The Transvaal Education Act confirmed the suspicions which the Free Staters had long been harbouring against the Transvaalers and their policy of conciliation. These suspicions, as we have seen, had deep roots in memories of the war and of Vereeniging, and in the temperamental and intellectual opposition between Steyn and Botha. Smuts followed Botha but his personal relations with Steyn seemed to be unimpaired and he may well have thought that he could build a bridge of understanding between the two leaders. When Steyn returned after his long absence in Europe, with improved but not restored health, Smuts began at once to write to him with news of his family and with news and views about the political struggle in the Transvaal and South Africa generally. Steyn responded 'with greetings from house to house' and with comments on political developments and prospects. Both men, meanwhile, were in correspondence with Merriman, and to some extent a united front came into existence between the nationalist politicians of Pretoria, Bloemfontein and Cape Town. This unity, nevertheless, was in some respects superficial. The letters exchanged between Steyn and Smuts lacked the warmth and spontaneity of the Smuts–Merriman correspondence. More than once, arrangements seemed to be in hand for an exchange of visits between the Smuts and Steyn families, but for some reason or another they always came to nothing. On Steyn's side, the letters give the impression of a persisting coolness, of something held back.

Smuts in his turn held something back. In December 1905, on the eve of his mission to Campbell-Bannerman, he gave Steyn to understand that he was going to England for the benefit of his health.[13] For the sake of good personal relations, it would have been better if he had avoided that small equivocation; but he may well have felt that for political reasons it was unavoidable. Certainly, that was not a time for slow committee work, cumbersome deputations and newspaper publicity. Smuts attempted a one-man *coup* and brought it off. It would be unfair to say that he was thinking only of the Transvaal's interests. As has been shown, his plea on the Free State's behalf was chivalrous, cogent and urgent. He bore no responsibility for the time-lag of a year in the granting of self-government to the Free State. That had two explanations: first, the disposition on the British side to make a start with self-government in a community where the two elements of the European population were evenly balanced, rather than in one with an overwhelming Afrikaner majority; secondly, the slow start which the Free Staters had made in organising themselves politically. Orangia Unie (inaugurated May 1906) was more than two years behind Het Volk (inaugurated January 1904). The constitutional time-lag was not half so long as that.

When all this has been said, it remains true that Smuts and Steyn were deeply divided emotionally and ideologically. In their hearts and in their heads they held conflicting conceptions of nationality. Smuts's conception has already been explained many times in his own words: in effect, it was a call for cooperation between Boer and Briton in service to their common country.* In the mixed population of the Transvaal that meant, inevitably, compromise and conciliation. Steyn hated compromise and he came to hate conciliation. He hated and dreaded everything that threatened to impair Afrikaner solidarity. There is a phrase which recurs like a refrain in his letters to Smuts: let Afrikaners stand together 'as one man'.

It was, of course, much easier for Steyn than it was for Smuts to take his stand as the uncompromising guardian of Afrikaner integrity. In the land between the Orange and the Vaal, English-speaking people were such a small minority that politicians had no real need to compromise with them. Besides, Steyn had ceased to be a politician. He was not the party leader of Orangia Unie. He was its oracle.

The party leader was James Barry Munnik Hertzog. He was the fifth son in a family of twelve and four years older than Smuts. The careers of the two men up to 1908 ran broadly in parallel, although on a lower level of achievement for Hertzog. Like Smuts, he came of farming stock in the Cape Western Province, but he had not enjoyed in his childhood those blessings of quiet security that were taken for

* See pp. 149, 163, 181, 199, 207 above.

granted in the Smuts family. During the agricultural depression of the 1860's and 1870's his father had accepted mortgages which proved too heavy for him to carry, so he had to give up farming and go on trek—first to the Kimberley diamond fields, where the family spent some restless and anxious years, and after that to Jagersfontein in the Free State, where he went into business as a butcher and baker. There at last his fortunes began to mend and he found himself able to give his children a good education.

The boy Barry did well at Victoria College, Stellenbosch, although he won none of the distinctions and prizes which Smuts gathered in a few years later. Instead of going to Cambridge on the Ebden scholarship he went to Leyden, where he took his doctorate of law in 1892. Like Smuts, he had a girl waiting for him at Stellenbosch; he married her in 1893 and took her with him to Johannesburg. There he lived quietly until 1895, when he was made a judge of the Orange Free State at the age of twenty-nine. At this period of his life his ambitions appeared more limited than those of Smuts and his mind seemed to move more slowly and on a narrower front, even in the legal studies which were one of his chief pleasures. It was the same when war came; like Smuts, he became a general and led a commando into Cape Colony, but he did not show comparable audacity nor win equal renown. At Vereeniging the two men were closely associated as legal advisers to the Assembly of the People, and again it was Smuts who played the more positive and decisive part. There is no evidence that Hertzog showed any chagrin at being so persistently outshone; but there is evidence of a widening divergence between the two men in their political attitudes and personal loyalties. Smuts followed Botha, Hertzog followed Steyn. And even here there was a difference. Various words could be used to describe the deep feeling of Smuts for Botha, but veneration, which was Hertzog's feeling for Steyn, would not be one of them. Hertzog venerated Steyn as the living symbol of Afrikaner nationhood.

With the advent of self-government in the Free State in 1908 Hertzog could have been prime minister; but he preferred to take office under Abraham Fischer, an older and more pliable politician. Once again, his temperament expressed itself in the concentrated pursuit of a limited objective. As Minister of Education he was determined to produce a policy which would contain all the virtues but none of the blemishes of the Transvaal Education Act. In his eyes, its chief blemish was its temporising approach to the language problem. He was willing to follow Smuts in opting for mother-tongue instruction in the early years of schooling, although even there he made provision for the gradual introduction of the second language. After Standard IV, he prescribed the use of *both* languages as media of instruction. This was not a matter that he was prepared to leave to the choice of parents. His purpose was not merely equality between the two language-groups but universal and complete bilingualism, imposed and enforced by the law of the land.

Hertzog's Education Act aroused a storm of protest and even of abuse among English-speaking South Africans. The word 'Hertzogism' soon became synonymous in the English press with 'racialism'. This was most unjust. Hertzog was not merely an Afrikaner nationalist but a South African patriot. His vision of a completely bilingual nation was imaginative and constructive. He was not seeking a position of dominance for his own language-group, but a real partnership of both groups on the basis of their full equality. It was his English-speaking tormentors who were the true 'racialists'. At that time, and for a long time to come, they thought it proper for other people's children to speak English but improper for their own children to speak Dutch. (Not to mention Afrikaans: as will be explained later, that language was destined to come into its own with Hertzog, not Smuts, as its political champion.)

When Hertzog found himself the target of these prejudiced and violent attacks he was at first genuinely surprised. Then he grew angry. He was always inclined in his speech-making to take colour from his audience, to let his emotions run away with him and to lose control over his words. Some of the things that he said in his speeches on educational policy lent colour to the accusations of his enemies. And so the genuine differences of policy and outlook between him and Smuts came to be exaggerated in the popular mind: Smuts was the statesman, Hertzog the fanatic: or—from a different point of view—Smuts was the compromiser, Hertzog the unfaltering champion of Afrikaner rights.

These origins of the long-continuing duel between Hertzog and Smuts are so important that an attempt has been made (rather sketchily, and not without some guesswork) to understand them from Hertzog's point of view. It is now time to take up the story again from the point of view of Smuts. His guiding purpose was different from Hertzog's and far broader. The objective that he had in mind was the Union of South Africa. He saw this objective endangered by the passions which Hertzog's educational policy was arousing. He had no love for British jingos and saw that they were largely responsible for the turmoil; but he also put part of the blame upon Hertzog. That man, he felt, had no sense of proportion and no sense of time; he lacked the patience to admit any distinction between a thing that ought to be done in due time and a thing that could be done here and now. There was no chance of even beginning to achieve bilingualism until the training colleges became ready to produce bilingual teachers. Hertzog was dooming himself to be thwarted, not merely by the prejudices of his enemies but by his own refusal to face facts. No matter how many inspectors he dismissed, he could not all at once make administrative impossibilities possible. If only he would practise a little patience!

When he considered his own act, Smuts felt no twinges of remorse. It secured for Afrikaner children throughout the Transvaal all the advantages that only a few of them had so far enjoyed in the most advanced C.N.O. schools.[14] It did this without exciting racial turmoil. It was a victorious, but also a peaceful liberation from Milner's house of bondage. It was a long stage of the journey towards the promised land—wherever that might be: Smuts was not so sure as Hertzog of its precise location. Of course, there would be new needs and demands to deal with later on. The act could then be amended. Meanwhile, it could be administered. It did not demand impossibilities from the teachers and inspectors. It did not make things too hard for the children. By and large, it satisfied the parents.

Smuts's educational policy must stand or fall with the general policy of his government. Certainly the Union of South Africa would never have been achieved if his act had pushed half the population of the Transvaal into passionate mutiny. Conceivably, it might not have been achieved if the full consequences of Hertzog's act had become apparent before the convention met at Durban. From this point of view, the time-lag of self-government in the Free State may have been a blessing.*

* The chronology (1908) runs thus:

April	Death of Campbell-Bannerman.
May	Intercolonial Conference.
June–July	Closer Union Resolutions approved in the four South African parliaments.
August	Hertzog's Education Act passed.
October	National Convention meets.

The decisive step towards closer union was taken in May 1908, a few weeks after the death of Campbell-Bannerman. 'The death of that good old man', wrote Margaret Clark to Smuts, 'turns one's mind very much to things which he helped to bring into life and to make to grow in the world.... In reading what the papers say, I often think of what you said constantly "that C.B. was a rock, and a long way your best friend"....I wonder if he realised how much he had done in S. Africa.' Smuts believed that 'the miracle' of his achievement was revealed to him before he died. 'The loss of C.B.', he wrote, 'we have felt severely, but really so far as South Africa was concerned his work was done. It is enduring work and will ever remain a monument to Liberal policy at its very best....C.B. and Louis Botha—both men of the same type and mould—will ever remain in history as co-workers of this miracle in South Africa. The one is dead and the other may not live to work still greater miracles. For we are now busy with closer Union, and if the stars continue to fight in their courses for us, there may yet be in a short number of years a United South Africa.'[15]

CHAPTER 13

UNION

AMONGST the many men who worked together to make the Union of South Africa Smuts was pre-eminent. From start to finish it was his strategy and tactics that dominated the campaign.

To say this is to contradict a familiar version of history which fathers the Union not upon South African politicians but upon English officials—upon the members of 'the kindergarten' who stayed behind when Milner left South Africa and, in the last months of Crown Colony government, drafted the Selborne Memorandum. That document, certainly, was a powerful plea for political union and it had a powerful effect, particularly upon English-speaking South Africans. Its authors, nevertheless, found themselves before long enrolled as auxiliaries to the politicians: above all, to Smuts. And that was as it should be. Union had been the goal of Smuts's endeavour years before Lionel Curtis and his friends discovered it as their great cause.[1]

Union may have been in his mind even at Vereeniging. The vision of it, or of something very like it, had suffused the closing passage of his great speech to the Assembly of the People: and this not merely as a mirage of rhetoric, but—so he testified later[2]—as an understanding deep within him of the way things would work out, an assurance of the future which fortified his spirit even in the frustrating years of Crown Colony rule. Imperialism, he told Merriman in May 1904, was a fever that was bound to pass, that was already passing.

I believe thoroughly in liberty, in patriotism and in those who are faithful to South Africa; the future is with them—and sooner than we think we shall find that Imperialism has spent its force and has come down never to rise again in South Africa.

...Don't you think as soon as the Liberals get into power we ought to make a move in the direction of Federation? That would perhaps take us out of the narrow rut into which we have been getting and supply a larger and ampler ideal for South African patriotism. You know with the Boers 'United South Africa' has always been a deeply-felt political aspiration and it might profitably be substituted for the Imperialism which imports Chinese, a foreign bureaucracy, and a foreign standing army'.[3]*

* See pp. 149, 199, 203 above.

In this letter he made no distinction between federation and union; some years were still to pass before it became rewarding for him or for any other South African to start work on constitution-making. His first preoccupation in May 1904 and throughout the next two years was to build Het Volk and to achieve self-government. Yet even then, national unity and self-government were joined together inseparably in his political strategy. He made this plain in the memorandum that he took with him to London at the end of 1905; he made it still plainer in an exposition of the memorandum which he addressed to Merriman in March 1906. 'It seems to me that in Federation or Unification lies the solution of our and your troubles. If Hoggenheimer has to do, not only with the crippled population of the Transvaal, but with the people of South Africa, there will be some chance of keeping him in his right place politically.' For the rest of that year he continued to hammer on the same theme. 'But after all', he wrote in August, 'I come round to my conviction that unless the power of the magnates in the Transvaal is broken by our entry into a Unified or Federal South Africa, the danger of their capturing supreme power here and so over the rest of South Africa (which they will rout piecemeal) will continue to exist....We must checkmate them by working for the only real and possible Union— viz. of all South Africa.' In December he returned to the charge again: 'Believe me, as long as we stand divided and separated in S.A. the money power will beat us....Let us...proceed to lay the foundation of a united South African people.'[4]

Merriman's response to these advances was not so forthcoming as Smuts would have wished. For one thing, Merriman distrusted the colour policy of the Transvaal and its 'democratic shibboleth' of manhood suffrage for white men; if he could have had his way, he would have established the Transvaal's franchise on sound Whig principles before proceeding to Union. But what counted still more with him was the timing of the unification movement and its tactics. From Milner's time to Selborne's he was constantly suspicious of an imperialist plot to unify South Africa 'from the top downwards' and to the profit of the capitalists, the Progressive party and his own particular *bête noire*, Dr Jameson. In 1904 and 1905 he had it in mind to fend off Lord Milner's designs by reviving the old understanding between the Cape and the Free State and leaving the Transvaal to 'stew in its own juice'.[5] In 1905 and 1907 he was just as much concerned to fend off Lord Selborne's designs. The Selborne Memorandum was conceived in October 1906, completed in January 1907, circulated to the four governments in the same month and published in July. Throughout this period, and perhaps for a little longer, it looked as if Lord Selborne and his young Oxonians were making the running. Merriman believed them to be hand in glove with Dr Jameson; that was annoying, but only to be expected. The unexpected and alarming thing was their successful propagandising of F. S. Malan, his own follower in Cape politics, the chairman of the Afrikander Bond and the editor of *Ons Land*.

Even before this climax of his anxieties, Merriman was all for going slow with Union until he and his political friends could take charge of the movement. '*Festina lente*', he exhorted Smuts and again, '*Timeo Danaos*—I do not want to see any union hastily patched up with a view of serving the ends of Imperialism. That the whole of S. Africa may have one neck in order to fit the yoke easier on to it.'[6] Smuts made the appropriate rejoinder to these Latin exclamations. He was just as much resolved as Merriman to prevent Lord Selborne and Lionel Curtis from running the movement; but he also saw the danger of playing party politics at the expense of the nation. He endorsed Merriman's plea for caution and held himself in some degree aloof from 'Curtis and Co.'; but at the same time he did his best to avoid pouring cold water on their enthusiasm. He agreed that sinister influences were at work, that Abe Bailey and other people wanted to run the movement 'as a sort of Barnum policy' for their own advertisement; but he added—'Still, the thing itself is very good, and if it is initiated in a proper spirit and from and on the right basis, a tremendous step in advance will be achieved. I would however wait till there is self government in the O.R.C. and a general election at the Cape has given the quietus to the Jameson crowd.'[7]

From January 1907 onwards, these tactics were agreed between Smuts and Merriman. But they were severely tested in July, when F. S. Malan broke loose and tabled some motions in the Cape parliament which led to the publication of the Selborne Memorandum, and might have led to a premature conference for the purpose of implementing its proposals. At this Merriman was so angry that he lost all sense of proportion. 'Now comes in Lord Selborne's windy effusion', he wrote to Smuts on 7 July. 'Surely the price of flunkeyism can go no further than the attempt to compare it with Lord Durham's report.' A week or two later he compared 'that mischievous pamphlet of Lord Selborne' to the apple of discord that was thrown between the guests 'on a certain famous occasion'. It was a disreputable capitalist plot to break up the South African party and to foist a bankrupt Rhodesia upon the unsuspecting South Africans. Merriman was so upset that he thought of dropping Union altogether and of trying for a 'Customs Parliament'. A retreat so ignominious would have left his opponents triumphant on the field.[8]

Smuts showed great skill in keeping Merriman on the straight road. He sympathised with him on having such 'disreputable' opponents to deal with but assured him that he would defeat their machinations by his wisdom and tact. A Customs Parliament, he said, was not the right answer to the problem; on the contrary, the existing Customs and Railways Union would face dissolution at the conference in May of next year. That would be the time to go all out for a real Union, the only worthwhile objective. Within a few months, he felt sure, Merriman would be in power in the Cape. Meanwhile, there was no need for him to worry about Malan's apparent defection.

I however rely on your wisdom and tactful handling to smooth away possible difficulties. Malan is an old friend of mine and I know his enthusiastic temperament all too well. You can moderate him and give wise counsel just as you are giving to me. Do not think that he has any vulgar ambition. I feel certain that if you do not get impatient and bring wisdom and sympathy to bear on the situation, you will find in him just the loyal lieutenant whom you need.... Your wisest course is not to be deflected from the South African national course by your antipathy to the rotten or disgraceful tactics of opponents. My own position is that Federation or rather Unification is a good and wise ideal....Do not throw cold water; but wisely guide a movement which, under favourable circumstances, *may* possibly lead to great things. I shall not be rushed. The Progressives wish to introduce Malan's motion here, but I have absolutely declined to join. To me the issue is sacred and ought not to be a party pawn. I shall write to Malan and give him brotherly advice. [9]

But it was fatherly advice, a stranger might well have thought, that Smuts was offering Merriman—his senior by twenty-nine years! Its effect was wonderfully calming. Before very long Merriman was telling Smuts about the ignominious failure of the attempts to sow dissension between Malan and himself. 'Malan's conduct has been beyond praise and his personal relations with myself have been marked by a generous affection that has placed me under a great obligation. I think that they have abandoned this line of attack and I hope and believe that the coming elections will show the beginning of a real fusion between English and Dutch S. Africans that will be following your lead. As to the importance of the issue I am quite alive. If we gain the day we may do much to lay the foundation for the future.'[10]

You will certainly gain the day, Smuts assured him. Indeed, there was a great forward surge of the popular forces around the turn of the year. In November, Orangia Unie won a sweeping victory in the Free State. The Cape elections—strung out for the Legislative Council and then for the Assembly from November to February—were less dramatic but similar in their effect. From their opening to their climax Smuts cheered Merriman to victory; you will win, he wrote, you are winning—you have won!

With like-minded governments holding power in three of the four colonies there was now a heaven-sent chance of uniting South Africa quickly. Once again it was Smuts who planned the operation and its timing. In June 1907 the Transvaal government had given notice of its intention to withdraw from the railways and customs agreement in its existing form but had also declared itself ready to negotiate a new agreement. Failing that, the customs union would break up on 30 June 1908. The decisive conference was due to be held in May 1908 at Pretoria. Then and there, declared Smuts, it would be now or never—forward to union or back into anarchy.

He had expounded this time-table to Merriman in July 1907, and again in September, as the elections were drawing near.[11]

Our wishes and prayers go with you; for much, very much for South Africa depends on your victory. By good fortune and hard work we have got together a majority here, which though apparently large is by no means stable. You will win at the Cape—and a unique opportunity will present itself for righting the situation in South Africa, an opportunity such as may not recur in our lifetime. The O.R.C. is all right, Natal has also a well-disposed government. There is the chance to neutralise all the evil effects of the war, to weld South Africa into a compact South African nation, and to rid ourselves of the internal discords which always and inevitably invite Downing Street interference.... The conference on Railway and Customs policy to be held next year will mark the cross roads; if by any possibility we could make that the starting-point for a united South Africa, no consummation could be better. Otherwise I am afraid we shall drift further apart and develop vested rights alien to the establishment of Union.

Once the Cape elections were over, Smuts wrote still more insistently about the urgent need for speed. During recent months, he said, a very dangerous movement had been growing in the Transvaal—'a movement for Separatism similar to that which existed before the war'. Farmers and industrialists were clamouring for a ring fence around their local markets to protect them against the rest of South Africa. General Botha and he had been stumping the country to combat this insane retrograde movement and perhaps they were still strong enough to control it; but any delay would be fatal: the alternatives were to hurry on Union or relapse into conflict: no middle course was possible. It may be that Smuts deliberately over-painted the picture for tactical reasons; anyway, his letter produced the effect that he was hoping for. Merriman and Steyn both expressed horror at his report of reaction in the Transvaal and insisted on the urgent need for action. Let us carry Union, exclaimed Merriman, by a *coup de main*![12]

It still remained to agree upon the procedure for bringing Union into being. The first step, said Smuts, was to get the forthcoming Customs conference to submit to the four governments and parliaments proposals for a national convention. But how would the convention be constituted? In a letter to Merriman on 3 March 1908 he set out the alternatives.

Are we going to adopt the Canadian or Australian procedure or combine the two? It will be a question of nice calculation whether the Parliaments or the peoples of the colonies will be more favourable and that time alone can show. I would favour the idea (as a first stage) of delegates being chosen by parliaments in our following sessions to a convention which will sit after the prorogation of parliaments and report before the sessions of 1909. The Constitution will be published and if favourably received might be pushed through parliaments, or referred to another Convention of parliamentary delegates for ratification. If parliaments are hostile and peoples more favourable, a referendum to the electorate might be taken for final confirmation.[13]

Merriman's ideas about procedure were not so flexible as those of Smuts and in particular he was insistent that the Colonies should be represented at the proposed convention in proportion to their white populations. Sir Henry de Villiers, Chief Justice at the Cape and the destined president of the National Convention, would have preferred equal representation of the Colonies; but in the end Merriman had his way.[14]

The upshot of it was that full agreement on immediate action existed in the minds of three of the governments—and Smuts felt sure that the fourth, Natal, would come into line—which met at Pretoria on 3 May 1908. Next day Smuts moved a long resolution to the following effect: that the best interests and permanent prosperity of South Africa could only be secured by an early union of the four colonies under the Crown of Great Britain; that provision should be made for the accession of Rhodesia at a later date; that the legislatures of the four colonies should be invited to appoint delegates to a National South African Convention; that this convention should consist of not more than twelve delegates from Cape Colony, eight from the Transvaal and five each from the Orange River Colony and Natal, and that it should meet as soon as possible after the next parliamentary sessions; that it should publish the draft constitution as soon as possible and should determine, in consultation with the governments, the further steps to be taken: that voting in the convention should be *per capita* and not by States.

The resolution was carried unanimously. Thereupon the conference agreed, on Merriman's motion, to tell the world of the proposals it was submitting to the governments, parliaments and peoples of South Africa.

In their long-drawn-out correspondence with each other Smuts and Merriman had reached agreement not only upon the tactics and procedures of constitution-making, but also upon the principles to be embodied in the constitution. On some of these principles they found themselves from the start to be of one mind. South Africa, they were both convinced, must be united under the Crown. Their reasons were in part practical—indeed, no alternative road to Union existed—and in part idealistic, for they both believed that this road, which the Canadians and Australians had followed before them, would lead their people also to freedom and nationhood. As a young Cape Colonist, Smuts had absorbed this doctrine in the school of Jan Hofmeyr and he had returned to it after his hard battering in the school of experience. Merriman had preached the same doctrine throughout his political life. His theory of the Crown was in the Whig tradition, under which the monarch must act on the advice of ministers responsible to parliament. In the setting of a united South Africa, this constitutional rule would exclude the interference of Downing Street. Did this mean the end of the Empire? To Merriman, it meant the advent of something more satisfying. As has been seen earlier, he chose the word Commonwealth as a true description of the political society that he saw emerging—a family of free and equal nations, living together fraternally within the circle of the Crown.*

Another matter upon which Smuts and Merriman were temperamentally and intellectually at one was the form of the South African constitution. Notwithstanding the Canadian and Australian precedents, they wanted it to be unitary and flexible, not federalistic and rigid. This had been Merriman's view for many decades past. Whether or not the view could prevail over the fears of English-speaking Natal and the scruples of such eminent men as Jan Hofmeyr and W. P. Schreiner was another matter; Lionel Curtis and his friends believed at first that a unitary constitution was too much to hope for. Smuts, however, became convinced during 1907 that a full-blooded Union was not only desirable but possible. Before the year was out, this had become the agreed programme of Merriman, Steyn and himself. His reasons can best be explained in his own words.

The federal system [he told the Transvaal parliament] is not only undesirable because it involves even more expense and means more machinery superimposed on the people of South Africa, which is already groaning under all this administration, but to my mind the great difficulty with federation is this, that it assumes that a number of independent parties come together into a compact, into an agreement, which is binding for the future....Is that the sort of Constitution we want for South Africa, a country in its infancy? Do we want a Constitution which will lead to civil wars as the American Constitution led to? No, we prefer to follow a different type—that of the British Constitution....We must not be prevented in far-off years, from going forward because we have an agreement which cannot be altered. What we want is a supreme national authority to give expression to the national will of South Africa, and the rest is really subordinate.[15]

Merriman used very similar arguments. There was, however, one question upon which he and Smuts did not reach agreement so

* See p. 203 above: also the draft of a letter (1905) from Merriman to the British Empire League [Merriman Papers, no. 119 (1905)]. 'The name Empire which is generally used to describe the various communities that acknowledge allegiance to the King of England may serve as a convenient expression for the somewhat undefined relation that hitherto existed between Great Britain and the self-governing colonies but if this relation is to be made the subject of any Constitution I venture to think that the word Commonwealth expresses the sort of relation that must exist in the future if the connection is to be a permanent one.'

easily. As has been seen earlier, Merriman was the ardent champion of a limited franchise which would deny the vote to poor and ignorant white men but would grant it to such non-whites as might raise themselves to a respectable European standard of prosperity and education. This was in essence the Cape rule, and its rejection by the Transvaal, although he agreed that it was inevitable, filled Merriman with foreboding. He never seriously entertained the hope that the northern politicians and peoples would embody in the new Union a principle which they had refused to accept in their own constitutions. Nor did he favour the representation of Natives on a separate electoral roll—a device which had been adopted by the New Zealanders for their Maoris, which had been commended to South Africa by Lord Milner's Native Affairs Commission, and which had some attraction for Smuts.[16] Considering all the circumstances, Merriman decided that the only thing to do was to allow each of the four colonies to carry its existing franchise laws into the Union. No doubt he hoped (for he too belonged to the sanguine age) that the Cape would ultimately come out on top in the ensuing competition of political philosophies; but he made preparation for the opposite contingency by demanding special safeguards for the Cape franchise. In February 1908 he suggested to Smuts that their difficulty might be resolved 'by leaving the question of the franchise to the provinces themselves and providing that the local franchise should not be altered except on a $\frac{2}{3}$ majority to be ascertained by a plebiscite of registered voters in the province'. Here was the idea of 'entrenchment', which was destined to embody itself, with some important procedural modifications, in the constitution of the Union.[17]

Merriman's proposal, or something like it, was needed, not only to appease South African contentions but also to assuage British doubts. These were reported to Smuts regularly and at length by Sir Richard Solomon, the defeated politician who had hoped at one time to lead the Transvaal government, but was now serving it as Agent General in London. From December 1906 to February 1907 Solomon had kept Smuts fully posted about British reactions to his dramatic first encounter with Gandhi—an encounter which ended, or seemed at first to end, with considerable applause for Smuts.* During the following months, Solomon gave news of the Milnerite campaign against the Transvaal's retrenchment policy, which, it was alleged,

* See below pp. 344 *et seq.*

was a shabby pretext for dismissing English-speaking civil servants. This unwarranted and unscrupulous attack fizzled out about the middle of the year.[18] From that time onwards Solomon's letters were full of news and views about Union. 'With regard to the Cape Colony Native franchise', he wrote on 17 July, 'why not follow what was done in Canada? Let each Colony elect its representatives to the federal parliament on its own franchise. Let the federal parliament have power to alter the franchise for each Colony with the view of making a uniform franchise for the whole of South Africa but make a proviso that the amendment of the Franchise by the Federal Parliament must be passed in the Assembly by a majority of $\frac{2}{3}$s, or else provide that the franchise of a Colony cannot be altered by the federal Parliament unless $\frac{2}{3}$ of that Colony's representatives in that Parliament agree.'[19] This shot was very nearly a bull's-eye.

Smuts was not ready as yet to endorse these proposals for entrenchment, but he must by now have been pretty clear in his mind about how best to handle the question of Native political rights in the National Convention. From the tactical point of view this was fortunate, for he knew from his friend J. A. Hobson that the question was troubling the consciences of many British liberals. He took particular pains to allay their anxieties.

My impression [he told Hobson] is that the only sound policy at this stage is to avoid any attempt at a comprehensive solution of the various questions surrounding the political status and rights of the natives. With the chaotic state in which public opinion on this subject is at present, any solution at present would be a poor compromise which might probably prejudice a fairer and more statesmanlike settlement later on. Public opinion in the majority of the South African States is against a native franchise in any shape or form, and while it cannot be denied that on this delicate subject responsible public men are probably in advance of the rather crude attitude of the people at large and would be prepared to consider the subject on its merits, still the fear of the people will be with them and they will probably shrink from any far-reaching innovation. The danger then is that a poor makeshift arrangement will be framed; and there is the further and graver danger that the people, who will have to ultimately ratify any constitution, may veto it on the ground that it confers the franchise on natives. This latter danger is a very real one, and will be a strong inducement to all who seriously desire to bring about a United South Africa to shelve this question at this stage in order to attack it under more favourable circumstances after Union has been brought about. My view is that the different franchise laws of the several Colonies ought to be left undisturbed and that the first

Union Elections ought to take place thereunder, and that the question of a uniform franchise law be gone into only after the Union has been brought about. You will then avoid the dangers I have referred to, and you will in the Union Parliament, representing as it will all that is best in the whole of South Africa, have a far more powerful and efficient instrument for the solution of the question along broad and statesmanlike lines than you will have in the Union Convention which is going to meet next October or November. The political status of the natives is no doubt a very important matter, but vastly more important to me is the Union of South Africa, which if not carried now will probably remain in abeyance until another deluge has swept over South Africa.[20]

Hobson did not challenge this argument; indeed he did not even acknowledge it until four or five months later. The report that he gave then of thought and feeling amongst his radical and liberal friends must have convinced Smuts that their interest in the rights and liberties of black and coloured South Africans would not be pressed to the point of interference with those articles of the constitution which should be agreed upon by South African politicians as fundamental.

Liberals in South Africa, few though they were in number, kept the problem in steadier focus than their fellows in England did. To W. P. Schreiner, at any rate, the order of priorities which Smuts envisaged was upside down. Union, Schreiner believed, was no doubt a very important matter, but human rights were vastly more important. 'To embody in the South African Constitution a vertical line or barrier separating its people upon the ground of colour into a privileged class or caste and an unprivileged inferior proletariat is, as I see the problem, as imprudent as it would be to build a grand building upon unsound and sinking foundations. The *freedom* to which all are born in a free land is as true as their alleged *equality* is false.... In our South African Nation there must be room for many free peoples, but no room for any that are not free and free to rise.'[21] These words had the warmth and glow of Schreiner's individual temperament and their doctrinal implications should not have seemed strange to Merriman. In theory, that old Whig still believed in the 'safety valve'; but in practice he was ready to compound for entrenchment of the Cape franchise. He made this clear on 19 July 1908 in a letter which he wrote in a more formal tone than usual, with the idea that Smuts might wish to send it on to Hobson.[22] In this letter he endorsed the programme of Union First. Steyn, whose hopes and expectations for the future were very different from Merriman's, gave the same endorsement a week or two later.

And so the last word in this long argument may fittingly be left with Smuts. 'On the question of the native franchise my mind is full of Cimmerian darkness and I incline very strongly to leaving that matter over for the Union Parliament. I also feel pretty certain that a native franchise imported into the Constitution would make Union impossible of acceptance by the people. Let us therefore adhere to the comfortable gospel of laissez-faire....'[23] But was that gospel destined during the next half century to prove so very comfortable?

Controversy over the franchise did not only involve the political rights of non-Europeans; it also involved the distribution of voting power amongst different sections of the European community. On the question of adult male suffrage, as has been seen, Smuts would not and could not agree with Merriman; but the two men were originally of one mind in their desire to weight the franchise in favour of the country population.* This was the system which prevailed in the two coastal colonies, and Smuts had done his best to get it established in the Transvaal. However, the West Ridgeway Commission had accepted, with a few practical mitigations, the Progressive party's slogan 'one vote one value'. Merriman hated this slogan, which equated the rabble of urban voters with those honest country-folk who, he believed, were the true backbone of the nation. He thought it intolerable that the Transvaal's error should be repeated in the constitution of the Union. But Smuts knew it to be inevitable: the English-speaking politicians of the Transvaal made it a condition of their support for Union. And did it really matter so much? 'I am interested', he told Merriman, 'in your protest against the new-fangled notions of equal voters' areas and automatic redistribution. Our Progressive friends, however, decline to consider Union except on such terms of "equal rights" and it may be that you will have to move with the times, however distasteful the process may seem to such an old-fashioned Tory. No doubt there is much in all this to justify your fears, but remember that we achieved victory in our last elections notwithstanding these doctrinaire aids to the manhood of the Rand.'[24]

Historical memories are short—or it may be that men misremember

* See above, pp. 209, 226.

facts which contradict their prejudices. Half a century later, when Smuts was dead and his party in eclipse, it became fashionable among a section of his former followers to put upon him the responsibility for their own ineptitudes or misfortunes. He had foisted upon the Union, they said, a franchise which enabled a minority of the white voters to achieve a majority in parliament.[25] The very reverse of this was true. Such weighting of the country vote as was embodied in the Union franchise was not the work of Smuts, who steadfastly supported Sir Percy Fitzpatrick and the other champions of 'equal political rights'. Indeed, he went even further than his Progressive allies demanded, and produced a new 'democratic shibboleth' which must have shocked Merriman. If he had had his way, proportional representation would have been written into the constitution of the Union.[26]

In the correspondence between Smuts and Merriman, one or two differences of attitude had been identified; but they were not held so strongly as to endanger the work of constitution-making. The really dangerous difference had not been mentioned; it was not a question of principle but rather of prestige—the location of the capital. This question apart, the two men were basically in agreement. Moreover, Steyn had made it clear that he was willing to go ahead with them.

The date agreed upon for the opening of the National Convention was 12 October. To Smuts, anticipation of that day was like looking forward in his student years to examination days, when he must go into action with all his facts assembled and all his thoughts in order. 'We who have taken up this issue', he told Merriman, 'have practically burnt our boats and may therefore not look back. If we fail, we shall be ruined politically, so that there is this additional inducement to do our best to achieve success within a reasonable time.'[27] Instead of 'we' he might well have written 'I', for he took upon his own shoulders almost the whole burden of planning and preparing. Indeed, there was no other political leader to shoulder the burden. The politicians of Pietermaritzburg were torn between their sentiments, which made Union seem alarming to them, and their interests, which made it seem inescapable. The politicians of Bloemfontein were well disposed to Union but unwilling to take any initiative except upon the language question, which at this very time was arousing turmoil throughout the colony, as Hertzog went ahead with his Education Act. The politicians of Cape Town were enduring turmoil of a different kind, as Merriman, unmindful of the advice that Smuts gave him,[28] doggedly set to work to balance his budget by measures of extreme rectitude, orthodoxy and unpopularity. Merriman's political position was not nearly so solid as his parliamentary majority suggested; for he was in the unhappy situation of having no footing in the strongest extra-parliamentary organisation of Cape Colony, the Afrikaner Bond. Apart from this, he was by temperament an individualist, averse from teamwork and happier by far in the cut and thrust of debate than in any systematic drudgery.

The initiative lay therefore in Pretoria. Here, as usual, the Botha–Smuts combination worked to perfection. Botha, the very embodiment of his own word, 'conciliation', charmed away the fears of Fitzpatrick and other English-speaking Transvaalers who had been bewailing their 'political helotry' and did much to persuade some of the Natalians that it might be safe for them to come quietly into Union. Smuts, meanwhile, set himself to the task of drafting the constitution. The labour would have been formidable even if he had been free to give all his time to it; but the parliamentary session did not end until late August, and, as chief spokesman for the government, the main burden of it fell upon him. On 24 August he wrote to Margaret Clark—'Saturday 22 Aug. our Parliament was prorogued after 10 weeks sitting and passing 40 bills, many of them long and complicated. Even today I feel more dead than alive with all the work and worry of the last few weeks....Nor will there be any rest yet. The Union Convention will meet on 12 Oct. and I shall have to set to work at once in order to prepare for that ordeal.'[29]

Actually, his preparations were already far advanced. On Saturday of the same week he sent to Merriman, de Villiers and Steyn a paper entitled *Suggested Scheme for South African Union*.[30] The paper was simple, clear and persuasive, and the letter introducing it was insidiously modest. If the main ideas in his *Suggested Scheme* were approved, he said, he would be prepared (merely to save time, that indispensable commodity) 'to proceed with the drafting of a Constitution on the lines sketched'. The offer might appear unassuming, tentative—but the constitution was already drafted! In that hectic last month of the parliamentary session, Smuts had drafted it twice over.

The first draft is in his own handwriting, heavily marked and corrected. It is not complete, but is a broad outline of the constitution under eight heads. No doubt it gave him the foothold he needed for tackling his second draft, a document of 133 consecutively numbered sections under ten heads, which he got into type and marked in his own handwriting 'August 1908, J.C.S.'.[31]

The *Suggested Scheme* and the two drafts are of great historical interest; but an analysis of them in detail would clog this biography.[32] All that can be done here is to look at them as a landmark along the road which Smuts was following at his furious pace. This, more or less, was how he looked upon them himself. He judged correctly that the time had come to give greater precision to the views which he had been exchanging with Merriman, de Villiers and Steyn. In doing so, he made clear the constitutional implications of the principles upon which they were all agreed. He also threw into relief the issues upon which they were divided.

In their comments on the *Suggested Scheme*, his friends reassured him on the essential matter: the area of agreement was large, the points of disagreement few and for the most part negotiable. However, Smuts had yielded more ground to the federalists than Merriman and de Villiers could approve; in particular, he had made provision for cabinet government in the Provinces. He had also carved two additional Provinces out of the Union. These lapses, it was clear, he would have to correct. On the other hand, it seemed unlikely that he would need to make many corrections to his proposals for the franchise and electoral system, for de Villiers applauded their 'mathematical' tendency as vigorously as Merriman assailed it. The colour-blind franchise of the Cape was a different matter; in his *Suggested Scheme*, Smuts had ignored Merriman's proposal for entrenching it, but Merriman now served notice that he intended the proposal most seriously. Nobody as yet had suggested the entrenchment of language rights. As to these, the *Suggested Scheme* contained only one short sentence: 'Equal rights will have to be accorded to the English and Dutch languages in the Parliament and Law Courts of the Union.' This was not nearly enough for Steyn. 'I am', he wrote, 'largely in agreement with your scheme. Many points, however, should be very seriously considered. I can say at once that I do not agree at all with one, i.e. the point about language. I think we should demand equal rights not only in the courts and parliaments but also in the *schools* and in the *public service*....' Steyn's letter continued and ended on the note of passionate commitment. Reading it in the lightning flashes of the storm Hertzog was raising, Smuts must have forecast stormy weather ahead. But not shipwreck.[33]

His friends across the Vaal and the Orange rivers refrained, perhaps rather pointedly, from taking up his offer to produce a draft constitution, so probably he never showed them the 133 clauses which he had already written down. Instead, from early September onwards he adopted a more flexible plan of work—the preparation, under the main headings, of alternative draft documents which could be drawn upon according to the development of the constitutional debate. In this task he gave himself the assistance of R. H. Brand, probably the coolest head amongst the Kindergarten, who not only served his political master well but rendered a great service to the historical record, for he made a collection of all the documents that were compiled from the time of his joining Smuts and linked them together in an explanatory narrative which he wrote soon after the Cape Town session of the National Convention. Merriman, it may be noted, could see no merit at all in Brand;[34] but then, Merriman had been quite unable to overcome his original prejudice against Milner's young men. Smuts, on the other hand, had discovered them to be most valuable allies, with many and varied aptitudes for helping the great cause—the propagandist fervour of Curtis, whose Closer Union Societies were mobilising opinion throughout South Africa; the analytical gifts of Kerr, who was soon to become editor of a new periodical, the *State*; the political and constitutional expertise of Brand, Feetham and Duncan; the diplomatic wiles of Malcolm, who as secretary to Lord Selborne was well placed to give early notice of difficulties that might arise with Imperial officialdom. Lord Selborne himself, having accepted the fact that he would neither preside over the National Convention nor in any other way play a public part of leadership, was eager to do all that his constitutional position permitted, both in keeping communications open between the national leaders and Downing Street, and in reassuring conservative doubters in Natal and elsewhere.

Smuts knew very well that preparations for the National Convention were not merely an intellectual but also a human task; assembling experts and building up briefs would not suffice without unity of spirit in the Transvaal delegation. It was a well-balanced delegation, five members from Het Volk and three from the Progressive party; among the former, Botha had wisely included de la Rey, who knew nothing about constitutional questions but held the affectionate trust of country-dwelling Afrikaners; among the latter, the mercurial and magnanimous Fitzpatrick was destined to play a more positive part than his stodgy leader, Sir George Farrar. Fitzpatrick was prepared to go wholeheartedly into Union once he was convinced that the franchise would be kept close to the Transvaal model, without the heavy loading against city voters that Merriman wanted. Here Smuts perceived the chance of a deal that might satisfy both Fitzpatrick and Steyn: equal voting rights in exchange for equal language rights. This certainly was the most important question (from the point of view of practical politics) that was discussed and broadly agreed upon during talks which the delegation held at Pretoria during the first week of October. Since the Progressive members had made no systematic preparations at all, the talks inevitably covered the ground as Smuts had mapped it out. Their upshot was the deepening of mutual confidence and a genuine agreement upon the ends to be pursued. The means were kept sufficiently flexible (Brand was given fresh work to do in drafting alternative documents) to anticipate the various contingencies that might arise.

Smuts by now had done as much as one man could do in preparing for the National Convention. He had mastered the small constitutional details and had faced the large political issues. He had made certain that three of the four governments—and consequently the great majority of the Afrikaner population—would speak with one voice on these issues. In support of Botha, he had done all that was humanly possible to assuage the fears of English-speaking South Africans. He had convinced Sir Percy Fitzpatrick and his colleagues that Union would be the fulfilment of the conciliation policy. And so the Transvaal delegation went to Durban as a united team with an agreed programme. They went with the confidence and prestige, which no other delegation possessed, of their colony's economic strength and political stability. They went also, for Smuts was leaving nothing to chance, with an expert staff of nineteen persons.

The following months—October to early November in Durban, mid-November to early February in Cape Town—were as strenuous for Smuts as the months of preparation had been. There was not one resolution of any importance that he did not make his personal concern, either as its mover, or as its promoter, or as a main participant in the public debates and private consultations by which agreement was wrung from contending parties. He had done his preparatory work so thoroughly that the Transvaal team became the centre upon which the National Convention continually rallied. He had invested in Union so much of his own reputation, intellect and conviction that he dared not fail to see the work through.

The meetings of the National Convention were the climax of his endeavour, the harvest-time of his faith and works for many years past. Consequently, it may seem strange that his biographer should take them at a leap. To follow them with patient watchfulness from one day to the next might seem at first sight the natural thing to do; but it would involve the detailed historical exposition of each of the 152 clauses of the emerging constitution. This task has been faithfully performed by Professor Thompson; to perform it twice over would be waste of effort. Besides, the work of the National Convention could not without distortion be compressed into one biography; it requires not a single portrait but a whole portrait gallery, with each figure in its characteristic attitude—de Villiers vigilant and positive in the chair, Jameson looking around for partners at bridge or golf, Fitzpatrick and Hertzog in conflict leading to agreement, Botha, like his Scottish counterpart Campbell-Bannerman, always 'the Rock'. There would be in all thirty portraits to paint: some of them, it is true, not ordinarily significant but each one of them transfigured in some degree by his participation in a significant drama.

If this new metaphor may be followed a little further, Smuts's part in the drama was the threefold one of actor, manager and producer. Often he took the centre of the stage but all the time he was watching the action develop as he had already produced it and acted it within his own mind. On the whole, it went more smoothly than he could have dared to hope. In the first act at Durban the unitary constitution took shape as he had foreseen with the definition of legislative and executive powers at the centre; in the second act at Cape Town the plan unfolded for the Provinces, the judiciary, the civil service, finance and the amending power. Both at Durban and at Cape Town crises occurred. At Durban the crisis was over 'equal rights'—not, be it said, the rights of Natives and the Coloured people: that part of the play ran too easily, with the Cape delegates achieving the entrenchment of their franchise but conceding the exclusion of non-Europeans from the national parliament, and with the Convention admitting as a consequence (which Smuts perforce had faced in advance) that South Africa could not have at one and the same time a political colour-bar and immediate transfer of the High Commission Territories. These decisions of October 1908 were momentous for South Africa's future; but the immediate crisis was over 'equal rights' for European voters and for the two European languages. When Hertzog submitted his uncompromising motion on language equality, it looked for a short time as if the passions which his Education Act had aroused in the Free State might wreck the National Convention. The danger was averted by a meeting of minds between Fitzpatrick and Hertzog: language rights and voters' rights, they agreed, must stand together. Their reconciliation scene, although he had envisaged its substance beforehand, possessed a special quality of drama which Smuts, as producer of the play, must have found exhilarating.

Yet it is possible that he failed to envisage beforehand the intensity of the crisis which arose in Cape Town over the location of the national capital. The Transvaal delegation, as it had agreed before the Convention met, was determined to claim the capital for Pretoria; but the Cape delegation was just as resolute in claiming it for Cape Town. After discussions which nearly split the National Convention the crisis was resolved by a judgment of Solomon: the executive to have its seat in the northern city, the legislature in the southern one. Smuts, who had been just as partisan as anybody else while the fight was on, accepted this compromise against the advice of Lord Selborne.[35] He would have thought it intolerable for the Union to founder on the rock of provincial prestige. By the end of January, that disaster had been averted, and on 3 February 1909 the members of the National Convention signed a unanimous report, which contained the full text of their draft constitution, and made recommendations for all the steps that must be taken towards its legal embodiment in a 'South Africa Act' of the Imperial Parliament.

In those February days the mood of the National Convention and of all South Africa was one of deep gratitude and exaltation.

In the creative Spirit of History [wrote Smuts] the blunders of men are often more valuable than their profoundest wisdom.... From the blood and tears of nations which human passions have caused she proceeds calmly and dispassionately to build up new nations and to lead them along new undiscovered paths of progress. And when the darkness of the night has passed at last and the light of a new national consciousness dawns, the scales fall from men's eyes, they perceive that they have been led, that they have been borne forward in the darkness by deeper forces than they ever apprehended to a larger goal than they ever conceived, and they stand silent in the presence of that greatest mystery in the world, the birth of the soul of a new nation.[36]

The nation, nevertheless, was not yet born, either politically or (to use a word that Smuts was fond of using) spiritually. Three more acts of the political drama still remained to be played before the Union of South Africa could come into existence. The draft constitution must be debated by the four colonial parliaments: the convention must meet again at Bloemfontein to examine such amendments as the parliaments might propose: and—assuming acceptance by the four colonies of the amended draft—a delegation must go to London to discuss such amendments as the British government might wish to make before embodying the constitution in an Act of the Imperial legislature.

When the draft constitution came to be discussed in the newspapers and debated in the parliaments of the four colonies, evidence soon piled up—although few people at that time understood its full significance—of profound contradictions that existed, beneath the surface of unity, in the definition of the new nation and of its programme. What destiny, to begin with, was envisaged for the Native and Coloured populations? Could they or could they not look forward to an expanding political future as citizens of the Union? What their white rulers were proposing for them here and now was not an expansion but a contraction of their political rights; persons of non-European descent could sit in the Cape provincial council but would be debarred from the parliament of the Union. Their leaders thought this an evil omen.[37] So too did W. P. Schreiner, who upheld their cause bravely but vainly, first in Cape Town and subsequently in London. Not so Merriman: he was preaching the doctrine of Union First with all the fervour of a convert, holding out hopes of a fair deal for Natives when the liberal Cape converted the whole Union—as it surely must—to its philosophy. Did he close his eyes to the evidence? 'All our speeches are boomerangs', he told Smuts, and begged him not to use arguments in the Transvaal which would weaken his own arguments in Cape Colony.[38] For this plea he had good reason: face to face with the prejudices of their constituents, the northern politicians were making promises clean contrary to those that Merriman and his followers were making. The entrenched Cape franchise, some of them declared, was only a temporary blot upon the constitution, which was bound to be rubbed out when the North converted the South—as it surely must—to its own philosophy.[39]

In the conflict of ideologies which was thus foreshadowed, the northerners were destined to prove themselves the more resolute fighters. Looking back half a century later upon the work of the National Convention, an Afrikaner historian has written: 'Particularly significant was the fact that the act and "compromise" of Union enabled the ex-Republics of the Transvaal and the Free State to indoctrinate the rest of the Union with their traditions and ideals. This was eminently true of the two great principles which counted as corner-stones of the national existence of the Afrikaner people; the first, republicanism and the second, the practice and theory of inequality between white men and black men.'[40]

In the hindsight of 1958, these consequences of the work of 1908 may seem clear; but could they possibly have been foreseen by the men of the National Convention? The word 'republicanism' was not so much as whispered among them—not even by Steyn. And if divergent views were recorded upon the proper relations between white men and black men, their discussion did not take up more than a few days of the four months of constitution-making. The whole emphasis of the discussion was upon a different problem: namely, the relationship between the two sections of the European population. And here there was no open clash of views. The ideal which everybody accepted, or seemed to accept, was 'the fusion of races'.

No doubt different views were held about the manner by which this fusion would come about. English-speaking South Africans were prone to imagine that it would happen by the natural progress of their language to a position of dominance. Similar dreams of tribal ascendancy may well have been stirring deep down in the minds of some Afrikaners. If so, it was no task of the National Convention to fish them to the surface; psycho-analytical investigations were not within its terms of reference. By making provision—as it believed that it had done—for the equality of voters and of languages within the framework of a unitary state, it had done as much as any constitution-making body could do for the creation of South African nationhood.

These reflections are relevant in considering the last crisis which the National Convention was called upon to resolve. It arose at the final session in May 1909, at Bloemfontein, when amendments coming from the Colonial parliaments had to be considered. Merriman, despite recent attacks that he had made upon 'the wreckers', put forward proposals which nearly wrecked the Fitzpatrick–Hertzog understanding and with it the whole constitution. Fitzpatrick had already conceded to the opposite side more, perhaps, than he realised, for he had accepted a substantial qualification to the principle of voters' equality—an allowance of 15 per cent above or below the standard quota of a constituency, in recognition (among other things) of sparsity or density of population.* Merriman and his followers now proposed to wring additional profit from this concession, by defining in advance, and to the maximum advantage of rural interests, the precise manner in which the 15 per cent bonus or penalty should be handed out. Botha and Smuts stood loyally by Fitzpatrick; but the united Transvaal delegation consented to buy off Merriman by surrendering proportional representation—a sacrifice which fell hard upon Smuts, for it was he who had proposed it, and he had been enjoying the congratulations which came to him from Lord Courtney and others of its champions.[41] Indeed, he had come to set great store upon it as a device for the protection of minority opinions.

All the same, the significance of this last crisis can easily be misunderstood. The familiar dramatisation of South African history as an ideological struggle between 'north' and 'south' is, in this instance at least, singularly inappropriate, for it was the northerners, not the southerners, who upheld the cause of voters' equality. Equally inappropriate would be its dramatisation in terms of the Afrikaans–English contest, for Smuts was proud to call himself a Boer and Merriman was more truly 'English' than any other politician in South Africa; besides, on this issue, Merriman had the support not only of the Afrikander Bond but of English-speaking Natal. He would, indeed, have been shocked and dismayed had he been able to foresee that his fanatical conviction of the superior worth of country voters would play a large part, forty years later, in the advent to power of

---

* See pp. 257–8 above. In the Transvaal constitution, variations from the standard quota of a constituency had also been provided for in accordance with certain criteria which did not, however, include sparsity or density of population.

a party which finally rejected principles deeply rooted in the history of the Cape: principles which he believed to be fundamental and essential to the peace, order and good government of his country.

Smuts and Merriman had been reading the books of André Siegfried and other students of Canadian nationhood, and they both expected their country to conform—federalism apart—to a Canadian pattern of growth. In politics, this would mean the continuance of a party system cutting across the linguistic and cultural barrier. This, indeed, was the general expectation and the general desire among members of the National Convention.

The final act of the drama contained no crises. In June the amended draft was accepted by the colonial parliaments and by a referendum of the Natal voters. In July a delegation of the National Convention went to London. It found the British government accommodating. The Imperial power paid no heed to Schreiner and the other advocates of racial impartiality and proposed no amendments except of a technical character. The Union of South Africa Act had a smooth passage through Parliament and received the royal assent on 20 September 1909. A royal proclamation of 2 December appointed 31 May 1910 as the day upon which the new constitution would come into effect.

More than any other national constitution within the Commonwealth, that of the Union of South Africa bears the imprint of one man's mind. This, however, was not generally understood until it was revealed by historical research half a century later. Smuts himself took care never to say a word which would reveal the immensity of his own labours.

CHAPTER 14

POLITICAL AND PRIVATE LIFE

REACTION was bound to follow the fraternal ardours and high-pitched hopes of 1909. Barely a year from the passing of the South Africa Act, a cartoonist of the *Cape Times* pictured the 'Convention spirit' as a miserable cat, left to starve in an empty room. This was too cynical; but the steep fall of the political barometer during those twelve months may be gauged by the violent swing of Sir Percy Fitzpatrick: in September 1909 he was all aflame for a 'fresh start' under Botha's leadership; in September 1910 he fought and beat Botha in the constituency of Pretoria East.[1]

Fitzpatrick's pamphlet, *The Union, A Fresh Start*, was published in March 1910. By that time, its message was already several months out of date. What Fitzpatrick wanted was a nation-wide political alliance of moderate and patriotic men. Botha and Jameson had discussed this idea together before their return from Europe and Jameson thereafter had popularised it in his slogan: 'a government of the best men'. Such a government would presumably include politicians of his own party, as well as the leaders of Het Volk, Orangia Unie and the South Africa party. This could only mean the obliteration of existing party divisions, whether by coalition or by the formation of a new party. Whether or no Botha had ever contemplated a change so drastic as this, he soon discovered that his old political friends and followers would have none of it. So, with the aid of Smuts, he composed a letter to Merriman explaining that he had never had anything more in mind than a merger of the three *governing* parties, under a new name and with a new programme that would attract English-speaking voters. This explanation left Merriman profoundly distrustful. Whom was Botha humbugging, he asked, his enemies or his friends?

These party manœuvres were intermingled with the conflicting personal ambitions of Merriman and Botha. Both men wanted to become the Union's first prime minister. Looking back from fifty years later, one may find it interesting to speculate as to whether or no the Union might have been given the better start under the leadership of an English-speaking South African so deeply rooted as Merriman was in the constitutional tradition of England and the liberal philosophy of the Cape; but, in 1910, Merriman never had a real chance. Although Steyn and some other Free Staters may well have preferred him to Botha, he lacked the support of a party organisation (for he did not belong to the Bond) and he had, besides, offended large sections of public opinion at the Cape by his austere financial policy. Botha, in contrast, had the backing of a strictly disciplined party; his prestige as a Boer leader was beyond all rivalry except from Steyn (who was debarred by ill-health from political office); his reputation as a conciliator (in contrast with Merriman, whom many British South Africans looked upon as a renegade or a crank) made him acceptable to moderate opinion; his friendship with Smuts made good the disadvantages he would otherwise have suffered from his lack of intellectual training. For all these reasons, there were few who doubted that Botha would be the choice of Lord Gladstone, the newly arrived governor-general. That choice was made on 21 May. On the last day of the month the Union was proclaimed and its first government took office.

Smuts had played so central a part in these manœuvres that he was lucky to come through them without losing the trust of some, at least, of the ill-assorted people who sought reassurance or encouragement from him. Political leaders in Natal, such as T. Hyslop, assumed that he would listen sympathetically to their complaints against the old parties and to their pleas for a fresh start. Political leaders in the Free State assumed the very opposite; the only thing that mattered, wrote Steyn, was to maintain a solid front of the Boer leaders and hold all Boers together 'as one man'. Political leaders in the Cape were not so forgetful as Steyn was of the 'fusion of races'— that is to say, the fusion of Boers and Britons in the crucible of nationhood, which had been the ideal almost universally acclaimed during the National Convention. But if the Cape politicians were agreed upon the end, they were divided about the means, and divided to such a degree that Merriman looked on Graaff and F. S. Malan as 'Judases'. And yet Smuts maintained intimate touch both with Merriman and Malan and preserved his friendship with them both.[2] Merriman's mother died at this time. 'May I drop you a line', wrote Smuts, 'to tell you how often you have been in my thoughts in these days of trial and bereavement? There are many things one feels but would not put on paper. I can only say in all sincerity that my heart has gone out to you in these days in a way I should not like to express bluntly. To you I shall always cherish feelings of the deepest attachment for what you have done for South Africa and even more for what you are. However you will understand.' His letter ended with a few sentences about the difficulties the new government had to face getting the administrative machine started. Merriman replied to him at once with deep gratitude. 'It was good of you to write mid all the thrutch of business. Yes, I have had many troubles public and private, but "Aequam memento rebus in arduis servare mentem" is very good advice.' He told Smuts that his mother had retained until the end her keen faculties and interest in public affairs, but mercifully had not lived long enough to learn of his political discomfiture. Then he began to chide him on some mistakes that the new government was making, to warn him against the navy propaganda of the imperialists and to advise him about his reading-list. Thus the old friendship continued as close as ever; but it was no longer a political partnership, for Merriman had refused to serve under Botha. His role in the first parliament of the Union was to be that of the elder statesman, the government's candid friend and on occasion its caustic critic. He called himself a 'musketeer'.[3]

From June to September the election fight was on—a puzzling battle, for the combatants were untidily grouped and the principles which divided them were obscure. There was a newly formed Labour party, led by Colonel Creswell, which was overwhelmingly English-speaking in its membership and had the distinction of being the first party in South Africa to make racial segregation a plank of its platform. There was a newly formed Unionist party, which brought together the old Progressive parties of Cape Colony and the Transvaal but failed to gain much support in Natal, where most of the political leaders preferred to stand as Independents. On the government side there was no similar amalgamation of the old colonial parties; but in the Transvaal Hull and his little group (the erstwhile 'Responsibles') accepted a merger with Het Volk, which now called itself the South African National party. To the majority of South Africans, the political drama took shape as a struggle between the Nationalists and the Unionists. Yet it was difficult to discover what the struggle was about, for the protagonists on both sides—with one exception—professed the same ideals and proposed similar policies.

The exception was General Hertzog, who would have played no part at all in the election if Botha had had his way. Botha found it difficult even to talk to Hertzog; when he was forming his government at the end of May he had used Smuts as his intermediary in trying to persuade him to accept a seat on the Supreme Court; but Hertzog was determined to stay in politics and Botha perforce had taken him into the government as Minister of Justice. From the election point of view nothing could have been more awkward, for the battle over Hertzog's Education Act was now at its height and Hertzog kept himself in the thick of it. There were other issues as well, such as immigration and the Imperial connection, where the tone of Hertzog's election speeches was in discord with the policy of his leader. To the Unionists, this was a godsend. At last they had a real target for their fire—'Hertzogism'.

Indeed, the cleavage between Hertzog and his colleagues went deeper by far than the division between the Nationalists and the Unionists. Hertzog, whether he knew it or not (his public utterances showed confusion of feeling and thought), represented the attacking force of Afrikaner nationalism, still intellectually uncertain about the future, but with deep emotional roots in the past, embodied and alive as it was in the Dutch Reformed Church, the language movement and a vivid historical mythos. We shall see later how these forces, under Hertzog's guidance, took political shape in a new party which appropriated the label Nationalist, leaving Botha's South African National Party (S.A.N.P.) to call itself henceforward the South African Party (S.A.P.). However, in 1910 this clash was still some years ahead; Hertzog as yet was not an open enemy but merely an embarrassing friend. His ambiguous support of the government probably cost it some seats, including Botha's;[4] but it did not decisively affect the election results.

Nationalists	67
Unionists	39
Labour	4
Independents	11

A close analysis of the voting would have shown that it still conformed closely to the 'racial' division of the white population; but Smuts did not realise this, or else did not realise how ominous it was for the future.

We have come fairly well out of the struggle [he wrote on 19 September] and will have a minimum majority of 20 in a house of 121. But the defeat of Botha, Hull and Moor has come as a nasty knock, and in other cases too we have expected better results. However, even this reverse may be a blessing in disguise as most misfortunes are. We shall continue our liberal South African policy undeterred by this apparent windfall to the extremists. . . . The thing that knocked us badly was Genl. Hertzog's Education policy in the Free State, which the English people resented as directed against their racial ideals. It is very hard that Botha and Hull should be punished for a policy which they have always stoutly resisted; but such is the logic of the crowd.[5]

In short, the Hertzog trouble did not so greatly signify. In the years ahead he was to learn his mistake.

Meanwhile, the government was granted a year or two of grace before this trouble grew to open schism. Its main task during this period was to complete the constitution by equipping the Union with the legislative and administrative apparatus requisite for a twentieth-century State. Smuts as usual took upon his own shoulders a great part of the load, including responsibility for the three important departments of the Interior, Mines and Defence. As Minister of Defence he was at work throughout 1911 and the first part of 1912 upon a Defence Act which proved to be of fundamental importance in the military and political history of South Africa. In his other two departments he had equally heavy work to do and in all three of them he felt the full impact of the disorders which afflicted the Union from 1912 onwards. On top of all this, it fell to him to plug the holes which from time to time appeared in the government; for example, when Hull resigned in May 1912 he took over the Ministry of Finance, and when Graaff fell ill he took over Posts and Telegraphs, together with the exacting task of negotiating a new mail contract with the Union Castle Line. And all the time he shouldered heavy responsibility for the general policy of the government and played a leading part in every political crisis, for he and Botha remained as close to each other in their work for the Union as they had been in the years of their Transvaal partnership.

Short of writing a full political history of the Union for these crowded and strenuous years it is impossible to record and explain all his tasks and troubles; but the most important ones will become the themes of later chapters. Meanwhile, this is a good place for looking at him as he appeared, or sometimes appeared, to his political opponents.

They were beginning to call him 'Slim'. This word is not easy to translate, for its connotation varies with the context in which it is used and the intentions of the users. Like the Greek adjective πολυμῆτις, which Homer commonly applied to Odysseus, it connotes a man who is crafty, astute, rich in stratagems and wiles. Whether such a man is judged worthy of praise or of blame may well depend on who does the judging; we may suppose that the comrades of Odysseus admired and acclaimed him for bringing them so cleverly through so many dangers; whereas the Cyclops and the Sirens cursed him. Similarly we may suppose that the men of Smuts's commando, after he had led them through one of the traps which half a dozen British columns were trying to spring upon them, congratulated each other on their good luck in having such a 'slim' general. But the British were bound to take a different view. As we have seen, no praise was intended in the Intelligence notes which from time to time described Smuts as 'the brains of the Boer side', the implacable and 'crafty' enemy of everything British.*

It would appear that he retained as a politician the reputation for astuteness which he had gained as a general. Or did English-speaking politicians persuade themselves that all Boers were 'slim'? Anyway, Smuts raised a laugh, as we have seen, in the debate on the Cullinan diamond, when he admitted that this splendid gift to the King might look like 'another question of slimness' although in fact it was deeply sincere. There were some people who found this hard to believe. They felt that the Boers, and Smuts in particular, were always outsmarting them. A few months before the National Convention met, Patrick Duncan, who had been Colonial Secretary in Crown Colony days and was destined to become a prominent Unionist politician and in later years governor-general of the Union, explained to Lady Selborne the doubts he felt about Smuts: 'I only wish I thought that his fine sentiments were more intimately hitched on to the springs which govern his actions. They do sometimes get turned on but they spend much of their time in the cupboard of his soul.'[6]

Doubts or insinuations so subjective and vague as these can hardly be brought forward as evidence for the prosecution. One looks about

* See pp. 147, 167 above.

for specific accusations of insincerity or double dealing. A resounding accusation was made by Sir Percy Fitzpatrick in a private letter which he wrote to one of the mining magnates during the National Convention.

Smuts has been twice caught and exposed in deliberate trickery, phrasing his resolutions with amazing cleverness so that they can mean the very opposite of what he appears to concede. But he has no feeling of shame or resentment, and resumes at once his too perfect air of camaraderie and overdone boyish frankness. By two totally wanton and short-sighted acts of duplicity he has managed to give every man in the Convention the same feeling of profound mistrust that dogs him in all he does. It is wonderful that so clever a man should not be clever enough to be reasonably straight. It almost convulsed me with laughter to see Sauer's look of speechless incredulity, and almost horror, when Smuts's little game was exposed— whether it was because of the audacity of the attempt and the cool-bloodedness of the deception, or the fact that he himself had been caught trusting, I don't know.[7]

Professor Thompson, who quotes this tirade, believes that Fitz-patrick had in mind the proceedings of two committees which reported rather confusedly on two important topics, the franchise and the Provinces' shares of representation in the House of Assembly. The first committee had nine members, the second thirteen. How far the inadequacies, inequities or obscurities of the reports may fairly be ascribed to one member of the committees would appear to be a pertinent question. It also seems pertinent to ask whether Fitz-patrick's explosion can be treated as well-weighed evidence? Professor Thompson mentions 'his tendency to exaggerate', but this is putting it mildly; Fitzpatrick was a pugnacious, romantic, lovable Irish-man who always saw everything in black and white and had a great gift for fluent and vivid prose portraiture, or caricature. The chances are that he saw Smuts in quite a different light a few weeks or even a few days after he had dashed off his exuberant tirade. Be this as it may, we know precisely what he felt and thought about him when all the alarums and excursions of constitution-making were finished and the Union of South Africa became at last an accomplished fact. He wrote to him on 25 August 1909—

You were asleep when I tried to see you on Friday morning to say goodbye and I did not see you at the close of the debate—on the stroke of midnight! Well, it's through now and I only wanted to shake hands on it and con-gratulate you on, and thank you for, all the earnest work you have put into it. Balfour struck the right note: someday a lot of people will realise what has been done. There are very few who do to-day.....Goodbye.....All I wanted to say to you is that—come what may in the future—it has been a great pleasure—and more than that—to have worked with you during this year for the Union of South Africa and I know that the work of the Transvaal is going to be 'blessed of our people'.[8]

Later on we shall make the acquaintance of another, much greater man whose final thoughts about the 'slimness' of Smuts were far different from his first thoughts. The conflict between Smuts and Gandhi will produce some evidence very relevant to the present discussion; but the examination of it must be postponed. Meanwhile, let us remember that to play straight with friends is frequently far more difficult than to play straight with enemies. Smuts was a friend both of Botha and of Merriman, between whom, as we have seen, there was bitter rivalry for the honour of being the first prime minister of the Union. Did he manage to play straight with both men? Professor Thompson quotes (without, be it said, endorsing) some evidence which may seem to suggest that he was deceiving one or the other. On 12 May 1910 the Attorney-General of the Transvaal, Jacob de Villiers, told Steyn that Botha would refuse to serve under Merriman and that Smuts and Hull would follow him. On 6 September, after the Governor-General's choice had fallen on Botha, Smuts told Merriman the very opposite: 'When Sauer was here at Pretoria in March or April', he said, 'I told him that I would be perfectly willing to serve under you and I told General Botha the same.'[9]

What Smuts said is better evidence than what Jacob de Villiers said. To begin with, de Villiers is believed to have disliked Botha and he may well have known in mid-May that Botha would never give him the place in the cabinet of the Union to which he aspired.[10] But even if his evidence were unprejudiced, it would be conclusive about nothing except his own opinion or guess; he did not claim to be quoting Smuts. On the other hand, what Smuts told Merriman about his own attitude was a categorical statement which Merriman could easily check by consulting Sauer, whom he had known intimately for many years. Whether or no he made this check, he never gave any sign of feeling aggrieved. Throughout the months of uncertainty it was Botha, not Smuts, whom he had accused of being 'slim', and when the uncertainty was concluded in a manner so painful to himself he continued his correspondence with Smuts just as warmly and zestfully as in the old days. In later years he took pains to defend Smuts against the accusations of excessive craftiness which other people brought against him. He wrote to Bryce in 1917, when Smuts was on his way to the Imperial War Cabinet in London, describing him as 'a philosopher ruthless and cultivated', but with 'a reputation for shiftiness which is, I think, in some measure undeserved, and which goes against him in this country'. It was not precisely a glowing testimonial and Merriman gave a list of all the points that could be made against Smuts. He blamed him for his handling of the Indians and of the labour leaders (matters which will be considered later) and for his appointments to the Defence Force, which, he said, were largely responsible for the rebellion of 1914. He declared him to be a poor administrator. The 'musketeer' was living up to his reputation for pungency as a critic, and even in his summing-up, which was warmly in Smuts's favour, there was a Tacitean sting: 'But he is, as I said, ruthless and determined, with very great intellectual gifts, a charming companion and perhaps a better friend than a counsellor.'[11]

Enough has been said for the time being on this subject, which it has been thought best to bring into the open. If evidence of double dealing should be found later on, it will not be concealed. Meanwhile, let it be agreed that Smuts, so far as we have studied his record in war and politics (much still remains to study), was 'slim' in the good, but not in the bad sense of the word. Nobody, surely, wants stupid soldiers and naïve politicians: one wants them to be single-but not simple-minded; one wants them to be men of honour but also men of resourcefulness, ingenuity, technical dexterity. People who lack that sort of 'slimness' had best keep out of politics, for they will never do any good there.

Smuts, of course, was so abundantly, indeed so abnormally endowed with these qualities that often it must have demanded extreme sophistication or deep simplicity to follow the operation of his mind. Sophisticated people were scarce in South Africa. Of the massively plain people, Paul Kruger and Louis Botha understood him and trusted him. It must be admitted that he allowed himself very little time for getting on terms of easy understanding with the ruck of ordinary people. Soon after his appointment as Kruger's State Attorney, Roderick Jones had discovered that he was not a man to suffer fools gladly.* His training in politics, it is worth noting, was unusual and in one important respect one-sided; he was never in all his life a back-bencher and a full quarter of a century went by after his first ministerial appointment before he ever found himself on the opposition side of a legislative body. These were conditions under which an able and masterful man might only too easily acquire arrogance, or at least the appearance of it. This particular charge against Smuts, however, was not formulated until the later 1930's, when Armstrong published his biography *Grey Steel: A Study in Arrogance.*

For the time being, at any rate, enough notice has been taken of these various attempts at external portraiture. It is time to return to our documents. Still, it has been healthy to remind ourselves that Smuts did pay a price for the appalling overwork which he inflicted upon himself. The demands which it made upon his time and energy made it impossible for him to share fully the easy-going, day-to-day give and take of political life. We must now inquire whether he suffered a similar abatement of the spontaneity and freedom of his private life.

His overwork was beginning to alarm his friends. Merriman warned him more than once that he was doing too much—but kept asking him all the same to give his personal attention to various odds and ends of work, such as the national archives or the public libraries, which other people were mismanaging. Emily Hobhouse kept scolding him for overstraining himself. 'I was quite horrified, seeing your handwriting this mail. You know I have grown very sensitive to the *writing* of my various friends since letters have become my chief or only link with them and I get to know their state of health or spirits, etc. by the variations which are shown. Now your handwriting— far more than anything you say or have said—shows me you are pretty well on your beam ends and *must* draw in your horns and take rest.' Smuts knew that his handwriting got worse when he was over-driven and sometimes asked his friends to forgive him for putting them to so much trouble in deciphering his letters. He admitted that he was overtired and that he longed to get away from people and their talk. 'Six months in the desert for me!' In June 1914 Emily Hobhouse advised him to take a sea-voyage to St Helena and back. As if he had a chance! The next time that he went on board ship

* See p. 80 above.

was when he sailed from Cape Town to take command of British forces in East Africa.[12]

Weary though he was at times, there was never any failure of his physical health and mental energy. How did he manage to stay the pace? A sound bodily constitution and the habit of vigorous exercise were part of the answer; during his first parliamentary session at Cape Town he discovered the joy of climbing Table Mountain and sometimes after a hard day in his office would rush up and down again within a few hours. Such violent spasms of bodily exertion were good so far as they went; but he also needed emotional and intellectual relief from politics. He found it in his family, his friends and his pursuit of philosophy. 'In my overwhelming troubles', he once told Wolstenholme, 'I may perhaps appear to forget my friends. But it is not so.' And again, as he watched the shadow of war coming near: 'I have done a great deal of hard grinding work in public life and my favourite relaxations are my family and that spiritual structure which has been reared by the thinkers of the ages.'[13]

The family by now was deeply rooted at Doornkloof, a farm superbly situated on the high veld at Irene, on the main line between Johannesburg and Pretoria. Smuts had been planning the move from the middle of 1909 but it took place while he was on his way to England with the delegation of the National Convention. A letter that he wrote to his wife from the ship makes it possible to give the precise date, 10 July 1909.[14]

There had been good reasons for them to shift house besides his preference for country over suburban life, for they had by now four children (a fifth was born in 1912 and a sixth in 1914) and as they grew up it would be good for the family to have more room, both inside and out-of-doors. All the same, Mrs Smuts hated being uprooted and made her husband promise that they would never move again. They never did. As the years went by, their new house and the old land took gradually a shape and colour which expressed the quality of life belonging to them as individuals and as a family. The farm was bare veld when they went there but they planted it with tens of thousands of trees. They planted trees along the banks of the little stream which flowed in the valley below and more trees to shelter and shade their house. Smuts called the house his 'tin palace'; it had weatherboard walls and a tin roof and had been built as a recreation hut for British officers of the Anglo-Boer War. He took the billiard room for his study and enclosed the verandahs on both sides to make new rooms which seemed to be almost in the out-of-doors. These rooms at first were for the children; but as they grew up and left Doornkloof to make homes of their own, Smuts annexed them to house his overflow of books and his botanical specimens and presses. It became his pleasure to sleep in a lightly partitioned and netted enclosure on the stoep outside his bedroom, furnished with an old-fashioned iron bedstead, with a small table beside it and on the table a reading-lamp, his Greek testament and his bedside book for the time-being.

Doornkloof is most easily recalled to the eye of memory in the appearance of its later years, when it was mellow and comfortable with age and the trees surrounding it were tall and its master was an old man and his favourite bedside book was the poetry of Emily Brontë. Peace was the spirit of the place. Whenever he returned to it after his journeys, his battles, his interminable labours, peace enfolded him.

All my wounds are healed, all my aches are gone, and I almost feel reborn in this atmosphere of peace and loving kindness....

No peace this side the grave like the peace of Doornkloof. The grand-children are in bed, the mothers and grandmother are attending to household chores in another part of the big house and here I sit in the study hearing only the dull subdued hum of silence in my head. This hum is now quite usual with me, and I suppose it is a sign of age, as I did not notice it before. It sounds like cicadas in the bush in the distance on a hot day, really quite pleasant if you happen to notice.... What memories this hum recalls....[15]

What memories indeed, going back over thirty years, when the sleeping children were his own and he and Isie were strenuously planning how to extend the house or where to plant the trees, and Doornkloof was still in the making; yet even then, a haven of rest and peace in a life of struggle and storm.

Children were an essential element of the peace which enfolded him in his home, and if a long absence were enforced upon him he sought the missing element in the families of his friends. One of them has written: 'Small children seemed to be necessary to his spiritual and mental health. The children and grandchildren of his friends and acquaintances supplied this need, when he was away from his own.... The youngest was always declared to be "the pick of the bunch".'[16] Fortunately, while his own children were small he was never absent from South Africa for any length of time until 1916, when he was called away for three and a half years (barring one short break) of military and political service, at first in East Africa and later in Europe. Up to that time he had enjoyed a dozen years or more of delight in his own family, broken only by the local absences which his political duties imposed upon him. These, to be sure, came too often and sometimes were long drawn out; but he had the feeling, even in a wearisome parliamentary session at Cape Town, that Doornkloof was not so far away and that perfect peace was awaiting him there. It was the simplicity of his home life which made it so restful: the busy but unhurried routine of farm and household, the comfortable plenty unadorned by urban or suburban pretensions, the dignified but informal hospitality proper to a Boer farm, the lively talk in the mother-tongue of the children with each other and with their parents: or, if he wanted serious talk, he had Isie, who never in her life possessed more than two or three dresses at the same time and was quite content to make Doornkloof her world, yet still remembered her German and Greek and found time for reading plenty of modern novels: or, if he wanted solitude, he had his great study with its enormous desk and the bookshelves steadily being filled from floor to ceiling with the purchases which Wolstenholme was making for him.

He lived at Doornkloof fairly continuously during the winter and spring months, travelling to his office in Pretoria by motor-car or train but occasionally walking the ten miles from Irene for the sake of exercise. In January he had to go to Cape Town for the parliamentary session, a bad arrangement, so Emily Hobhouse used to tell him (as if he could alter it!), for he needed better company and care than he could get in his club. Still, this rackety life produced as a by-product advantages for his biographer in the form of the letters that he wrote to his wife and children during the months of separation. These letters sometimes contained political news but for the most part their themes were domestic and their tone playful and tender, as if he were emptying his mind of political cares and living in imagination the simple and joyous life of his family at Doornkloof.

After his family, his friends. Although it has often been said of him (indeed, in times of strain he used sometimes to say it of himself) that he had no time for people, it would be truer to say that he had little time for many people but a great deal of time for some people. His friendships were a main anchorage of his life. They cannot all be brought to life again in this book, because he so seldom had occasion to write to the friends (Louis Botha, for example) who were close not only to his affections but close to him geographically. The pattern of friendship which he wove around him can only be reconstructed here and there from his correspondence with the absent friends.

His letters to Emily Hobhouse have nearly all been lost: but her letters to him are so vibrant with feeling, intelligence and wit that a vivid picture emerges of their pathetic and glorious friendship. He could always tell from her first words of address what mood she was in. Usually she began quietly, 'Dear Oom Jannie'; but if she were deeply moved by his kindness to her she would write 'Dear, dear Oom Jannie', 'My dear kind Oom Jannie', 'My dear generous but ever naughty Oom Jannie': if she had it in mind to scold him she would invent a mocking address—'Oom! Super-Oom!': if she were deeply grieved by his tragic mistakes in politics (as she conceived them to be) she would address him like this—'Ah, dear Oom, dear Oom— What are you all about? I can't write much for I feel too strongly, but oh...!'—and then she would explode.

Her letters to him from the time of Union to the Kaiser's war reveal both a deepening of their friendship and a growing divergence of their political views. She was a pacifist—or nearly a pacifist, for she always felt a thrill at the victory of a little nation over a big one, even if her measurements of bigness and littleness were a bit out of date: the British, she appeared to believe, were perpetually big; whereas the Germans by comparison were quite little. She was an anarchist, or nearly an anarchist, as is apparent in the following imaginary conversation between Smuts and herself.

Yes Auntie and you have the natural disposition of the Irishman who defined his politics as being 'always agin the government'. And I should reply—that also is true. No government pleases me, for I am a Celt, I must move on to better ideals that open out before me in vistas at every step, while a government represents the brake on the wheels of Progress and the enforcement of outgrown laws.[17]

Since Smuts belonged to a government he was bound to find himself the target of her disapproval. She told him that he was getting too high and mighty, rushing about in his motor-car (which anyway was bad for his health) and telling people what *they had* to do instead of letting them tell him what *they wanted* to do.

I wish you would give up that motor and take to the healthier exercise of the saddle. You should ride daily at least *one* way to Pretoria and you would regain something of the health and vigour you gained during the war. And then all Sunday you should ride about your farm, and have a pony for the children in turn to ride with you. Motors are so modern and I think on the whole degenerating physically and mentally. In our crowded Europe motorists become quite inhuman, and to the poor of all classes they are a pest of noise dirt and danger and smell. Don't be spoilt, mind and body, by a mere motor, a horrid monster of tubes and oil.

Yes, I think you are very wrong to be so impatient with Parliament, which is after all, however talkative, the voice of the rank and file of the people thro' their representatives, and peoples have to be brought on little by little, and reasoned with and persuaded, till it comes to be in reality 'Government *by* the People'. Now you want to be an autocrat, a Czar. Having thought out a matter and decided it is best, you just want to rush it through without criticism. You must go and live in Russia.[18]

But even czars have their ridiculous side, and it delighted her to have the chance of writing to Mrs Smuts—'You astonish me, this news that a dignified statesman of mature years has *measles*. It is quite infra-dig, a childish disease like that.' Then she began to worry about the damage he might suffer to his eyes and begged Mrs Smuts to see that he took care of them.[19]

She often scolded him for wearing himself out in politics. 'This photograph is *very* like you, that you have so kindly sent me, though it is not well taken. Still it is you yourself grown, however (I will not say *older*) but more *mature*. . . . And oh! dear Oom Jannie, you look *very, very* stern. Is South Africa so very difficult to govern? Must you stiffen your will to such rigidity to manage the people? Or is it those Indians that prove ungovernable and demand your greatest determination?'[20] She told him that he was doing violence to his nature by forcing it into the narrow mould of politics. When would he give himself time for the simple pleasures of life and for the books of history and philosophy that he had wanted to write? Yet she was quick to protest if ever he showed any sign of taking her at her word. 'So you imagine you are going to slide gradually into the background, satisfied with having completed *Union*! You dream of a peaceful country life and teaching your daughters and writing a history of your great Campaign. I fear me if you took to the bucolic life you would always be half asleep from the effect of much open air and your brain would not work. However that may be, you and Botha can't retire until you see others coming on who are competent to take your places.'[21]

And yet she never had much good to say to him about the way in which he and Botha were tackling their job. She attacked them for their subservience to monarchical flummery. 'Why on earth did you let Sir Henry de Villiers take a peerage? Surely the first Colonial who has ever done so. It is unworthy of him.' And after reading the Honours list for 1911 she wanted to know—'How many more titles are you going to give?...Well well you are all very prosperous smart and important people, too grand for me to write much to or to associate with....' Then there were the new Union Buildings— awful to look at, she complained, and a bigger waste of money than anything ever perpetrated in Milner's day; but the most dreadful thing of all was to invite royalty out to open them! She suspected that it was all a part of Botha's misconceived policy of conciliation (hateful word!).[22]

By this time Hertzog was out of the government and schism was rending the ranks of Afrikanerdom. It was also rending the mind of Emily Hobhouse, who was trying to decide whether or no to go to Bloemfontein to unveil the monument to the Boer women who had died in the concentration camps. She had received the invitation from President Steyn; but Botha—so she was told—was holding himself aloof from the ceremony. Had the monument been raised to symbolise and perpetuate national division and racial hatred? She could not believe anything so ignoble. Who then was to blame for the division between Steyn and Botha? She chose to put the blame upon Botha. If only Smuts would persuade him to do the magnanimous thing and go to Bloemfontein! The unveiling would then become what it ought to be, a truly national occasion of pious commemoration, forgiveness and dedication. 'So dear Oom Jannie your work is cut out to bring them all to reason.' That sentence reveals her trust in him; she might scold and reproach him and grieve over his errors, but she had an unshakeable belief in his goodness and in his power to make the good prevail. Sometimes she demanded impossibilities from him; for example, she called on him a few years later to make peace among the warring nations. He could not perform that miracle; but in December 1913 he did achieve all that she expected of him.

He and she together raised the ceremony at Bloemfontein to the level of spiritual greatness.[23]*

On 16 December 1913 she was with him at Bloemfontein in spirit; but her broken-down body was still at Beaufort West. 'Why oh! why', she asked him, 'did you urge such a derelict, such a broken-up wreck to come so far? Here I am, held up by that incapable organ, my heart.' For many years past her battle with *angina pectoris* (if that was the correct name for her disease) had absorbed most of her strength. The disease had driven her from South Africa to England but before long the cold and wet of London drove her to Rome. There she found the dust just as insupportable as London fogs and used to wake at night half dead with suffocation. After a time she moved to a flat high above the street where she was able to open her window at night; but she had to hire a man to carry her up and down the ninety-six steps and a cab to take her through Rome. She could afford to do this once a week at most and so found herself condemned to lie month after month on the sofa in her lonely room. 'The view from this house is beautiful', she told Mrs Smuts, 'but the isolation is terrible and I don't quite see yet how I shall bear it. When days pass together without my speaking to anyone I feel the solitude almost driving me mad, and I am not strong enough to do much reading or writing.... It is a terrible thing to be a solitary invalid woman, but there are thousands of us in the world and it is a mere matter of holding on till Death!'

Her agony in Rome lasted for a year or more, until somebody told her about a miracle-working doctor in Florence who used inhaling machines and electrical pumps and other wonderful instruments for bringing enlarged hearts back to their proper sizes. Her trouble was how to pay him. She was living from the rent of her home in South Africa and the income from some small investments which Smuts and his solicitor, Jim Roos, were looking after, without too strict a regard for business method, for they constantly forgot to debit her account with the cost of the house repairs and the other expenses that they incurred on her behalf. Smuts had offered from time to time to lend her money and she now asked him for £50 at 6 per cent interest, carefully explaining all the little shifts she would be able to make (such as letting her flat in Rome and living in a *very* cheap place she had heard of) so that he could feel quite sure of getting his money

* See pp. 181, 362–3 for her message and for Smuts's speech at the unveiling.

back. He sent her by return of post his cheque for a much larger sum.

What am I to say [she exclaimed]? What am I to do? Your generosity is so overwhelming and so startling and in spite of what I have written I do not like to send this cheque back to you because I can't bear to vex you, and you say it is a 'joy' to send it. But remember you have three very costly things to prey upon your resources (far ampler than mine though they be as you say) and these three things are *Family, Farm, Fame*. Hence I cannot feel otherwise than that you have done this generous thing at personal sacrifice and if that makes it the harder to accept it also makes it more precious, when I recollect the feeling that prompted it.

A year or two later, when she was telling him about the economies she was making to pay him back, she discovered that he had recently paid out of his own pocket the bill for installing electricity in her South African house. 'Dear Oom, such things must not be. You are generosity incarnate, but indeed I must not let you do such things. Think of the 5 you have to educate and put out in the world and how all your money will be needed for them. And I don't know what to do. If I send this poor cheque I fear for its fate at your hands.'[24] As well she might.

Smuts annoyed her by calling her Florentine doctor a quack; but the new treatment did her so much good that she thought of Olive Schreiner, whose sufferings were so like her own. How wonderful it would be to put her on board ship and carry her to these miraculous springs of healing in Tuscany! Her idea was to raise the money, 'without any annoyance to her feelings', as a gift of gratitude from her friends and admirers in South Africa and England. She made Isie Smuts her partner in the plot and it succeeded. Olive Schreiner sailed for Europe in December 1913, after sending Smuts a farewell message through Isie—'Give my love to Neef Jan. Tell him to take care of my Indians and Natives for me while I'm away.'[25]

When the war took Smuts to England four years later, the two women were still alive, still suffering the pain of their bodies and suffering in their minds the pain of humanity, still expecting him to set the world to rights. They were perfectionists and he was in the groove of politics; they were pacifists and he was fighting the war. They were a plague to him when he was desperate with the pressure of work; but they were his friends, often infuriating and impossible but always the salt of the earth.

His friendships were seldom an exclusive relationship between two persons but were apt to sprout and ramify until a variety of persons found themselves joined together within their intricate pattern—Emily Hobhouse, Olive Schreiner, Margaret Clark, Wolstenholme (even that old recluse was not so completely alone as he used to be) and often their brothers, sisters or husbands, most notably Arthur Gillett, who married Margaret Clark in May 1909. He was a partner in a late-surviving country bank, Gillett's Bank, Oxford, which was destined to be absorbed later by one of the Big Five. He had been her contemporary at Cambridge and belonged, like her, to the Society of Friends and the English liberal tradition. 'I don't know how much you would like him,' she told Smuts when announcing their engagement, 'but I believe Mrs Smuts would like him very much, and I know he would like you both. He is not clever like you, and it is not his lot in life to be a statesman. But our happiness in life is built on this, that when we were at Cambridge at the same time years ago we made friends because we felt the same way about the war.' When they had been married a few weeks she received a letter from Smuts telling her that he would soon be arriving in England with the delegation of the National Convention and that he hoped that she would go with him to the theatre just as in the old days and that Mr Gillett would not be jealous 'to see on what terms we are'. He managed during his stay in England to pay two visits to their home at 102 Banbury Road, Oxford, where Arthur Gillett remembered him walking up and down the garden exclaiming 'What a world it is!' By this he meant—for the sanguine age was at its zenith—that the world was a happy and glorious place. This certainly was the conviction of Arthur Gillett. Each man thought the other a splendid fellow and Mrs Gillett found cause before long to chide Smuts for addressing all his letters to her husband rather than to her. After all, she had known him first![26]

In 1911 the Gilletts had their first son and named him Jan. More children were born in the following years and the letters from 102 Banbury Road to Doornkloof contained all the news of these and other family events as well as news and views about what was happening in the great world. These letters were never caustic or sharp like those of Emily Hobhouse: how could they be, when the Gilletts were leading a life so peaceful, poised and deeply rooted? Like 'the Missus',* they expected Smuts to achieve great things in

---

* A good many years back, Smuts and Margaret Clark had invented this affectionate nickname (sometimes written 'the Mrs') for Emily Hobhouse.

making a better world; but if his deeds fell below the level of their expectations they were concerned to understand rather than to upbraid him. Sympathetic understanding, deep enough to touch his heart and broad enough to satisfy his intellect, was the keynote of their friendship with him. And so they drew him out. Letter answered letter, until in the fulness of time the Smuts–Gillett correspondence became a continuous and comprehensive record of almost everything that he had at heart and in his head.

This unique correspondence, from its origins in the 1900's to its close in 1950, has been preserved complete, without the loss on either side of a single letter, saving perhaps a few casualties of war. It is bound to become a main source of this biography. But, like the friendship which sustained it, its riches accumulated with the years. Up to 1912 it contains no record of the philosophic quest which Smuts had been pursuing since his undergraduate days. In 1912 that quest reached a climax, which is recorded in the correspondence between Smuts and Wolstenholme.

CHAPTER 15

PHILOSOPHY

SMUTS so far had found no companion except Wolstenholme in his adventure of ideas. His broad-based course at Stellenbosch had included some elementary philosophy; but at Cambridge Professor James Ward had refused him admission to his lectures, presumably on the ground that law students had better stick to their law. In philosophy he remained perforce to all intents and purposes self-taught. But the self-teaching had been spontaneous and ardent, with living roots in the wonder and bewilderment of his boyhood, when he first discovered his own duality—as a fragment of the natural world, akin to the animals and plants and stones around him: and yet an exile from this world, because he, Jan Smuts, was a person, with a power of standing apart from the world and making images and ideas of it, and of himself, within his own mind. This wonder and puzzlement remained with him throughout his undergraduate years, when he wrote some essays on the theme of evolutionary 'emergence' (although he did not hit upon that word) and began his study of Walt Whitman. His book on Whitman, if he had found a publisher for it, would have had some significance in the history of ideas; it would at least have merited an occasional footnote in other people's books, for it studied Whitman as an exemplar of personality and studied personality as an exemplar of 'the whole'. From this time onwards, The Idea of the Whole—he wrote it in capitals—took possession of him.*

Nobody except his wife and Wolstenholme realised that he was thus possessed. Even Wolstenholme underrated the strength of his determination to embody his idea in a philosophical work: in the Cambridge days, when they were reading Goethe together or talking interminably on their afternoon walks, he had not taken very seriously the philosophical speculations of his ardent young friend. And what chance had he had of pursuing them further in the years of hectic action that followed? Wolstenholme was not to know that the years of campaigning on the veld had contained weeks and months of

* See pp. 49–50 above.

inaction, which Smuts had spent in strenuous combat with Kant and other great philosophers.

After the war, it became Wolstenholme's chief satisfaction in life to renew and deepen his friendship with Smuts, to act as his agent with the Cambridge booksellers, to guide him in making up his book-lists and to give him news and views about events and tendencies within the academic world. Even so, the books which they discussed and the ideas which they exchanged with each other were as often as not political or sociological rather than philosophical. Whenever Smuts showed signs of venturing any distance into the territory of philosophy it was Wolstenholme's first impulse to warn him off, for he did not believe that a man with so little training could achieve anything there. Consequently it must have been with surprise, if not with apprehension, that he heard from Smuts in July 1911 that he had nearly completed a work of philosophy and would be sending it over for criticism early in the coming year.[1]

The book duly arrived in March 1912. A quick glance at the preface and synopsis confirmed Wolstenholme's worst fears. It was a matter of wonderment to him, he told Smuts, how a man so overloaded by political burdens could manage to produce any work of philosophy at all; consequently he was not surprised—he hinted this very delicately—at the work's shortcomings. He begged Smuts not to rush it into print. 'Don't go before the public before you have the best and ripest of which you are capable to put before them.' Then he asked to be excused from the task of reading and criticising the book and begged his friend to look for somebody more in sympathy with his point of view and method. All the same, he kept the book by him for six months and managed during that time to read the first two chapters and part of the third. Then he gave up. On 18 October he wrote to Smuts: 'I have not been able to get your MS. arranged and packed to go this week, but I will despatch it by next week's mail. I have not been able to read any more of it; I have read almost nothing for several months of a kind requiring severe mental application. I doubt whether I shall ever do much more now of this kind of reading; it is too great a strain.'[2]

Smuts might almost have asked himself whether he had made Wolstenholme ill by sending him his book to read. Has any ambitious author ever suffered at the hands of a friend so dismal a reception of his work? Smuts took it very cheerfully. After the anti-climax of

Wolstenholme's first comments on his manuscript he wrote to him in his usual vein about some books that he wanted and concluded, with unconscious irony—'Goodbye, my dear old friend. I wish you a speedy recovery and good health.'[3] Nothing that Wolstenholme said could shake either his friendship or his conviction that he had something immensely important to say in philosophy.

He called his book *An Inquiry into the Whole*. In the preface he described it as 'an unpretentious essay', but it contained about ninety thousand words and was systematically arranged in two parts and thirteen chapters.

A typewritten copy survives with some pencilled comments and exclamation marks in the margins recording Wolstenholme's strenuous endeavour to read the book. His strength gave out at page 45; but up to then one feels the excitement of listening in to a debate between the ardent author and his crusty critic. Besides, these early pages are of particular importance, for they raised two questions which Smuts regarded as fundamental:

1st. Is there a Whole, either conceptually or existentially? If so, how can it be defined or explained?

2nd. Is the Whole (if it can be said to exist) knowable, and how?

In approaching the first question, Smuts declared that the Idea of the Whole had fallen out of fashion in modern times. The philosophers of classical and medieval times used to believe in it; but their unitary universe had been riven by the modern separation of subject and object. Hegel had attempted to close the rift, but his dialectic, with its presiding Absolute, seemed to Smuts too abstract to be satisfying. So he felt himself summoned to strenuous and realistic combat with the philosophical dualism which had been in the ascendant among philosophers since Descartes.*

This meant that he had also to wrestle with the scientists, for their world-picture had become suffused with the Cartesian philosophy, just as philosophy in its turn had become saturated with the method of science. 'The most important concept of science', wrote Smuts,

---

* Of course he oversimplified and over-dramatised the situation. The 'idea of the whole', as formulated for example by Bradley and Bosanquet (although some Cambridge philosophers were at work to undermine their influence), was still very far from being out of fashion. As to philosophical dualism, it had been vigorously attacked not only by Bradley and Bosanquet but by Hobhouse, Ward, William James, Bergson and many others.

'was what is commonly called the mechanical view of nature and it was fully realised by Descartes and by him transplanted from physical science to philosophy.' Now, if the natural world was just like a machine, the obvious method of studying it was to take it to pieces, to examine its constituent parts, to measure their movements mathematically, describe them in strictly mechanical terms, without invoking the aid of ghosts, forces, influences, causes or any other animistic survival. Smuts agreed that the application of this method had purged the human intellect of many errors, fancies and superstitions, and he did full justice to its glorious achievements in the field of scientific discovery. Nevertheless, he did not believe it to be a sufficient method for the discovery of truth.

He dealt specifically with two of its shortcomings. The first of them might be called 'reductionism'. Smuts did not hit upon this word, any more than he hit upon the word 'emergence', but he expounded the idea which it connotes. People often talk of reducing a thing to its simplest elements, but this, he said, was not a sufficient way of understanding it: for example, the simplest elements of Jan Smuts, like those of a stone, were physico-chemical; but Jan Smuts differed from a stone in many things, such as the power of self-propulsion which he possessed. Could Jan Smuts be understood, then, by 'reducing' him to the living cells of which his body was composed? Certainly, the examination of cells is an indispensable method of gaining knowledge not only in botany and zoology but also in physiology; but it is not a sufficient method of discovering the differences between a plant, an animal and a man. All three are akin to each other in virtue of their capacity for growth; but the plant cannot move itself about any more than the stone can, and the animal cannot frame equations any more than the plant can; whereas a man can do all these things. Consequently, it seems to follow that there is something more in the man (as in the animal, the plant and possibly even the stone) than can be discovered by the process of reducing them to their simplest elements. It was Smuts's main purpose in writing his book to inquire into this 'something more'. For the time being, however, he was content to make a simple point about method: 'To reduce the lowly organisms at the beginning of life to pure mechanism', he wrote, 'is as wrong as to explain them on the assumption of their having a complete personality like human beings.'

This sentence, and a good many similar ones, anticipated the thought and almost the very words of Lloyd Morgan's Gifford Lectures on *Emergent Evolution* which were delivered eleven years later.[4]* There was, however, one difference of terminological habit between the two men: whereas Lloyd Morgan usually spoke about the lower and the higher stages of the evolutionary process, Smuts often preferred to speak about its outward and inward aspects; a man, he liked to think, possessed more inwardness than an animal, seeing that he could guide his conduct by conscious will and thought, just as an animal possessed more inwardness than a plant and a plant than a stone. It was a matter of degree: Smuts had been at Cambridge during the dawn of microphysics and realised that powerful energies were at work inside the chemical atom. He believed them to be at work throughout the entire cosmos and regarded the evolutionary process as the record of their progressive intensification. Where Lloyd Morgan spoke of higher stages he preferred to speak of deepening interior reaches.

From this angle of approach he had a second specific objection to make against the analogy between a machine and the universe, or rather against the misuse of this analogy in scientific and philosophical method. It restricted itself, he said, to examining and measuring external motions. Nobody need ever trouble himself about the inwardness of a machine, for it is a man-made thing which can be sufficiently understood by examining it from the outside; but man himself, and the universe to which he belongs, have an inside as well as an outside.

These specific objections to the mechanistic habit of thought—its reductionism and its externality—were aspects of a more fundamental objection. In trying to understand a machine, the proper procedure is to examine it part by part; but Smuts did not believe that this was

---

* 'Emergence' was also a favourite word of Samuel Alexander, but probably it was Lloyd Morgan who put it into general circulation. It had been used earlier by J. S. Mill but subsequently dropped. Lloyd Morgan, it should be remembered, had developed his general ideas (as indeed had Smuts: see pp. 10, 29, 49 above) long before he gave his Gifford Lectures. 'Reductionism' and 'inwardness' were also quite often discussed early in the twentieth century: for example by James Ward and Lord Haldane. I owe to Professor John Passmore, among much other bibliographical information and critical comment, the following reference to Haldane's *Pathway to Reality* (London, 1905), p. 143: 'Life discloses itself as something totally different from mechanism. In mechanism you have got mere externality and separability of the parts from one another. In life that externality is superseded, is overcome; the whole is present in each of the parts.' (Not that Smuts would have accepted so sharp an antithesis between mechanism and life.)

a sufficient procedure for trying to understand the universe: 'You may add up your infinite series as long as you like, and you will never reach the Whole. The partial does not contain the cement for the Whole....From the Whole you can go down to the parts, from the parts as such you can never rise to the Whole; and if you are in search of the whole truth, it is hopeless to begin with partial truths, however important and useful they may in other respects be.' And so the Whole, with its confident capital letter, took the centre of the stage before Smuts had answered—indeed, before he had explicitly posed—his question as to whether or not it existed.

But not without emphatic protests from Wolstenholme. Opposite the sentence, 'The partial does not contain the cement for the Whole' he scribbled in the margin 'a confused and ambiguous expression'. And when Smuts expounded his favourite idea that the Whole was more than the sum of its parts and consequently could not be understood merely by adding up the parts, Wolstenholme interjected, '*No one* attempts it. The scientific man studies the parts as parts of a whole, *so far as* at his stage of inquiry he can recognise a whole.' But Smuts by now was sweeping forward to an attack upon the analytical psychologists who broke up the human person, so he complained, into a heap of bits and pieces—percepts, concepts and other mental phenomena—without recognising any 'I' to bind these phenomena together. 'Far too summary!' interjected Wolstenholme. And lower down the page he repeated his protest in a longer note: 'Psychologists are more cautious and speak of the "psychological ego"; a metaphysical ego will be far more disputable.'

Wolstenholme concluded his reading of the first chapter with the conviction that Smuts was unendurably slapdash. He wrote at the bottom of the last page: 'You seem to me to make charges against "men of science" wh. hold good against only some of them, and then to withdraw them on the ground of a limitation of "science" which I for one cannot accept.' But worse irritations were awaiting him in chapter 2. Smuts opened it by stating, rather belatedly, his two 'fundamental questions'* and then by essaying a working description of the Whole.

What then is the Whole? In a rough and general way we may begin by saying that the Whole includes whatever is, the entire universe, material and immaterial, whether considered as an outward visible system, filled

* See p. 291 above.

with motions and energies, or as containing the infinite phenomena of life and mind; the Whole includes the totality of being or experience both actual and possible; in short, whatever is, either to the inner or outer experience of man. Whatever objects, material or immaterial, form the subject matters of the various sciences from physics to psychology, fall within the Whole, although as we shall see they do not exhaust the meaning of the Whole.

The Whole is the All, but not in an arithmetical sense. We shall not arrive at the Whole by adding up all the items of experience.... If we add together in the most perfect order all the dead cells of a dissected corpse, we shall be no whit nearer the living organism. If we had the mental vision, our object would be to penetrate to that concept of the Whole, which is no mere aggregation or sum total or compound of parts, but which is itself one and indivisible, a real vital organic unity of which the multiplicities of the universe are not the constituent parts, but the aspects, phenomena or manifestations.

An idea so vast and vague as this might appear useless for all practical purposes, but Smuts proceeded (with Wolstenholme still protesting) to demonstrate its pragmatic value in psychology, cosmology and epistemology. The psychologists, he said, were already beginning to understand that they were getting nowhere by following the old method, which they had taken over from physics and chemistry, of examining isolated fragments of mental experience— percepts, concepts and so on—and then trying to compound them into a system by the 'law of association'. Nowadays, the best of them were favouring an evolutionary approach, assuming at the start within the still unborn child a diffuse, undifferentiated continuum of experience, tracing its gradual differentiation into the sensations, feelings and volitions of post-natal experience, and following its later differentiations through adolescence and the adult life, 'until on the one hand all the manifold objects of the External World are formed and on the other the inner world of the subject self, the world of the will and the emotions, the spiritual world, stands revealed in all its richness and complexity'. At this point Wolstenholme, panting helplessly in the wake of Smuts, begged him to read a treatise by Professor Höffding. But Smuts by now was making a still bolder leap, eliminating the time-factor in his imagination so that the end of the evolutionary progress became visible at its beginning and all the unfolding complexities of personality were gathered into a single, timeless Whole. 'I can put no *meaning* into this', interjected Wolstenholme.

No matter what Wolstenholme might say, Smuts believed that his conception of personality as a unified structure, 'with the capacity of organic growth latent in it', was more realistic than the aggregative constructions of association-psychology. Confident that he was on the right track, he proceeded to consider cosmology from the same synoptic and evolutionary point of view. He emphasised both the continuity and the creativity of the evolutionary process; from the first primordial stuff to the mind of man its march was unbroken; yet it was marked from time to time by the emergence of new and more 'inward' forms—life, mind, personality.

Smuts tried to picture to himself the nature of the primordial stuff of the universe. Modern science, he thought, was tending more and more to conceive it as 'modes of motion of infinitesimally small centres of energy'. He found himself wondering whether motion might not originally have been diffused throughout space as a sort of continuum and have condensed later on in specific centres, rather as the nebular stuff was supposed to have condensed into planetary systems. All this was anathema to Wolstenholme. 'What is motion', he asked, 'without *things* that move?' And again: 'I can just as easily think of a continuum of grins without the cat (Alice in Wonderland).' But Smuts was now discussing life, picturing it as 'a sort of new creation', not a negation of motion but quite superior to it and 'using motion as a means to achieve its own ends': perhaps, like motion before it, it had been diffused as a continuum throughout the universe before becoming condensed into minute organisms. 'What is life', interjected Wolstenholme, 'apart from living *things*? Life isn't a *substance*!' As for the condensation of a 'continuum', he could just as easily conceive the condensation of 'saccharinity, before there is any sugar!'

His interjections grew more frequent and tart as Smuts expounded the evolutionary process as an unfolding of inner potentialities, a movement 'from the external to the internal', and then (as he had done in his psychological reconnaissance) eliminated the element of time in order to contemplate as one Whole the majestic march of the universe.

Smuts. The Whole we have reached both by the psychological and cosmological processes has all the fulness of the concrete universe, and all the unity and simplicity of an ideal thought-construction blended into one. The Many are contained and held in the One, not mechanically, not added together in their separateness, but as it were in solution, all their separateness swallowed up in the one indivisible Whole.

Wolstenholme. These formulations are as unrealiseable to my mind, as having 'meaning', as the Christian Trinity.

Indeed, Wolstenholme by now was nearing the end of his patience. Smuts, however, had still to do battle with the most obdurate enemy of the Whole—the conscious thought of man and the schism which it had created between subject and object. The epistemological problem, as he saw it, was to reconcile unity, which he believed to be a precondition of all experience, with the discontinuous flow of sensations, feelings, conations and volitions which are the experience of the subjective mind. 'To explain how out of these flux elements, these ephemeral unsubstantial subjective phenomena, there arise or can arise the unchanging laws of the moral and material universe, the grand constancy of the processes of nature and that objective reality which the mind posits as the substratum of all this subjective phenomenalism—this is the great problem of all metaphysics.'

In approaching this problem, he started with the Kantian categories of universality, necessity, etc., with which the human mind is equipped in advance for ordering and unifying 'the chaotic flow of sensations'. This gift of whole-making—so he argued—does not belong merely to the subjective minds of separate individuals; if that were so, different individuals might reach different results by adding or multiplying two and two, and no valid basis would exist for the multiplication table, or for truth of any other kind. No, he declared: the order which exists within the mind of an individual must be the exemplar of a larger order. He quoted Kant's *bewusstsein überhaupt*, which he understood to signify 'a universal consciousness, of which all cases of individual consciousness are fundamentally identical specimens'. But even this seemed to him an insufficient basis for knowledge: all men might be in agreement about the multiplication table, but all men might be wrong. Universal opinion, which might turn out to be universal delusion, could not by itself support 'the grand constancy of the processes of nature'. The certainty and universal validity of knowledge could not be established, even as a possibility, without positing unity not merely between the experiencing subjects, but also and as much between these subjects and the experienced objects. 'Knowledge is only possible on the basis of a unity of experience which embraces not merely the individual subject, nor merely all subjects, but also the entire objective universe. The harmonies of nature, the grand sweep of natural law throughout all time and all space, the great ideas and the vast syntheses of thought which embrace the interior spiritual world no less than the external visible universe, all have their origin and find their last explanation in that ultimate unity which is the essence of the Whole and without which all the heterogeneous elements of experience would fall asunder and chaos would take the place of cosmos.'

Opposite this purple passage one may still read in faint pencil Wolstenholme's grey comment. Knowledge, he observed, need not be absolute but is a matter of degree: absolute chaos and absolute cosmos are not the only alternatives. Wolstenholme thought Kant *démodé* and much preferred the meritorious Professor Höffding; but Kant, at any rate, was an antagonist whom one could pin down in argument, whereas he saw no way at all of pinning Smuts down. Yet he tried to fight one last battle with him before reporting himself sick. For Smuts was coming to grips at last with the second of his 'fundamental' questions. In his first two chapters he had demonstrated to his own satisfaction the real and necessary existence of the Whole; in his third chapter he attacked the problem of how it can be known.

He began by recalling the explanation given by the psychologists (although Wolstenholme complained that he was mis-reporting them) of how knowledge is acquired: experience penetrating into consciousness through the five senses, and 'the discursive intellect' building it up first into percepts and concepts and thereafter into judgments. This apparatus, he said, was capable of explaining a great deal of our rational life, but it could not lead to knowledge of the Whole: first, because the five senses yielded 'only small supplies of experience with enormous, dark, unfathomable gaps between them': secondly, because the discursive intellect, as ordinarily understood by the psychologists, was 'a discrete function', capable of breaking wholes up but not of constituting them. 'This is mere assertion!' exclaimed Wolstenholme. 'I know of no means of knowledge', he added, 'except *perception*, in the broadest sense, and *conceptual judgment*, "intellect", or reason. We thus stand on such different ground that there is hardly any basis for discussion in detail.' His comments for the next page or two were chiefly exclamation-marks. Then he gave up.

This was a pity, for Smuts was just about to embark upon a vigorous debate with Kant. It was his purpose to prove that the analytic intellect of the psychologists, with its incapacity for conceiving the Whole, did not really exist but was itself a fabrication of the intellect. The original mistake, he considered, was the artificial, unnecessary and erroneous separation of sense from intellect. This separation had been made by Locke and Hume and taken over by Kant, through whom it had become part and parcel of modern philosophy and psychology. No doubt the distinction between sense and reason was useful for the purposes of psychological analysis; but it created a great deal of unnecessary confusion for philosophers in dealing with ultimate issues. Smuts believed that it had entangled Kant himself. 'For after his final separation and (one might almost say) alienation of sense and intellect, the former of which is synthetic and creative, the latter analytic, formal and barren, he is as a result forced to the conclusion that all knowledge is only of phenomena, or to use our own language, of the parts; that knowledge which transcends the phenomenal, as we would say knowledge of the Whole, is impossible and unattainable.' And yet Kant proceeded to consider certain ideas—God, the Cosmos, the Soul—which transcended the realm of the phenomenal and seemed to depend on some knowledge of the Whole. As neither sense nor intellect could account for the existence of these ideas, Kant was forced to invent for their accommodation a new and distinct faculty of the human mind: the Reason. But this desperate expedient, declared Smuts, would have been quite unnecessary had it not been for his original analysis of the mind into sense and intellect 'as two separate and almost hostile powers'.

The same original error, Smuts believed, vitiated Kant's treatment of the intuitive understanding. Since this was the climax towards which Smuts was driving his argument, it is worth while quoting him at some length.

Kant attributed knowledge to the two sources we have already indicated—sense or intuition and intellect or understanding; according to him intuition supplied the contents and understanding the conceptual forms of knowledge. Such knowledge, however, representing the imperfect combination of contributions from two quite different sources, cannot but be itself imperfect. The ideal of perfect knowledge could only be reached according to Kant by an intelligence possessed of the power of *intuitive understanding*.

Kant had felt himself constrained to deny this power to mortals and attribute it to Deity alone. But why? asked Smuts. Simply and solely because of the false start he had made by his artificial separation of sensation from intellect, intuition from conceptual thought.

In fact, mind is one, and experience is one; they may indeed be analysed for theoretical purposes, but the results of the analysis are mere abstractions and not independently existing factors of mind or experience. The intellectual intuition which Kant reserves to the Supreme Being, is shared in by the humblest of His thinking creatures....It varies in clearness and power in different men; the genius has more of it than the ordinary man; the mystic aspires to cultivate it to the exclusion of his separate mental functions. But in one degree or another it is possessed by all sane men; and it is the function by which each human being in some degree or other has a glimpse and glimmering of the Whole.

Smuts believed that this power of intuitive understanding was so spontaneous, so deeply rooted in the common experience of mankind that one might almost call it common sense. He began to play with that phrase and all at once found himself envisaging the existence of a sixth sense, a *sensus communis*—

which takes up the deliverances of the other senses in one common intuition, which is not a composite aggregate of sense-experience but a unique unity of experience....This *sensus communis* is the source of our power of intellectual intuition; it is the origin of the Whole; by it we do really, albeit vaguely and indefinitely, apprehend the Whole, or any Whole; by it the Whole in an indefineable way is held together in experience, where nothing else could hold it together. And our knowledge of certain Wholes which lie beyond the limits of discrete sensuous experience, such as God, the Cosmos, the Soul, originates in this power of the mind to act as a Whole—in this *sensus communis* of our Personality.*

After this ardent leap forward, he withdrew fleetingly into a mood of unaccustomed caution. The *sensus communis*, he admitted, would appear problematical to some people. Even so, they would possess, if only in a shadowy form, an intuitive understanding of the Whole, which they could amplify and enrich by studying some of the parts *sub specie totius*. In any case, a man's knowledge of the Whole must always fall far short of the reality, since he himself is so immeasurably smaller than it is. We see through a glass, darkly. Our human task is not to try to transcend our faculties but 'to read reality aright with those human faculties with which we are endowed'.

* Of course, the idea of a *sensus communis* is as old as Aristotle, to whom it signified precisely that which enables a man to perceive what is common, or distinct from the sort of specific object perceived by sight, hearing, etc.

These words might have been written by Wolstenholme; but Wolstenholme held a severer view than Smuts of the limitations of 'human faculties'. He recognised no instruments of the human understanding beyond perceptions and conceptual thought. 'Your method', he told Smuts, 'is that of speculative metaphysics, and runs riot—like Bergson's—in the "hypostatization of abstracts", which to me is *anathema maranatha*'. When Smuts invoked intuitive understanding he could bear it no longer and begged to be excused from reading any further.[5]

Wolstenholme had read less than one-quarter of the book: three chapters only of the thirteen. As one turns the pages further and looks in vain for his pungent criticisms in the margins, one cannot help feeling a sense of loss. Smuts himself must have felt it, for a prickly companion is surely better than no companion at all. Wolstenholme's desertion condemned him to pursue his adventure of ideas in unrelieved loneliness.

It may seem that his biographer also is deserting him, for no attempt will be made in what follows to accompany him chapter by chapter to the end of his book. Still, a strong defence may be made against the charge of desertion. To begin with, the plea of impossibility may be advanced. This biographer did in fact study in close detail every chapter and every page of the book: he read the books of many other writers on the same theme, but he found himself in the end composing a treatise on the history of ideas, which could not possibly be fitted into this or any other biography. He spent days, if not weeks, in struggling with this problem of logical and aesthetic proportion, before he discovered that the struggle was quite unnecessary. All the main themes of the book had been announced, if not developed, in those first three chapters through which he had been guided by the peering and carping Wolstenholme. Should a biographer peer into every page, sentence and word? Might it not be better to stand back some distance, to look at the shape of the wood instead of scrabbling among the trees, to contemplate 'holistically', as Smuts himself would have put it, *The Inquiry into the Whole*?

One can but try. And—not to be too ponderous—one may begin the attempt by asking two slanted questions. Was the book a mistake? Was it wicked?

Wolstenholme had no doubt that it was a mistake. In a letter which was quite merciless in its unpremeditated cruelty he complimented Smuts upon his literary talent and advised him to employ it for the future in writing the history of his campaigns.

> The turn for literary style, which I think your MS. shows to be well worth cultivation, leads to the suggestion that you should apply yourself to history rather than to philosophy. In the latter I think you are attempting the, in your circumstances, impossible, and in my view, the überhaupt impossible. It would be little short of a miracle if a busy statesman and man of affairs should be able to do as a parergon what some of the keenest intellects have vainly essayed to do with the full devotion of a whole lifetime. Your work must perforce always remain that of an amateur, and it would take years of study and work before you could write anything that could command the attention of philosophers *vom Fach*. But if you carried out the design you once mentioned to me, of writing a history of the war, you would at once get a hearing, and might succeed in adding one more to the not numerous classics of history. It is worth considering.[6]

In other words, professors should write for professors.* The kingdom of philosophy is private property: no admittance except on business. Smuts, to be sure, was a trespasser, as anybody could easily see from his strange philosophical clothes; but otherwise there was not so very much to distinguish him from some of the eminent proprietors. Among these were Professor Lloyd Morgan (a biologist with some philosophical sophistication) and a much greater man, Professor Samuel Alexander, O.M.

Alexander published his *Space, Time and Deity* in 1920, eight years after Smuts had posted to Wolstenholme the complete typescript of his *Inquiry into the Whole*. Alexander received wide and well-merited acclaim for his book, whereas Smuts persuaded only one man to read only one-quarter of his. Yet the two books, widely separated though they may be in linguistic sophistication and philosophical *savoir faire*, are closely akin to each other both in theme and method.

Alexander's argument has been portrayed diagrammatically[7] as a pyramid: its base is Space-Time, its apex is Deity: from the centre of the base a straight line (*Nisus*) thrusts its way upwards through successive levels of evolutionary complexity (Matter, Life, Mind) towards the apex. No intervention takes place from the outside; each successive quality, from Matter all the way to Deity, emerges within the pyramid.

---

* The present writer is aware that dreadful crudities are sometimes perpetrated when professors do *not* write for professors.

This diagrammatic summary may seem unforgivably terse; but it may serve for the comparison between the viewpoints of Alexander and Smuts. To consider first the base of the pyramid: Smuts did not postulate anything so apparently precise as Alexander's 'point instants in Space-Time'. These point-instants, however, turn out to be patterns of motion which contain the potentiality of physical and chemical structure and combination. There is not much difference here from Smuts's 'modes of motion of infinitesimally small centres of energy'. There is, moreover, a close similarity between the attitudes of the two men towards Time: Alexander reproved philosophers for failing 'to take Time seriously' and Smuts criticised Kant for representing Time in terms of Space. Both men emphasised the separate reality of Time because they both needed it as the vehicle of their evolutionary process: if Time did not exist, the universe could have no history.

In their conception of the successive forms emergent within the pyramid the two men were closely akin. They both laid great emphasis upon the observable fact of progressive structural complexity: a stone is a relatively simple structure, a man is a highly complicated one; between stone and man stretches a long procession of increasingly complex forms. Smuts, as we have seen, was not content to view this procession merely from the outside; to him, the progressive structural complexity observable in life, mind and personality expresses the intensification of inward activity. If any difference existed between him and Alexander on this issue, probably it was merely verbal.

The apex of Alexander's pyramid was Deity. Only the apex? Sometimes he conceived Deity in contrast with the opening phrase of the Book of Genesis—he could have written 'in the *end* God'—but at other times he seemed to conceive it as a presence and activity permeating the entire universe here and now: Spinoza's *Deus sive Natura*. On this issue, Smuts was more explicit than Alexander. In his pyramid, the Whole was both the end and the beginning, the apex and the upward thrust. 'The Whole then includes, (1) all realised experience; (2) a process by which reality and experience are being extended; (3) an ideal towards which that process of realisation is tending.'

As to the upward thrust, Alexander and Smuts were broadly in agreement; but Alexander did not lay so much emphasis upon whole-making and was, besides, more skilled in the use of words. He chose one splendid word, *nisus*, and used it with unvarying consistency. Smuts, in contrast, was far too free with his words. Sometimes, particularly when he was deeply moved, he used the language of his Christian upbringing; at other times—as in the sentence quoted above —he used the weak word 'ideal'. Yet he believed with almost too much fervour in a word of his own creation. In his seventh chapter, after making an immense generalisation about the 'activity of the Whole', he cast about for a word which would express his meaning. The activity of the Whole, he declared, expressed itself throughout all space and time in 'the cosmic process of individuation': that is to say, the continuous creation of 'lesser wholes' in its own image. 'If ever an operative factor deserved a name of its own, this self-developing, self-realising power of the Whole deserves it. Hence I propose for it the name of Holism (from ὅλος = Whole) with special reference not only to it as the activity of the Whole, but more especially to its *holizing* or whole-producing tendency in the sense above explained. Holism then is the ultimate activity which prompts and pulses through all other activities in the universe. . . .'

Gilbert Murray told Smuts some years later that he found his word Holism and its proliferations etymologically correct and logically appropriate but aesthetically unpleasing.[8] Alexander, it may be supposed, would have felt the same. Perhaps he would also have felt that the contrast between his own *nisus* and Smuts's *holism* raised other issues besides the aesthetic one. Yet surely he would never have thought it a mistake for Smuts to attempt a book so closely akin—not of course in its academic sophistication and analytical discipline, but in its emotional and intellectual drive—to the one that he himself had in his head.

Be this as it may, the time was not far distant when philosophers of Wolstenholme's breed would be calling the tune in English universities. When that time came, Alexander's own work would be labelled 'nonsense' and his advocacy would be of no help to Smuts. Surely it is a mistake to get 'nonsense' into print? Smuts, however, did succeed at last (with not too much time to spare) in getting into print a book which—although it said only half of what he had said in 1912 and was still wanting to say to the end of his life—received a welcome which would have dismayed Wolstenholme as a philosopher but delighted him as a friend.[9]

If Wolstenholme could have lived into the mid-twentieth century, he would have found the ideas of his friend amazingly and (from his own point of view) disconcertingly alive. In Cambridge, to which Smuts and Wolstenholme both belonged, all kinds of people—theologians, astronomers, geneticists—had become infected, whether they knew it or not, by the holistic virus.*

The story of how this infection spread may be worth a chapter or two in a later volume. Meanwhile, we may ask ourselves whether 'infection' (which for most people has unpleasant associations) is the appropriate word? This means facing our second slanted question about *The Inquiry into the Whole*. Was the book wicked?

A distinguished professor of philosophy has chosen to depict holism as the creed of tribalism and collectivism, a devilish totalitarian invention for the glorification of the State and the enslavement of the individual.[10] It is proper to inquire whether or no this violent attack is grounded upon solid evidence. In 1933 the word which Smuts had minted gained admittance to the supplement of the *New English Dictionary*, where its definition, although rather inadequate, possessed none of the nasty features enumerated by the professor. Nor are any of these nasty features discernible in the examples cited by the *N.E.D.* from *Holism and Evolution* or from reviews of that book. Nor are they discernible anywhere at all in the published writings of Smuts. The presumption is that the professor did not study these writings and that he did not even consult the *New English Dictionary*. It just happened that he hated tyranny (which is proper) and loathed Plato (which is permissible) and looked about for a label that would discredit these two arch-enemies. But the word holism, however unpleasing it may have sounded to some people, was never thought

---

* Here are three Cambridge examples: (1) Sir Ronald Fisher, in *Creative Aspects of Natural Law* (Cambridge, 1950: Eddington Memorial Lecture) deals both critically and sympathetically with Smuts's *Holism and Evolution*. (2) Professor C. E. Raven, in his Gifford Lectures (*Science and Religion*, Cambridge, 1953), takes throughout a consistent and explicit holistic position, which he amplifies in note xiii, 'On the Holism of General Smuts'. (3) Professor Fred Hoyle, in *Man and Materialism* (Allen and Unwin, 1957), shows himself to be an ardent but probably unconscious holist (see especially pp. 158–9). However, despite his acceptance in the concluding pages of *Deus sive natura*, he might be resistant to the 'inwardness' which Smuts emphasised so strongly.

A critical history of the holistic trend of thought (of which the three men cited are only examples) would be rewarding, if a philosophical historian of good quality would undertake the task. No doubt it would show that Smuts was more in debt, whether he realised it or not, to various predecessors and contemporaries than the present biographical study has indicated.

discreditable until professors began twisting its meaning. Of course, anybody is free to argue that holistic views, whatever the intentions of their proponents may be, lead inevitably to totalitarianism and all its iniquities. With Smuts, the man who introduced the word into the English language, that simply did not happen.

Nobody, of course, has imputed wickedness to *The Inquiry into the Whole*, an unpublished work which probably has never even been seen by more than half a dozen people. All the same, the book offers basic evidence in reply to the accusation that holistic theories lead inevitably to the denial of political and personal freedom. It reveals the deepest convictions of its author on the great questions of truth and error, good and evil, freedom and necessity.

Smuts wrestled with those questions not only in the chapters which he devoted specifically to problems of moral philosophy but from the beginning to the end of his book. He realised, for example, that his discussion of the relation between the Whole and its parts and his exposition of the evolutionary process had a direct bearing upon the problem of freedom. It might seem at first sight that any philosophy which emphasises the primacy of the Whole, both in its formal relations with the parts and in movement and growth, must necessarily deny to the parts the possibility of self-determination. But suppose that the parts are themselves wholes? In the philosophy of Aristotle, where every thing has its specific end, and in that of St Thomas Aquinas, where a hierarchy of 'partial wholes' leads upwards to God, this apparent paradox exists. There is no direct evidence that Smuts had studied Aristotle and there is direct evidence that he had *not* studied Aquinas, but his thought is saturated through and through with their teleology. He did not find it incompatible with evolutionary theory: on the contrary, evolution as he conceived it was 'a cosmic process of individuation' which produced *individuals* progressively complex in structure. Structural complexity, in his view, had an inward as well as an outward aspect. Inwardness signified the power of self-direction. The plant has more of this power than the stone, the animal more than the plant, the man more than the animal.

Consequently, the freedom of the human person has its roots deep down in the condition of things. From 'dark beginnings' in the deep, unconscious levels of the cosmic process, man has grown to the stature of a 'legislative being', striving by conscious will and thought to realise his own wholeness and his union with the Whole. It is in this striving that he finds his freedom. The man divided within himself has no power of self-determination; he is not free, he is hardly a person, but a bundle of jangling parts. Personality, freedom and wholeness are correlatives.

To summarise this teaching in a sentence or two makes it sound too smooth and easy; but it is a warrior's creed. A man cannot make himself whole and free save by perpetual combat with pain, error and evil. Nor can any man—unless he be also more than a man—ever win this battle completely. For pain, error and evil are not mere appearances, as the idealists maintain; they are realities which must belong to the very constitution of things so long as successive forms of reality continue to co-exist and to collide with each other in the unfolding movement of the universe.

Nay, Evil will increase, just as and in proportion as Good increases with the progress of that movement; because with the deepening intensive movement the resulting imperfect wholes become ever more sensitive and intolerant of their own limitations and imperfections and strive with ever more painful intensity to emancipation and realisation of their ideal destiny as wholes. Indeed, so close is the association of Evil with progress that to us human beings it appears to be one of its main incentives and guarantees and that stagnation must ensue if the goad of Evil were withdrawn from the slow weary movement of life and mind. With great historical progress Evil in its grosser more external forms may diminish, only however to be felt with all the more anguish by the more sensitive and highly strung nerves and the larger more delicately attuned souls which mark the intensive progress of the holistic movement. Hence the greatest men are usually the least happy in the ordinary sense. But here again the Whole exerts its wholesome beneficent influence and as a compensation they know a blessedness which is unintelligible and unrealisable to smaller natures.

Let it not be forgotten that Smuts felt and knew both 'anguish' and 'blessedness'. For him, the sanguine age was not the superficial age. By an immense effort of intellect and will he had gained a coherent faith to live by.

His book contains the record of this effort. Hard driven as he was by all his tasks of State-building, it was foolhardy of him even to attempt it; just as foolhardy as it had been to attempt the invasion of Cape Colony with his ragged commando. Both operations were exuberant, slapdash, unprofessional, epical. Both operations, to all outward seeming, ended in failure; for one would normally suppose that a soldier has failed when he agrees to surrender, and that a philosopher has failed when he cannot find even one person to read his book through. And yet, the last chapter of Smuts's book has a triumphal ring, as he describes, sometimes in St Paul's words, sometimes in his own, what it means to a man to discover his own significance within the universe.

He walks straight from darkness into light

CHAPTER 16

THE STRANGER WITHIN THE GATES

NATIVE POLICY

THROUGHOUT his whole life and in despite of changing fashions Smuts clung to the time-hallowed conception of philosophy as comprehensive knowledge, man's endeavour to understand the universe and his own place within it. In 1912 he accepted Wolstenholme's verdict upon his *Inquiry* to the extent of refraining from any attempt to get the book published, but not to the extent of cutting the losses that he had incurred in writing it. So far from considering it waste labour, he was determined to make it—sometime, somehow—the starting-point of a new book on the same theme. Meanwhile, the immense effort that he had put into it helped him to clarify and strengthen his own mind and will. The sanguine years were running out, the age of confusion was drawing near, but he had explored and explained the foundations of his belief, as if in preparation for the storms ahead.

His philosophy reinforced his native sense of realism, of proportion and of purpose. It helped him to explain, but not to explain away, the sombre powers of pain, error and evil, such as had overwhelmed his own country ten years earlier and were destined soon to overwhelm Europe. He knew these powers to be formidable but he did not admit them to be sovereign: evil, he used to say, might triumph in the short run but good was the long run winner. How long, oh Lord, how long? In the times of peril and struggle which filled so much of his life, this cry was wrung from him often; but never in despair. His philosophy contained both the time-scale of modern science, which he had discovered in evolutionary theory, and the doctrine of the sovereignty of God, which his uncle Boudewyn had preached in the little church at Riebeeck West. Which of these two phraseologies he chose for expressing his meaning was largely a matter of circumstance with him. *Homo sapiens*, he used sometimes to say in his private letters, had come such a long way, when one compared him with the other mammals, that one could not imagine him petering out in failure. At other times he used to say that God must be given time to

309

work out his purposes. He did not mean by this that individual men and women could leave everything to the evolutionary process or to the Divine plan: on the contrary, it was through their active participation that the process and the plan found fulfilment. The human person—whether one regarded him as the highest achievement, so far, of 'the cosmic process of individuation' or as a creature made in the image of God—was so much in the centre of the stage that without him the play could not go on.

Philosophy, as Smuts tried to understand and to practise it, gave him firm anchorage. What it could not give him was a ready recipe for politics. It is only in retrospect and by superficial analogy that some people (his enemies as well as his friends) have pretended to discover a precise translation of his philosophical tenets into his political loyalties: the Union of South Africa, the British Commonwealth, the League of Nations, each in its turn a bigger and better whole—or a bigger and worse one, from the point of view of narrow nationalism.[1] As if he had ever conceived the holistic process in terms of expanding size! On the contrary, he had discovered immensity in the beginning, and from that 'vague undifferentiated continuum' had postulated the progressive emergence of individual wholes, above all, the human person, which were both more intricate in structure and *smaller* in size. Similarly, his political striving revealed no vulgar correlation between value and scale: whereas in South Africa whole-making had meant the creation of a larger polity, in the British Commonwealth it meant the creation of many smaller ones. His political ideal for the Commonwealth, and, indeed, for the world, envisaged the multiplication of sovereign States, constituted on the principle of nationality. On the other hand, nationality was never an absolute for him; he postulated a correlation between the rights and the duties of nations, between independence and interdependence, and for this reason he made himself the advocate of Commonwealth and League, associations which tempered the *sacro egoismo* of sovereignty. This, to be sure, was in accord with his philosophical teaching, in which the individual whole was differentiated, but not alienated from the Whole; but it was equally in accord with Mazzini's teaching—indeed, with the main current of liberal doctrine from Mazzini to President Wilson, not to mention John X. Merriman. Smuts had no need to write a philosophical treatise in order to discover his political ideals. The converse is just as probable—that he discovered those ideals in the prevailing climate of western thought and in his own experience of South African politics, and then carried them with him into his philosophical inquiry.

In the theory and practice of European nationalism one insistent question remained unanswered: how could a territorial State, constituted upon the national principle, satisfy the interests and aspirations of the diverse communities—ethnic, linguistic, religious, cultural— intermingled in close neighbourhood upon its soil? In South Africa, this question was even more insistent than it was in Europe. It had been for generations past the very stuff of South African history. How to make a Boer state acceptable to the British, or a British state acceptable to the Boers? Or, if Boer and Briton became partners at last in a new South African nation, how to reconcile their joint freedom with the interests and rights of the Bantu, the Cape Coloureds and the Indians?

This last question is the theme of the present chapter. The older Smuts grew, the more intractable it became: when he died in 1950 it appeared even further from a solution than it had been forty years earlier, when he was establishing the Union. Inevitably, a good many people have been prone to put upon him the blame for those years of lost opportunity. After all, he held power (although not always the supreme power) for three-quarters of this period. Besides, there appears to be a glaring discrepancy between his holistic philosophy and the jarring racial discords of South Africa. Satirists have been quick to seize upon this paradox as an opportunity for their barbed wit.

Here, obviously, is a problem of central importance for this biography. The biographer, however, cannot find any short cut to its solution; in particular, he cannot identify any particular scheme of race relations as the proper counterpart of the *Inquiry into the Whole*. As a philosopher, Smuts employed the cosmological time-scale; as a politician, he had to reckon time from one election to the next and sometimes from one day to the next. His cosmological outlook, reinforced in later life by studies of palaeontology and pre-history, excluded the crude doctrine of the inequality of races; but it contained no quick cure for the racial prejudices of his constituents, still less for those stubborn, factual inequalities that were rooted so deeply in the history of his country. It pleased him, twenty years later, to place European Man and the South African Bushman upon the same branch of humanity's family tree; to be sure, the European had developed his latent powers while the Bushman had remained isolated and static; but this was the luck of the evolutionary game.[2] Unfortunately, the game had been played in cosmological time and its results could not easily be reversed in politician's time.

For the Bushman, this was true. But what about the Bantu? The cosmological time-scale was hardly appropriate in Bantu studies and it may have predisposed Smuts to take too seriously the talk about 'child races' which was fashionable in the early twentieth century. Certainly, he underestimated the capacity of black Africans to adapt themselves at speed to western ways. But was it their proper destiny thus to adapt themselves? Among his contemporaries, there were not many who would have asserted that it was. In South Africa, some people, such as John X. Merriman, wanted to admit a minority of black Africans to European politics, but wanted also to exclude the masses from European industry; while other people, including almost every white man on the Rand, wanted precisely the opposite. In England, liberals were losing confidence in the old missionary slogan, 'Commerce and Christianity', and were disposed to favour new slogans and devices, such as 'Trusteeship' and 'Indirect Rule', in the hope of safeguarding Native cultures from the disruptive impact of western civilisation. Academic support for this new outlook was soon provided, whether intentionally or not, by the rising school of social anthropologists. Both in England and in South Africa it became fashionable to advocate a policy which would encourage Native communities 'to develop upon their own lines'.[3] Such a policy might well have appeared to Smuts nearer than any other to his own principle of 'individuation'; but one may doubt whether it had a strong attraction for him.[4]

Indeed, it was in the main abstract theorising, far removed from the economic, sociological and political realities of South Africa. It was an academic exercise which has been worth noticing because it set the tone of public discussion for some time to come and got some people into a bigger muddle than they would otherwise have been in; but really there was nothing new in it; at most it provided some new arguments for the old habit of treating people of different colours in different ways. To understand how that habit grew up and gained ascendancy one needs to look a little more deeply into South African history.[5]

The habit—or policy, or ideology, or whatever description is most appropriate—has expressed itself from time to time in different slogans; round about the 1920's *segregation* was the favourite word; in the late 1930's *apartheid* began to be used. Here it will be best to choose a word which possesses no emotive associations. *Separateness* will serve the purpose. From that day, three centuries and more ago, when the first governor, Jan van Riebeeck, decided to plant his hedge of wild almond (its line can still be traced) to separate his Dutch settlers from the surrounding Hottentots, the separateness of Europeans from the other breeds has remained, right up to the present day, the central theme of South African history.

There have been, however, two distinct and often conflicting versions of this theme. One version became the official policy of the governors, Dutch and British, and their political masters, first in Amsterdam and later in London. The separateness which they aimed at was territorial. Their purpose, reaffirmed through successive centuries, was to draw a fixed boundary line to contain the expansion of European settlement and the consequent strife between Europeans and the other peoples. Their motives were various. One motive was peace. Another was economy, since wars and administration cost money. Another was compassion, for they realised that the Native peoples were the weaker party and needed protection against the whites. This last motive (contrary to the assumptions of some cynical historians) was operative almost continuously from early times to the era of self-government, at first for the protection of the Hottentots and later—from the 1770's onwards—for the protection of the Bantu. The growth of missionary activity and humanitarian sentiment from the late eighteenth century onwards powerfully reinforced the compassionate impulse by creating strong pressure-groups (for example, the London Missionary Society and the Aborigines' Protection Society) in the political metropolis. From those days to the present time, the policy of territorial separateness has never been merely repressive, but has always been able to win some support from idealists who have hoped to find in it a means for the protection of Native interests and rights, beginning with land ownership.

The European settlers, however, were insatiable land takers. From very early times, they had responded to their historical and geographical situation by developing an extensive pastoral economy with an innate propensity to sprawl.[6] No matter what boundaries their governors might draw on the map, they remained determined to trek further on. Their version of separateness—we may call it the voortrekker version—was not territorial but social and political. They wanted the land. They wanted Native labour to work the land. They wanted to be masters both of the land and the people. This last motive was reinforced by their horror at the policy of legal equality and racial impartiality which the British government, from the 1820's onwards, began to impose upon their brethren who had remained behind in the areas of old settlement. *Gelykstelling*—the equality of persons, irrespective of colour, in the courts of law, to begin with, and later in the franchise—was anathema to them. Their reply was *baasskap*—the white man's dominance.

The contemporary map of South Africa records some important consequences of the conflict between the official and the voortrekker programmes of separateness. The official policy has found permanent embodiment in the sizeable Native Reserves of eastern Cape Colony and Natal, not to mention the three High Commission Territories, which still remain under British sovereignty; but in the Transvaal, Native Reserves are scattered,* and in the Orange Free State they are almost non-existent. Even so, the map does not tell the whole story, for the voortrekkers annexed not only their own territories but also the minds of many white people in neighbouring territories—in the colony of Natal, for example, where *baasskap*, which at times was paternalistic and kindly, would be too kind a description of what the white men did to the Zulus between 1906 and 1909, or of their niggling, malicious mishandling of the Indians over a much longer period.

Obviously, it was not membership of a particular language group or citizen body that made men opt for social and political rather than for territorial separateness. The *uitlanders* of the Rand abhorred Boer rule but absorbed the racial attitudes of their rulers and adapted them to their own special requirements. The great capitalists were just as hungry as Boer farmers were for Native labour and they found ways and means of drawing it from great distances. To be sure, their persistent struggle to keep down labour costs held the threat of *gelykstelling* in the economic sphere, for the colour-bar was likely to prove incompatible with maximum efficiency of the

---

* Up to 1936 the Transvaal Reserves were also small in total area. After the legislation of that year they were considerably added to.

labour force. Their white employees, on the contrary, were intransigent champions of the colour-bar: £1 a day for the white man and £1 a week for the black—this had been the slogan of the white miners when they and their skills still possessed scarcity value; it still remained the rule (subject to changes in money values) even when the white miners grew plentiful and their black subordinates acquired skill. The subordination of black to white—*baasskap*—had no more passionate advocates than these English-speaking miners. Here in the making was a political alliance destined to play an important part in South African history. The Hertzog–Creswell pact of the 1920's was foreshadowed forty years earlier in Paul Kruger's republic, where the Mines and Works Act of 1885 embodied the industrial colour-bar in the law of the land.

Early in the twentieth century, a synthesis began to take shape between the two versions of separateness. It found expression (to cite one notable example) in the *Report of the Native Affairs Commission, 1903–1905*.[7] The appointment of this commission was prompted by Lord Milner and his young men, working through the Customs Conference of March 1903. The commission's terms of reference were ineptly framed, for they showed no awareness of the profound economic changes, more deep-seated even than the wartime upheaval, which were transforming South African society in city and town. These changes cannot be analysed here; but one feature of them at least—the rural exodus—should have been plainly visible even at that time. In the white farming areas, agricultural change was driving from the land scores of thousands of *bouches inutiles*— 'poor whites' and poor blacks; in the Native Reserves, agricultural stagnation, combined with population pressure, was producing the same effect. In consequence, whites and blacks were becoming jumbled together, particularly in the cities, to a degree and in a fashion which threatened the dogma of separateness both in its territorial and its social aspects.

The *Report of the Native Affairs Commission*, widely acclaimed though it was as a masterpiece of wisdom, was really a superficial document. It made no attempt to get to the roots of the problem or to treat it as a whole but dealt chiefly with bits and pieces of it, quite often the less important bits and pieces. For example, apart from advocating residential segregation, the report said nothing of note about the influx of Natives into the cities; but it made a great fuss about the occasional purchases of land which a few Natives had made—singly or in combination—outside the Reserves. Here it gave a new twist to the old policy of territorial separateness, which from this time onwards became just as much a matter of keeping the 'white areas' white as of keeping the 'black areas' black. On this issue the commissioners were frank. 'It will be far more difficult', they declared, 'to preserve the absolutely necessary political and social distinctions if the growth of a mixed rural population of landowners is not discouraged.'[8] They proposed to discourage it (if that is the right word) by defining once and for all the area of the Native Reserves and prohibiting by law Native purchases of land outside that area. At the same time, they proposed vigorous action to expel the Native squatters (though not as yet the labour tenants) from their holdings on the farms of white landowners.

The commissioners had it in mind that what the Natives lost by these curtailments of their existing legal rights and customary privileges might be made good to them by extensions to the Native Reserves; but they left to the future—as it turned out, a postponed and precarious future—the precise definition of these extensions. It is to be inferred from this, as from the general tone of their report, that they valued territorial separateness primarily as a means of protecting European interests. The same inference may be drawn from their advocacy of political separateness. In Cape Colony, they said, 'Native interests have secured a considerable amount of attention because of their political power, which is sufficient not only to influence elections but even to turn the balance in certain constituencies, and to affect the general policy'.[9] They thought this situation intolerable and called for the abolition of the Cape franchise. In its place, they proposed—not only for the Cape but for all four colonies—a system of separate voting by Native electors for a fixed number of representatives, 'the number not being more than sufficient to provide an adequate means for the expression of Native views and the ventilation of their grievances, if any, and not to be regulated by the numerical strength of the Native vote'.[10] They did not define sufficiency and adequacy in numerical terms but suggested that the Native voters should have 'at least one seat' in each colonial legislature.

The doctrine of separateness, as now defined under Lord Milner's auspices, could get along quite comfortably with *baasskap*. Lord Selborne made this perfectly clear in a long memorandum which he sent to Botha and Smuts in January 1908.[11] The most interesting thing about this document is the picture it paints of its author's state of mind; Lord Selborne obviously regarded himself as a practical idealist, a down-to-earth but also a forward-looking thinker. He began with a plea for giving the Coloured People 'the benefit of their white blood'; for it was sheer folly, he argued, to classify them with the Natives and thereby force them, against their natural inclinations, into making common cause with the Natives against their white masters. As for the Natives: the government should formulate its policy towards them with three objects in view: first, the preservation of peace; secondly, the promotion of Christianity and civilisation; thirdly, the destruction of tribalism. Lord Selborne was a strong believer in the economic motive as a means of bringing black people 'from tribalism into the atmosphere of civilisation' and he was hostile to all restrictions upon economic mobility, such as the pass laws and the industrial colour-bar. He argued his case with humanity and liberal fervour—mixed, however, with some racial complacency. 'Before pursuing the subject of native policy further, I should like to face a question which is constantly being asked, and that is, can the black man be allowed to become a rival to the white man? I have no hesitation in answering that question, because I believe the idea to be simply a nightmare. The black man is absolutely incapable of rivalling the white man....No one can have any experience of the two races without feeling the intrinsic superiority of the white man. All history in addition proves it.'

How sure people felt in those days—Boers, Britons and all of them —about what history proves! Lord Selborne confidently pictured the passage of the Natives from tribalism to civilisation—on the Reserves, on European farms, in town locations—everywhere working their way upwards, although never any higher, it would seem, than manual labour or domestic service. He was eager to give them the educational facilities they needed to qualify themselves for these callings, provided they paid for them £ for £. There was only one place where he drew the line on their behalf. He disbelieved in politics for them and poured scorn on their 'absurd', 'futile' and 'dangerous' participation in the elections of Cape Colony. Here, however, he found himself in a dilemma, for he also believed that 'the worst form of government for natives is direct government by a Parliament of white men'. His way of escape from the dilemma was to advocate a strong Department of Native Affairs, consulting with half a dozen tribal councils. A single Native Representative Council might have appeared more in accord with his passion for detribalisation, but he feared that it might prove dangerous. As a safety valve, he was prepared to give votes—or rather, fractions of votes[12]—for the white man's parliament to such rare and exceptional Natives as might be certified by three Judges of the Supreme Court to have achieved the white man's standard of civilisation.

Imperial Britain, as represented by Lord Selborne, had by now absorbed pretty thoroughly the ideas of the conquered Boers. There were, of course, some significant points of variance—on the industrial colour-bar and the pass laws, for example—but by and large agreement had been reached between the British establishment, the local politicians and the two sections of the white population. This agreement, tempered here and there by compromise, took constitutional and legislative shape under the leadership of Botha and Smuts. The compromise on the franchise was embedded in the constitution; a good many years were to pass before General Hertzog ventured openly to assail it. The industrial colour-bar was sacrosanct on the Rand and it received from the Union parliament the same measure of legal endorsement as had been granted to it by the republican Volksraad.* The most important new departure was the Natives Land Act of 1913, which established territorial separateness precisely in the manner recommended in 1905 by the Native Affairs Commission. The Act made it illegal for Natives to purchase land outside the existing Reserves (enumerated in the schedule at a total of 10,422,935 morgen); but, in recognition of the fact that this area was insufficient for their needs, made provision for the demarcation of additional areas where they would be 'released' from the ban against purchase. Here was a promise. Twenty-three years were to pass before the Union of South Africa did anything at all to honour it.[13]

What did Smuts have to say to all this? Hardly a word. This silence on his part was a new departure. In the years preceding Union, as we have seen, he had disputed pertinaciously with Merriman about the franchise. When the South Africa Act was passed, he defended the clause which restricted the right of sitting in parliament to persons of European descent.[14] But in his election speech of 10 August 1910 he spared only a few sentences for the Native question and for the

* See p. 320 below.

next four years, if not for longer, he had not a single word to spare for it. At any rate, he said nothing at all about it in Parliament. Nor did he discuss it in his private letters.[15]

In view of this astonishing silence, it seems worth while to quote the relevant passage—crude though the reporting of it may have been—of his speech of 10 August 1910.

He personally was not against the native, but was against the policy of oppression. He would help the native in every legitimate way in accordance with his present requirements; but he could not forget that civilization had been built up in this country by the white race, and that they were the guardians of liberty, justice and all the elements of progress in South Africa. The franchise was the last argument; it was more powerful than the sword or the rifle, and the day that the white race gave away the final protection they possessed they would have to consider very carefully what they were doing. They had received a heritage of civilization from their fathers, which he hoped they would hand on intact and unspoiled to their children. If those children found an opening to extend the rule of liberty and political rights in this country, they could do so; but to his mind it would be one of the most dangerous things for the white race, constituted as it was, in South Africa, to take any such steps today.[16]

There can be no doubt that these sentences represent faithfully the views that Smuts held on that question at that time. Probably they were a good deal more moderate than the utterances of most of the other parliamentary candidates in the Transvaal; they did not contain the fatal word 'Never', but left at least a chink of the door open for a future time. In effect, and allowing for the differences of emphasis that were called for in a personal discussion and an electioneering speech, they repeated the argument which he had urged upon Merriman: there was an order of priorities in time; the uniting of white South Africans here and now, the settlement of the Native question later on. He did not face the fact that the decisions taken here and now might predetermine the decisions to be taken later on.

It seldom happens in politics that an entrenched minority shares its political power with the majority, except under pressure, and under the constitution of the Union no effective means existed outside the Cape Province, whereby the excluded majority could bring pressure to bear. Lord Selborne, all unconsciously, had stated the essential facts of the situation when he argued that Coloured and Native voters were able to influence the course of public policy in the Cape because they possessed power—limited though it was—to swing the elections. The moral which he drew from this was that they should be deprived of the franchise which gave them this power. Other people might have drawn the opposite moral. They might have argued, using Lord Selborne's own words, that it was 'absurd', 'futile', 'unwise', 'dangerous' for any government to deny to important classes of its subjects effective means for defending their interests and expressing their aspirations. This, indeed, was Merriman's argument, when he warned Smuts in letter after letter that it was dangerous to 'close the safety valve'.

How dangerous it was may be seen from the debate on the Mines and Works Bill of 1911, which Smuts himself, as Minister of Mines, piloted through parliament. Clause 15 of the bill, when one views it in the long perspective of South African history, was explosively political, for it provided the means of embedding the industrial colour-bar in the law of the Union.* Yet Smuts told parliament that the bill was purely technical. That, no doubt, was how he saw it. No speaker arose to point out his mistake. It may well be that the members of the other Provinces looked upon the bill as a domestic concern of the Transvaal, while the Transvaalers were so used to the colour-bar that they took it for granted. Yet the time was bound to come when it could no longer be taken for granted, either by the mine-owners or the white trade unionists or the Native miners. The clause which parliament did not think worth debating contained the seed of revolution.

Smuts had said in his student essays and many times since then that 'the Native problem' was immensely more important than anything else that his country had to face; it was, he declared, *the* South African problem. But in what dimension of time? The cosmological time-scale was too long, for the Native problem would certainly not wait for settlement until the next Ice Age; the politician's time-scale was too short, for the problem could so easily be ignored in the day-to-day business of parliament. There was nothing to prevent politicians from letting it drift, thereby making it more intractable for the years ahead. Lord Selborne and his like were

---

* Act no. 12 of 1911, clause 15, imposed penalties on any person endeavouring fraudulently to obtain 'a certificate of competency'. Regulations under this clause provided that persons operating or attending on machinery must be competent and also (in the Transvaal and Orange Free State) white.

surely wrong when they said that the best way of solving it was by
'taking it out of politics'. Unless it were put into politics it would
never be faced.

Later in his career, Smuts twice 'put it into politics' in the sense
of giving his political opponents the opportunity of making 'the
Black Peril' their main electioneering cry. In consequence, he and
his party suffered defeat at the elections of 1929 and 1948. That
double experience illuminates the problem that would have faced
any forward-looking South African: how to create a public opinion
that would tolerate any observable change in the relation of European
and African without producing a torrent of European fears. In the
early years of Union, Smuts decided that the problem was not his
business but that of his colleague Sauer, the Minister of Native
Affairs and a man reputedly pro-Native. But the only solutions that
Sauer had to offer were a few that he selected from Lord Selborne's
repertoire. His selection was uninspired. Would Smuts have done
any better if he had been in Sauer's place? Suppose that he had
chosen, or had been compelled by circumstances, to make the Native
problem his urgent business? Would it have made any difference to
the history of his country? It might have done, for hitherto he had
made something of every task that he had tackled. On the other
hand, it might not have done; the historical forces that have been
examined in this chapter were possibly too powerful to be deflected
even by his energy and intelligence. Still, the answer to the question
need not be left quite so indecisive. Circumstances *did* compel him
to make the Indian problem his business. It will be instructive to
see how this happened and what emerged from it.

SMUTS AND GANDHI

To say that circumstances compelled Smuts to treat Indian grievances
seriously would be to put the matter too impersonally. It was Gandhi
who compelled him. The encounter between Smuts and Gandhi was
an experience of deep significance in both their lives, but was also far
more than that; it was an event of world-historical significance,
prophetic both of the impending conflict and the eventual reconciliation between Britain and India.

At a time when Smuts appeared to be seeing no further than the
petty and embittered politics of the Transvaal, he received from his
old friend at Cambridge a reminder of the deeper issues.

You look at home [wrote Wolstenholme], and are content to hope that the agitation with you is 'dying out', but its reverberations in India and its embarrassing effect on the English govt. of India, its effect on the relations of East and West, will not readily die out....A perfectly 'epoch-making' change is taking place in the relations between East and West. Less than half a generation ago the European peoples were calmly discussing the possibility of an agreement among themselves for the 'partition of China' and the policing and commercial exploitation of the oriental peoples generally. That has all been quietly dropped now, as a grotesque mistake. ...Many of these 'inferior peoples' are showing themselves by no means inferior in capacity, and only need the teaching and training which the Japanese have already in a great measure secured, and which even the negroes of the U.S.A. are striving after, to enable them to take up competition on equal terms with the older nations, which are coming to see that they will have to bestir themselves in order to keep their place in modern progress. And it would surely be wise statesmanship, as well as good human fellowship, to concede in time and with a good grace what is sure eventually to be won by struggle.[17]

One is astonished that so shrewd an appraisal of the shape of things to come should have emerged from those secluded lodgings at no. 5, Oxford Road, Cambridge. Yet even from Wolstenholme's insight some things remained hidden, most notably the spiritual and political force of Gandhi and the power of the new weapon, *satyagraha* or 'non-violence', which he was forging.

Gandhi and Smuts had been born within a year of each other and under the same flag, but at first sight there would appear to be little else that they had in common by inheritance and upbringing.[18] Between the Calvinist family in the spacious farming land around Riebeeck West and the Hindu family in the tiny principality of Porbandar, on the north-western coast of India, the spiritual gulf might have seemed to be even more unbridgeable than the geographical distance. While Smuts was tending his father's herds and attending his uncle's church, Gandhi was experimenting with some transitory divagations, such as smoking and meat eating, from the strict rule of middle-caste Hinduism. While Smuts was feeling the first stirrings of his speculative impulse, Gandhi was learning his lessons by rote in the village school. While Smuts was discovering the delights of study in Mr Stoffberg's house at Riebeeck West, Gandhi was losing a year of his schooling in the excitement and upheaval of a Hindu child-marriage. Gandhi at that time was only thirteen years old. Five years later, in 1887, the paths of the two young men began to converge a little, for Smuts was finishing his matriculation year at Stellenbosch when Gandhi said farewell to his wife and children and took ship for London, with the intention of qualifying himself as a barrister. He left England four years later just when Smuts was getting ready to go there. In the meanwhile, his experience as a stranger in London had been similar in some respects to that awaiting Smuts as a stranger in Cambridge: a similar loneliness, a similar reliance upon his own resources, mitigated by a similar good fortune in finding a few friends. Yet how different those friends were from the ones that Smuts found a little later! None of them possessed scientific or philosophical sophistication but all of them belonged to the experimental, not to say the cranky fringe of English Protestantism —vegetarians, theosophists and such-like good people who encouraged their protégé to pursue his experiments with *ahimsa* (non-violence), *bramacharya* (chastity) and similar precepts or practices of his spiritual inheritance.

Between the young Indian and the young Boer the gap might have seemed to be as wide as the distance between the civilisations of East and West. But might not the orthodox of both civilisations be prone to exaggerate that distance? From their separate bases of ancestral belief Gandhi and Smuts were both exploring the simplicities of divinity and of morality, and if they sometimes discovered opposite norms of conduct—opposite convictions, for example, about the place of chastity in marriage or of force in politics—they could at least mutually understand the purpose of each other's quest. Moreover, they both knew themselves to be deeply in debt to their English teachers; Smuts carried the discipline of the Cambridge Law Tripos into his tasks of State-building, while Gandhi—more surprisingly—grafted *Snell on Equity* on to the *Bhagavadgita*.[19] Gandhi, if anything, was more deeply in love than Smuts was with the British constitution and the British habit of compromise, which he believed to be harmonious with the basic values of his own civilisation. 'Hardly ever have I known anybody', he wrote in 1927, 'to cherish such loyalty as I did to the British Constitution. I can see now that my love of truth was at the root of this loyalty.'[20] And again—'But all my life through, the very insistence on truth has taught me to appreciate the beauty of compromise. I saw in later life that this spirit was an essential part of Satyagraha. It has often meant endangering my life and incurring the displeasure of friends. But truth is hard as adamant and tender as a blossom.'[21]

Here, then, were two men who might have been thought destined to work with each other rather than against each other. Yet circumstances condemned them to meet in conflict.

It was an unlikely accident which brought Gandhi to South Africa and thereby to his unpremeditated mission in life. Unlike Smuts, he had cherished no youthful visions of public fame and would have thought himself utterly unfit for a political career, for he was too shy to stammer out even one sentence on a public platform. In 1891, when he returned from England to India, he had no higher ambition of worldly advancement than to earn the means of maintaining his family and repaying his brother the expense of his English education. Even these modest hopes seemed to be beyond his powers, for his attempts to establish himself in the legal profession were a failure and he discovered no other ladder of advancement. It was a great stroke of luck for him when his brother secured him an invitation to go to South Africa and take part in a court case involving two rich and litigious Indians in Paul Kruger's republic.

On the day of his disembarkation at Durban he visited a magistrate's court and was ordered to take off his turban; rather than submit to this affront he left the court and saw himself next day advertised in the newspapers as 'an unwelcome visitor'. On his journey from Durban to Pretoria (in those days it was by rail and road) he was pushed about by the ticket-collector on the train and pushed about again by the driver of the coach. In Pretoria he was pushed from the pavement into the gutter. His white tormentors, if only they had known it, were pushing him into politics, with consequences incalculable for the history of South Africa, of India and the world.

For a time he did not fully realise the change that was taking place within him. The insults which he had suffered did not make him resentful, but they puzzled him. He wanted to know whether his own experience was peculiar or whether it was the usual thing. His shyness slipped away from him and he found himself calling meetings to discuss the situation of the Indian community in South Africa. Not that he had any plans for action; it was still his intention to leave South Africa as soon as his legal work was finished; indeed, he was on the very eve of taking ship from Durban when he heard by accident that the Natal legislature was about to debate a franchise bill which would exclude Indians from voting on the grounds of race. Then and there he made up his mind to cancel his passage and to organise a petition of protest to the legislature. When the petition failed he organised a new one to the Secretary of State for the Colonies. In May 1894 he founded a permanent political organisation, the Natal Indian Congress, to defend Indian rights in Natal and to arouse public opinion both in India and Britain.

Imperial Britain was under precise obligations to maintain Indian rights, not only in Natal but in all the other territories of the Empire, chiefly tropical or sub-tropical, where white capitalists had imported their labour from India under the indenture system. This system had been the sequel to slave emancipation and the consequential famine of plantation labour. The great Act of emancipation was passed in 1833; in 1834 the sugar colony of Mauritius, where the planters found themselves faced with ruin, led the way in procuring Indian 'coolies'. Sturdy abolitionists in England suspected the reintro- duction of slavery under another name. Brougham, Fowell Buxton and others secured in 1840 the appointment of a commission to investigate the conditions and consequences of indentured labour. The commission condemned the system by a majority of 3 to 1; but the House of Commons voted to continue it under safeguards. Throughout the next three generations there flowed to the colonies a steady trickle from India's vast reservoir of labour: between 1842 and 1870 Mauritius received 351,401 indentured labourers; British Guiana 76,691; Trinidad 42,519; Jamaica 15,169. Natal, which did not enter the market until 1860, received only 6448 labourers during the next ten years; but by 1891 her Indian population was 35,000 and by the end of the century it had passed the total of the white population.[22]

As time wore on, public opinion in India grew increasingly suspicious of this traffic. The government of India did its best to ensure that freedom of contract between the buyers and the sellers of labour would not be abused at the expense of the weaker party. It demanded, and it received, unambiguous assurances that Indian labourers would receive fair and equal treatment when their indentures expired; 'they would be in all respects free men', declared Lord Salisbury in 1875, 'with privileges no whit inferior to any other class of Her Majesty's subjects resident in the Colonies'. In the tropical territories, which were destined to remain for a long time under Crown Colony government, this pledge could be made good; but it could not be made good in the territories of white settlement which were advancing rapidly towards self-government. The white settlers had been insistent upon importing Indian labourers to help them out of their economic troubles; they were no less insistent upon denying to these labourers—and to the 'free settlers' who followed in their wake—those opportunities of political, economic and social advancement which they claimed for themselves. They had begun by treating the Indians as human instruments; they continued by resenting them as economic competitors; they ended by imposing upon them a status of legal and political inferiority.

It is a measure of Gandhi's greatness that he was able to understand and even to sympathise with the white settlers' point of view. 'Our different ways of living,' he wrote in 1927, 'our simplicity, our contentment with small gains, our indifference to the laws of hygiene and sanitation, our slowness in keeping our surroundings clean and tidy, and our stinginess in keeping our houses in good repair—all these, combined with the difference in religion, contributed to fan the flame of antagonism.'[23] Understanding all this, Gandhi felt no call to go crusading for complete and immediate equality. He believed that he and his fellow Indians had duties as well as rights and that the remedy for their relative backwardness in hygiene, in civic seemliness and similar matters, lay largely in their own hands. But he could not agree that it lay wholly in their own hands. While they were doing their best to improve their social habits, the State should do its best to help them to help themselves. At the very least, it should refrain from putting obstacles in their way. Yet that, precisely, was what the white rulers of South Africa seemed set upon doing.

In the Orange Free State, Indians were debarred by law from farming, from trading, from every kind of work except the most menial; but in practice this hardly mattered because they had been debarred from entry at an early date and their numbers were in consequence negligible. In the Transvaal, they were debarred by law from citizenship and land ownership and they were compelled to pay a registration fee of £3 and to give their fingerprints before being allowed to trade.* In Gandhi's view, such laws were not merely economically injurious but morally indefensible, since they embodied the principle of racial discrimination. The British government held the same view and addressed repeated protests to President Kruger's

* Law no. 3 of 1885. Fingerprinting was not mentioned in the law itself but was imposed on the Indians by administrative regulation under the law.

government.[24] Admittedly, it could do nothing to make its protests effective, short of going to war with the South African Republic. However, it still possessed both the legal power and the moral obligation to reject the doctrine of racial discrimination when it found embodiment in the legislative proposals of British colonies. Such proposals were the immediate sequel to the grant of responsible government to Natal in 1893. The franchise bill to which Gandhi objected was avowedly discriminatory. The British government rejected the bill in form but accepted it in fact, for it advised the Queen to disallow the original bill and then permitted the colonial legislature to achieve its original purpose under a different form of words. Still, the principle was saved and Gandhi did not press his objection. He was not so easily satisfied with the handling of a taxation bill which the Natal parliament debated in 1894. The purpose of the bill was to drive the indentured labourers back to India on the expiry of their indentures, by imposing upon them a discriminatory tax which they could not possibly pay—£25, which was more than the annual earnings of many of them. The Natal Indian Congress launched a vehement campaign against the bill and the Viceroy of India was dragged into the dispute. On his representations, the figure was reduced from £25 to £3. Gandhi believed that the Viceroy had failed in his duty, for it was wrong in principle to endorse a tax based upon racial discrimination, whatever the figure might be.

In 1896 Gandhi spent six months in India, where he published a pamphlet on the condition of the Indians in South Africa and proposed a resolution on that subject at the annual meeting of the Congress. He took great pains to explain the difficulties of the situation not only from the Indian but from the European point of view, for, as he said later—'My experience has shown me that we win justice quickest by rendering justice to the other party'.[25] What he won on this occasion was misrepresentation in the press and a near lynching by a rabble of white men on the day of his return to Durban. He had anticipated something of the kind and talked about it with the captain of his ship. 'I hope God will give me the courage and the sense', he said, 'to forgive them and to refrain from bringing them to law. I have no anger against them. I am only sorry for their ignorance and their narrowness. I know that they sincerely believe that what they are doing today is right and proper. I have no reason therefore to be angry with them.'[26]

327

Already he was discovering the principle of self-suffering, which lay at the root of his technique of non-violence; but ten years were still to pass before he discovered and employed the technique itself. Meanwhile, he found himself more frequently at odds with his fellow Indians, whom he was trying to convert to habits of cleanliness and good sanitation, than with the Europeans. These were the years in which he was moulding his personal life to the rules of chastity, poverty and menial service. His political ideas remained extremely simple; as a loyal subject of the British Empire he felt that he had duties to perform as well as rights to claim and on the outbreak of war in 1899 he organised an Indian ambulance corps and served with it under fire around Spion Kop. After that he spent a year or two in India, where Gokhale became his mentor in the movement for national freedom. Yet the most important years of his South African apprenticeship still lay ahead of him. At the end of 1902 he was summoned back to prepare a brief on the Indian claims and present it to Joseph Chamberlain. That commitment led him on to others and ultimately to his conflict with Smuts.

For some years to come it was in the Transvaal rather than Natal that the Indians felt themselves to be most damaged in their material interests and self-respect. As has been seen earlier, the British government had addressed strong protests to President Kruger's government against its treatment of the Queen's Indian subjects resident in the Transvaal; but after it had won the war it permitted Lord Milner's government to treat them in precisely the same way. Inspired by Gandhi, the Indians protested against this breach of faith. 'What the Indians pray for is very little. They admit the British race should be the dominant race in South Africa. They ask for no political power. They admit the principle of restricting the influx of cheap labour, no matter from what source it may come. All they ask for is freedom for those that are now settled and those that may be allowed to come in future to trade, to move about, and to hold landed property without any hindrance save the ordinary legal requirements. And they ask for abrogation of legislation that imposes disabilities on them because they wear a brown skin.'[27] They asked, in fact, that the British administration in the Transvaal should make good the professions and the promises of the British government. Lord Milner, Lord Selborne and other high officials admitted that these promises had been made but argued that it would be folly to fulfil them: for what future would the Transvaal have if it were given over to 'a horde' of Asiatics?[28]

So the laws of the old Republic were kept on the statute book and enforced against the Indians with an efficiency which had never been known in republican times. Their enforcement was entrusted to a specially created Asiatic Department, from which emerged in 1906 a new code of extreme stringency. It was embodied in the Asiatic Law Amendment Ordinance, named by the Indians 'the Black Ordinance'. Its purpose was to close the Transvaal against new Indian immigrants and to clear it of all Indians illegally resident there; its method was to compel every Indian to take out a new certificate of registration, to carry it on his person and to produce it on the demand of any official or policeman. This code was far more stringent, both in its detailed provisions and in the penalties which it imposed, than the pass laws imposed upon the African population or the drastic laws directed against criminal tribes in India. This, at least, was Gandhi's belief: 'I have never known legislation of this nature', he declared, 'being directed against free men in any part of the world.'[29]

A few months earlier, Gandhi had once again been demonstrating his loyalty to the British Crown by serving with an Indian ambulance unit in the so-called Zulu rebellion; but the manner in which the rebellion was put down impressed upon him (as it did, for that matter, upon Merriman and Smuts)* the distinction between the principles and the perversions of British justice. Gandhi by now was in the frame of mind to assert the right of resistance against unjust laws. This was revolutionary doctrine; but not of the classical English stamp, for Gandhi made a distinction between the right of resistance and the right of rebellion. This distinction found expression in the fourth resolution passed by a representative meeting of Indians on 11 September 1906. All those present pledged themselves under oath, as individuals and as a body, 'not to submit to the Ordinance in the event of its becoming law in the teeth of their opposition and to suffer all the penalties attaching to such non-submission'.[30]

'Not to submit': these words have the ring of revolution. 'To suffer': these words proclaim a new revolutionary technique. It was a technique which Europeans would find hard to understand until it had demonstrated its efficacy in action. A benevolent magnate of

* See p. 224 above.

Johannesburg, Mr Hoskens, revealed the depth of European mis-understanding at a public meeting which he called on the Indians' behalf. Introducing Gandhi to the meeting, he declared that the Indians had had recourse to 'passive resistance' because they had no other means of resistance. They had no arms. They had no votes. They were few in number. They were weak. They had taken to passive resistance as the weapon of the weak.... Gandhi listened with astonishment to this travesty of his thought and instead of delivering the speech which he had prepared stood up to contradict his chair-man. He denied that the Indians were passive. He denied that they were weak. They were active and strong. The force which they pro-posed to use was the strongest force of all. Gandhi called it 'soul force' and contrasted it with that inferior instrument of conflict, 'brute force'. He felt that the words 'passive resistance' were apt to give rise to a terrible misunderstanding and looked about for a better name for the non-violent use of force. He opened a competition in his newspaper and awarded the prize to a competitor who proposed the name *sadagraha*. He changed this into *Satyagraha*, which for him contained the following meaning: 'Truth (Satya) implies love, and firmness (agraha) engenders and therefore serves as a synonym for force. I thus began to call the Indian movement "Satyagraha", that is to say, the Force which is born of Truth and Love or non-violence.'[31]

In September 1906 Gandhi still hoped to forestall the need for non-violent resistance. He persuaded the Indian community to appoint him, and one other representative, as a deputation to the Secretary of State in London, where he hoped to get the Black Ordinance disallowed on the ground of racial discrimination. At Madeira, on the return journey, he received a cable informing him that his deputation had been successful. He soon realised that it was only an empty success. The Transvaal was on the eve of receiving self-government, and Lord Elgin had made it clear to the political leaders there that, while he must advise Her Majesty to disallow the Ordinance, he would not feel bound to give the same advice if they passed through their new parliament a bill precisely in the same terms. And so it came to pass. Within a few months, the Black Ordinance became the Black Act, with force of law as from 1 July 1907.[32]

The time for registration under the Act, after being extended once or twice, was fixed finally as 30 November. When that day came, only about five hundred Indians had registered. An appreciable number, so the officials believed, knowing themselves to be illegally domiciled in the Transvaal, had slipped quietly across the border; but this still left approximately nine thousand, who by their own deliberate action—or inaction—had set themselves against the law. What could the government do with these people? It had assumed the legal power to deport them. But could it deport them all? Or could it prosecute them in the courts and have them all sent to prison? Or could it send the heads of families to prison and leave the women and children unprovided for?

It fell to Smuts to answer these questions. There were other members of the government—Botha, as Prime Minister, or Jacob de Villiers, as Attorney-General—whose responsibility might have been thought equal to his; but he took the main burden upon his own shoulders. He thought it would be best 'to strike at the head, not at the tail', that is to say, to take legal action against the leaders; but before committing himself to this policy he wanted to explore the possibilities of compromise. With this purpose in view he sought the advice of Lord Selborne, whose responsibility for the trouble was at least equal to his own, seeing that the Black Act simply repeated Lord Selborne's own Ordinance of the previous year.

Lord Selborne confessed that he had never anticipated such passionate resistance from the Indians. It filled him with foreboding, because the coloured people and the educated natives were watching the struggle, realising 'that they have an instrument in their hands—that is, combination and passive resistance—of which they had not previously thought'. For this reason alone he believed it essential to restore the authority of the law as quickly as possible. But how? He drew a distinction between the essential parts of the legislation, which must be preserved at all costs, and the inessential ones, on which compromise might be possible. The restriction of future immigration was essential; it was, indeed, 'the whole object of the legislation'. Registration was equally essential, because the government could not control Asiatic immigration unless it knew how many Asiatics were already in the Transvaal. The methods of registration, however, were merely a matter of convenience: fingerprinting, for example, could be dispensed with provided an alternative method of identification could be discovered. It followed from all this that the government should be ready to amend, but not to repeal its legislation. Lord Selborne thus continued—

But the Asiatics, through the mouth of Mr Gandhi, demand the total repeal of the existing Act. This, in my opinion, would never be permitted by Parliament, and ought never to be permitted by Parliament. The Asiatic is a very bad person from whom to run away, and I do not think that any such repeal would be consistent with the self-respect of the Government or of Parliament. But, if the Asiatics are, at the last, prepared to be reasonable, then I would make the way easy for them. The one simple object of the Government is to get them registered so that the Government may control future immigration. I would advise the Government to accept any proposals which the Asiatics may make which *really* would effect this object, even should it require a supplementary Act on this subject next Session. But the movement must come from the Asiatics to the Government, and it must come in a form which the Asiatics cannot afterwards repudiate. It must be on paper and vouched for by men who undoubtedly represent the Asiatics.[33]

Similar advice came to Smuts from Sir Richard Solomon, the Agent General in London, who took very seriously the protests of the government of India and the outspoken comments of the British press. Nor was he clear in his conscience that they were undeserved.

You have great strength [he told Smuts], and I am sure you will use it wisely with every regard for the feelings of these unfortunate Asiatics, keeping only in view the main object of the law, that is to have the Asiatics in the Colony registered in such a way as to prevent evasions of the Immigration Act.... When I read over the Act I can't help thinking that it might have been toned down a bit without affecting its main object, but it was initiated and drafted by officials (Lionel Curtis etc.)* who though very clever do not understand human nature and can therefore never be legislators.

This, by and large, was the opinion of Winston Churchill, who as Under-Secretary of State gave Solomon his views for transmission to Smuts.[34]

It was also the opinion of Merriman, who protested that he had no love for Asiatics; but neither could he abide petty persecution.

Rightly or wrongly [he wrote], a certain number of these people have been allowed to settle down, acquire property and carry on their avocations. Is it worth while to harry them by imposing what may be considered vexatious regulations, provided that you can obtain a registration that will secure you against any further influx by other means? Does it not savour of the yellow cap of the Jew, or the harrying of the Moriscoes by Spain?...If you persist, as you are entitled to do, you will succeed, but

* Curtis was head of the Asiatic Department.

I much fear that you will alienate the bulk of liberal opinion in England, you will give the Imperial government a most serious blow in her most vital part—India, and you will above all furnish a pretext for a great deal of mischievous interference in native matters.... Would there be any loss of dignity on your part if you said that in deference to the expressed wish of Gt Britain and solely with a view to *her* interests you would withdraw the obnoxious provisions on the clear understanding that you would be protected or would be allowed to protect yourselves against any further influx and that measures for the strictest registration would be carried out?[35]

This advice was cogent and Smuts was ready to follow it, if and when the opportunity should arise; but, in the meantime, he felt bound to uphold the law as it stood. In Christmas week, 1907, Gandhi and some other prominent Indians were summoned before the magistrate's court to show cause why, having failed to apply for registration under the law, they should not be ordered to leave the Transvaal within a certain period, which in Gandhi's case was defined as fourteen days. On 10 January 1908 Gandhi was again called upon to appear in court to receive sentence. 'I had some slight feeling of awkwardness', he wrote later, 'due to the fact that I was standing as an accused in the very Court where I had often appeared as counsel. But I well remember that I considered the former role as far more honourable than the latter, and did not feel the slightest hesitation in entering the prisoner's box.' Much to his disappointment, he received a lighter sentence—two months' simple imprisonment— than the majority of his companions.[36]

By the end of January 1907 about one hundred and fifty Satyagrahis were in prison. Meanwhile, Mr Albert Cartwright, editor of the *Transvaal Leader*, had been keeping touch both with Gandhi and Smuts, in the hope of bringing them to a compromise. In a speech at Pretoria on 28 January, Smuts foreshadowed an amicable settlement. Next day he received a letter, also dated 28 January, from Gandhi and two of his associates.[37]

Our opposition [they wrote] has never been directed so much against the fingerprint requirements Regulations under the Act, in as far as such fingerprints were deemed necessary for the identification of Asiatics who could not very well be otherwise identified, as against the element of compulsion in the Act itself. On that ground we have repeatedly offered to undergo voluntary registration if the Act were repealed. And even now at this late hour we would urge on the Government the adoption as far as possible of the course more than once proposed by us. We recognise that it is not possible during the Parliamentary recess to repeal the Act, and we have noted your repeated public declarations that there is no likelihood of the Act being repealed. We would, however, point out that the periods fixed for registration by the various Government notices have expired and that therefore any registration would necessarily have to be that of a voluntary nature which we originally prayed the Government to concede. Under these circumstances we should once more respectfully suggest to the Government that all Asiatics over the age of 16 years should be allowed within a certain limited period, say, three months, to register themselves, and that to all who so register the Act be not applied, and that the Government take whatever steps they deem advisable to legalise such registration. Such mode of registration should apply to those also who being out of the Colony may return and otherwise possess right of re-entry.

The letter contained some further suggestions about the details of registration, including the exemption of certain classes from finger-printing. These suggestions never became matter for controversy, because Smuts felt able to accept them and, if anything, to improve upon them, to the advantage of the Indians. However, the passage quoted above did very soon become relevant to an accusation brought against Smuts of breaking faith with Gandhi. It was said then, and has been said many times since, that he pledged himself to repeal the Black Act. It should be noted, therefore, that the signatories of the letter of 28 January never brought themselves to the point of demanding that the Act be repealed; on the contrary, they took note of the 'repeated public declarations' which Smuts had made about the unlikelihood of its being repealed. Certainly, no promise of repeal was contained in the letter of reply sent to them on Smuts's behalf on the following day. The letter took note that they had stated the legal position correctly and pointed out 'that the Colonial Secretary can only accept registration in a form similar to that prescribed by Act and subject as regards the regulations to the small alterations you mention, and lay the matter before Parliament at its next session'.[38]

There is, therefore, no evidence in the official record to support the contention that Gandhi asked for the repeal of the Act and that Smuts promised to repeal it. The evidence is plainly to the contrary. However, the exchange of letters on 28 and 29 January was the prelude to a personal meeting between Smuts and Gandhi on the 30th. No record was taken of what the two men said to each other; but they got on well together and Gandhi left the meeting not only a free, but also a happy man. He called his people together and told them that he had reached an honourable understanding with General Smuts, that the Black Act would be repealed and that the Indians could now register themselves voluntarily without suffering any stigma.

There were some people, particularly among the small community of Pathans, who could not understand this sudden change of direction. They felt that Gandhi had been fooled, if not bought, by Smuts. On the morning of 10 February, the day appointed for registration, Gandhi was set upon and severely beaten by two Pathans as he was leading his people to the Registration Office. He was taken to the house of Mr Doke, a Baptist clergyman and one of his staunchest supporters amongst the Europeans. There he had the registration official brought to him so that he might still be the first to register.* By and large, the Indian community followed his lead, so that registration was nearly complete when the stipulated three months expired on 9 May. There still remained, however, some Indians with a pre-existing right of domicile who were absent from the Transvaal and therefore unable to register. Gandhi claimed, but Smuts denied that voluntary registration had been meant to apply to them also, irrespective of the time limit. This was not the only point of contention between Smuts and Gandhi, nor the chief one. The government introduced legislation to validate the voluntary registrations, but did not repeal the Black Act. Gandhi asserted, but Smuts denied that this was a breach of faith.

What are the rights and wrongs of this matter? As has been seen (although Gandhi did not always see it),[39] Smuts was acting in strict accord with the exchange of letters of 28 and 29 January. The only question, therefore, is whether or not he made additional promises to Gandhi at their unrecorded meeting on 30 January and at a second meeting between them four days later.[40] It seems worth while calling to witness the onlookers at the game, particularly the highly trained and critical onlookers of the Colonial Office and the India Office. The former were satisfied from the beginning that the agreement was contained in the exchange of letters. Gandhi's subsequent complaints did not impress them. In a despatch of December 1908 the Secretary of State for the Colonies declared in the most explicit

---

* He insisted, although he need not have done so under the amended regulations, on giving full fingerprints.

terms that he could see no ground at all for the accusation of a breach of faith.[41] The Secretary of State for India did not challenge this conclusion. His attitude was most clearly stated in a letter of 3 September 1908 from the India Office to the Colonial Office.

With regard to the general attitude of the Transvaal Government, I am to say that Lord Morley has not sufficient information before him to justify a decisive expression of opinion. It is of course clear that Ministers are fully entitled to abide by the letter of the documents in which the settlement of February last was embodied. At the same time it is most unfortunate that the Asiatic community in the Transvaal, together with the large and influential body of their fellow-countrymen in India who sympathise with their claims, should have formed the opinion that the Transvaal Government have failed to observe the spirit of that agreement. Lord Morley must not be understood to support that opinion, but, so far as he is in a position to judge, the misunderstanding on the part of the Indian community is quite genuine.[42]

'Misunderstanding' is the appropriate description of what occurred. A complete explanation of how it occurred is probably beyond attainment, and would in any case demand a far more detailed study of the course of events than is possible here. However, Smuts himself provided a useful clue in a statement which he made in parliament on the second reading of the bill to legalise the voluntary registrations. He said that he had more than once discussed with Gandhi the possibility of bringing the whole machinery of registration under the Immigration Act (no. 15 of 1907). By this procedure, the 'Black Act' (no. 2 of 1907) would have been repealed and there would have been no need to introduce a special bill to legalise the voluntary registrations. Smuts made no promise to follow this procedure; but he did tell Gandhi that he had it in mind as a possibility. Gandhi may have interpreted this statement as a promise. As things turned out, Smuts got so far as having a bill drafted and was disappointed when he found himself unable to proceed with it. Among the obstacles which prevented him, was the opposition which arose on the Indian side to the Immigration Act itself.[43]

Gandhi and Smuts were hopelessly at cross purposes with each other. They were meeting each other for the first time. In the art of political negotiation, Smuts was already an old hand but Gandhi a novice. The two men were attracted to each other and had so many things in common—for example, their basic political loyalties and their belief in compromise, not to mention *Snell on Equity*—that one may too easily forget their differences of upbringing and outlook. They both set great store upon the virtue of keeping faith; but they would have given different definitions of what constitutes a breach of faith. Gandhi, for example, had promised his mother when he set out as a young man for London never to eat meat, and had remained uncertain for some time thereafter whether or no he was under pledge to abstain from milk and eggs as well; in the end he had resolved his doubt by applying two 'golden rules'—first, to accept the interpretation put upon a pledge by the person administering it, and, secondly, to accept the interpretation of the weaker party.[44] Smuts knew by bitter experience what it meant to be the weaker party; but, even so, he would have found Gandhi's criteria inapplicable to the conduct of public business.

Smuts accused Gandhi of submitting new demands and thereby enlarging the area of conflict. Gandhi denied the charge. Upon the evidence, his denial appears justified, and yet it is easy to see why Smuts found it unconvincing. Beneath the dispute about words there lay a conflict of principle. Gandhi envisaged a higher degree of equality in the society of South Africa than Smuts was willing or able to concede. Smuts tried to hold a static position. Speaking on the bill to validate the voluntary registrations, he declared, 'We must have some finality'. Gandhi, in contrast, was dynamic. He claimed on his people's behalf 'partnership with the white people of this country'.[45] Admittedly, he had no intention of presenting the full claim all at once. He made it a point of honour to stand firm upon the original ground of contention. But what would then become of his dynamic programme? In serene confidence, Gandhi entrusted it to the march of events and the mistakes of his enemies. He left it to the government to enlarge the area of conflict, as an unjust government was bound to do.

My experience has taught me [he wrote later] that a law of progression applies to every righteous struggle. But in the case of Satyagraha the law amounts to an axiom. As the Ganga advances, other streams flow into it, and hence at the mouth it grows so wide that neither bank is to be seen and a person sailing upon the river cannot make out where the river ends and the sea begins. So also as a Satyagraha struggle progresses onward, many another element helps to swell its current, and there is a constant growth in the results to which it leads. This is really inevitable, and is bound up with the first principles of Satyagraha. For in Satyagraha

22 337 HS

the minimum is also the maximum, and as it is the irreducible minimum, there is no question of retreat, and the only movement possible is an advance. In other struggles, even when they are righteous, the demand is first pitched a little higher so as to admit of future reduction, and hence the law of progression does not apply to all of them without exception. But I must explain how the law of progression comes into play when the minimum is also the maximum as in Satyagraha. The Ganga does not leave its course in search of tributaries. Even so does the Satyagrahi not leave his path which is sharp as the sword's edge. But as the tributaries spontaneously join the Ganga as it advances, so it is with the river that is Satyagraha.[46]

There was little chance that Smuts, or for that matter any other politician of western upbringing, would understand reflections such as these without first getting to know the man who made them. Smuts called Gandhi 'cunning'.[47] As will appear below, the time was to come when he would discover the inappropriateness of that epithet.

Similarly, the time was to come when Gandhi would have second thoughts about Smuts. In 1908 he accused him of committing 'a breach of faith'; but twenty years later he printed that phrase with a question-mark after it. It is worth while quoting in full the sentences which record his retrospective doubts:

Even today, I look upon the incident as a breach of faith from the Indian community's standpoint. However, I have placed a mark of interrogation after the phrase, as in point of fact the General's action did not perhaps amount to an intentional breach of faith. It could not be described as a breach of faith if the intention was absent. My experience of General Smuts in 1913–14 did not then seem bitter and does not seem so to me today when I can think of the past events with greater detachment. It is quite possible that in behaving to the Indians as he did in 1908 General Smuts was not guilty of a deliberate breach of faith.[48]

But at the time Gandhi felt no doubt at all that Smuts had deceived him and thereby had given him good cause for renewing the conflict. It flared up dramatically on the afternoon of 16 August 1908, when more than two thousand Indians assembled under Gandhi's leadership in the grounds of the Hamidia Mosque at Johannesburg and flung their certificates of registration into fires that had been lit in two immense African cauldrons. Battle was joined again that day. It was destined to continue for the next six years.

As one studies the unfolding conflict from 1908 until 1914, one has the feeling that Gandhi could see in advance what course it would follow, whereas Smuts, time and time again, was taken by surprise. The government did not reply to the dramatic act of resistance of 16 August; it refrained from arresting Indians who had burnt their certificates of registration. But it could not refrain from arresting the Satyagrahis who chose deliberately to challenge the Immigrants Restriction Act. Gandhi had made careful selection of the challengers—all respectable residents of Natal who, for one reason or another, had a claim in equity for admission to the Transvaal but were excluded under the law.

The Government would become an object of ridicule if it allowed such a large troop to enter the Transvaal, and was therefore bound to arrest them. So they were arrested, and on August 18, 1908, brought before the Magistrate who ordered them to leave the Transvaal within seven days. They disobeyed the order of course, were rearrested at Pretoria on the 28th and deported without trial. They re-entered the Transvaal on the 31st and finally on September 8 were sentenced at Volksrust to a fine of fifty pounds or three months' imprisonment with hard labour. Needless to say, they cheerfully elected to go to gaol.[49]

Indians in the Transvaal were not content to allow their friends in Natal to have the monopoly of resistance and suffering but looked about for ways and means of breaking the law and getting themselves into gaol. Before long more than seventy Satyagrahis, Gandhi amongst them, were serving prison sentences, while others were being deported to neighbouring territories and even—illegally, as it turned out—to India.

So the struggle continued with its ups and downs while the white South Africans were drafting the constitution of the Union. In the second half of 1909, when the delegation of the National Convention went to London, Gandhi, having served his prison sentence, also went there as leader of a two-man deputation whose small voice, he feared, was likely to be drowned 'in the loud roar of British and Boer lions'. Nevertheless, he had the support of many prominent people, including Lord Ampthill, an ex-Governor of Madras, and was able to exert strong pressure, direct or indirect, upon Botha and Smuts. They, for their part, were anxious to get themselves in the clear with the British government and British public opinion. After consultation with Sir Richard Solomon,[50] Smuts decided that some substantial concessions could be made to the Indian point of view, saving always the main principle of immigration restriction. These concessions satisfied Gandhi's fellow delegate, but not Gandhi. By now, Ganga had been joined by many tributaries as it flowed towards the sea.[51]

Gandhi had begun to see his South African battle in the wider perspective of the Indian national struggle. On the return voyage to Cape Town in November 1909 he composed his pamphlet, *Hind Swaraj*, and from that time onwards he maintained close and continuous contact with the Indian nationalists, above all with Gokhale. Meanwhile, his diminished band of Satyagrahis carried on the fight with undiminished fortitude, year in year out. Life for many of them had lost almost all regularity except the movement in and out of gaol, with the result that it became impossible for them to earn a continuous livelihood. Gandhi solved this problem with the aid of one of his European supporters, a well-to-do German South African named Kallenbach, who gave him the use of a farm about twenty miles from Johannesburg. There he gathered his Satyagrahis into a community of mutual aid and simple living which he named Tolstoy Farm.

As the months went by life on Tolstoy Farm fell into a peaceful routine which grew ever more remote from the exciting drama of defiance and repression. Enemies or doubting friends of the Satyagrahis said that they were finding their cooperative commonwealth too comfortable; but the real reason for the *détente* was different. Smuts was striving hard for a legislative settlement acceptable to Gandhi.[52] Moreover, he was himself beginning to acquire some Gandhian skills and was training his officials and police in the art of *not* getting Indians into gaol. From Gandhi's point of view no development could have been more unwelcome than this, for he knew that his movement would wither away if it ceased to grow. The time came when his force of Satyagrahis fluctuated between a higher limit of sixty-six and a lower one of sixteen. He needed some new and exciting issue to arouse enthusiasm among the masses, but his principles forbade him to manufacture one: in Satyagraha, the minimum must also be the maximum; a deliberate extension of the conflict beyond the objectives professed at the beginning would be a violation of truth.

However, he held that his rule of self-restraint would cease to be binding should the government on its side violate truth by some new act of wrong. This, in his view, was what happened in 1912. The incident occurred in a changing historical context, namely, the steady advance both of South Africa and India towards a position wherein they might be said to have international relations with each other. The advance was still masked, on the Indian side particularly, by the constitutional forms of Imperial sovereignty; but the surge of nationalistic feeling was already so powerful that the Viceroy found himself compelled to protest against the disabilities imposed upon Indians overseas, especially in South Africa. In 1912 it was agreed between the governments of the Union and of India that S. K. Gokhale, the respected leader of moderate Indian nationalism and a member of the Viceroy's Legislative Council, should visit South Africa to study the condition of the Indians there.

Gokhale met a good reception everywhere, from the white people as well as the Indians, and on the eve of his return home he held constructive talks with the government. Their sequel was legislation introduced into parliament early the next year to transfer the regulation of Indian affairs from the Provinces to the Union and at the same time to rationalise and humanise the system.[53] The Transvaal's Black Act, which had been the original occasion of Satyagraha, disappeared at long last. The power to restrict Asian immigration was to be based explicitly and exclusively on economic and social grounds. All this, surely, was a great step forward in removing the causes of conflict? Gandhi would not admit it. By the mere process of consolidating provincial legislation, he argued, the parliament of the Union was committing new aggressions: for example, although in practice it left the Indians of the Free State in precisely the same position as before, it was putting the stamp of national endorsement upon their disabilities. But the Indians of the Free State were a mere handful, and the legalistic argument which Gandhi advanced on their behalf was unlikely to arouse the masses. Gandhi needed a slogan which would strike right home to mass emotions. He found it in the discriminatory £3 tax imposed upon the Indians of Natal nearly twenty years earlier.

Gandhi had not felt justified hitherto in making the £3 tax an objective of his campaign, for that would have taken him beyond 'the maximum' which he had stated. However, he now convinced himself that the government itself had thrown the tax into the arena of conflict. Smuts, he declared, had promised Gokhale that the tax would be repealed. He had broken his promise, just as he had broken his promise in 1908 to repeal the Black Act.

In the ensuing controversy, there were strong differences of emphasis in the statements issued on the one side by Smuts and Botha, and on the other side by Gokhale; but there was sufficient agreement on the facts to make possible a reconstruction of what probably happened. Smuts said:

Government never gave such promise as Gokhale alleges, either to Gokhale or anybody, anywhere. Gokhale, at interview with some members of Government, made strong point of repeal of £3 tax in Natal. Government replied that £3 tax was unimportant from revenue point of view, but was imposed as matter of policy in Natal. Government promised to consult members Parliament Natal, and if they had no objection on grounds of policy, Government would take question of repeal into favourable consideration. Government carried out their promise by consulting Natal members, majority of whom objected to repeal of tax otherwise than as affecting women and children....

Botha declared that he, Fischer and Smuts had all taken part in the interview with Gokhale and that 'he agreed with and endorsed every word spoken by General Smuts in regard to that interview and in regard to what took place'.

Gokhale's considered summing up of the controversy contained the following passage.

I was assured that the Government realised the iniquity of the £3 licence Tax and that from a financial point of view its proceeds were negligible, and that the earliest opportunity will be taken of abolishing it. On my asking for the authority to announce this, I was told that it was necessary for the Ministers to mention the matter to Natal members, and I should, therefore, merely announce in general terms that the Ministers had promised their most favourable consideration to my representations in the matter and that I had every confidence that the tax would be repealed in the new Parliament.

Gokhale went on to give his own explanation of the ensuing anticlimax: the government, he believed, would have taken prompt action to repeal the tax, had it not felt compelled to refute the accusations of General Hertzog, who was denouncing it for truckling to the Indians and for submitting to Imperial dictation.[54]

It is quite clear from the foregoing that Smuts and his colleagues, in their interview with Gokhale, aroused expectations which they failed subsequently to fulfil. It is equally clear that they stopped short of giving a binding pledge to repeal the £3 tax. As Gandhi himself put the matter later, Gokhale, when he left the interview, 'supposed' that the tax would be repealed. Between a supposition and a pledge there is a deep gap. But, at the time, Gandhi felt no doubt that a pledge had been given and broken. The *élite* whom he had been training at Tolstoy Farm were ready for action. The masses were ready to follow him. He launched his great attack.

It was not only an attack against the £3 tax. The Supreme Court of the Cape Province had recently delivered a judgment which had the effect, so the Indians believed, of invalidating Indian marriages and bastardising Indian children wholesale. 'As if unseen by anyone', Gandhi wrote later, 'God was preparing the ingredients for the Indians' victory and demonstrating still more clearly the injustices of the Europeans in South Africa.'[55] With a brilliant mastery of tactics, Gandhi chose a select band of women to lead his forces into action. The women aroused the Indian coalminers at Newcastle in Natal and they came out on strike. The mine-owners cut off their water and light. Gandhi arrived on the scene and gathered them by thousands into an open camp. But how could he feed them? He solved this problem by passing it on to the prison authorities. In the Transvaal they would be illegal immigrants; Gandhi organised them as an army of 'pilgrims' and marched them across the border. There the government arrested them, as it was bound to do.

Gandhi himself was arrested on 8 December and sentenced a week later to three months' imprisonment; but he felt confident that the government would soon be forced to yield. By now, fifty thousand Indians were eager candidates for imprisonment. As Gandhi put it later: 'The Union Government had not the power to keep thousands of innocent men in gaol. The Viceroy would not tolerate it, and all the world was waiting to see what General Smuts would do.'[56] The Viceroy's protest on behalf of India was prompt, public and emphatic, and the Union government could see no answer to it except 'in the dignity of silence'.[57] On 18 December Gandhi was released from gaol and Smuts announced the appointment of a commission to inquire into Indian grievances. Gandhi, however, denounced the commission because it contained no representative of the Indian community. He boycotted its proceedings and declared his intention of starting a new march of Satyagrahis.

To Smuts, the situation must have been looking more hopeless than ever, when an offer of help reached him from an unexpected quarter. It will be recalled that Emily Hobhouse had come to South

Africa to unveil the monument to the victims of the concentration camps, but had collapsed on her journey from Cape Town to Bloemfontein.

Probably an invalid like myself [she wrote to him on 29 December], who has hardly come back from the brink of the grave, ought in your opinion to lie quiescent and not mix in public affairs. But somehow I was not born that way and if once one has started a public conscience one can no more silence that than one can a private conscience.

And we women, you know, *are* developing public consciences at a surprising pace. Well dear Oom Jannie this is my excuse for invading your New Year's peace with a political letter, on a subject that is only my business in the sense it is everybody's and upon which therefore I should not presume (since you are a Minister) to write to you, had it not been that Gandhi has *asked* me to do so and that gives a sort of right to do what might otherwise be deemed interference, were we not such old friends.... Now, dear Oom, having thus cleared the ground and defined our mutual attitudes, can't we do something to adjust this matter, so that I may go hence feeling that all is well and at peace in South Africa....You see Jan. 15 is the date now proposed for another march. *Before then* some way should be found of giving private assurance to the leaders that satisfaction is coming to them. Their grievance is really *moral* not material and so, having all the power of the *spiritual* behind him, he (Gandhi) and you are like Mrs Pankhurst and McKenna and *never never never* will governmental physical force prevail against a great moral and spiritual upheaval. Wasted time and wasted energy dear Oom Jannie....You see the gravity of the situation is that India keeps it going with her money and *will* till all handle for doing so is withdrawn, because she is using you or rather the position here as a convenient whip to beat the *old* horse with. Not being South African or Indian but in fullest sympathy with both it just struck me, since Gandhi asked (and the name of Hobhouse is so reverenced in India) that I might be of some use, so use me or refuse me or abuse me just as pleases you dear Oom. I am too old and benumbed to mind throwing myself down as a paving stone and being trodden upon as the result.

I do so as Gandhi has asked me to do what I can....[58]

Whether or no it was Miss Hobhouse that brought them together, Gandhi and Smuts met a few days later and began the negotiations which led to a settlement. Gandhi made about this time a public gesture of good will by calling off the march of his Satyagrahis, so as not to embarrass the government at a time when it had on its hands a great strike of European miners and railwaymen. Smuts made it clear to Gandhi that he proposed to work for a complete and permanent settlement, using the commission on Indian grievances as leverage. This time, he was determined, there must be no imprecision, no mental reservations or misunderstandings on either side, but everything agreed between them must be tested word by word to make sure that their language was in complete accord with their thought. While the commission was doing its work they kept close touch with each other and at the end of June they accepted its main recommendations as the basis of a settlement. By the Indian Relief Act which passed quickly through parliament in July 1914 the £3 tax was abolished and the validity of Indian marriages was affirmed. Other matters were left to administrative action, on the understanding that the 'vested rights' of the Indian community would be maintained.[59]

Gandhi did not accept this settlement in final satisfaction of all the just demands of his people; on the contrary, he gave notice that they would have other objectives to strive for, including franchise rights, at some future time. He did, however, agree that his own claims and those of the Satyagrahis had been fully and fairly met. He felt that he had finished his work in South Africa and sailed for England on his way to India on the eve of the outbreak of war.

'The saint has left our shores,' wrote Smuts, 'I sincerely hope for ever.'[60] And so it proved to be. Yet Gandhi's separation from South Africa did not involve a severance of the ties that had been so strangely and strongly knit between Smuts and himself. As the years went by he found himself thinking of his old enemy with affection; he used that word in his letters and there can be no doubt of his sincerity. He had never imputed racial prejudice to Smuts nor underrated the political pressures which limited his freedom of action. Probably he received information about the part which Smuts had played in 1917 when the question of granting commissions to Indians came before the War Cabinet, and of the words in which he recalled that episode two years later in Durban: 'I strongly supported the proposals for granting commissions to Indians. When it was pointed out that this would create an anomalous position and that there might be a possibility of Europeans being placed under Indians, I replied: "Why not, I would be proud to serve under an Indian officer, if he were able."'[61] A few years later, when the grievances of the Indians were being ventilated in the Imperial Conference, Gandhi received a letter from Smuts explaining, if not justifying, the line of argument which he felt compelled to follow:

When I was about the same time as you studying in England, I had no race prejudice or colour prejudice against your people. In fact, if we had known each other we should have been friends. Why is it then that now we have become rivals we have conflicting interests? It is not colour prejudice or race prejudice, though some of our people do ignorantly talk in those terms, but then there is one thing which I want you to recognise. It is this. I may have no racial legislation, but how will you solve the difficulty about the fundamental difference of our cultures? Let alone the question of superiority, there is no doubt that your civilisation is different from ours. Ours must not be overwhelmed by yours. That is why we have to go in for legislation which must in effect put disabilities upon you.

Gandhi's comment on this plea was characteristic of him: 'I understood what he said.... If, therefore, we wanted to live in South Africa we must adopt their standard of life, so long as it was not against morality.'[62]

The temptation must be resisted of anticipating too much the story of tension and friendship between Gandhi and Smuts in later years. There is, however, one episode of the Gandhi–Irwin discussions of 1930 which casts retrospective light upon the seven-years conflict between Gandhi and Smuts in South Africa. Gandhi had demanded drastic restrictions upon the activities of the police, and the Viceroy was expecting trouble when he rejected the demand, as he felt bound to do, on the plain argument of public security. But Gandhi surprised him—'Ah,' he exclaimed, 'now Your Excellency treats me like General Smuts treated me in South Africa. You do not deny that I have an equitable claim, but you advance unanswerable reasons from the point of view of Government why you cannot meet it. I drop the demand.'[63]

Smuts never quite learnt to take Gandhi for granted nor to disentangle the feelings of fascination, admiration and irritation which Gandhi's words and actions aroused in him at different times. The nearest he came to a studied estimate of him was in 1939, when he contributed an essay on *Gandhi's Political Method* to a commemorative volume celebrating the Mahatma's seventieth birthday.[64] The essay offers some penetrating observations upon 'the principle of suffering' which lay at the root of Gandhi's technique, but the following quotation is taken from the autobiographical passage with which it opens—

It was my fate to be the antagonist of a man for whom even then I had the highest respect.... I must frankly admit that his activities at that time were very trying to me. Together with other South African leaders I was then busily engaged on the task of welding the old Colonies into a unified State.... It was a colossal work which took up every moment of my time. Suddenly in the midst of all those engrossing preoccupations Gandhi raised a most troublesome issue. We had a skeleton in our cupboard....

Smuts went on to describe the Indian grievances and the technique which Gandhi had invented for getting them redressed. He told the story of their struggle and of the little personal touches that kept it sweet—for example, of Gandhi setting to work in prison to make him the pair of sandals which he had worn 'for many a summer since'. Those sandals! Gandhi's biographers like to tell how Smuts returned them to the Mahatma on the occasion of his seventieth birthday, but all he sent was a photograph of them; they were still 'a treasured relic' in his possession on that day, nine years later, when he heard the news of Gandhi's death and exclaimed: 'A prince of men has passed away and we grieve with India in her irreparable loss.'[65]

CHAPTER 17

SCHISM

THE distinction that needs sometimes to be made between State-building and nation-building found expression, round about 1860, in the aphorism of Massimo D'Azeglio, a great Italian patriot: 'Now that we have made Italy,' he exclaimed, 'we must set to work to make the Italians.'

A South African patriot, at the time of Union, could hardly have formulated so succinct a programme, for he would have been compelled first of all to face the question, 'Make whom into what?' No agreement existed as yet about either the membership or the character of the future South African nation. The most ardent advocates of racial impartiality, such as W. P. Schreiner, took it for granted that a long time must elapse before the *disjecta membra* of the territorial population could be gathered into a single body national. Across the barrier of colour, no leader had arisen as yet whose programme could be called national, rather than communal. Gandhi's nationalism—if a man of such universal humanity can even be called a nationalist—was Indian rather than South African and in his long debate with Smuts he propounded no theory or programme of South African solidarity in which 'the negroes' (as he called the Native Africans) would acquire the same equality of status as he envisaged, if only in the long run, for the Indians. *Mutatis mutandis*, the same was true of Abdurahman, the most prominent spokesman of the Cape Coloureds, and of Jabavu, the most prominent spokesman of the Natives; both of them spoke only for their own communities. In this situation, the European masters of South Africa might well have regarded *divide et impera* as a superfluous maxim. They might well have considered their non-European dependants to be sufficiently self-divided by their separate cultural inheritances and sufficiently remote from modern conceptions of nationality. A few thoughtful politicians, it is true, expressed uneasiness about the future of the Coloured people, arguing that it must be moulded, for reasons both of prudence and justice, into the European rather than the Native

348

form of life.* This reservation apart, almost everybody took it for granted that South African nationhood was for Europeans only.

The Europeans, however, found themselves unable to formulate a definition of South African nationhood upon which they could all agree. They did not, at the outset, search self-consciously for an agreed definition; but they soon discovered the difference which exists between a unitary constitution and a united nation. Within a few years of Union, the united front of white South Africans, to which universal lip-service had been paid at the National Convention, was rent and riven.

The rift, to begin with, was between two Afrikaner leaders, Botha and Hertzog. Smuts, it will be recalled, had been Botha's intermediary in trying to persuade Hertzog to accept a judicial rather than a cabinet appointment, and had subsequently held 'Hertzogism' responsible for Botha's defeat at Pretoria East and for the other disappointments of the first Union elections.† Here was a poor look out for harmony within the first government of the Union. The opposition was quick to probe the sensitive spot and on 24 November 1910 Colonel Crewe, the Unionist member for East London, introduced a motion alleging an incompatibility between the Free State Education Act and the principles of freedom and equality of opportunity embodied in the new constitution. In the retrospect of half a century, Crewe's argument appears completely untenable, for nothing could have been better designed to safeguard the future of the English language in South Africa than the compulsory bilingualism which Hertzog had at heart. The English-speaking section of those days, however, thought it a monstrous imposition that their children should be compelled to learn Dutch. Botha's political position was difficult: if he supported Hertzog, he would antagonise many of the English-speakers on whom he depended for his majority; if he supported Hertzog's opponents, he would split his Afrikaner following. He dexterously extricated himself from this dilemma by moving for the appointment of a select committee to report upon the question of bilingualism in the educational systems of the Provinces. The committee presented a majority report of seven of its members and a minority report of one (General Beyers). Neither report endorsed

* See p. 317 above for Lord Selborne's opinions about the Coloured people: they continued to win wide acceptance until after the Second World War.
† See pp. 269, 273 above.

the principle of compulsory bilingualism, although Beyers came close to doing so. The majority report recommended mother-tongue instruction up to Standard IV (with parallel use of the other language if the parents desired it) and thereafter parents' choice of the language to be taught as a subject and used as the medium of instruction. The government announced its acceptance of the majority report and parliament then approved it with only one dissentient vote. Since school education remained an affair of the Provinces, the Union government and parliament could do no more than recommend the report to them. The Transvaal immediately adopted the report and put it into effect. The other three Provinces took no action.

Hertzog had signed the majority report and voted for it in parliament; but he continued to nurse a grievance against the Transvaal on the score of its educational policy, past and present. Moreover, he showed himself profoundly suspicious of the national policies which his prime minister and his colleagues in the government were following. To begin with, he disliked their immigration policy, although he would have found difficulty in making a well-reasoned case against it. According to the census of 1911, the European population of South Africa was approximately 1,280,000 and the Native population 4,161,000; the former had increased at the rate of 14·44 per cent, the latter at the rate of 16·19 per cent since the previous census in 1904. These figures, it is true, were disputable in detail, but Botha and Smuts drew the moral from them that South Africa ought to welcome more European immigrants. Hertzog might have drawn the same moral, had there been any prospect of getting most of the immigrants from Holland, or even from Germany; but he knew that they would be predominantly of British origin. Why should a nationalist government imitate the immigration policy of Lord Milner? It would be playing the old game of British imperialism!

Not so many years had passed since Botha and Smuts had led the outcry against imperialism. It was hard for them now to have the opprobrious word flung at themselves. Did they deserve such treatment? The question cannot be answered with precision because imperialism cannot be defined with precision; it is a chameleon word which constantly changes its colour while one is looking at it. Nevertheless, it had, temporarily, a fairly precise connotation at the Imperial Conference of 1911, which Botha attended on behalf of South Africa. At this conference a plan for federating the British Empire was put forward by Sir Joseph Ward, the prime minister of New Zealand. Ward, it is true, was a muddled man who did not even understand his own argument; but Lionel Curtis, who had prompted the argument, understood it very well. His purpose was to combine Great Britain and the self-governing Dominions into an 'organic' State with a single government and parliament, speaking with a single voice on foreign policy and possessing the legal and financial power to back this policy by armed force. The idea was not a new one; it had been formulated (although never so systematically) in the latter decades of the nineteenth century and had been discussed intermittently at previous Imperial gatherings. Amongst the statesmen of the overseas Empire, Sir Wilfrid Laurier had been its most pertinacious and clear-headed opponent. He held Imperial federation to be inconsistent with the rights of self-government which Canada and her sister Dominions had inherited from the past and with the status of nationhood which was their claim upon the future.

Where did Botha and Smuts stand in this debate? The answer emerges crystal clear in the letters which Botha wrote to Smuts from London while he was attending the Imperial Conference. He wrote on 3 June: 'Just a short survey of our work. We easily quashed the Imperial Council of State. Ward, the proposer, read a three-hour speech but never got to the Council of State. In the document it was called an Imperial Parliament, above all parliaments, with 297 members of which the dominions together will have 77 and South Africa only 7 representatives—I have never heard of a more idiotic proposal and he also cut a poor figure, never studied his case and as far as I can see Lionel Curtis is really the proposer—when he was in New Zealand.'[1] On 15 June Botha made it clear that he had joined forces with Laurier to defeat the Ward–Curtis plan of Imperial federation: 'Yes, Jannie, Laurier and I have renewed our friendship, and he and I have spent last week quietly on Harcourt's country estate. Of course we talked much there. He and I agree about everything.... The Conference work is going quite well. We have destroyed root and branch the proposal for an Imperial Council of State or Parliament and we have succeeded in keeping the Conference as a round table affair. Of course, the Conservatives are dissatisfied, but all that is nothing and we have, in my opinion, done good work.'[2] Good work indeed, granted the assumption that the proper destiny for South Africa was sovereign independence!

Hertzog was destined, from 1926 onwards, to play a significant part in the transformation of the Empire into the Commonwealth. His biographers (including the latest of them, Oswald Pirow) have told the story as if the whole credit belonged to him and none of it to his predecessors. But this is quite untrue. As will be shown later, Hertzog merely dotted the *i*'s and crossed the *t*'s of a policy which Botha and Smuts had already formulated both comprehensively and in detail.* Even in the early days of Union, as appears quite clearly in the above-quoted letters, Botha and Smuts were following the path which led to the sovereign independence of South Africa; even before Union, as we have seen already in the Smuts–Merriman correspondence, they were envisaging the Commonwealth whose advent Hertzog acclaimed many years later.† To call these men Imperialists would seem to be impossible, except by ignoring the familiar categories of political science and constitutional law.

These categories, however, do not contain the whole of political reality: it is contained also in the actual policies which were pursued by the overseas members of the Empire (or Commonwealth) as they advanced along the road towards national sovereignty. There was nothing to prevent those policies bearing the isolationist, or (to adopt a word which came later into fashion) the 'neutralist' stamp. On the other hand, they might bear the stamp of cooperation. In the latter case, it would be open to any party leader of 'neutralist' inclinations to oppose cooperation and to call the cooperators by any name that seemed likely to damage them. Botha and Smuts were convinced cooperators and Hertzog began to call them Imperialists.

Merely to attend the Imperial Conference was an act of cooperation. To begin with, it made the visiting statesman a participant in the social and political round of London and the ceremonies of monarchy, which in 1911 were particularly brilliant owing to the coronation of King George V. 'Social life reaches its peak this month', wrote Botha in early June, and added '—unfortunately for us. Dinner, lunch, church service, Coronation day—all Commands in uniform and one feels so unhappy in the uniform, which is not only uncomfortable but also dear and stiff and I can tell you it is all very difficult.' Throughout the rest of the month he continued to grumble

---

* See pp. 429–32, 469, 496–7, 521–2 below. (The detailed proposals formulated by Smuts in 1923, which are in substance closely akin to the decisions of 1926, will be examined in a later volume.)   † See p. 204 above.

at the incredibly high prices of London, the discomfort of his uniform, and the seven or eight hours of purgatory which he would have to endure in Westminster Abbey. But when it was all over he felt that it had been worth while: 'The Coronation is over, and was particularly beautiful; it was brilliant in the highest degree and well regulated. I and my wife had good seats in the Abbey. The ceremony lasted seven hours. At half-past eight everyone had to be in his seat and at half-past two we came out, stiff as boards. You will understand my feelings, in a stiff heavy uniform all that time, but one must admit that they understand how to make this sort of thing beautiful, tasteful and brilliant and so orderly too....'[3] In London, the splendid ceremonial of monarchy was so appropriate that it would have seemed churlish not to enjoy it; but how would it appear when reported at second hand to Afrikaners nostalgic for the *vierkleur* and the old republican simplicities? Pomp and vain-glory of Empire!

Moreover, attendance at the Imperial Conference involved the representatives of South Africa and the other Dominions in discussions of foreign policy. In 1911 they were taken into the full confidence of the Foreign Office and the Committee of Imperial Defence. Botha found this most interesting but Hertzog would have considered it most insidious. To become the recipient of confidential information, it is true, did not create any new obligations. Asquith, Botha and the other speakers at the conference of 1911 were all agreed that the British government must continue to bear undivided responsibility for the conduct of foreign policy.[4] Consequently, it must continue to bear undivided responsibility for implementing this policy in the event of war, leaving each Dominion 'at liberty'—the words are Laurier's —'to act or not act, to interfere or not interfere, to do just as she pleases...'.[5] That doctrine, surely, ought to have satisfied Hertzog? But the freedom of decision which it ascribed to the Dominions was to a considerable degree illusory. According to the law of that time, when the King was at war, all his subjects were at war: this meant that a Dominion could not possibly be neutral; it could be at most a 'passive belligerent'. But suppose the enemy should find it convenient to wage active war against this unbellicose Dominion? Or suppose its own people, or a section of them, should catch the itch of active belligerency? Or suppose its leaders should feel themselves bound in fact, if not in form, to support a policy whose secrets they had shared in advance? All these contingencies were in the minds of Botha and the other members of the Imperial Conference of 1911. They were in the mind of Smuts, as Minister of Defence, when he studied the resolution of the Defence Conference of 1909: that 'each part of the Empire is willing to make its preparations on such lines as will enable it, should it so desire, to take its share in the general defence of the Empire'.[6] The phrase, *should it so desire*, emphasised the voluntary principle so dear to Sir Wilfrid Laurier; but this principle, if one considered it realistically, was far more apt than were the grandiose plans of the Imperial Federationists to elicit Dominion support for British wars. Here was the crux of Hertzog's complaint against Botha and Smuts. He wanted to keep South Africa aloof from the approaching war; he suspected that their policy was likely to end in participation. Perhaps it was a pity that he did not say so clearly, instead of talking in a vague way about the iniquities of imperialism.

Of course, as a member of Botha's cabinet, Hertzog was bound to keep some of his suspicions to himself and to maintain some appearance at least of solidarity with his colleagues. Even so, the tradition of the collective responsibility of the cabinet was not so firmly established in South Africa as to restrain a strong-willed minister from saying and doing many contentious things on his own account. Botha was enraged when news reached him in London that Hertzog had made a senior (and in Botha's opinion unsuitable) judicial appointment without consulting him. He was beginning to think that the same government could not contain both himself and Hertzog. The time was fast approaching when the Transvaalers would have to resign: 'I feel something is coming,' he wrote to Smuts, 'but am not yet certain what.' He had talked his troubles over with Sir Wilfrid Laurier, who was suffering similar provocation at the hands of a self-willed French Canadian, Henri Bourassa. If Bourassa were to have his way, Laurier believed, a complete cleavage would be made between the French and English sections of the Canadian nation and the prospects of the Liberal party and its unifying task in Canada would be destroyed for all time. Botha felt that much the same thing would happen in South Africa if Hertzog were to have his way.[7]

Nevertheless, on his return to South Africa, he and Hertzog patched up a truce with each other. Against all expectation, it was

Hull, not Hertzog, who caused the first open rift in the government. Hull had been a leader of the old 'Responsibles' (later called 'Nationalists') and had no quarrel at all with the government on ideological grounds; but he was a stickler for financial and constitutional propriety and thought it intolerable that Sauer, the Minister of Railways, should incur heavy expenditure without authorisation from the Treasury, or, indeed, from the cabinet. In May 1912 he handed in his resignation.

In reconstructing his cabinet, Botha shifted Sauer from Railways to Native Affairs. It looked for a time as if the cabinet would be wrecked by a mutiny of its Cape members.[8] But it was Hertzog and the Free Staters, not Sauer and the Cape contingent, who took the limelight and fired the powder. The Free Staters had found the balance of power tilted in their favour after Hull's resignation and Hertzog may well have thought that his chance had come for committing the government to the true nationalist doctrine. In a speech at Nylstroom in early October he proclaimed the doctrine to a wildly applauding Afrikaner audience. What the reaction was among English-speaking South Africans may be seen from a letter which Botha wrote to Smuts from Maritzburg on 10 October: 'The whole of Natal feels insulted by it—in newspapers, club, streets, houses or wherever one goes. There is unprecedented excitement which, as you can understand, is doing us much, very much harm. Yesterday I met our party here, and believe me they also feel so strongly that one can hardly speak to them. Whatever I say and do I get only one answer: they are regarded as uitlanders. So, Jannie old chap, I must say I have no idea why Hertzog goes so far, although I do not want to condemn him because I do not know and can also not find out from the newspapers the actual words that he has used. Is it so bad?'[9]

From the point of view of a political theorist, it might not have seemed so bad: but from Botha's point of view as prime minister and party leader it could hardly have been worse. There was nothing at all shocking in the doctrine that Hertzog preached; but the manner in which he preached it was a shock to party unity and a challenge to Botha's leadership. In the Nylstroom speech and others that followed it, Hertzog was trying to explain that South African life could flow in 'two streams' of language and culture without detriment to the bonds of territorial citizenship and political loyalty which held the Union together. Here was a valid distinction—although Hertzog did not express it clearly—between cultural nationality and political nationality, two ideas which may usefully be kept distinct upon a planet whose population has been so arranged as to debar this nation or that from possessing a territorial State all to itself. To be thus debarred is not the ultimate disaster; the Swiss, for example, have not felt it as a deprivation, but have used it as an opportunity for new experiments in civic virtue and human fraternity. Alas, in Hertzog's exposition, the spirit of fraternity was absent. He denounced his English-speaking opponents, particularly Sir Thomas Smartt, the Unionist leader, as 'foreign adventurers' and 'bastard sheep', and said that he wanted to make the Afrikaner master ('baas') in South Africa.

To be sure, Hertzog declared himself ready to accept as an Afrikaner anybody, whatever his language, who put South Africa first in his love and loyalty. This was not heresy, but orthodoxy; old Jan Hofmeyr had often said the same thing in almost the same words.* Hofmeyr, however, had said it in a tone of persuasion; whereas Hertzog appeared to be saying it in a tone of accusation. It had been Hofmeyr's purpose to widen the circle of South African patriotism; it was Hertzog's purpose to expose the unpatriotic. Hertzog won a dialectical victory against Sir Thomas Smartt, the leader of the Unionist opposition, who let himself be manœuvred into the position of putting the Empire before South Africa. Such a man, declared Hertzog, was only a 'foreign adventurer'. Yet Smartt had served South Africa faithfully.

It is widely agreed amongst psychologists that people who feel that they and their group are treated as inferiors are apt to develop emotions of aggressiveness towards the dominant group and to strive in their turn not merely for equality but for dominance. Hertzog himself, although his impulses and his tongue sometimes ran away with him, was not really aiming at Afrikaner dominance; his political record over a long period of time is sufficient proof that his aim was true equality between the two sections of the European population. There were other Afrikaners, however, who shared his impulses but not his principles. Amongst these people, his nationalistic logic could easily become the instrument of aggressive and exclusive ambitions. To put South Africa first might be a fair enough test of civic virtue; but the test could too easily be applied in a hectoring

---

* See pp. 24–5 above.

and intolerant manner that would cast an imputation of civic guilt upon the English-speaking section. Afrikaner rectitude could be taken for granted, for the Afrikaners proclaimed increasingly their complete separateness from Holland, their European motherland, in language, literature and everything else. English-speaking South Africans, however, continued to take pride in the language of Shakespeare. How then could they be wholly rooted in South African soil? How could they escape their inherited curse of a double loyalty?

Botha and Smuts believed that Campbell-Bannerman's act had redressed the verdict of the Anglo-Boer War, or had, at any rate, given full power to the South Africans themselves to redress it. Hertzog, on the other hand, at least in moments of excitement, felt himself still to be fighting the war. Botha and Smuts believed that the wounds of war, as well as the passions which had caused the war, could best be healed by emphasising the things which the two sections of the European people held in common; but Hertzog felt himself specially called to assert the rights of the section which had suffered defeat. Hertzog's quarrel was not merely with the English-speaking journalists or politicians who ignored or belittled Afrikaner claims, but with his own leader, who refrained from paying these people back in their own coin. Why should Botha conciliate them? It was his business to fight them!

The word conciliation stuck in Hertzog's throat. In a speech at De Wildt on 7 December 1912 he declared: 'I am not one of those who always talk of conciliation and loyalty: they are idle words which deceive no one. I have always said that I do not know what this conciliation means.' This angry and contemptuous thrust could have had no other target than Botha, who for so many years past had made conciliation his watchword. After the De Wildt speech, there could no longer be room for Hertzog and Botha in the same government. The crisis was precipitated by the resignation of Colonel Leuchars, the representative of Natal in the Union Cabinet. But Hertzog refused to resign. Did Botha deny, he asked, that South African interests came first? Botha did not deny it. Nor did Colonel Leuchars deny it. Then why could they not all work together, demanded Hertzog, seeing that they were all agreed that South African interests came first? The dialectical exercise might have continued interminably, had not Botha cut it short by handing in his own resignation to the Governor-General. The same day, he received the Governor-

General's invitation to form a new government. In forming it, he shed Colonel Leuchars (without any noticeable consequences) and General Hertzog—with consequences which have continued to pile up from that day to this.

The rest of the cabinet remained solid for Botha. Hertzog's own colleague from the Free State, Abraham Fischer, decided that it was his duty to remain in office. In parliament, Hertzog found only five members out of one hundred and twenty-one to support him. The parliamentary vote, however, was not a true reflection of feeling in the constituencies. The Afrikaners of the Free State rallied to Hertzog and a party congress at Bloemfontein, in March 1913, gave him a vote of confidence by 47 to 1. As the year wore on, the Hertzogite opposition to Botha found leaders beyond the borders of the Free State—Tielman Roos in the Transvaal and D. F. Malan in the Cape. At the national conference of the party at Cape Town in November 1913 the opposition to Botha mustered 90 votes out of 221. The minority decided to call a conference of their own. It met at Bloemfontein in January 1914 and founded the National party with Hertzog as its leader. And so the nationalist label, which Botha and his friends had used in the first elections of the Union, became henceforward the property of Botha's Afrikaner enemies.*

In the rapid sketch which has just been made of the emotional, ideological and party-political conflict, attention has been focused upon the two Afrikaner protagonists, Botha and Hertzog. It is now time to examine the point of view of Smuts and the part that he played in the conflict. On his farm Doornkloof, he was not so close as he had once been to the old and new centres of Afrikaner nationalism. So long as he had been in Pretoria, he had remained a churchgoer (although perhaps not a regular one), but when he moved to the country he began to spend his Sundays in reading and writing, in recreation with his family, and in the enjoyment of life out of doors.†
The Dutch Reformed Church by now was moving into a strong reaction against the liberal theology and tolerant politics of his

---

* The South African National Party (S.A.N.P.) became the South African party (S.A.P.).

† But not as yet systematic botanising. As to churchgoing, Mrs Gillett (*née* Margaret Clark) had remarked on the absence of it during her visits to the family; but on his voyage to England to see Campbell-Bannerman, Smuts wrote to his wife and children 'It is now Sunday morning and as I can not go to Church today I shall spend the time usefully in writing to you three' (17 December 1905).

boyhood and youth, and the fundamentalist and nationalistic sermons which he was likely to hear from the new generation of *predikante* would have displeased his uncle Boudewyn or Professor Marais as much as they displeased him. Nor was the estrangement all on one side: whereas his spiritual mentors in the old days at Stellenbosch would have applauded him for the ardour and the true piety of his *Inquiry into the Whole*, their successors a generation later would more likely have censured him for his unorthodoxy and presumption.

Other people might have censured him—he did in fact receive such censure when he published *Holism and Evolution* in the mid-1920's —for writing in English. The language question was moving into an important new phase and it is necessary to define his attitude towards it. There had been very little change from the opinions which he had held during his student years. In his essay of 1892 on *The Conditions of Future South African Literature*[10] he had given his considered estimate of Afrikaans, or (as it was still commonly called at that time) the *taal*. 'It is exceedingly simple and flexible in structure, with even less inflectional forms than are found in English; and it is said to be very easily acquired by foreigners. It is not yet sufficiently developed and refined to express high intellectual conceptions and complex relations and may therefore not yet be called a literary medium. But for expressing wit or humour as well as the primary emotions of the human heart—and in this it reveals the character of the people—it is scarcely second to any language with which we are acquainted.' His years of education in England did not bring about any change in these opinions. At the annual prize-giving ceremony of the *Zuid-Afrikaansche Taalbond* in 1895 he reviewed the history of the language question since the British occupation of Cape Colony and called upon his audience to resist the policies of linguistic denationalisation and to stand fast in loyalty to their ancestral tongue. 'Then our children and children's children for many years to come will speak the language of their forefathers—the language in which we formulated our national ideas, in which we talked with our mothers and friends, in which, stammering, we honoured the God of our fathers.'[11] That, in essence, was what he was fighting for in the years when Milner was straining every nerve to force the English language upon Boer children. That, in essence, was the victory which he and his wife and his children embodied and symbolised in their way of life at Doornkloof.

What more could be demanded of him? Something more *was* demanded. While the issue of the struggle against Milner still remained undecided, Gustav Preller, one of the champions of Afrikaans as a literary language, wrote to Mrs Smuts thanking her for some encouragement she had given him and expressing regret that he had received no similar encouragement from the General. 'It has always been my wish and I flatter myself with the hope of one day being able to know what you and the General think about the intrinsic value of the language question in connection with our nationality. I have never yet heard the General speak about this.'[12] He spoke about it too little for his own good. Seven years later, he refused an invitation to give the inaugural address to the Language Academy at Stellenbosch on the plea that he already had an appointment to inspect the fortifications at Durban.[13] It was an appointment which he would have done well, in his own interest and that of his party, to postpone. By 1912 the movement of Preller and his fellow enthusiasts was already gathering the strength which was destined in the early 1920's to put Afrikaans in the place of Dutch and alongside English as one of the two official languages of the Union. The Afrikaans language movement, more than any other, contained the dynamic force of Afrikaner nationalism. Smuts stood aside and permitted Hertzog to gather the prestige and power which was certain to accrue to the politician who made himself its champion.

His aloofness from the zealots of Afrikaans can be explained in part by the same objective conditions as were emphasised when the Smuts and Hertzog Education Acts were under discussion: in the Free State, with its 90 per cent Afrikaner majority, the propaganda for Afrikaans proved to be an electioneering asset; in the Transvaal, with its 50-50 division between the two language groups, it would have been an electioneering liability. This, however, was not the only, nor the most important factor in determining the attitude of Smuts towards language and the politics of language. In his patriotism, love of the mother-tongue was one, but only one of many interweaving strands. His love of the soil of South Africa (and that was a passion which English-speaking South Africans could share) was just as strong. Moreover, he felt, as his old political teacher, Jan Hofmeyr, had felt, that a good South African could and should be a good European also. He did not want (and here he found himself in straight conflict with the separatist zeal of Afrikaner nationalism) to tear up his roots in Europe. In religion and theology he clung to his heritage of the Dutch Bible, which symbolised the continuing presence and piety of his Dutch forefathers; he did not wish—nor, for that matter, did the majority of *predikante* wish at that time—to see it ousted by an Afrikaans Bible. In politics and political journalism he remained constant to the conservative teaching of 'Onze Jan' and preferred the simplified Dutch of *Ons Land* to the forthright Afrikaans of the *Volkstem*.[14]* In philosophy he retained the stamp of his Stellenbosch teachers and continued to express himself in English. What else could he do, short of giving up his search for the scientific and philosophic understanding of nature and man? He could not conceive that nationalism would ever demand from him that sacrifice. The South African nation whose coming of age he so much desired would have something distinctive, something adult to contribute to the culture of the western world and the self-critical wisdom of humanity.

To sum up: his theory of South African nationality was never exclusive, separatist or narrow, but in all its aspects comprehensive and spacious. There is hardly need to emphasise yet again the practical application of his theory which he made in the sphere of party politics. He set himself the task of demonstrating that two linguistic groups could just as easily come together within a single party in South Africa as they did in Canada. He accepted, just as readily as Botha did, the example of Laurier, the great French-Canadian leader. He welcomed, as eagerly as Botha did, the reinforcement of numbers and strength which European migration would bring to the young South African nation. In the flush of his enthusiasm and confidence following the National Convention he declared: 'The whole meaning of Union in South Africa is this: We are going to create a nation—a nation which will be of a composite character, including Dutch, German, English and Jew, and whatever white nationality seeks refuge in this land—all can combine. All will be welcome.'[15] It is hard to imagine any words more out of tune than these with the urgent, reiterated summons of Steyn to all Afrikaners 'to stand together as one man'. The theory of nationality as one intermingling stream stood confronted with the theory of the two separate streams.

As we have seen, it was Steyn's disciple Hertzog who translated this conflict of theories into a party-political conflict. In the crisis

* See p. 25 above.

following Hertzog's De Wildt speech of December 1912 Smuts had done his utmost to avert an open break between Botha and Hertzog; but the temperamental and ideological cleavage between them was too wide to be bridged. Of course, he took his stand with Botha when the break came. He told Arthur Gillett that he had to see it through, painful though he found it to fight his friends of former days.[16] In the bitter fights of 1913 his strength proved more resilient than Botha's. By the end of that year Botha had fallen into a mood of deep depression. Some people were putting the rumour around that he was angling for a job in England. That was the last thing that he had in mind, but he was beginning to doubt his capacity to hold the government together. On 23 December he wrote to Smuts from his farm—'In any case, Jannie, peace with *honour* or no peace. One thing that I will *never* do is to accept a job in England. It is an insult. No, I want peace without committing murder. Then I prefer above all my farm, Rusthof, and a seat in Parliament and if there (is) a good government, without Hulls, Hertzogs, Fichardts in it, I may be able to support it heartily—especially if you (are) at its head.'[17]

But Smuts was bending all his energies to supporting his leader and friend, not to supplanting him. A week earlier, on Dingaan's Day, he had spoken for his government and spoken from the depths of his own heart at the unveiling of the monument in Bloemfontein to the women and children who had died in the concentration camps. It would have been so easy for him to make the wrong speech, either by 'forgetting too easily' the sufferings and sacrifices of his people or allowing their commemoration to become an incitement to hatred and revenge. Against the tragic and heroic background of Afrikaner history, he gave the stark figures of the national disaster of the last war: more than 4000 women and 22,000 children dead in the camps, a total of 26,251 deaths.[18]

When one remembers [he said] that the whole population of the Republics —man, woman and child—who stood on the Republican side, probably did not number many more than two hundred thousand souls, then one realises the terrible, overwhelming meaning of these figures. What misery, what anxiety of soul must have filled the hearts of most of those women in those dreadful days! And yet, we who remained in the field know it; from the women's side, with a few exceptions, no attempt was ever made to persuade the men to surrender.... These women were indeed worthy descendants of their brave mothers and grandmothers. Our descendants will point to these women with rightful pride. A people that has produced such mothers cannot and never will degenerate! The cost of this monument was, as you know, met from modest gifts from all parts of the country. It can therefore claim to be a national homage to our heroines—a homage that is paid, so we hope, without bitterness in the heart and only out of pure love and respect for the noble women and their children who were the victims of a struggle between the two white races who have peopled this part of the world. Without bitterness....I know, every honest person knows and realises, that this is to ask much. For those among us who recognize in the long list the names of wives, mothers, daughters or children— and many of us do so—great self-control and austerity is demanded to rid oneself of all feelings of bitterness. We are profoundly moved and our throats tighten when we remember everything, especially when we think back to the suffering and hardship...and yet I say it is our duty to cherish no bitterness or hate....We may and we must teach our children to try to be worthy of such mothers. Not only may we do all this—it is our sacred duty....But the bloodshed in our past is not one of the things upon which we must fashion our future. God has not willed that one should exterminate the other. After all that misery and that bloodshed of the past, both races are still here—may we not, must we not believe that it is His will that we try to walk another road—the road of love and peace?

What can one say about these words of Smuts? Perhaps it is enough to say that they were in the spirit of the letters that he had written to his wife in 'the darkest time' of the history of their people.*

They were in the spirit, too, of the message which Emily Hobhouse sent to Bloemfontein from Beaufort West, where she lay stricken and struggling for life. He and she together set the tone of the ceremony, nor did anybody mar it by words of narrow partisanship. And yet, 'the road of love and peace' which Smuts envisaged might well have appeared a mirage. With the approaching New Year, each separate conflict afflicting South African society approached its climax. Hertzog was at work on his manifesto of Afrikaner protest. Gandhi was mobilising the Indian masses for their march to prison. Smuts himself was preparing a drastic counter-stroke against the turbulent labour leaders of the Rand and Natal. 'Love and peace'— these blessings were nowhere visible, except, perhaps, amongst the Natives.

To many intelligent observers of that time, the nationalistic schism appeared of small account in comparison with the conflict of classes. The leaders in that conflict on both sides were almost entirely

* See pp. 160, 164 above.

English-speaking, for Afrikaners had not as yet achieved the front rank either in the capitalist or in the labour world; nor had they achieved substantial representation even in the rank and file of industry. In December 1912 sixty-seven mines on the Rand were employing about 194,000 Natives and 23,000 white workers: of the latter, nearly two-thirds had been born in the United Kingdom and an appreciable number had come from Australia or other countries of the British Empire. To the deeply rooted Afrikaners, these white miners appeared a rootless, restless tribe—not without reason, for the figures of labour turnover were fantastically high. This was due in large measure to the contract system, under which a man's earnings depended upon the amount of rock he broke, with the result that men were constantly on the move in search of easier or more rewarding rock. Moreover, the men quite often followed their managers from one mine to the next, while the managers, for one reason or another, had the same restless disposition as the men; it was quite exceptional for a manager to stay three years in the same post and some mines had a new manager every year or oftener. The industry was anchored to a small area of the country; but its population was perpetually on trek. Although it was an industry of 'big propositions', highly developed in its financial structure and capital equipment, it was primitive in its social relations. It permitted a catastrophic waste of human life through miner's phthisis. It was resistant both to governmental control and trade unionism.

In 1913 there existed only one small craft union which the mine-owners recognised; but industrial unionism was making rapid progress, not only among the miners but among the railway workers. Nearly all the leaders were foreign born and some of them were apostles of syndicalism, the vanguard of proletarian revolution in pre-Bolshevik days. But, in South Africa, syndicalism wore its revolutionary dress with a difference; if some of the leaders remained revolutionaries, few of them remained proletarians. A faithful and sorrowful Marxist once described their programme thus: 'The wages system for ever—provided ours are high and yours are low; an injury to one is an injury to all—unless he's black. Down with capitalist exploitation—of Europeans only.'[19] This description was satirical; but in the uprising on the Rand after the First World War the revolutionary commandos inscribed on their banner these words: 'Workers of the world fight and unite for a White South Africa.'[20]

One or two idealists fought a rearguard action for proletarian revolution, irrespective of colour; but the rank and file and almost all the leaders, whether syndicalist or not, were implacable defenders of the white man's high standard of living against the competition of masses of low-paid Natives. For this reason, a strike which began with high revolutionary fervour could easily degenerate into a race riot.

To complete this picture of industrial anarchy one should add something about the economic pressures to which the mine-owners were subjected, particularly their incessant, inescapable struggle to strike a balance between cost and profit in handling the low-grade ores of the Rand. One should emphasise, too, the mental unpreparedness of government, parliament and community for the problems of industrial conflict. South Africa did not as yet possess a single fully grown university, although she was hoping to create one. The scientific study of economic and social behaviour had scarcely begun. The Chamber of Mines understood the accountancy and technology of the mining industry, the miners understood their own grievances, the labour leaders possessed a theory of syndicalist revolt; but there existed no mediating body of instructed and humane public opinion. Within the government itself, there was no group of men genuinely expert in industrial problems; the Department of Mines was staffed predominantly by clerks and engineers whose understanding and imagination were confined within their customary routines. As a consequence of all this, the political leaders could only too easily miss the underlying causes of industrial unrest and reduce the complexities of labour revolt to the elementary problem of law and order. Even within this narrow range, the government was singularly unprepared to shoulder its responsibilities, for the Union Defence Force created by Smuts's Act did not become a going concern until late in 1913. Consequently, the government could not in a crisis maintain public order except by calling in Imperial troops.

So much for the background of the industrial upheaval. It will also be necessary to describe with some care the aftermath. But the chronicle of events has been repeated so often and in such great detail that a bare outline must suffice here. The chronicle falls into two successive chapters, each of which reaches its climax in a day of high drama: 5 July 1913, when Botha and Smuts risked their lives and swallowed their pride to patch up peace with the leaders of a victorious mob: 27 January 1914, when the government's successful counter-stroke was symbolised in the summary and arbitrary deportation from South Africa of nine defeated labour leaders.

The first chapter opened with a dispute between a new mine manager and some of the white miners at New Klipfontein. In itself it was a trivial incident, but out of it grew a demand for the recognition of the white miners' trade unions and a struggle which engulfed and enflamed the whole Rand. The government tried at first to stand aside but the wild men among the miners and violent elements of the white population broke out of control; there was burning, shooting and imminent danger of worse to come. The government, with its own Defence Force not yet organised, called in the Imperial troops. Fortified by their presence, it tried, too late in the day, to stop a mass meeting. Rioting broke out more violently than ever. The Imperial troops opened fire, but did not resolutely persist. The mob remained master of Johannesburg. Botha and Smuts then entered the city and parleyed with the miners' leaders. They promised reinstatement of the strikers, a judicial committee to inquire into the miners' grievances, recognition of their trade unions. The strikers had won.

The judicial committee reported that the miners had real grievances and the government made systematic preparations for their redress. Six months after the wild days of July 1913 it had in draft no less than six bills for improving the conditions of white labour. Unfortunately, the more extreme syndicalist leaders had pushed the moderate men into the background and the wilder elements among the rank and file had persuaded themselves that violence paid dividends. Throughout the last six months of 1913 there were mutterings and rumblings and in January 1914 a violent eruption of industrial militancy, which began in the coal mines of Natal, spread to the railways and the Rand and culminated in the proclamation of a general strike throughout the Union.

The classic instrument of syndicalist revolution was now being tested in South Africa. But the industrial and social conditions of South Africa, as has been seen, were special; in a separate stratum deep below the white man's level lay the unorganised, unindoctrinated, unconsidered black proletariat. It was not as yet so clear as it became in the 1920's that the white miners were passionately negrophobe; a few syndicalist doctrinaires may have hoped, just as the government feared, that white victory would open the gates to black victory. That thought was certainly in the mind of Smuts.

As happened so often during those years, Merriman was hard at work telling Smuts what he ought to be thinking and doing. He kept harping upon the humiliating surrender of 5 July and upon the need to restore the authority and prestige of the State.

What people do really feel [he wrote on 8 September] is the fact that on the first occasion, despite a lavish expenditure, the government of the Union should have proved itself incapable of protecting persons and property or of keeping law and order without the aid of the Imperial forces. As I with you had much to do in framing the Act of Union this is the bitterest pill of all. . . . Perhaps my musings in Arcadia make me take a more serious view than you seem to do of the situation. We may laugh at the ravings of the syndicalists but the dangerous thing is that they are appealing—not I fear without success—both to the poorer Dutch and to the Natives. . . and do recollect that the maintenance of law and order is the great question before the country.[21]

It was Merriman's habit about this time to begin his letters to Smuts with expressions of solicitude about his health and his excessive burden of work, and then to ask him to take responsibility for some extra task which nobody else could be trusted to perform—something to do with the museums, perhaps, or the public archives. Smuts must do something about these things, he would say, and he must do something about the larger questions of public policy which were being mishandled. Above all he must do something to reassert the authority of the State. Words were not enough. Action was wanted!

I do not like to tender any advice [he wrote on 10 January], as my essays in that direction are not happy, but my dear Smuts it is of no sort of use the Prime Minister shaking his fist, figuratively speaking, at the labour agitators from Paulpietersburg, unless it is followed by some action. I have read with indignation the reports of the speeches of Messrs Waterston and Mason 8 Jan. in which they use the most violent language. Surely under the Common Law of any civilized country these men are liable to arrest for using language calculated (even intended) to provoke a breach of the peace, and arrested they should be unless the law is a farce.[22]

And so the bombardment of protest and well-intended advice continued. Smuts endured it patiently. Then on 22 January, he replied: 'Many thanks for your note which has just come to hand. Do not think that we have not followed your advice. I am only afraid you will say we have done so too well, when the matter comes before parliament.'[23]

Instead of writing 'we' Smuts might well have written 'I'. At the turn of the year, when everything was coming to its climax—Afrikaner schism, Gandhian non-violence, syndicalist violence—Botha was sick in body, depressed in spirit and brooding over his retirement. Smuts took charge. Between July 1913 and January 1914 he had brought his Union's Defence Force into being as an efficient military organisation. On 10 January he called it to action stations under the command of his old friend and leader de la Rey. On 14 January he issued a proclamation of martial law. Then de la Rey rode into the Rand with his commandos. 'The shadow of the burgher' lay over Johannesburg. This time, there would be no shooting into the air. De la Rey trained his cannon on the Trades Hall. The strikers capitulated.

The syndicalist bubble was pricked. The general strike collapsed. Order was restored with the loss of two lives. But Smuts did not leave it at that. With no legal authority beyond that which the proclamation of martial law may have conferred on him, he gave orders for the deportation of nine labour leaders. On 27 January, under conditions of extreme secrecy and haste, the police hustled them on board the steamship *Umgeni*.

When parliament met on 4 February, Smuts defended the action of the government from start to finish of the crisis, in a speech which lasted five hours. The general strike, he declared, had been 'a deliberate attempt to starve the public into surrender'. Revolutionary syndicalists had led the unions into 'a declaration of war' against the State and—'. . . naturally, the Government answered it in the proper way, not only by calling out those large forces, but by proclaiming Martial Law—and I think if ever a declaration of Martial Law was justified it was justified under the circumstances which existed at that time'.[24] None of the government's critics confuted this argument, and some of them—Hertzog, for example—took special pains to endorse it. Nor did anybody challenge the appeal which Smuts made to the verdict of events: what might have been a 'tremendous tragedy', had indeed passed off with negligible bloodshed. Then why spoil the record? If peace was already restored, what need was there for the deportations? 'Why wipe away all the credit', exclaimed Merriman, 'by this one false step?'[25]

The explanation, if not the justification of the deportations must first of all be sought in a document contemporaneous with the event

—in the minute which the ministers addressed to the Governor-General on 26 February. It contained the following passage:

It is, in Ministers' opinion, essential to the interests of the future peace, order, and good government of the Union that an example should be made of some of the most dangerous amongst these men and that they should be removed from the sphere where they have been working so much harm.

Ministers are of the opinion that expulsion from the Union will have the desired effect, as it will not only deprive these persons of further opportunity for fomenting unrest and working harm in this country, but should also act as a strong deterrent to their followers from ever again embarking upon a course of action which has proved so inimical not only to the best interests of the European labouring classes themselves but to the welfare of the Union.

The deportations, then, were squarely based upon the theory of deterrence. At the same time, the government knew that it had no chance at all of getting this theory accepted either in the courts of law or in parliament. So it acted arbitrarily, secretly and in haste.

Smuts admitted this in parliament with astonishing frankness. He laid great weight upon the argument of deterrence, and equal weight upon the impossibility of making it effective either through the courts or in parliament.

Now I wish to say [he asserted] that, after comparative quiet had been restored in the country, the Government had to consider most seriously not only the situation then existing, but any future situation that might arise in this country. Hon. members must understand that it is impossible for the Government of the country to have to face a situation like this every six months. In the last six months we have had three deliberate attempts made to work up a general strike....[26]

He reminded parliament of the special reason South Africans had for crushing the trouble-makers once and for all.

We are [he said] a small white colony in a Dark Continent. Whatever divisions creep in among the whites are sure to be reflected in the conduct of the native population, and if ever there was a country where the white people must ever be watchful and careful, and highly organised, and ready to put down with an iron hand all attempts such as were made on the present occasion, that country is South Africa. The Government felt that, and has acted accordingly.

If it had not acted at once, he said, it would have found itself powerless to act at all. He accepted no blame for breaking the law, but blamed the law for being out of date.

We had to deal in a case like this [he said] with entirely novel developments of the most recent character. Our criminal law does not really fit in
with such conditions....The only crime which fits this state of affairs is
high treason. But you attempt to indict these people for high treason and
see what will be the result....No; I think that the Government have
acted properly and in the public interest, and that the Government were
the best judges of the public interest in a case like this, far better judges
than any judge or jury in a court of law could possibly be.[27]

Far better judges, too, than members of parliament could possibly be!
For they were not in session during the strike and were hardly likely
to pass an Act of deportation later on, when the excitement and
passion were cooling down.

No sir; my view is this, and I submit it was the correct view, that it was
necessary in the public interest to expel these people, that it should be
done while these events were occurring, and, as a matter of public necessity,
by the authorities, and not wait until the fires had gone down, until a
different state of feeling had arisen....In January I felt that the deportation had to take place while the country was still in arms and the revolutionary state of affairs was prevailing, or not at all.[28]

It was open to anybody to retort that 'not at all' was the proper
choice if the alternatives were as Smuts described them. In effect,
Merriman made this retort when he accused Smuts of preaching
'a Latin Republican doctrine and not the doctrine of a free country
where Englishmen and Dutchmen live'.[29] Merriman did not deny
that the government, and Smuts in particular, had been contending
against great dangers; but they had flouted the constitution and
thereby had set a precedent fraught with evil and danger to the
future of the country. Hertzog and Creswell said practically the
same thing with the same conviction and force. As Hertzog put it—
'The strongest condemnation of the whole case came from the mouth
the Minister himself, when he admitted that he had superseded the
of courts because the courts would have had to find the people not
guilty. Then he had superseded Parliament because it would not
have condemned these people in cold blood.'[30] To this accusation
the government spokesmen had no defence to offer except the
argument of *salus populi*. 'It was an extreme measure,' Botha
admitted, 'but it was a measure for the safety of the country—and
the well being of the country was the highest law.'[31]

On this basis, the leader of the Unionist opposition decided to
make common cause with the government. Sir Thomas Smartt

had been reading the recently published report of the July disturbances,[32] and it had convinced him that the labour leaders were dangerous revolutionaries. Admittedly, the government had had no right to send them away, but he was not going to vote to have them back. He would support the government, not from a legal but from a practical point of view.[33] Smartt's speech, although not very inspiring, was significant of the shape of things to come. So, indeed, was the whole debate, for it foreshadowed the opposing political forces of the 1920's: on the one side, a coming together of the Unionists with the South African party, under the leadership of Smuts: on the other side, an alliance of Labour with the Nationalists, under the leadership of Hertzog.

This realignment of political forces might have occurred very much earlier, had not the outbreak of war in Europe aroused other passions and raised other problems. Some people have even argued that, if only world peace could have been kept, the realignment would have come not only earlier but—from their point of view—more hopefully, with Creswell's Labourites rather than Hertzog's Nationalists setting the pace of radical politics and guiding their course. This argument, perhaps, represents wishful retrospection; but early in 1914 the trend of events did seem to be in that direction. Provincial elections in March swept Labour to power in the Transvaal. On the Rand, the rout both of the South Africa party and the Unionists was complete, and they suffered heavy losses in Pretoria also. A very astute political commentator, F. T. Krause, told Smuts that his deportations were chiefly to blame. They had, for example, 'scared the *Jew* and made upon him the impression that Russian methods are not unknown in South Africa and may possibly be applied in the future'. And what about those Boers who had given their votes to Labour? 'With regard to our *own people*', said Krause, 'the result has been surprising. But if one considers what a very large percentage of Afrikanders are now working in the mines and that these men have been compelled to join the Miners' Association and consequently are politically and financially supporting that Association, and that therefore they would support their new leaders, one can easily understand why they voted against us.'[34]

Krause did not take the setback in the constituencies too tragically. He believed that Labour had reached its peak, he had hopes of gathering the Hertzogites back into the party fold and, anyway, he thought that a rearrangement of parties along lines of class (he did not use that word, but it was what he meant) would be quite a healthy development. Smuts may have been reassured by these optimistic forecasts. All the same, when he took stock of the Transvaal elections and similar signs of the times, he could hardly fail to regard the deportations as an immense political blunder.

It was also a personal trouble to him with some of his friends. Merriman had not voted against the government but he had walked out of the house when the division was called. The Liberal government in England had resisted the pressure put upon it—not wholly without reason*—to defend the rights of British subjects; but Liberal opinion in the country was almost unanimous against the deportations. Amongst the newspapers, *The Times* was the only powerful supporter of the Botha government, and its support was a poor recommendation in many Liberal families. Smuts began to receive letters of anxious inquiry from his English friends. Lady Courtney confessed that she was 'a bit troubled'.[35] Mrs Gillett, with the best will in the world to believe him in the right, confessed that she had doubts about the deportations.

It seems to me so much better [she wrote on 20 February] to *prevent* bloodshed than to have soldiers in when damage is done, that I feel quite calm when our good friend the Manchester Guardian finds fault with you, and our well-intentioned but less weighty and rather excitable friend The Nation denounces you. But I must confess I could no longer see what you were at when the deportations were done and were made prospective as well. Then I began to feel your political foundations a bit shaky. . . . It *has* been a bad time with you, and I do indeed sympathise. . . . When all is quiet again I do hope you will *all* come over here and have a good holiday.[36]

Such affectionate solicitude did not temper Wolstenholme's disapproval. The deported men, he told Smuts, would be welcomed in England as heroes and martyrs, even by people who did not approve either their tactics or the characters of some of them. He was afraid that the Government's lawless action would still further inflame the lawless temper of the workers. 'And the more the struggle is shifted on to this plane the worse it will be for all parties, and for civilization. No one now denies the right of excluding "undesirable aliens", including that of deportation of those who may have slipped in—within a moderate period; but I think that general public opinion here is

---

* A legal argument of the time was that the deportations involved the assumption of extra-territorial powers which the South African government did not possess.

right in disapproving of the new "ostracism". Suppose we deport Sir Edward Carson or Mrs Pankhurst, and pay their passage to South Africa?' Wolstenholme continued at some length in this strain and concluded with the hope that the gods might give Smuts wisdom in dealing with the questions of world-wide bearing that were before him.[37]

However one looks at it, Smuts's attempted master-stroke had turned out for him as badly as could be. Whatever had induced him to attempt it? One recalls some words that President Kruger was supposed to have said to him long ago: 'Smuts, you crack your whip too loud.' In politics, as in war, he was temperamentally disposed to follow the enemy in hot pursuit and sometimes to overshoot the mark. Yet he had also in his temperament a strain of caution and patience, which tended to gain the upper hand over his impetuosity as he gained experience. We have already seen, however, how little experience of labour problems existed in South Africa in 1914. Nor had trade unionism become as yet a regular and familiar part of social machinery. If Smuts had been able to get to know the labour leaders at first hand, as he was getting to know Gandhi at first hand, it might have made a big difference, for they were in reality a mixed lot, idealists and time servers, saints and villains, moderates and extremists.* Perhaps he had in his mind's eye a composite picture of them all in the likeness of Thomas Bain, the violent and triumphant demagogue whom he and Botha had confronted with his riotous mob in Johannesburg on 5 July 1913.

Be this as it may, the strain which he had to bear at this time was almost insupportable. He snatched time to write brief letters to Wolstenholme and Arthur Gillett, and began each letter with a few words of apology and explanation: 'In my overwhelming troubles I may perhaps appear to forget my friends. But it is not so.'[38] He was now very much alone. Given Botha's mood of acute depression, it had fallen to him to handle at one and the same time Hertzog's secession, Gandhi's civil disobedience and the syndicalists' general strike. Merriman did not forget this when he rose in parliament to perform the painful duty of giving his friend a trouncing. 'As usual', he declared, 'the whole business of the Government—as seems generally to be the case—was left on the patient shoulders of the Minister

---

* 'Saint', the only disputable term in this list, does seem appropriate to the character of S. P. Bunting.

of Finance, and when one criticises his actions one is filled with admiration for the undaunted pluck and courage he has shown since last April. That he makes errors of judgment is, unfortunately, too true.'[39]

Well, he had made his error of judgment, or his temperamental blunder, or whatever one chooses to call it. It now became his task to mitigate its effects so far as he was able. In the original bill, it had been provided that the men named should be deemed permanently to be undesirable inhabitants of the Union. The deletion of this clause had been the only substantial concession which the government had offered during the debate to its parliamentary critics: an important concession, as things turned out, for next year the men were given permission to return. By the irony of fate, one of them, the Hollander Poutsma, became later on a supporter of Smuts and general secretary of his South Africa party! But these events lay the other side of the great watershed of August 1914. This side of the watershed, the success which Smuts achieved in re-establishing within himself the rule of patience was demonstrated most strikingly by his long, careful and successful negotiation with Gandhi.

Looking back from the eve of war along the road which South Africa had travelled since Union, he could at least feel sure that the work of State-building had been well done. He still hoped, despite the gloomy evidence of recent events, that the work of nation-building would be accomplished in due time. But what if the gift of time should be withheld? The infrequent letters which he wrote to his friends during these months reveal a growing uneasiness at the growth of violent attitudes and policies, in Ulster and among British Unionists to begin with, but soon, and far more dangerously, in Europe. On 30 July he wrote to Wolstenholme:

Yesterday the news arrived that Austria has declared war on Serbia and we have been officially warned by the Imperial Government that the position is most grave. I do hope it will be possible to stave off a general conflict which is bound to put Europe back 50 or more years and to bring untold suffering and loss in its train. If Serbia goes under it will be impossible to keep Russia out of it, and with Russia stepping in the business will become a dreadful one.... What times we live in and what fate is in store for our day and generation! I had never thought of seeing the general break-up in my time.[40]

PART IV

WAR AND PEACE, 1914–19

CHAPTER 18

THE WAR IN AFRICA

1914

WHEN war broke out Smuts felt immediate and deep concern for its effects upon the destinies not only of South Africa but also of Europe and of humanity. His friends in Britain were prone to put the blame upon the British government, first for their failure to prevent it, secondly for becoming entangled in it. The crash has come, wrote Emily Hobhouse, and 'our wretched Imperialists' have brought it about: 'for pity's sake don't let South Africa be dragged in'. The speeches of Asquith and Grey, wrote Margaret Gillett, with their 'hypocritical theories as to why we are at war...left me cold and indignant'. Wolstenholme declared himself too broken-hearted to write at length about a catastrophe 'so entirely without cause or reason'; but he was disposed to put the blame upon the faults of a bad system, rather than the wickedness of a few individuals, and he clung to the hope that a 'Concert of Nations' would emerge from the conflict in place of the old system of diplomacy, whereby 'a small clique' determined the issues of peace and war. Arthur Gillett wrote in simpler vein; he was a Quaker, a liberal, a banker, just as distressed as the others were at the ruinous folly of the war and just as aloof as they were from vulgar jingoism: 'But fight we must, and so four clerks have gone, and I should like to go into some corps or at any rate get trained for the days that may come.'[1]

It was in his reply to Arthur Gillett that Smuts revealed his innermost thoughts about the significance of the war and, consequentially, about his own duty.

Let us remember the deeper import of the events through which we are passing and not simply curse our statesmen. It is difficult for me to see what other alternative there was for English statesmen. In 1907 the great C.B. made a move towards limiting armaments and war preparations. Germany made not the slightest response. As the burden became too great for England, tacit arrangements came to be made with France, and her fleet was taken to the Mediterranean to protect also British interests, and England became morally responsible for the northern coasts of France. I don't think England could have done otherwise then, nor could she without infamy have backed out now. I love German thought and culture and hope it will yet do much for mankind. But a stern limit must be set to her political system which is a menace to the world even worse than Bonapartism was. But I must admit the future is to me very dark. If Germany wins—but what if Russia wins! Let us do our duty according to our best lights and leave the ultimate issue to that Providence which somehow turns evil to good and makes poor erring humanity reap 'the far-off interest of tears'. We are also fighting in the awful desert of German S.W. Africa and will lose many valuable lives there. But such was the wish of the English Government and Botha and I are not the men to desert England in this dark hour. Many Boers cannot forget the past and bitterly disapprove of our action. But I think we are doing our duty. Goodbye, dear Arthur. Remain calm, knowing that there is more in this than man's blundering.[2]

When Smuts wrote these sentences in late September he did not even yet foresee that the path of duty, as he and Botha conceived it to be, would become within a few weeks the path of fratricidal strife between Afrikaner and Afrikaner. It is necessary to explain briefly how this happened; but something must first be said about the historical sources. In March 1915 a 'Report on the Outbreak of the Rebellion and the Policy of the Government with Regard to its Suppression' [U.G. 10 (1915); also Cd. 7874] was presented to parliament. It was followed next year by a 'Report of the Judicial Committee Relating to the Recent Rebellion in South Africa' [U.G. 46 (1916)]. The first report, which was written by Professor Fouché of the Transvaal University College, was argumentative in tone and uncritical in method; but it printed in an appendix some essential documents, including the telegraphic correspondence of Botha and Smuts with ex-President Steyn. The second report, as might be expected from the fact that three judges of the Supreme Court were its authors, is more objective in its handling of the evidence. In addition to these and some other official publications, the student of the rebellion needs to consult secondary printed material, including the general histories of the rebellion and the biographies (which vary greatly in quality) of its leading personalities.[3]

On the basis of this material it is not difficult to construct a clear chronology of events. The story opens on the day Great Britain declared war, when the Union government sent a cabled message through the acting Governor-General to the Secretary of State for the Colonies, announcing its willingness 'to employ the defence force of the Union for the performance of the duties entrusted to the Imperial Troops in South Africa' and thus to release these troops for service elsewhere. In a cable of 7 August, accepting this offer, the Secretary of State raised a fateful question: 'If your Ministers at the same time desire and feel themselves able to seize such part of German South-West Africa as will give them command of Swakopmund, Lüderitzbucht, and the wireless stations there or in the interior, we should feel that this was a great and urgent Imperial service.' On 10 August the Union government notified its willingness to participate in an expedition for this purpose, 'the naval part to be undertaken by the Imperial authorities and the military operations to be undertaken by the Union Government'. Next day Smuts, as Minister of Defence, issued a press notice announcing the government's intention to organise adequate forces (including four volunteer regiments which would be raised forthwith) 'to provide for contingencies'.[4]

The government soon discovered that the action which it had in mind would be unpopular with many of its own supporters and even of its official servants. Two years previously, Smuts had appointed his old war-comrade and rival, Christiaan Frederik Beyers, to command the Union Defence Force; but he had felt cause more than once since then to wonder whether his action had been wise: in particular, he had consented very reluctantly to some of the military appointments and postings which Beyers had urged upon him.[5] On 14 August, at a meeting of officers held in Pretoria, Beyers showed strong aversion from the proposal (although it was not officially under discussion) for the invasion of German South-West Africa. The same aversion was shown by two other important officers, Maritz and Kemp.

However, Beyers gave no sign during the following four weeks either of allowing his personal feelings to interfere with his military duty or, alternatively, of sending in his resignation. The chief anxieties of Botha and Smuts during these weeks were aroused by their old friend de la Rey, who was under the influence of a famous prophet named van Rensburg, whose apocalyptic visions awakened wild hopes of England's imminent downfall and the resurrection of the Republics. Within a few days of the outbreak of war, de la Rey issued a summons to the Boers of the Lichtenburg district to assemble at Treurfontein, mounted and armed, on 15 August. Two days before that date de la Rey was persuaded to come to Pretoria for a talk with Botha and Smuts. He was in an almost distracted state of mind, broke off continually into prayer and always kept reverting to van Rensburg's prophecies. Still, the influence of his friends prevailed upon him, and at the meeting of 15 August at Treurfontein a resolution was passed expressing complete confidence in the government to act in the best interests of South Africa.

Before committing itself to action in South-West Africa, the Union government sought the approval of parliament, which met in special session from 9 to 14 September. In moving the address of loyalty and support to the King, Botha affirmed the solidarity of South Africa with the Empire. In virtue of her allegiance to the Crown, he declared, South Africa was involved automatically in the war. In law, that doctrine was universally accepted at that time; but in politics, the implications of the doctrine were wide open to debate. Botha acclaimed the Empire as South Africa's shield against the storms and perils of international conflict and he accepted the moral obligation incumbent upon South Africa, as a faithful ally, to make a contribution of her own to the common security. This brought him to the problem of German South-West Africa. It may seem surprising that he did not follow a frankly realistic line and emphasise the value of that territory as an acquisition to the Union. Territorial expansionism was a persistent element in the political tradition both of the Cape and of the Republics; in the 1880's, Cape politicians had done their utmost to prod the Foreign Office into forestalling Bismarck's annexation of territory on their north-westerly borders, and nothing could conceivably have been more expansionist than the old Republican slogan: 'Then shall it be, from Simonsberg to the Zambesi, Africa for the Afrikanders!' In retrospect, too, it is clear that all parties, and not least the Afrikaner Nationalists, have regarded South-West Africa as a valuable, indeed an indispensable acquisition, blemished only by the League of Nations strings which in 1919 were so regrettably—as most of them thought—attached to it. In 1914, however, the government's case was grounded upon the argument of German aggression; consequently, it would have been too embarrassing for it to avow aggressive purposes of its own. In his discussion of South-West Africa, Botha did not introduce the argument of national interest except in the form of a question: What would the Union's position have been, he asked, if the occupation of the territory had been entrusted to Australian or Indian troops? The question was a relevant one; for nobody with any knowledge of naval strategy could believe that German South-West Africa, with its ports and powerful wireless station, could possibly be left undisturbed on the flank of an important sea route.[6]

Afrikaners, however, were a land-minded people and in Hertzog's newly formed Nationalist party no knowledge existed at all of naval strategy. In the debate, Hertzog followed a clear line; without denying the Union's legal belligerency, he upheld its political and military neutrality. He laid great stress on the risks of an active war policy: What would happen to the Union, he asked, if the Germans should win the war in Europe? 'Why should South Africa undertake a thing which could lead to nothing else than to bringing the country into the same condition as Belgium?' Realising that he might seem to be concurring in the moral indictment brought against Germany, he hastened to express every sympathy for Belgium but refused to condemn Germany for an unjust aggression, 'as it might be shown afterwards that it was no such thing'. He ended with a note of warning. 'The government', he declared, 'would very speedily find that they had to deal with a population which felt that something was being done which ought not to be done.'[7]

Smuts, who spoke next day, met Hertzog's arguments squarely. He pinned upon Germany both the general offence of militarism and the particular offence of aggression. The question, he declared, was 'whether the military autocracy is going to be "baas"' or whether freedom would prevail. As to aggression, he declared that Germany had committed it not only in Europe but in South Africa, for she had already sent her forces across the Union's frontier at Nakob. He declared also that the government had in its possession 'information which clearly showed that the German government had had its eyes on South Africa for many days...and was still having very eager eyes on the Union'.[8]

The issue of the debate was never in doubt. Supported not only by Smartt, the leader of the Unionists, but also by Creswell, the leader of the Labour party, the government carried its motion by 92 votes to 12. That same night, 14 September, the first troopships sailed for the ports of German South-West Africa.

The voting in parliament, however, did not accurately reflect the feeling of the country. Smuts had disquieting evidence of this in his own mail. For example, while the debate was still proceeding, Deneys Reitz, who was practising law at Heilbron in the Free State, wrote to warn him that the Hertzog party was making capital out of the South-West Africa expedition and that the Boers were in commotion throughout the Heilbron district. Of course, if the government could make a clean job of the expedition with its existing forces, the public would soon come to see the matter in a different light; but at the moment the situation was nasty. 'Hertzog's address was a sheer electioneering speech with an eye to the next election. He is too petty even in these days to sink his personal interests, but nevertheless the fact remains that his oration has aroused the people amazingly and if the Free Staters, or at any rate the Heilbronners, are called up, a serious mutiny will certainly develop the results of which will undoubtedly be far-reaching.'[9]

Reitz was a partisan who saw chiefly the 'petty' motives of leaders on the other side, but in the dissension which he reported there was a tragic element. The tragedy became embodied and symbolised in the last days and in the death of General de la Rey. On 12 September he had made in the Senate a brief speech which revealed the confusion and conflict within his own mind.

Let them remain calm [he pleaded]. He was wholly against war....As to neutrality, as the Prime Minister had said, there could be no possible doubt about their being neutral [*sic*]. When the speaker signed the Treaty at Vereeniging he never thought that if Britain were involved in war he was binding his own country to make war....He wanted to see the German power broken because if so his country was free of danger, but if the British power were broken what would happen to this country?...As far as the final result was concerned what they did in South Africa would be as a drop in the ocean; and why then should they put their country in danger?

He declared that he would rather live under the British than under the German flag and that he would be ready to fight if South Africa were attacked; but he could not vote for the motion, 'not because he had anything against the government, but because he had conscientious scruples'.[10]

Parliament rose on 14 September. On the 15th, de la Rey and Beyers set out after nightfall for the western Transvaal. According to what Beyers said later, it was their intention to address people in the towns, urging opposition to the government and its attack on German South-West Africa. It happened that the police had been alerted that night to prevent the escape from Johannesburg of some dangerous criminals known as the Foster Gang. Two cars were shot at when they disobeyed the order to stop and two men were killed, a certain Dr G. Grace and General de la Rey. The bullet which killed de la Rey had been aimed at a back tyre of his car but had ricocheted after striking the hard road. That was the finding of a judicial inquiry; but a story was put about that the shooting of de la Rey was a deliberate act of murder perpetrated by the government.[11]

'We were almost brothers', Smuts said, 'before the war, during the war and after the war. He has departed this life under tragic circumstances without a stain on his character.'[12] Smuts must have found some consolation in the knowledge that de la Rey's widow showed no abatement of her trust and affection towards him. Two months after her husband's death she wrote him a tragic letter.

You will be surprised to have a letter from me. It is because my heart is wrung about our condition. Ah, in the last bitter struggle in our land we were as brothers although there were also Afrikaners who went against us. Because they were weary and did not know what to do, it was not so terrible as it is now. Ah Jannie, it was not for nothing that Oom Kosie said to me that the future was so dark for him that he said to God: Lord, take me, but think of the People and show them the good road. Ah Jannie, and when it happened that he was really taken away in such a marvellous manner, and I see every day how terrible things are, his words become more solemn in my mind....Now it seems to me as if I stand in the midst of the two parties, the one is as precious to me as the other and as yet I see light on no side and we do not know on what side the light will shine, and as I have told you, I feel as if I stand between the two parties, have the welfare of both very much at heart.

She had just received news that one of her friends had captured her husband's brother, Adriaan de la Rey. '...Ah, Jannie, I shall be a pleader for him, hope that you will do the best for him, for, as I have said, I am as sorry for one as for the other. I do not see whom I can shut out. If it is necessary I can do the same for you, so my heart feels for us all....Ah Jannie, I cannot forget my husband and cannot imagine that it is so. Ah, once and for all it is so; may the Lord strengthen me; He has done it so often and will do it further. How are Isie and the children? I hope all well....'[13]

This noble letter contains all the agony of fratricidal strife. Warning of its approach had been given on the day de la Rey died. Before setting out with him for the western Transvaal, Beyers had resigned his commissioned rank and his post as Commandant-General. His letter of resignation was a polemical document, which was given to the press before it reached the Minister of Defence; but Smuts employed the press censorship to have it held back until his own reply could be published with it. There is no profit in quoting verbatim from the two documents. Beyers made it clear that he had disapproved from the start of the proposed expedition but had been counting upon parliament to reject the proposal, which he considered to be unconstitutional, rash and unnecessary, seeing that the war (and with it the fate of the German colonies) would in any case be decided in Europe: moreover, he rejected British pretensions as a champion of small nations and recalled British outrages against the Boers only a few years ago. Smuts, in his reply, reminded Beyers that he had been the recipient from the outbreak of war of all the military information which the government possessed and that his advice had been followed, both in making the plans for the invasion of South-West Africa and in appointing and posting the senior officers: consequently, his resignation had come rather late in the day. The decision of parliament, so far from being an excuse for resignation, should have kept him at his post. His reference to the barbarous acts committed by the British during the South African War could not justify Germany's crime against Belgium and could only sow hatred and dissension among the people of South Africa. Since those days, the British people had helped South Africa to achieve national freedom. Beyers had spoken of duty and honour: those virtues, Smuts retorted, were not to be found in 'a policy of lip-loyalty in fair weather and a policy of neutrality and pro-German sentiment in days of storm and stress'.[14]

In retrospect, it is clear that the war of words was a prelude to the war of bullets; but at the time neither side desired this and both sides hoped to avoid it. On 20 September Botha, Smuts and Beyers appeared together at a great gathering in Lichtenburg to commemorate General de la Rey. Speaking after Botha, Beyers disavowed any idea of rebellion. Parliament, he said, had decided on a campaign in German South-West Africa and consequently 'every Afrikander should do his duty or we should lose our freedom'.[15] But what was duty? Next day, Beyers appeared again in the market-place of Lichtenburg with the Free State hero, General de Wet. The platform was General de la Rey's car and the chairman was Major Kemp, another officer who had resigned his commission. A resolution was passed calling upon the government to withdraw the citizen forces from the German borders before the end of the month, and a further meeting was arranged to consider the government's reply.

In this crisis Botha rose to his full stature as a political and military leader and as a man. He had by now quite thrown off his earlier depression and throughout the anxious months ahead he was always clear-headed, resolute and masterful. On 20 October he made two important decisions: first, to use only volunteers for the invasion of South-West Africa; secondly, to take the field himself as military commander.

Smuts had the task of administrative and military organisation at the seat of government in Pretoria. He still had good hopes that the expedition could be carried through without any serious trouble on the home front. On 22 September he gave Deneys Reitz the reassuring news that there would be no 'commandeering' for South-West Africa and continued: 'There is much, very much talk. Some are afraid of a revolution or civil war. I am not. Nevertheless I shall be glad if you will keep your ears and eyes open and keep me informed of what goes on in your parts. You will see, when all is over and German South-West Africa again forms a part of our Afrikaans heritage, feeling will quickly swing round and our action be generally approved.'[16] On 2 October he wrote rather more dubiously, but still in the main optimistically, to Merriman. 'This is indeed a difficult time. What with people's genuine dislike to this German West operation, the survival of old anti-British feeling, and the recent luxuriant growth of factions, our troubles are great. But I have faith in South Africa and in the end it will all come right.'[17] On 10 October he wrote to his wife in a different strain. The police considered it unwise for him to travel in the evenings to Doornkloof. For the present he would have to stay in Pretoria and he asked her to send his clothes there. 'Maritz has rebelled and joined the Germans with his commando; there are 200 Germans with him and I expect an attack on Coen Brits at Upington. Do you think I should hire a house here or do you prefer to stay out there? I think here is better.'[18]

The memoirs which Maritz published a quarter of a century later revealed him as a man gnawed at and eaten away by many pathological hatreds.[19] In 1939 it was the Jews, in 1914 it had been the British, who were the main object of his hate. Such a man should never have been entrusted with the command of troops on an enemy frontier in time of war. Smuts had sanctioned the posting only under intense pressure from Beyers[20] and from late September onwards had been doing his best to correct the mistake without driving Maritz into the arms of the Germans; but he failed. Early in October Maritz made his deal with the enemy and when he crossed the frontier to join them he handed over to them as prisoners of war the men of his commando who would not fight on their side. Then he promoted himself to be a General and proclaimed the independence of South Africa and declared war against England. On 10 October he sent an ultimatum to the government to say that he would invade the Union next day unless permission were given to Generals Hertzog, de Wet, Beyers and some others to come and confer with him.[21]

Rightly or wrongly, the government decided that this challenge could only be met by declaring martial law and by commandeering men to deal with the threat of a rebellion supported by the Germans. In justification of these measures it published Maritz's ultimatum—an act which Hertzog bitterly resented, on the ground that he and the other persons named in that wild document would appear to be in collusion with Maritz. But the government was in a dilemma: if it acted too mildly, it would be accused of allowing the country to drift into civil war: if it acted too sternly, it would be accused of provoking that same disaster.

Certainly, commandeering as a precaution against rebellion proved to be just as unpopular in the disturbed areas as commandeering for the invasion of German territory. In the Free State, the reply of General de Wet was to raise commandos of his own in a counter-mobilisation to uphold a counter-policy. In the western Transvaal, Beyers made the same reply. Up to the third week of October, both these generals would have denied that they were in league with Maritz and in revolt against the Union: all that they were intending, they would have argued, was a demonstration in force to compel the government to change its policy. Indeed, the *gewapende protest* (protest in arms) had deep roots in the habits and traditions of early republican days; but those days had passed for ever; a modern State had been set up, and its rulers, whoever they might be (Botha or Hertzog, it would make no difference), would always assert their lawful authority against unauthorised military force. Even if a line still existed between armed protest and armed rebellion, de Wet and Beyers came close to crossing it on 22 October, when they met at Koppies and demarcated their respective zones of military operations. But they never reached such close agreement on their political objectives. Six days later, de Wet was speaking for himself, but not for Beyers, when he told an audience at Vrede what his intentions were: to procure arms from Maritz and then 'to trek to Pretoria, to pull down the British flag and to proclaim a free South African Republic'.[22]

All this time the government remained inactive. So, at least, it seemed to Merriman, who wrote to Smuts on 8 November a letter of furious complaint.

What I wanted to express was the feeling of myself and a good many others, Dutch as well as English, that this palavering with avowed rebels has gone altogether too far. Just look at the facts. On the 26th Oct. de Wet at the head of a band of ragamuffins, collected, not on the spur of the moment, but by a carefully prepared plot, destroys the railway, inflicting severe loss and damage on public property. On the 28th, having in the interval stolen (commandeered!) arms and property he appears at Reitz, makes a ridiculous and seditious harangue, damages public property, seizes private goods and proclaims that he is in rebellion. All this time palavering is going on. You are sending his avowed confederate to him, and above all you are giving him plenty of time to increase his forces and to unite them with the other bands of malcontents. Decent respectable farmers are living in terror of having their stock stolen by these ruffians....All the time you are parleying with the ringleader. *Is* there no law? Are the crimes of robbery, sedition and public violence merely venial eccentricities when committed by a certain section of the community?...I feel most strongly that unless the malady is extirpated, not smoothed over, and the authors, aiders and abettors soundly punished, there will be little respect for the law in the future and that the condition of South Africa will be that of Mexico or Peru.[23]

'Do pray remember', Merriman exclaimed in a later letter, 'that there is a party of law and order and that it is the majority of the community.'[24] Botha and Smuts knew this well enough; but they also knew the passionate feelings which swayed the minority. The palavering and parleying which so incensed Merriman were their attempts, pursued patiently and at great risk throughout four successive weeks, to re-establish the authority of the State by persuasion instead of by coercion. Botha opened the attempt on 11 October with a telegram to Steyn which concluded—'A word from you will go far'. He wanted Steyn publicly to condemn the rebellion and appeal to the men in the commandos to return to their homes. But this Steyn declared himself unable to do in such simple terms: not that he would find it hard to reprobate treason and condemn the action of Maritz; but he would feel called upon equally to condemn the government and its plans for the invasion of German territory. On 22 October Botha appealed to Steyn again; he asked him to use his influence with de Wet and Beyers to avoid bloodshed and told him that the danger was now so near that he had a responsibility no longer to keep silent. Steyn declined once again to commit himself publicly; but he responded to Botha's appeal to use his influence with the rebellious generals. His plan was to invite them to his home, Onze Rust, to discuss the disbandment of their forces upon terms agreed upon with the government. For this purpose he used his son, Dr Colin Steyn, as his intermediary and personal representative.

Between 24 October and 10 November Colin Steyn travelled continuously to and fro between Bloemfontein, Pretoria, the rebel camps in the Transvaal and the Free State and back again. His arduous journeys can be followed from day to day in the letters and telegrams of that time and in the narrative which still remained vivid in his memory forty-five years later. He never spared himself and deserved the generous praise which Smuts gave him for his 'fine and patriotic' conduct. But the all-out effort which he made came to nothing.[25]

Colin Steyn still retained in his old age a piece of paper on which Smuts had written down in his presence the terms which the government was prepared to offer to the rebels. Both at that time and in retrospect they seemed to him milder by far than the terms he had been expecting. His friends in Pretoria had advised him to see N. J. de Wet, the Minister of Justice, whom they regarded as a more pliable man than Smuts; but Colin Steyn had the reverse experience; he found de Wet unyielding and stern, Smuts accommodating and mild. What Smuts actually wrote down was (translated into English) as follows:

For C.S.

1. Government is not prepared to make any proposal or take any step in regard to which they are not assured that effect will be given to it.

2. If any proposal must be made such as C.S. suggests (i.e. freedom from punishment for all who within a given time lay down arms at local

magistrates against issue of a certificate and go home) then it must come from the other side as a proposal that the dissatisfied burghers are prepared to make.

3. In that case government will be inclined to take such a proposal into the most serious consideration as they ardently desire to prevent bloodshed.

4. It is not clear why burghers think they will be called up for German South-west Africa as Prime Minister has already officially declared that this will not happen and only volunteers will be used for it.[26]

These four clauses were the basis of the proposed talks between President Steyn and the rebel generals; but it proved impossible to bring the generals together with Steyn at Bloemfontein. To begin with, Beyers refused to go unless he were assured that de Wet and Kemp would also go. Then many days were lost by Colin Steyn when he set out with Hertzog in an attempt to locate de Wet. When he was tracked down at last he promised to be with President Steyn on 5 November, but as that day approached he found reason for postponing the appointment and said that he would write a letter instead. Colin Steyn made more journeys to Pretoria and to the rebel camps and some days after the lapsed appointment of the generals with his father found himself again looking for de Wet. As he approached Doornberg on the Sand river he saw a track of dust on the other side and soon he heard the sound of shooting. He took shelter while government troops passed close by in swift retreat. Then he found himself between the two forces until de Wet came charging by 'agter die klitsgras aan' (after the government troops). Among the men who were killed in that skirmish was de Wet's son Danie. Colin Steyn knew then that there was no longer any chance of peace. In his old age he recalled what Smuts had said to him: 'Ek gee jou baie kans maar intussen trek de Wet voorentoe en dit maak die wêreld vir my baie moeilik' ('I gave you a good chance but in the meantime de Wet marches forward and this makes the situation very difficult for me').

Even after the engagement at the Sand river on 9 November, President Steyn still hoped against hope that the fighting might be stopped. Next day Beyers, whose forces had recently been scattered by government troops in the Transvaal, made a belated appearance at his house. Thereupon Steyn telegraphed to Smuts asking him to arrange a safe conduct for Beyers to visit de Wet in his camp. At the same time he reproached the government for hardening its terms.

But Smuts by now was convinced that the negotiations had been protracted up to and beyond the limits of safety. In a forthright telegram to Steyn on 12 November he brought them to a full stop.

Had I expected any good result from the interview I would certainly have given Beyers a pass. He is discouraged and depressed and de Wet is firmly resolved and determined to proceed and only result of meeting between them in your absence would be that de Wet would talk Beyers round. We delayed active operations in Free State in expectation of conference until at last de Wet had 5000 men in the field, until he was openly saying in his speeches to the commandos that he thought it strange that the government should be so anxious to negotiate with rebels, and until after temporizing for a long time he finally refused to attend conference. We could wait no longer and unless he is convinced by force I do not believe he is more likely to listen to argument. It is therefore in the highest interests of country and people that we discharge our duty as a government.[27]

That same day Botha began military operations in earnest. He fell upon de Wet's forces at Mushroom valley and heavily defeated them. De Wet managed to escape with a few men but on 2 December he was caught in British Bechuanaland while he was trying to get through to Maritz and the Germans. Kemp did succeed in getting through with 500 men and was not rounded up until early February next year, after the failure of a joint attack which he and Maritz had made across the border. All the other leaders—excepting Maritz, who finally escaped to Angola—were dealt with before the New Year. But before the fighting was over there occurred another dramatic tragedy. On the night of 8 December, Beyers was drowned as his horse was shot under him while he was trying to escape across the Vaal river.

The story which has been told may seem too short for history and too long for biography; but no other way could be found of explaining the thought and action of Smuts in this crisis. At the time, he felt called upon to defend himself in his correspondence with Merriman and later in parliament against the accusation that he had been dilatory and weak in allowing the negotiations to go on so long.[28] Steyn, on the other hand, believed that he should have let them go on longer. He in turn believed that Steyn and Hertzog should have taken their stand publicly against rebellion. 'But not a finger was stirred. The oracles of nationalism were dumb, and the poor dupes went to their doom.'[29]

The fighting was almost entirely between Afrikaners because Botha took great pains to keep English-speaking South Africans out of it. The casualties were far lighter than might have been feared. According to some figures prepared by Smuts the government forces had nineteen men killed and eighty-two wounded; there was, besides, an appreciable toll (over fifty) of deaths through disease or accident. On the side of the rebels the total of deaths was 124 and of wounded 229. About 5000 rebels were captured and about 400 surrendered.[30]

What was to be done with these men? On 29 October Emily Hobhouse had written to Smuts pleading passionately for mercy.

I cannot *bear* to think that dear de Wet and Beyers and Kemp will meet a rebel's death. You have asked too much of human nature, or rather London has; I believe the pressure came from there—and I write in a hurry to implore you if these men are captured to ask General Botha to consider these facts and *not* to shoot them unless in open fight. The issue might be awful—an internecine struggle—an enmity never forgiven. They are brave good men. Keep them in prison if you will till the end but do not execute them, do not, *do not*, DO NOT.... I can't write, have no time, and you are too busy to read. Only once more I beg and pray you to *spare those men* for in opposing a war of aggression they were surely right, even if the means taken have been wrong. Oh! that Defence Force of yours, how often I wrote to you that it would lead to trouble and that if you had it you would not stop at Defence, but begin to invade, and so it is.[31]

Almost, if not precisely on the same day as Emily Hobhouse was writing this letter, Smuts was writing down for Colin Steyn the mild terms under which he hoped to end the strife without any bloodshed at all. More than a week went by after that before he felt obliged to warn President Steyn that the deliberate procrastination of de Wet and Beyers had so changed the situation that a complete amnesty 'in the case of the more prominent leaders' might no longer be possible. On 12 November the government issued an edict calling upon all rebels to surrender themselves and their arms, after which they would be allowed to return to their homes. Those rebels who failed to comply with the edict would be dealt with by law. The amnesty would no longer apply to persons who had taken a prominent part in the rebellion. The government reserved its right to deal with such cases on their merits.[32]

This edict, coinciding as it did with de Wet's debacle at Mushroom valley, probably played a large part in undermining rebel resistance. The government had every intention of interpreting its provisions with restraint and on 9 December Botha issued a statement calling for a spirit of 'forgive and forget'. Special courts were set up for the trial of certain categories of rebels. Of the rank and file, all had been set at liberty before the end of 1915. The leaders had fines imposed upon them and were given prison sentences of from two to seven years; but their fines were paid by public subscription and all of them had been released before the end of 1916.

To this wise clemency there was one exception. Commandant Joseph Fourie had gone over to the rebels in his officer's uniform and without resigning his commission in the Defence Force. In late December, when resistance had collapsed everywhere else, he was still fighting fiercely and was only captured after he and his men had inflicted heavy casualties upon a force commanded by Colonel Pretorius, a grandson of President Pretorius and his own cousin. Fourie was tried by court martial and condemned to be shot. A deputation of his friends went to Doornkloof to plead with Smuts to remit the sentence. Smuts was not to be found and the deputation asserted that he had avoided them. Challenged with this in the House, he said that he had been out walking when they arrived; he had neither made an appointment with them nor had he avoided them.[33]

If they had succeeded in their attempt to see him it would have made no difference, for he would not have remitted the sentence. He believed that it was just and he affirmed his belief publicly. And yet, as the years went by, he must have asked himself sometimes whether it had been necessary or wise to let the sentence take its course. For the name of Jopie Fourie became almost at once enshrined in the martyrology of nationalist Afrikanerdom. Along with the victims of Slagter's Nek and the other tragic heroes of Afrikaner legend he became a symbol of the piety and the sacrifice, the exultation and the defiance of his people. Marvellous and significant things were told about him: he had been captured on Dingaan's Day and shot on a Sunday; he prayed that the cup should pass from him but when his moment came he offered his breast to the bullets with a serene faith in his God and his people; if he allowed himself to be blindfolded, it was only to make easier the task of his executioners; he died singing a psalm. These stories were passed at first from mouth to mouth but soon they appeared in published print.[34]

The tragic deaths of de la Rey and Beyers lent themselves similarly, if not quite so poignantly, to the myth-creating genius of a pious people. There was the vision which had been vouchsafed to the prophet van Rensburg of 'the number 15 on a dark cloud, from which blood issued, and then General de la Rey returning home without his hat'. There was the symbol of Beyers dying with a full bandolier as his horse was shot under him in the Vaal river: Beyers, the martyr-patriot, who had never intended the shedding of Afrikaner blood. Who then had intended it? The mythus of the rebellion, as it burgeoned spontaneously or was fabricated purposefully[35] from year to year and from generation to generation needed not only innocent but also guilty men. Who else than Botha and Smuts could carry the burden of guilt?

During the closing months of 1914 anonymous letters began to be delivered at Doornkloof. Some of them were in English (possibly from angry syndicalists who had refused to follow Creswell in his support of the war); others were in Afrikaans. Most of them were venomous through and through; but there was an Afrikaner woman who said that she would have signed her name had not her husband prevented her from doing so and who mingled sorrowful reproof with her anger: 'For just as there is no murder and killing', she reasoned, 'in the household of a father who knows how to rule his family, so there is none under a government that rules its people justly.' From another anonymous Afrikaner Mrs Smuts received a different kind of letter. What, the writer asked her, would Slim Jannie do when the Germans conquered the country? Let him trek to England with the other traitors and with his wife and children and let them all stay there. 'The Germans will clear this country of the English and rubbishy (*vuilgoed*) Afrikaners who run after the English. Go and trek!' Among the effusions in English was one addressed to 'Mr Turncoat Smuts' by 'Republican'. It assured the 'Sneaky Reptile Turncoat Smuts' that the Germans would be hailed as deliverers from mean skunks like him who were sucking South Africa's blood. Another person wrote in English to ask him when *he* would be off to the front? But perhaps he was 'too funky'.[36]

From 1914 right up to the year of his death Smuts was reminded from time to time by anonymous abuse of this kind that some people —he might hope only a few—had made him the object of their pathological hatred. The record of this hatred has a place, though

393

not an important one, in his biography. Does it have any place at all in the history of his country? Smuts would not have given it one, and probably he would have been right to reject the ignoble evidence of anonymous letters. All the same, he was over-optimistic in his rejection of other evidence. He persuaded himself that the rebellion was no more than an episode, a fleeting impediment to the growth of the nation which would leave it stronger than before. 'These difficulties through which we have passed', he told Parliament, 'have helped to consolidate the people of South Africa and to weld them into a strong united people....The foundation of the Union of South Africa today is much more solid, permanent and enduring than it was before.'[37] The outlook was not quite so rosy as that.

1915

As soon as they had the home front under control Botha and Smuts switched their energies to the front in German South-West Africa. They had lost three months of precious time which they were determined at all costs to retrieve. Some of the troops which had been despatched the previous September and October had had to be recalled because of the rebellion and at the New Year the Germans still held the whole country except for the two ports of Swakopmund and Lüderitz.

Botha described the country as 'a natural fortress on a huge scale'.[38] It was three-quarters the size of the Union, a vast tableland from 4000 to 5000 feet in height, much of it fair grazing country but all of it encircled by deserts or semi-deserts: to the east, the Kalahari; to the south, the arid wastes of Namaqualand where Smuts had fought in 1902; to the west, a barren and almost waterless coastal plain 40 or more miles wide. For the defence of this fortress the Germans had 2000 regular troops and about 7000 reservists, a total of less than 10,000 against the Union's total of 43,000;[39] but they also had good railway communications along the spine of the territory from north to south, whereas their enemies had the most intractable difficulties of communications and supply. These being the conditions, the Germans might well have proved the equals of their enemies in battle if only they had possessed (as in East Africa they did possess) a commander who could match the drive and skill of the Boer generals.

Botha arrived in Swakopmund in the second week of February

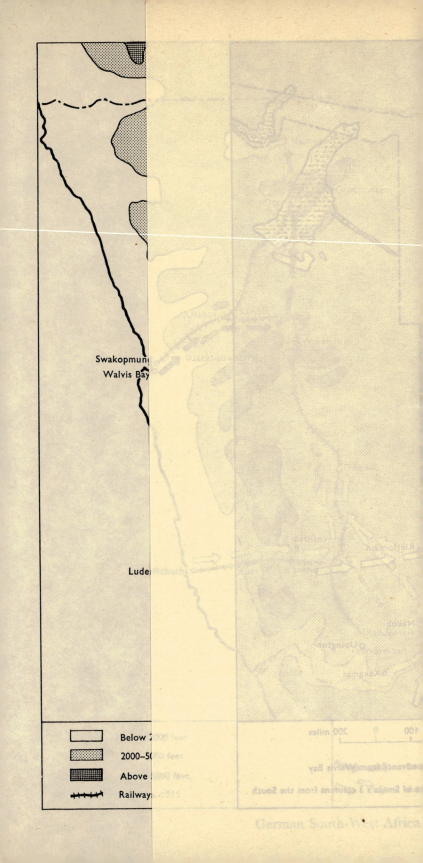

Swakopmun
Walvis Bay

OJackhais

Lude

Below 2000 feet
2000-5000 feet
Above 5000 feet
Railways

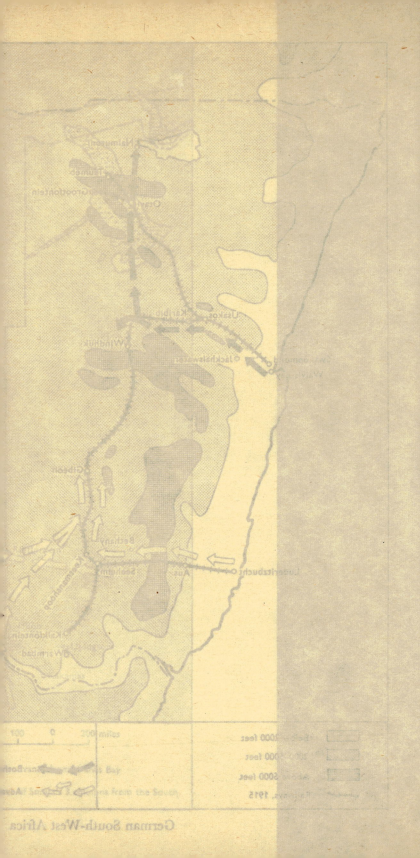

and threw himself at once into the work of clearing up the muddle which he found there. His most urgent problems were transport and human relations. From Lüderitz and Swakopmund the Germans had built connections with the main north–south railway-line; but as they retreated from the coast they tore up the track. Fortunately, they failed to demolish the earthworks, and Botha found when he landed at Swakopmund that a start had already been made in laying new sleepers and rails—far too slow a start, in his opinion; but he now drove the work forward furiously. Meanwhile, his forces as they fanned out were dependent for their supplies chiefly upon mule-drawn waggons; Botha found that the mule-teams were too small— only ten mules, whereas twelve were absolutely essential for a team in such difficult country. The mules, like the horses and the men, could not do their work without water; but the wells were sparse and the Germans were putting Cooper's sheep dip into them;* Botha set hundreds of men to work at digging new wells. And all the time he and his staff were sending a stream of telegrams and letters to impress upon the Defence Department in Pretoria their transport needs—engines, rolling stock and other railway equipment, motor-vehicles (the best answer of all to the transport problems of open and arid country), waggons and the mules to pull them, horses for the cavalry and the mounted infantry.[40]

The trouble that Botha was having about horses became a symbol of the trouble that he was having with human beings. Units which were supposed to be mounted had been shifted from Cape Town without horses, but with the assurance that horses would be waiting for them at the remount depots at Swakopmund and Walvis Bay. And then it transpired that these depots did not contain a single animal. Botha was furious when he discovered this bungling and more furious still when he found out that officers of the remounts and transport depots were in collusion with each other to steal horses from such Boers as had the good fortune to possess them.

Now, Jannie [he wrote on 7 March], you must not mind if Collyer and I sometimes send you strong telegrams. It is necessary, for, believe me, there is a lot of wrong-doing that has to be put right, and, Jannie, there are a whole lot of little misplaced junior officers in Remounts and Transport

---

* An outcry was raised against the Germans in the press for poisoning the wells; but sheep dip, which was their favourite means of making the water undrinkable, is not usually classified with the poisons: moreover, the Germans normally gave notice when they had spoiled a well.

who treat the boers badly. Take it from me that it is so. To show you with what contempt Commandants are treated, Commandant Trichardt will serve. He received all his horses in the Cape. On arrival at Walfisch the vet ordered that 12 of his horses were to go to the sick line Remounts. This was done on a receipt being issued. Now that I have ordered the Brigade to march further, he sent to fetch the 12 horses and was told that the horses have been given out to others.

Botha's answer to this sharp practice was to have the officers responsible for it sent back to Cape Town and to put Remounts under the direct control of a member of his own staff.[41]

About the same time he asked Smuts to take additional steps for the satisfaction of his soldiers. Many of them, it needs to be remembered, were conscripted men, for Botha had decided that his pledge to employ volunteers only was no longer binding in the changed circumstances when Maritz joined forces with the Germans.[42] Conscripts or volunteers, the men were irked by some of the postal and censorship arrangements.

You know we decided long ago that the Commandos could post letters free, but the wives or people in the Union were to use stamps. The result is that the wives don't understand this—they post free and then the letters are not delivered and the men do not hear from them. Do allow the wives to post free as well; the men are making great sacrifices for land and people and they deserve it. Also see Roland and have his censorship instructions modified—they are entirely based on European conditions and letters are censored for all kinds of nonsense....See that there are enough people so that the censor does not hold up the letters so long.[43]

Amongst the survivals of the twenty years' correspondence between Botha and Smuts the letters that Botha wrote from South-West Africa are a precious series: they reveal most vividly the simplicity and subtlety, the prudence and the daring, the patience and the gusto of a great leader of men. While he was attending most meticulously to the innumerable details of administrative preparation Botha all the time was pushing his forces forward to hustle the enemy and 'give them a good fright'. He felt no doubt of his ability to finish the business quickly as soon as he got into 'the grass and water country'. Unfortunately, he soon discovered that General MacKenzie, 'the old chap' who was in command at Lüderitz, was unwilling to stir from his base and attack Aus, the German position above him on the plateau, until he had an overwhelming superiority of men and heavy guns and all the paraphernalia for battering down a fortress. But Botha was convinced that his own thrusts from the north had already compelled the Germans to evacuate this so-called fortress. He would have liked to send MacKenzie back to Durban; but once again he had to consider the human implications of his military problem; MacKenzie's men were English-speaking South Africans who would feel aggrieved if their general were treated too roughly. In the end, Botha decided that he had better make a personal visit to Lüderitz to unravel this tangle.

Well [he wrote on 30 March], I have had a long and serious talk with MacKenzie. I have told him very plainly that there can be no more waiting and that he must do more with such a big, costly army; that, if he wishes it, both you and I would want to help him with everything that he still needs, that I am even inclined, if he wishes it, to take command and attack Aus. I cannot say more because the position is delicate. Were I to go further, he would resign. Now this...would not be wrong, but the consequences of it may be wrong, because his mounted Commandos are all Natal men and they will misunderstand MacKenzie's resignation and stand by him— so let us do nothing now.[44]

But Botha had a clear idea of what needed to be done soon. Three weeks earlier he had written to Smuts asking him to hurry through the parliamentary session and then come himself to the southern front to get things moving. 'Well Jannie, I wish you all success. Stand fast and hurry through and come in yourself at one end—then we shall finish everything by May.'[45] Nothing could have pleased Smuts better than this summons and he began at once to make his plans. They failed to satisfy Botha.

Jannie [he wrote], this is an amazingly big country in which to wage war. I have given much attention to all the plans of invasion and attack and especially your plan to advance in the south to Seeheim. May I hope that you will allow me to give you a little advice. Allow me first to assure you warmly of my delight that you are coming to take command in the south. It will be and is very necessary. We have, in the first place, to do with an army which consists of two races and the desired cooperation depends on who is in command, and as soon as the various commandos in the south are nearer together, which we hope will soon happen, then, Jannie, you are absolutely indispensable there. We have no one else to send there, so no one will welcome you more heartily to these plains of Moab than I. Now as regards your plan—it is definitely wrong.

The understanding between the two friends was so complete that they need never mince words with each other for fear of giving offence. At the beginning of the campaign, Botha's sharp demands upon the Ministry of Defence had aroused the resentment of an over-driven official, who had drafted a querulous reply which, by some mistake, was telegraphed to Swakopmund as from Smuts himself. Botha's reply had been characteristic of him. 'I shall always be the last to take it amiss if you, with all your worries, become a little impatient, but Jannie, if you want to rap me over the knuckles, do not let it go via all the clerks at both ends.' Now that he in his turn was giving Smuts a rap he did it forthrightly; but after arguing for a different plan which seemed to him much better, he concluded: 'I want you therefore to consider this plan thoroughly—and if it does not appeal to you, think no more of it.'[46]

Smuts dropped his own plan in favour of Botha's. After all, the change was chiefly one of emphasis, for the broad outline of operations in the south had already been agreed upon. It was to be an attack in three columns: the first, under Berrangé, moving in from the east through British Bechuanaland; the second, under van Deventer, striking north across the Orange; the third, under Mac-Kenzie, advancing from Lüderitz through Aus to the central railway. Smuts had intended at first to reinforce van Deventer and to direct operations from the south; but Botha persuaded him that van Deventer's column was already quite big enough for the transport which was available and that he would do much better to give the extra drive to the advance from the coast.

You should come direct to Lüderitz, form two wings out of the cavalry now under MacKenzie in one brigade, and let MacKenzie take command of them alone. He does not understand infantry and should be head of a smaller mounted force only. You then take command over him and the others in the south and after Aus is occupied you will have a big open country for operations. From Aus there is much grass and water to Bethany and this is the correct flank movement. After such a movement Seeheim, Kalkfontein, Warmbad and the outlying places must fall of themselves, and then you are in a position to do a great deal of important work. It will help me tremendously, for if the enemy is really concentrating near me, I shall soon be in very serious fighting. And I am convinced that the heaviest work lies north.

So, more or less, it fell out. By the second week of April Smuts was at the front. After assembling his staff at Aus he moved it forward to Keetmanshoop, 'a charming little town with lovely public buildings',[47] on the central railway just beyond its junction with the

Lüderitz line. His three columns had converged upon each other with excellent timing and were chasing the Germans north. Smuts, as usual, did a great deal of scouting ahead. He called on his columns for a special effort to catch the fleeing Germans and on 25 April their rearguard suffered heavy losses at Gibeon. But the main body escaped north. There was nothing more for Smuts to do. After three weeks of blazing action he returned to his political and administrative treadmill. Still, he allowed himself the luxury of a few days with his family.

I have finished my job [he told Arthur Gillett], and occupied all that country up to Windhoek and have now returned to the Union after disbanding part of my force and handing the balance over to General Botha who continues the campaign in the north. Tomorrow I proceed to Pretoria and to the dear family from which I have been separated for many anxious months. You can understand that, in spite of cares and worries, I feel like a schoolboy going home for the holidays.[48]

Actually, it was Botha, not Smuts who occupied Windhoek. At Jakhalswater, where the river Swakop breaks out of the plateau into the coastal plain, Botha had set up his advanced base and coiled the springs for his thrust in full force into the interior. On 6 May a long leap took him to Karibib, on the central railway. Two weeks later he was in Windhoek, conferring with the German governor and the commander-in-chief. They made the wholly unacceptable proposal that hostilities should be suspended, with the two military forces retaining respectively the areas that they now held, until the future of the colony should be decided at the peace conference. The governor blustered: 'Do you', he asked Botha, 'want to embitter 70,000,000 people against you when you have only 40,000,000 behind you?' But Botha had already flung his patrols forward in pursuit of the 4000 Germans who still remained at large in the north. It irked him that he could not set out at once with his main forces to make a clean finish; but his horses, through being tied up each night without fodder, had become too weak to use and he was getting through only 20 tons of supplies per day as against the 130 tons he needed. The Germans had destroyed the bridge at Usakos, dismantled the railway workshops and done everything else they could think of to put the transport system out of action, and everything seemed to be going wrong with the attempts his engineers were making to get it working again. On 23 May he told Smuts: 'I have already made all sorts of plans, but it is now becoming clear to me that our forward movement is only being delayed by the clumsy feebleness of a bunch of engineers...it is damned discouraging and has a bad effect on the burgers and gives the enemy every chance to make the already difficult and hard positions before us still more difficult. However, by the time you receive this, I hope to get sufficient fodder.' By 2 June he felt confident that he would be able to move within eight days and reckoned that he would be able to finish the whole business within a month after setting out. It proved to be an accurate reckoning, for he received the German surrender on 9 July.[49]

A few opinions on this brilliant campaign are worth citing. The *Official History* describes it as 'a unique instance of strategical operations culminating in an engagement that completely destroyed the enemy as a fighting force in the entire theatre of operations'.[50] A markedly unofficial opinion was quoted many years later by Deneys Reitz, who had been at first with Smuts and then with Botha on their forced marches; the German commander-in-chief, he says, exclaimed, as he saw the Boer horsemen appearing in apparent disorder out of the bush all around his troops: 'This is not a war, it's a hippodrome.'[51] Finally, some words which Smuts used contemporaneously are worth quoting. In an address to the burghers at Potschefstroom in the closing stages of the campaign in the north, he said:

I have had some difficult work in my time, but I have never seen any accomplishment that was more successful or more expeditiously carried out than this work of yours in German South West....If you tell them of the march from Nonidas to Karibib they will not believe you; if you tell them how little water you drank and how few biscuits you ate, they will not believe you. Everything ends well, however, and it has been my experience in the world, and no doubt it has been yours as well, that there is always success on the road of duty.[52]

On 12 July Smuts issued a general order acclaiming the conquest of German South-West Africa as 'the first achievement of a united South African nation, in which both races have combined all their best and most virile characteristics'.[53]

Nevertheless, Botha had been harassed to the very end by tension between the English- and Afrikaans-speaking elements of his army.

This tension proved to be a special curse when the time came to make provision for the administration of the conquered territory. It was of the greatest importance to the Union that the administrators should be men of high quality, seeing that the case for dispossessing the Germans permanently had to be built up chiefly on the ground that their administrators were men of low quality who had failed to treat the Native population justly. Merriman put this argument to Smuts with great force.[54] Botha, however, was preoccupied with arguments of a quite different kind. He felt (and often he may have been quite right) that he could not appoint English-speaking South Africans to administrative posts because of their bitter feelings towards the Germans and towards the resident Boers, most of whom had sided with Maritz. He also felt that it would be a great help in the approaching elections if the word went round among his Boer soldiers and their relatives and friends at home that the conquered territory would offer plenty of openings for farmers 'as well as openings in the police and administration, etc.'. He was lucky in finding an experienced colonial administrator named Gorges to put in charge of the territory; but in the years ahead Gorges was to feel himself constrained many times to complain to Smuts about the poor quality of his subordinates in the administration and police.[55]

The same tensions as were expressing themselves so ominously in South-West Africa were rending the Union. Smuts might acclaim the recent victory as the achievement of a united nation; but the two European communities were drawing further apart from each other: or, at least, powerful sections within each community were doing so. Smuts had not been back from the front more than a week or two before the news of the sinking of the *Lusitania* became the occasion for a wild outbreak of anti-German rioting in the English-speaking cities. He thought this jingoistic hysteria cowardly and contemptible but his government was compelled to temporise with it. The effect was to weaken the government's position among Afrikaners, whom Smuts himself quoted as saying: 'The rebels are being shot down and kept in prison but the Jingo favourites escape scot-free.'[56]

Victory in South-West Africa had done nothing to win over that section of the Afrikaner community which had opposed the campaign and sympathised with the rebellion. A movement called *Helpmekaar*, which had been launched to pay the fines imposed upon the rebels, spread far and wide and so prodigiously overshot its target that money became available for endowing Afrikaner cultural associations of many kinds. In the sacrificial flame which the rebellion had kindled, or rekindled, the language movement became aglow with a new splendour; Leipoldt and Celliers began to write in Afrikaans their poems on the Boer War and the martyrs of 1914. Before 1915 was out, Merriman told Smuts that a poem was in circulation about Jopie Fourie which depicted him as an Afrikaner Andreas Hofer. The new wine of passionate nationalism was fermenting in the Church, the universities and the schools. In the Church, perhaps, the balance was still evenly held between the supporters and the opponents of the government; but the conflict was so bitter that cases occurred of dissident congregations splitting off from their parent synods. Amongst Afrikaner students, the rebels quickly got the upper hand; at Stellenbosch, the student body, whose pride it had been in happier years to send messages of congratulation and encouragement to their greatest graduate, now rejected Smuts bitterly and irrevocably. In the schools, if Merriman was to be believed, the tone was set by 'imperfectly educated teachers whose whole idea of instruction consists in fostering an anti-English propaganda'. Merriman declared that he had never, in all his forty-six years of public life, known 'such a feeling between English and Dutch, so bitter, so absolutely impossible.... What is going to be the end of all this?'[57]

The Nationalist party was fully conscious of the great surge of emotion which was driving it forward. By now the party was well organised and actively at work, not only in the Free State, the home of its oracle Steyn and its leader Hertzog, but also in the Transvaal and the Cape, where it had found effective local leaders in Tielman Roos and D. F. Malan. These men were looking forward aggressively to the impending elections. The idea came into Smuts's head, or rather was put there by some of his colleagues (Botha at the time being still in South-West Africa), that there might be something to be said for declaring a moratorium upon elections in wartime, as the British government was doing. He asked Merriman to consider this suggestion carefully and to let him know what he thought about it.[58] Merriman saw nothing at all to be said in favour of it. Nobody, he confessed, disliked elections more than he did, but up to the present no substitute for them had been found and to postpone them *now*, after armed rebellion had been put down and party warfare was taking its place, would be to give the disaffected party a just ground of grievance which they lacked at present. Besides, despite all the noise they were making the Nationalists were a disunited and ineffectual crowd who would make a poor showing once they were brought into the open.

The only bond of union is a professed hatred of Botha and yourself, which if you sift to the bottom, where it does not come from jealousy, is based, not on your mistakes and errors, but on your good deeds. . . .But you must have courage and take the job in hand, organise! organise!. . .The one stream policy will carry the day if you explain it. . . .Go round! Get some missioners going! Remember the old proverb 'Softly stroke a stinging nettle and it wounds you for your pains, Grasp it like a man of mettle, and it soft as silk remains.' Just so with this Hertzog faction. Their cause is based on personal jealousy, race hatred and narrow-minded exclusiveness, and it is bound to fail if we grapple it properly.

That was the advice that Smuts had been hoping for. He told Merriman that the battle would be opened as soon as Botha came back from South-West Africa and that he for one had no doubts about its outcome. News had just come through of the German surrender and it was having a depressing effect on the local Hertzogites. Poor things! they had been looking all the time for news of a serious reverse. Just wait till Botha's stalwarts came home![59]

They came home in July and August and the elections were fixed for October. Underneath the confusing slogans the practical issue before the country was quite clear: whether or not it would continue to support the war. The South African party supported it and so did the Unionists; the Nationalist party opposed it; the Labour party was split between the war-supporters led by Creswell and the war-opposers led by Andrews. In terms of tactics, the most awkward decisions which the South African party had to make concerned their relations with the Unionists; it would be folly to fight them in constituencies where a Nationalist candidate was likely to become *tertius gaudens*; but elsewhere it would be folly not to fight them, since the appearance of a deal with them would drive many Afrikaner voters into the opposite camp.[60]

As the pattern of electoral conflict became clear and the fighting grew hot Smuts felt his confidence rising. He wrote at the end of August: 'I read the future as follows: Labour and N.P. 40, Unionists 30, S.A.P. 60. I shall be much surprised if we do worse than that.' On 23 September an extremist Labour mob broke up a meeting that he was addressing at Newlands in Johannesburg and he narrowly escaped being murdered. To a telegram from Merriman he replied: 'Many thanks for wire which greatly appreciated. Political effect will be excellent.'[61]

Merriman, however, was shocked by this act of violence and was beginning to revise his earlier opinion about the beneficial effects of bringing political enemies into the open. If the country escaped civil war, he said, it would be only because the Nationalists lacked fighting men. He wanted Smuts to take legal action against his slanderers, some of whom were saying in so many words that Botha and he had murdered de la Rey.

You have not done the things you ought to have done in not exercising some vigilance over this propaganda of poison, or in omitting to publish vital documents. I write plainly but I feel strongly. It makes me extremely angry to hear these Afrikaner nationalists booing the hero of Spion Kop and cheering such sorry fellows as Malan (not Francy)* and Hertzog. What ignorant ingratitude!! And of course you come in for your share. Do be careful about sending men out of the country. We shall want them all when the Civil War comes as come it will, if things go as they are now going.

In his reply to this outburst Smuts showed natural resentment against the rowdyism and abuse and slander which Botha and he had to endure but he refused to prosecute the slanderers.

I can understand your anger against the lampooners and libellers. There is a stream of this anonymous filth which the censors are stopping in the press but some copies circulate privately.... Of course the Nationalists are now resuscitating all the episodes from our greater past and appropriating credit to themselves although most of them did precious little to build up that tradition. They were the handsuppers and national scouts in those times, and I fear the only thing which is 'national' about many of them is their connection with the national scouts.

Of course, he was being unfair to Hertzog and the majority of his followers, but the cap fitted some of them. And their libels were indeed 'most gross'. Still, to prosecute them on the eve of the elections would only have the effect of making martyrs of them.[62]

Polling-day was in the fourth week of October. Smuts professed himself satisfied with the results, and it was true that the majority in favour of fighting the war was as large as the one that he had

---

* He meant 'Fransie', that is, Senator F. S. Malan, editor of *Ons Land*, as distinct from Rev. Dr D. F. Malan, editor of *Die Burger*.

counted on in his forecast of late October. Its distribution, however, was very different. The figures were:

South African party	54
Unionists	40
Nationalists	26
Labour	4
Independents	6
	130

He had thought that his own party would win at least 60 seats and that the Nationalists and Labour between them would win 40; whereas the Unionists would win only 30. What he had not counted upon was, first, the almost total collapse of Labour in urban constituencies, with consequential gains to the Unionists: and secondly, the great advance of the Nationalists in rural constituencies, chiefly at the expense of his own party.

According to a contemporary analysis,[63] the distribution of votes among the parties, in the 122 seats which were contested, was as follows:

	S.A.P.	Unionist	Nation-alist	Labour	Inde-pendent
Cape	46,215	28,136	34,773	6,502	6,603
Transvaal	30,159	17,815	25,049	14,683	2,424
O.F.S.	9,530	—	16,597	—	—
Natal	8,413	3,668	1,767	3,259	1,510
	94,317	49,619	78,186	24,444	10,537

The detailed commentary upon these figures called for considerable discrimination: for example, they seemed to suggest that the Unionists were considerably over-represented in parliament, until it was remembered that five of their members had been returned unopposed, and that they could, besides, have easily added to their total poll if they had chosen to contest more constituencies. The figures for the Free State were a surprise, showing as they did that the South African party, although it had not won a single seat in this Nationalist stronghold, had nevertheless polled 36 per cent of the votes. On the other hand, the Nationalists had found themselves in a similar position in many constituencies of the Transvaal and the Cape. They might well consider themselves unlucky to have gained only 26 seats from their 78,000 votes. That figure represented 30% of the poll. If one eliminated Natal, where Nationalist support was negligible, it represented 43 per cent of the poll—not so very much below the 49 per cent of the South African party. And nearly all the Nationalist gains were in the country districts, which had seemed in 1910 the unconquerable fortress of the Botha government. That fortress by now was more than half in enemy possession.

Smuts did not believe that they would hold their gains. He felt sure that the conception of national interest and duty which he and Botha represented must in the long run prevail over General Hertzog's conception. The Nationalists, he said, must realise that they were by far in the minority, 'and this being their high water mark, it will be useless for them to proceed along a path of isolation and impotency'.[64] All the same, there were some disturbing portents. In December, when the government released over a hundred of the imprisoned rebels, Deneys Reitz wrote to say that it was 'a damned disgrace' and had made life in Heilbron so intolerable that he and his friends were resigning in a body from the South African party. About the same time, Smuts received an anonymous letter: 'On the anniversary of the murder of Jopie Fourie we wish the murderer happy Christmas.'[65]

That was only the opening bar of the hymn of hate. But Smuts by now was getting used to being hated. Despite all the strain and worry and weariness of the past year (such a year, he said, as he hoped never to have to go through again) he was looking forward to a peaceful, happy Christmas with his family at Doornkloof. But what kind of Christmas would families in Europe be having? He wrote to Arthur Gillett: 'What a Christmas that of 1914, and what a Christmas this one is, and what will the next be like? It is terrible and depressing to see all the great discoveries and scientific achievements of our race turned like so many daggers against the heart of the race. Do you see any daylight? I am always thinking of these things and yet always trying to stifle my thoughts.'[66]

Throughout the past year he had felt isolated from the wider world. He had written hardly a dozen letters to his friends in Europe and had not received many more. On the eve of his departure for South-West Africa he had received from Emily Hobhouse a letter which he thought 'curious'—as well he might, for she was setting out in a state of intense nervous exaltation for a Women's Peace Conference in Holland, an occasion which she was able to combine (so incomplete, even in 1915, the apparatus of total war still remained) with a visit to Germany and German-occupied Belgium. She believed herself to be enlisted in a great crusade of Womanhood to rescue humanity from the hell into which it had been flung by men; by men like Smuts.

We have to try and *un*do all that you and those like you have done, the woe, the ruin, the misery you have wrought.... Men have indeed shown their absolute inability to guide and govern this fair world, without women's civilizing and moderating influence to guide them.... So you see we have nought in common. You and General Botha had a glorious opportunity—*and you did not take it*.... We believe, not in narrow Nationalism, but in Internationalism, the Brotherhood of Man, and we recognise *no* enemies, all humanity are our friends and our interests everywhere are one and the same. Preach this and you will be a great statesman.[67]

...A great evangelist, Smuts might well have said to himself; but no longer a statesman. And yet, in his own way, he felt as deeply as Emily Hobhouse did that statesmanship of the old stamp was powerless to save the world. In South-West Africa he came across a copy of Houston Stewart Chamberlain's *Grundlagen des 19ten Jahrhunderts*, which moved him to reflect upon the long road that the Germans had travelled from Kant and Goethe. What the statesmen of the world did or tried to do could never reach a higher level of sanity and humanity than the intellectual and spiritual levels of their peoples. Could those levels be raised? With the directness of a perplexed student addressing his old and wise tutor, Smuts put the question to Wolstenholme. 'Will mankind, sick of all this horror, turn inward and purify its spirit, or will it become debased and demoralised and brutalised by its horrible experience? Please answer these questions in your next letter.' Wolstenholme, in his reply, said that they were questions which could never be answered, except by a God. 'And there isn't one—not even a vague "something not ourselves that makes for righteousness".' He packed into a single sentence his total repudiation of the sovereignty of God, the progressive realisation of the Whole—the entire system of faith and thought which Smuts, by whatever name he called it, had made his sheet anchor. To Wolstenholme, all this was 'reasoning of the heart', not of the head; in other words, it was self-deception and delusion. He told Smuts that the universe was sublimely indifferent to the struggles of men for things like 'happiness' or 'holiness'; it just left it to each man 'to fight it out for himself or, as most men do, to let it go by default'. Different men, he said, would make different decisions according to their temperaments; his own preference was for putting up a fight. And that brought him to the doings of Smuts. It was reported that he might be coming over to London with other Dominion leaders for an Imperial War Conference. Wolstenholme could hardly believe that anything so good could happen—'but I wish it could, and would bring you once more, before I go, to these four walls in which my existence is ebbing away in a strange mixture of despair, resignation and at times something that looks like the ghost of happiness and hope'.[68]

The suggestion had been put to Smuts more than once in 1915 that he ought to go to London. The Union's High Commissioner, W. P. Schreiner, told him that Canada was represented in London by a minister and that the day would come when all the Dominions would follow the same practice.[69] Smuts, however, could not at that time conceive that his duty could possibly be outside South Africa. Or, at any rate, outside Africa. In November he found himself compelled to consider seriously an invitation from the British government to take command of the much-frustrated army in East Africa.

His government was conscious of having a strong interest in the course of the war there. When the fighting was finished in German South-West Africa the question had arisen of employing elsewhere such men as were willing to serve beyond the Union's frontiers. A volunteer force (which included Smuts's secretary, Ernest Lane) had already been raised for Europe; but, apart from the difficulties which arose from the different rates of soldiers' pay in the British and South African forces, there were some people who argued very strongly that German East Africa was the proper arena for the Union's next effort. The argument was put by Merriman to Smuts, who accepted it, not only on military, but also on political grounds. 'If that country were conquered by us', he said, 'we could probably effect an exchange with Mozambique and so consolidate our territories south of the Zambesi and Kunene.'[70] From the strictly military point of view, the invitation to him to undertake this conquest himself came at an appropriate time; for in November the Union government was making arrangements to send 20,000 men to East Africa. From the political point of view, however, the invitation came at a bad time, when the country had not yet settled down after the elections. It happened, however, that General Smith-Dorrien, who had been given the appointment after Smuts's refusal of it, fell ill at Cape Town on his way to the front. Early in the New Year the British government again offered the command to Smuts. This time, under the urging of his colleagues and 'with many a pang and many a grave misgiving', he accepted.[71]

1916

A year earlier, when Botha had gone to take command in German South-West Africa, Smuts had remained behind in Pretoria to see that his military needs were supplied and to hold the political front. Those roles were now reversed. 'My heart and soul are with you', wrote Botha on 23 February, 'and I shall do everything to help you, be assured of that. Just tell me what can be done.... Your going has everyone's approval and I can only wish you God's best blessing. Be careful and let van Deventer always keep a captaincy with you. If I can do anything for you here, privately or officially, you have only to say so. God bring you back safely to us will always remain my prayer. May your work be blessed.'[72] When Botha wrote this letter, news had just come through that Major-General Tighe, Smuts's predecessor, had taken 'a good drubbing' at Salaita hill. People were perturbed at the casualties, which in a few hours' fighting had reached between one-third and one-half the total of the six months' campaign in South-West Africa.* However, 'now that you are there', said Botha, 'everything feels relieved'.

Up to the time of Smuts's arrival, nothing had gone right with the British campaign in East Africa. Von Lettow Vorbeck, the German commander, had proved himself to be a man of superb resolution and skill. In November 1914 he had repulsed with ignominy and heavy loss a much more numerous force which had attempted to capture Tanga from the sea. In January 1915 he had attacked and routed a force assembled at Jassini, on the coastal road, for an invasion by land. Throughout the next twelve months it was he, not the British, who seized the initiative. From firm bases in the rampart of mountains guarding the northern boundary of the German colony he raided British territory and threatened its lifeline, the railway from Mombasa to Nairobi. Meanwhile, steadily and methodically, he

---

* In South-West Africa there were 113 killed and 311 wounded; at Salaita hill total casualties were 172, of whom 133 were South Africans.

built up and trained his military forces and organised their communications and supplies for a long and bitter struggle.

Von Lettow Vorbeck had had trouble at first with Dr Heinrich Schnee, the Governor of German East Africa, who was ready to yield without fighting the coastal towns of Dar-es-Salaam and Tanga. For psychological, if not for strictly military reasons, that would have signified general defeat. Still, one can sympathise with Dr Schnee, for it was not easy to see how the colony could be successfully defended. Not only was it blockaded by sea but it was hemmed in on all sides by hostile territories: British to the north, Belgian to the west, British again to the south-west, Portuguese (although Portugal's belligerency was belated)* to the south. The colony's isolation—military, economic and political—was total.

Von Lettow, nevertheless, was not at all downcast. As he explained later, he had made up his mind that the fate of the German colonies would be decided on European battlefields and had set himself the task of pinning down in East Africa as large a volume as possible of the military power which otherwise would have been available to the enemy on those battlefields. When he looked at the map, he considered his chances of making himself useful in this way to be very good. The area of German East Africa was 384,000 square miles, not so far short of the combined areas of the Hohenzollern and Habsburg Empires. Its population was only $7\frac{1}{2}$ million, of which by far the greater part was concentrated in the more favoured hilly districts, only about one-fifth of the total area, which had adequate supplies of water. A great deal of the country was economically, militarily and politically expendable. Anyway, an attempt to defend every frontier against every enemy would be quite hopeless. 'The best protection for the whole territory', von Lettow Vorbeck believed, 'consisted in taking a firm hold at one point.'[73] That 'point', when Smuts arrived, was in the north-easterly region, where the colony's economic resources and European population were in large measure concentrated, where the mountains and bush offered wonderfully strong positions, and where the Germans had an immense advantage of communications over their enemies.

The mountains stretched almost unbroken from the narrow coastal strip to Kilimanjaro. Behind them, parallel with the Pangani river for most of its course, was a railway linking the port of Tanga

* March 1916.

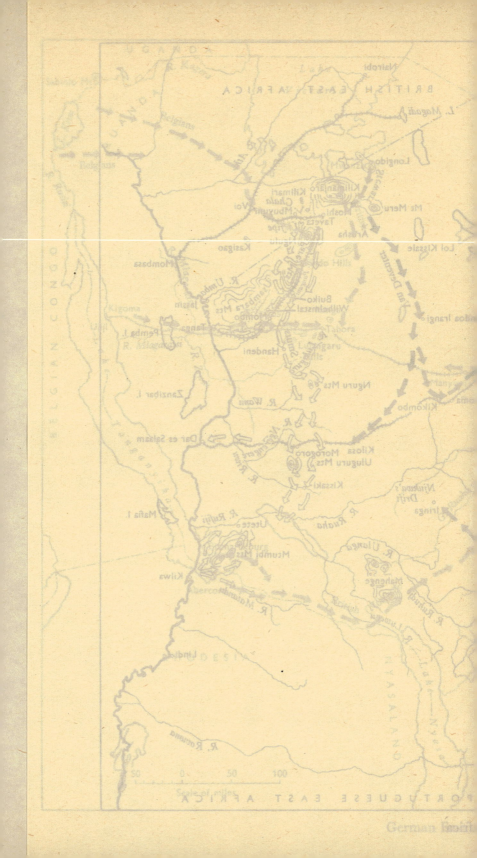

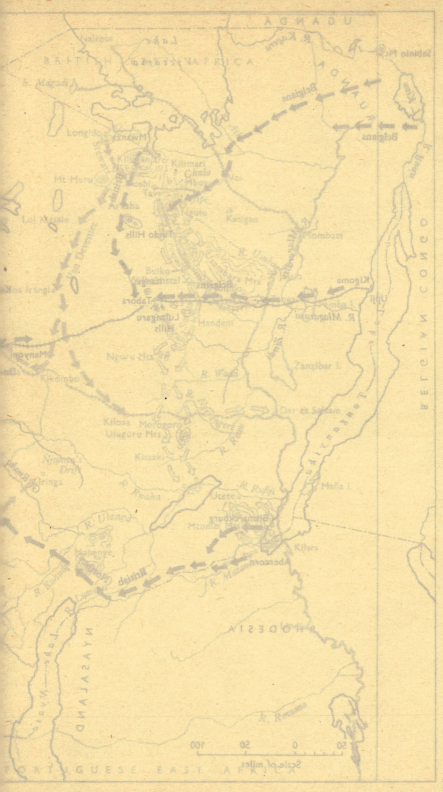

German East

with Moshi in the Kilimanjaro foothills. To the south, at varying distances (only about a hundred miles at the coast, but much further inland) ran the central line, from Dar-es-Salaam nearly 800 miles westwards to Kigoma on Lake Tanganyika. Von Lettow Vorbeck had taken great pains to improve communications between the two railway systems; from Wilhelmstal in the Usambara Mountains to Handeni in the plain behind the northern railway he had the use of an efficient trolley line and he had also built a number of military roads. They were unmetalled, but for him that was a positive advantage; the enemy forces, if they broke through, could not possibly use motor transport on them except in the dry season, whereas his own native porters could use them in all weathers.

The inferiority of the Germans to their enemies in numbers and technical equipment was not such a handicap as might at first sight have appeared. When Smuts arrived in February 1916 he found at his disposal for an attack on the mountain rampart two fully equipped divisions and an additional mounted force under van Deventer, his comrade in the invasion of Cape Colony fifteen years earlier and in South-West Africa the year before. To withstand the expected attack, von Lettow Vorbeck had built up a force of 3000 Europeans and 11,000 Askaris. They were welded closely but flexibly together in company formations and had the high morale of men who trusted their commander and had proved themselves in action; whereas their enemies were a polyglot army of Indians, East Africans, West Africans, South Africans, Rhodesians, West Indians and British* whose confidence had been shaken by past failures and who did not yet know their new leader. Nor did he as yet know the country into which he would be leading them; nor its weather. These were von Lettow's most powerful allies. He was free to concentrate his forces in the healthier regions, whereas the attacking forces would be compelled to traverse tracts of country where the malarial mosquito and the tsetse-fly would inflict terrible casualties on men and animals. His men had acquired a high degree of immunity to fever and he had no need to use animals for transport. He affirmed later

---

* Some of these units arrived later in the year. According to the British Official History, the ration strength on 22 March 1916 was just below 45,000, of whom 25,500 were white troops (including approx. 19,000 South Africans): 14,000 were Indians and 5000 Africans. These numbers included administrative, transport, medical forces, etc.: consequently, the numerical superiority over the enemy was not quite so great as has been generally assumed.

that it was no exaggeration to say that he had had 'hundreds of thousands' of native porters working for his troops. For his purposes, they were probably as efficient as the motor and animal transport which Smuts used; for the motor-vehicles were immobilised in the rainy season and the animals in all seasons died by thousands and tens of thousands.[74]

Nevertheless, despite the windfalls which had accrued to the Germans from blockade running and despite their successful improvisations of *ersatz* production,[75] Smuts enjoyed over his opponent a strong superiority of weapons and supplies, as well as of men. What use he made of this superiority has become a matter of controversy. The critical summings-up in both the Official Histories are emphatically in his favour;[76] but some unofficial writers, most notably H. C. Armstrong, have denounced his campaign as a costly failure.[77] The present writer must excuse himself from repeating the detailed researches which kept the British official historians at work (and even they did not finish their job) for more than twenty years; all that he can hope to do is to present some of the pros and cons of the contemporary argument. On the con side there are the diatribes of the Nationalist opposition in South Africa, which denounced the ruinous cost of the campaign in men and money and steadily opposed recruitment and supply to support it; there are also some echoes of the disdainful grumbling which came from senior British officers who hated having to serve under an amateur and a Colonial. On the pro side, there is the testimony of, among others, Francis Brett Young, Louis Botha and von Lettow Vorbeck.

A senior British officer who, to begin with at any rate, was ranged on the con side was Colonel R. Meinertzhagen. His evidence has to be taken seriously, for he was in charge of military intelligence, a man of great gifts and completely free from the rancour and jealousy of some of his colleagues.[78] What follows are some extracts from his diary dated 23 February and 5 March.

One cannot talk to Smuts without being attracted by his personality.... He is a fascinating little man and one leaves him after an interview with the impression that he has a first-class brain. He has that wonderful trick of never forgetting faces or names. I found it such a pleasure to run over the situation with him on a map after the laborious processes and artifices one had to resort to with Tighe. Smuts grasps points at once and never wants telling a second time. Yes, I like Smuts and we shall get on well together.... Smuts is quite determined to avoid a stand-up fight. He told me openly that he intends to manœuvre the enemy out of positions and not push them out. He told me he could not afford to go back to South Africa with the nickname 'Butcher Smuts'. Manœuvre is a peculiar form of war which I do not understand and which I doubt will succeed except at great expense in men and money. Every man killed in action means 10 invalided with disease, therefore it is all-important to bring the campaign to a close as soon as possible.... Von Lettow is concentrated here and ready for a fight, but of course he is not going to risk a decisive action against vastly superior numbers. Smuts should bring him to battle and instead of manœuvring him out of position should endeavour to surround and annihilate him, no matter what are our casualties.

For an appreciation of this criticism it is necessary to take stock of the position held by von Lettow Vorbeck. The mountainous rampart which defended the German colony from a northern attack could only be penetrated at three points: on the coastal strip, where the attempted British invasion of January 1915 had been smashed; at Ngulu, a narrow gap in the Pare mountains; and at the much broader Taveta gap, between the precipitous escarpment of the Pare mountains and the majestic mass of Kilimanjaro. There was, in addition, a back-door approach from Longido, on the far side of Kilimanjaro, southwards across a wide waterless plain into a valley leading between mounts Meru and Kilimanjaro to the fertile German plantations around Arusha and the railhead at New Moshi.

Von Lettow Vorbeck had concentrated his main forces for the defence of the Taveta gap, including the advanced position at Salaita hill; but his good railway communications gave him the ability to reinforce quickly such other points as might be threatened. It seems a fair interpretation of what Colonel Meinertzhagen wrote in his diary that he wanted Smuts to concentrate his forces for a frontal attack through the Taveta gap. Meinertzhagen was certainly right in thinking that Smuts was reluctant to accept the heavy losses that these tactics would have entailed: a long list of battle casualties would at that time have been something new in Afrikaner military experience (or, for that matter, in the experience of English South Africans) and there is plenty of evidence in Smuts's correspondence that it would have raised an outcry at home. However, Smuts had additional and probably better reasons for adopting a different method of attack. For one thing, British forces in East Africa had hitherto failed in all their attempts at direct assault and only four weeks earlier their failure at Salaita hill had been resounding. For another thing, von Lettow, as his book makes quite clear, was determined under no circumstances to let his forces be pinned down and destroyed in a pitched battle. The only possible chance of destroying them (and at the best, with such a competent commander in such difficult country, it was only an outside chance) was by a combination of frontal pressure with rapid flanking movements aiming at encirclement.

By and large, this was the plan which Smuts found already drafted when he arrived at the front on 20 February. He added to it one crucial element: speed. On 23 February he cabled to the War Office to the effect that an immediate offensive was both possible and desirable and two days later he 'received the sanction of H.M. Government for his contemplated operations'.[79] The frontal advance through the gap was entrusted to the first division under Tighe, with van Deventer's mounted brigade sweeping across the Kilimanjaro foothills on the right flank. The wide encircling movement from Longido southwards was entrusted to the first division under Stewart. The first division had farthest to go and set out at night on 4 March; but it moved forward with a cautious deliberation which must have infuriated Smuts. The attack on Taveta, which had been preceded by a series of probes and feints from Ngulu northwards to test the enemy's strength and to keep him guessing, was launched on 8 March. Four days later the enemy had been cleared out of the gap and on 12 March the front-door and the back-door forces made contact in the Arusha–Moshi area. It was too late for the smashing victory that Smuts had been aiming at. To achieve that, Stewart would have needed to move faster and advance farther than he managed to do, so as to cut off the Germans in their retreat from the Taveta gap.

Nevertheless, the military position in East Africa had been completely transformed within a bare month of Smuts's arrival at the front. The German threat to the Kenya–Uganda railway had been eliminated. The gateway to German East Africa had been forced. The rich lands around Kilimanjaro had been conquered. The whole area served by the Tanga–Moshi railway had been brought under immediate threat. All this had not been by any means the 'effortless' operation which in retrospect it appeared to Smuts; at the time, he was fully conscious of the hard fighting which had been called for in the Taveta gap and of the casualties which his 'little Afrikaners' had suffered. He told his wife that the South African troops were 50-50 British and Boer and that all of them had fought splendidly.* He told her also that the excellent beginning to the campaign would greatly encourage the whole army and strengthen his own position, which had been very difficult. Letters of congratulation began to crowd his mail. Most welcome of them all must have been the one he received from Botha, his friend, his political chief and his master in the art of war.

I received your letter from Nairobi yesterday, for which my best thanks. What you wrote in it before the attack, you have carried out beautifully. I have shown the letter to various people to indicate to them how, in so short a time, you have made yourself master of the situation. Allow me then to congratulate you sincerely, also on behalf of your other colleagues and all friends, on the success achieved. We all admire what you have done, because we know that your work there is a gigantic task which is accompanied by the greatest difficulties. Your victories have also contributed much to the development of a better spirit here.[80]

Smuts had been hoping to strike a second blow before the enemy had time to reorganise his forces; but the rains came. They were continuous throughout the second half of March and most of April. Then they started again. On 2 May Smuts wrote: 'Outside a tremendous downpour of rain is proceeding. I have never in all my life dreamt that rain could fall as it does here on the slopes of the Kilimandjaro (sic)....The rivers are full, the country is one vast swamp between the mountains; and my advance troops are 220 miles from here where the railroad is at present and have to be fed and provided somehow.'[81] He had used his enforced time of waiting to bring the railway, which branched from the main Uganda line at Voi and had been supplying the forces in front of Taveta, through the gap to Moshi, where it joined the line running down the Pangani valley to Tanga. Another thing which he had done in preparation for his next attack was to make a drastic reorganisation of his army. In the place of two divisions under two British generals, Tighe and Stewart, there emerged three divisions under three South African generals, Hoskins, van Deventer and Brits. This reorganisation could be justified by the fact that the great majority of European soldiers

---

* Three South African battalions took part in the action together with Indian, African, and Rhodesian units (Hordern, *Official History: East Africa*, pp. 243–6).

under his command were South Africans; but the strongest case for it was his need to have divisional commanders who held his confidence. So, as Merriman would have put it, he grasped the nettle.

Action could begin again in the drier country west of Kilimanjaro while it still remained impossible in the rain-sodden country to the east. Far away on Lake Victoria at Nyanga a small force based upon Uganda began to advance southwards; farther away still Belgian forces began to advance eastwards from Lakes Kivu and Tanganyika. About the same time a Rhodesian force led by General Northey began a thrust north-east towards Iringa. Of these peripheral movements, only the last could possibly have any effect upon the main struggle.

The second phase of this struggle had opened in the first week of April, when Smuts sent van Deventer's men on a long ride into the seemingly dry south-east. On 6 April they captured nearly 500 of the enemy at Lol Kissale and from there 'a famous forced march' took them to Kondoa Irangi, two-thirds of the way from Kilimanjaro to the central railway. They occupied the town in the third week of April. The return of the rains made Smuts very anxious about keeping them supplied; but it did not deter him from persisting with his strategic plan. Van Deventer's thrust was intended to be the right prong of the offensive; the left prong would be his own march down the northern railway and then south towards the central line. On his birthday, 24 May, he received a telegram from Botha wishing him good luck. Two days before that he had launched his attack.

Once again, his strategy aroused Colonel Meinertzhagen's strong disapproval. Meinertzhagen did not feel confident that Smuts had strength enough to sustain the offensive on both its prongs and felt that he was dangerously exposing van Deventer's force. On 28 April he wrote in his diary

Information points to von Lettow having decided to hold the Usambara Railway with a weak detachment while concentrating the bulk of his forces against our Mounted Brigade at Kondoa. Such would be his correct course and we can rely on him to do the right thing. Smuts's strategy again places von Lettow on interior lines and von Lettow will only be too ready to profit by any mistake Smuts may have made. Smuts should strengthen Kondoa to a division at once so as to give von Lettow a good smack should he attack before we are prepared to move on the Central Railway.

Africa, he continued, was 'our worst enemy' and, so long as the rains lasted, von Lettow, with his porter transport, possessed a great advantage of mobility. Now was his chance.

Smuts did in fact reinforce van Deventer just enough to enable him to fend off the enemy's counter-attack on Kondoa; but not enough to take the power out of his own drive to the south. It would be tedious to follow in detail the advance of his columns; but a vivid impression of its headlong speed and of the force which propelled it has been given by Francis Brett Young, an English medical officer and novelist who was 'marching on Tanga' under Smuts's command. The thing that most sustained the troops, Brett Young wrote, was their complete confidence in their leader. 'That he was a fine strategist, the move on Moshi, in spite of the failure of the northern enveloping column, had shown us. Of his personal courage we had been assured by the incidents of the Lumi fight; but there was yet another fact—in this case one might almost have called it a personal attribute—in his success which demanded our confidence, and that was the luck which has followed him throughout his career. Everyone believed in his fortune no less than his attainments.'[82] There was still another 'factor' which the troops soon became familiar with— the physical presence of their leader amongst them and ahead of them when things were going badly. Brett Young describes how the force on the right bank of the Pangani was held up by the impossibility of forcing the men and animals any further across the deep ravines and through the dense bush. A rest was ordered while the pioneers were sent ahead to cut the track; soon they came back with the news that the only thing to do was to retire for some miles and then strike out in a new direction. 'The order had been given to retire and all of us were thankful....But no sooner had I loaded my pack-mules and inspanned my bullocks...than we heard rapid hoofs ascending the track, and three horsemen pushed by.' One of the three was Smuts, and in his swift passage the men realised with extraordinary clarity the force that was driving them on. 'He had not been gone five minutes when the order came back to us to advance. Wheeled transport was to be left behind, but, for all that, the brigade must move on. Fifteen hours of marching had made us tired, and yet I do not think there was a man in the brigade who was not cheered and stimulated by this order.'[83] The leader had given his men the feeling that Africa had not beaten them and that it would never beat them.

Later, when the men had hacked and fought their way through the dense bush into more open country, they became used to the sudden appearances of 'the grey Vauxhall with shining, painted radiator' in which their General scouted ahead. Brett Young never records having seen him escorted by the bodyguard which Botha had urged him always to have with him.

The risks which he ran with his life and his constant determination to see with his own eyes what was holding up the advance appeared to some professional soldiers, perhaps to the best of them, to be a serious fault. 'Smuts has made a mistake', wrote Colonel Meinertz-hagen in his diary,[84] 'in mixing himself up with local situations. They obscure the general and larger situation. During an advance he is usually with or in front of the advance guard. During an action he is often in the firing line and loses control of the fight. His staff have often pointed this out but it falls on deaf ears.' In his defence, Smuts would have said that leadership and drive were the supreme requisites for a campaign in which the really dangerous enemy was not von Lettow and his Askaris but the sickness, the slovenliness, the lassitude of tropical Africa. And who would provide these requisites if not the commander-in-chief? Twenty-one years later, when General Collyer, his chief-of-staff in East Africa, wrote a book about the campaign, Smuts admitted it to be a competent work of military history—'and yet he misses the real matter of it all. And that is the immense personal drive that kept that machine going, against all the forces of nature and weaknesses of human nature.'[85]

Brett Young's narrative depicts vividly the headlong rush of late May and early June, which far outstripped the supply services. All the same, it was not quick enough to offset the advantage of communications which the enemy possessed. Leaving behind him his *bouches inutiles* at Wilhelmstal in the Usambara foothills, von Lettow got his main forces away to the south. Still, Smuts by his lightning stroke had conquered the northern railway and the port of Tanga. When the engineers and supply columns had done their work he would be well poised for his third leap forward, this time to the central railway. That was how the campaign went: a series of deep thrusts, which a determined and skilful enemy always tried to blunt and delay on ground chosen by himself, followed at intervals by pauses for re-equipment and supply.

It was towards the end of one of these pauses, in late July and early August, that Botha paid a brief visit to the front. The pleasure which he had expressed in his letters at the progress of the advance became deep admiration now that he could see with his own eyes the obstacles with which it had to contend. In his farewell letter from Kilindini he wrote, 'Well, my good friend, tomorrow I return and so I would, before I leave, like to tell you that now that I have seen all your operations here and understand your difficulties, I admire it more than ever that you have done so much in the time. I am proud of your work, old chap, and on leaving I can only say that all my weight is at your disposal, and be assured, Jannie, we pray for your success and safe return.'[86] About the same time Colonel Meinertzhagen revised his estimate of Smuts—not of his character, which he had always found attractive, nor of his strategy and tactics, which he continued to criticise forcibly, but of the whole mixture of virtues and defects which belonged to him as a commander.

We lunched with Smuts at Nderema near Handeni. The more I see of the little man the more I like him. He has great charm and he has already won my affection. Always cheerful, witty and prepared to make the best of things. He is, of course, no soldier, for, as 'Truth' said some weeks back, he is an amateur. His knowledge of human nature, his eye for country, his exceptional power of imposing his will on others, his remarkable personality, reckless disregard of difficulties and very remarkable brain, compel one to respect and admire him. Perhaps it is wrong to say he is no soldier. He is a bad tactician and strategist, an indifferent general but in many ways a remarkable soldier.[87]

Good or bad, the same strategy as before served Smuts for his final thrust to the central railway. In mid-July he let van Deventer's force loose far away to the west. By the end of the month it had made the long leap from Kondoa Irangi and had gained control of the railway for a stretch of about 200 miles. The effect of this coup was to close the west of the colony to von Lettow's forces; henceforward their only possible way of retreat was southwards towards the border of Portuguese East Africa. That, however, was still some hundreds of miles distant, with a great deal of difficult country in between. Smuts, no doubt, had hopes of van Deventer coming in from the west to cut off the retreat, for he delayed his frontal advance until 6 August. By 26 August, after a good deal of fighting in and around the rugged Nguru mountains and after much bridge-building and similar engineering work, his troops reached the railway at

Morogoro. The enemy, as usual, managed to slip away; for the age of armoured cars and aeroplanes was still in its infancy and German East Africa, with its mountains and scrub and immense distances, was a good place for playing hide-and-seek in.

Smuts, nevertheless, flung his forces across the railway in hot pursuit of the enemy. The letters which he was writing to his wife every week reveal what was in his mind at every stage of the march south. On 16 August he had told her about the loss of time he had to endure through having to rebuild the innumerable bridges which the enemy had burnt or blown up, but he was hopeful that many of the Askaris would refuse to continue the retreat further south and that von Lettow would be left with only a remnant. On 3 September he told her that he was across the railway and that within a fortnight he would be at the Rufiji river, which was as far as the British government had asked him to go: all the same, he had it in mind to stay a few months more to see if he could finish the business. On 26 September, however, he told her about the obstacles which the country and its climate were putting in his way.

You cannot imagine how dangerous the rains become in this country. An old missionary informs me that the 40-mile plain between Kissaki and the Rufiji River becomes one continuous sea of water in the rainy season. How am I to pursue the enemy thence? And if I do so and the rain comes, how do we get food and what will become of us, cut off from the world on the Rufiji? But everything will come right, and I shall make other plans. This 40 miles is now an arid desert, so that there is not enough water for the troops should they now go forward. So it is a case of nothing or too much. We are having a terribly hard time. But how much harder a time the fleeing Germans and Askaris are having! So let us be patient and persevere to the end.[88]

He had to resign himself to another period of waiting. There was urgent engineering and administrative work to be done—many hundreds of miles of railway track to be repaired, the wrecked ports to be re-equipped, the economy of an immense territory to be got working again and its government restored. In addition, the military forces were due for a drastic reorganisation. Smuts would never admit that he had demanded too much of his South Africans; they had been the spearhead of an attack which had conquered an immense area, including almost all the economically useful districts of the Colony. Their wastage by disease would have been almost as heavy even if they had not been driven so hard. All the same, this wastage was at a rate which could not be accepted indefinitely. Between October and December from 12,000 to 15,000 patients were evacuated from the hospitals and sent home.[89] From this time onwards, the burden of the campaign would fall increasingly upon soldiers from East and West Africa and other countries whose peoples had acquired a higher degree of immunity to tropical diseases.

All these formidable tasks of reorganisation were carried far within the next few months and by the New Year the leap across the Rufiji was an accomplished fact. Smuts by now had completed the work which the British government had asked him to undertake. Nevertheless, his letters to his wife show him torn between his longing for home and his hankering to stay on just a little longer. Repeatedly, he looked forward to just 'another few months'.[90]

Between his violent spasms of action he had given himself time for reflection. East Africa was making a deep imprint upon his imagination; he thought it an appalling country to make war in and asked his little son to picture him at grips with two terrible monsters, Pangani and Rufiji; but it was a grief to him that he had never climbed Kilimanjaro (twenty-three years later, he felt vicarious triumph when his eldest son climbed it) and he looked forward one day to bringing his wife and family to the lovely Nguru mountains. The East African vegetation fascinated him and he collected some seeds which he hoped would stand transplantation to Doornkloof.[91]

In the evenings, he made time for reading some at least of the books which Wolstenholme sent him. Among them was *The Realm of Ends*, by James Ward, the professor of philosophy whose lectures he would have attended, had permission been granted him, when he was an undergraduate at Cambridge. He thought *The Realm of Ends* 'a fine piece of philosophic thought, however barren the ultimate results'—an opinion which quite upset Ward when he came to hear of it. Smuts was still revolving the holistic theory of which Wolstenholme thought so little and tried once again to explain to his old friend what he was searching for. 'Please think about this', he pleaded, 'and don't merely pooh-pooh what I say. There is something in it.'[92]

The letters which came to him from Merriman and from his colleagues in the Cabinet, especially Botha and Watt, suggested that South African affairs were now in a far better state than they had been in 1915. The habits of settled government seemed to be re-establishing themselves in the country. A foolish plot for 'a second rebellion' had been exposed and publicly denounced by no less a person than General de Wet. The death of Steyn was the occasion for national mourning and the removal of a restraining influence; but Hertzog, although he denounced the government's 'imperialist' ideas and opposed its proposals for continuing the war, was guiding his party along the road of constitutional opposition. Botha, meanwhile, remained in good health and spirits. He felt, quite rightly, that he still had a large and devoted following among Afrikaners and he did not waver in his policy of reconciliation. His parliamentary position was comfortable and he had no trouble in getting through a large programme of legislation. By and large, Smuts found his South African mail encouraging. 'Unless things miscarry in Europe', he told Merriman, 'we ought to see a much better spirit develop in South Africa after the end of the war.'[93]

Unfortunately, the news from Europe was bad. After the terrible fighting at Verdun and on the Somme there seemed no prospect of breaking the stalemate on the western front. And all the efforts which had been made so far on other fronts seemed to have ended in disaster. From time to time there was talk about the future peace settlement; but to Smuts most of this talk seemed barren, if not positively dangerous. On the one hand, he repudiated the punitive economic programme which Mr Hughes of Australia and the Northcliffe Press were trying to foist upon the allies; on the other hand, he feared 'an inconclusive peace'.[94]

In December 1916 it seemed to Smuts that he was just as well employed in East Africa as anywhere else. There appeared no urgent need in the Union for his services and it had not occurred to him that they might be required in Europe. Perhaps he had allowed his personal duel with von Lettow to become something of an obsession. As 'a proof of the mutual personal esteem and chivalry' which united them, he sent him towards Christmas a message of congratulation upon a decoration awarded him recently by the Kaiser.[95] He still looked forward to catching him within a few months and thus making a clean finish of the campaign. Of course it was an illusion. Von Lettow was never going to be caught. And what did it matter? In the undeveloped wastes south of the Rufiji and across the frontier in Mozambique he could keep his reduced forces in being but he could do no serious damage to the British Empire and its allies. In so far as they wasted their energies and resources in trying to round him up, the more fools they.

At the end of the year Smuts encouraged his wife to expect him home soon. But did he really mean it? Certainly, his longing to see her was growing intense. On 21 December he wrote: 'Tomorrow is your dear birthday, and I wish you all possible good fortune for it. Many more of them in health and surrounded by those who love you. A pity that this time one of them is so far away, but I hope that this is the last time, and that we shall in future not be so much separated as in the last 16 years. Yet...I doubt if you will see me now before March, 1917....But bear it bravely; time is now flying fast. Tomorrow I leave for the Mgeta front.' Six days later he wrote: 'But I shall come back one day, Mama, and then not go away so quickly again.' He told her that he hoped to be back for the parliamentary session in March and that in the winter he might perhaps be able to keep his promise of taking the whole family for a few weeks of peace and quiet on Rooikop, their farm in the bushveld.[96]

Alas for these hopes. His letter had a postscript to say that he had just received a telegram from Botha asking him to be the Union's representative at an Imperial Conference to be held shortly in London.

CHAPTER 19

LONDON, 1917

IMPERIAL COMMONWEALTH

SMUTS showed no eagerness to go to London but told Botha that *he* should go himself. He promised to be back in South Africa in time to take charge of the next session. Botha, however, insisted that he could not possibly leave South Africa and that Smuts must go in his place. The ministers were all away on Christmas holidays, but Botha consulted them by telegram and early in the New Year summoned them to a special meeting of the Cabinet. In a series of telegrams he impressed upon Smuts the importance of the London meeting, the impossibility of his own attendance at it and the unanimous desire of the Cabinet that Smuts should go. Smuts consented to 'step into the breach' and on 11 January wrote to his wife to say that he would be back at Doornkloof by the end of the month, but only for a week. 'So get ready for a sort of honeymoon week. But I wonder how many honeymoons we have already had after long separations and hope fervently that this will be the last, or the second last, when I get back from England.' What a hope! All his forecasts and calculations proved wrong. He told her that he would be 'home for good' by next May at the latest but it was not until July 1919 that he returned. She had told Botha that what the Chief decided was always right ('altyd vir die beste'), but she did not foresee that she and her husband now had in front of them a separation longer by far than the one they had endured during the Boer War.[1]

Smuts had not welcomed the advent to power of Lloyd George and he disliked the look of the new British government, which included, among others, his old antagonist Milner. He told Merriman that he was going to London 'with some misgivings' and only hoped that he would not be 'overborne' by other members of the conference to acquiesce in schemes which would be good neither for South Africa nor for the Empire. Merriman retorted that he must not allow himself to be overborne. 'Do, I implore you, make head against the gasbags! Do not give way to them....Do not be *forced* to anything;

you can be dour enough if you choose. . . . I fancy I see you surrounded by the "Kindergarten" revolving round those twin luminaries, Milner and Northcliffe. . . .'[2] The old man's foresight was uncanny. Smuts landed in England on 12 March and the same day received an invitation from Milner to dine at Brooks' and meet five or six influential persons with whom he would be closely associated during the coming weeks. As Merriman had foretold, Northcliffe also was waiting for him—with an inscribed copy of a book that he had published recently and an invitation to talk things over. The bankers, the bishops, the industrialists, the political hostesses—they were waiting for him in droves. Invitations came to him from Lord Cunliffe, the Archbishop of Canterbury, Lady Brassey, Lady Winchester, the Duchess of Rutland and a host of others. Sir Arthur Steel Maitland invited him to All Souls, Lady Astor to Cliveden. Mrs Asquith pursued him with a fierce, possessive ardour. 'I have made a new friend,' she wrote to him on 23 March, 'and as one is able to stretch the power of love so much the more grateful we should be. You are sane, clever and kind (a rare combination) DON'T go away just yet. . . .' She said that she and her husband would be so happy if he would visit them at their country house at Sutton Courtenay and she hoped that he would write something in 'the most precious and private book' which she kept there.[3]

Honours came crowding in on him. London, Plymouth, Cardiff, Manchester, Bristol and other great cities offered him their Freedoms. The Middle Temple and the Society of Law Teachers elected him to honorary membership. The Royal Geographical Society made him a Fellow. Universities put him on their lists for degree conferrings next June. The King made him a P.C. and a C.H. 'People make rather much of me here', he wrote to his wife, 'but I am keeping a little apart from everything in order to avoid too much attention. I don't want to make the same blunder here as Australia's Hughes.'[4] He had one candid friend who told him that he could not possibly avoid the blunder, no matter how hard he tried. On his arrival in London he had found waiting for him a letter from the caustic pen of Emily Hobhouse. The Press, she told him, was stuffed with lies, but all the same she felt inclined to believe that its announcement of his advent was true.

So off this goes to welcome you. . . . Years ago I prophesied to you that the day would come when your name would be seen in big print in the 'Times', that mighty organ that emulates Divinity for 'it putteth down one and setteth up another'—and I further said that I should live to see you Earl of Irene and Lord of Doornkloof and lo! are not these words fulfilling themselves? in essence if not the letter?

For I know from of old that honours come showering down upon those who tread 'Imperialist' paths. Still I hope something of the old 'Oom Jannie' yet remains, enough to enjoy association with the Pacifist and Anti-Imperialist I am prouder than ever to be.[5]

Smuts encouraged Emily Hobhouse to come to London, the better to look after his soul. He sought out another of his old comrades, Olive Schreiner, whom he found ill and overwrought; 'she is bewildered at the condition of the world', he told his wife, 'and just bursts into tears when we talk; but I cool her down'.[6] He took her with him to Cambridge, whither he went to see Wolstenholme within the first fortnight of his arrival. During the same week-end he sought out Alice Stopford Green, the widow of a famous historian and herself an historian of distinction, whose main preoccupation at this time was the redress of Irish wrongs. Very soon he went to Oxford to stay with the Gilletts at 102 Banbury Road. Their visitors' book records that he spent with them that year more than a dozen week-ends, not counting his shorter visits and the expeditions which he made with them to the Downs in midsummer. It is plain that he had no intention of spending his leisure time with the important new acquaintances who tried to take possession of him. He spent it with his old Liberal friends—the Hobhouses, Hobsons, Courtneys, Clarks, Gilletts: especially the Gilletts. In their quiet Quaker household he found a second home.

It was a strange background to the warrior's life that he was leading. The business which had brought him to London was first and foremost war business. As Lloyd George had put it in a statement to the House of Commons on 19 December—'We feel that the time has come when the Dominions ought to be more formally consulted as to the progress and course of the war, as to the steps that ought to be taken to secure victory, and as to the best methods of garnering in the fruits of their efforts as well as of our own'. In his *War Memoirs*, Lloyd George reveals himself to have been deeply moved by the rallying of fighting men from all parts of the Empire: as well he might be, seeing that India raised over one and a quarter million men for overseas service and the Dominions little short of a million men out of a combined total population well below fifteen million. By 1917 their mobilisation, like that of Great Britain, was approaching its peak. Lloyd George wanted to get from them the extra ounce of effort. To this end, he thought it essential to confront them with the immediate perils and opportunities of the war and of the peace settlement that would follow it. The gathering which he had in mind would be a war-and-peace conference of the whole Empire. And something more than that. Lloyd George wanted the statesmen of the Empire not merely to exchange information and ideas but also to make decisions. They were meeting, he told them, not merely as an Imperial War Conference, but also as an Imperial War Cabinet.[7]

To some people, this seemed to be an implausible claim. In British constitutional custom, a cabinet was hardly conceivable except as a body of men collectively responsible to a parliament. Various attempts were made to explain the Imperial War Cabinet as an intelligible exception to this rule. Sir Robert Borden, the Prime Minister of Canada, called it 'a Cabinet of Governments'. Mr L. S. Amery used often to protest in later life that it was bound together 'by a common sense of responsibility for a common cause' and there- fore deserved its title 'as fully as any Cabinet I have ever attended'.[8] Such pleading failed to satisfy the constitutional purists. In par- ticular, it failed to satisfy the Round Table reformers, whose views had recently been defined by Lionel Curtis in his book, *The Problem of the Commonwealth.*

These people believed that the British Empire had no choice between federation and disintegration. In 1917 they were envisaging their either–or as a now-or-never. They thought themselves well placed for pushing their scheme through. Milner, their educator and inspirer, was a member of the new War Cabinet. Philip Kerr (later Lord Lothian), who was, perhaps, the most brilliant graduate from Milner's 'Kindergarten', was the Prime Minister's personal assistant. Moreover, they had planted groups or cells of the Round Table in all the Dominions and believed that their ideas had taken root there. They expected one or other of the Dominions to take the lead in the demand for constitutional reform (by which they meant federation) of the British Empire.

This was the situation which Smuts had in mind when he told Merriman that he was going to London 'with some misgivings'. On the eve of his departure news had come through which he considered disquieting. According to the original plan, the meeting in London was to be a small and realistic 'war and peace conference'; but under pressure from the southern Dominions the British government was now expanding both its membership and its agenda. In New Zealand, Sir Joseph Ward (the muddled apostle of federalism at the Imperial Conference of 1911)* was threatening to break up the wartime coalition unless he were permitted to go to London with his premier, Mr Massey. The situation in Australia was different; conditions there were so disturbed by the conscription quarrel that Mr Hughes could not get away; all the same, he backed up the New Zealanders in demanding that the agenda should include long-term problems which had nothing to do with the war, such as the future constitution of the Empire and its commercial and industrial policy. Botha, meanwhile, had given a public assurance that such far-reaching discussions, which might place 'the freedom of my people in bondage', would not be held. He now made a formal protest.[9]

The damage had been done already; but it proved to be far less serious than Botha and Smuts had feared. The problem of the swollen agenda was handled without difficulty. Two sets of meetings were held in parallel. On the one hand, there were the meetings of the Imperial War Cabinet, presided over by Lloyd George, where the Dominions and India joined with the British War Cabinet in handling day-to-day administrative problems, in deciding upon measures for the conduct of the war and, finally, in examining the reports of two important committees upon peace terms. On the other hand, there were the meetings of the Imperial War Conference, presided over by the Secretary of State for the Colonies, which dealt with the miscellaneous problems. On some days it was the Imperial War Cabinet which met, on other days the Imperial War Conference. The British War Cabinet continued to meet on the days when the overseas statesmen were engaged at the Conference; it also met separately, in order to deal with domestic affairs, at the conclusion of most of the meetings of the Imperial War Cabinet.

Usually, Smuts found the Cabinet meetings far more satisfactory than the Conference meetings. While there was so much urgent work to be done, he thought it a waste of time to discuss either the little questions which had been crowded on to the Conference agenda or the big questions which had better have been postponed until the

* See pp. 351-2 above.

war had been won. When the former were raised he sat in silence, when the latter were raised he protested. For example, he said that it was wrong to bring forward a resolution that the Empire and the allies should have a first claim upon certain scarce raw materials when the war was over; such a resolution contained the threat of a vengeful peace and its effect might well be to prolong the war unnecessarily. He made a similar protest against a proposal that was brought forward to prohibit all imports from enemy countries for a stated period after the war. There were various other proposals—about double income tax, for example, and an Imperial Mineral Resources Bureau—which he said should be postponed until after the war, when more time and thought could be given to them.

When the constitutional question came up he adopted different tactics. He said in effect that the question was so big that it could not be settled now and so crucial that it must be settled now: settled, that is to say, in principle. These two affirmations, at first appearance so contradictory but in reality so coherent, are both contained in a resolution of the greatest historical importance which Smuts drafted, and carried through the Imperial War Conference on 16 March 1917.

The Imperial War Conference are of opinion that the readjustment of the constitutional relations of the component parts of the Empire is too important and intricate a subject to be dealt with during the War, and that it should form the subject of a special Imperial Conference to be summoned as soon as possible after the cessation of hostilities.

They deem it their duty, however, to place on record their view that any such readjustment, while thoroughly preserving all existing powers of self-government and complete control of domestic affairs, should be based upon a full recognition of the Dominions as autonomous nations of an Imperial Commonwealth, and of India as an important portion of the same, should recognise the right of the Dominions and India to an adequate voice in foreign policy and in foreign relations, and should provide effective arrangements for continuous consultation in all important matters of common Imperial concern, and for such necessary concerted action, founded on consultation, as the several Governments may determine.[10]

The decisive phrases in this resolution were 'self-government', 'consultation', 'such necessary concerted action...as the several Governments may determine'. Speaking in support of the resolution, Smuts rammed home the truth that these phrases embodied a principle completely incompatible with Imperial Federation.

If this resolution is passed, then one possible solution is negatived, and that is the Federal solution. The idea of a future Imperial Parliament and a future Imperial Executive is negatived by implication by the terms of this Resolution. . . . Here we are, as I say, a group of nations spread over the whole world, speaking different languages, belonging to different races with entirely different economic circumstances, and to attempt to run even the common concerns of that group of nations by means of a Central Parliament and a Central Executive is, to my mind, absolutely to court disaster.

Smuts did not envisage or desire the disruption of the British Empire. He envisaged and desired its transformation. It was founded, he said, upon principles which appealed to the highest aspirations of mankind, the principles of freedom and equality; but those principles were still too much obscured by the legal clutter of a past age, with its obsolete theories of Imperial sovereignty and colonial subordination. The clutter would have to be cleared away. The theories would have to be recast. What would emerge when this work of tidying-up was done? Not a super-State, but an international polity of novel design and of great hope for the future of mankind. People were talking, he said, about a league of nations; but the British Empire was already taking shape as 'the only successful experiment in international government' that the world had yet seen.[11]

'At any rate', one of his South African colleagues wrote to him (rather inelegantly), 'you have put the lid on Messers Lionel Curtis & Co.'[12] He had indeed. Two doctrines of Imperial destiny had long been confronting each other: the doctrine of Colonial Nationalism, as expounded by Richard Jebb, and the doctrine of Imperial Federation, now reinterpreted and systematised by Lionel Curtis. There is still room for a reflective study of this battle of theories, which is bound in many respects to acquire new significance as the perspective lengthens; but there can be no doubt that the resolution passed by the Imperial War Conference on 16 March 1917 will always remain a decisive landmark. From that day onwards, the road ran straight to the Statute of Westminster in 1931, and beyond it to the Commonwealth of the mid-twentieth century.

Smuts and Merriman, as we have seen, had used the name Commonwealth many years earlier to describe the emergent family of equal, cooperative nations which they envisaged.* Subsequently,

* See p. 203 above.

the name had been appropriated by 'Curtis & Co.' to describe the
federated super-State of their dreams. Smuts believed that this was
a misappropriation. He made up his mind to take the name back again.

On the evening of 15 May he addressed a meeting of both Houses
of Parliament. He began his speech by discussing the war situation.
The Germans (he said in effect) seem to think that they are winning
the war but they are wrong. They may have been winning the
victories but we are winning the war. From the four corners of the
world we are gathering our strength. *We*—but who are *we*? He
answered his rhetorical question with a shattering paradox. We are
not an Empire, he said. We are not British.

I think that we are inclined to make mistakes about this group of nations
to which we belong because too often we think about it as one State. We
are not a State. The British Empire is much more than a State. I think
the very expression 'Empire' is misleading, because it makes people think
that we are one community, to which the term Empire can appropriately
be applied. Germany is an Empire. Rome was an Empire. India is an
Empire. But we are a system of nations. We are not a State, but a community of States and nations. We are far greater than any Empire which
has ever existed, and by using this ancient expression we really disguise
the main fact that our whole position is different, and that we are not one
State or nation or empire, but a whole world by ourselves, consisting of
many nations, of many States, and all sorts of communities, under one
flag....We are a system of States and not a stationary but a dynamic and
evolving system, always going forward to new destinies.

If we are not an Empire, he went on, why call ourselves one? If we
are something new, we had better give ourselves a new name. Let
us take the name of Commonwealth.

Smuts believed the Commonwealth to have its roots deep down
in the soil of British freedom. When one looked at it in the context
of legal and constitutional history, it was British and would remain
so. But it was no longer British when one looked at it in the context
of cultural and national history.

All the empires we have known in the past and that exist today are founded
on the idea of assimilation, of trying to force human material into one
mould. Your whole idea and basis is entirely different. You do not want to
standardise the nations of the British Empire; you want to develop them
to fuller, greater nationality. ...This is the fundamental fact we have to
bear in mind—that the British Commonwealth of Nations does not stand
for standardisation or denationalisation, but for the fuller, richer and more
various life of all the nations that are comprised in it.

431

There, in a few vivid strokes, we have it—the picture of the Commonwealth as it came fully into being before Smuts died, a polity of many sovereignties and many cultures. But how in the world can such a polity be held together? Smuts put this question frankly and gave a confident answer. There were three things, he said, which would hold the Commonwealth together: common loyalty to the Crown, the technique of conference, common values. To the champions of Imperial Federation, these must have seemed flimsy links. Before his death, Smuts was destined to see and to lament the weakening of some of them. But in 1917 he believed them strong enough to ensure unity in diversity and to keep the Commonwealth great—'far greater', he declared, 'than any Empire that has ever existed'.

BRITISH WAR CABINET

Smuts had assured his wife that he would be home by May at the latest, but when his colleagues from the other Dominions left he stayed behind. His reasons for staying will be examined later on, but it is necessary first of all to state why the British wanted him to stay. To put it bluntly, they felt that he could not be spared. As Lloyd George wrote later—'So deep was the impression that General Smuts made at this time upon his colleagues, nay, upon the nation, that we would not let him leave us when the Conference ended. We insisted on keeping him here to help us at the centre with our war efforts.'[13] What kind of help did they hope to get from him? From early April onwards Lloyd George had this question much in mind. He thought of Smuts as the man to settle the Irish question. He thought of him as the man to beat the Turks in Palestine and drive them out of the war. He thought of him as a reinforcement to the central directorate of the war, that is to say, the War Cabinet.

Following the Easter Rebellion, the executions by court martial and the alarming exacerbation of Irish nationalism, Lloyd George was planning to reconcile and pacify the conflicting passions by means of an Irish Convention. What better president could it have than Smuts, who was proved by his record to be all the things which a true Irishman might claim to be and hope to be: nationalist, rebel, reconciler, State-builder? From the early days of his arrival in London, Smuts had shown himself to be deeply concerned with the Irish situation. As has been seen, he had paid an early visit to Mrs Green, a great champion of Irish freedom, who at once put him into touch with a circle of Irish idealists who shared her views: amongst others George Russell ('A.E.'), Colonel Moore (brother of George Moore, the writer) and James Douglas, a member of the Quaker community in Dublin.[14] The pressure which they put upon him to expend his energies and abilities upon the cause of Irish reconciliation was reinforced by the pleading of his old friend Wolstenholme.

I do not think [he wrote] there is a man in Britain who could do this work better, or with a better chance of success, than you; and I hope that so far as depends on yourself, you will give all your trained powers and experience and your great *human* as well as statesmanlike gifts to the final settlement of this tangled affair. You will certainly earn the eternal gratitude of the whole British people, and establish more firmly still the position you are making, which may place you in the history of these sad times as the greatest and wisest force at work for the honour, for the beneficent influence in the world, and for the true welfare of the British Commonwealth. I am sure you and the Irish people would get on together admirably; you would appeal to them humanly and temperamentally as hardly any Briton could.[15]

Never before had Smuts received from Wolstenholme so eloquent, so fervent a letter as this; but he received a very different letter from an old acquaintance who had better claims than Wolstenholme to advise him about Ireland. This was John Gregg, who had shared lodgings with him at 13 Victoria Street when they were fellow undergraduates at Christ's and was now Archbishop of Armagh. The Irish problem, Gregg wrote, had broken many hearts, and nobody could hope to make any progress at all with it unless he had lived in Ireland, North and South, and had drunk in some of its spiritual atmosphere. 'If you want to do what everyone in British politics has hitherto failed to do, here is an opportunity. But the essential prerequisite is—come and live amongst us for a little, and then you will learn the nature of the problem.'[16] Smuts did not go to live amongst the Irish. He was destined, nevertheless, to intervene decisively in Irish affairs. But not yet.

Lloyd George did not make his various proposals *seriatim* and Smuts still had the Irish possibility in his head while he was making up his mind whether or no to accept the command in Palestine. A little time (but not much labour) must now be spent upon killing a legend, which has been embalmed in the limpid prose of L. S. Amery.

When the Imperial War Cabinet broke up in May, 1917, Lloyd George had proposed—my suggestion, I believe—that Smuts should take command on the Palestine front. The idea had greatly appealed to Smuts, but he eventually dropped it giving the very good reason that he could not rely on any consistent support from Robertson once he got there. A more private reason, which may also have weighed with him, was a jocose reply from his Prime Minister, Botha, whom he consulted: 'Don't do it, Jannie, you and I know you are no general.'[17]

This story had first been printed some years earlier in Armstrong's *Grey Steel* and may have been floating about even before that. Amery thought it a good joke, nothing more; but many people have taken it *au pied de la lettre*. Smuts, they have said, was no good at commanding armies and Botha told him so.

We have already seen what Botha thought of Smuts's generalship in East Africa and it is hard to believe that he had changed his opinion since then. Actually, we have the full record at first hand of Botha's thoughts about the Palestine proposal, because he took pains to share them with Mrs Smuts. He wrote to her on 4 May— 'I hear from old Jannie every week. He is well and is making a big impression on the English. A high honour was shown him in the form of the Palestine command. It looks as if the battles on all fronts are becoming impossible, hence the new front. I enclose herewith for your strictly confidential information first, telegram A, from Jannie, ditto B, telegram from me, and C, from Jannie. These telegrams speak for themselves....' Indeed they do. The text of telegram B from Botha to Smuts runs as follows:

I regard the offer by the Imperial government of the Palestine command as a great honour, not only to you but also to the people of South Africa. Please accept our congratulations. As regards the wisdom or advisability to accept this offer, this will depend upon the scale on which the operations there are to be carried on. If on a large scale it would be difficult to refuse the offer. I have no doubt that South Africa will appreciate with thankfulness this personal sacrifice by you. It is true that your colleagues will miss you greatly, but we are anxious to give you all facilities....

Botha went on to ask Smuts for his views about the effect this new duty would have upon his position in the South African cabinet; probably it would be best for him to remain a member of it as Minister without Portfolio, and thus to remain on the payroll of the Union, rather than of the British government.[18]

Smuts cabled back that he had asked the British government to review its whole military programme so that he might measure the scale of the effort proposed in Palestine; it would be wrong, he said, for him to go there unless the operations were 'treated as first class campaign in men and guns'. He and Botha were fully agreed that this was the crucial question. The answer to it has been recorded by Lloyd George. Sir William Robertson, Chief of the Imperial General Staff, made it quite clear to Smuts that in the view of the War Office Palestine was an obsession of the Prime Minister's and at best 'only a sideshow'.[19] So Smuts declined the command. All the same, he was destined to play an important part in the overthrow of the Turkish Empire. And here L. S. Amery comes again into the story. In one respect, Amery's recollections in old age of this affair were precise; it was he who had first thought of Smuts, the only soldier who 'has not got trenches dug deep into his mind', as the man to lead the offensive against the Turks. A year later, when the War Cabinet sent Smuts on a military mission to the Middle East, he in his turn thought of Amery. Together they produced the plan which was the prelude to Allenby's master-stroke.[20]*

It was on 31 May that Smuts declined the Palestine command. He thought that the time had now come for him to go home, where he would be 'on the reserve, to be called up in time of need'; but Lloyd George had put it to him a month earlier that he might be needed in the War Cabinet and now returned insistently to this proposal. Smuts cabled again to Pretoria for Botha's advice, he spent a day in Cambridge talking the matter over with Wolstenholme and on 9 June he wrote to his wife to say that he had accepted the proposal and would not be returning home this year.[21]

His appointment to the War Cabinet was constitutionally and politically anomalous. He told his wife that he had been asked to 'attend' it. Attendance is a different thing from membership and there were some people in England who took the difference seriously. Among them was Mrs Asquith, who wrote on 19 June asking him to deny the report that he was throwing in his lot with Lloyd George.

I hope you will not let this statement remain uncontradicted. All the Ll. Georgites—anti-Asquithites—and Tories are *overjoyed* and say to me 'There you see *how* wrong you were! he has *joined Ll. G.* after all!!' You might write a short note to *The Times* saying you are only doing what you and all the Imperial Conference Premiers and representatives do—go to the War Cabinet when you are asked to, but that you have *not* joined it.

* See p. 472 below.

This would delight my husband.... You have a fine loyal nature.... He is the *most* loyal man in the world.... Dear friend do make your position *clear*.

To help him make it clear she enclosed for his signature a letter of four terse sentences to *all* the newspapers.[22]

Her attitude might appear excessively proprietorial but she had raised a serious question: how could a South African politician join the British government without becoming a British politician? It could not be argued that the Imperial War Cabinet was still in session, or that it had left behind it one of its members to represent it in the British War Cabinet; ideas of this kind had been discussed in its closing sessions and flatly repudiated by Sir Robert Borden and by Smuts himself. Consequently, no other Dominion except South Africa was concerned in any way with Smuts's membership of the British War Cabinet. It was his own prime minister and his own colleagues who gave him leave to join it, as they had a perfect right to do. But was it not odd that the British parliament and people should tolerate in the government of their country a person who stood quite apart from the rules and conventions of the United Kingdom? The thought of it gave Lloyd George himself some squeamish moments. Towards the end of September he tried to persuade Smuts to take a seat in the House of Commons. Smuts, after consulting Botha, refused and the question was never raised again.[23]

From the British point of view, it did not really matter; in a time of national emergency nobody was likely to make a fuss about these constitutional and political niceties; even Mrs Asquith resigned herself to the *fait accompli* and sent Smuts her affectionate greetings for Christmas.[24] From Smuts's point of view, however, the decision was difficult. On the one hand, he could exert no effective leverage upon British political action—and the time might well come when he would want passionately to do just that—unless he became an M.P.[25] On the other hand, he could not become an M.P. without tearing up his roots in South Africa.

He found a middle course. In effect, he joined the War Cabinet on long loan from his own country and government. The price he had to pay proved to be a heavy one, not only in the prolongation of his loneliness and homesickness but in being cut off from the sources of political strength both in South Africa and in England. It may well be that he did not discover until two years later how high and dry he would be left; but even if he had foreseen his agonies at the Paris Peace Conference he might still have decided that London—but *not* as an M.P.—was the place for him.

He had assured his wife that he would not go the same way as Australia's Hughes, and neither he did; but he could not keep himself from quoting to her an article which described him as the most 'romantic' figure in the country; yes, he told her, his story was romantic indeed—the lonely Cambridge undergraduate, the passionate Boer patriot, the enemy of England and her Empire now returning to help them in their hour of need.[26] Smuts had his romantic streak. But he was also a realist, and his realism played a larger part than his romanticism in bringing him to a decision.

To begin with, he knew his own powers and could never be at peace unless he was exercising them to the full. His tasks in South Africa were easy in comparison with the immense labours awaiting him in London. He looked forward to them with zest. Moreover, he believed, and so did Botha and his other colleagues, that it was to the interest of South Africa for him to be in London. South Africa's claims could be enumerated under two heads: status and security. Smuts had already struck a strong blow for status when he carried the resolution which put Imperial Federation out of court; but that blow needed to be followed up. 'I want very much to see', he told his wife, 'that in future our position in the Dominions is improved; I cannot and never shall forget that we were free republics.' He looked forward to the day when even Hertzog and the Nationalists would admit that Botha and he had led South Africa along the right road, indeed, the only practicable road, to national sovereignty.[27] That day would come when the Peace Treaty was signed. The Peace Treaty must also establish South African security. Botha and Smuts had made up their minds to tolerate no dangerous neighbours on the frontiers of the Union. They had conquered German South-West Africa and meant to keep it. Moreover, they had hopes, as has been seen, of persuading the Portuguese to accept a deal whereby the Union would receive Delagoa Bay and its hinterland in exchange for some of the territory which Smuts had conquered as commander of the Imperial forces in German East Africa.*

To advance the frontiers of the Union in this way at the conclusion of a victorious war would be in full accord with the existing rules and

* See p. 408 above.

customs of international politics. Smuts, however, had also running through his head a different train of thought. His correspondence with Wolstenholme and other friends shows him to have been deeply conscious from the first days of the war of the immense disaster which had fallen upon Europe. The existing rules of international politics had been unavailing to fend off this disaster and may well have been its underlying cause. The idea took hold upon him that the nations of the world, taught by their suffering, might be willing to accept new and better rules at the end of the war. His speeches at the Imperial War Conference suggest that he was looking for a connection between the Commonwealth of Nations which was already emergent in fact and the League of Nations which was taking shape on paper. Was it his romanticism, or was it his sense of reality, which prompted him to believe that he might play a decisive part in this work of creative transformation? His attempt to play such a part will be examined later on; meanwhile, it is necessary to say that his concern for South African interests was not his only motive in joining the War Cabinet. He felt that his service there might have some effect in shortening the span of the world's suffering and of preventing its recurrence. When he wrote to tell his wife that he would not be coming home before the end of the year he said that it was very hard on them both; but—'...We have learned the lesson of "weary waiting" long ago and often, and mankind is in a terrible state and stretches out its hands for help and rescue. God alone can rescue, but all can help.' He told her later in the year that he considered himself to be 'on active service for humanity'.[28]

His service, whatever its compelling motives might be, was compacted of three main elements. He had an important part to play in strategical decision, in war organisation, in preparations for the peace settlement. In the later sections of this chapter and in the two following chapters, strategy and peace-making will be our main concern: here let us consider the work of Smuts as a war-organiser. Two examples will be considered: first, the reorganisation of British air power; secondly, governmental control of industrial production.

Lloyd George has revealed in his *War Memoirs* that Smuts, more perhaps than any other man, has the right to be called the father of the Royal Air Force.[29] To document the complete story would demand a long chapter; but the salient facts can be set down in a few pages. As the summer of 1917 wore on uneasiness grew about Britain's response to the rapid development of air warfare. At the popular level, the people of southern England, Londoners in particular, were taking very ill the German air-raids. At the higher levels of government, grave doubts were becoming manifest about the control of air operations, which was still divided between the army and the navy, and about the formulation of policy for the use and production of military aircraft. In July the War Cabinet commissioned two of its members, the Prime Minister and Smuts, to examine, in consultation with various experts: (1) home defence against air-raids; (2) the existing organisation for the study and higher direction of aerial operations.

Lloyd George has made it clear that he left it to Smuts to direct the committee's work.[30] Smuts pushed it ahead at high speed. Within the first fortnight the committee produced a drastic report on home defence against air-raids: London, it said, was the nerve centre of the Empire but might find itself within the next twelve months in the front line of battle: the present measures for its defence were ineffective and hopelessly dispersed: exceptional measures must be taken as a matter of urgency. The committee recommended: first, concentration of executive command in a senior officer of first-rate ability, under the control of the Commander-in-Chief, Home Forces; secondly, immediate attention to the concentration and disposition of A.A. guns; thirdly, the rapid completion and training of air squadrons to fight in formation; fourthly, the provision of sufficient air-defence units to cope with the attacks on London.[31]

All these recommendations were promptly approved by the War Cabinet. Meanwhile, the committee was hard at work on the long-term problem. At the end of August it presented a second report which was even more drastic than the first. It said that the day was not far distant when air operations might become the decisive branch of warfare, to which old-style military and naval operations might well become subordinate. With events moving so fast in this direction it was intolerable that the control of British air power should still be split between the R.N.A.S. and the R.F.C., that is to say, between the Admiralty and the War Office. To be sure, an Air Board had been set up to link these separate powers and it had achieved some useful work in the field of design and supply; but it had no powers of decision; it was only a conference. In waging war, conferring was no substitute for command. Britain would lose the race for air power unless she established a single authority to command and control both operations and supply. The war was becoming increasingly a war of arms and machinery. The side that commanded the larger industrial resources and exploited them to the full would win in the end. Britain had the power to win the war next year, if she mobilised her inventive and mechanical genius for the production of sufficient aircraft to strike hard at the enemy's communications and deep into his homeland. This was a task for an independent Air Staff backed by an independent Air Ministry.

The report tried to do justice to the old Fighting Services; but it insisted that a new, independent service was essential. Its main recommendations were as follows:

1. An Air Ministry to be set up as soon as possible.

2. An Air Staff (analogous to the Imperial General Staff) to be set up as soon as possible.

3. Arrangements to be worked out for amalgamating the R.N.A.S. and the R.F.C.

4. The Air Service to keep the closest touch with Army and Navy.

5. The Air Staff to attach to the Army and Navy the air units necessary for military and naval operations.[32]

The War Cabinet accepted these recommendations in principle but the task of making them effective was immense. Lloyd George left it to Smuts. He became chairman of a new Air Organisation Committee appointed by the War Cabinet and in this capacity he chose as his chief assistant Sir David Henderson, a member of the Air Board who had sent him in July a powerful memorandum urging amalgamation of the R.F.C. and the R.N.A.S.[33] With Henderson's aid, he kept a close rein on the proliferating sub-committees; he maintained a steady pressure upon the two Service Ministries, particularly the affronted Admiralty; he employed all his arts of persuasion upon all the rebellious interests and dignities and reported in the New Year that the following subjects had been dealt with:

(1) Legislation needed for the establishment of an Air Force and an Air Council to administer it. [This legislation was passed in November.]

(2) Constitution of an Air Council; its membership and the apportionment of duties among members.

(3) Organisation of an Air Ministry and rates of pay and duties of its officials.

(4) Nomenclature of the Air Force.

(5) Supply in all branches of the Air Force.

(6) Rates of pay, allowances, conditions of service and pension rates of all ranks in the Air Force. System of payment.

(7) Relations between the Air Ministry and Air Force on the one side, and on the other side the War Office, Admiralty, Army and Navy.

(8) Operation of an administrative branch of the Air Force.

(9) District Organisation of the Air Force in the United Kingdom.

(10) Arrangements about lands and buildings and works services for the Air Force.

(11) Medical organisation for the Air Force.

(12) Peace establishment of the Air Force.

By next April all these tasks had been completed and the Royal Air Force was in operation. Granted that Smuts had first-rate assistance, one is still astonished that he, a newcomer to Whitehall, amidst all the other tasks thrust upon him, should have made himself within a few months so much the master of English administrative procedure.

For a brief interval, Smuts had entertained a view which some of his colleagues held, namely that the root and branch reorganisation of British air power might well be left until after the war; but in the autumn of 1917, with German air-raids on London growing heavier and Haig's offensive bogged down in Flanders mud, he felt that it was now or never. He did not believe that the artillery barrage and the fighter squadrons were a sufficient shield for London; counter-attack against the enemy's airfields was the best means of defence.[34] By now he was thinking not merely of defence. The idea of a great air offensive was taking shape in his mind. The navy did not look like winning the war on its own. No more did the army, nor the navy and army in combination. Their combined power needed to be reinforced by air power on a massive scale.

That was a task, in the first place, for British industry. Smuts reported to the War Cabinet on the progress of two programmes of aircraft production which it had authorised: an earlier programme to provide 106 service squadrons for the R.F.C. and a later one to provide 200 squadrons. He told the War Cabinet that even the earlier programme was endangered by lagging production. This lag must at all costs be made good and at the same time the sights must be raised to the extended programme and the massive air offensive against Germany. To achieve this, the War Cabinet must authorise 'the fullest and most complete priorities' for aircraft production.[35]

Some differences of opinion emerged about the facts and the War Cabinet referred them to a new committee, the Aerial Operations

Committee, again with Smuts as chairman. This committee at its first meeting asked to be made a standing committee of the War Cabinet with power to determine all questions of industrial priority. It was an unheard-of demand. To grant it would make the committee the arbiter on vital matters which hitherto had been determined by the War Cabinet itself. But why not, provided that all interested departments were represented on the committee and possessed *in extremis* a right of appeal to the War Cabinet? There was another proviso—that a member of the War Cabinet should be the committee's chairman. That meant Smuts.

On these terms the Aerial Operations Committee became the War Priorities Committee, with full powers to determine all the conflicting claims of the Services upon British industrial resources—upon factory space, plant, raw materials and (up to the limit set by the incomplete controls of that war) industrial manpower. These powers were exercised through an elaborate structure of official sub-committees which it would take too long to describe here. By and large, the devolution of power proved so successful that the main committee did not need to meet very often. Had it been otherwise, Smuts might well have found himself loaded with all the work of a Minister of Production. By his genius for concentrating upon essentials he saved enough of his time and energy for the many other urgent tasks which, as we shall see, were thrust upon him.

It was an immense burden of work that he was carrying. Still, it was not beyond his physical strength nor did it depress him. He lived his full life with a gusto which sometimes had its comic side. It was the habit of Emily Hobhouse at this time to attack almost everything that he was doing and she had some tart observations to offer about his anti-aircraft barrage.

As to your defence of London by this infernal Barrage I do trust you will stop it, as it is a remedy worse than the disease. We have lived under showers of this odious shrapnel (purely home-made) and it is costly in life and property. A woman close to me was killed in bed thereby!

The German bombs will be fewer and more local, and if you must shoot at them pray do so only as they cross the coast line, so that this mischievous shrapnel (which all criticise) may fall only into the sea.[36]

No more did Smuts (although he could hardly admit it) think very much of his barrage. All the same, he looked forward to the clear moonlight nights when the German bombers would come over and Alice Clark would be with him at the window of his sitting-room in the Savoy to enjoy the fireworks and the noise. She was Margaret Gillett's sister, the fourth child of the family at Street and a director of C. and J. Clark Ltd. In a life much interrupted by illness she had contrived to make herself an expert in the shoe manufacture and trade, a capable and creative business executive, and a woman of affairs with an experience which embraced both industry and politics. After a long battle with tuberculosis of the throat and lungs and a journey of convalescence in the Middle East she had joined Millicent Fawcett, Maude Royden and other distinguished women on the executive of the Union of Suffrage Societies, which set systematically to work to force the lagging Liberals to make good their promises about women's suffrage. When the war came she took a course in midwifery, with the thought that she might join her sister, Dr Hilda Clark, in the hospital which the Society of Friends had established at Châlons. But her work lay in London, on the Friends' committee for the relief of war victims and in a systematic study of labour problems which, later on, bore both academic and practical fruit, in a published study of the *Working Life of Women in the Seventeenth Century* and in the progressive policies of labour relations adopted by the firm of C. and J. Clark Ltd.

Alice Clark, it is plain, was a woman of unusual independence and ability but she was many other things besides—a beautiful woman with a rare sensitiveness to beauty, a lover of little things as well as of great causes, a clear thinker and writer and a student of life and books, with a genius both for sympathetic and critical understanding. Smuts had brought with him to England the typescript of his *Inquiry into the Whole*, with Wolstenholme's caustic comments on the margins of the first fifty pages. He lent it to her and she took it with her one week-end to Street, read it through steadily and reflectively and wrote to him a thoughtful letter about it. At last, he had found somebody who could understand his philosophical quest and the central place it held in the manifold activities and interests of his life. On the nights of the full moon, when the German aircraft had dropped their bombs and the guns fell silent, they discussed with each other, in the Quaker language of 'Thou' and 'Thee', the agony of the nations, the aspirations of the workers, familiar places in Somerset or on the Downs and the philosophy of the Whole.

443

THE STRUGGLE

Smuts, as we have seen, had joined the British War Cabinet without entering British politics. Of the struggle for political power in Great Britain, which some historians have found more interesting than the struggle against Germany and her allies, his papers contain no record at all. They contain no information at all about his personal relations with his colleagues in the War Cabinet. From the evidence of L. S. Amery and others we know that these relations were easy and friendly at the business level; but apparently they went no deeper than that. Outside working hours, Smuts kept himself aloof from British politicians, including Lloyd George himself. At any rate, he never went with Lloyd George, as other people did, for a week-end to Churt and his correspondence contains no exchange of ideas between them except upon the problems of war and peace.

There can be no doubt that Smuts admired Lloyd George as a war leader. If ever he recalled his own brilliant paper on the eve of the Boer War, he must have been struck by the similarity between his outlook in 1899 and that of Lloyd George in 1917.* Both men had the gift of envisaging the problems of war comprehensively, not just as a heap of bits and pieces. They both possessed a sense of urgency and a fiery determination. Before Lloyd George came to power, it had seemed so easy to postpone urgent tasks or to declare them insoluble. The land could not be ploughed up. The ships could not be controlled or convoyed. Hesitations such as these were finished with when Lloyd George took control. Difficult things could be done, they must be done, they were done. Lloyd George, like Smuts, was audacious, experimental, resilient. Both men possessed the gift of coming fresh to the work of each successive day. But beyond that? Whereas Smuts was never content unless he could see his day-to-day tasks in deep perspective, Lloyd George was intent upon the immediate foreground. Smuts, so Merriman had said, was a 'ruthless philosopher'.† Nobody had ever accused Lloyd George of being philosophical.

These intellectual and temperamental differences between the two men were bound sooner or later to come to the surface; but throughout 1917 they remained hidden. Smuts, as we have seen, had an important part to play in the reorganisation of war government that

* See pp. 110–12 above.   † See p. 227 above.

had been set in train by Lloyd George. The change of leadership in December 1916 had announced the arrival, late, but not too late in the day, of order and system at the centre of government. In Lloyd George's War Cabinet of four to six members was vested the supreme power of decision. The War Cabinet took into its direct service the machinery and techniques which had been built up during the past ten years by the Committee of Imperial Defence and its wartime heirs. Brain-power and will-power were brought together at the centre of government. Simultaneously, devolution was achieved at the focal points of the nation's danger by the creation of new ministries—for Shipping, Food, Labour, Blockade, Propaganda and (as we have seen) for Air. These and the older ministries, in so far as their areas of responsibility intersected, were kept in step with each other and with national policy by strong committees of the War Cabinet. Smuts and his War Priorities Committee controlled scarce industrial resources. Milner and his Shipping Committee controlled the scarce resources of tonnage which were vital for the life of the nation as a great importer of food and raw materials, for the despatch and supply of British forces overseas, and for the transport of American and Dominion forces to Europe. Milner and Smuts both served on the *ad hoc* manpower committees which, although they never achieved the meticulous 'budgeting' of the Second World War, played an essential, if controversial, part in matching the available supplies of manpower with the demands which came in from the fighting services, the munitions industries, shipping, land transport, mining, agriculture, consumer goods and all the other industries and services that had to be kept going, for the sake not only of military efficiency but also of national health and morale. The pattern of War Cabinet control, focused as it was upon the fundamental shortages which, without good management, might have wrecked the British war effort, was comprehensive and realistic.[37]

There remained, however, one deplorable gap. Lloyd George was always conscious of it and Smuts identified it with precision in a paper which he wrote in September 1917. He would have liked to see set up, under the aegis of the War Cabinet, a supreme War Staff to co-ordinate all the plans and direct all the activities of the separate naval, military and air staffs, so as to secure the maximum of energy and efficiency in operations. He admitted that so large a work of reorganisation could hardly be achieved in wartime, but he thought it essential to devise 'some interim makeshift arrangement' for advising the War Cabinet on the many pressing questions of strategy which came to it for decision. 'I would therefore suggest', he wrote, 'the creation of an Advisory War Committee consisting of the Chiefs of the Naval, General and Air Staffs, and presided over by a member of the War Cabinet, whose function would be to advise the War Cabinet on all developments and operations in which the three Services or any two had to collaborate and on all questions involving priority as to their respective requirements.' Here we have in a single sentence the design of the Chiefs-of-Staff Committee, which was set up in the early 1920's and was destined throughout the Second World War to render faithful and efficient service to the War Cabinet of Winston Churchill.

Lloyd George had no such tempered and disciplined instrument to serve him. Conflict between 'the top hats and the brass hats', with consequential incitement to political conflict, became his plague. Smuts never became personally involved in this conflict; but as a member of the War Cabinet he played his part in the making of decisions which affected its course and outcome.

To understand the strategical questions which came up for decision it is necessary to review briefly the war situation early in 1917. British strategy was conforming, albeit with some sinister divergences, to a pattern or model which elucidates the experience of the British people in all their big wars from Napoleonic times (to go no further back) right up to Hitler's day. Its salient features can be set down as follows:

The war opens with defeat. Britain's enemies heavily outmatch her in military power. But they cannot move in to the kill because of British naval power. Behind her naval shield, Britain mobilises her economic and military resources. She makes war on the enemy's resources by naval blockade. Her navy gives her the advantage of strategic mobility and surprise. She raids the enemy coasts. The raids grow more massive as she builds up her striking power; they grow into campaigns of the Peninsular War type. Meanwhile, the British are conducting political warfare. They make themselves the rallying-point of mighty coalitions. At last—it may be after four years, or after twenty—the balance of military power swings against the enemy. He meets his Waterloo.

The strategy which fits this pattern of experience has been aptly named 'the strategy of the long haul'.[38] However, it would be erroneous to affirm that British governments in all their big wars have fully understood and consistently pursued this strategy, or that —in so far as they have understood it—they have found it an infallible guide to the changes and chances of each successive war.

Many persons of great authority, including Lloyd George, Churchill and Amery, believed at the time and have argued since that the long haul of 1914–18 could have been shortened immeasurably had not the British government been persuaded or overborne by bad professional advice into surrendering the advantages of strategical mobility which it derived from its command of seapower. They have argued that victory could have been won two years earlier at least if only a small fraction of the men and material hurled against the German trenches in France had been added to the scanty forces in the Near East—to destroy Turkey, link up with Russia, rescue Serbia, rally Greece and Bulgaria and strike north through the Balkans against Austria-Hungary, while the Russians were striking south. By the end of 1915, it had become too late. 'There was nothing left now on land but the war of exhaustion. No more strategy, very little tactics; only the dull wearing down of the weaker by exchanging lives; only the multiplying of machinery on both sides to exchange them quicker.'[39]

That is the thesis of 'the Easterners'. 'The Westerners' would reply that the deployment of force on the scale required for victory in the east would have been paid for by a German victory on 'the main front' in France. This controversy is too large a one to be entered into here: suffice it to say that Smuts arrived in England at a time when the Germans appeared impregnable in the west and all-conquering in the east. While he was chasing von Lettow across the Rufiji river, Rumania had been overwhelmed. While he was still on board ship for England, Russia stopped fighting. Some opportunities for the strategy of indirect approach still remained on the periphery of the Turkish Empire; but Germany's victories in the east seemed bound to loosen the pressure of the naval blockade and to release large numbers of men for employment, sooner or later, on the western front. It looked as if 'the haul' would be both long and grim. Yet even this was not the worst thing to be feared. There could no longer be a haul of any kind if the naval shield were broken. On 31 January 1917 the Germans proclaimed their determination to break it by the weapon of unrestricted submarine warfare. Within a few weeks they were sinking merchant shipping at the rate of half a million gross tons a month.

There were, of course, some favourable items on the balance sheet. Russia was not yet irrevocably out of the war and the Americans looked like coming in. The new submarine campaign so alarmed and angered the American people that on 2 April President Wilson declared a state of war to exist between the United States and Germany. A little later, Greece became an active ally instead of a blockaded and suspected neutral. There was some evidence, too, of food shortages and deteriorating morale in the enemy countries, at any rate in Austria-Hungary. Most important of all, there was evidence that Britain herself was settling down purposefully to the long haul under a leader who understood the meaning of that grim task.

In this uneasy balance of apprehension and hope it seemed all the more necessary to employ British power prudently. Lloyd George, a convinced Easterner, would have left it to the Germans to hurl their troops against the barbed wire and machine-guns in France while the British and their allies took the offensive on one or more of the other fronts. His professional advisers, however, were convinced Westerners and were already deeply committed (although the War Cabinet did not as yet know it officially) to the project of a great British offensive in Flanders.

Lloyd George had hopes that Smuts would help him to resolve this conflict in the way he thought right and in early April persuaded him to go to France to study and report upon the military situation and prospects there. This was asking a great deal of Smuts. For one thing, the Palestine command was under offer to him and his acceptance would depend upon the size of the forces made available for Eastern service; it was hard for him to have to consider at one and the same time his personal problem and the impersonal pros and cons of the strategical controversy. Moreover, his military experience was exclusively colonial and the professionals were likely to consider him an amateur soldier. Nor did he possess as yet the authority of War Cabinet membership; he was merely a visiting South African statesman who had been in England a bare month, not nearly long enough for him to master the political, economic and military elements of the strategical problem. Nor did he have time enough in France for more than a superficial study of the situation there. Despite all this, he expounded his views with great clarity and power, first in a letter to Sir William Robertson in mid-April and secondly in a long report to the War Office at the end of the month. That report, according to Lloyd George, produced a great effect: although not altogether the effect that he had been hoping for.[40]

The major premiss of the report, affirmed at the outset and reaffirmed in successive contexts, was the primacy of the political over the military factors. The objectives for which the war was fought would determine its course and character. Smuts insisted that those objectives were limited. From this limitation two consequences followed: unconditional surrender (Smuts had good reason to dislike that concept) need not be aimed at: a purely military victory need neither be desired nor expected. 'A military position', he declared, 'which is hopeless in view of a large and ambitious political programme may yet be quite hopeful and reassuring if that programme is severely cut down to the essential minimum of our war aims and of the victory we consider necessary to realise them.' He believed that the Imperial War Cabinet at its recent meetings had in fact produced a sufficiently realistic programme: first, elimination of the threat, by means of the German colonies, to the sea communications of the Empire and—by means of Turkey—to its power in Asia: secondly, evacuation by Germany of the conquered territories of Europe and the limitation (*not* the destruction) of her military power on that continent. The threat to the Empire's sea communications had already been eliminated; but achievement of the other objectives depended upon the defeat of the enemy in Europe and the Middle East.

I have already told the War Cabinet and I repeat here my frank opinion that that will not be merely, or even entirely a military defeat.... This war will be settled largely by the imponderables—by the forces of public opinion all over the world which have been mobilised by German outrages, by fear on the part of the governing classes of Central Europe of the dark forces of revolution already gathering in the background, by the gaunt spectre of want or even starvation already stalking through the land; and by all those consequential factors of morale to which even Napoleon attached more military importance than to the prowess of his armies.

Starting from these assumptions, Smuts had something to say about 'methods of barbarism'—(did he recall the origin of that phrase?). The British, he pleaded, must not allow themselves to be drawn into reprisals which would mirror German frightfulness. They must look beyond the war to its political consequences. If only they could be brought to see it, they had far more to gain from the advance of democracy in Central Europe than from military victory.

He admitted, none the less, that 'a substantial measure of military success' was essential. How could it be achieved? Some brilliant opportunities which had existed earlier in the war—no doubt he had the Dardanelles in mind—were no longer open; but the allies must be ready to seize such new opportunities as might offer themselves; they must equally be ready to ward off any unexpected thrusts that the enemy might make. To achieve these ends they must at all costs establish a strong strategic reserve.

The Germans probably have great reserve forces which they could fling either against one of the existing fronts or into some new diversion into which they may be driven in order to achieve success.

If any such diversion is made by the enemy where is our force to meet it? If, again, any great diversion planned by us may, at some later stage of the War, present the promise of decisive success, we shall be impotent to execute it because we shall have left no reserve force in our hands to play with....A great force, such as ours, which has no strategic reserve, is running grave risks. The German strategic reserve last December could deal with Roumania as soon as the danger of her invading Transylvania arose, and we should be in a similar position of security against unforeseen developments.

Why was it that no strategic reserve existed? From what fund of power could a reserve be created? In answering these questions, Smuts appeared at first sight to be aligning himself with Lloyd George and 'the Easterners'.

I have always looked upon it as a misfortune, no doubt inevitable under the circumstances, that the British forces have been so entirely absorbed by this [the Western] front. The result now is that in a theatre mainly of the enemy's choosing, the two most important armies of the Entente are locked up in front of almost impregnable positions. It is essential to our ends that we should keep the initiative and offensive, but both are enormously difficult in the situation in which we are placed on this front. I have no confidence that we can break through the enemy line on any large scale. No doubt with our predominance of heavy artillery we can batter in any selected portion of the enemy line, but in every case so far we have been unable to advance for more than a comparatively short distance, and there is no reason to think that this state of affairs will materially alter in the near future unless some unforeseen calamity overtakes the enemy. I found the spirit of both our officers and men on this front magnificent in its confidence and determination. But my visit has only strengthened my impression that a decision on this front can only be reached by a process of remorselessly wearing down the enemy. And that is a very slow, costly and even dangerous process for us no less than for the enemy and threatening both with exhaustion of manpower as the process of attrition goes on. Victory in this kind of warfare is the costliest possible to the victor.

The British, he went on, had locked up too many of their resources in this unprofitable warfare. They had been shouldering too large a share of what was essentially the French burden—the defence of French soil. They must shed part of this load in order to create their strategic reserve.

Having created this reserve, where should they look for its employment? Smuts began by looking eastwards. Not to Salonika: he thought it a misfortune that France was the senior partner there and saw no prospect of a profitable offensive unless—as seemed unlikely—Bulgaria could first be detached from the Central Powers. Not to Mesopotamia: General Maude should be content for the time being to establish a strong position covering Baghdad. The great opportunities, in Smuts's view, were to be found in Palestine. A strong offensive there would be the biggest threat that Turkey had had to face since the Gallipoli campaign and would give to the Palestinian front 'an importance eventually second only to that of the Western front'.

So far, everything that Smuts had written—except for his belittling of the Salonika expedition, which the Prime Minister was disposed to favour—was grist to Lloyd George's mill. But suddenly the argument took an unexpected, an inconsequential turn. The shining hopes of a death-thrust against the Turkish Empire grew misty. The troops to be withdrawn from Salonika were destined, so it began to seem, for France instead of Palestine. The general reserve to be created by shortening the line in France would be assembled in the north for action in Flanders, possibly even in Holland, which seemed to be under threat of a German invasion. All this, after the strong case which Smuts had made for a big effort in Palestine, looked like a complete *volte-face*. For this there was only one explanation that Lloyd George could see. Smuts must have been carried away by the ardour of Sir Douglas Haig.

Ever since the previous autumn, Haig and his staff had been at work on their plans for a great offensive to smash the German front in Flanders and let the cavalry through to Ostend, Zeebrugge and beyond. These plans had the backing of the C.I.G.S., Sir William Robertson. They had not as yet been submitted to the War Cabinet but Smuts was given a preview of them. In their immensity of mass, their meticulous detail and their self-confidence they may well have appeared impressive to a fighter whose experience of campaigning had been confined so far to Africa. On the other hand, Smuts had always been opposed to frontal attacks and a great practitioner (it was part of his 'slimness') of flanking movements. He had already emphasised the costliness and sterility of frontal attacks on the Western front. He felt that a special case would need to be made for the assault that Haig had in mind. Army Headquarters had their special case ready, point by point: the need to bolster up the French, the need to anticipate a German invasion of Holland, the need to drive the submarines from their advanced bases. This last argument had the emphatic support of the Admiralty, which was still resisting convoys but felt that Ostend and Zeebrugge must be captured at all costs.

Smuts listened to all this advocacy but did not yield to it. He did not recommend Haig's plan to the War Cabinet but recommended that it should be examined, along with any alternative plans. The conclusion of his report was:

...that the time has come, or is coming soon, when the strategic situation, both military and naval, in relation to our resources and diplomacy, should be reviewed as a whole and, so far as is possible, definite policy should be laid down on the points raised in this memorandum as well as on others which I have refrained from referring to. Unless the First Sea Lord and the Chief of the Imperial General Staff have the clear guidance of the War Cabinet on general questions of policy, it is impossible for them to obtain the highest and most efficient power out of the war machine they are directing.

Early in June the War Cabinet set up a small committee—the War Policy Committee—to go into all the facts of the military, naval and political situations and present a full report. The members of the committee were the Prime Minister, Curzon, Milner and Smuts. Before long, Bonar Law also was attending the committee regularly.

At this time the French army was badly shaken after the failure of General Nivelle's offensive on the Chemin des Dames. Haig and Robertson believed the British army to be by far the most formidable fighting force on the allied side. They admitted no doubts about its ability to break through in Flanders. Lloyd George felt then, and has argued since, that they held back essential information from the War Cabinet.[41] There is no space, nor is there any need, to reopen this controversy here: all that we are concerned with is the part that Smuts played in the discussions which led to the agony of Passchendaele. These discussions took place on 19 and 20 June, when Haig and Robertson were summoned to the War Policy Committee. Lloyd George probed their evidence searchingly: again and again he asked them to reconsider their plans in the light of his objections and of the alternatives he placed before them. They held fast to their plans. Jellicoe was called in and gave them his uncompromising support. Of the ministers, Milner and Bonar Law shared the Prime Minister's misgivings; Curzon inclined hesitatingly to the side of the generals; Smuts spoke in their favour. 'General Smuts', Lloyd George wrote later, 'was strongly of the view that the Generals had made out their case for at least having a good try. Personally, he thought the chances were highly favourable.'[42] What Lloyd George has not made clear is the emphasis which Smuts laid upon two conditions: first that the French should give a guarantee to hold on their front all the enemy divisions and reserves already located there; secondly, that Haig should slacken or stop his offensive if he found it impossible to complete his full programme without excessive losses. On these conditions the War Cabinet gave its consent to the offensive after the discussion had swayed to and fro for another day. The preparatory bombardment had been unleashed four days earlier.

Smuts would have been surprised if anybody had called him a Westerner; even during the June meetings he had had the needs of the Italian front prominently in mind and he never ceased to urge the opportunities of offensive operations in the Levant (he had in mind at that time a landing at Alexandretta in support of Allenby's thrust northwards). However, the deep commitment of British power to the Flanders offensive rendered these schemes illusory. Smuts had been wrong in his expectation that this commitment would or even could suddenly be cut if its costs proved to be excessive. Military balance-sheets of costs against gains, or hoped-for gains, are frequently matters of dispute; sometimes of legitimate dispute.

There can be no doubt that Smuts bitterly regretted the War Cabinet's decision of June 1917 and his own part in making it. By the end of July he was convinced that the offensive in Flanders had proved a disastrous mistake. He set himself deliberately to envisage the worst that might follow and drew up a list of possible (not probable) disasters which included the collapse, one after the other, of Britain's continental allies. Even so, he declared, the strength of the British Empire, with America to back it, was so great and the issues at stake were so vast that it was impossible 'even to contemplate a peace which will in effect mean a defeat'. A satisfactory peace, he thought, might not be achieved until 1919 or 1920. Nor would it be achieved even then save by hard fighting, relentless economic warfare, skilful diplomacy and—last but not least—telling the truth to the British people.

...I think the time is coming [he declared] when the British people should be told the truth. The newspapers create a false mirage of illusions. The people think we are on the road to break Germany and many good Christian souls are filled with pity for her fate. They do not realise that the danger is all the other way and that at the end of the third year of war everything is still in the balance and that the balance appears to be inclining the wrong way. The people should be calmly and judiciously told the truth. They will stand the truth: it will strengthen instead of weaken them.

From the time of his arrival he had steadily maintained that 'the imponderables', and chief among them the conviction and staying power of the British people, would count just as much in determining the issue of the war as the measurable, material factors. Believing this, he considered speech-making to be an essential part of his contribution to victory. 'The cause I fought for fifteen years ago', he would begin, 'is the cause which I am fighting for today': and then he would tell the story of that earlier war, of Vereeniging, of Campbell-Bannerman and the Union, merging with the story of Belgium, of the Commonwealth, of the much desired League of Nations. The applause had always come quickly—too quickly and too easily, he now thought. From the later summer and autumn of 1917 his speeches became more sombre in tone; but also more bracing.[43]

In all the suffering nations, 1917 was a testing-time for accepted ideas and traditional loyalties. The Russian revolution, even before its November climax, was shaking Europe. In Britain, most working-class leaders and radical intellectuals were resistant to Marxist theory but not to Marxist slogans, particularly to those that had their roots in liberal thought: for example, 'No Annexations! No Indemnities!' Painful tensions arose within the minds of many thoughtful men and women who were anxious to do their duty both to their country and to humanity. Socialists who felt themselves thus torn between their patriotism and their internationalism found it hard to make up their minds whether or no it would be right for them to support the peace conference at Stockholm which the Second International was trying to organise. Anxieties such as these invaded even the British War Cabinet and led to the resignation of Arthur Henderson, as good a patriot as anybody. No wonder, then, that they spread among the shop stewards and the workers in mines and factories, who by the third year of the war were vexed by many grievances and fears, both at work and in their homes.

Towards the end of the year these discontents rose to a climax, with strikes or threats of strikes in many parts of the country. In October the situation in the South Wales coalfield became particularly serious owing to organised resistance to any combing-out for military service of men engaged in the industry; a ballot was shortly to be held as to whether a strike should be called in protest. The War Cabinet felt that it must face this challenge to its authority. The mines represented the last remaining large pool of manpower available for military recruitment. Besides, there was no knowing how far the disaffection might spread if it were not scotched in South Wales. The War Cabinet was prepared at need to arrest the ringleaders and fight the strike. It decided, however, to make one last effort at persuasion. It asked Smuts to go to the coalfields and address the men.

He set out on 29 October. The War Cabinet was due to meet that day to discuss the Italian disaster at Caporetto and Smuts had found time the previous night to write a strong letter to the Prime Minister setting out his views. Thus he went straight from an urgent military crisis to an equally urgent crisis of the home front. How he handled it was recorded contemporaneously by a careful local official, who had been expecting the tour to be the signal for widespread disorder.[44] But none occurred. In the audience at Tonypandy there were many pacifists, syndicalists and other opponents of the government. When Smuts entered the hall they greeted him with whistles instead of cheers but they fell silent when he began to speak. At the end they cheered him. From Tonypandy to the other towns his tour became a triumph.

He got his Welsh audiences singing. When Curzon heard of it he went up to Smuts and exclaimed, 'Ah, Smuts, you are a crafty fellow!'[45] (A South African would have called him 'slim'.) Many years later, Lloyd George told the story of the singing at Tonypandy as he had heard it from Smuts.

I started by saying: 'Gentlemen, I come from far away as you know. I do not belong to this country. I have come a long way to do my bit in this war, and I am going to talk to you tonight about this trouble. But I have heard in my country that the Welsh are among the greatest singers in the world, and before I start, I want you first of all to sing to me some of the songs of your people.'

Like a flash, somebody in that huge mass struck up 'Land of My Fathers'. Every soul present sang in Welsh and with the deepest fervour. When they had finished they just stood, and I could see that the thing was over....[46]

Smuts returned to London with the knowledge that there would be no trouble in South Wales but with deep anxiety about the Italian front. The letter which he had written to Lloyd George on the eve of his Welsh tour is worth quoting in full.

The extent of the Italian disaster is not quite clear to me from the telegrams which I have seen but must in any case be great and may yet assume dimensions which may well frighten the Italians out of the war, with very far reaching results for the whole Allied cause. We have not appreciated the danger in time and it is clear now that Cadorna's fears were justified and that our General Staff was not properly informed about the troop movements from the Russian to the Italian front. But late as it is, I think we should do our duty and not let the Italians entertain the despairing feeling that they are left alone to bear the onslaught of both the Austrian and German armies. The Italians will hold on more firmly if they are assured in time that we stand by them not only on the Western but also on the Italian front. I suggest that we declare at once to the Italian Government our readiness to send 4 or 5 divisions (if they are required) with a great proportion of heavy artillery to their assistance as fast as the movement can be effected, and that if our offer is accepted, the French government be asked not to press for our taking over any of their front line while these divisions are in Italy. The French might prefer to join in our Italian undertaking but in view of the continual friction between French and Italians I consider it important that the reinforcements should be under British command.

The transportation arrangements should be pushed with the greatest energy.... We must not add Italy to our Serbian and Roumanian disasters.[47]

No sooner was Smuts back in London than Lloyd George annexed him for an allied conference which had been called in urgency at Rapallo. There the two men made arrangements with their Italian and French colleagues for assistance to Italy along the lines sketched by Smuts. They also made arrangements for a Supreme War Council, a notable step forward towards the co-ordination of strategy between the allies.

And so this terrible year ended without irreparable disaster. Russia was out of the war but the Americans at last had their first division in the trenches, with the expectation of many more to follow. The agony of Passchendaele had come to its close in November. By early December the Italian front was re-established in strength on the Piave. By Christmas, Allenby's men were in Jerusalem. The home front held firm.

On 15 December Smuts told his wife that he had 'a feeling'—no more—that the war might be ended satisfactorily by next spring. He also told her about the death of Wolstenholme, whom she had grown to love almost as much as he did, although she had never met him.

I saw him about four or five days before his death and took leave of him in spirit as I knew that I should never see him again....I had been his best friend and he expected that I would still do much great work, but he was glad to leave this evil world, and no one felt the war more than he. He talked much of you and the children, and had your books in a big parcel, and this will now be sent on by his sister. May his soul now rest in peace.[48]

THE AIM

What kind of victory, what kind of peace was Smuts aiming at? In an unsystematic way, these questions have already been raised in various contexts: for example, in the discussions of his reasons for joining the War Cabinet, of his advice on strategy, of his views about the Commonwealth. It has been seen that he was asserting South African national interests under the two heads of status and security; that he was the advocate of limited objectives in war and the primacy of politics over military strategy; that his picture of the peace settlement contained a League of Nations created in the image of the British Commonwealth. All these scattered observations, however, are bound to leave a blurred impression unless some attempt is made to pull them together. But how? Smuts discussed the problems of war and peace with a good many of his friends, whom it is tempting to treat as types: practitioners of *realpolitik*, perfectionists, reformers: or—to use different labels for the same variants—power-mongers, peace-mongers, constitution-mongers. Or again, to adopt a gentler terminology, the three types may be described as advocates respectively of established practice, of a change of heart, of institutional change. Unfortunately, the classification breaks down in practice because few if any of his friends belonged exclusively to any one of these types and Smuts himself appeared at times to belong simultaneously to all of them. Still, it may bring some system into the inquiry if we keep the types in mind while we are exploring the exchange of views between Smuts and his friends.

So let us, to begin with, look for a *realpolitiker*, or the nearest approximation to one whom we can find. We should naturally expect to find him in the War Cabinet had we not discovered already that the relations between Smuts and his British colleagues, outside the official business which they shared, have left only a scant deposit of record. Fortunately, a rich record has been left of the relations between Smuts and L. S. Amery, who at that time held an important post under Sir Maurice Hankey in the War Cabinet secretariat. Smuts had first met Amery when he came to South Africa on the eve of the Boer War as correspondent of *The Times*. It would have seemed inconceivable then that the two men could ever become friends, for Smuts was looking for 'another John Bright', whereas Amery was a zealous Chamberlainite. Smuts, however, showed himself throughout his life always ready to modify his judgment of people as the passage of time and his own deepening experience revealed that the labels which he had once pasted upon them did not completely fit. As the years went by, he discovered the existence of many bonds between himself and Amery. They both loved physical exercise and out-of-doors life, and this despite an original implausibility; for Smuts had been a puny stripling and Amery was a midget, appropriately named Leo—his little body contained the courage of a lion. They both had a special love for the high mountains. They both pursued philosophy.[49] They both devoted their lives— Amery with constant cheerfulness, Smuts with intermittent groaning —to the practice of politics.

The Amery of 1899 had appeared the very opposite to Smuts in his political views; but the Amery of 1917 was in some respects close to him. When Smuts made his great speech about the Common-wealth, Amery wrote him a letter of enthusiastic approbation, for he was just as much opposed to Imperial Federation as Smuts was and was destined in his later political career to render signal service to the cause of sovereign equality and national freedom in the Dominions and India. He possessed a generous ardour of disposition which recalls, not so much the political master whom he professed to follow, Joseph Chamberlain, as that earlier exemplar of progressive conservatism, George Canning. Like Canning, he was a great caller-in of the New World to redress the balance of the old. Like Canning, he was the inveterate enemy of the busybodies of foreign policy; he wanted his own nation to defend its own interests and carry its own responsibilities; he was willing for other nations to do the same. 'Every nation for itself and God for us all': Amery might well have said that. But there Smuts would have parted company with him.

In March 1917, when Smuts landed in England, Amery was quick off the mark in giving him his personal views on the urgent questions that would come before the Imperial War Cabinet. These fell under two main heads: the conduct of the war and the terms of peace. As to the former (which included Amery's pet scheme of a great offensive in Palestine with Smuts in command) enough has been said already. As to the latter, Amery was already at work on a memorandum enumerating the strategical requirements of Imperial security.[50] The menace of hostile bases must be removed; that meant holding on to the conquered German colonies. Air communications must be safe-guarded no less than sea communications; that meant British control over the land bridge from the Mediterranean to India—an objective which could only be achieved by dismembering the Turkish Empire. Did not all this signify a punitive peace? Not necessarily. A century earlier, the British had taken from the defeated French all the territories they needed for the security of their overseas Empire, without denying to France a position of power and influence in Europe. Amery had it in mind to mete out similar treatment to Germany. Thirty years later, he recalled the sudden and sweeping victories of 1918 which destroyed not only the enemy's will to resist but the allies' will to practise moderation. It may have been unavoidable, but—'All the same, looking back over all that followed from the fragmentation and balkanisation of Central Europe, the temptation offered to Germany to reassert her influence by violence, and the present enslavement of Central Europe behind the Iron Curtain, one may wonder whether a more limited settlement of the issues of the First World War might not have secured greater stability for Europe and for the world'.[51]

A century earlier, a peace settlement such as Amery desired would have been considered highly respectable. The statesmen of those days would have called it 'a just equilibrium'. Alas! the idea was taking root in the democracies of the twentieth century that equilibrium and justice were contradictory concepts. The old system of the balance of power, the peoples were being told, was 'forever discredited'. Smuts did not completely agree. We have already seen, and shall see in fuller detail later on, that he went a long way along Amery's road. His plans for South African expansion fitted admirably into Amery's new Imperial map. His insistence upon limited objectives in Europe was harmonious with Amery's ideas about a just equilibrium. However, he differed from Amery in looking forward to a new and improved system of international organisation. The balance of power seemed to him useful so far as it went (at any rate, some of the alternatives to it were terrifying), but it was an insufficient safeguard for international liberty and order. Smuts, as we shall see later, believed that he had an individual contribution to make to the League of Nations. Amery, on the other hand, was satisfied with the existing habits and practices of international politics. He told Smuts that his proposed League was moonshine.

Smuts was criticised from a different angle by his perfectionist friends. Among them were those two glorious battlers, Olive Schreiner and Emily Hobhouse, who in their different ways had cast him for the role of the world's saviour and lamented his backsliding when he failed to live up to their expectations. Olive Schreiner used literally to fall to the ground before him and clasp his knees and beg him with tears to stop the slaughter—as if he could.[52] Emily Hobhouse hailed him as 'the man great enough to make peace' and proposed that he should send her as his agent to Switzerland to arrange preliminaries with the Germans. When he rejected the proposal she told him that he had frozen her Peace Soul and that humanity no longer had anybody to look to except the Bolsheviks. He gave her more of his time than he could properly spare, but this did not stop her from writing him a scolding letter at least once a week—'Super Oom. Super Oom. What are you about? What mischief are you up to? The bloodstained weeks creep on—the world is weary—the winter is dreaded....' She told him that he was just as disastrous as any other member of the Ruling Class; but all the same she still kept looking to him for the great deliverance and began her last letter of the year to him with the words, 'Dear Angel that Openeth Prison Doors'.[53]

She was thanking him for services that he had rendered in securing better treatment for conscientious objectors. Some of their champions, notably Lady Courtney and Mrs L. T. Hobhouse, had pleaded with him to come out openly on their side. This he could not do without breaking the constitutional convention of collective cabinet responsibility; but he promised to give what help he could from inside the War Cabinet.

He believed in 'liberty for tender consciences' but did not exalt it into an absolute principle of political morality.

There is already so much suffering in the world. My mind stands still and dazed whenever I stop to think of it. Why add to this suffering gratuitously? Of course suffering is contagious. The spirit is spreading among good people, and as Quakers are debarred from the suffering of war action, they tend to draw suffering from other sources. But in this we may go very far wrong, just like those early Christians whose one passion was to imitate the Lord and become martyrs. C.O.ism is an exaggeration to great intensity of the individualism latent in the whole....The individual has his just claims, so has the whole, so has society: so have the ordinary police arrangements of a society up against the gravest dangers. Goodbye my child. Good be with you.[54]

These sentences, which reveal his undogmatic approach to the problems of individual conduct raised by Christian pacifism, occur in one of his letters to Mrs Gillett. She, although firm in her pacifist convictions, was equally undogmatic in her attitude to the political problems which she knew him to be grappling with. Writing to him on 4 December 1917 she referred to Lord Lansdowne's 'peace letter' in the *Daily Telegraph* and Gilbert Murray's comments on it in the *Daily News*—'I wonder a great deal', she continued, 'about your position and my wondering always ends in plain old fashioned praying'.[55]

No wonder Smuts found himself at rest at 102 Banbury Road, Oxford. The Gillett family provided an outlet for his inner need to be able to express himself without fear of being quoted or argued with or 'interviewed' or made responsible in any way. He could say what he liked without fear of emotional disturbances or embarrassing consequences. Besides, there were always the children to play with and good walking country close at hand: still better country when midsummer came and the Gilletts rented Breach House, a few miles from Streatley, in easy reach of the high open Downs over which Smuts used to go striding, and of quiet stretches of the Thames where he used to go swimming.

The idiom in which he spoke and wrote to the Gilletts is different from the idiom of his communication with Amery. In the vocabulary of *realpolitik* force is a matter-of-fact word: force exists, whether or no it is used with prudence: the problems arising from its existence are entirely problems of application. But in the language of Christian doctrine force is an evil—an evil which man may be condemned to suffer *propter peccatum*, but one against which he is called upon to struggle. To govern force, and thereby to transcend it, is the Christian problem.

Smuts was living his life in both these universes of thought and speech. His experience in this respect was not unique; for example, J. M. Keynes, although his pacifist friends were not Christian, was faced with similar problems of language, thought and conduct. This similarity of experience may explain in large measure the friendship which grew up later on between the two men. For the relief, or at least the mitigation of their moral and intellectual difficulties, they both looked forward to a peace settlement which would save mankind from the excessive and barbarous use of force exemplified by modern war.

If this aim were to be achieved, two things were necessary: a prudent and just settlement of existing international disputes and the creation of a new international order. Aspirations such as these were characteristic of the third type that was enumerated earlier on—the reformers who looked for salvation to a change of institutions. As we have seen, this hope had found expression from the first days of the war in the correspondence between Smuts and Wolstenholme.* It was shared by many of Smuts's old friends, such as J. A. Hobson, and his new friends, such as Gilbert Murray. Some of these men were playing an active part in the Union of Democratic Control, whose guiding spirit was E. D. Morel. When Smuts arrived in

* See pp. 374, 377 above.

England, no time was lost in putting before him the programme of the U.D.C., which Morel had summarised in four 'cardinal points':

1. No transfer of populations from one sovereignty to another without a plebiscite.

2. No treaties without parliamentary sanction.

3. No military alliances under any circumstances: instead, an International Council to guide and control the relations of states.

4. Reductions of armaments.

Later on—after the Allied Economic Conference which met at Paris in June 1916—an extra cardinal point had been added:

5. No economic warfare.

Smuts examined these points critically. The first one, which in effect asserted the principle of nationality, corresponded closely with his own ideas; but he saw that its beneficence would depend upon the manner of its application: for example, he believed (and thought it a good thing) that its effect would be to give to France part, but not the whole of Alsace-Lorraine.[56] The second point, with its demand for democratic control over foreign policy, was based on the assumption that wars are made by governments against the wishes of their subjects—an assumption which Smuts came increasingly to question.* The fourth and fifth points he accepted wholeheartedly. It was the third point which commanded his deepest attention. Underlying it was the assumption that wars arose from the system of alliances and the conflicting policies of military and economic aggrandisement which the rival combinations pursued. As G. Lowes Dickinson had put it, the root cause of wars, including this present war, was not the peculiar wickedness or folly of any particular government but the 'International Anarchy' in which all governments conducted their foreign policies. It followed that the cure for war was 'International Government' (Hobson's phrase) to be embodied in a new institution, which Lowes Dickinson had named the League of Nations. There is no need to state again how strong an appeal this argument held for Smuts. All the same, he did not accept it uncritically. Within a few weeks of his arrival in England he was invited to appear on a public platform in support of the proposed League of Nations. He accepted the invitation, on condition that he was not expected to endorse any of the particular arguments or schemes that had been put forward but only the general conception of the League.[57]

* See below, p. 504.

The ideas of the U.D.C. crossed the Atlantic, where they were adopted with enthusiasm by President Wilson.[58] With such powerful backing, they were bound to play an important part in the negotiations for peace. Smuts welcomed this development, although he was well aware that the enunciation of general principles would not by itself determine the content of the peace treaties. That would depend also, among other factors, upon the balance of military force at the end of the war.

The radicals of the U.D.C. had this last consideration very much in mind. They were afraid that an overwhelming victory by either side would lead to a peace governed by the old concepts of national interest—as expressed, for example, in the secret treaties—rather than by the concepts of national right and international solidarity which they were promulgating. They looked to President Wilson to extract from all the belligerent powers public statements of their war aims, such as would commit them to a peace grounded on moral principles. This the President endeavoured to do in December 1916. They also looked to him to bring about a negotiated, instead of a dictated peace. This he endeavoured to do in his famous speech of 22 January, calling for 'Peace without Victory'.

Smuts was willing to go some of the way with Wilson, but not the whole way. We have seen already that he had advised the War Cabinet to enumerate British war aims in order of priority, so that it might be ready, if opportunity offered, to secure an early peace which would achieve essential objectives, instead of prolonging the war in the hope of achieving additional objectives which were not essential.* We shall see later that he wanted the war to end with some balance of military power still surviving between the belligerents. He said emphatically that he did *not* want 'overwhelming' victory. He said just as emphatically that he *did* want victory. He did not accept the sharp antithesis between a victorious and a negotiated peace; what seemed to him important was the degree of victory and the timing and procedure of negotiation. This, he realised, depended just as much upon the Germans as upon the allies. He agreed with Lord Lansdowne upon the advantages of accepting something less than twenty shillings in the pound in consideration of prompt payment; but he was aware that the Germans, in their present mood, so far from being willing to pay

* See p. 449 above.

anything at all, were determined to make their enemies pay to the last farthing. This was equally evident in their arrogant peace note of December 1916 and in their ruthless handling of the Russians, a year later, at Brest-Litovsk.

President Wilson gave up talking of peace without victory from the moment that he declared the United States to be in a state of war with Germany. Smuts, as we shall see, continued to talk, alike in his private correspondence, his official memoranda, and his public speeches, of precise and limited peace objectives, with a precise and limited victory as their sufficient prelude. This assumed that the Germans could be brought to the point of admitting a precise and limited defeat. It assumed that a spirit of moderation existed, or could be brought into existence, not only in Britain and the allied nations but also in the enemy countries. Smuts could produce no evidence of the existence of this spirit and therefore could make no practical suggestions for getting peace talks started. In September 1917, when Lord Loreburn pleaded with him to make a personal effort, with the assistance of somebody like Lord Bryce, to get into touch with the German government, he thought it worth while to circulate Lord Loreburn's letter to the War Cabinet but replied to it with depressing realism.

While I largely agree with what you say I am at the same time profoundly impressed with the enormous difficulties and perplexities surrounding the whole subject of peace. Difficult as it has been to wage this terrible war, I am not sure that the making of peace will not be an even more difficult business, requiring greater courage and statesmanship and far-sightedness.

Germany is manœuvring in order to get all the belligerent Governments around a conference table, as she knows that that motley crowd is sure to disagree among themselves and perhaps to break up, and that she will win at the Conference Table more than she has won in the field....[59]

At this very time, the War Cabinet was considering what response to make to an indirect approach made to it by von Kuhlmann, the German Foreign Minister, with a view to starting peace talks. Had they been entered into, they might well have produced the disastrous results which Smuts feared, for in September 1917 everything appeared propitious for Germany—Russia had ceased to count as a military power, America had not yet begun to count, the French offensive had failed, the British offensive was held, the U-boats were still a dangerous threat to allied sea communications, there were many signs of exhaustion and indecision among the allied peoples.

Despite all this, Smuts told Lord Loreburn that a chance might come of trying out his idea when the fighting season closed in the winter. The chance did seem to come in December. Since the death of the Emperor Franz Josef twelve months earlier, it had become plain that the Habsburg government, to say nothing of its subjects, would welcome an opportunity to end the war. From January to July Prince Sixte de Bourbon, brother-in-law to the Emperor Karl and an officer in the Brussels army, had sounded opinion among the allies, particularly the French. These soundings had come to nothing, chiefly because the Austrians could not bring themselves to consider any substantial concessions to the Italians; but by the end of the year, despite Caporetto, their condition had grown much worse and their need for peace urgent. Early in December word came to the War Cabinet that Count Czernin, the Austrian Foreign Minister, was willing to send Count Mensdorff to Switzerland to discuss the prospects of peace with a British representative. Mensdorff was an able and upright diplomatist who had made himself respected and well liked when he was ambassador in London. The War Cabinet sent Smuts to talk with him.

Smuts interpreted his instructions as follows:

First, to instil into the minds of the Austrians that in case they freed themselves from German domination and made a fresh start in sympathy with the British Empire they would have our full sympathy and support; and, secondly, to gather as much information as possible while declining to enter into a general discussion of peace terms so far as the Germans were concerned....A third object which I had in mind was, if possible, to induce the Austrians to conclude a separate peace; but the subject was from many points of view a risky one to open, as I was anxious to avoid laying ourselves open to the charge in future of having intrigued with the Austrians for a separate peace.[60]

Mensdorff saved Smuts that awkwardness by declaring at the beginning of their talks that his government was ready to do anything to secure an honourable peace short of deserting its ally: in no circumstances could it discuss a separate peace. From time to time he tried to lead Smuts into discussions of a general peace, but Smuts fended him off. He told Mensdorff plainly that the British people saw no prospects of a free and peaceful Europe so long as German military domination remained unbroken.

I explained to him how deeply impressed the British people were with the dangers to the future political system of Europe, if Germany survived as a sort of military dictator, and that we meant to continue the War until either victory had been achieved or the dark forces of revolution had done their work in Germany as they had already done in Russia. We were in a good position to go on...if necessary, to go on indefinitely as we had done during the Napoleonic Wars....He replied that that would indeed be the end of Europe. Was it really worth while?

Smuts insisted that it was not only worth while but absolutely necessary, if ever Europe and the world were to win the chance of a new and hopeful start. He explained his conception of the League of Nations and of the British Empire's destiny as an intermingling League. A similar destiny awaited the Austro-Hungarian Empire, once it broke free from German domination.

The best way to strengthen the bonds of sympathy between the British and Austro-Hungarian people was to liberalise as much as possible the local institutions of Austria-Hungary. We had no intention of interfering with her internal affairs, but we recognised that if Austria could become a really liberal Empire in which her subject peoples would, as far as possible, be satisfied and content, she would become for Central Europe very much what the British Empire had become for the rest of the world. She would become a League of Free Nations, very largely free from the taint of militarism, and she would have a mission in the future even greater than her mission in the past.

He spoke with the conviction of personal experience. In the growing community of the Commonwealth he was finding release from the tension between his two political languages—the languages of power and right, of interest and obligation, of necessity and aspiration. He envisaged a similar release for the Danubian peoples and their rulers. Alas for them, and for Europe: the Habsburgs could not break the chains binding them to the Hohenzollerns and the still stronger chains binding them to their own past.

All the same, Smuts returned from his talks with Mensdorff greatly encouraged. He felt that he had met a man of like mind with himself and had won his agreement to principles upon which the liberty and peace of Europe could be grounded. He did not under-rate the immediate obstacles to British–Austrian cooperation but believed that the chance might come later on of overcoming them. Mensdorff had pleaded with him to do his best to keep the two governments in touch with each other and had asked for a new statement of British war aims which would make it clear to the nations of Europe, including the Germans, that the allies were not aiming at their ruin. Lloyd George had been under strong pressure in recent months from British radicals and the Lansdowne group of conservatives to make such a statement. As soon as he received Smuts's report he brought it before the War Cabinet, which was also much concerned about the statement which the enemy had just issued on the peace negotiations at Brest-Litovsk. The War Cabinet decided on an early declaration of British war aims which would go to the extreme limit of concession and prove to the world that the destruction of the enemy nations was not an object of British policy. It entrusted the task of drafting to Smuts, Kerr and Lord Robert Cecil.

Smuts felt hopeful that the Austrians would do their best to persuade the Germans to accept peace. His talks with Mensdorff had convinced him that they were close to the limits of their endurance. Philip Kerr, who had accompanied him to Switzerland, and had held parallel talks with a prominent Turkish politician, felt equally sure that the Turks had little more fight left in them. Although 1917 had been a bad year for the allies, Smuts was hopeful of their winning through in 1918.

The war situation [he told his wife] is far from favourable but equally far from despair. The fall of Russia means that we shall have to fight longer and harder; and the defeat of Italy was a great disappointment. The nations are becoming dead tired and are giving in one after the other. I hope the Turks will give in now after the fall of Jerusalem; but it is difficult to be sure. The Austrians are also very exhausted. The world will heave a sigh of satisfaction when this bitter slaughter is over for good. I sometimes feel as if the end is no longer far and as if this winter or spring will see the end. But this is a feeling and perhaps I am wrong.[61]

CHAPTER 20

LONDON, 1918

IN 1918, as in 1917, Smuts kept himself aloof from British politics. He did not write or receive a single letter bearing upon the political struggles of February and May, in which Lloyd George emerged victorious over his enemies. Throughout the year the issues of war and peace remained his exclusive and intense concern. He was able in some degree to narrow and at the same time to deepen the front of his activities. He had no new tasks of organisation to perform comparable with his prodigious labours the previous year in establishing the Royal Air Force and the War Priorities organisation— no new committees to guide, until he was made responsible in late autumn for the British Peace Brief and demobilisation policy; no new ministries to establish, although he put forward proposals at the end of the war for a Ministry of Communications and a Ministry of Supply, as permanent parts of the peacetime machinery of government. He had no repetition of last year's annoyance at the overgrown agenda before the Imperial War Conference; he made certain of this by drafting the agenda himself.* Adding one relief to another, he found it much easier during his second year in London to concentrate his energies upon the tasks which he considered crucial.

There were two sides to his work, he told Mrs Gillett: the side that she was in sympathy with, the side that she was out of sympathy with; his work of peace-planning and his work of war-winning. Actually, he looked upon these two activities as two aspects of a single task, belonging just as much together 'as President Kruger's two cheeks'.[1]† Still, it was quite possible to let the accent fall more heavily upon one aspect than upon the other and in Smuts's thought peace came first and strategy second. He began the New Year with a prayer for peace. 'May the peace be, not a German peace or an English peace, but God's peace enveloping all the erring nations as with the arms of

---

* The Imperial War Conference gave practical application to the principle of sovereign equality asserted at the conference of the previous year, by recommending that official communication between Great Britain and the Dominions should be henceforward direct from government to government, instead of through the Secretary of State and the Governors-General.   † See p. 480 below for the parable of the cheeks.

an Everlasting Mercy. To that sort of peace I would contribute my last scrap of strength.'[2] *When* God's peace would come—if indeed it was destined to come—he felt unable to forecast. In successive letters to his wife he laid bare his alternating hopes and fears. Sometimes he felt that the end could be 'no longer far' and that he would be back at Doornkloof with her and the children before the year was out; sometimes he felt that the war would drag on for another winter, or longer—unless the good tidings of peace should come unexpectedly, 'like a thief in the night'.[3] In his New Year letter to Alice Clark he dramatised these conflicting hopes and fears as the thrust and counter-thrust of battle between God and Satan. 'I wish you all that is Good. I pray that Heaven may be kind to thee, and hear thy prayers. There is only one prayer rising today from tens of millions of human hearts, and if as I believe there is creative power in intense longing or praying, then there is no doubt that the end is drawing near. How long, O Lord? I do believe the Lord is really on the move. I only hope that in moving to meet Him we may not make the wrong moves. For Satan is also on the move.'[4]

The thought and imagery of this letter were characteristic of Smuts. 'How long, O Lord, how long?' was a cry wrung from him often in times of struggle. It was customary for him to picture the struggle as one between the Lord and Satan, with the soldiers of the Lord 'moving to meet him' when he was on the move. He never doubted that the Lord was 'the long-term winner'; but no more did he doubt that it depended upon men to determine the time of each particular victory and, in large measure, its content. What he did not make precise in his letters and talk was the composition of the opposing armies: who was on the Lord's side and who on Satan's. He never imagined (not even in the Second World War when he put Hitler among the really nasty devils) that all the Germans were on Satan's side and all the British and all their allies on the Lord's side: on the contrary, he could think of many eminent persons—in Fleet Street, for example—who were doing a good job for Satan. Nor would he have thought it completely inconceivable that General J. C. Smuts, if his will should falter or his intelligence fail, might find himself lending a hand to Satan. The battle between the City of God and the City of Satan, as he pictured it, was not merely or chiefly a battle between visible powers, but a silent, incessant, truceless struggle within the minds of men.

470

All the same, he knew that minds belonged to bodies and men to States; one had to consider men and States as wholes, making up one's mind in each particular crisis what *on the whole* they were standing for—whether they were on the Lord's side or on Satan's. In the crisis of 1918 he felt no doubts. 'A German mastery over the world', he wrote, 'means a deflection from the true paths and an era of coercion for the human spirit just when we were beginning to dream of liberty.'[5] That was an evil not to be endured.

The year opened with the Prime Minister's speech to the trade-union leaders at Caxton Hall enumerating British war aims. Smuts had good reason for approving the speech, seeing that it was based in large measure upon the draft which he had prepared. It was couched in the language of moral and political principle, accented and exemplified in such a manner as to satisfy the interests which Great Britain, the Dominions and the allies considered essential, but at the same time to reassure the enemy countries that the allies were not aiming at their destruction. There is no space for giving details: suffice it to say that the speech anticipated in its essential particulars (except for 'the freedom of the seas') the fourteen points enunciated by President Wilson a few days later. That declaration also gave Smuts great satisfaction. He was inclined at this time to put too much faith in the enunciation of points, particulars and principles. He felt that a clear stand had now been publicly taken for 'limited objectives' and against 'the knock-out blow'.

The two speeches did, at any rate, bring the British and American governments into close alignment with each other and with their peoples. Policy had been declared; strategy must now be defined. Smuts became deeply involved in this task. He was a member of the War Cabinet's committee on manpower, which completed its work in January 1918. The government acted on its recommendations.[6] On the basis of the estimates submitted hitherto by the War Office the allocation of strength to the Western front was adequate; but the War Office kept changing its estimates as its fears grew of a massive German attack. In mid-January Smuts went to France at the Prime Minister's request to report upon the condition of the British defences. His report revealed undertones of anxiety. Although he was satisfied that the army's morale was good he had found the troops greatly in need of rest after the Flanders battle. He had also found them in need of training. But the defences still needed a vast amount of work put into them and this must fall chiefly upon the troops, at the expense both of their rest and their training. Still, Smuts reported that a very strong defensive system would be completed within about six weeks and the Germans appeared hardly likely to make their big attack before then.

Consequently, he felt no deep forebodings about the Western front when he set out on 5 February with a small staff (including his friend Amery, his private secretary Lane,[7] and Brigadier-General Stewart, a Canadian railway expert) to study the war situation in the Middle East and report to the War Cabinet on the opportunities and means of driving the Turks out of the war. He and his staff allowed themselves the luxury of a little sight-seeing at Luxor, but they worked at a terrific pace and had their report ready at the end of the month. Like every document for which Smuts took responsibility, it laid stress upon the political no less than upon the military aspects of strategy: upon the need to assure the Turks that Constantinople would not be taken away from them and that they would be given every help to organise themselves as a national State comprising all the territories in which they possessed a numerical majority: upon the need to assure the Arabs that their national claims were accepted in good faith and would not be prejudiced either by the Balfour Declaration on Zionism or by the Sykes–Picot agreement, which they regarded as an attempt to turn a great part of Syria into a French colony. In this political context the report gave clear guidance on the military problem. It rejected the plan of two converging offensives, one from Mesopotamia, the other from Palestine, in favour of a massive concentration in Palestine and a break-through to the north. It expounded the logistics of this operation—troops, supplies, railways and rolling-stock, port facilities, shipping—and offered suggestions about tactics. Smuts had kindled Allenby's enthusiasm for a hammer-blow to smash the Turkish lines and a 'cavalry raid' to mop up their armies—a dazzling dream which had decoyed Haig into the mud of Flanders but beckoned Allenby to glory in Palestine. Only in two particulars did Allenby's action depart from Smuts's conception: he broke through on the seaward, not the landward flank of the Turks: he broke through in the late summer, not in the early spring.[8]

Indeed, so far from receiving the early reinforcements which he and Smuts were budgeting for, Allenby soon found himself compelled to surrender two of his best divisions to the Western front. When Smuts returned to England at the beginning of March he found that military and political events were moving fast. There was, to begin with, a new flutter of peace talks with the Austrians. As Lloyd George tells the story,[9] Smuts was sent away to Switzerland with Philip Kerr to conduct them; but this can hardly be so, for Smuts did not sign any report about them and is, besides, on record as having been in London for the whole period (7–16 March) when Kerr was in Switzerland. This raises a curious problem, but not an important one, for the talks with the Austrians were foredoomed to failure whoever conducted them. The days of grace were past for the Habsburg monarchy, whose political servants had decided to stake everything upon the great offensive which the Germans were about to let loose in France.

They let it loose in the last week of March. There is no need here to give the chronology of their two terrific blows against the British in March and April and their furious assault against the French from late May to mid-June. From Smuts's point of view, the fighting of these three months constituted a single crisis in which the fate of the war and of the world hung in the balance. Smuts wanted to throw his own weight into the balance but could find no direct way of doing so. It was Milner, not he, who attended the two conferences of late March and early April which established the military pre-eminence of Marshal Foch. Smuts felt himself to be no more than an onlooker, a role most repugnant to him.

Throughout these three months his resolution never faltered. Late at night on 26 March he wrote a characteristic letter to Mrs Gillett. The Germans had just struck their first smashing blow and the allied leaders were conferring at Doullens. Haig was envisaging a British retreat northwards to the Channel ports; Pétain was making preparations for a French retreat southwards; Foch was insistent upon holding the united front. Smuts did not know what shape the discussions were taking but instinctively he took his stand with Foch.

The Germans [he wrote] are within sight of victory but the little distance between them and their desires may be large enough for the Miracle once more to be wrought. If not, then in our day anyhow the Devil triumphs, and this generation will drill and prepare and scheme for the greater wars which will engulf the next generation. The Spirit ever resides in a body, and the spiritual which you cherish is conserved in the material which is now being tested to the uttermost. May it not break! A German victory which will mean for the West what it has meant for Russia will be horrible to contemplate. May God give strength to our boys who are standing in the breach.[10]

His craving to stand there with them can be read between the lines of many of his letters and in some of them is revealed openly. In early May he told his wife the tragic and heroic story of the South African brigade.

Here there is still heavy fighting but I think the worst is still to come. Never in history has blood flowed on such a scale. May God speedily grant an end to this anguish. The South African brigade was first destroyed at Bon-chavesnes and then again at Messines, and still the remnants continue to fight on. Their fame is unequalled, but the losses are bitterly heavy. How long, O Lord![11]

In early June he reported the continuing progress of the German thrust across the Marne towards Paris.

Yesterday the enemy took Chateau Thierry, and for the next few days at least the intense pressure in the direction of Paris will continue. This is a very critical time. So much hangs in the balance. I want no overwhelming victory, but a certain measure of military victory is so necessary to ensure the victory of what we all hold dear.... I sometimes chafe bitterly at having to sit here instead of being where the struggle is and so much hangs in the balance.[12]

In his imagination and will he shared the suffering and fortitude of the soldiers in France; but it was not so simple for him as for them to know where his duty lay. He was at one and the same time resolute and perplexed. He wrote on 8 May—

It is much to know that where you are struggling in the night loving spirits encircle you and embrace you. For the path is very dark indeed. I have never in all my life been so perplexed as to the right thing to do. Always in the darkness there has been the clear steady light of duty to guide one. But now I am not clear even as to that. But I am in no worse plight than millions today.

> 'O lonely grave in Moab's land, O dark Beth-Peor Hill
> Speak to our troubled hearts and teach them to be still.'[13]

By misremembering these lines just a little Smuts gave them a poignancy which they did not originally possess. The poetess had written 'curious hearts'; he changed it to 'troubled hearts'. What can it have been that was troubling his own heart? Why was he unable, despite his unfaltering resolution, to see 'the clear steady light of duty'?

Let us consider in turn three problems which were troubling him at this time. The first was Ireland; the second was the state of public opinion in relation to the great issues of war and peace; the third was the inactivity of the American army. From his point of view each of these problems was intensely personal. Each demanded a decision by himself.

Two events had brought the Irish question to a crisis: first, the military emergency, which forced the government, if only to satisfy British public opinion, to bring Ireland within the conscription law: secondly, the report of the Irish Convention, which forced it to face the problem of Home Rule. From the outset, Smuts took his stand upon the principle 'Home Rule before Conscription is applied'.[14] He hoped that this principle had been sufficiently safeguarded by making the application of the conscription law to Ireland contingent upon an Order in Council; but some people thought differently and wanted to conscript the Irish even when it became clear that there was no chance at all of producing a Home Rule Bill acceptable both to North and South. Meanwhile, the nationalist Irish were falling into line behind Sinn Fein and moving rapidly into rebellion. On 8 May Smuts had found himself unable to see the 'steady light of duty'; but next day he took his stand on the Irish question in a forceful letter to Lloyd George. He insisted that there was no justification at all for 'throwing this apple of discord in front of the people and undermining their confidence in the judgment and wisdom of their rulers'; Irish home rule, he declared, would have to be dropped for the present and with it Irish conscription.

My advice in regard to this matter was not followed before, viz.: not to touch conscription in Ireland till Home Rule was an accomplished fact. Even so I would again tender you advice. Inform Parliament that before introducing the Home Rule Bill which the Government have prepared you are trying to obtain the adhesion of both Irish parties to it, as at such a time you do not feel justified in asking Parliament to divert their attention from the war to a Home Rule Bill which does not meet with a substantial measure of agreement from the people of Ireland as a whole. Inform Parliament also that this is a question on which you are anxious to consult the Imperial War Conference meeting next month....In the meantime conscription would not be enforced; but that will be no unmixed evil, as I do not consider the enforcement of conscription a practical measure in the present temper of Ireland; and I doubt whether, when its real inwardness is realised, the British people will allow it to be done. You remember the sensation produced by the shooting of a few rebels in the last rebellion. In respect of Man-Power the Americans must make good the failure of the Irish.[15]

The War Cabinet decided in June to follow this advice. Notwithstanding all the troubles that lay ahead, Smuts no longer had any need to feel immediately perplexed about his duty towards Ireland.

Anyway, in the early summer of 1918 he considered the Irish situation 'a trifling matter compared to the war situation'.[16] He was beginning to see the war map in a perspective which most of his contemporaries did not find intelligible until a generation later. During the 1940's, the war of 1914–18—'the Great War', as it had been called hitherto—was given a new name; the Americans, in particular, decided to call it the First World War. This name, however, described not what it was, a European war of the traditional type with subsidiary operations overseas; but what it might have become, a world war engulfing all the continents and oceans. Following the Brest Litovsk treaty Smuts saw a real danger of its becoming precisely that. The Germans were keeping military control over the territories carved out of Russia-in-Europe and seemed to have designs upon Russia-in-Asia. Smuts understood very well the threat contained in this enlargement of Germany's *lebensraum*: it could defeat the blockade; it could vastly extend the economic base of German military power; it could threaten the British position in India. And now the Germans were straining every nerve to break through in the west as they had done in the east. Supposing they succeeded? Supposing they made themselves the masters of the whole European land mass? Smuts had a prophetic, nightmare vision of the real world war, the war which the British Commonwealth, twenty-one summers later, found itself fighting—and might conceivably have found itself fighting in 1918.

Smuts did not anticipate his nightmare vision coming true; but he faced the possibility of its coming true. Should he or should he not speak out? He found this a difficult question to answer. If he warned the British people, he might have to reproach himself thereafter for having created alarm and despondency without sufficient reason; if he did not warn them, he might have to reproach himself for having failed to put them on their guard. But that was not the whole of his perplexity. He had the faculty of envisaging alternative sets of possibilities at the same time. In the summer of 1918, while he was enumerating the worst possible consequences of a German victory, he was also enumerating the worst possible consequences of an allied victory. What he particularly feared was that the allies, after having repelled the German offensive, might be tempted to prolong the war until they had achieved 'the knock-out blow'. He feared that they would let themselves slide into the unlimited use of force for unlimited objectives, regardless of the agony of the nations and the shattered fabric of European civilisation.

Victory we must have, but not overwhelming victory: let us be ready, if we must, to prolong the war for years: let us be ready, if we may, to end it this year—altogether, Smuts had in his head at one and the same time too many ideas for a single speech to a popular audience. Nevertheless, he made up his mind to deliver that speech on 17 May, when he was due to appear in Glasgow to receive the Freedom of the City. When that day came he spent the morning visiting the shipyards and docks and had already made half a dozen short speeches before he arrived at the City Hall for the civic ceremony and the principal speech of the day.

Resolution was the dominant note of his speech. He began by giving a full and clear account of the fighting in France. He gave many cogent reasons for expecting the German offensive to be held and broken—the heroism of the British army, which was bearing the brunt of the fighting, the achievement at long last of unity of command under General Foch, the inspired leadership of Lloyd George, the unflinching temper of the British people, the awakening of the American people.

Ludendorff's offensive has been like a blinding flash of lightning on a dark night. In that way he has done this people the greatest service possible.... The blow which has been struck against the British Empire has not shattered it as the Germans expected, but it has only laid bare the soul of the nation in all its heroic fibre....Ludendorff has not only awakened the British people, but he has awakened the Americans. Not only are you speeding up as you never speeded up before, but the American Army is speeding up....

So far, the speech had been no more than a good example of the usual wartime blend of exaltation and exhortation. There followed the usual denunciation of German ambitions, the usual defiance— and then, suddenly, a lifting of the veil.

...But they were not satisfied with peaceful penetration of the world—they wanted to become the dominant military power—they wanted to smash other nations, to finish other countries and to stand out as the final arbiter. That plan they have adhered to all through this war. That plan is now culminating in this great offensive which they are waging against the British Army today in France, that offensive is intended to smash our Army, to smash us, to smash the Empire, to smash the world. That is the German view of victory. Will they achieve it? No, they will never achieve it.

Suppose for the sake of argument—I do not for a moment look upon it as a possibility—that they do succeed in their present offensive, and they do take the Channel ports, and they do sever our connections with the French Army, and they do encircle us there. Would that be the end of us? No, if the last British soldier is driven from France the Germans will be in no better position than Napoleon was in the day of his pride and glory. If the Germans want to win in this war, to achieve the victory they are after, they have to win not only on the land, but they have to win on the seas. That is the bedrock of the situation. They will have to beat our Navy on the seas, and they will have to get control of the seas. As long as we stand with our Navy intact, with America on our side, in command of all the communications of the world, in command of all the raw materials which are required for the modern industries of the world, so long it is impossible for the Germans to win—even, I say, if they have that measure of success of driving us out of France.

There we have it, the preview of 1940, of an embattled Britain face to face with the whole Continent and ready to work and fight, 'if necessary for years', to liberate the conquered nations.

Then, quite suddenly, Smuts moved into his second theme. He had asked his audience to face the worst that might happen; he now reaffirmed his conviction that it would not happen. The Germans, he said, would fail—were failing already—to break 'the iron wall' in France. That meant, he declared, that they were already losing the war. He contrasted the German and the allied conceptions of victory: the Germans were fighting an offensive war for unlimited objectives, the allies a defensive war for limited objectives: the Germans must march to Paris, the allies need not march to Berlin.

...Our view is an entirely different one. We have not gone into the war with any aggressive or offensive spirit. When this nation made its great choice in August, 1914, it went into the war as a war of defence, of defence of the liberties of mankind, of the rights of small nations, and of the public law of Europe. That is what we are out for. That is our idea of victory. That is our war aim, and for that we shall fight until we have succeeded and until we have won. We are not out to smash any country or Government. We are not making this war drag on uselessly in order to attain some impossible victory. We have a limited object. . . . When we talk of victory we don't mean marching to the Rhine, we don't mean marching on Berlin, we don't mean going on with the war until we have smashed Germany and the German Empire, and are able to dictate peace to the enemy in his capital. We shall continue this war until the objects for which we set out are achieved, and we will continue on a defensive basis to the very end.

Whether or not the objectives enumerated in President Wilson's Fourteen Points and in Smuts's own draft for Lloyd George's Caxton Hall speech were all 'defensive' may well be disputed. Still, Smuts was justified, by his interpretation of them, in calling them 'limited'. And he was well justified in emphasising, as he now proceeded to do, the dangers of prolonging the war for the sake of undefined objectives and in a blind passion for total domination.

The result may be that the civilisation we are out to save and to safeguard may be jeopardised itself. It may be that in the end you will have the universal bankruptcy of government and you let loose the forces of revolution, which may engulf what we have so far built up in Europe, because civilisation is not an indestructible entity. Civilisation is a structure built up by the generations before us, slowly built up for hundreds of years, and as it has been built up, so can it be broken down, and you revert to barbarism just as after the Roman Empire the world reverted to barbarism.

Smuts could never forget the extra year of agony and ruin inflicted needlessly upon his own country, so he believed, by Milner's insistence at the Middelburg negotiations of 1901 upon total victory and domination.* He wanted, if it were possible, to spare Europe from a similar, indeed a far more ruinous prolongation of the war. As will be seen later, he overestimated Germany's capacity to prolong it; but even if he had not made that miscalculation, he would still have been an opponent of the knock-out blow, an advocate of diplomatic explorations, the sooner the better, with a view to ending the war. There was, however, a practical question to be decided: how were these explorations to be made and how were the ensuing discussions to be conducted?

The slogan 'peace by negotiation' seemed to him vague and dangerous. Six months earlier he had told Lord Loreburn that the enemy would like nothing better than to get the allies into discussions around a table without any preliminary definition of the basis of the discussions.† He could now point to the disasters which the Russians had suffered through walking into that trap at Brest-Litovsk.

* See p. 128 above.   † See p. 465 above.

That is another of the great eye-openers of history, the Russian peace...
the most abject and humiliating and disgraceful and impossible peace
which history has ever recorded....Now here you have a case not of
Alsace-Lorraine but of a whole Empire being torn to pieces and being
enslaved and treated in a way which must perpetuate future wars on a
much larger scale than in the past....But I hope that if we stand firm we
shall be able not only to save ourselves, but we shall also save the weary
Russians, who are a great object lesson to us in how not to do things.

Smuts was trying to make his audience understand that a middle
way was possible between throwing in the sponge, as the Russians
had done, and fighting the war 'to a smash up'. He made his point
by telling them a story about his old President. 'I remember a very
wise thing said to me many years ago by President Kruger when I
was very young and inclined of course to be very aggressive. He said
to me one day "That is not the way to deal with your opponent.
The way to deal with him is to smack him hard on the one cheek
and to rub him gently on the other."' The practical application of
this advice which Smuts now made was as follows. The Germans
must be 'smacked' hard enough to make them concede 'the principal
terms' of the allies as the basis of negotiations. Their willingness to
concede these terms must be ascertained by informal soundings.
After that, the negotiations could begin. Diplomacy, he declared,
must help military power in bringing the war to a victorious end.

Now how are you going to bring it there? I conceive that you have fought
up to a stage when the enemy is prepared to concede your principal
terms; the terms you consider essential. But if there is no informal conference, how are you to know that he is going to concede them? It seems
to me to go into a peace conference is one of the most dangerous things
you can do before you know your principal terms are going to be conceded.

The diplomatic sequence which he had in mind was: first, informal
soundings such as he and Kerr had conducted with the Austrians
and Turks; secondly, acceptance by the enemy of preliminaries of
peace embodying the essential allied demands: thirdly and finally,
a formal peace conference to fill in the details.

His speech at Glasgow on 17 May was independent and courageous, but so complicated in its argument that it lent itself to
manifold and contradictory misunderstandings. It needed to be
reported as a whole or not at all. The majority of British newspapers
made no serious attempt to report it. Two and a half months later,

however, Lord Lansdowne gave it belated publicity by quoting the
sentences in which Smuts had declared that the allies had no need
to march to Berlin.[17] Lord Lansdowne in effect claimed the support
of Smuts for his own programme of peace by negotiation. What that
programme amounted to in practice, and to what extent it was in
conformity with the 'essential objectives' upon which Smuts never
ceased to insist, are important historical questions which cannot be
investigated here: suffice it to say that large sections of the British
public judged Lord Lansdowne merely by the slogan which came to
be associated with his name. 'Peace by negotiation' was anathemat-
ised by the jingos and applauded by the pacifists. This anathema
and applause began now to fall on Smuts's head. Jingo journalists
smelt the blood of a defeatist in the British War Cabinet.[18] Emily
Hobhouse, on the other hand, wrote to Smuts begging him to make
just another such speech and he would bring down Lloyd George.
'A strong Man', she declared, 'who will snap his fingers at the Press
and who has a Policy for Peace could be Prime Minister of England
before Christmas!'[19]

Faced with such fantastic misreadings of his mind Smuts took up
his pen. He did not complain of being quoted out of context, nor did
he discuss the Lansdowne programme (which, no doubt, was different
from the Emily Hobhouse evangel); but he recapitulated his Glasgow
argument in terms so clear that nobody any longer could have any
excuse for misunderstanding it. There is no need here to repeat again
the distinctions which he had made at Glasgow and on many other
occasions between an offensive and a defensive war, between limited
and unlimited objectives, between victory and 'the smash up'. He
said all these things again and said them forcibly. That done, he
threw the main stress upon what seemed to him most urgently
necessary: to elucidate once again the procedures whereby a peace
settlement, embodying the essential allied demands, might be
brought into being.

In previous speeches I stated my objections to a peace by negotiation.
There are matters which we can never negotiate about. The evacuation and
restoration of Belgium is such a matter. For us Belgium is not a subject for
discussion at all, it will not be redeemed from Hertling's pawnshop, but
must be unconditionally restored as a preliminary to a formal peace
conference. Then again, there are other matters vital to us and our Allies
which must be settled in principle before we are prepared to discuss and

work out details round a Conference table. Finally, there are the numerous matters and details which are fit subjects for discussion and negotiation at a Conference.

The view which I developed at Glasgow was that the belligerent peoples who are bleeding and wasting away are entitled to look to their governments to find out, through those informal channels which are always at their command, when the enemy has been brought to a frame of mind in which he will concede our essential terms.... This is not peace by negotiation; nor is it a confession of failure; it is sound business procedure which the wise victor resorts to even more eagerly than his baffled opponent.[20]

Some verbal confusion may still have remained (for 'peace by negotiation' meant different things to different people), but the interweaving threads of the argument which Smuts had expounded at Glasgow and reiterated subsequently formed a logical pattern. The argument was intellectually and morally coherent. But was it practical politics? Smuts wanted to break the rhythm of totalities—total war, total victory, total punishment. He forgot that the force required for total war is generated by passions which it is easier to arouse than to allay. He, the warrior of two campaigns, the founder of the R.A.F., the controller of war industry, the man who had packed as heavy a punch as anybody on the British side, was laying himself open to the accusation of pulling his punch just when it ought to be smashing home. British people in the mass were bound to find his attitude puzzling. As for the Germans, the alternatives of total victory or total defeat were built into the military, financial, political and psychological structure of their Empire.

Between 28 May and 14 June the Germans made their last violent bid for total victory. Their threat to the French army and to Paris brought to a head the third of the perplexities which had been troubling Smuts. Since the opening of the great offensive at the end of March he had felt often that the firing line was his proper place. He had felt also that it was the proper place for the Americans. He now offered to lead the Americans into battle.

This offer is contained in a letter of 8 June to Lloyd George which is worth examining with some care. Smuts began by expressing a doubt whether the war would last till next summer. He thought it possible that the Germans might make a peace offer in the winter. They might well think it good policy, in view of their great conquests in the east, to propose a moderate settlement in the west. They might begin by giving an undertaking to evacuate Belgium and northern

France. Smuts did not see how the allied governments could refuse an invitation to a peace conference on such a basis.

The result would be that we go to a peace conference under the shadow of the great military achievements of the enemy in the spring and summer of this year and conclude a peace which, however favourable to us in other respects, leaves the German military prestige dominant for the future. That would in reality be a great disaster for us and the world. How is this to be avoided?

The American Army will in the late autumn be a first class instrument of action, and an unexpected blow could be struck with it before the end of the year, which might regain the initiative for us and reverse the military situation completely. The effect on the enemy after their efforts this summer might be far-reaching, and they might be anxious to conclude a really good peace—good for us—before it becomes too late.

The American Army will be there, but it will be without a reliable Higher Command. Pershing is very commonplace, without real war experience, and already overwhelmed by the initial difficulties of a job too big for him. It is also doubtful whether he will loyally cooperate with the Allied Higher Commands....What is to be done?

I would propose that we suggest to President Wilson a re-organisation of the American Command. Their army is becoming a business too large for one man to control if he is to direct operations in the field. Let Pershing remain in charge of all organisations in the rear (bases, supplies, training camps, transport, etc.) but let the fighting command over the American Army be entrusted to another commander.

This is a very delicate matter, as every risk of hurting American pride should be avoided. But I do not think they have the man, and we cannot afford to waste time on experiments. It is doubtful whether they will be willing to accept an English or French commander....

I am naturally most reluctant to bring forward my own name as you can well understand. But I have unusual experience and qualifications to lead a force such as the American army will be in an offensive campaign. I think if American *amour propre* could be satisfied I could in that capacity render very great service to our Cause.

But of that as well as of the question whether it is expedient to make any such suggestion to President Wilson you will be a better judge than I am, and I must leave the matter in your hands....If you do not yourself look upon my suggestion favourably, I trust it will not go beyond you.[21]

Lloyd George did not let the suggestion go beyond him, either at that time or when he published his *War Memoirs* many years later; it was not until 1954 that it became widely known.[22] By that time, the Americans had achieved a pre-eminence of military power in the world which only the Russians could challenge. In such a context,

Smuts's proposal was bound to appear presumptuous, if not down-right silly.

It takes on a different appearance when one examines it in its own historical context. Lloyd George himself has painted the background in his *War Memoirs*. To reproduce the lurid colours in which he has contrasted American promise and performance in war production, sea transport and military deployment might create an unpleasing impression of British patronage; but, on a matter which touches the reputation of a South African soldier and statesman, an Australian writer may permit himself some comment. Australia during the First World War had a population below 5 million, America a population above 103 million; but the Australian army suffered heavier battle casualties—not in proportion to its numbers, but absolutely—than the American army. This discrepancy arose not merely because Australia was in the war much longer than America (a matter of historical circumstances, not lending itself to praise or censure), but because the Australian government and army showed themselves far more ardent than the Americans did for action. After they had been in the war for six months, the Americans did not have a single division in the line. After they had been in the war for ten months, they still had only one division in a quiet sector of the front. From an Australian or New Zealand point of view that record does indeed appear poor. After only eight months from the outbreak of war two divisions of Anzacs had fought their way across the beaches and up the hills of Gallipoli.[23]

As late as the spring of 1918 General Pershing was still complaining about the dilatory dribble of American troops across the Atlantic; but he was in no hurry to blood them when he got them to France. He was intent upon training them. When the Germans launched their shattering offensive and the fate of the world was trembling in the balance he fought a series of stubborn battles, not against the enemy but against his allies and even his own government. At last, after many weeks of weary argument, he consented to have some of his divisions trained alongside allied formations close to the fighting front. And there, on 8 July, an unforeseen incident occurred. General Monash, commander of the Australian Army Corps, had been planning the classic counter-stroke at Hamel which proved to be the hinge upon which the campaign turned. The Americans who were training alongside the Australians believed that they would be

allowed to join the fighting; but a message came down from Headquarters to remind them that training, not fighting, was still their
business. Lloyd George has told what followed:

When the Americans heard of this order a wave of disappointment spread
over their camp, and some of them passed the sad news to their Australian
comrades. The latter promptly scoffed at the idea that they should be
diverted from their purpose merely because an order had come from
Headquarters, and they told their American comrades: 'You don't mean
to say you take any notice of those blighters?—we never do.'
The Americans agreed with this view, went into action and by all
accounts I heard they fought with great dash and spirit. The only comment
of the Australians was: 'They are fine fighters, only rather rough.'[24]

General Pershing gave the strictest instructions to prevent anything similar happening again. There is, of course, a great deal to be
said on his side. He was building the foundations of the powerful,
independent American army which from mid-July onwards played
an indispensable and ever-increasing, if still subordinate part in the
last battles of the war. The enemy might not have thrown in his hand
so completely that autumn had he not recognised Pershing's army as
a visible sign of the wrath to come. Still, Smuts had no more fore-
knowledge than anybody else of the events of that autumn. It was
in early June that he made his suggestion to Lloyd George and there
was still no sign of the German onslaught slackening. Nor was there
any sign of the Americans going into action. They had been in the
war fourteen months without taking part in a single battle. They had
been lookers-on during the bitter fighting of the past three months.
In those early weeks of June, when the fate of France and the issue
of the war hung in the balance, they still remained lookers-on.

Smuts was not peculiar in concluding that they needed more
spirited leadership. Nor was he arrogant in offering himself as their
leader. He was, perhaps, romantic: we have already seen that the
romantic image of his own career was familiar and pleasing to him
and that the vision of himself as leader of a new crusade in Palestine
had appealed to his romantic sense.* In Palestine he would have
been commander-in-chief, just as he had been in East Africa. But
he did not propose himself as commander-in-chief of the American
forces in France. He proposed himself as combat-chief. This was a
distinction deeply rooted in the tradition of his own people; the

* See pp. 434, 437 above.

Boers had their *Generals*, who carried the main administrative burdens, and their *Vecht Generals*, who led the commandos into battle. Of course, this distinction was not always observed in practice; Smuts himself had not observed it in East Africa, where he carried heavy administrative burdens but still retained the spirit of a *Vecht General* and used to go scouting ahead of his troops....What substitute for those forays, one wonders, would he have found in France?

The real motive which prompted Smuts to offer himself as *Vecht General* of the American army was his passion for action and for personal commitment in a cause and at a crisis which he thought crucial. The real obstacle to the acceptance of his offer was American pride. Smuts himself was afraid that this obstacle might prove insuperable; but he did not lay himself open to the charge of tactlessness. After all, he was writing a private letter to Lloyd George and if he had anything worth while saying he might as well say it forcefully; Lloyd George could be trusted to supply the tact if and when he took up the proposal with President Wilson. Lloyd George decided, no doubt realistically, to let the proposal go no further.

Smuts indulged no further his craving to put on field uniform again. From mid-June onwards his mood became more relaxed than it had been during the previous months. A main reason, no doubt, was the improvement in the war situation which began about this time, but there was also another reason which can be discerned in the following letter written in late May by Mrs Gillett to her mother.

We, after Oom Jannie had played with the children, set off at about 11 for our old haunts on the Downs, to see if we could get the use of a deserted cottage in some woods, as a point d'appui for camping. Alice knows the place, it is just on the edge of a wood, with the open ground sloping away from it. We called on the keeper's wife, an old friend of ours, and the keeper met us there and showed us round with great enthusiasm. It will do very well and if we have any luck we shall have lovely times there.

We walked over those much beloved Downs and at the end of the afternoon swam in the Thames, got tea at the Beetle and Wedge, and interviewed the Landlord of the countryside for permission to use the cottage, all most successful and then we went on the Down tops again in all the beauty of the evening and the moonrise, and only came down at 9.30 to take the car and return to 102 for a big rice pudding, coffee and bed. Oom Jannie left us at 6.45 this morning.

He did immensely enjoy himself. So did we. The greatest excitement to me however was seeing a pair of badgers in our wood! Just think! I never saw badgers before.

Smuts and his friends had various names for their sylvan refuge—the Sleeping Beauty's house (because it was so hidden away in the woods), 102 A (on the pretence that it was an annexe of the Gillett's home at 102 Banbury Road, Oxford), Paradise Plantation, or just Paradise. The cottage stood in an open glade of Ham Wood with great beeches on three sides of it and a broad grassy ride leading downhill towards the valley of the Thames and the wooded Chilterns rising from the opposite bank. It was roomy and in good repair, for it had been the home of one of the gamekeepers until he was called away on war service. In the large kitchen there was an old-fashioned raised hearth with an oven underneath the bricks and above them an iron kettle hanging from a chain fixed to a bar or hook in the chimney. The atmosphere of the place was one of permanence and peace. Forty years later, everything was still the same—the cottage, the wood, the glade, the grassy ride, the view across the Thames valley to the Chilterns—and memories still lingered among Moulsford people of the soldier-statesman who had taken his rest there during the Great War.*

He took his rest strenuously. Hard physical exercise was always a necessity for him and in London he used to take it by walking before dinner round and round Hyde Park at a cracking pace, with a companion if he could get one; sometimes it would be his tall secretary, Captain Ernest Lane—'the Long Lane'—sometimes one of the Clarks or Gilletts up from Street or Oxford to stay with him in the extra room which the management of the Savoy kept at his command. On Friday night he would drive to Oxford, stay the night at 102 Banbury Road, play with the children next morning and then set off for Paradise Plantation with the Gilletts and sometimes one or two other friends. On warm summer nights they would sometimes take their mattresses from the cottage out into the glade and under the trees. In the mornings there would be the milk to fetch from a neighbouring farm, a few chores to do in the cottage, and after that walking, morning and afternoon, through the woods and over the downs, with an evening bathe in the quiet river and then the evening

* The owner of Moulsford Manor in 1918 was a Mr Mills, who showed the greatest kindness and consideration towards his eminent and unconventional guest.

meal and talking, or sometimes poetry reading or singing; but often silence: and so to bed.

Saturday, 22 June 1918. Arranged for going to Ham Wood. Jannie and Alice came about 4.30 for us. We took the children. The others bathed while I installed the children. They slept indoors and we four outside, moonlight, light wind.

Sunday, 23 June 1918. A sunny morning and lovely day of blue and cloud. Breakfast late. A. and I went to fetch milk. Then Jannie and I walked Lowbury and Temple. Dinner about 3. Jannie and I bathed and Alice cooked a wonderful supper. Another great night of full moon. The evening very clear....

Sunday, 1 September 1918. A most beautiful day. Clear air and blue and white sky. Blackberrying and going for milk a.m. Jannie and I walked along S. edge of wood as far as the other Down and sat there a bit. He, May and I went bathing. Singing at night....

Sunday, 27 October 1918. Jannie to Cabinet returned to cottage.[25]

So it continued from June to October—a magical holiday, not in length of days (the sum total of Saturdays and Sundays spent at Paradise was twenty-one),* but in fullness of days. For Smuts, their fullness depended first of all upon the power he possessed throughout his life to empty his mind of the cares and complexities of government and to employ his faculties in apprehending and enjoying the simple things of life—the play of children, the company of friends, physical exercise, food, fun and nonsense, a lovely landscape.

He had a clear and powerful memory for the structure and colour of a landscape and from the summer of 1918 until his death he could open at will and spread out within his mind a map of Paradise Plantation and the woods and valleys and Downs. He could put this map alongside his boyhood's map of Riebeeck West and know himself to be in love with two soils.

Familiarity and repetition were another source of his pleasure that summer—always the same place and the same people. If somebody new did from time to time appear at Paradise Plantation he or she was sure already to have a place somewhere within the circle. Smuts had got to know the Gilbert Murrays through League of Nations projects and their mutual acquaintance with the Gilletts, and once or twice a daughter of the family, Agnes, joined the party in the woodland cottage. A more frequent visitor was May Hobbs, a

* Only two week-ends in this period were spent elsewhere, one at Oxford (from where Smuts was recalled to London), the other at Street.

co-worker and friend of Margaret Gillett's in the Women's Movement and the wife of Robert Hobbs, famous among English farmers
for his herd of dairy shorthorns at Kelmscott. She was born an
Elliot of the Scottish Lowlands and her head was full of Border
ballads and songs. If there was singing in the woods on warm summer
nights or around the fire on the raised hearth when the autumn chills
set in, she was sure to be leading it—an ardent, vivid spirit, full of
light and shade.

Arthur Gillett was almost always there and male relatives of the
Gillett, Clark and Hobbs connections sometimes appeared, but the
atmosphere of Paradise Plantation was predominantly feminine. It
was besides radical and pacifist, or near-pacifist. Both in its femi-
ninity and its pacifism (but not in poverty) it suggests memories
of the circle which Gandhi had formed around himself in South
Africa. Gandhi, however, was able to make his life—political, social,
religious—all of one piece, whereas Smuts seemed almost to be living
two separate lives based on two separate sets of assumptions. He
felt strongly impelled to bring them into unity but the task was not
easy. He was drawn to the Society of Friends and used sometimes to
say that he would become a Friend himself—except for having to
fight. Every Monday morning he returned to his other world, to the
masculine society of Whitehall and to the business of war.

From July onwards the Imperial War Cabinet was in session.
Smuts was there in a dual capacity. As Minister of Defence for South
Africa he reported on his country's war effort; as a member of
the British War Cabinet he introduced the debate on the war
situation.

In the discussions of the Imperial War Cabinet his themes and
arguments were substantially the same as those of his public pronouncement at Glasgow. There were, of course, some differences
which followed inevitably from the turn of the tide in France: no
need any longer to steel one's will for the worst that might
befall, German domination over all Europe and a long implacable
war of the continents and oceans. All the same, Smuts believed the
enemy's strength still to be formidable. Looking to the past, he made
out a balance-sheet of failure and success: on the debit side, Passchendaele and its grievous consequences: on the credit side, unity of
command, the defeat of the submarines, the arrival of the Americans,

the unconquerable spirit of the British people. Looking to the future, he felt no doubt at all of victory.

Where and how would victory come? Not, he thought, by frontal assault in France. He agreed with Milner that the Western front was a candle which burnt all the moths that entered it. We should not reinforce it, as the War Office proposed, at Allenby's expense. Rather should we concentrate our military and diplomatic offensive upon those points where the enemy was weakest. The Western front and the German army were not, in his view, weak points; Austria, Bulgaria and Turkey were. Smuts took his stand with the Easterners.

When would victory come? That depended, he believed, upon the kind of victory we aimed at. Throughout the discussions of July and August he took his stand upon the principle which he had affirmed and reaffirmed, in private and in public, in season and out of season, ever since his arrival in England: for Britain, the Commonwealth and their allies this war was and must remain a war of limited objectives. To win such a war it was necessary to beat the enemy, but not to smash him.

In developing this argument, Smuts made the same tactical mistake as he had made in Glasgow. He might have contented himself with standing upon principle, of arguing, as he sincerely believed, that the knock-out blow, even if it could be delivered, was in itself an evil and would produce evil consequences. He argued instead that it could not be delivered, except by ruinously prolonging the war. He took his stand upon the facts as he saw them; but he saw them askew. They slipped away from under his feet.

In his errors of military forecasting he was in eminent company. On 25 July the Imperial War Cabinet began to discuss a paper on long-term strategy submitted by the C.I.G.S., Sir Henry Wilson. Lloyd George has dwelt at length and with disdain upon the exaggerated pessimism of this paper, which listed five alternative possibilities in 'descending order of calamity' and, at the very time when the Germans were beginning to give way in France, contemplated their victorious advance to the gateway of India. Smuts, Lloyd George has added, put too much trust in the wisdom of the military experts.[26] The criticism has point. All the same, it might be said in reply to it that in July nobody of any authority, not even Foch or Lloyd George himself, envisaged the collapse of the Germans and their allies before the winter. Everybody assumed that they were strong enough to prolong the war to 1919, if not 1920.

A month later the situation was different and Smuts stood almost alone in overestimating the strength of the enemy. The discussion on this occasion was opened by Balfour, who argued that the British must take pains to avoid coming out of the war with any substantial increases of their overseas territories; but also recommended large alterations of the European map, which assumed, among other things, the dismemberment of Austria-Hungary. This programme, by and large, was the very reverse of the one which Smuts had always advocated. He now fought it strenuously.

As regards Africa and Asia, he saw little merit in Balfour's proposal to bring in the Americans (who, anyway, had not been consulted) to govern large territories held hitherto by the Germans and Turks. At the same time, he was aware of the strong American opposition to colonial annexations. In his search for a middle way he hit upon some ideas which had a future. Possession, he said in effect, might be nine points of the law but need not be the whole law. For Central Africa he sketched the outlines of a new system, with the possessing powers still in possession, but with the United States presiding over a Development Board under the aegis of the League of Nations. Schemes such as that, he suggested, might reconcile the needs of the Commonwealth for security with American aspirations (and British aspirations too) for a better world. They might take the place of the old competitive Imperialism.

As regards Europe, Smuts insisted that Balfour's proposals went far beyond the essentials for which Britain had gone to war. She had not gone to war to break up the Austrian Empire. She had her obligations to her allies; but this did not mean underwriting all their claims; they might have to be talked to about scaling their claims down.

Smuts could well have grounded his argument upon the British interest in maintaining 'a just equilibrium' in Europe or upon Britain's obligation to stand by her declared peace aims. Instead, he repeated his mistake of laying the heaviest stress upon the military situation, as he understood it. Balfour's programme, he said, assumed a complete and final defeat of the enemy; but so far the allies had recovered only one-third of the territory the Germans had taken in the spring. No more great operations were likely in 1918 and it was unlikely that a decision would be reached even in 1919, despite American aid. If there was no decision in 1919 must the Imperial War Cabinet look forward to 1920? By prolonging the war the British Empire could make sure of smashing the Germans but might find itself at the same time reduced to the status of a second or third class power. The leadership of the world would have passed to America. Europe would have fought herself to a finish. Why fight the war to a finish which would be as fatal to us as to the enemy? Instead, as soon as the military tide had turned (and it was turning now) and as soon as the enemy came to us ('as I am sure he will') with an offer to concede our essential demands, then we should be prepared to make peace, even though the German armies had not been smashed to the extent some people would like.

In the discussion which followed some speakers agreed and others disagreed with the outline of a peace settlement which Smuts had sketched; but nobody agreed with his conception of how the war would—and should—end. Speaker after speaker answered him back in terms which he must have felt to be ominous. We must go on hammering till Germany was beaten. We must bring Germany to a right frame of mind. We must make sure that no other nation would ever be tempted to repeat Germany's crime. We might not be able to beat Germany in 1919 but we must make sure of beating her in 1920. We must go on fighting till we could dictate terms which would symbolise humanity's reprobation of Germany's crime and thereby give the League of Nations a good start.

So the Imperial War Cabinet fell into line behind the policy of the knock-out blow.

The Germans were not so rational as Smuts conceived them to be. It was to their interest, if only they could have seen it, to keep in being such an equipoise of military power as would make it impossible for their enemies to prolong the war except at a high cost; but this they could not do unless they made the decision to cut their losses of conquest and prestige. They had open to them two rational alternatives: either to admit a limited defeat and try to get moderate peace terms (as Smuts thought them likely to do) while their armies still held strong positions on enemy territory: or else to withdraw their armies in good order to their own frontiers and rally their people for a war of national defence. Either way, as Lloyd George admitted later on,[27] they could have made things very awkward for their enemies; but neither way was congruent with their philosophy. So they fought on until the soft under-belly of their power was ripped open and its hard carapace cracked.

As summer merged into autumn the allies found within their grasp that 'overwhelming victory' which Smuts had repeatedly declared that he did not want. What did he think of it when it arrived? He was slow to admit that it had arrived. Although he told his wife on 10 October not to be surprised if he were home by Christmas, he warned her a fortnight later that his return might be a good deal later than that.[28] On 23 October, in two successive memoranda for the War Cabinet, he asserted that it might take another year to beat the Germans.

And yet Prince Max of Baden had told President Wilson on 4 October that Germany accepted his principles of peace and wanted him to arrange an armistice. How then could Smuts possibly anticipate another year of fighting? Because the allies, in his view, were trying to get the wrong peace settlement in the wrong way. President Wilson was discussing with the Germans, but not with his allies, the principles, but not the terms of peace; the allies were discussing with each other the terms of the armistice. It was the President's main purpose to get his Points, Particulars and Principles accepted; it was the allies' main purpose to assert their military power. As Lloyd George later put it: 'It was not sufficient for Germany to express readiness to negotiate on the basis of the Fourteen Points unless we were in a position to insist on her accepting our exegesis of the sacred text.'[29]

Foch was principally responsible for the allies' armistice proposals and Smuts believed (this time with the opinion of Haig to back him)[30] that he was overcalling his hand. The proposed terms were so drastic that there was a risk of the Germans refusing to accept them. They might prefer to fight a war of national defence on their own frontiers, thereby putting the stigma of aggression upon the allies and leaving them to argue among themselves who was responsible for prolonging the war. This was a risk, said Smuts, which Britain and the British Empire should not accept. Their mobilisation was now at its peak. It was principally their effort, on land, at sea and in the air, which had achieved the dramatic victories of the summer and autumn. The peace, if it came now, would be a British peace. If it were postponed for another year it would be an American peace. Smuts, no doubt, was arguing *ad hominem* and not with any jingoistic intent; he proceeded at once to show that it was not the predominance of America but the fate of Europe which he had in the forefront of his mind. Nations and States, he said, were falling to pieces from the inside even before their armies were beaten. It had happened in Russia, it was happening in Austria. Autocracy, the enemy of yesterday, was dead or dying. The new danger was anarchy. Right across eastern Europe there would stretch a chain of discordant fragments from the Baltic to the Adriatic. If the war continued much longer, no League of Nations could hope in the future to prevent a wild war dance of these so-called free nations. The disorder would be such that autocracy would once again lay its heavy hand on Europe. Germany might one day make herself the policeman of this chaos and dominate the heterogeneous mass and in another generation plant her foot just as firmly as before on the neck of Europe. Nor would the evil stop with Europe. It would engulf the world.

Smuts was writing at white heat. His military forecasting was soon proved wrong, for the Germans accepted the armistice terms. But his political forecasting?

Smuts had a proposal to make about procedure. He argued that the negotiations had followed the wrong road and that it was a matter of urgency to get them back on to the right road. While President Wilson had been seeking the agreement of the Germans to the Fourteen Points and Foch had been seeking to impose upon them armistice terms equivalent to unconditional surrender, nobody had given any attention to the actual terms of peace. Smuts proposed that the allies should make it their first objective to get Preliminaries of Peace concluded.

He enumerated the main heads of the Preliminaries of Peace: to begin with, the whole programme of British Commonwealth security which he had agreed with Amery eighteen months earlier: then the evacuation and restoration of all the occupied countries, east and west: the evacuation of Alsace-Lorraine, to be followed by a plebiscite of some kind: cession to Italy of the Trentino and some other territories: complete autonomy of Bohemia in a federal or confederate Austria (unless Austria broke up in the meantime): complete self-determination of Yugoslavia: independence of Poland with access to the sea: revision of the treaties of Brest-Litovsk and Bucharest: establishment of the League of Nations.

These, he said, were the 'bedrock terms'. In proposing to get them embodied in a preliminary treaty he had two purposes in view: first, to achieve a speedy peace settlement; secondly, to achieve it while a military and political balance still to some degree survived in Europe. To state his second purpose is to give a sufficient explanation of why his proposal was rejected.

Smuts felt deep misgivings but he forgot them in the exhilarating November days. 'Things are moving at a tremendous pace', he wrote on 7 November, 'and appeals are made to us to come and occupy Austria and Hungary to keep the peace and feed the starving. Much of the German fleet is in the hands of a Sailors' Soviet. Perhaps peace is very near. Pray God it is.'[31] On Sunday, 10 November, he was with the Gilletts in Oxford, but in the afternoon he felt that he must get back at once to London. At midnight he wrote to Arthur Gillett—

It is all over. As I said to you on leaving, this was the last Sunday of the war. The new revolutionary German Government have accepted the Armistice terms. The war is over, but as to peace in this hour of falling worlds who could say? A great task is ahead of us. As I said to the Prime Minister tonight, it is for us now to be large and generous and to send food at once to the famished millions on the Continent. We shall reap a rich reward not only in the gratitude of the starving people but in the words of that great Judgment which now will come truer than ever before (Matt. 25: 31–46). May God in this great hour remove from us all smallness of heart and vitalise our souls with sympathy and fellow feeling for those in affliction— the beaten, weak, and little ones who have no food. I write in remembrance of this great day.[32]

A great Englishman was thinking the same thoughts that morning. It was the first thought of Winston Churchill to send the food-ships from London to Hamburg.[33]

Armistice Day brought no relief to Smuts but added to his burden of work, if that were possible. Towards the end of October he had been entrusted by the War Cabinet with two formidable tasks which now became urgent—to guide and control the demobilisation plans of all the British departments and to assemble the British brief for the Peace Conference. The *omnia opera* of Smuts contain the materials for many monographs; his biographer must leave these specialist investigations to future historians and content himself with selecting from the mountainous record of immoderate labour such evidences as best reveal the impulses and purposes which drove and guided Smuts. About his work on the Demobilisation Committee, let it suffice to say that he took the chair at twenty-one meetings between 31 October and 9 December and submitted proposals of his own which possessed both long-term and immediate significance: proposals for the permanent improvement of governmental machinery* and for making sure that the return to 'normalcy' was not made in a rush at the expense of the working man.† About his work on the Peace Brief rather more must be said. It had an organisational side: the selection of subjects upon which memoranda were required, the commissioning of these memoranda from a dozen or more departments of government and, finally, the choice of experts to assist the political delegates at the Peace Conference. Under these heads, the work of Smuts on the Peace Brief need not be discussed. But his work had also an intensely personal content which will repay careful examination. By mid-December he had achieved an intellectual synthesis (whether or not it was firm enough to stand up to criticism and the pressure of events will appear later on) of the various elements of his thought on the problems of peace.

We have seen that his first concern when he reached England in the spring of 1917 had been with the status of his own country. In his view, the Nationalists oversimplified the problem of status by envisaging it as something to be achieved *against* and outside the British Empire; whereas he believed that the most effective and rewarding way of achieving it was within and through the British Commonwealth. He now found himself working towards this end in partnership with Sir Robert Borden of Canada and Mr W. M. Hughes of Australia. The three men proved an effective combination —Borden making the running in the Imperial War Conference, Hughes raising a clamour in the press, Smuts using his position at the centre of power to slip in the right memorandum at the right

* See p. 469 above.
† For example, Smuts insisted that the government must fulfil its pledges to the trade unions by introducing a bill to restore pre-war practices in industry and he resisted the Treasury's proposal to restrict out-of-work payments to the men covered by State insurance: the State, he argued, had been lavish with war expenditure and it was unreasonable to rush suddenly to the other extreme.

time.* The object to be achieved was the recognition of the Dominions at the Peace Conference in their own legal and political right; the main obstacle was the resistance of other nations, particularly France. The story of how this resistance was overcome need not be told again; but it is worth while recalling the arrangements which were finally made. They were as follows:

1. Separate representation of the Dominions (two members each for the larger ones, including South Africa, one member each for New Zealand and Newfoundland) at the Peace Conference, with full rights of attendance at plenary sessions and of representation on committees.
2. Voting power to reside in the British Empire as a whole, which had five votes at the Conference. The Dominions became formal participants in the voting power by means of the panel system; from a realistic point of view, they enjoyed greater power still through their membership of the British Empire Delegation (the Imperial War Cabinet under another name) which was in continuous session in Paris.

There can be no doubt that South Africa and her sister Dominions gained far more influence under these arrangements than they could possibly have gained as separate entities—more influence, indeed, than any except the largest of the European nations. It was an early demonstration of the principle, 'Independence *Plus*'. Smuts had good warranty in the facts for writing to his wife, on the eve of the first plenary session at Paris—

While the Nats. make a noise about our independence we have obtained this—that South Africa takes her place at the Peace Conference among the nations of the world. This is the second time that I appear at a Peace Conference—but how different is the situation in Paris from that of Vereeniging in 1902! There we had to drink the cup to the bitter lees; here South Africa is a victor among the great nations! I am thankful that it has been granted to me to do my part in this great work and to help lead my people out of the painful past into the triumphant present.[34]

The programme of South African security, as Smuts envisaged it, depended just as much as the programme of status did upon fellowship with the Commonwealth. Smuts considered the isolationist path too dangerous for his country to tread, and he could foresee no artificially constructed pacts which would give such effective support

* On 25 November he produced an effective paper advocating the panel system as the means whereby Dominion Prime Ministers could be represented on the British Empire Delegation.

as South Africa could claim already from Great Britain and the Dominions. As we have seen, he also thought of security in territorial terms and was resolved to resist any move to bring German sovereignty back into South-West Africa. Here he found himself automatically aligned with the Australians and New Zealanders, who had formed similar resolutions with regard to New Guinea and Samoa. This formidable combination easily got its way with Great Britain and the other members of the British Empire Delegation. They were not willing, however, to underwrite every South African demand or desire; in particular, the Imperial War Cabinet had made it quite clear as early as 1917 that pressure would not be put upon Portugal to cede Delagoa Bay to the Union in exchange for territory in German East Africa.*

At the end of 1918 Smuts felt convinced that German East Africa should remain under British control. His programme of South African security, as we have seen, had become interlocked with the programme of British Commonwealth security expounded by L. S. Amery, who thought it essential to retain strategic control of the routes from Cairo to the Cape and from the Mediterranean to India. This programme, however, ran into opposition from two quarters: from the French, who had conflicting interests of their own and, so far as the Middle East was concerned, could cite their recognition in the Sykes–Picot Agreement: from the Americans, who believed that the old rules of the game of international politics—secret diplomacy, balance of power, territorial annexation—were 'for ever discredited', and that the time had now come to establish new and better rules.

Smuts tried to think this problem out on two planes: on the plane of the old rules, which he was bound to reckon with unless and until they were superseded; and on the plane of the new rules which he hoped, just as much as President Wilson did, to see established. The balance of power, whether or not the President was right in proclaiming it to be eternally discredited, was still a fact of international politics and Smuts opted in the most emphatic terms for America in preference to France as a weight or force to keep the balance safe. It must be admitted that his judgment of France was unkind. The French, he said, would try to keep the Germans in a state of humiliating subjection which would create a hopeless atmosphere for future

* See p. 408 above and p. 553 below.

peace and international cooperation. The French had done well for themselves, too well, from the generosity of the British, who had promised them the best of Germany's colonies in West Africa and had made them by the Sykes–Picot Agreement the principal heirs of the Turkish Empire. According to Smuts, that had been a hopeless blunder of policy and every effort must be made to get free of it. America could help in that: the Sykes–Picot Agreement was in flagrant contradiction to the principles proclaimed by the President and he should be urged to veto it. From the very start of the Peace Conference we should work with America and give to the President the maximum support consistent with our interests. Our true line of policy for the foreseeable future must be to link the destinies of the two great Commonwealths which, by their community of language, ideals and interests were marked out for political comradeship with each other. For the Dominions this was obviously true: as a great naval power in the Pacific, the United States would become more and more the protector of Australia and New Zealand against the dangers of attack from Asia. For Great Britain it might prove to be just as true: if militarism were ever to revive in Europe, American support might come to mean even more to the British than it had meant during the recent war.

All this, although it had flashes of generous aspiration, was argued in the language of *realpolitik*. President Wilson, however, conducted the foreign policy of his country in the language of moral principle. And there could be no doubt that he had objections on grounds of principle to some of the peace aims of Great Britain and the Dominions: for example, to the transfers of territory in Africa upon which Smuts himself set such great store. But perhaps his objections could be met by reforms of the colonial system which, short of abolishing sovereignty, would take the sting out of it? Smuts wrote down under two main headings a brief list of duties which might properly be made obligatory upon the rulers of tropical dependencies:

(1) Native interests: repression of slave trade, prohibition of sale of firearms and spirits, prohibition of raising armies, etc.

(2) International trade: free trade and navigation, prohibition of fortifications, etc.

These items were not at all an original discovery of Smuts. They were quite familiar, for example, to Sir Frederick (later Lord) Lugard, who probably was at work at this very time on his book,

The Dual Mandate in West Africa. Mandate was a word which some of Smuts's friends, J. A. Hobson, for example, were using. Smuts himself, as we shall soon see, had the word in the forefront of his mind. For good practical reasons—what, for example, would be the reaction of his Australian colleague, Mr Hughes?—he was not inclined as yet to apply it to the territories which the Dominions had conquered from Germany or, in general, to African territories. And yet, in the proposals which he had made only a few months back for economic aid to Africa under the aegis of the League of Nations, he had already adopted the mandatory idea, if not the name.*

By following this train of thought Smuts was making good progress in bridging the gap of ideology or phraseology between the British and the Americans and also between the realist and idealist elements within his own mind. He completed the bridge by an impressive achievement of intellectual engineering in which three theories were firmly interlocked: a theory of Imperialism, a theory of the Commonwealth and a theory of the League of Nations.

His intense mental activity at this time, it is worth explaining, was expressing itself in a series of letters and memoranda which were, so to speak, codified in a great State paper on the League of Nations which he submitted to the Imperial War Cabinet on 16 December.[35] His theories of Imperialism, of the Commonwealth and of the League may be illustrated by the following quotation from that document:

Nations in their march to power tend to pass the purely national bounds; hence arise the empires which embrace various nations, sometimes related in blood and institutions, sometimes again different in race and hostile in temperament. In a rudimentary way all such composite empires of the past were leagues of nations, keeping the peace among the constituent nations but unfortunately doing so not on the basis of freedom but of repression. Usually one dominant nation in the group overcame, coerced and kept the rest under. The principle of nationality became overstrained and over-developed, and nourished itself by exploiting other weaker nationalities. Nationality overgrown became imperialism, and the empire led a troubled existence on the ruin of the freedom of its constituent nations. That was the evil of the system; but with however much friction and oppression, the peace was usually kept among the nations falling within the empire. These empires have all broken down, and today the British Commonwealth of Nations remains the only embryo league of nations because it is based on the true principles of national freedom and political decentralisation.[36]

* See p. 491 above.

This paragraph suggests at one and the same time so many trains of thought that it is hard to know where to begin; perhaps it will be best to begin with down-to-earth *realpolitik* and to recall the intense desire of Smuts to bring America into the balance of power as a decisive makeweight. But how to overcome the isolationist prejudices so deeply rooted in American tradition and doctrine? We can do it, said Smuts in effect, by supporting the President in his plans for a League of Nations. He looks upon the League of Nations as the key to the future. Let us help him to fit and turn the key. His ideas about the League are vague; let us help him to give them substance. They are theoretical; let us convince him that the League has practical and urgent work to do here and now.

Realpolitik, it is often said, wears the cloak of lofty aspirations; but the contrary can also happen; or perhaps both things can happen at the same time. Certainly, Smuts looked to the League as a means of inducing American participation in world politics; but he looked just as much to American participation in world politics as a means of establishing the League. That was an end which he pursued with sincere and passionate conviction. He himself believed the things which he wanted Wilson to believe.

His belief that urgent practical work was awaiting the League here and now followed logically from the exposition of Imperialism which has just been quoted. The old Empires, whatever their perversions, had performed the function of keeping the peace within wide areas of economic and political interdependence. The war had destroyed these Empires and some new system was urgently needed to take their place. The territories which they had ruled were inhabited by many nations weak in resources and untrained in self-government. If they were looked upon as loot to be shared out among the victorious nations the future of the world must be despaired of. The only statesmanlike course was to make the League of Nations 'the reversionary', in the broadest sense, of the shattered Empires. This did not mean that it would exercise direct sovereign rule. Various ways would be open to it, in accordance with the variety of circumstances, of performing its tasks of salvage and guidance. In the area covered by the Sykes–Picot Agreement, for example, it could solve some of the knottiest problems confronting the international community by delegating its powers to agents or mandatories. Thus it could devolve upon State *A* its tutelary powers in territory *X*, subject to such rules as might be laid down to fit the varying needs (including always the need to respect local wishes in choosing the mandatory)* of the various territories and peoples.

These proposals about mandates occupied a full third of Smuts's paper and were an important contribution to the Covenant of the League. Equally important was the contribution which Smuts made to the problem of organisation at the centre. Needless to say, he had very much in mind the exemplar of the only Empire which had survived the war—if indeed, the British Empire had done this, for it had transmuted itself into something different, into a Commonwealth, a league of nations on less than world scale. The new universal League of Nations, he declared, must profit by the Commonwealth's experience, avoiding on the one hand the presumption of the super-State and on the other the futility of the debating society. Above all, it must leave room for natural growth in response to practical needs.

The grand success of the British Empire depends not on its having followed any constitutional precedent of the past but on having met a new situation in history with a creation in law; and as a matter of fact the new constitutional system grew empirically and organically out of the practical necessities of the colonial situation. So it will have to be here. And above all let us avoid cut-and-dried schemes meant as a complete definitive and final solution of our problem. Let us remember that we are only asked to make a beginning, so long as that beginning is in the right direction; that great works are not made but grown; and that our constitution should avoid all rigidity, should be elastic and capable of growth, expansion and adaptation to the needs which the new organ of government will have to meet in the process of years. Above all it must be practical....[37]

He meant, the sceptical French might well have objected, that it must be British! But that would have been too cynical. It was Smuts who made the suggestions which took shape later on as the Council and Assembly of the League; but in making them he drew upon his experience, not only of the Commonwealth, but of inter-allied cooperation, as exemplified, above all, by the Supreme War Council.

It would be out of place here to try to measure the precise influence of Smuts's paper on the Covenant of the League; that task has been attempted by David Hunter Miller and other authorities. Sufficient

* Here *realpolitik* re-entered the argument (although not its printed and published exposition) since Smuts expected as a matter of course a fortunate coincidence to arise between British desires to become the mandatory Power in 'Territory *X*' and the desires of the people in that territory to choose Great Britain rather than any other Power.

to say that the influence was profound and that the paper has been accepted universally as a work of exceptional ability.

The document he turned out [wrote Lloyd George] is one of the most notable products of this extremely able man. It is pellucid in style, eloquent in diction, penetrating in thought and broad in its outlook. It contains one or two striking phrases which will live in the literature of peace. It is difficult to summarise, for every sentence is full of fruitful suggestion and couched in language of stately impressiveness. This ideal State paper will have its place in history, not only for its intrinsic merit, but as the model on which the Covenant of the League was built.[38]

Smuts had written not merely an 'ideal State paper' but a tract for the times, vibrant with faith and hope. And yet, when the work was done, his mood became gloomy. He was with the Gilletts at Oxford on 16 December, the day his paper was published, but next day he wrote to them from London—'It looks an age since I was last at 102. And the days are so beautiful. But the world is just rotten.'[39] ...But why? Perhaps he was feeling 'just rotten' himself? For a good many weeks past he had been suffering from severe headaches, but they had not damped his zest for work and life; indeed, illness seems seldom if ever to have had a depressive effect upon him and there were times (for example, September 1899, December 1918, March 1919) when it positively stimulated his creative energy. Besides, it was not his habit to fall into nervous collapse even after his fiercest spasms of effort and there is evidence in his letters that his health began to improve after he had finished his paper on the League.

But while he had been writing his paper he had been withdrawn from the world of events. He now re-entered it and found it to be a very different world from the one that he had been imagining. Within his own mind he had achieved coherence; in the world surrounding him he saw chaos. In Europe, the national States which had emerged from the ruined empires were showing no disposition to wait for the helping hand of the League but were rushing to stake out their claims not only against their old oppressors but against each other. In America, Congress was showing no sign of shedding its isolationist habits but was giving the worst possible send-off to the President on his voyage to Europe to redeem the world. In Britain, the people were showing a temper clean contrary to the one which Smuts had credited them with.

Three days after the Armistice, Smuts had addressed a gathering of American journalists on the theme of British magnanimity—'Remember that this people has borne unexampled burdens for nearly four and a half years. They have striven and fought and laboured in a war effort which has no parallel in history....And today you see them rejoicing in the same great spirit in which they have laboured and suffered. Not a tinge of bitterness or vindictiveness mars their rejoicings....No hymns of hate, no tramplings on a prostrate foe.'[40] But when Smuts had finished his pamphlet on the League he had time to study his newspaper cuttings of election speeches. A day or two later (18 December) he could study the election results. They bore witness to the triumph of a different spirit.

The election has no doubt been blamed for many evils which had a different cause; but all the same, among its prominent themes were hanging the Kaiser and making Germany pay for the war.[41] Smuts, as we have seen, had been at work upon themes of a different kind. But what effect would his work have? By his decision fourteen months earlier not to enter British politics he had forfeited the chance of fighting for his cause by the most direct means. In the first great crisis of the peace, as in the last great crisis of the war, he felt himself for a time to be merely an onlooker.

But only for a time. He had already (14 December) sent in his resignation from the British War Cabinet; but he still had his anchorage in South Africa. Botha was now on his way to England and together they would represent their country at the Peace Conference.

CHAPTER 21

PARIS, 1919

HISTORICAL study of the attempt to make peace at the end of the First World War still remains what Sir Harold Nicolson called it nearly twenty years ago, 'a study of fog'.[1] Here and there little pools of light—the books, monographs and articles produced by careful and reflective scholarship—mitigate the murk; but for the great beam of light which some day will sweep through it we still await the great historian. His task will be immense: to master the complex detail of five main treaties and many subsidiary agreements, the processes and procedures whereby this detail was shaped, the guiding ideas, the driving passions and, above all, the conflicting criteria of judgment which confronted politicians at that time and still confront historians.

What follows is a chapter of biography rather than of history. It is not to be expected that Smuts, the second delegate of a small country, should have mastered all those intractable problems which troubled the men who carried the main burden of responsibility. Smuts did, nevertheless, passionately and persistently search out and probe the issues of crucial importance. From January to June he wrote almost every day a letter or memorandum which reveals his mind at work upon the things that mattered most. In this record, which will now be examined both sympathetically and critically, there is likely to be a good deal to interest the great historian who will one day arise.

Smuts, as we have seen, was in a pessimistic mood when he went to Paris. The proposal that he had made in the last weeks of the war —to reverse the order of priorities and make a preliminary treaty the first objective of policy—received the retrospective approval of three experts in diplomatic history and procedure, Sir Ernest Satow, J. Headlam-Morley, and Harold Nicolson;[2] but in October and November 1918 Smuts showed some naïvety if he seriously expected to get it accepted. The contrary procedure was insisted upon both by President Wilson, who wished to get his speeches accepted by both sides as the *pactum de contrahendo*, and by Marshal Foch, who wished to make sure that the allies possessed a monopoly of military power before they started conferring with their enemies: if, indeed, they conferred with them at all; for, as things turned out, the allied and associated Powers conferred only with each other until they had ready a complete draft treaty for presentation to the Germans. This procedure, it has been suggested, may not at the beginning have been deliberately intended: certainly, there is no indication that Smuts foresaw it. But then he was no longer, since his resignation from the British War Cabinet, at the centre of information and decision. He knew, of course, that the President's Points, Principles and Particulars —twenty-three items in all—had been accepted as the basis for the Treaty, subject to two reservations stipulated by the allies: the first on 'the freedom of the seas', the second on 'restoration' or, as it came to be called, reparation. He knew also that reparation was acknowledged by all the parties concerned to be due for all the damage caused to the civilian population of the allies and their property by Germany's 'aggression'. He probably did not know that the word 'aggression' had taken the place (whether or not by deliberate purpose) of the more matter-of-fact word 'invasion', which had been used in an earlier draft. He probably was not told, any more than the Germans were told, about the 'Interpretation' of Wilson's speeches with which Colonel House had reassured and comforted the principal allies: it would enable them, so House said, to establish any point they wanted against Germany. But all this, had he known it, would only have confirmed the mood of foreboding in which he went to Paris. He feared that the military monopoly established by Foch was likely to have a good deal more to do in shaping the peace settlement than the principles established by Wilson.

And yet, from the time of his arrival in Paris, Smuts found his hopes predominating over his forebodings. His hopeful mood found expression after the first plenary session on 18 January, and this despite the disgust which he felt at the opening speech by President Poincaré.

What a farce that first meeting was! You should have heard the smug Poincaré roll out his periods about Justice!...What a poor beginning! Here is a world waiting for the Word: for some crumb of comfort to fall from the table of the great and the wise. And we had nothing to say except punishment for war crimes with which our tempers are already worn threadbare through the agonies of five years! However, things may improve; nor must we expect too much. Next time we start with the League of Nations and our sentiments may improve. The League has been pushing to the fore very rapidly like a child being born.[3]

In the next plenary session on 25 January it was resolved that a League of Nations should be created 'as an integral part of the Treaty of Peace' and that a committee should be appointed to draft its constitution. Wilson was chairman of the committee, Smuts and Lord Robert Cecil the representatives of the British Empire. Lloyd George had told Smuts when he arrived in Paris that Wilson had been studying his pamphlet and adopting its ideas as his own. Who cares, exclaimed Smuts, so long as the work gets done? Who cares whether it is Paul who plants or Apollos who waters? When the committee got to work he kept himself deliberately in the background so that other people more influential than he was (he meant President Wilson) could take the credit for bringing the League to birth and thereby feel all the more committed to making a success of it.[4]

Before the end of the month, the committee ran into trouble over mandates; Wilson wanted to extend the mandatory system to Africa and the Pacific Islands but was opposed by the French and the three southern Dominions. As we have seen, Smuts had played the leading part in formulating the mandatory system but had not intended it to apply to Africa. At least, that had been the stand which he took in his treatise on the League; we also know that in official discussions he had gone a good distance in adapting the mandatory principle to African circumstances.* His letters from the Peace Conference show him to have been equally satisfied with the forthright speech which he had made at the beginning in favour of direct annexation of the German colonies, and in the leading part which he played at the end in achieving an orderly retreat from this position. The chief opponents of compromise were, on the one side, the Australian Hughes and the New Zealander Massey: on the other side, President Wilson. It was Botha who assuaged the President's doubts by an appeal which Lloyd George declared to be more moving than any speech which he had heard so far at the Peace Conference. It was Smuts who moved the long resolution on mandates which became subsequently, without any substantial change, article xxii of the Covenant of the League of Nations.[5]

The letters which Smuts wrote at the end of January and early in February show him to have been in good heart at that time about the progress and prospects of the Peace Conference.

* See pp. 491, 499 above.

We are of course having great trouble and delays over many things. Fortunately the things that really matter are progressing....Our work is beginning to speed up. There are many things I don't like. There is a bad spirit about, mostly of course among the *other* fellows! I feel sometimes deeply concerned: but I do hope and trust and pray that the things which really matter will be all right, and will in the end pull the rest through.[6]

That remained his mood throughout the first four weeks of the conference. When the Armistice was renewed towards the end of January he reported—erroneously, as it turned out—that the food blockade was lifted at last.[7] He also reported that means of supplying raw materials to the enemy countries were being studied. He thought that he could see daylight at last for Europe and broadening prospects for mankind. He recognised a good many 'nasty' problems but thought that they were only transient difficulties which would be forgotten in history. 'Whether the boundary is just here or just there', he said, 'leaves me stone cold.' The thing that really counted was the capital progress that was being made with the League of Nations. On 16 February he announced that the draft of the covenant was already in public print.[8]

That date may be taken as the close of the first phase of his feeling, thought and action at the Peace Conference—the phase of hope predominating over foreboding. It so happened that a break occurred about this time in leadership at the conference. Although its directing body, the Council of Ten, representing the five principal Powers, continued regularly in session, the chief political personalities were temporarily scattered: Wilson went to America to try to placate the Senate, Lloyd George went to London to damp down 'the industrial powder magazine', Clemenceau went to hospital with the bullet of an assassin in his body. Smuts was not an important person in the official hierarchy; as he put it himself, he was 'only the second representative of South Africa';[9] but he possessed such high personal prestige that his absence may fittingly be recorded along with that of the big political leaders. On 15 February he crossed to England to straighten out some muddles of South African demobilisation and attend to other urgent business. And there he fell ill.

He had quite shaken off the headaches which had troubled him in December and had seemed to be thriving on the excitement of seeing the covenant take shape and on the exhilaration of the long fast walks which he took every evening in the Bois de Boulogne; but on 11 February he had a violent gastric attack during a visit in bitter weather to the old front on the Marne. When he crossed the Channel he carried 'a microbe' with him. He spent his first week-end with the Gilletts in Oxford and there he was laid low with influenza. He got up too soon and on his return to London suffered a serious relapse. Alice Clark came up from Somerset to nurse him but it was not until 17 March that his physician, Sir Bertrand Dawson, allowed him to leave his room and it was not until 23 March that he returned to Paris.[10]

While he was cooped up in London he brooded over the papers which Lane, his secretary, sent him from Paris. The conviction began to grow upon him that the work there was taking a bad turn. In so far as this was true, it was due in large measure to the fact that the conference lacked a united purpose and firm guidance. The Council of Ten (and later the 'Big Four') might have acted as an effective steering committee if only they could have made up their minds what shore to steer for. They had inherited the functions of the Supreme War Council and spent much of their time treating the symptoms of European disorder without diagnosing its causes. Seemingly, they began with the vague idea that they would call in the Germans later on to negotiate the treaty (a 'congress' to follow the 'conference'), but they allowed the idea to drop out of mind. Meanwhile, they invited the resurgent nations of central and eastern Europe to stake out their claims in written memoranda and oral argument. They permitted the territorial committees to immerse themselves in the intricacies of map-making without sufficiently defining their powers and terms of reference. Thus the treaty began to take shape in bits and pieces, without any central focus—unless the French were giving it one. While the British and Americans were groping in the fog, the French had a clear view of what they wanted. It was their passionate desire to assure, if they could, their own security by perpetuating the present military and political inferiority of Germany. For this reason they supported the efforts of the new States in eastern Europe to reverse the predominance of power which the Germans of the Habsburg and Hohenzollern Empires had hitherto possessed there. At the same time they aimed at asserting their own predominance in the west by means of a varied assortment of prohibitions, servitudes and territorial rectifications—above all, by pushing the Germans east of the Rhine. In March this ancient ambition of their nation was voiced by Foch and Tardieu with the desperate urgency of Now or Never.

When Smuts returned to Paris on Sunday, 23 March, he had a general idea in his head of the way things had been shaping during his absence. The only talk he had in Paris that night was with W. M. Hughes, whom he found disgruntled because the authorities would not allow Mrs Hughes to bring her baby to the hotel and because progress with the question of reparation was so slow. Smuts offered his sympathy, went to bed and read 'Spinoza on Blessedness'. Next morning he found the world bursting into spring and the newspapers announcing a revolution in Hungary. He spent the day 'trying to get the hang of things' and to find out what progress had been made by the innumerable committees.[11] He pursued these inquiries the following day and on Wednesday, 26 March—the third day after his return to Paris—he set down in a letter to Lloyd George his reflections on what he had learnt.

This letter of 26 March[12] marks the opening of the second phase of his activity at the Peace Conference. In this phase his foreboding became predominant over his hopes and all his endeavours became bent upon securing radical alterations to the emerging draft treaty before it was presented to the Germans. His letter to Lloyd George gave emphatic notice of this intention.

Since my return to Paris last Sunday I have tried to get into touch with the present state of our peace preparations. May I trouble you with some of the reflections stirred in me by what I have learnt? I fear it won't be pleasant reading to you, but even so my criticism is well-meant, and may prove helpful to you.

I am seriously afraid that the peace to which we are working is an impossible peace, conceived on a wrong basis: that it will not be accepted by Germany, and, even if it is accepted, that it will prove utterly unstable, and only serve to promote the anarchy which is rapidly overtaking Europe. I say nothing about the long delays of the Conference work, and the rapid growth of dissatisfaction in all the Allied countries. Our daily communiqués with their record of small details which appear to the world to be trivialities and futilities, are enough to raise great discontent. But it is about the sort of peace we are preparing that I am alarmed.

To my mind certain points seem quite clear and elementary:

1. We cannot destroy Germany without destroying Europe.

2. We cannot save Europe without the cooperation of Germany.

Yet we are now preparing a peace which must destroy Germany, and yet we think we shall save Europe by so doing! The fact is, the Germans are, have been, and will continue to be the *dominant factor* on the Continent of Europe, and no permanent peace is possible which is not based on that fact. The statesmen of the Vienna Congress were wiser in their generation; they looked upon France as necessary to Europe. And yet we presume to look down upon them and their work! My fear is that the Paris Conference may prove one of the historic failures of the world; that the statesmen connected with it will return to their countries broken, discredited men, and that the Bolshevists will reap where they have sown.

Viewed superficially, this passionate diatribe contained a glaring contradiction: Germany, Smuts said, was being destroyed; Germany, he also said, was bound to remain the dominant factor in Europe. However, the contradiction is resolved when one looks beneath the surface. Writing at white heat, Smuts telescoped his views of the short-term and long-term prospects. He wanted to stress both the harshness of the punishment meted out to Germany and its inevitable impermanence. As to the former, he cited, among other examples, the proposal to restrict the German army to 100,000 men; the British, he said, needed more soldiers than that 'in poor unarmed Ireland' and to fix so low a number for a nation of seventy millions, with its intolerable internal conditions and urgent external dangers, was simply to invite anarchy. And after the anarchy—what? Smuts did not believe that the penalties imposed upon Germany or the precautions taken against her would prove effective in long term. The Germans were bound sooner or later to break free of them and to take their revenge—starting with the new States which were being built up at their expense.

The fact is, neither Poland nor Bohemia will be politically possible without German goodwill and assistance. They ought to be established on a basis which will secure German cooperation in their future success; and Germany ought to undertake definite liabilities in the peace treaty to assist and protect them militarily and otherwise against Russia and Hungary and against each other. Instead of dismembering and destroying Germany, she ought in a measure to be taken into the scope of our policy, and be made responsible for part of the burden which is clearly too heavy for us to bear.... My view is that in trying to break Germany in order to create and territorially satisfy these smaller States, we are labouring at a task which is bound to fail. We shall get no peace treaty now, and Europe will know no peace hereafter. And in the coming storms these new States will be the first to go under.

Turning to the economic aspects of the treaty, Smuts argued that the allies should not demand a large indemnity unless they were prepared to supply the Germans with the raw materials and other facilities that would enable them to pay in goods. This to him was elementary prudence. Indeed, his whole argument up to this point had been prudential—a realistic argument for maintaining the European balance, couched in language singularly free from moralising. It was not until he came to his last paragraph that he introduced ethical considerations—and with them an addition of ill-omen to the vocabulary of politics.

To conclude: even at this late hour I would urge that we revise our attitude towards Germany, and while making her pay heavily and also making her undertake burdens for the defence and assistance of Central Europe, which we have neither the men nor the means to undertake ourselves, treat her in a different spirit from that in which our proposals have so far been framed; avoid all appearance of dismembering her or subjecting her to indefinite economic servitude and pauperism, and make her join the League of Nations from the beginning. Her complete economic exhaustion and disarmament would prevent her from becoming a military or naval danger in this generation, and her appeasement now may have the effect of turning her into a bulwark against the on-coming Bolshevism of eastern Europe. My experience in South Africa has made me a firm believer in political magnanimity, and your and Campbell-Bannerman's great record still remains not only the noblest but also the *most successful* page in recent British statesmanship. On the other hand I fear, I greatly fear our present panic policy towards Germany will bring failure on this Conference, and spell ruin for Europe.

Appeasement was the new word which Smuts put into circulation. It was used once or twice again during the acrimonious Franco-British disputes of those days[13] but did not become common currency until the false dawn of hope at the Locarno Conference of 1924. *Apaisement* from that time onwards was Briand's favourite word, the symbol of a policy towards Germany entirely opposed to that which Poincaré had been pursuing. In the Briand–Stresemann era the word, both in its French and English versions, signified reconciliation. Unfortunately, the word can also signify the satisfaction of immoderate appetites. During the 1930's statesmen like Simon and Halifax continued to intend the first meaning while Hitler and Mussolini were intending the second. During the 1940's, a final stage was reached of etymological degeneration. Appeasement became a word of abuse. A long journey had been made by then since 26 March 1919, the day when Smuts put the word into circulation. He had in mind the example of Campbell-Bannerman and the magnanimity of the strong towards the weak, not the folly of paying Danegeld and the grovelling of the weak before the strong.[14]

At the end of March 1919 Smuts believed that he had come back to Paris and made his appeal to Lloyd George 'in the nick of time'. The tone of his letters to his friends in Oxford was rather more self-approving, and more patronising to Lloyd George, than the facts of the situation at that time warranted.

I find the P.M. still leans on me more than I thought he was doing as we had tended to drift apart since the General Election and its orgies of wild statements and doings. However the still small voice is always there....

I have talked over the whole matter with the P.M. who largely agrees with me. He appears even prepared to face the situation boldly and go under if necessary. I have told him that that is preferable to surrender on the great things. He feels acutely the truth of my remarks which were expressed with perhaps undue severity.

I can see that phrase about 'broken and discredited men' is rankling. But he knows it is sincerely meant and is probably true. He is at present leaning on me again, but one never knows the orbits of minds like his. As usual when I am pressing very hard on his conscience, he wants to send me on some distant mission.[15]

Lloyd George may well have felt that he did not deserve just then to be lectured to. It is one thing to listen to the 'still small voice' within oneself, but another thing to have its dictates poured into one's ear by an earnest colleague at the very time when one is already trying to do the very things the colleague exhorts one to do. Lloyd George had been alarmed for some time past by the way things were going at Paris: both by the procedural shortcomings of the conference, particularly the leakages of news from the Council of Ten, and by the substantial dangers which seemed to him to be arising from the cumulative imposition upon Germany of punishments and burdens. In the last week of March he successfully tackled the procedural difficulty by getting the Council of Four (Clemenceau, Wilson, Orlando and himself) put into the place of the Council of Ten as the central directorate of the conference. At the same time he made a supreme effort to state the fundamentals of a just and durable peace and to ensure that the draft treaty was built upon these fundamentals. His effort took shape in the famous Fontainebleau Memorandum, which was dated 25 March and discussed at the Council of Four on 27 and 28 March.

The pre-history of the Fontainebleau Memorandum can be traced back to the night of 18 March, when Sir Maurice Hankey had a talk with the C.I.G.S., Sir Henry Wilson, whom he found to be deeply concerned at the spread of military and political anarchy from east to west across Europe.[16] The sequel to that talk was a memorandum produced next day, almost certainly by Hankey, emphasising the potential expansionist force of Bolshevism and the flimsiness of the 'line of outposts' immediately confronting it—that is to say, the chain of new States or would-be States strung out along the western borders of Russia. If the outposts were weak, what barrier lay behind them? The Habsburg Empire, for all its faults, had once been an effective barrier but it no longer existed. Only the German barrier remained. What folly, therefore, to pursue towards Germany a policy which would leave her helpless in face of Bolshevist attack and political subversion: or, alternatively, draw her in desperation to make common cause with the Bolshevists. For Germany was just as well placed, the memorandum insisted, to become 'the head and brain of Bolshevism' as the barrier against its westward expansion.

A copy of this memorandum is preserved among Smuts's papers with a note from his secretary Lane, dated 26 March: 'With Sir Maurice Hankey's compliments. He sent this to the P.M. a week ago.'[17] There is no direct evidence to show whether or no Smuts had written his fiery letter of 26 March before he received this memorandum or learnt about its sequel, the discussions at Fontainebleau. Lloyd George has said that he took with him to Fontainebleau Wilson, Hankey, Kerr and Smuts; but so far as Smuts is concerned there is a plain incompatibility between Lloyd George's recollections and the recorded chronology.[18]

> 22 March: arrival of party at Fontainebleau; discussion opened.
> 23 March: discussion and drafting.
> 24 March: final draft completed.
> 25 March: signature by Lloyd George.

As we have seen, Smuts said goodbye to the Gilletts in London on 23 March and did not arrive in Paris until the evening, when he talked with nobody except W. M. Hughes. He spent the next two days 'picking up the threads' in Paris. It is barely possible that he went to Fontainebleau on the morning of 24 March, just as the party was getting ready for the return journey to Paris: but it is hardly likely. Indeed, it is almost inconceivable that his letter to Lloyd George next day could have contained, among other things, its reference to 'broken and discredited men' if he had had any understanding of what Lloyd George had just committed himself to.

He had committed himself to a good part of the programme which Smuts was urging upon him. The Fontainebleau Memorandum was divided into two parts: first, 'Some Considerations for the Peace Conference before they finally draft their Terms' and secondly, 'An Outline of Peace Terms'. It would be out of place here to summarise the memorandum; but its general tendency was drastically to scale down the demands which the French were striving to have enforced against Germany. It was realistic, besides, in offering to the French an alternative means of ensuring their security—a British and American guarantee of their frontiers, instead of the ruthless pushing back of German frontiers in the west as well as in the east. Smuts had pleaded with Lloyd George not 'to surrender on the great things'. So far was Lloyd George at this time from surrendering, that he had already committed himself to a violent and acrimonious struggle with the French.

Smuts was probably right in believing that the Prime Minister was feeling ruffled by his letter of 26 March and in the mood to send him on 'some distant mission'. The suggestion was put to him that work of great importance awaited him in Syria. He would not have accepted that; but he did accept with alacrity a proposal that he should go to Buda Pesth to negotiate with the communist government of Bela Kun.[19] He set out with his small party on the evening of 1 April.

Right up to then his days and nights were crammed full of business: not only the great debate on treaty-making in the large, but detailed questions such as the future capital of the League and the Japanese attempt to get racial equality affirmed in the covenant: while all the time he was handling the thorny problem of South African demobilisation. And then, as if this were not enough, he let himself be dragged into the centre of the controversy over reparation. On the night of 30 March, with his Hungarian adventure already looming up, he was hard at work preparing 'a legal opinion' on Germany's liability to pay reparation. The document he submitted will be examined later:* suffice it to say here that it has done more damage to his reputation than any other document that he ever produced in his whole life. He had not been a member of the reparation

* See pp. 540 ff. below.

committee, he possessed no expert knowledge and he made a big mistake by allowing himself to be hustled into giving a snap opinion upon a crucial question which he did not at that time understand.

His mind was upon other things. On the day of his departure for Hungary he proposed to Lloyd George that the Russians should be invited to meet him at Buda Pesth; he felt sure that he could make recommendations which would 'lead to peace with Russia and thus round off the work of this Peace Conference'.[20] As we have seen, he had been deeply concerned a year earlier with the extension of Germany's *lebensraum* in Russia following the Treaty of Brest Litovsk. At that time he had been an advocate of military support to the Russians who were still resisting the German invaders; he had also made it quite clear that his object was 'to save the weary Russians' as well as the western allies.* He had not foreseen in the spring and summer of 1918 that the centres of resistance to the Germans would become in the process of time centres of resistance to the Bolshevik government; when that happened, he supported Lloyd George in his resistance to the pressures put upon him by the anti-Bolshevik interventionists. Before long, he felt himself moved to deliver a personal and public warning, in the most explicit terms, against intervention in the domestic affairs of Russia.† There had been an attempt early in 1919 to assemble a conference of *all* the Russian factions, the 'whites' as well as the 'reds', on an island in the Sea of Marmora; but there can be no doubt that it was the Bolshevik leaders and them alone whom Smuts was hoping to meet when he set out for Buda Pesth on 1 April. His spirits rose as he envisaged the magnitude of the issues at stake. He told his Quaker friends that the situation was desperate but all the same—'miracles *do* happen'. He found running through his head the words of a hymn that he had been used to sing in his pious youth, '*Yet there is time*'.[21]

Nothing came of these hopes of bringing the Russians into the talks and the mission lasted only eight days instead of the full month that Smuts had been budgeting for. A full narrative of the mission was compiled by his secretary Lane and some of its dramatic episodes are recorded in the diary that was kept by Harold Nicolson, one of the young men seconded to Smuts by the Foreign Office. Nicolson, when he woke up in the train in Austria, felt that his 'plump pink

* See p. 480 above.   † See p. 547 below.

face' was an insult to the starved people whom he saw crowding the railway stations, and recorded with delight the rebuke given by Smuts to the British military attaché in Vienna, who had arranged an expensive lunch for the whole party at Sacher's restaurant. 'Smuts is furious. He ticks Cunninghame off sharply. He calls it a gross error in taste. He decrees that from now on we shall feed only upon our own army rations and not take anything from these starving countries. His eyes when angry are like steel rods.'

At Buda Pesth, Bela Kun had requisitioned the Hungaria Hotel for Smuts and his party but Smuts refused to budge from his train and summoned Kun to confer with him there. On 4 and 5 April the two men conferred four times. They came close to agreeing upon the definition of a military frontier between Hungary and Rumania and some other urgent matters, but when Kun tried to haggle for extra concessions Smuts ordered the train to start at the precise time that he had notified for his departure. 'We glide out into the night, retaining on the retinas of our eyes the picture of four bewildered faces looking up in blank amazement. We then dine. Smuts is delightful, telling us stories of the Veldt with a ring of deep home-sickness in his voice. A lovely man. Our rations are even more Spartan than before, since we gave all our chocolates and condensed milk to our liaison officers.'

The newspapers proclaimed the mission to have been a fiasco but Nicolson did not agree with them;[22] he thought it all to the good that Smuts had dropped the grandiose plan of using Bela Kun as a liaison with Moscow and he enumerated some useful gains that had been made, including 'a conviction that Austria-Hungary *is* an economic unit and that these trade barriers are fatal'. For Smuts, the economic dilapidation of the dismembered Empire and its appalling human consequences became 'an ineffaceable memory'. The day after his return he wrote to the Gilletts:

Nothing so burns up every particle of self as the sights I have passed through during the last week. And this afternoon after I had written to you Keynes came to see me and I described to him the pitiful plight of Central Europe. And he (who is conversant with the finance of the matter) confessed to me his doubt whether anything could really be done. Those pitiful people have little credit left, and instead of getting indemnities from them, we may have to advance them money to live! And what will Northcliffe and Bottomley and Beelzebub say? Ah, yes, and what will God say? For there is the rub.[23]

Smuts, perhaps, was rather too prone at that time to imagine that he had the answer to his last question; but he sought the most practical human advice that he could find and in combination with Keynes worked out a scheme for getting the Danubian wheels to turn again by means of an international loan guaranteed by all the Powers.

In the second week of April, when Smuts returned from Buda Pesth, he still had hopes of a draft treaty emerging which he would be able to support. Lloyd George was fighting hard for the Fontaine-bleau programme and achieving some measure of success, particularly in the defeat of the French plans to detach the Rhineland from Germany and make it into a buffer State. That was the form of security which Marshal Foch wanted; but Clemenceau said that he would accept the alternatives of an Anglo-American military guarantee, demilitarisation of the Rhineland and military occupation for a period of up to fifteen years of three zones west of the Rhine, and their bridgeheads. Lloyd George, with strong encouragement from Smuts, resisted Clemenceau's proposals for the military occupation. He also resisted the strong pressure put upon him at this time by W. M. Hughes and others to turn the reparation screw harder than he thought prudent. In conversation with Smuts he expressed the fear that this pressure would soon prove too strong for his resistance; whereupon Smuts wrote him a letter, dated 11 April, congratulating him on his success so far and urging him to stand firm.

You said something to the effect that unless the representatives of the British Empire were unanimous on this question of reparation, as well as the other peace terms, you possibly would have to support the view of the 'whole hoggers' (if I may use the word) and that would probably mean that all the work of the past four months would be in vain, and perhaps no peace at all be signed.

This remark constrains me to express my high appreciation of the herculean efforts you have made in surmounting difficulties which to any thoughtful observer were stupendous, and to convey my best congratulations upon the results so far achieved.

My sole reason in writing is to encourage you in the firm stand you have made, and to assure you of my whole-hearted support of the peace terms in so far as they are settled.[24]

This letter was the last of the hopeful ones. From Smuts's point of view, the situation now changed rapidly for the worse. One reason, which he can hardly have foreseen, was the change of attitude by

President Wilson, who on 15 May accepted Clemenceau's proposals for the military occupation of Germany and from that time onwards, whether by coincidence or not, enjoyed immunity from attacks in the French newspapers. Meanwhile, Smuts had been fitting his proposals for getting the wheels of Danubian industry to turn again into the Keynes plan for a general financial settlement in Europe, shored up by an international loan. These ideas were ahead of their time; the allies were intent upon squeezing reparation out of the conquered countries, the Americans were intent upon getting paid for the money they had hired to the conquerors, the little nations were intent upon their game of grab against each other. On 23 April Smuts expounded his proposals to the Supreme Economic Council but failed to win its support. 'That is another talking shop', he exclaimed, 'which does nothing. Will the Lord never rid us of these useless debating societies? Oh for an ounce of action, but I find myself in a world where despair seems already to have settled on men's souls. Despair, and a solemn belief in words and talk.'[25]

Towards the end of April Smuts was hard at work reading the reports of the commissions as they were sent in for incorporation into the draft treaty.* His feelings about some of them fluctuated from time to time; he thought at first that the reparation clauses were better than they might well have been—'no amount fixed, a commission to work out the matter at leisure, reparation only for damage to civilians, pensions and reparation allowances, and a long time to pay'—but when he went through them again with Botha he found them 'impossible'.[26] That, by and large, was what the two friends felt about the whole document. Botha hated its 'pinpricks', Smuts its 'petty, small spirit'. 'And of all shortcomings that is the worst. There is something of value even in vindictiveness, but in the merely small and trivial we seem to reach an absolute zero and limit which leaves me in a most unhappy, impatient mood.' Adding the 'pinpricks' to the heavy penalties, Smuts began to think that the Germans would refuse to sign the treaty, or, if they did sign it, would fail to carry it out. But what could he do? He did not want to attack his own side while the negotiations (if the procedures followed by the allies could be so described) were still going on; but afterwards it might be too late. He wished that he did not worry so much over the troubles

---

* It had not been expected originally that the reports of the commissions would be accepted, as they mostly were, without further criticism, discussion and amendment.

of the world or have such a strong itch to set everything right. What he would have liked to have, he said, was 'a *good* heart in a *thick* skin'.[27]

He decided at last to write a letter to Lloyd George summarising his objections to the draft treaty. This letter, dated 5 May, was moderate in tone but in substance it was far more drastic than the previous letter of 11 April. Smuts maintained that important changes could be made in the document without changing its 'structure or main contents'; but the cumulative effect of the changes which he proposed would have been sweeping. He emphasised the tactical advantage of making these changes before the draft treaty was published or handed to the Germans and proceeded to enumerate them under eight heads: the territorial clauses, the occupation terms, the denial to Germany of all aircraft, the destruction of all aerodromes behind her frontiers, the reparation clauses, the provisions as regards rivers and railways, the occupation provisions. Under each head he wrote a few terse words giving the grounds of his criticism and stating his remedies. With these principal alterations and with the removal of many small pinpricking provisions which served no useful purpose, he believed that the draft treaty could still be made a reasonable and acceptable document. Otherwise, he said, the Germans would probably refuse to sign it.[28]

His appeal produced no result. Two days after he had composed it the ceremony of presenting the draft treaty to the Germans took place at Versailles. Smuts went there in his frock-coat and top-hat along with all the other allied delegates. He saw Clemenceau rise from his seat and welcome the German delegation in a brief and courteous speech. He saw Count Brockdorff-Rantzau read his reply sitting down—an act of apparent discourtesy which shocked the conference. 'Isn't it just like them!', exclaimed Wilson. But Smuts was intent upon what Brockdorff-Rantzau was saying. He heard him repudiate Germany's sole responsibility for the war. He heard him assert that President Wilson's Fourteen Points, as modified by the Lansing Note of 5 November, were binding upon the victors and vanquished alike.[29]

The ceremony of presentation, like the document that was presented, seemed to Smuts 'to have been conceived more in a spirit of making war than of making peace'. Yet the mood which found expression in two letters which he wrote the same night was not rebellious, but resigned, almost fatalistic.

Behind the petty stage on which we pose and strut and play-act at making history there looms the dark Figure which is quietly moving the pieces of world-history. So has it ever been. In May 1902 we were called to Vereeniging to receive the British terms. And within 5 short years what had become of them? The Boers were once more ruling the country and the same Boer leaders were the Government. May the same great and wise Spirit guide us through the dark times ahead of the world.[30]

Then he told himself that it was not good enough for men to wait for 'the dark Figure' to do their work for them in some indefinite future, when Europe was falling to pieces here and now. But what could men do? Smuts was unable that night to think of anything that *he* could do.

Poor Keynes often sits with me at night after a good dinner and we rail against the world and the coming flood. And I tell him this is the time for the Griqua prayer (the Lord to come himself and not send his Son, as this is not a time for children).* And then we laugh, and behind the laughter is Hoover's terrible picture of 30 million people who must die unless there is some great intervention. But then again we think things are never really as bad as that; and something will turn up, and the worst will never be. And somehow all these phases of feeling are true and right in some sense.[31]

This mood of passivity did not last long. Even on the day of the presentation ceremony it was, probably, merely superficial. The period from 7 May to 29 May—the day when the Germans delivered to the allied and associated Powers their observations on the draft treaty and their counter-proposals—marks the third phase of Smuts's activity at the Peace Conference. Urgent warning was the dominant note of everything that he wrote during those three weeks.

He believed that the treaty, if it were not drastically amended, would lead to a second big war in the future and he took counsel with Botha about how best to warn Lloyd George that in such a war Great Britain could no longer count upon South African support. Even before the draft treaty had been presented to the Germans, Botha had fired this warning shot across the British Prime Minister's bows. In a letter of 6 May, drafted by Smuts, he had asked for an assurance that South Africa was not committed by the proposed treaty

---

* Throughout his life, if ever the future looked hopeless, Smuts was apt to say that there was nothing for it but the Griqua prayer. He had once heard the story of an old Griqua chief who saw his tribe beset by great dangers and prayed: 'Lord, save thy people. Lord, we are lost unless Thou savest us. Lord, this is no work for children. It is not enough this time to send Thy Son. Lord, Thou must come Thyself.'

promising British military support to France in the event of a German attack. When Lloyd George gave him this assurance he wrote a second letter on 12 May, again on a draft prepared by Smuts. Two sentences of this letter contain a trenchant summary of the advance in the status of the Union achieved during and after the war by Botha and Smuts. 'One result of the perfectly correct exclusion of the Dominions from the obligation which it is proposed to lay on the British people may well be that in some future continental war, Great Britain may be at war and one or more of the Dominions may stand out and maintain their neutrality. But that result is inevitable, and flows from the status of independent nationhood of the Dominions.'[32]

These two sentences were pregnant for the future of the Commonwealth. They may also have had some bearing upon the future of Europe, as a sign of the New World's growing detachment from European affairs and, therefore, a justification for the nationalistic policies of security favoured by the French. Smuts, however, hoped that they would give extra weight to a letter of warning and appeal which he sent on 14 May both to Lloyd George and President Wilson.

The more I have studied the Peace Treaty as a whole, the more I dislike it. The combined effect of the territorial and reparation clauses is to make it practically impossible for Germany to carry out the provisions of the Treaty. And then the occupation clauses come in to plant the French on the Rhine indefinitely, even beyond the already far too long period of fifteen years, under an undefined regime of martial law. East and West blocks of Germans are put under their historic enemies. Under this Treaty Europe will know no peace; and the undertaking to defend France against aggression may at any time bring the British Empire also into the fire.

I am grieved beyond words that such should be the result of our statesmanship. I admit it was hard to appear to fight for the German case with our other Allies, especially with devastated France. But now that the Germans can state their own case, I pray you will use your unrivalled power and influence to make the final treaty a more moderate and reasonable document. I fear there may be a temptation to wave aside objections which will be urged by the Germans, but which will be supported by the good sense and conscience of most moderate people. I hope this temptation will be resisted, and that drastic revision will be possible even at the eleventh hour.

Democracy is looking to you who have killed Prussianism—the silent masses who have suffered mutely appeal to you to save them from the fate to which Europe seems now to be lapsing.

Forgive my importunity; but I feel the dreadful burden resting on you, and write from motives of pure sympathy.[33]

As will appear below, Smuts's warnings and appeals, then and later, made some impression (although he did not know it at the time and it proved to be far less than he thought essential) upon Lloyd George.* President Wilson, however, was now showing himself most unreceptive of criticism. He thanked Smuts for his 'earnest letter' and told him that he need offer no apology for writing it. He admitted that the treaty was 'in many respects harsh' but did not believe it to be 'unjust in the circumstances'. He agreed that real consideration should be given to the objections raised by the Germans but added that their criticisms so far had been addressed only to points which were substantially sound. He emphasised the need to punish the Germans for their crimes.

...I feel the terrible responsibility of this whole business, but inevitably my thought goes back to the very great offense against civilization which the German State committed, and the necessity for making it evident once for all that such things can lead only to the most severe punishment.

I am sure you know the spirit in which I say these things, and that I need not assure you that I am just as anxious to be just to the Germans as to be just to anyone else.

With unaffected thanks for your letter,

Cordially and sincerely yours,
Woodrow Wilson.[34]

In later years Smuts many times defended the reputation of Wilson against its detractors; but at the time he found this arid and unctuous letter utterly disillusioning. He told his Quaker friends that Wilson had failed him. He told them that he was completely isolated—'And yet not isolated. For they are never alone who labour for the Good. They are accompanied by the aspirations of all the good souls; they are borne forward on the sighs and prayers of those who long for better things; and who knows whether they may not reach their goal?'[35] Smuts, in his different idiom, could be just as unctuous, though never so arid, as Wilson; but he usually had some salt of humour and the saving grace of doubting his own infallibility. Two days after he had received Wilson's letter he wrote to Margaret Gillett—'I am still looking at that Porcupine of mine, I mean the Peace Treaty, and considering what to do with the damned thing. You can see it is not improving my temper. Nor does my temper affect it sensibly. So something else will have to be done, but just exactly what?'[36] Two

* See p. 530 below.

days later again he told Alice Clark that he wished he could see more clearly because then he would act more resolutely: however, he would 'grope along'.[37] And then, on 20 May—that is to say, only six days after Wilson's disillusioning letter—he suddenly saw daylight. He wrote a letter to his wife warning her that he would refuse to sign the treaty unless important alterations were made in it.

It is a terrible document [he told her], not a peace treaty but a war treaty, and I am troubled in my conscience about putting my name to such a document. Under this treaty the situation in Europe will become intolerable and a revolution must come, or again, in due course, an explosion into war. Germany is being treated as we would not treat a kaffir nation. I have already protested against this, and I shall, if necessary, go further in my resistance. My children must never be ashamed of their father's signature. Is that not so, Mamma? It would be hard for me to have to say publicly that I do not feel free to sign such a peace, and it will cause a great fuss not only in South Africa but in the whole world. I feel my responsibility greatly, and that is why I first want to do my best to get the treaty altered.... If the Germans do not accept, the hunger blockade will again be produced, even though countless women and children have to die. I shall fight against this whatever the cost; that is why I want to make the treaty more acceptable to the Germans. I tell you this so that you may be informed in advance of things that may appear later in the newspapers. I want to keep my conscience clear in this great matter. General Botha also feels very depressed about these peace terms, but does not go as far as I want to go. It is not a pleasant feeling to stand alone, and you will understand how much I long for my dear ones in such dark days. But we shall see each other soon now, for I think that everything will be finished in June. If the Germans refuse to sign, I shall very probably set a campaign going in the press and on the platform in England and America, and then you will not see me before the end of the year. But let us pray that it will not come to that. In any case we are both ready to make any sacrifice for the future peace of the world and for truth and right. The Germans behaved disgracefully in the war and deserve a hard peace. But that is no reason why the world must be thrust into ruin. If necessary, I shall resign as Union minister and sell Goedgevonden* to get money to keep us going in the meantime. I hope all that will not be necessary. But, Mamma, you have a right to know all my plans and thoughts. So I write in good time....

But surely everything would come right and they would soon be together again at Doornkloof? He told her that he often saw the farm in his dreams. The trees would be tall by now. Santa and Cato

---

* Goedgevonden was one of the farms that he had bought before the war in the western Transvaal on the advice of General de la Rey.

would already be big girls and the little ones were growing up. Yes, there would be great changes after his two and a half years of absence —'But however much I long for you and the children and for precious South Africa, I must do my duty to the end, should this become absolutely necessary'.[38]

No sooner had he posted this letter than he began to ask himself whether he had made it clear that he was preparing her only for what *might* happen. So in the evening of the same day he wrote her a second letter to report that he would not take such drastic action unless he failed in his attempt to get large changes made in the treaty and the Germans refused to sign it.

But if it is absolutely necessary, I shall do it, and I know it will be with your entire approval. Everything will soon come to a head and when you read this letter everything will probably have been already decided.... Well, 'come weal come woe', we shall try to stand faithfully by what is best and highest in our view of life and leave the rest in God's hands. My heart remains overflowing with the richest love for you, my faithful life's companion, and the Higher Hand will not be withdrawn from us.[39]

Having thus raised his personal stakes he renewed his efforts to get the draft treaty recast. In a letter to Lloyd George two days later (22 May) he enumerated the most important provisions which in his opinion called for amendment. The items were broadly the same as those he had listed in his letter of 5 May,* but he arranged them in a different order. He also gave more space, though still with a severe economy of words, to justifying his criticisms and producing his alternatives. Not that he imagined that he had all the correct answers already in his own head; some of them would not emerge clearly until the Germans had been brought into the discussion. He set the greatest store upon bringing them in.

I am very anxious, not only that the Germans should sign a fair and good Peace Treaty, but also that, for the sake of the future, they should not merely be made to sign at the point of the bayonet, so to speak. The Treaty should not be capable of moral repudiation by the German people hereafter. And for this purpose I consider it important that we should as far as possible carry the German Delegates with us, that we should listen to what they have to say, that we should give all necessary explanations to them, and that where our Clauses appear really untenable, we should be prepared to accept alterations or compromises. In order to do this, it will be necessary to meet them in oral discussion. And the suggestion

* See p. 520 above.

I would make for this purpose is that a small Committee of minor delegates be appointed to meet the Germans after they have handed in their final note on the 29th May, and confer with them in regard to the Treaty as a whole. This Committee to make a report to the Supreme Council of the alterations they recommend after hearing the German side. In this way the Supreme Council will avoid direct negotiations with the German delegates, but will have before them the recommendations arrived at after full cognisance has been taken of the German case. Necessarily much will depend on the personnel of this Committee. I would suggest that it consist of three delegates, one nominated by the United States, the British Empire and France respectively. It is essential for rapid work that the Committee be as small as possible, and Italy and Japan are not sufficiently interested in the German Treaty to make it worth while overloading the Committee with two additional representatives. If the three Delegates are carefully selected, their work may be of first class importance, not only in securing the necessary modification in the Treaty, but in listening to and considering the German case, and thereby removing from the making of the peace all appearance of one-sidedness and unnecessary dictation. The moral authority of the Treaty will be all the greater and more binding on that account.[40]

In his heart, Smuts must have wanted to be put on this committee; but the question never arose, because the Big Four would not contemplate in any shape or form the idea of oral discussion with the Germans. Even if they had done so, Lloyd George would not at that time have proposed Smuts as the man to speak for the British Empire. The growing tension between the two men was now close to breaking point.

On 26 May Smuts replied to a letter from Lloyd George inviting him to serve on the Commission on Austrian Reparation.

The imposition of reparation on a broken, bankrupt, economically impossible State like Austria, or a new friendly allied State like Czecho-slovakia...seems to me a hopeless policy, which could only lead to the most mischievous results. I am against payment of all reparation by those countries for damage done by the dead and dismembered Austro-Hungarian Empire. And if it is (as it appears) your policy to exact reparation in these cases, I hope you will excuse me from serving on the Commission.

Lloyd George replied the same day asking Smuts whether he was proposing that Great Britain and South Africa should bear a crushing burden of debt for the next thirty or forty years while the States that they had liberated, to say nothing of enemy States like Austria and Hungary, got off scot free? He did not see how he could justify such a policy to Parliament and he thought he would be rendering poor service to his fellow countrymen by leaving them, burdened as they would be by the tremendous costs of the war, to compete against the industries of the new States which had been 'freed by our deliberate action from any equivalent burden'. This argument made no impression upon Smuts. In his answer to Lloyd George next day he said that no matter what abstract principles of liability might be affirmed, the attempt to apply them to the countries carved out of the former Austrian Empire would lead to nothing but trouble, friction and economic floundering, and would probably drive all those countries some day 'into league with Germany against us'.

If my advice had been followed after my visit to Austria-Hungary, and an Economic Conference of all those States had been called (as they were unanimously asking for) we would today have had a scheme, evolved on the spot, on which a statesmanlike basis could have been laid for the economic cooperation and reconstruction of those countries. A Customs Union of those States might have emerged, and part of the proceeds of their external Tariff might have gone into a Reparation Fund. Now we are working absolutely in the dark.[41]

Once again, Smuts refused to serve on the commission.

On 28 May, the day before the Germans submitted their observations and counter-proposals, Smuts received a message through Kerr and Lane to the effect that the Prime Minister was thinking a good deal about his views but could not explain at present. Smuts was not in the mood to let himself be wheedled by Lloyd George.

I believe the fact is, he is trying to deceive one or other of the opposing parties, and is at present unwilling to show his hand. There may be a great volte face or there may not. I am taking ordinary precautions against being the victim. The P.M. wants to ride to heaven on the back of the devil, and he hails me by the way: 'My dear General, you get hold of the tail of this fellow and he will carry us a good way. If we come across Christian walking *another* way to heaven, we can let go and join Christian's company.' I fear Christian will not be met on that road at all. . . . I had a letter from Isie yesterday in which she condemned the harshness of the terms and added that someone had told her that a peace with which 'our two Generals are associated could not contain unfair or harsh terms'. *That* is quite the hardest thing that has yet been said to me, but you know how hard she can be—God bless her.[42]

The next day opened for Smuts a fourth and final phase: furious revolt. As soon as he saw the German answer to the allied peace terms—'a portentous document, quite the size of our prodigious Peace Treaty'—he made its basic argument his own.

They raise the point to the very forefront which I have always considered vital, viz. that we are bound by the correspondence of last October and November to make a Wilson peace—that is, one within the 4 corners of the Wilson Points and Speeches. This was a solemn international engagement which we must keep. It would be dreadful if, while the war began with a 'scrap of paper', it were also to end with another 'scrap of paper' and the Allies' breach of their own undertaking. I am going to fight it out on this basis.[43]

He began to fight it the same day in a letter to President Wilson which raised the same issue in the same words: what was the treaty going to be, a 'Wilson peace' or a 'scrap of paper'? Subject to the two reservations which the allies had made before the armistice, he held the President's Points and Principles to be binding upon victors and vanquished alike.

The question becomes, therefore, most important whether there are important provisions of the Treaty which conflict with or are not covered by, but go beyond, your Points and Principles. I notice a tendency to put the whole responsibility for deciding this question on you, and to say that after all President Wilson agrees to the Treaty and he knows best what the Points and Principles mean. This is most unfair to you, and I think we should all give the gravest consideration to the question whether our Peace Treaty is within the four corners of your Speeches of 1918. Frankly I do not think this is so....

He gave some illustrations, and ended with a warning of the terrible disillusionment which would follow a peace built upon so flagrant a breach of faith with the world and the repudiation of 'a formal agreement deliberately entered into'. Such a peace, he concluded, might well become 'an even greater disaster to the world than the war was'.[44]

In a reply of eight lines, Wilson held out the hope that some of the conclusions embodied in the draft treaty would be re-examined; but he ignored altogether the main argument of Smuts's letter. The correspondence between the President of the United States and the second representative of South Africa was from this day closed.[45]

The only means which remained open to Smuts of getting his views taken seriously by the Big Four was to prevail upon Lloyd George to be their advocate. For this purpose, impassioned personal appeals such as he had been making ever since mid-March were not enough;

he could not succeed unless he won over his colleagues of the British Empire Delegation to his point of view and persuaded them to embody it in firm instructions to Lloyd George upon the stand that he must take on behalf of the British Empire.

The deliberations of the British Empire Delegation at the Peace Conference deserve some day to become the theme of a specialist monograph. In particular, the three meetings which were held after the Germans had submitted their counter-proposals possess extraordinary importance. They were attended by nine principal members of the British Cabinet, by all the Dominion Prime Ministers and the other overseas statesmen attending the Peace Conference. According to Lloyd George, they constituted 'one of the most remarkable Cabinet Councils ever held by the British Empire'.

The account of their proceedings which Lloyd George published nearly twenty years later is reasonably full; but it contains some inaccuracies of fact and is in some degree slanted to support the arguments which he himself favoured and caused to prevail.[46] There was quite a lot to be said for these arguments. Lloyd George, Balfour and other experienced politicians must have been acutely aware of two opposite dangers: on the one hand, the danger of being so harsh with the Germans that they would refuse to sign the treaty and thus force upon the Allies the odium of reversing the machinery of demobilisation and starting the war again: on the other hand, the danger of being more complaisant towards the Germans than Clemenceau, Wilson and the other allied leaders would agree to, and thus destroying the united front of the victorious Powers. Lloyd George was trying to find a passage between these two dangers. Of the two, the second seemed to him to be the greater.

Smuts was ready, if the choice had to be made, to face the second danger. At the meeting of 30 May and again at the morning meeting of 1 June, he expounded his thesis forcibly and at length. Lloyd George has given an account of some particular criticisms which Smuts made against the draft treaty but not of the strong stand which he took upon the ground of fundamental principle: the pre-armistice correspondence, he declared, constituted a solemn agreement: it bound the contracting parties to make 'a Wilson peace': if the allied and associated Powers now did the opposite, the war would have ended, as it had begun, with a 'scrap of paper'. Smuts did not win the meeting's assent to that proposition; but for many of his proposals he won stronger support than would appear from Lloyd George's narrative. That narrative reproduces *in extenso* Lloyd George's own speech at the conclusion of the third meeting; he called it a summing-up of the discussion; but it was hardly that, for his purpose in making the speech was not to review the main arguments and proposals that had been put forward but to identify those proposals which he was prepared to urge upon the Big Four. They fell under the following main heads: modification of the clauses in the draft treaty dealing with Germany's eastern frontier (including provision for holding a plebiscite in Upper Silesia): earlier entry of Germany into the League of Nations: modification of the clauses dealing with the army of occupation: modification (although the method and extent of it were left very vague) of the reparation clauses. Lloyd George asked the British Empire Delegation to give him the authority to maintain these proposals with the full weight of the British Empire, even to the extent of refusing to take any part in further naval and military operations against Germany.

In this programme there were some items, for example the proposed plebiscite in Upper Silesia, which satisfied Smuts; but the programme as a whole, although it was destined to provoke Clemenceau and Wilson to strong opposition, fell far short of what he considered necessary. Moreover, he was not satisfied with the manner in which the business of the British Empire Delegation had been conducted. At the final meeting on Sunday, he had made no reply to Lloyd George's concluding speech. That, perhaps, was a mistake of tactics; but there was no resolution before the meeting. A resolution was drafted subsequently by the secretaries and circulated on Monday, 2 June. That same day Smuts wrote a strong protest to Lloyd George. He declared that the very restricted amendments to the peace terms contained in the resolution failed to do justice to the views expressed the previous day by half a dozen speakers in the morning session, and those expressed by General Botha in the afternoon session.

No proper regard appears to have been paid to the general feeling of the meeting, and the limitation of the resolution to recording unanimity in accepting the proposals submitted by yourself at the end of the afternoon meeting though perhaps strictly accurate cannot be allowed to pass unchallenged.

In any case, so far as I myself am concerned, I wish to make it clear that I cannot agree to anything less than the very drastic course I proposed at the beginning of the meeting, viz.: that the Peace Treaty should be recast and transformed, so as to be more in accord with our solemn undertakings, our public declarations, and the requirements of a reasonable and practicable policy. In particular I specified the immediate entry of Germany into the League of Nations, the abolition of the Occupation, the removal of provisions which are not in accord with the Wilson formula, as well as of the numerous pin-pricks in the Treaty; the thorough revision of the Eastern boundaries settled for Germany, and the fixing of a reasonable though high amount for reparation payable by Germany, partly by way of services rendered in the restoration of devastated areas, and the balance to be now divided in definite proportions between the Allies; the powers of the Reparation Commission, which constitute a serious invasion of German sovereignty, to be thoroughly overhauled.

This programme I must stand by....[47]

Precisely how did he propose to stand by it? He was by now in open conflict with Lloyd George. What chance did he have of bringing the stronger force to bear? He could not bring it to bear through Parliament. For some time past he had been asking himself whether he had been right when he had refused the seat in the House of Commons which Lloyd George had urged him to take in the autumn of 1917. 'I now begin to think', he wrote on 19 May, 'I made a mistake in 1917 when I did not plunge right into British politics so as now to occupy a position at the centre instead of on the periphery. For I am now only the second representative of South Africa.'[48] But supposing that he had taken the plunge in 1917, what chance would he have had in December 1918 of stemming the tide which ran so fast and high in the elections? And in the months which followed, when the only parliamentary revolts against Lloyd George came from members who thought that he was not hard enough upon the Germans, what members of the House of Commons except Colonel Josiah Wedgwood and Commander Kenworthy and perhaps one or two others would have approved his plea to treat them more gently? Even to ask these questions is to suggest that Smuts was able to exert more leverage upon Lloyd George from his base in South Africa than he could have exerted if he had exchanged it for a base in Great Britain.

As we have seen, he had from time to time exerted considerable leverage and had achieved appreciable results. Those results, however, had fallen far short of what he was aiming at. The meetings of 1 June had demonstrated that to him finally. But what could he do about it? The statesmen of the British Empire had gone along with him part of the way; but they had also made quite clear that they were not prepared to support the second representative of South Africa in an open revolt against the British Prime Minister. Not even Botha, his chief and his friend, was prepared to support him in that.

He was isolated. Whatever stand he took he had to take alone. The only plan of action which he could envisage was the one that he had outlined to his wife in the two letters he had written to her on 20 May: to resign his position in the government and parliament of the Union, to raise money by selling some of his land and to wage his own war against the treaty by a campaign in the press and in public meetings throughout Great Britain. If he were to do that there was one essential decision that he must make first: whether or not to sign the treaty.

To sign or not to sign: the record of the battle which he fought within himself is contained in the letters that he wrote from the beginning almost to the end of June to his wife, to Alice Clark and her sister Margaret Gillett, to Keynes and to Botha.[49] An attempt will be made to follow quickly the central current and the main swirls of his thought; but first it has to be remembered that doubt still remained up to the fourth week of June as to whether or not the Germans would sign. On the 16th their counter-proposals were rejected by the allies. On the 22nd they accepted the allied terms with reservations. On the 23rd, under the pressure of an ultimatum, they accepted them unconditionally. The Treaty of Versailles was signed on 28 June.

On 2 June, Smuts recapitulated his demands of the previous day at the British Empire Delegation and warned Lloyd George: 'This programme I must stand by.' He told Mrs Gillett next day that he 'was not budging an inch'; but he also told her how hard he was finding it to make up his mind what action to take.[50] That was the theme of a letter he wrote on 10 June to Keynes. Two days previously Keynes had done what the trekking Boers used to call *kop uittrek*; he had slipped his neck out of the yoke, walked away from the hated ox-team of Paris and by now was enjoying the good green grass of Sussex. Smuts reproved him gently for absconding and then went on to discuss the future. He wanted Keynes to write an account, not for the specialist but for the plain man, 'of what the financial and economic clauses of the Treaty actually are and mean'. After that, they could discuss together and decide what course of action to take.

Indeed I have not yet made up my mind on the matter. The Treaty will in any case emerge as a rotten thing, of which we shall all be heartily ashamed in due course. But it is necessary to have a formal peace in order that the world may have a chance; which it will not have so long as the present state of affairs continues. And it may well be that with peace, and the better knowledge of what it all means, a great revulsion will set in and a favourable atmosphere will be created in which to help the public virtually to scrap this monstrous instrument. I am still considering both the time and the manner of doing the thing, as very much is at stake, and no tactical mistakes should be made. But I want every preparation for the attack to be made in advance.[51]

In this letter to Keynes Smuts appears committed within his own mind to a campaign for the revision of the treaty, if not to any detailed plans of campaign; but in a letter the same day to his wife he appears still undecided. He told her that it was his wish, his ardent wish—

to get out of it as soon as possible and return to home and country. But the cause here weighs heavily on my mind and I am not yet sure what I am going to do. Sometimes I feel as if this death sentence on Europe must be torn to pieces and as if I must set the work going before I return to my dear ones. And then again I feel what is the use of all this toil? It will and must all soon collapse anyway. Leave this Treaty to its own devices, and it will soon come to an end. So my mind swings from one side to the other.[52]

About this time he showed himself well aware of the state of public opinion in Great Britain and the other allied countries. It had usually been taken for granted among his Liberal friends that the peoples of the world, as distinct from their governments, were peace-loving; but Smuts now concluded from all the evidence before him that 'the plain Englishman' was just as much behind his government as he had been at the general election and would back it up even if it used force of arms to make the Germans sign the treaty.[53] In contrast with the majority opinion at Paris, he was not expecting the Germans to give way. 'Everybody here', he wrote on 13 June, 'thinks the Germans will sign. I don't.... And if they don't sign, and Foch resumes his march to Berlin and the British Navy resumes the Hunger Blockade, things will really begin to move....But as I say the Lord himself may appear—and it may be *not* in a still small voice.

And the opening of the floodgates of Famine will be the beginning of the greatest storm that has ever raged.'[54]

Three days later (the day the allies rejected the German counter-proposals) his thoughts were less cataclysmic, but his mind no more made up. He felt completely isolated in Paris and the only news that he was getting came to him through 'the turbid channels of the Paris press'.[55] He relapsed for a time into his quietist mood.

The League of Nations is the only bright spot in a situation of unrelieved gloom. But my work there is done, and the mustard seed will grow through the coming ages. What more could I do to help? I am not a good critic, I am not a 'Bolshevist' and I look to the coming years to undo the evils of our present work. I believe in consuming one's own smoke. I believe in time and tide in the great affairs of the world, and the present time seems inopportune for the things I could say. And I have a quiet but fundamental faith in God, the regenerative creative spirit. And I have no ambition and no mission. Under these circumstances is it wrong of me to slink away like a wounded animal without great cries of distress or fuss of any kind?[56]

That mood did not last long. In the third week of June the allies made their preparations for renewing the war if the Germans refused to sign; the Royal Navy was ready, Foch went to his headquarters. Smuts believed this time that the Germans would give way. For himself he would not give way. On 21 June he sent a telegram to General Botha: 'Signature of Treaty by Germans appears most probable. As I shall not be able to sign I wish you to think over question whether I shall simply refuse signature at proper time or shall previously resign as South African delegate so as not to embarrass you in signing. In any case my mind is fully made up not to sign.'[57] He realised that his refusal would produce the most serious consequences for his friend and his country; but conscience, he said, was 'a rotten business'. He had that affliction and what could he do about it? He could not under any circumstances see himself putting his signature to the treaty. 'I am not going to sign it on any account. What the consequences of my act will be I don't know and to some extent I don't care.'[58] But within three days he had swung right round. On 24 June he wrote to Mrs Gillett, 'After all I am going to sign that Treaty'. On 28 June he wrote to her, 'Yes, I have gone and done it'.[59]

Why did he do it? Some of his motives have already become apparent but it will be profitable to identify them systematically and in doing so to exchange the narrative form for a critical examination of the strength and weakness of his position.

He had a strong sense of reality and he must have become aware, although his letters do not say it in so many words, of the impossible strain he was putting upon himself in trying to be a politician in two continents. In 1917 he had refused to enter the House of Commons. Could he make a belated entry in 1919? And if so, under whose banner? Under Asquith's? Or Ramsay Macdonald's? Or his own? But where would his followers come from? Did he need followers? Suppose he stopped being a politician and made himself an evangelist? But how would he support his family while he was trying to save the world? And where would the family live? Could he uproot them from Doornkloof? Could he live without them in England? If so, for how long?... Probably he never got so far as formulating questions like these; there was no need; the answers to them were so obvious. All the answers were contained in two sentences which he wrote in mid-June—'I have been long from home, far away from the base which I have to rely on. I have not been big or effective enough in the last two years to work to a new base and to appeal from a world platform.'[60] If only he could have seen it—and in the end he did see it—his one chance of gaining a world platform was by remaining a South African politician.

He made the right decision when he clung to his home base. That meant, however, that he had to accept the responsibilities of his nationality, his office and his own past. He had been linked inseparably with Botha in making the Union and bringing it to its present position in the world. Could he now separate himself from Botha? There could be no doubt at all that Botha *had* to sign the treaty, for otherwise South Africa would be left in the limbo; she would lose her mandate over South-West Africa, her membership of the League of Nations, her new status within the Commonwealth and in international law. And what would be the consequences on the home front? Everybody in South Africa would say that either he or Botha must be wrong. For Smuts to take a separate road might give him in the eyes of some people a spurious halo of sanctity; but it would split the party and ruin all the work of State-building which he and Botha had achieved from Vereeniging to Versailles in seventeen years of patient and loyal fellowship with each other.[61]

Smuts held the conviction (although it was already heretical among

535

Afrikaner nationalists) that it was possible at one and the same time to be concerned for the well-being both of South Africa and Europe. When he made up his mind at last to put his signature to the treaty, he did it for Europe's sake as well as for South Africa's. The drift of his thought about Europe has already been seen in the quotations that have been given from his letters to his friends. He thought the treaty abominable, but he also thought it necessary. As he put it to Keynes, a formal peace was needed to give Europe and the world 'a chance'—a chance, that is to say, of regaining stability and making a fresh start. And the League of Nations would be there to help. For Smuts, that consideration by itself would probably in the last resort have been decisive. The League was embodied in the treaty: no treaty, no League—and therefore no 'grain of mustard seed' from which might grow the freedom and peace of mankind.

Smuts believed also in the recuperative powers of human societies. Again and again in his letters from Paris he had recalled the almost miraculous recovery which his own people had made after a cruel war and a ruinous defeat. Might not Germany repeat the miracle? Might not the Danubian countries and all Europe repeat it? But first they must have peace signed and sealed in a treaty—even a bad treaty.

The treaty of Versailles was only one of a series but it was the one above all to whose making Smuts had committed himself, intellectually and emotionally. He never budged from his conviction that it was a bad and baneful piece of work. Was he right? That is a question far too large even to be raised in one chapter of one man's biography. There are, however, two smaller questions which can profitably be raised. What criteria did Smuts employ in forming his judgment of the treaty? And what degree of consistency do we find in his own conduct when we judge it by his own criteria?

As we have seen, Smuts reproached President Wilson, Lloyd George and the whole British Empire Delegation (including himself) for failing to make 'the Wilson peace' to which, he declared,[1] they had pledged themselves in the pre-armistice correspondence. Was this reproach well grounded in fact? Historians have given the most wildly divergent answers to this question. On the one hand, Sir Harold Nicolson has written: 'Of President Wilson's twenty-three conditions, only four can, with any accuracy, be said to have been incorporated in the Treaties of Peace.'[62] On the other hand,

Professor Brogan has said that Ludendorff and the other German leaders had not studied the President's Points, Principles and Particulars and did not realise when they accepted them what onerous peace terms were implied in them.[63] Wherever the truth may lie between these two extremes, there can be no doubt that Lloyd George was right when he declared that the predominant military power which the allies possessed was bound to determine 'the exegesis of the sacred text'.* Smuts, as we have seen, had feared precisely that. It was one of his main complaints against the treaty that it embodied interpretations of Wilson's principles which were consistently biased in favour of the victors and, in their cumulative effect, indefensibly harsh to the defeated countries.

And yet the principle of nationality, which was perhaps more heavily underlined in the President's speeches than any other, was bound, however it was applied, to work against the traditional predominance of the Germans in central Europe; indeed, it had found embodiment even before the Peace Conference met in the emergence of many new non-German States. How could Smuts object to that, seeing that he himself had consistently upheld the principle of nationality? But he had never upheld it as an absolute: he had always insisted that it must find expression within some wider system, which he defined at times in terms of the balance of power (a most un-Wilsonian concept) and at other times in terms of political obligation. He had no objection to make in principle against any of the new States; but he did not believe that the political, economic and moral environment created for them by the Treaty of Versailles offered them good prospects of a long and happy life. He believed their prospects to be bad because he believed the treatment of Germany to be bad. From the beginning to the end of his struggles in Paris, he had insisted that the treatment to be meted out to Germany was the most important problem before the Peace Conference, and the main reason for the long battle he had had to fight within himself before he signed the treaty was his conviction that the terms which it enforced upon Germany were too harsh.

Was this conviction well grounded? Here again we have a question far too sweeping to be faced in a single biographical chapter—a question, besides, upon which the widest differences of opinion still persist between historians; some of them argue that the

* See p. 493 above.

537

Germans were treated far too harshly, others that they were treated far too mildly.

In these controversies the degree of subjectivity which the contending historians display is intolerable and a reproach to the historical guild. Have the guildsmen no common standards, no agreed criteria of judgment? Let us recall Machiavelli's criteria. If you see your enemy in the water up to his neck, he once said, you will do well to push him under; but if he is in it only up to his knees, you will do well to help him to the shore. He made the same point in his terse antithesis: *o spegnerle o carezzarle*—either annihilate them or win their consent.*

Smuts was not a student of Machiavelli and he never formulated alternatives so brilliantly, so brutally extreme; nevertheless, similar alternatives were in his mind throughout those months at Paris, when he said again and again that it was impossible to keep the Germans down permanently and that it was necessary in consequence to produce a treaty which they could sign and execute in good faith. He had prudential reasons for his revolt against the Treaty of Versailles. He believed that it was destroying the old balance of power in Europe and creating a new balance which was bound to prove impermanent. It contained many stipulations which were bound sooner or later to provoke German attack; but it did not contain defences which would be sufficient in long term to forestall or repel that attack.

Smuts based his case against the Treaty of Versailles not only upon prudential but also upon moral grounds. In a letter to the Gilletts on 28 June he quoted the words which Botha had written on his agenda paper after he had signed the treaty—

28 June 1919. In the new dawn the laws of God will be justly meted out to all peoples, and we shall persevere in the prayer that they will be applied to humanity in love and peace and in the spirit of Christ. Today I recall 31 May 1902 (Vereeniging).†

'I could only join in that prayer', Smuts told his friends.[64]

* Machiavelli was here talking about nations. He made the same point (*Discorsi*, II, ch. XXIV) in a discussion of how to treat a captured city: *o farsela campagna o disfarla*—either make it your associate or destroy it. A half-and-half policy (*via del mezzo*) always seemed to him foolish.

† 28 Junie 1919. Gods rechten sal op alle volkeren rechtvaardig toegepast worden onder de nieuwe son, en wy zullen volharden in het gebed dat dit op den menschdom in liefde en vrede en christelikheid worde toegepast. Vandaag gedenk ek 31 Mei 1902 (Vereeniging).

In the Treaty of Versailles he could see very little of 'love and peace and the spirit of Christ'. But had he really expected those virtues to be embodied in that document? Neither he nor Botha had discovered much sign of them seventeen years earlier in the Treaty of Vereeniging. His memory did not deceive him about that; but it bore the far deeper imprint of his meeting, five years later, with Campbell-Bannerman. That meeting, he believed, marked the real peace settlement between Boer and Briton. Writing to Lloyd George on 26 March 1919 he reminded him that he, as a member of Campbell-Bannerman's government, had been a party to it. He reminded him, too, of the stamp it bore and in which its greatness consisted— the stamp of magnanimity. He called upon Lloyd George to treat the Germans as Campbell-Bannerman had treated the Boers. He called for a magnanimous peace.*

Whether or not the Germans would have made the same response to magnanimity as Botha and Smuts (but not all their fellow Afrikaners) had made is a question which cannot be pursued here. Let it suffice to say that Smuts had set a very high standard of conduct for Lloyd George and the other statesmen who bore the heaviest responsibilities at Paris. Consequently, the question arises whether Smuts himself, with the far lighter responsibilities which fell to him, succeeded in living up to his own standard. Lloyd George compelled him to face this question when he replied on 3 June to the letter of passionate protest which he had received from him after the three crucial meetings of the British Empire Delegation on 30 May and 1 June. 'Are you prepared', he asked, 'to forego the claims for pensions and so confine compensation to material damage?' That question cut very close to the bone. Lloyd George followed it up with another which probed just as deep. 'The Germans', he reminded Smuts, 'repeatedly request the return of their colonies. Are you prepared to allow German South-West Africa, or German East Africa, to be returned to Germany as a concession which might induce them to sign the peace?'[65] (he might have added: 'and to keep the peace?').

In his book on *The Economic Consequences of the Peace* which Keynes, with strong encouragement from Smuts, was writing at this very time the problem of war pensions and separation allowances took a

* See p. 512 above.

prominent place. Keynes believed that the inclusion of these categories in the bill for reparation was indefensible and that its consequences would be calamitous. He knew also that his friend Smuts had prepared a document whose purpose it had been to persuade President Wilson that their inclusion was proper.

This document has more than once been printed *in extenso* and it will be sufficient here to quote its concluding paragraph, which opens with a reference to the reservation contained in the Lansing Note of 5 November 1918, whereby the obligation was put upon Germany, and accepted by her, to make compensation for the damage done to the civilian populations of the allies and their property by her 'aggression' by land, by sea and from the air. In contradiction of the advice given to President Wilson by his own experts, Smuts maintained:

The plain, commonsense construction of the reservation, therefore, leads to the conclusion that, while direct war expenditure (such as the pay and equipment of soldiers, the cost of rifles, guns and ordnance and all similar expenditure) could perhaps not be recovered from the Germans, yet disablement pensions to discharged soldiers, or pensions to widows and orphans or separation allowances paid to their wives and children during the period of their military service are all items representing compensation to the civilian population for damage sustained by them, for which the German Government are liable. What was spent by the Allied Governments on the soldier himself, or on the mechanical appliances of war, might perhaps not be recoverable from the German Government under the reservation, as not being in any plain and direct sense damage to the civilian population. But what was or is spent on the citizen before he became a soldier, or after he has ceased to be a soldier, or at any time on his family, represents compensation for damage done to civilians and must be made good by the German Government under any fair interpretation of the above reservation. This includes all war pensions and separation allowances; which the German Government are liable to make good, in addition to reparation or compensation for all damage done to property of the Allied peoples.[66]

An attempt must be made briefly to put into its true perspective this argument, which has been the occasion of comment running to many thousands of pages of published print. In doing so, it will be as well to make two historical points before passing to the biographical ones. In the first place, there can be no doubt that the inclusion of war pensions and separation allowances, as categories under which reparation payments were due, had the effect of greatly increasing the sum (although the reparation chapter of the treaty left its total menacingly vague) which the Germans might be called upon to pay. In the second place, the document which Smuts composed played a much smaller part than has been commonly supposed in creating this situation, for there is some evidence to show that President Wilson was already disposed to include war pensions and separation allowances in the reparation account before he had seen Smuts's arguments in favour of including them.[67]

To return to biography: the charge levelled against Smuts as the man allegedly responsible for imposing upon Germany the cost of allied war pensions and separation allowances was first put into circulation in 1920 (although more in sorrow than in anger) by the *History of the Paris Peace Conference*, edited by H. W. V. Temperley. Circulation grew very rapidly and before long Smuts was being accused by the Nationalist opposition in the Union Parliament of having multiplied by three the staggering bill imposed upon Germany (so the orators declared) by her conquerors.

Smuts defended himself both in letters to his friends and in a public statement to the newspapers. He laid great stress on the fact that he had had no part in the political decision but had merely given 'a legal opinion' which, he said, had won the approval of 'the greatest jurists at the conference'. This defence was not very convincing, partly because the jurists were divided into two camps (the Americans against the English), partly because Smuts went on to offer a second defence which by implication contradicted the first: 'If, however, pensions had been excluded from civilian damage, France would have got practically the whole indemnity, whatever it was, as she had suffered by far the most devastation. That would have been quite unfair.'[68] One may agree: indeed, anybody who knows anything at all about the economic effort and the economic effects of war must agree; but the proposition amounts to much more than 'a legal opinion'; it is essentially political.

Given the fact that reparation was to be paid by Germany (and that was an obligation which the Germans had accepted in the negotiations which preceded the armistice) it would have been ludicrous economically and indefensible morally for the British Empire to be denied some benefit from it while being left to bear the main burden (with America the ultimate beneficiary) of the inter-allied war debts. But the inclusion of war pensions and separation allowances in the reparation account was a bad means (although in the intellectual and emotional muddle of that time it would have been hard to win acceptance for a better one) of achieving distributive justice.

Some part of the responsibility for choosing this bad means, if only a small part, rested upon Smuts. As we have seen, he had been remote from the complexities of the reparation problem up to the time when he wrote his memorandum. He wrote it in a hurry on the eve of his departure for Hungary. He made a bad mistake.

After his return from Hungary he did his utmost to retrieve the mistake. That was the period in which he got coaching from Keynes upon the financial and economic problems of peace-making. In the last weeks of May and the early weeks of June he conducted a furious campaign for the drastic revision of the Reparation Chapter, both by fixing a total for Germany's liability and by agreeing upon a ratio of apportionment among the allies.

The last word in this long argument may fittingly be left with Keynes. When the *History of the Paris Peace Conference* appeared to put upon Smuts the main responsibility for the war pensions proposal, Keynes wrote a letter of protest to Temperley and enclosed a copy of it in a letter to Smuts. 'It looks', he said, 'as though they are going to saddle *you* with the responsibility for the Big indemnity, which is absurdly unfair to anyone who knows the facts—though I am not sure it won't serve you right for writing that memorandum!'[69] Two years later, when Smuts had been stung into defending himself in the press, Keynes wrote again: 'You know already my views about the opinion you gave on the legality of including pensions. I have always regretted that this opinion was given, more than I can say. But it is monstrous that anyone should give the public to believe that you were anything but the leading champion for views of sanity and reason on this issue at the Conference.'[70]

The answer which Smuts gave to the first of the two questions addressed to him by Lloyd George on 3 June has been indicated in the foregoing discussion: fix the total sum for reparation (quite a stiff total) and the ratio of apportionment. That would make possible (as Lloyd George was well aware) dropping the claim for pensions.[71]

His answer to the second question—about the German colonies in Africa—requires a brief introductory discussion. As we have seen, Smuts had insisted, ever since his arrival in England, that the expulsion of the Germans from South-West Africa was essential for the security of the Union and their expulsion from East Africa essential for the security of the British Commonwealth's communications. He laid great stress on this argument in the resolution proposing mandatory rule which he moved on 29 January in the Council of Ten; Germany's submarine bases, he asserted, constituted a menace 'to the freedom and security of all nations'. He also argued that Germany's record of colonial administration made it incumbent upon the allied and associated Powers to ensure 'that in no circumstances should any of the German colonies be restored to Germany'.[72]

Given the pre-existing rules and customs of international relations, there was a great deal to be said for the argument of security. But was not Smuts making an attempt to institute new and better rules and customs through the agency of the League of Nations? He was indeed; but the League of Nations had still to be created and to prove its efficacy. A good statesman may perhaps distribute his weight between the world which exists and the world which is struggling to be born; but he had better be ready to shift his whole weight back on to the first world, if the second fails to be born. Along lines such as these, Smuts might have made out a strong case for the South Africans and British dispossessing their defeated enemy of large areas in Africa. But could not the French and the Poles make out just as strong a case along the same lines for dispossessing the same enemy of small areas in Europe? Subject to such restrictions as were imposed by the Mandates, the South Africans, like the Australians and the New Zealanders, were doing very well for themselves in the game of territorial grab. By what standard could they be judged more virtuous than the French, Polish or Italian grabbers? Not, certainly, by the standard of magnanimity, which Smuts was urging Lloyd George to recognise and uphold.

In Smuts's argument about Germany's bad record of colonial rule in Africa there was some truth; but it still remained to be proved that the Union's record would be better.* Besides, this argument brought him dangerously close to the people who imputed special wickedness to the Germans—people such as President Poincaré, whose speech at the opening session of the Peace Conference had so disgusted him.† Once again, magnanimity was not his standard. Was it his standard, then, only when the interests of other nations were concerned? To

* See p. 401 above.   † See p. 506 above.

say that would be unjust. When Lloyd George asked him straight out whether he was ready to restore South-West Africa or East Africa to Germany, he gave a straight answer: No, he was not ready to restore either of these territories to German ownership; but he was ready to recognise Germany as a potential mandatory Power.[73]

Lloyd George had told Smuts in effect that there was a beam in his own eye which he had better cast out before plucking out the mote in his neighbour's eye. But really, there was no longer any need for this admonition, for Smuts had been discovering for some time past the appalling complexities of the task of making peace amidst the mental, emotional and material chaos brought about by four years of slaughter and destruction. In a letter of 14 May to Mrs Gillett he had launched himself upon one of his passionate tirades and then reproved himself—'But I must not go on like this. I really have nothing practical to suggest, as the dimensions of the problem are beyond me, perhaps beyond human power.'[74] He was beginning to discover how hard it was to achieve coherent thought, and how much harder to impose coherent thought upon chaotic material. He was beginning to mingle self-criticism with his criticism of others; to ask himself whether *he*, a man so far removed from the centre of power, would have been able to do so much better if *he* had been carrying the great responsibilities of Lloyd George? 'Prime Minister,' he wrote on 3 June, 'do not for a moment imagine that I write in any other but a most friendly and sympathetic spirit, which I am sure you will not resent. Perhaps the main difference between us is that you are struggling in the water, while I shout advice from the shore.'[75]

When he made up his mind to sign the treaty he was mindful of his own responsibility, of the mistakes which he himself had made, not only at the Peace Conference but throughout the years of war which had been its prelude. 'It has been an awful thing', he told Alice Clark, 'making up my mind to sign the Peace Treaty with which I so thoroughly disagree. But I have gone through the war of which this is really merely the end, perhaps the inevitable end; and I feel I am no better than the others, and that I must stand in the dock beside them. And God be merciful to us poor sinners.'[76] That became his settled conviction. Eighteen years later he was invited by Lord Lothian and others to come to England to help 'make peace' in Europe. He saw no point, he replied, in ploughing the sands again; he lacked not only the position for undertaking such a task but also the strength and the wisdom. His mind went back to Paris in 1919, where, he said, 'I was as bad as the rest, as I was also partly responsible for some of the mistakes made in that awful time of confused thinking and counselling'.[77]

For Smuts, the sanguine years may be said to have closed with this discovery that intractable human material is resistant to the patterns which men of liberal intelligence and goodwill attempt to impose upon it. To say this is not to suggest that the Paris Peace Conference marks a sudden watershed of his experience and thought: on the one side great expectations, on the other side deep disillusionment; on the one side over-confidence, on the other side extreme mistrust. The contrast was not so sharp as that. In his philosophic thought, Smuts had always emphasised the real existence of pain, error and evil; in his personal life, he had experienced and absorbed the tragic element. Still, he had never faltered in his faith that good was sovereign over evil. No more did he falter now, or in the years ahead; but he did become more critical than he had used to be of his own formulations and predictions; he was not so certain that he could foresee, and in appreciable measure determine, in what manner and within what dimensions of time the sovereignty of good would assert itself. His second experience of war and peace had made him less prone than in the past to expect great advances in his own lifetime or the lifetime of his children. Temperamentally, some rearrangement was taking place (although from time to time there were bound to be reversions) in the ingredients of his disposition; the ingredient of patience, which had always co-existed with the ingredient of ardour, steadily acquired more consistency and weight.

This new balance which he was finding within himself between faith and criticism, hope and wariness, found expression in two public pronouncements which he made on the work of the Peace Conference. The first of them appeared in the British newspapers on 29 June, the day after the Treaty of Versailles was signed. It has been called 'a protest', and in retrospect Smuts himself sometimes called it so; but, at the time, he called it a 'statement'. It would be incorrect to say that he had signed the treaty under protest; he had signed it in the conviction that it was, things being as they were, the only thing that he could do. Its signature marked the end of the war. It did not mark the achievement of peace. 'The real peace of the peoples', he declared, 'ought to follow, complete, and amend the peace of the statesmen.'

Smuts had recently shown himself aware that the peoples were behaving no better than their statesmen; but he was now appealing from Philip drunk to Philip sober. He gave a list of amendments which he believed would prove necessary and, in the years to come, would become possible, as 'a new spirit of generosity and humanity' sprang to life in the heart of the peoples. It was the familiar list which he had enumerated so often in his memoranda of the past three months—territorial settlements to revise, guarantees to waive, punishments to forego, indemnities to scale down, 'pin-pricks' to remove—a full revisionist programme. Its achievement, he said, depended upon two things: upon the Germans proving themselves ready to fulfil the treaty so far as they were able: upon the allies recognising that God had given them the victory to use not for their selfish ends but for the highest ideals of humanity.

There had been a moment when Smuts had allowed himself to cast doubt upon the validity of everything which he had believed in and fought for since the outbreak of the war. On 3 June he had written to Mrs Gillett: 'The last battle of the war is being fought out in Paris and we look like losing that battle and with it the whole war. That would appear to justify the view you have held all through of its futility.'[78] But it would have been contrary both to his temperament and his philosophy for him to have sunk himself in total disillusionment. In his statement of 29 June he repudiated the idea that the past four years of war and peace had been altogether futile. Two great achievements, he declared, had been wrung from all the struggle and suffering: the overthrow of militarism and the establishment of the League of Nations. 'But the League', he added, 'is as yet only a form. It still requires the quickening life, which can only come from the active interest and the vitalising contact of the peoples themselves.'

Smuts had made his statement 'not in criticism but in faith'. Some of the newspapers applauded it, some ignored it, some attacked it. Among the latter was the *Globe*, which published an article under the heading, 'In his True Colours'. The British people had always suspected, it said, that they had an enemy in their midst; now they knew.[79] It may well be that Smuts had the *Globe* in mind when he wrote his farewell message on 19 July, the very eve of his departure, to the British people.[80] Modestly but firmly, as one who had played his full part alongside them from start to finish of the war, he claimed the right to remind them of some truths which some of them might find unpalatable. The first truth, of which his own presence and work among them had given them proof, was that the enemy of yesterday could become the friend of tomorrow. Pleading with them to look forward, not back, he gave them his own thoughts on some of the issues which would confront them.

On Germany. The brutal fact is that Great Britain is a very small island on the fringe of the Continent, and that on that Continent the seventy-odd million Germans represent the most important and formidable national factor. You cannot have a stable Europe without a stable, settled Germany....

On Russia. Leave Russia alone, remove the blockade, adopt a policy of friendly neutrality and Gallic-like impartiality to all factions....If we have to appear on the Russian scene at all, let it be as impartial, benevolent friends and helpers, and not as military or political partisans.

On the Dominions. The successful launching of her former colonies among the nations of the world, while they remain members of an inner Britannic circle, will ever rank as one of the most outstanding achievements of British political genius. Forms and formulas may still have to be readjusted, but the real work is done.

On progress in India and the other Imperial Dependencies. It is a task to be approached in an open mind and with the fixed determination here too to realise those principles of freedom and self-government without which this Empire cannot continue to exist in the new time.

On Ireland (most urgent of all). Unless the Irish question is settled on the great principles which form the basis of this Empire, this Empire must cease to exist.

If the British people showed themselves willing, Smuts concluded, to attack these tasks with courage and openness of mind and willingness to learn and to try new methods, they would discover that they had not fought the war in vain.

Before he took ship for home Smuts wrote a letter of farewell to Keynes. In his new mood—'not in bitterness but in faith'—he had changed his mind about the advice he had given Keynes barely four weeks earlier to launch a frontal attack on the treaty. 'Better to be constructive', he now told him. '...You will find many opportunities to help the world, especially when the real trouble over the Reparation and Financial clauses begins with Germany.'[81] Keynes did not follow this advice. Would it have been better had he done so? His book, when it appeared a few months later, produced a shattering effect. It crystallised thought in the English-speaking countries upon the revision of the peace settlement. On the other hand, it damaged international confidence. In Germany, it provided ammunition for the enemies of the policy of fulfilment. In America, it provided ammunition for the isolationists. In France, it roused resentment against 'perfide Albion'. In England it led, among other things, to the exclusion of Keynes himself for many crucial years from the confidence and counsel of the British government.

Smuts had chosen a different road. He was returning home to share in the government of his country and, very soon, to lead it.

CHAPTER 22

THE DEATH OF BOTHA

In March 1917, when Botha sent Smuts to London to speak for South Africa at the Imperial War Cabinet, his first thought was for the woman upon whom was inflicted once again a painful separation from her husband.

Yes, Mrs Smuts [he wrote], the friendship between Jannie and me is an unbreakable bond which will persist throughout our lives. We have never had an irreparable difference which could not be resolved, and there was never a difference which, having been resolved, left a feeling behind, and that is why I love him as much as and more than my own brother. We have gone through deep waters together, and even through mud, to save our people, and although there are many who only want to curse us, there never were two people who have worked harder and more honestly for our people and who have done more than Jannie and I. Well, Mrs Smuts, my wife and I have never, in the friendship with you and Jannie, had anything but affection and pleasantness, and today the bond goes much deeper than friendship, and that is why we pray together every evening for his safe landing on the other side.[1]

Such love and trust excluded the possibility of misunderstanding or resentment, however heavy the burden might be which Botha was left to bear alone.

Usually, he found it well within the compass of his strength. He no longer had any anxiety on the score of public order. At the end of 1915 the government had felt strong enough to release the chief leaders of the 1914 Rebellion and next year no less a person than General de Wet had denounced a 'plot' (if, indeed, the foolish talk of a few hotheads had gone so far as that) to start 'a second rebellion'. General Hertzog was leading the Nationalist party along the path of constitutional opposition. He accepted as a regrettable fact the Union's participation in the war and deduced from this fact a constitutional doctrine for which he could (and did) quote the authority of Lionel Curtis: self-government is only a sham if it stops short of the nation's right to make its own decisions upon the supreme issues of peace and war. Upon this foundation of doctrine he built a programme: the sovereign independence of South Africa, externally as well as

549

internally. As he put it in a speech to the students of Stellenbosch in May 1917: 'We stand in no way under Great Britain or its Parliament or Government. The only bond which binds us together is our Common King, but under him we each stand separately and independently of each other.'[2] This pronouncement raised a great fuss in parliament and in the newspapers, but really there was nothing shocking in it; it was an affirmation of the same principle which Botha and Smuts, as we have seen, effectively vindicated two years later, when the issue of the military guarantee to France came up for discussion and they exacted from Lloyd George an acknowledgment of the Union's right to remain neutral in a British war.* Hertzog, if he had only realised it, was contending for a principle which his political opponents were applying in practice. From the narrow tactical point of view, he made the mistake of appealing to President Wilson's speeches instead of to the constitutional evolution which was already taking place within the Commonwealth. Taking his stand upon the principle of self-determination, he demanded that the stolen independence of the two Boer Republics should be restored to them. But that would have meant the dissolution of the Union, which nobody in South Africa really wanted.

Botha never had any reason to fear that Nationalist propaganda on these issues would shake his position in parliament. Rightly or wrongly, he felt also that it was failing to make much headway in the country, except when his opponents were able to interweave it with their denunciation of immediate grievances.[3] Of those, however, there were plenty: for example, the discontent of the white trade-unionists at the failure of wages to keep up with prices and the indignation of the farmers at the terms offered by the British War office for the bulk purchase of South African wool. Still, these difficulties could be and in fact were straightened out without too much trouble. Botha would never have felt them to be unendurable had he not fallen ill.

In September 1917 his friends became alarmed at his state of health. He was suffering from carbuncles, an enlarged liver and a painful swelling of the legs which was caused, the doctors said, by heart trouble or possibly dropsy. He was finding it hard to follow the instructions the doctors gave him to discipline his diet, and to take regular exercise. He fell into deep depression and felt that the

* See p. 522 above.

burden of politics was growing too heavy for him to bear. 'Als Jannie maar hier was!',* he groaned. Lord Buxton, the Governor-General, thought it his duty to send Smuts a telegram of urgent warning. He doubted whether Botha would be strong enough to face the next parliamentary session. If that proved to be so, the government could hardly get through without Smuts. But Smuts at this time was in the midst of his labours on establishing the Royal Air Force and the War Priorities organisation. 'Lord Buxton has wired to me (he told Mrs Gillett) that I should now return to South Africa in view of the local situation. Lloyd George and Bonar Law tell me that it will be "a disaster" if I go at the present juncture.' Smuts felt at one and the same time that he could not possibly return and that he must at any cost return; but he was spared the agony of decision by a second telegram from the Governor-General announcing Botha's almost miraculous recovery. Lord Buxton had never seen 'such a wonderful change for the better in so short a time'. In a letter giving fuller news he reported that Botha himself had been as much distressed as Smuts must have been by the decision which had seemed to be thrust upon them both. 'He was a good deal worried as to what was best; and he is very glad now that it is definitely settled that you should remain as he immensely appreciates all you are doing there.'[4]

For the next ten months or more Botha's health continued to be reasonably satisfactory. He brought his diet under better control, took regular exercise and reduced his weight. On 3 February 1918, Mrs Botha wrote to Smuts:

Louis is much, much better and so that must not trouble you. At one time I honestly did feel that I would have to write to you that he could not go on, for he really was seriously ill, but he rallied marvellously and is once more as 'game' as he possibly can be. His leg still worries him occasionally, but he is able to play golf again and that helps him to keep fit bodily. His colour is also clearer and his eyes brighter and he takes a keen interest again in everything concerning the country, and he is ready for the 'Wool' debate which takes place on the 7th and what is more he feels that you are a power of strength to him working as you are for our interests in England.

She went on to say that sometimes still she heard Louis exclaim, *Als Jannie maar hier was!*; but in a further instalment of the same letter a week later she reported his complete victory in the wool debate.

* If only Jannie were here!

Their two families were keeping close together and her daughter Helen was helping Isie in the great work she was doing for soldiers' comforts and in the military hospitals on Roberts Heights. 'Isie is looking thin, Jannie, but bright and full of energy. She has done wonderful work during your absence and is untiring in her endeavours to help in every way and fill up your place where she is able to do so. She is just a brick. She and Helen are great friends. Helen loves her and tries to play her "lieutenant".' The Bothas, however, were worrying about their boy who was serving with the South African forces in Europe. Smuts had been doing all he could for him when he was on leave and Mrs Botha begged him to go on treating him 'as a son'. She expressed a mother's anxiety at the rising toll of battle casualties. Recently she had been in Cape Town when a transport had berthed on the return journey from England to Australia. 'The last Australian lot of wounded men was...an eye-opener. There were so many maimed amongst them.'[5]

On 26 February Botha wrote a long letter to Smuts giving him the political news. On the whole he thought it good. The government had come fairly well out of the wool debate. They were having some trouble with the Unionists, who sometimes resented the task allotted to them of supporting the government on its war policy without having any share in making the policy; they kept talking of a coalition, which Botha thought 'impracticable'. So indeed it was, from the point of view of the South African party, which had already lost about half the Afrikaner votes and would certainly lose many more if it joined forces with the English-speaking Unionist party. As things were, Botha thought that the Nationalists were losing ground in the country. Their growing frustration had revealed itself the previous day in an embittered attack which they had launched against Smuts on the ground of his long absence in London. Botha made it quite clear that he wanted Smuts to stay on there for the approaching session of the Imperial War Cabinet; he himself had been invited to attend but did not want to go.

My colleagues and I are truly satisfied with your work, nay more, I am proud of the way you are defending and representing us there. And it seems to me that, if I go there now, it can have only one effect and that is to weaken your position or possibly to make it uncertain. I understand something of war and of your work there, and fully confirm what you are doing....I have only one desire and that is to be there when peace is discussed, for then I shall support you in person in getting many things and seeing difficulties solved for which we shall perhaps never have another chance—especially the question of Mozambique.* Jannie, there is no doubt about it—this is a matter which we must bring up and settle in our favour. . . . Then there is German West—we must keep this, for we and the Germans will not again live together on a friendly footing if they keep German West.

Botha continued with reflections on the war (he emphasised the danger of fighting it to a smash-up) and with home news, both political and private. Like his wife a few weeks earlier, he ended his letter by commending his son to the affectionate and wise care of his friend.[6]

Things worked out as Botha wished; he stayed at home while Smuts remained in London. But in early August, just when the tide of battle was turning and Smuts was contending in the Imperial War Cabinet for the policies of war and peace which he and his chief both had at heart, the Governor-General cabled news of an alarming recurrence of Botha's illness. The cables were followed by letters from Lord Buxton and others. Botha was not only seriously ill but deeply depressed. He kept saying that his father had died at 56 (which would be his own age next year) and so had his brother, and that he himself would not go beyond that age either. His clear bright eyes had grown dull, his breathing was laboured and he was apt to drop off into a doze even while he was talking with his friends. His doctors said that he could not possibly live much longer unless he went away on a long holiday; but this he would never be induced to do until Smuts was back in South Africa.[7]

Once again, Smuts seemed to be faced with an agonising decision; in August 1918 he would have found it even harder than in the previous September to leave London. But once again reassuring news soon followed the first sombre telegrams. From mid-August onwards the improvement in Botha's health and spirits was so great that Lord Buxton felt moved in early November to protest that his telegrams three months earlier had not been 'alarmish'.[8] On 16 December Botha landed in England, in fulfilment of his determination to attend the Peace Conference. 'I was really glad [Smuts wrote to his wife] to see old Louis looking so much better. He is not at all so fat and looks strong. I hope he will not tire himself too much and lose ground again during his stay here.'[9]

* See pp. 408, 498 above.

553

Smuts made it his particular concern to see that this did not happen. He shielded his friend from the pressure of social engagements and took upon himself the main burden of work both at the Peace Conference and in such South African business as had to be transacted in Paris or London. All this without intruding upon Botha's position as head of the government: as has been seen already, on various critical occasions it was Botha who said the decisive word for his country. Admittedly, Smuts put a great strain upon the strength and patience of his friend during those days of late June when he insisted that he would never sign the peace treaty. 'Jannie is baie koppig' (is very stubborn) Botha used sometimes to say, and his stubbornness over the treaty contained the threat of calamitous ruin to a great partnership and friendship. But in the end that evil was averted.

During their six months together Smuts must have realised that he had been too optimistic in his first estimate of Botha's state of health. At Paris Botha began to put on weight again. Often he could not bear the confinement of clothes and collars but would sit in his hotel room in his dressing gown playing bridge, if a four could be got together, or patience, if he were alone. His secretary, Frank Theron, used to take him walking for exercise in the Bois de Boulogne but Botha found these excursions painful and Theron felt sometimes that they were hazardous. Despite all these trials and difficulties, Botha's sturdy intelligence and nobility of character made a strong impression upon the Peace Conference. This impression, which is reflected in the published writings of Lloyd George and others, found expression one day in a conversation between Smuts and Theron: 'Who do you think [asked Smuts] is the biggest personality here? I thought of Woodrow Wilson, Lloyd George, Clemenceau (the Tiger), Foch, etc., even of Smuts himself, but without waiting for an answer, and obviously thinking aloud, he said, "Our own Oubaas Louis—no one amongst these people can hold a candle to him".'[10]

After the treaty had been signed Smuts had to spend a week or two in London; but he encouraged Botha to take an earlier ship to South Africa and wait quietly in Cape Town until they could both travel north together to their families and to the official duties which awaited them. Smuts himself set sail in the third week of July. His letters from the ship to his friends show him to have been brooding too morbidly (although it would be harsh not to make allowances for

VII. Botha and Smuts, July 1919

him) upon the defeats which idealists such as himself had suffered at the Peace Conference; but mingled with his disillusionment were strands of hope, and deep gratitude for the friendships which had enriched his life in England.

Your letters [he told Alice Clark] always make a strange appeal to me— and yet not strange, considering what a comradeship of the spirit we have enjoyed in these terrible years. A little circle of peace and blessedness inside the raging storm....I have spent a quiet happy time on board, mostly in reflections on the past and broodings on the things which the future may still have in store for us. What a tremendous past it has been with all its wild romance, all its agonies and exaltations! Is anything still left? Will they ever come again, the long long dances?*

I arrive at Cape Town on the morning of 4 August and at a moment when the Union will be busy with its Peace Celebrations. Isn't that a curious double coincidence? I have been 5 complete years in the war; and with the almost 3 years of the Boer War that makes 8 or almost $\frac{1}{6}$ of my life spent in this sort of business.† I pray at any rate that this long dance will not come again....Who can tell? So let us continue to work and pray, in faith that over this great darkness the light will yet shine even if we do not live to see it. The feeble light of Reason has burnt very low during this period, but it may revive into a great illumination of the nations, or at least of the souls of millions now groping about in darkness and despair.[11]

In Cape Town and all along the thousand miles of their journey northwards Botha and Smuts were welcomed as conquering heroes. These celebrations, which soon became an arduous ordeal, were the foretaste of more to follow elsewhere in the Union. But in the third week of August Smuts enjoyed a few days of rest with his family. He told the Gilletts that:

...the home-coming to Doornkloof was the best. Even little Louis‡ had learnt English to speak to me as she said that I would surely have forgotten to speak in Dutch! Isie and the children were great; and Doornkloof was a dream. And the air, and the nights and the days! I have simply plunged into it all with all my heart, and it is soaking into me like a blissful opiate, and making me forget the great world of sorrow and suffering I have left behind me.[12]

---

* An echo from Gilbert Murray's translation of Euripides's *Bacchae*.

† Of his political life (even without making any deduction for the five years of Crown Colony government) the war years amounted to eight out of twenty-one; approximately two-fifths. If one reckoned back from 1950, the year of his death, the proportion would be comparable: fourteen war years in fifty-two years of political life, more than one-quarter of the total.

‡ The youngest daughter of the family, named Louis Annie de la Rey Smuts (later McIldowie).

Surely, he exclaimed, these feelings were healthy and natural, like 'the return of the savage to his natural life,...of the native to his tribe'. He had forgotten that there was 'such a dream of a climate' and revelled in the cold frosty mornings followed by exhilarating warmth as the sun climbed higher in the heavens. One afternoon he drove with some friends to his bushveld farm, 80 miles away— 'and there we slept in a magic circle of sicklewood trees that night. The trees grow in a circle and inside we made a fire on which we prepared our supper in Paradise fashion and afterwards we made our beds in the circle, radiating out with our bodies from the fire in the centre which kept burning all night. It was truly grand.'[13] Next day he was back at Doornkloof and riding over the farm with his manager and his daughter Santa on her beloved chestnut stallion Comet. Alas, on the following morning he had to set off with Botha to a reception and party conference at Bloemfontein.

His rest at home had lasted only from the Thursday evening to the Monday morning. The business at Bloemfontein took nearly a week. After that, Botha and he were expected in Natal. Botha dearly loved those mountains and valleys of his birth and upbringing; but he allowed himself to be persuaded by his doctors and his friend to take a rest from the travelling and the speech making. On 25 August Smuts set out alone. He knew that the strain had been telling upon Botha but did not know that his last illness was now at hand. On his second day in Durban he received an urgent telegram from Louis Esselen, the friend of them both and the secretary of the South African party, reporting that Botha was failing rapidly. He took the train the same night for Pretoria. Early next morning at Volksrust the conductor of the train wakened Captain Theron and handed him a telegram addressed to Smuts. It said—

GENERAL BOTHA DIED AT MIDNIGHT OF HEART
FAILURE. PASSED AWAY PEACEFULLY.

Theron woke Smuts who said, 'It is bad news? Is it about General Botha?' Theron said, 'Yes, he died about midnight'. Smuts took the telegram, groaned and turned his face to the wall.[14]*

Mrs Smuts met the train next morning at Irene and together they drove to Botha's house to give such poor comfort as they could to the family and to discuss the arrangements for the funeral.

* See p. 592, reference 10.

Writing to Arthur Gillett that same night Smuts said simply, 'He was South Africa's greatest son and among men my best friend'.[15] Of the many letters of sympathy which he received, perhaps the most moving was from Winston Churchill:

Botha came to see me here before he sailed, and I did what I have so far done for no other visitor—escorted him downstairs and put him into his carriage myself. Almost immediately after (as it seemed) while the impression of his presence was strong with me I learned that he has gone. I know what a loss this will be to you, and believe me I felt a keen personal pang as if someone I had known all my life has passed away. He was one of the truly great men of the world, and thank God of the British Empire.[16]

Botha was buried on 30 August. After the church service the funeral procession was formed, at its head hundreds of cadets, each carrying a wreath; then the old brigade of burgher commandos with General Brits at their head; then some hundreds of Botha's intimate friends and colleagues in mourning dress; then the hearse, followed by Mrs Botha and the family and by members of the government and other distinguished persons in their carriages. So the procession moved slowly along Church Street West which was lined for nearly a mile by soldiers with arms reversed and behind them the silent, reverent people who bared their heads as the coffin passed. At the graveside Smuts spoke some simple and deeply moving words about Louis Botha as soldier, statesman and friend. He concluded by reading aloud the words which Botha himself had written on his agenda paper the day the Treaty of Versailles was signed.

Three days later Smuts arrived in Cape Town for the special session of Parliament which had been summoned to ratify the peace treaty. By that time, he held the Governor-General's commission to form the new ministry. Nobody had ever doubted that this honour and burden would fall upon him. He had not doubted it himself. At Botha's graveside he had said: 'Great in his life, he was happy in his death; for his friend was reserved the hard fate to bury him and to remain with the task which even for him was too much.' Writing to his wife from Cape Town on 3 September he said the same thing again in slightly different words. Yet his letter contained a spirit of resolution comparable with the 'colossal responsibility' which he had inherited: 'May I have strength and courage to do the work. Your help and belief in my star will help me greatly and have already helped me greatly on the long travelled road. When I think of the future and all that will have to be done I feel most uneasy. But these mountains of troubles, when they are nearer and "closer seen are but gigantic flights of stairs". We shall see.'

How far was Smuts fitted by his temperament, training and intellect to take charge of South Africa's destinies? The clues pointing towards an answer are scattered throughout this narrative of his life up to 1919. It would be a mistake to enumerate them too systematically; but one or two of them may be scrutinised with profit. And to begin with, it will be worth while considering his qualifications for the three separate offices which he now assumed.

In the new government he was Minister of Defence, Minister of Native Affairs and Prime Minister. His qualifications for the first office may be taken for granted; he had already proved them. But the second office? He had insisted in his student years that the Natives of South Africa were *the* South African problem; but as a politician he had never tackled this problem. In point of magnitude he had put it first, but in point of time he had put it second; in his order of priorities, reconciliation between Boer and Briton had stood at the head of the list. A few phrases about the Natives come to mind from his correspondence in the pre-Union years with Merriman: 'I don't believe in politics for them': 'My mind is in Cimmerian darkness': 'Put it on the ampler shoulders of the future'. But now, as Minister of Native Affairs, he was putting the responsibility upon his own shoulders. It was a responsibility for which he had not yet prepared himself. The Union by now had been in existence for nine years, but he had not spoken a single sentence in parliament about Native policy. In May 1917 he had referred to it in one of his London speeches,[17] but only in a superficial way— a medley of the traditional South African slogans; of the neo-liberal phrases about the development of parallel communities, each on 'its own proper lines'; of Lord Selborne's self-contradictory notions. In these abstractions there was nothing inherently bad nor—for that matter—good; their value would be determined by the manner of their application and modification in the particular circumstances of time and place. For this, Smuts was now accepting the responsibility. In other fields, he had given sufficient proof of his capacity for disciplined thought, his resolution and his aptitude for the flanking movement where no prospect existed of a frontal advance. In the field of Native policy these qualities of his would now be put to a hard test.*

About his qualifications to be Prime Minister a note of questioning could be detected in the newspapers, both in South Africa and overseas. Almost without exception they agreed that no other choice was possible; but in many of them a doubt was expressed about the capacity of Smuts to fill the gap which Botha's death had left. The two men had complemented each other and together they had been a wonderful partnership: nobody doubted that; but for that very reason it seemed to many people too much to expect from Smuts alone the leadership which Botha and he had given jointly. Botha, many writers suggested, had constituted the human, Smuts the intellectual element of the partnership. Smuts lacked 'the bonhomie' of Botha. He lacked 'that homely insight into the hearts of his own people' in which lay Botha's strength. He was 'not so liberally endowed with the gracious patience which made Botha's personality so winsome'. He could not suffer fools gladly. He had no gift for popularity. He possessed an 'icy coolness', 'a rather hard brilliancy'; but simple folk did not feel towards him that 'fraternal warmth' which they had always felt for Botha.

The unflattering implications of these quotations need not be heavily emphasised, for most of the commentators ended upon a note of confidence: Smuts, they agreed, was a great man who would grow to the measure of his new responsibilities.[18]

Amongst all this comment, only one reference has been found to the 'slimness' that was at times attributed to Smuts. 'In his conduct of public business [wrote the *Cape Times* on 3 September] he has been apt to resort to rhetorical and administrative sleight of hand: on the principle, or want of principle, that anything is good enough to grease the wheels of the clumsy machine of popular government.' That observation might well have led to some impersonal reflections upon the training which Smuts had had in the arts of parliamentary government. In one respect it had been both unusual and unsatisfactory. Since his entry into politics twenty-one years ago he had never once been a back-bencher. He had never once been in opposition. If from time to time he showed impatience with the procedures and processes of parliamentary government it could just as plausibly have been ascribed to his training as to his temperament.

* See above, pp. 30, 221, 225, 255 ff., 318 ff.

And yet he himself felt that he had certain temperamental deficiencies. On 6 September he wrote to Mrs Gillett: 'I am now Prime Minister but my heart is not in the thing and only an overwhelming disaster brought me there. Botha's loss to this country is quite irreparable. His was just the role which I temperamentally could not play, and you know how necessary that role is in the world. I shall do my best without being sanguine about success.'[19] He wrote in the same vein to Alice Clark, who replied with sisterly affection and frankness:

I have a photograph of you taken 14 years ago. Two strongly developed characters are mingled there, striving for the mastery—the Creative and the Instrumental. Seldom are the two so evenly balanced in one nature. I am very fond of that photograph; it is so like you. Nevertheless, the strife should have an end and out of the strong must come forth sweetness. It is the very excellence of your instrument which sometimes clouds your faith in creative power, for you never meet your equal in intellectual force.... But remember that creative power has its scope in the hearts of men and women, not in the machinery of Government, and that you have power to move those hearts. Don't tie yourself up with offices so that you have not time for sympathetic meeting with the common people.[20]

A few weeks later she wrote to him again in the idiom of Quaker intimacy: 'Thou art fond [she told him] of speculations on the Meaning of Good. Thou keeps them as a refuge from the clamouring demands of the political existence. Like Marcus Aurelius thou retires to that little farm of thy own mind where a solitude so profound may be enjoyed. But that is no place from which to draw creative force.' The only place to draw it from, she told him, was 'simple honesty'. She challenged him to look with clear eyes into his own mind and heart and to ask himself whether he had yet achieved unity and simplicity of character? There were some people whose instincts and emotions were better than their conscious thoughts but she did not think that he was one of them. His was a developing and progressing character and his conscious thoughts were apt to be too far in advance of his subconscious emotions. For example, might not those simple folk be right who felt that he was hankering after a more spacious theatre of action than he could find in South Africa? With his conscious mind, he realised that there were great issues to strive for there just as much as in Europe; but subconsciously was he not impatient with the day-to-day trivialities of South African politics?[21]

Indeed, he had not been Prime Minister many weeks before he began to rebel against the incessant petty calls which were made upon his energies and time. He began to fret at the deprivation from home life to which he seemed perpetually condemned. Of his first forty days in South Africa after an absence of over two years he had been able to spend no more than three at Doornkloof. His wife wrote to him to say that she hoped to see more of him in the life to come. But would she? He and she might be travelling, he reflected, to different destinations![22]

It was good that he could sometimes make a jest about his troubles and difficulties. He had no illusions about them; in the years immediately ahead he knew that they would become legion. For the past thirteen years, he reflected, he had been continuously in office and all the mistakes and misdoings of government for all those years would be visited upon him. Upon his head would be heaped the blame for the aftermath of war which South Africa would soon be suffering—the slump, the strife, the disillusionment. All this he saw clearly.[23] But if ever he had imagined that he could step aside and leave somebody else to bear the brunt of it, he had only to read the letter which Mrs Botha had written to him after her husband's death. It had always been Louis' wish, she said, that he would become Prime Minister and she felt as sure as Louis had done that God would give him the guidance and strength and wisdom to bear the burden.

I just want to say once more [she continued] many, many thanks for all your loving utterances in honour of the man who loved you so greatly during his lifetime. You never had a truer or more faithful friend and brother; and he thought the world of you and always said that you were the greatest man in our country, the coming man of the age. I thought I would tell you this—although I know you must often have realised what his thoughts and opinions were of you.

I cannot tell you all I wish for you—and I shall just end by saying again—God bless Jannie, Louis' faithful friend in storm and calm.[24]

There were doubtless many motives and forces which led and drove Smuts to become Prime Minister—ambition, duty, the habit of hard work, realism, idealism, love of power, love of country. To this list one compelling motive needs to be added: loyalty to Louis Botha.

REFERENCES

In the Smuts Archive, private letters are arranged in volumes with arabic numerals, official letters and memoranda in volumes with roman numerals, miscellaneous papers in boxes marked by capital letters. In referring to these series I have usually found it sufficient to cite the numbers or capital letters without further description.

CHAPTER I

1 Mrs Smuts wrote down the genealogical tables in a book, together with similar tables for her own family (Krige), which was as predominantly French in its descent as his was predominantly Dutch—a matter for mutual teasing.

2 The document granting permission to Michiel Cornelis Smuts (fourth in descent from the original *stamvader*) to occupy with his cattle 'de plaats genaamt Zoutfontein gelegen in 't Swartland' is dated 16 April 1786.

3 Cf. the books of Professor P. J. van der Merwe, particularly *Trek* (Kaapstad, 1945), a study of geographical mobility among the pioneering Boers. Van der Merwe's work is discussed by the present writer in the *Economic History Review* (1957), pp. 331–9. No social or economic history of the Swartland has been published but there is a short Church history, *Gedenkboek van die Nederduitse Gereformeerde Gemeente Swartland...1795–1945*, deur A. P. Smit (Kaapstad: Nasionale Pers, 1945).

4 The transfer was made to Michiel Nicolaas Smuts on 10 June 1818. Ongegund was a substantial property (3004 acres in 1856), but it was progressively subdivided and Smuts's grandfather held only a fourth share of it. I am greatly indebted to Mr V. C. H. R. Brereton, who in his profession as surveyor is familiar with Ongegund, for investigating its history from 1708 to the present day and writing a full account for my use.

5 The late Mr L. S. Amery told me that when he came to South Africa as correspondent of *The Times* on the eve of the Anglo-Boer War he had a lively interview with Mr J. A. Smuts, who had been elected to parliament the previous year (1898).

6 I have drawn particularly on the recollections of the late Boudewyn de V. ('Bool') Smuts, younger brother of General Smuts, and of Mrs T. C. Stoffberg, widow of Senator Stoffberg, formerly schoolmaster of Riebeeck West. Mrs Stoffberg communicated in Afrikaans a written statement entitled 'Jan Smuts', from which the above quotation was taken. An account of Mr (later Senator) T. C. Stoffberg was published in the *Rand Daily Mail*, 11 February 1931.

7 Vol. 23, no. 214 (26 July 1920); vol. 55, no. 178 (2 May 1937).

8 The descriptions in this paragraph of the life at Klipfontein are based chiefly on the recollections of General Smuts's younger brother, the late

562

Mr Boudewyn ('Bool') Smuts, who inherited the farm and lived on it until his death in 1953. I have been told (1960) that white children on some Cape farms still play with Coloured and Native children.

9 This paragraph, excepting the phrases in inverted commas, which are direct quotations from letters written in later years, represents an interpretation of evidence which, though indirect, scattered and retrospective, seems to the writer as clear as Wordsworth's *Prelude*, or W. H. Hudson's picture of his boyhood in *Far Away and Long Ago*.

10 'Misskien omdat hy so woorderyk was.' A possible translation of *woorderyk* is 'verbose', and perhaps Mev. Stoffberg chose this word with a slight touch of malice, because she could not in her later years give to Jan Smuts her unqualified approval.

11 Delicate (*tingerig*) not sickly (*sieklik*), his brother 'Bool' used to insist in later years in protest against the exaggerations of some biographers.

12 Interview of Dr Malan with the author, April 1951.

13 From the preface to *Libellus de Lacte* by Conrad Gesner, a German naturalist of the sixteenth century, quoted by Charles E. Raven in *Science and Religion* (Cambridge, 1953), p. 88.

14 Speeches, no. 271 *a*: the draft of a speech dated 30 May 1950. It was to have been a 'thank you' speech to Cape Town for its proposed present of a cottage on Table Mountain; but he fell ill before he could deliver it.

CHAPTER 2

1 These paragraphs are based on the memories of three of the Krige sisters—Minnie (Mrs Rust), Ella or 'Queenie' (Mrs Louw) and Isie (Mrs Smuts).

2 Vol. 60, no. 231 (to Mrs Gillett, 16 November 1939).

3 I am grateful to Mr Rodney Davenport, of the University of Cape Town, for writing me a study of Victoria College, and another of the Dutch Reformed Church, at that time.

4 Box *D*: Poems and Essays, 1886–9.

5 *Die Liberale Richting in Suid Afrika, 'n Kerk-Historiese Studie*, by T. N. Hanekom (Stellenbosch, 1951), pp. 432–4. Hanekom's list is for the year 1862, and he suggests that Rev. Boudewyn de Vries (Smuts's uncle) is to be classed with the pre-1850 type of liberals, i.e. the more moderate ones. His papers, including the full texts of twelve sermons, are in the Archives of the N.G. Kerk at Cape Town.

6 See especially F. S. Malan, *Ons Kerk en Professor du Plessis* (Cape Town, 1933).

7 OM TE STAAN VER ONS TAAL, ONS NASIE EN ONS LAND.

8 *The Life of Jan Hendrik Hofmeyr (Onze Jan)*, by J. H. Hofmeyr in collaboration with Hon. F. W. Reitz (Cape Town, 1913), *passim*.

9 *Ibid.* p. 599. Speech at Stellenbosch on 6 March 1905 on occasion of re-starting the Taalbond. In 1890 the original Taalbond had voted by 48 to 37 for High Dutch as against Cape Dutch; but Hofmeyr moved with the tide and in 1893 defined 'our language' as *both* 'the language of old Holland' *and* Cape Dutch (*The Life of Jan Hendrik Hofmeyr*, p. 446).

10 *Ibid.* p. 524.

11 He once said that he would 'rather see 5 Englishmen than 100 Cape Dutch' join the Africander Bond.

12 *The Life of Jan Hendrik Hofmeyr*, p. 236.

13 *Ibid.* p. 524.

14 *Niet de Wet, maar de Persoon, 't hoogste is.* The essay was printed in *Het Zuid-Afrikaansche Tijdschrift* (June 1899).

15 He did not complete this essay until after his arrival in England. He dated it July 1892 and wrote on it his name and address, 'J. C. Smuts, 13 Victoria Street, Cambridge'. In contemplation of publication, which never happened, he chose a nostalgic pseudonym: *Philomesembrias*, Lover of the South.

16 Vol. 12, no. 88 (J. X. Merriman to J.C.S., 10 January 1914).

17 Vol. 54, no. 263 (Carel J. van Zyl, J.P., to J.C.S., 3 March 1936).

18 Vol. 36, nos. 233 and 252 (to Mrs Gillett, 19 May 1926 and 13 October 1926).

19 *A Catholic View of Holism,* by Monsignor Kolbé, D.D., D.Litt. (London, 1928), p. 5.

CHAPTER 3

1 Vol. 46, no. 215; vol. 50, no. 199.

2 Vol. 36, no. 249.

3 *Portraits from Memory and Other Essays,* by Bertrand Russell (London, 1956), p. 68.

4 Vol. 63, no. 121 (22 October 1940).

5 Vol. 1, no. 10*a* and Box *S* (containing a notebook called CHIPS, in which he wrote the draft of his letter to Christ's).

6 Vol. 1, nos. 54–62.

7 Bergson's *L'Évolution Créatrice* was published in 1907; Lloyd Morgan's *Instinct and Experience* in 1912 and his *Emergent Evolution* in 1923; Alexander's *Space, Time and Deity* in 1920.

8 Vol. 23, no. 203 (J.C.S. to Ward, 8 December 1920).

9 Russell, *Portraits from Memory*, p. 40.

10 For the correspondence with Ethel Brown (or referring to her) see vol. 15, nos. 84–6; vol. 19, no. 42; vol. 25, no. 13; vol. 49, no. 248. I am particularly indebted to the late Chief Justice N. J. de Wet for giving me the clue to this correspondence, as well as for information about the 'Afghan Princes', the Presbyterian Church, Boat Race Day, and other persons or matters referred to in this chapter.

11 Vol. 15, no. 1; vol. 47, no. 51.

12 Vol. 45, no. 66; vol. 55, no. 205.

13 Letter to the author from O. R. Hobson (son of Professor Hobson), 2 January 1952, and from E. G. B. Atkinson (the professor's nephew), 21 November 1951 and 29 November 1951.

14 On Wolstenholme see the biographical note by Professor James Ward in the *Cambridge Review*, 21 January 1918. Ward had possession for a few weeks of Smuts's letters to Wolstenholme and then returned them to Wolstenholme's niece: unfortunately, it has proved impossible to track them further. Wolstenholme's letters to Smuts for the period 1902–17 have been preserved in the Smuts Archive and are the main basis for this brief sketch of his character and ideas.

15 Cf. vol. 4, no. 121, in which Wolstenholme expounds to J.C.S. his disbelief in the existence of moral values outside the subjective intelligence, and adds, 'Hence my utter repulsion to the very idea of a personal God'.

16 Vol. 2, no. 141.

17 Vol. 1, no. 45 (15 June 1894).

CHAPTER 4

1 Vol. 1, nos. 57, 58, 103. He kept an account of the reading he did at Strasbourg in a small black book.

2 The master copy, in the beautiful handwriting of Mrs Smuts, is preserved in the Smuts Archive.

3 Vol. 69, no. 261 (26 December 1942).

4 Smuts adapted the Baconian concept of *form* (really it was an Aristotelian concept, although Bacon would never have admitted it) to the study of personality. He held that in every man there exists a *form of the personality*, that is, a principle of development, from the *posse* of original endowment towards the *esse* which a man creates from this endowment under the pressure and stimulus of circumstances. He reaffirmed this theory in chapters x and xii of *Holism and Evolution* (London, 1926), using at times the identical phrases that he had used thirty-one years earlier in his book on Whitman.

5 Vol. 1, nos. 15, 105, 106. In recent years, inquiries have been addressed to the present writer by a number of publishers who profess themselves anxious to publish Smuts's book on Whitman.

6 'Een Reisje Naar de Transvaal. De Sluiting Der Driften en Andere Politieke Vragen' (26 October 1895).

7 Box *D*. Political Articles 1895/7. Manuscript entitled 'S.A. Nationality'.

8 *Diamond Fields Advertiser*, 30 October 1895, and *Not Without Honour. The Life and Writings of Olive Schreiner*, by Vera Buchanan-Gould (Hutchinson, 1949), pp. 153–4.

9 Vol. 1, no. 92.

10 Vol. 1, no. 73 (Olive Schreiner to J.C.S., 1 January 1896). The italics and exclamation marks are hers.

11 Box *D*. Political Articles 1895/7. *De Toekomstige Afrikaner Politiek* (date uncertain).

12 'Afrikaansche Toenadering', in *Ons Land*, 12 March 1896; cf. 'Adres aan de Paarl', 8 September 1896.

13 'Judgment' in *South African Telegraph*, 18 July 1896.

14 Box *D*. *The British Position in South Africa*, undated manuscript (about mid-1897).

15 Vol. 1, no. 74.

16 *The British Position in South Africa*.

17 Vol. 1, no. 60. In September 1896 he went to the Transvaal on an exploratory visit.

18 Vol. 1, no. 108 *b*. In his letter of application (4 March 1896) he said that his testimonials had been destroyed in the University Chambers and this was his excuse for quoting them from memory. The electoral Committee was a strong one (it included Chief Justice Sir Henry de Villiers and W. P. Schreiner). The application of the chosen candidate, A. J. McGregor, in contrast to that of Smuts, was contained in two lines (see *The History of the Faculty of Law, University of Cape Town, 1859–1959*, by D. V. Cowen: reprinted from *Acta Juridica*, 1959).

CHAPTER 5

1 J.C.S. to J. Hayman, 30 October 1898. He quoted Ulpian's famous definition of law as *ars boni et aequi*.

2 Vol. 1, no. 27. Smuts had been accused in the *Critic* of taking money from Rhodes and thought of bringing a libel action, but was dissuaded by J. H. Hofmeyr.

3 *Volkstem*, 23 May 1898; *Standard*, 27 May 1898; *Star*, 27 May 1898 and 2 June 1898; *The Milner Papers*, ed. Cecil Headlam (London, 1931), I, 336.

4 Vol. 1, no. 48.

5 *The Memoirs of Paul Kruger…told by himself* (trans.: London, 1902), II, 299.

6 I am particularly in debt to Professor D. V. Cowen for guidance through the extensive literature, both contemporary and retrospective, dealing with this affair, which he proposes to discuss in a chapter of a book now in preparation. Up to the present, the best published account is by Hon. B. H. Tindall in his introduction to Volume 2 of Kotzé's *Memoirs and Reminiscences* (Cape Town, 1934).

7 *Notulen van den EERSTEN VOLKSRAAD der Z.A. Republiek*, 25 February 1897. Cf. *Constitutionalism in the South African Republics*, by L. M. Thompson in Butterworth's *South African Law Review* (Durban), 1954, pp. 50 ff.

8 Headlam, *The Milner Papers*, I, 226, 231.

9 The quoted phrase is English in the original (Dutch) letter.

10 Vol. 99, no. 41.

11 An unsigned article 'Raad and Bench', which Professor D. V. Cowen considers very able, appeared in the *Cape Law Journal* of 1898 and may possibly have been written by Smuts.

12 The writer has had the privilege of reading in typescript *The Fall of Kruger's Republic*, by Professor J. S. Marais, now being published by the Clarendon Press.

13 *The South African League,* by M. F. Bitensky (M.A. thesis of the University of the Witwatersrand).

14 Headlam, *The Milner Papers,* I, 287.

15 This Credo was found among Milner's papers after his death and with Lady Milner's permission was published in *The Times,* 26 July 1925.

16 Headlam, *The Milner Papers,* I, 243–6.

17 *Ibid.* I, 246.

18 *Ibid.* I, 214, 217, 221–2, 226–9, 233, 236–7.

19 I am greatly indebted to Mr S. H. J. Krüger for making on my behalf a courageous reconnaissance of this material (which he was the first person ever to open) and for writing me a report on it. For the most part, Mr Krüger confined his research to letters and drafts in Smuts's handwriting.

20 *A Life in Reuters,* by Sir Roderick Jones (London, 1951), p. 33.

21 *The Standard and Diggers' News,* 29 September 1898.

22 *Ibid.* 18 November 1898; *Leader,* 14 June 1899.

23 Vol. I, no. 63; *Pretoria News,* 16 August 1899.

24 English in original.

25 Vol. XCVI, no. 5 (trans.).

26 Vol. I, no. 75.

27 Vol. I, no. 65.

28 Vol. I, no. 109.

29 Vol. I, nos. 67 and 110.

30 Headlam, *The Milner Papers,* I, 321–8, 331.

31 Vol. 20, no. 60: enclosure (trans.). Leyds wrote to Smuts on 23 January 1918 enclosing this letter of nearly twenty years before and asking his leave to print it in a collection of documents—not for immediate publication, since he did not wish to give a handle to German propaganda.

32 Headlam, *The Milner Papers,* I, 349–53.

33 Vol. I, no. 95.

34 Hofmeyr Papers, draft telegrams of 6 May 1899 and 10 May 1899 (or vol. 99, nos. 2 and 4).

35 Hofmeyr Papers (or vol. 99, no. 5) (trans.).

36 Vol. I, no. 29 (trans.).

37 Vol. I, no. 96.

38 Vol. I, no. 78.

39 Headlam, *The Milner Papers,* I, 378, 385, 396, 398, 400–3.

40 Vol. I, no. 96.

41 Vol. I, no. 110*a* (trans.).

42 All the quotations in the two paragraphs above are taken from Headlam, *The Milner Papers,* I, ch. XV.

43 Headlam explains (*op. cit.* p. 427) that in Milner's view 'henceforth the alternative lay between an appeal to arms and surrender by Great Britain of her position as Paramount Power in South Africa'.

44 *Ibid.* I, 439.

45 The quotations given below from the Hofmeyr–Smuts exchange of telegrams and letters are, unless otherwise stated, translated from the Dutch.

46 Vol. 1, no. 95.
47 Vol. 1, no. 111.
48 Vol. 99, no. 66.
49 Vol. 1, nos. 51, 68, 97.
50 Vol. 99, nos. 28–32.
51 Vol. 99, no. 33.
52 Headlam, *The Milner Papers*, 1, 457.
53 *Ibid.* 1, 465–6.
54 *Ibid.* 1, 468–9.
55 *Ibid.* 1, 471.
56 *Ibid.* 1, 474.
57 Vol. 99, nos. 34, 35.
58 Headlam, *The Milner Papers*, 1, 475.
59 Vol. 99, no. 37, 38.
60 Headlam, *The Milner Papers*, 1, 488–90. On 14 September, Smuts made a full report to his government on all his talks with Greene since late July, especially the crucial talks of 12–14 August. This report was published in the S.A.R. Greenbook, no. 10 of 1899. A translation was printed in the *Transvaal Leader* and reprinted in the British Blue book, Cd. 43 of 1900.
61 Hofmeyr Papers, vol. 11 (telegram: Steyn to Hofmeyr, 14 August 1899).
62 Vol. 1, no. 86.
63 Govt. Archives, vol. xcvi, no. 95; *The Military Position of the South African Republic in the Probable Event of War* (4 September 1899). The manuscript that survives is in Isie Smuts's handwriting. Quotations are from Dr Jean van der Poel's translation.
64 This story is told with spirit in Chapter x of *This War Business*, by Arthur Guy Enock (London, 1951). It follows faithfully a very full report which Enock wrote in Durban shortly after the outbreak of war. But the published chapter and the Durban manuscript both differ in one significant detail from the account that Enock wrote down on 3 October, immediately after the interview with Kruger and his advisers. In retrospect, Enock ascribed to Kruger the nostalgic reference to the England of John Bright; but the note that he made on the very day ascribes it to Smuts.

CHAPTER 6

1 *History of the War in South Africa, 1899–1902*, by Major-General Sir Frederick Maurice (London, 1906–10). Henceforth referred to as *Official History*.
2 *Memoirs of the Boer War*, of which four chapters only of the twenty-one which he planned were revised and copied (in Deneys Reitz's hand) although six others were written in a spirited first draft in his own hand. He wrote in English.
3 Govt. Archives, Pretoria, vol. xcvi, no. 95.

4 This is the English translation of the Dutch title, *Een Eeuw van Onrecht.*
I have followed the testimony of Mrs Smuts (see the Johannesburg *Star* of
8 March 1951) in describing how Smuts composed it. F. W. Reitz, as
State Secretary, issued it with departmental authority.

5 Vol. xcvi, no. 95 (quotations translated from the Dutch).

6 *A Life in Reuters*, p. 55.

7 Staats Procureur's Office, 221 (Smuts to Jacobsy, 6 December 1899).
I owe this reference to Mr G. H. J. Krüger.

8 Vol. 2, no. 105.

9 *Memoirs of the Boer War*, ch. 1.

10 Mrs Smuts showed them to the present writer when he and his wife
were staying with her at Irene in April 1951. At the same time she told
him many stories of that time, including the ones recounted above.

CHAPTER 7

1 *Memoirs of the Boer War*, chs. II and III.

2 Cf. the British Official History (*History of the War in South Africa*, by
Major-General Sir Frederick Maurice, London, 1906–10), IV, 128. 'In
ordinary warfare to break up the enemy is a victory; in South Africa it
usually only doubled the difficulty of subduing him.'

3 L. S. Amery in *The Times History of the South African War*, V, 77.

4 Draft for the preface to *Memoirs of the Boer War.*

5 *Memoirs of the Boer War*, ch. VII.

6 Vol. xcvi, no. 171. *Buitengewone Staats-Courant, Zuid-Afrikaansche
Republiek,* 17 July 1900.

7 *Memoirs of the Boer War*, ch. III.

8 The account of the action at Nooitgedacht (*Memoirs of the Boer War*,
ch. IX) is a superb battle piece, as vivid and exciting as anything published
by de Wet or Reitz or any of the other memoirists, and possessing besides the
wider strategic and human vistas which the others missed. The account of
the ceremony on Dingaan's Day is in ch. X. Smuts got no further than that
in drafting his book.

9 Cf. Government Archives, xcvi, no. 28.

10 Vol. xcvi, no. 183 *a*.

11 Vol. xcvi, nos. 185, 188, 192, 193, 295, 298.

12 Vol. 2, no. 106 *a*.

13 Vol. xcvi, no. 301. Smuts's claims are substantially endorsed in
Official History, IV, 128.

14 Vol. xcvi, no. 186.

15 Vol. xcvi, no. 304. A more immediate advantage of declaring Cape
independence would be to give the 'Colonial Rebels' legal military
status. Cf. *Official History*, IV, 75.

16 *De wonderlijke combinatie van bidderij en buiterij door zijn legermacht geprak-
tiseerd* (vol. 2, no. 107 *a*, Smuts to N. J. de Wet, 28 February 1901). The
above narrative is based on the correspondence of Smuts between

December 1900 and February 1901 with de la Rey, Botha, General de Wet and N. J. de Wet. Vol. xcvi, nos. 186, 298, 299, 302, 304, 306, 307, 308; vol. 2, nos. 107, 107 *a*.

17 *Official History*, iv, 91.
18 Cd. 663 of 1901, p. 10.
19 Vol. 9, no. 4.
20 Vol. 2, no. 104.
21 *Correspondentie, 1900–1902*, by W. J. Leyds, i, 248–54. The Deputation, consisting of A. Fischer, C. H. Wessels, and A. D. W. Wolmarans had gone to Europe in March 1900.
22 Vol. 2, no. 29.

CHAPTER 8

1 *Official History*, iv, 60.
2 *Ibid.* iv, 349–50.
3 Hely-Hutchinson to Chamberlain, 2 July 1901, 24 July 1901, 3 October 1901. C.O. Confidential Print: *African (South) No. 650. Papers (1901) Relating to South Africa.* Serial nos. 25, 27, 40.
4 *Ibid.* no. 217. Milner to Chamberlain, 2 September 1901.
5 *My Picture Gallery, 1886–1901*, by Viscountess Milner (London, 1951), p. 238.
6 *Official History*, iv, 268.
7 C.O. 48/560: Cape no. 20571. Hely-Hutchinson to Chamberlain, 6 May 1902, enclosing two captured and translated Reports by Smuts, (1) the Expedition of the Transvaalers to the Cape Colony; (2) report regarding the situation in Cape Colony. The minuting and correspondence quoted above are on Report no. 1. This report was published in the original Dutch in Holland.
8 *Official History*, iv, 268.
9 Vol. xcvi, no. 328. Copies of these two reports and some other documents were captured and translated by the British and are to be found among papers of the Colonial Office and the War Office: 32/877, files 8271, 8854.
10 As regards the Transvaalers, he had authority already, pending de la Rey's arrival (which never took place). As regards the Free Staters, a letter of General C. R. de Wet dated 8 February 1902 gave him the necessary authority in succession to Comdt. Kritzinger, recently reported dead (*Official History*, iv, appendix 3 (pp. 579–80)).
11 Comdt. J. S. Allemann and other officers slipped through very quickly to Holland early in 1902, carrying important papers (Leyds, *Correspondentie*, ii, 197f.).
12 Vol. xcvi, no. 334. 'Algemene Order van de Legermacht onder bevel van Ass. Comd. Genl. Smuts in de Kaap Col.'
13 Some of the depositions were taken down by Smuts's secretary, P. S. Krige, who protested many years later when H. C. Armstrong repeated the legendary version of this affair in his book *Grey Steel*. (Deneys

Reitz had already popularised the version, but P. S. Krige told the writer in April 1954 that Reitz was on duty elsewhere in the Cape at the time of the trial.) Anyway, the records of the *Military Court held at Aties in the case of the State* v. *Lambert Colyn* (Govt. Archives, S.A.R. (1902), vol. CI, notebook C, doc. 41) are clear beyond dispute.

14 Vol. CII, no. 6. Proclamation of 2 January 1902.

15 Leyds, *Correspondentie, 1900–1902,* II, 207–11. A copy was captured by the British and their translation is in W.O. 32/878.

16 *Nouveau Rapport de Général J. C. Smuts*...Mis en vente par le Comité pour l'Indépendance des Boers...(47 Rue Taitbout, Paris). The British Ambassador in Paris, Sir Edmund Monson, enclosed the pamphlet with some terse comment in a despatch of 30 May 1902 (F.O .Print no. 62, Africa).

17 Vol. 2, no. 108 (4 January 1902).

18 C.O. 48/555–61: Governor's despatches enclosing weekly intelligence reports. (To be found also in Royal United Services Institution, A 3. Intelligence Papers South Africa, 1901–2.)

19 Vol. CI, no. 36. Notebook A, containing copies of letters (see especially nos. 32–6) written by General Smuts.

20 C.O. 417/361. Letter of D.M.I., Pretoria, 20 April 1902. On the British side the Concordia affair is fully documented in W.O. 32/887, Files 288, 8806, 9037 (evidence and proceedings of a Court of Enquiry) and 9450.

CHAPTER 9

1 Royal United Services Institution, A 5, p. 116.

2 Vol. 2, nos. 109, 141, 145.

3 R.U.S., A 3, p. 342.

4 Among the Smuts papers are three diaries kept by men of the commando during the Cape Colony campaign.

5 Vol. 1, nos. 8–10; vol. 2, nos. 20–4.

6 *The Boer's Love of his Country* (unpublished).

7 Vol. 99, no. 167 (4 January 1902) and enclosure.

8 *The Peace Negotiations between Briton and Boer in South Africa* (London, 1912). Translation from Dutch original. Kestell was chaplain to Steyn and de Wet, van Velden was formerly minute writer to the Volksraad of the S.A.R. Other accounts are given by Kestell, *Through Shot and Flame* (London, 1903), and de Wet, *The Three Years' War* (London, 1902). The negotiations will be discussed by Professor G. H. L. Le May in a chapter, which I have had the privilege of reading, of his forthcoming book, *British Policy and Afrikaaner Nationalism, 1899–1910.*

9 Hertzog pointed out that the governments would be punishable under Roman-Dutch law if they did so 'meddle'. Moreover, Wet no. 13, 1897, of the O.F.S., and Wet no. 16, 1898, of the S.A.R., contained a direct legislative prohibition against either Republic making a separate peace.

10 There was no verbatim report of this first conference at Pretoria; but an account of its proceedings was dictated immediately afterwards to the Rev. J. D. Kestell by General Hertzog (who also dictated some personal impressions).

11 General Hertzog, in dictating the record to the Rev. J. D. Kestell (*Peace Negotiations*, p. 40), added an interpretation of his own—that the governments assumed that 'the People to a man would say: "We want to retain our Independence and if England does not agree to that, we shall go on with the war."' If some of the leaders nourished this hope, it was a dangerous illusion.

12 *Commando*, ch. xxvi.

13 I have called this book 'the surrender notebook' because it contains various notes of conversations, headings for speeches, quotations, etc., etc. that he wrote down during the Vereeniging period. See *The Smuts Papers* (Creighton Lecture for 1955, Athlone Press).

14 Vol. 2, no. 109.

15 *Through Shot and Flame*, p. 318.

16 Vol. 2, no. 109 *a*.

17 See *Adventure*, by J. E. B. Seeley (London, 1930), p. 91. I owe this reference to Professor G. H. L. Le May.

18 The complete manuscript of the speech survives among his papers but it is unlikely that he wrote it out in advance. The probability is that van Velden, in preparation for the publication of *The Peace Negotiations between Briton and Boer in South Africa*, showed Smuts the report of the speech which he had made from his shorthand notes. On this basis Smuts wrote out the version which, with a few unimportant changes, was published.

19 The very last entry notes the title of a recently published book on Personality.

CHAPTER 10

1 Vol. 2, no. 110.

2 Vol. 2, no. 110 *a*: 26 June 1902. This letter was the first that he ever wrote to her in Afrikaans—the language which they used invariably from this time on in their correspondence with each other.

3 Vol. 2, nos. 116 and 124.

4 Vol. 3, nos. 111, 114, 118.

5 Vol. 2, nos. 82–96.

6 Letters of 20 August 1905 and 18 November 1905 from Margaret Clark to her mother. Contained in M. C. Gillett's *Narrative of Going to South Africa 1905–1907* (Box *X*). The letters and papers, to be donated to the Smuts Archive by Mrs Gillett (*née* Clark), are a wonderfully rich collection, of which extensive use will be made throughout this biography.

7 The Rand Water Board Case. See vol. 3, no. 101.

8 See *Jan Christian Smuts*, by his son J. C. Smuts (Cassell, 1952), p. 121.

9 Professor James Ward of Cambridge saw these letters after Wolstenholme's death and perhaps a slight hope may be cherished even now of their eventual reappearance.

10 It became his custom to settle his book-purchase account with Wolstenholme about twice a year.

11 Vol. 2, nos. 141–6, vol. 3, nos. 117–22; vol. 4, nos. 117–26.

12 Headlam, *The Milner Papers*, II, 407.

13 *Ibid.* II, 503. Address to the Navy League at Johannesburg, 28 May 1904.

14 Headlam, *The Milner Papers*, II, 242.

15 Vol. 3, no. 94.

16 Headlam, *The Milner Papers*, II, 243.

17 Cd. 1163, p. 147, quoted in *The First Phase of Hertzogism*, by A. E. G. Trollip, ch. 1 (M.A. Thesis, University of the Witwatersrand).

18 Vol. 3, no. 59.

19 Article 6.

20 C.O. 241/41. Tel. 39233/5, Chamberlain to Milner, 26 September 1902. Half a century later, Lord Brand told the present writer that he and some other members of the Kindergarten once asked the Registrar of Deeds to dinner in mistake for the ex-State Attorney, and from that time always referred to him as 'the other Mr Smuts'.

21 *Emily Hobhouse*, A Memoir compiled by A. Ruth Fry (London, 1929).

22 For a useful review of the history of the camps see *Imperial Policy and South Africa, 1902–10*, by G. B. Pyrah (Oxford, 1955), appendix II. Mr Pyrah's estimate of total deaths in the camps is 26,000: others give lower estimates.

23 Fry, *Emily Hobhouse*, p. 290. (The more exact quotation from Marcus Aurelius would have been 'Dear City of Zeus'.)

24 Vol. 3, nos. 26–8.

25 Vol. 3, no. 83.

26 Vol. 3, nos. 84, 85, 88, 91.

27 Vol. 3, no. 32 (29 May 1903).

28 Vol. 3, nos. 88 (from J.C.S.) and 29 (from E.H.).

29 Vol. 3, no. 88.

30 Vol. 3, no. 92.

31 Vol. 3, no. 98.

32 Vol. 2, no. 218.

33 Vol. 2, no. 44 *a*.

34 Vol. 2, no. 131.

35 *Ibid.*

36 Vol. 3, no. 96 (17 July 1904).

37 Margaret Clark to her mother (5 March 1905).

38 Vol. 2, no. 116 (26 July 1902) and no. 29, for Graham's convincing reply.

39 Vol. 2, nos. 59–62. There were two interviews.

40 C.O. print: *African (South no. 681)*, no. 321: agreed minutes of meeting (11 December 1902).

41 Vol. 2, no. 12. The copy of the letter in the Smuts papers is marked 'Mr Hobhouse', but it was Leonard Courtney who had it published (as Smuts intended) in the English press.

42 Vol. 2, nos. 7–9, 68–71. The main letters between Milner and the Boer leaders were published by mutual agreement (*The Leader*, special edition, 13 February).

43 Vol. 2, no. 11 (1 June 1953).

44 Printed broadsheets, containing the heads of agreement, with some differences of emphasis, were issued simultaneously by the two parties in the two languages.

45 Vol. 3, no. 98.

46 Vol. 3, no. 40.

47 Vol. 3, no. 53. Headlam, *The Milner Papers*, II, 541–2.

48 Vol. 2, no. 124 (2 August 1902).

49 Vol. 2, nos. 56, 58, 130.

50 Vol. 2, no. 134; vol. 3, nos. 45, 46, 58, 82, 87.

51 Vol. 3, no. 57.

52 Vol. 3, no. 93.

53 Vol. 3, no. 48 (4 June 1904).

54 Vol. 3, no. 48.

55 Vol. 3, no. 53.

CHAPTER II

1 Box *G*, no. 1: 15 quarto pages of double-spaced typescript with an additional page of figures.

2 Vol. 4, no. 84.

3 From the Diary of Helen P. Bright Clark (Mrs W. S. Clark).

4 Vol. 4, no. 117.

5 Vol. 4, no. 102.

6 Vol. 4, no. 13 (1 February 1906).

7 Vol. 4, no. 102.

8 *Glasgow High School Magazine. Campbell-Bannerman Centenary* (June 1948).

9 *Ibid.*

10 Vol. 4, no. 30; vol. 6, nos. 10 and 102.

11 See Lord Riddell, *More Pages from My Diary* (London, 1934), p. 144, for Lloyd George's account of the Cabinet meeting.

12 Vol. 4, no. 103.

13 Vol. 4, nos. 104, 111.

14 *Memo. of Points in reference to the Transvaal Constitution*, para. 1, and Smuts to W. T. Stead, 18 March 1907, in Joseph O. Baylen, 'Notes and Documents: A Letter on the Hopes of Smuts', *The Journal of Negro History*, XVI (January 1956), 69–70.

15 Vol. 4, no. 53.

16 Vol. 4, no. 88.

17 Vol. 4, no. 54.

18 Vol. 4, no. 55.

19 Vol. 4, no. 55 (30 March 1906).

20 Vol. 4, nos. 56, 91, 107.

21 Vol. 4, no. 56.
22 Vol. 4, nos. 24, 91.
23 Vol. 4, no. 118.
24 Vol. 4, nos. 91, 92, 110, 111.
25 Vol. 4, nos. 60, 61, 66, 67.
26 Vol. 4, nos. 26, 27. No report from the Commission was published.
27 Vol. 4, no. 94.
28 Vol. 4, nos. 96, 113; vol. 5, no. 54.
29 Vol. 5, no. 56.

CHAPTER 12

1 Vol. 5, no. 55.
2 See, for example, Box *N*, Political Notes by J.C.S. 1899–1950, no. 50.
3 Vol. 11, no. 27.
4 Vol. 4, no. 95 *a*.
5 Vol. 5, nos. 25, 26, 28, 29, 57.
6 *Transvaal Legislative Assembly Debates*, 1907, col. 2517.
7 *Ibid.* col. 1305 (Governor's speech, 21 March 1907). When the government took office (March 1907) the number of Africans in the mines was 81,000: at Union (August 1910) it was 185,000.
8 Vol. 5, nos. 28, 39, 40, 58; vol. 6, nos. 43–5.
9 Vol. 6, nos. 62, 64.
10 Vol. 5, nos. 20, 62, 64.
11 *Transvaal Legislative Assembly Debates*, 1907, col. 362.
12 See *Education in South Africa 1652–1921*, by E. G. Malherbe (Cape Town, 1925), p. 336.
13 Vol. 99, no. 47.
14 Vol. 99, no. 56. Smuts told Fischer (16 June 1907) that the best C.N.O. practice was now 'transplanted' into the State system.
15 Vol. 6, nos. 10, 102.

CHAPTER 13

1 See *The Selborne Memorandum*, ed. Basil Williams (Oxford University Press, 1925) and *The Unification of South Africa*, by L. M. Thompson (Clarendon Press, 1960), ch. 11. Thanks to Professor Thompson's book, which is indispensable for the student of South African history and politics, this chapter can be kept reasonably short.
2 Vol. 6, no. 102.
3 Vol. 3, no. 93.
4 Vol. 4, nos. 88, 96, 100.
5 Merriman to Steyn, 27 October 1905, quoted in Thompson, *The Unification of South Africa*, p. 73.
6 Vol. 4, no. 69 (30 December 1906).
7 Vol. 5, no. 54 (25 January 1907).
8 Vol. 5, nos. 31, 33.

9   Vol. 5, nos. 60, 61 (15 July 1907 and 1 August 1907).
10   Vol. 5, no. 35 (3 October 1907).
11   Vol. 5, no. 62 (28 September 1907).
12   Vol. 6, no. 87, J.C.S. to J.X.M. (18 February 1908). He wrote in similar terms to Steyn. For the replies, see nos. 26 and 82.
13   Vol. 6, no. 88.
14   Vol. 6, nos. 27–9.
15   *Transvaal Legislative Assembly Debates,* 23 June 1908, cols. 180–1, quoted in Thompson, *The Unification of South Africa.*
16   Vol. 6, no. 93.
17   Vol. 6, no. 26 (24 February 1908).
18   Vol. 6, nos. 72 *a,* 74, 76, 77.
19   Vol. 6, no. 73.
20   Vol. 6, no. 93 (13 July 1908).
21   Vol. 6, no. 59 (2 August 1908).
22   Vol. 6, nos. 35 and 36.
23   Vol. 6, no. 99 (2 October 1908).
24   Vol. 6, no. 99.
25   See, for example, *Cape Times,* 18 May 1955 and 20 June 1955, letters from Arthur Barlow and others.
26   See Thompson, *The Unification of South Africa,* pp. 133–4. It was R. H. Brand who had convinced Smuts that P.R. would be of great practical value in mitigating 'racial' cleavage.
27   Vol. 6, no. 91 (10 June 1908).
28   *Ibid.*
29   Vol. 6, no. 104.
30   Vol. 6, no. 96 (29 August 1908) and enclosure.
31   Vol. CVI, nos. 15, 16, 18.
32   The analysis of these drafts—and indeed of all the subsequent drafts, resolutions, debates and proceedings from which the constitution of the Union emerged—will be found in Professor Thompson's book, whose existence has made possible the perfect division of labour between biographer and historian: so at least the present writer believes.
33   Vol. 6, no. 5 (de Villiers) and no. 84 (Steyn).
34   Vol. 6, no. 32.
35   Vol. 7, no. 90.
36   Box *D.* This fragment is from one unfinished article called 'The Closer Union of the South African Colonies'.
37   See, for example, *Resolutions of the South African Races Committee in reference to the draft South Africa Constitution Bill,* (Smuts Papers, vol. 7, no. 99).
38   Vol. 7, nos. 58, 59.
39   See Thompson, *The Unification of South Africa,* pp. 316–17.
40   *The Age of the Generals,* by D. W. Krüger (Dagbreek Book Store, 1958), p. 10.
41   Vol. 7, no. 23.

CHAPTER 14

1 Professor Thompson (*The Unification of South Africa*, ch. 8), has given a careful account of South African politics from the South Africa Act to the first Union Parliament, thus making possible brevity here.

2 Vol. 7, nos. 44, 105; vol. 8, nos. 53, 54, 59, 60, 62, 101, 103, 104 (letters from or to Hyslop, Steyn, Malan, Merriman).

3 Vol. 8, nos. 66, 108.

4 Botha was opposed in Pretoria East by Sir Percy Fitzpatrick, despite an attempt by Smuts to persuade both men to call off their contest (Box *N*: Political Notes by J. C. Smuts, 1899–1950, no. 48).

5 Vol. 8, no. 118.

6 Quoted Thompson, *The Unification of South Africa*, p. 32, note 73.

7 *Ibid.* p. 232, note 68.

8 Vol. 7, no. 32, and see p. 87 above for an earlier opinion of Fitzpatrick on Smuts.

9 Vol. 8, no. 113 and Thompson, *The Unification of South Africa*, p. 455.

10 *Not Heaven Itself*, by M. Nathan (Durban, 1946), p. 219. Manfred Nathan was a well-known lawyer who had had his office in the same building as Smuts and de Villiers before the Anglo-Boer War.

11 I owe to Professor G. H. L. Le May a transcript of this letter which is in the uncatalogued Bryce Papers in the Bodleian.

12 Vol. 11, no. 76; vol. 12, nos. 117, 134.

13 Vol. 12, nos. 113, 134.

14 Vol. 7, no. 108.

15 Vol. 69, no. 233 and vol. 77, no. 255, to Mrs Gillett (7 May 1942 and 22 July 1945).

16 Mrs Gillett to the author, 28 November 1958.

17 Vol. 11, no. 37.

18 Vol. 9, no. 29.

19 Vol. 8, no. 47.

20 Vol. 11, no. 20.

21 Vol. 9, no. 36, vol. 11, no. 20.

22 Vol. 8, no. 41; vol. 9, nos. 24 and 26; vol. 11, no. 27.

23 Vol. 11, nos. 21, 27, 34.

24 Vol. 9, nos. 34, 36; vol. 10, no. 32; vol. 12, no. 69.

25 Vol. 9, nos. 36, 42; vol. 11, no. 48.

26 Vol. 6, no. 11; vol. 7, no. 125; vol. 8, no. 27; vol. 11, no. 12.

CHAPTER 15

1 Vol. 9, no. 97.

2 Vol. 10, nos. 104, 107.

3 Vol. 10, no. 83. Nearly all the letters from Smuts to Wolstenholme have been lost, but by a lucky chance this letter of 29 May 1912 has been preserved, together with one or two others of the same period.

4 *Emergent Evolution*, by C. Lloyd Morgan (London, 1923), p. 298 and *passim*.

5 Vol. 10, no. 104.

6 Vol. 10, no. 108.

7 See Lloyd Morgan, *Emergent Evolution*, p. 11. See also *The Listener*, January 1959, for a vivid picture of 'Alexander and his Ideas', by Professor Dorothy Emmet.

8 Vol. 36, no. 30 *a*.

9 *Holism and Evolution* (London, 1926) was for the most part philosophy of science; whereas the *Inquiry into the Whole* had been both philosophy of science and philosophy of religion, with a great deal else in between. For many years after *Holism and Evolution* appeared, Smuts continued to hope that somehow or other he would find the time to produce a second volume, expounding the moral, political and religious significance of holism.

10 K. R. Popper, *The Open Society and its Enemies* (Routledge and Kegan Paul, 3rd ed., 1956), I, 80.

CHAPTER 16

1 See, for example, *South African Nationalism or British Holism*, by A. C. Cilliers (Stellenbosch, 1938).

2 See his *Climate and Man in Southern Africa* (Paper to the S.A. Association for the Advancement of Science, 1930).

3 See, for example, *The History of Native Policy in South Africa* by E. H. Brookes (Cape Town, 1924), *passim*. In his later writings, the author returned to a more robust liberal philosophy.

4 On the evidence of Mrs Gillett (letter to the author, 22 July 1958) Smuts used to say that 'the Natives learnt more of our civilisation in working together with us than in being sheltered and taught civilisation separately'.

5 The literature is immense. In preparing the rapid sketch which follows, I have used chiefly my own *Survey of British Commonwealth Affairs*, vol. II, part 2. I have also been stimulated by Professor C. R. Lovell's article, 'Afrikaner Nationalism and Apartheid' (*American Historical Review*, January 1956).

6 See 'Trek' by W. K. Hancock (*Economic History Review*, 2nd ser., vol. X, no. 3, 1958) and the works of P. J. van der Merwe there discussed.

7 Cd. 2399 of 1905.

8 *Ibid.* p. 25.

9 *Ibid.* p. 67.

10 *Ibid.* p. 69.

11 Vol. 6, no. 61, Selborne to Smuts, 9 January 1908, enclosing 'Notes on a Suggested Policy towards Coloured People and Natives'.

12 See *The Inner History of the National Convention* by Sir Edgar H. Walton (Cape Town, 1912), pp. 147–8. Lord Selborne proposed that every non-European who had reached the age of 31 and proved his possession of the civilisation qualification before an impartial tribunal should be given a vote equal in value to one-tenth the vote of a European citizen. His son on reaching the age of 30 and similarly possessing the civilisation qualification would receive a vote equal in value to one-ninth the vote of a European...and so on, until in the tenth generation a non-European might attain at the age of 21 a vote of full value.

13 Act no. 27 of 1913. See *Survey of British Commonwealth Affairs*, vol. II, part 2, 72 ff.

14 *Transvaal Leader*, 4 October 1910.

15 In 1917, in a speech in London, Smuts discussed the Native question in very general terms. See p. 558 above.

16 *Transvaal Leader*, 11 August 1910.

17 Vol. 7, no. 128 (14 May 1909).

18 The ensuing narrative is based chiefly upon the following sources: (*a*) On Gandhi's side, his two autobiographical books, *Satyagraha in South Africa* (Madras, 1928) and *My Experiments with Truth* (2nd ed., Ahmedabad, 1940), together with material in *Mahatma*, by D. W. Tendulkar (vol. I, Bombay, 1951) and in other biographies; (*b*) on Smuts's side, material in the Smuts Archive; (*c*) printed official material, especially in the following British Blue-books running from 1904 to 1914: Cd. 2239, 3308, 3387, 3982, 4327, 4584, 5363, 5579, 6283, 6940, 7111, 7265; (*d*) documents in the Public Record Office, which have recently become open for research up to 1910. I am indebted to Mrs P. Inman, who used this new evidence for checking my draft. She tells me that it only occasionally adds anything of significance to the voluminous material contained in the Blue-books.

Space is lacking in the present chapter to discuss in full detail all the intricacies of the Gandhi–Smuts controversies. I hope that Mrs Inman may be persuaded to publish an article discussing them further.

I should add that the present chapter corrects one or two inaccuracies which I committed in my study of non-violence, contained in *War and Peace in this Century* (Cambridge, 1961).

19 *My Experiments with Truth*, pp. 323 ff.

20 *Ibid.* p. 212.

21 *Ibid.* p. 184.

22 These facts are taken from the *Report of the Committee on Emigration to the Colonies and Protectorates*, Cd. 5192 of 1910.

23 *My Experiments with Truth*, p. 194.

24 *Papers relating to the grievances of Her Majesty's Indian Subjects in the South African Republic*, C. 7911 of 1895. Cf. C. 7946 of 1896.

25 *My Experiments with Truth*, p. 225.

26 *Ibid.* p. 235.

27 Cd. 2239 of 1904, p. 21 (from a memorial of the British Indian Association of Johannesburg).

28 *Ibid.* p. 28, despatch of the Lieutenant-Governor of the Transvaal (Sir Arthur Lawley), 13 April 1904. Cf. Cd. 3308, no. 3, despatch of Lord Selborne, 9 June 1906. At this time the number of Indians in the Transvaal was somewhere between 10,000 and 13,000 (the census returns giving the lower, the permit returns the higher figures).

29 *Satyagraha in South Africa,* p. 100 and Cd. 3308 of 1907, especially pp. 17–18. Women did not have to register, although this had been originally proposed.

30 *Satyagraha,* p. 102.

31 *My Experiments with Truth,* p. 389 and *Satyagraha,* p. 109.

32 Act no. 2 of 1907. The bill was rushed through all its stages at a single sitting on 21 March 1907. In fairness to Lord Elgin it should perhaps be said that, while assuring Botha that the Act would not be disallowed, he asked him to look into the question of its operation, with a view to removing some objectionable features. See Cd. 3887, no. 7; C.O. 291/116, no. 13940; C.O. 291/123.

33 Vol. 5, no. 46 (30 November 1907). Cf. no. 48 (9 December 1907). Some Indian grievances (e.g. fingerprinting) could have been met by amending the administrative regulations, while leaving intact the Act itself.

34 Vol. 5, no. 52 (6 December 1907); vol. 6, nos. 67a (17 January 1908), 68 (24 January 1908); Cd. 4327 of 1908, no. 3.

35 Vol. 6, no. 25 (13 January 1908).

36 *Satyagraha,* p. 149.

37 *Legislation Affecting Asiatics in the Transvaal,* no. 3 of Cd. 3982 and no. 16 of Cd. 4327. Gandhi's co-signatories were Leung-Quinn (representing the Chinese) and T. Naidoo.

38 *Ibid.* no. 16.

39 Cd. 4327, p. 15.

40 No. 1 of Cd. 4584. Gandhi here refers to a second meeting between him and Smuts on 3 February. He also refers to a meeting of Indian leaders with the Registrar of Asiatics who, he says, repeated the promise to repeal the Act: he says that he is producing affidavits in support of this statement. A search has been made in the P.R.O. for these affidavits; but without result.

41 No. 32 of Cd. 4584.

42 C.O. 291/131. I am indebted for this reference to Mrs Inman.

43 *Satyagraha,* ch. xxv: *Transvaal Legislative Assembly Debates,* 1908, cols. 1869ff.: nos. 11, 16, 23 of Cd. 4327. The Indian objections to the Immigration Act were on the ground of principle, namely that the doors of the Transvaal were bolted against the entry of educated Indians, thereby demonstrating that the bar to entry was racial.

44 *My Experiments with Truth,* p. 78.

45 Cd. 4327, p. 38.

46 *Satyagraha,* pp. 208–9.

47 *Ibid.* p. 208.

48 *Ibid.* p. 291.

49 *Ibid.* p. 218.

50 Vol. 7, no. 100.

51 Cd. 5363 of 1910, nos. 42, 64, 115, and C.O. 291/141, no. 27075. The Transvaal Government was prepared to accede to two of the Indian demands: (*a*) To repeal Act 2 of 1907; (*b*) to admit into the Transvaal a limited number of educated Asians under permanent certificates instead of temporary ones. But it refused a third demand—(*c*) to treat Asian immigrants under the Act like any other immigrants and limit their total number only by administrative means.

Because of the failure to agree on the third point, the Government, contrary to the advice of Lord Crewe, took no action on the first two points.

52 Cd. 5579; Cd. 6283, nos. 2, 15, 17; Cd. 7285, p. 16, all referring to an attempt to regulate immigration by Union legislation.

53 Act no. 22 of 1913. Act to Consolidate and Amend the Laws in force in the various Provinces of the Union relating to Prohibited Immigrants, to Provide for the Establishment of a Union Immigration Department, to regulate Immigration into the Union or any Province Thereof, and to Provide for the Removal Therefrom of Undesirable Persons. Cf. note 52 above, giving references to earlier attempts by Smuts to legislate in the same sense.

54 See Cd. 7111 of 1913, *Correspondence relating to the Immigrants Regulation Acts*, especially no. 46, Enclosures 7 and 55, for the statements of Botha and Smuts. For Gokhale's statements see *Johannesburg Star*, 1 November 1913, and *The Indian Review*, November 1913, p. 925 (I owe this reference to Mr S. R. Mehrotra). Cf. *Satyagraha*, p. 276. *The Report of the Indian Enquiry Commission* (U.G. 16 of 1914, p. 14) disposed of the controversy as follows: '...it is sufficient for our purpose that the Indians have been led to believe that such a promise had been made, and that on failure to produce the expected legislation there was considerable feeling on their part against the government'. It is curious that there is no reference at all to the £3 tax in a hasty but systematic enumeration of the items of discussion which Smuts wrote down in pencil on Prime Minister's Office notepaper under the heading 'Gokhale Nov. 14'. Perhaps it was his agenda for the discussion, not his summary of it. See Box *N*, Political Notes by J. C. Smuts 1899–1950, no. 52*a*.

55 *Satyagraha*, p. 273. The complicated legal background of the Searle judgment, which was not so arbitrary as the Indians believed, is considered in the *Report of the Indian Enquiry Commission*, pp. 18–24.

56 *Satyagraha*, p. 321.

57 Vol. 11, no. 13 (Gladstone to Smuts, 9 December 1913).

58 Vol. 11, no. 37 (29 December 1913).

59 Act no. 22 of 1914. Act to make provision for the redress of certain grievances and the removal of certain disabilities of his Majesty's Indian Subjects in the Union and other matters incidental thereto. Cf. Cd. 7644 of 1914, *Correspondence relating to Indian Relief Act*.

60 Vol. 12, no. 139. To Sir Benjamin Robertson (21 August 1914).

61 *Indian Review*, October 1919, p. 714.

62 Tendulkar, *Mahatma*, III, 117.

63 *Fullness of Days*, by the Earl of Halifax (London, 1957), p. 148.

64   *Mahatma Gandhi. Essays and Reflections on his Life and Work presented to him on his seventieth birthday, 2 October 1939,* ed. S. Radhakrishnan (London, 1939).
65   Vol. 88, no. 217 (Henry Cooper to Mr C. Shulka, 11 December 1948).

CHAPTER 17

1   Vol. 9, no. 3.
2   Vol. 9, no. 4.
3   Vol. 9, no. 5.
4   Cd. 5745 of 1911, pp. 97 ff.
5   *The Dominions and Diplomacy,* by A. G. Dewey (Longmans, 1929), I, 235, quoting a speech of 6 February 1900.
6   Cd. 4948 of 1909, pp. 29, 38.
7   Vol. 9, nos. 4 and 6.
8   Vol. 10, no. 92.
9   Vol. 10, no. 7.
10   Box *D*.
11   *Adres aan de Paarl* reported in *Ons Land,* 2 September 1896.
12   Vol. 3, no. 59. The letter, which is undated, probably belongs to 1904.
13   Vol. 99, no. 63. To Mrs Steyn (24 August 1912).
14   Vol. 3, no. 59.
15   *The Leader,* 10 February 1910.
16   Vol. 11, no. 81.
17   Vol. 11, no. 3.
18   Box *H*, no. 3. The figures were inserted in his manuscript in another hand. As elsewhere, I have used the translation of Dr Jean van der Poel.
19   *S. P. Bunting. A Political Biography,* by Edward Roux (Cape Town, 1944), p. 50.
20   *Loc. cit.* See also *Comrade Bill. The Life and Times of W. H. Andrews, Workers' Leader,* by R. K. Cope (Cape Town, 1945[?]). Cope defends this slogan as historically necessary from the revolutionary point of view.
21   Vol. 11, no. 38.
22   Vol. 12, no. 88.
23   Vol. 12, no. 112.
24   H. of A. Deb., 5 February 1914, col. 112.
25   *Ibid.* col. 275.
26   *Ibid.* col. 117.
27   *Ibid.* cols. 120, 123.
28   *Ibid.* col. 123.
29   *Ibid.* 11 February 1914, col. 273.
30   *Ibid.* 12 February 1914, col. 319.
31   *Ibid.* 13 February 1914, cols. 339–40.
32   Report of the Witwatersrand Disturbances Commission, Cd. 7112, December 1913.
33   H. of A. Deb., 18 February 1914, col. 491. Smartt told his followers that they could have a free vote and they voted on different sides.

34 Vol. 12, no. 82.
35 Vol. 12, no. 16.
36 Vol. 12, no. 53.
37 Vol. 12, no. 170.
38 Vol. 12, nos. 113, 160.
39 H. of A. Deb., 11 February 1914, cols. 263–4.
40 Vol. 12, no. 134.

CHAPTER 18

1 Vol. 12, nos. 49, 54, 73, 176.
2 Vol. 12, no. 162 (27 September 1914).
3 I am indebted to Mr R. Davenport for a study which he prepared for me of this literature. The most useful general history is *Die Rebellie, 1914–15*, by G. D. Scholtz, who is also the author of a biography of General Beyers. Mr Davenport also refers to an unpublished thesis of the University of Cape Town which I have not seen: *The Rebellion, 1914–15*, by L. J. E. Retief (1959).
4 Cd. 7873, *Proposed Naval and Military Expedition against German South-west Africa*, nos. 1, 4, 6. Also vol. 12, nos. 33, 135.
5 U.G. 10 (1915), p. 7.
6 Union of South Africa. Both Houses of Parliament, Fifth and Extraordinary Session, 1914: 9 September, cols. 57–9; 12 September, col. 12.
7 *Ibid.* 9 September, cols. 77–8.
8 *Ibid.* 10 September, cols. 84–5, 89. The statement about Nakob, although based on official information, was open to challenge (vol. 13, no. 173).
9 Vol. 12, no. 103.
10 Fifth and Extraordinary Session; 1914: 12 September, col. 20.
11 U.G. 48 (1914): *Judicial Commission of Inquiry into the Circumstances leading up to and attending upon the deaths of Senator General the Honourable J. H. de la Rey and Dr G. Grace: Report of the Commissioner the Hon. Mr Justice Gregorowski.* On the imputations against the government, see U.G. 46 (1916), pp. 10, 18. These imputations or insinuations have been repeated by later writers.
12 H. of A. Deb., Sixth Session, First Parliament, 3 March 1915, col. 78.
13 Vol. 12, no. 44, 9 November 1914.
14 U.G. 10 (1915), p. 56.
15 U.G. 46 (1915), p. 11.
16 Vol. 12, no. 143 *a*.
17 Vol. 12, no. 145.
18 Vol. 12, no. 147.
19 *My Lewe en My Strewe*, by S. G. Maritz (1939).
20 U.G. 10 (1915), p. 7.
21 U.G. 10 (1915), pp. 7–24.
22 U.G. 46 (1916), p. 98. Beyers denied responsibility for the actions of de Wet (U.G. 10 (1915), p. 35). In a document of 20 October, supposedly

signed jointly by him and de Wet, the doctrine of *gewapende protest* is still affirmed: however, there is reason to doubt whether de Wet had any share in composing this document or did in fact sign it.

23 Vol. 12, no. 92.

24 Vol. 12, no. 95.

25 The most important letters and telegrams exchanged between Pretoria and Bloemfontein are printed in an appendix to U.G. 10 (1915). At the request of Dr Jean van der Poel, Colin Steyn recorded his memories in March 1958 and subsequently corrected a typed script of the recording in March 1959.

26 Box *G*, no. 1 *b*.

27 U.G. 10 (1915), p. 75.

28 H. of A. Deb. Sixth Session, First Parl., col. 82.

29 Vol. 12, no. 157 (to Merriman, 19 December 1914).

30 Box *N*, no. 53.

31 Vol. 12, no. 75.

32 U.G. 10 (1915), p. 46.

33 H. of A. Deb., 9 March 1915, col. 200.

34 *Jopie Fourie: 'n Lewenskets*, by C. A. Neethling and J. M. de Wet (1915; new edition by the latter in 1940). *Jopie Fourie en ander Nuwe Gedigte*, by Jan F. E. Celliers (1920).

35 It is significant that during the Second World War there began a new outpouring of literature about the rebellion and its heroes, some of it popular and hagiographical, some of it careful historical work.

36 Vol. 12, nos. 2, 3, 5, 6, 9.

37 H. of A. Deb., 3 March 1915, col. 77.

38 Vol. 13, no. 11.

39 *Union of South Africa and the Great War, 1914–1918. Official History* (Pretoria, 1924), p. 29.

40 Cf. vol. 13, nos. 9, 10 (with enclosures), 11, 58.

41 Vol. 13, no. 11.

42 U.G. 46 (1916), p. 76.

43 Vol. 13, no. 11.

44 Vol. 13, no. 15.

45 Vol. 13, no. 11.

46 Vol. 13, nos. 10, 15.

47 Vol. 13, no. 144 (J.C.S. to his wife, 24 April 1915).

48 Vol. 13, no. 173.

49 Vol. 13, nos. 16 and 18.

50 *Official History*, p. 30.

51 *Trekking On*, by Deneys Reitz (London, 1933), p. 100.

52 *Potschefstroom Herald*, 11 June 1915.

53 *Rand Daily Mail*, 13 July 1915.

54 Vol. 13, no. 91.

55 Vol. 13, nos. 16, 18; vol. 16, nos. 140, 143; vol. 19, nos. 102, 103.

56 Vol. 13, nos. 79, 80, 149, 173.

57 Vol. 13, nos. 79, 89.

58 Vol. 13, no. 152.

59 Vol. 13, nos. 49, 85, 154.

60 Vol. 13, nos. 49, 85, 154.

61 Vol. 13, nos. 154, 155, 156.

62 Vol. 13, nos. 97, 99, 161.

63 *Round Table*, VI (January 1916), 359–61.

64 Vol. 13, no. 164.

65 Vol. 13, nos. 1, 113.

66 Vol. 13, no. 174.

67 Vol. 13, nos. 56, 173.

68 Vol. 13, nos. 146, 187.

69 Vol. 13, no. 50.

70 Vol. 13, nos. 89, 154.

71 Vol. 14, nos. 39, 42, 140, 206.

72 Vol. 14, no. 10.

73 *My Reminiscences of East Africa*, by General von Lettow Vorbeck (2nd ed., London, 1920), p. 63.

74 *Ibid.* p. 24. Cf. *General Smuts' Campaign in East Africa*, by Brigadier-General J. H. Crowe (London, 1918), p. 268. Crowe gives the following figures of the wastage of animals from mid-September to mid-November 1916: horses, 10,000; mules, 10,000; oxen, 11,000; donkeys, 2500.

75 'The War Economy of German East Africa', by W. O. Henderson, *Econ. Hist. Rev.* XII, nos. 1 and 2, pp. 105–10.

76 *Official History of the War. Military Operations. East Africa*, by R. C. Hordern (London, 1941), vol. I: for a broad appraisement of Smuts's leadership, see p. 324 (vol. II of this history was never completed). Cf. *Union of South Africa and the Great War*, p. 69.

77 *Grey Steel*, by H. C. Armstrong (London, 1937), pp. 261 ff.

78 Throughout his active life Colonel Meinertzhagen kept a full and vivid diary, and the present writer is deeply indebted to him for permission to take copies of those entries which refer to Smuts. Colonel Meinertzhagen has begun to publish extracts from his diary. (*Kenya Diary, 1902–6* and *Middle East Diary, 1917–56*).

79 Hordern, *Official History: East Africa*, p. 234.

80 Vol. 14, nos. 14, 145, 147. Also Crowe, *General Smuts' Campaign in East Africa*, preface by Smuts, pp. vii–viii.

81 Vol. 14, no. 207.

82 *Marching on Tanga*, by Francis Brett Young (London, 1917), pp. 4–5.

83 *Ibid.* p. 58.

84 18 October 1916.

85 Vol. 55, no. 197 (29 October 1937). Cf. no. 208.

86 Vol. 14, no. 19.

87 Diary, 28 July 1916. It is curious that Col. Meinertzhagen so often called Smuts 'the little man' whereas in Brett Young's mental picture of him (*Marching on Tanga*, p. 58) the dominant features are heaviness, hardness and masterfulness.

88 Vol. 14, nos. 173, 177, 181.

89 Crowe, *General Smuts' Campaign in East Africa*, p. xiv. Cf. Hordern, *Official History: East Africa*, pp. 377, 393, 521. In place of the South African troops who were sent home there was a big expansion of the King's African Rifles (East Africa) plus substantial forces from West Africa and a contingent from the West Indies.

90 Vol. 14, nos. 177, 191, 203.

91 Vol. 14, nos. 145, 163, 173, 199, 203, 207.

92 Vol. 14, nos. 160, 189; vol. 23, no. 203.

93 Vol. 14, no. 157.

94 Vol. 14, nos. 117, 160, 207.

95 Von Lettow Vorbeck, *My Reminiscences of East Africa*, p. 170.

96 Vol. 14, nos. 199, 203.

CHAPTER 19

1 Vol. 14, nos. 23, 24; vol. 15, nos. 61, 63, 150.

2 Vol. 17, no. 104; vol. 18, no. 163.

3 Vol. 15, no. 26.

4 Vol. 18, no. 202.

5 Vol. 16, no. 190.

6 Vol. 18, no. 202.

7 *War Memoirs of David Lloyd George* (London, 1934), vol. IV, ch. LV.

8 *My Political Life*, by L. S. Amery (London, 1953), vol. II, p. 107.

9 Vol. 15, nos. 106–7.

10 Cd. 8566, p. 45. Amery (*My Political Life*, II, 109) says that Smuts was 'the main author' of this historic resolution.

11 Cd. 8566, pp. 46–8.

12 Vol. 18, no. 385. The writer was T. Watt, a representative of Natal in the Union cabinet who took great pains to keep Smuts up to date with South African political news.

13 Lloyd George, *War Memoirs*, IV, 1766.

14 Vol. 16, nos. 151, 153; vol. 18, nos. 220, 335.

15 Vol. 18, no. 398.

16 Vol. 16, no. 155 *a*.

17 *My Political Life*, II, 136.

18 Vol. 15, no. 67: cf. no. 76.

19 Lloyd George, *War Memoirs*, IV, 1830 ff.

20 Vol. 15, no. 2; vol. 19, no. 12.

21 Vol. 18, nos. 235, 281, 336.

22 Vol. 15, no. 27.

23 Vol. 15, nos. 77, 109 *a*; vol. 18, no. 346.

24 Vol. 15, no. 29.

25 In a letter of 2 October 1917 Mrs Gillett told him that she was puzzled to see how he could 'develop and concentrate a public opinion any other way than as M.P.' and on 6 October 1917 she said that to her mind the question was how he could become 'the strongest for winning the best out of the struggle with the rallying round you of all the best in England'.

26 Vol. 18, no. 235; cf. vol. 22, no. 154.

27 Vol. 18, nos. 207, 249.

28 Vol. 18, nos. 281, 318.

29 Lloyd George, *War Memoirs*, IV, ch. LXVIII. See also H. A. Jones, *The War in the Air* (Official History of the War: Oxford, 1937), vol. VI, ch. I.

30 Cf. Jones, *The War in the Air*, p. 32.

31 *Ibid.* pp. 41–4 and appendices, no. VI.

32 The report is printed in Jones, *The War in the Air*, appendices, no. II.

33 The official history of *The War in the Air*, while agreeing elsewhere with Lloyd George in giving Smuts the main credit for establishing the R.A.F., emphasises the outstanding services of Henderson to the Air Organisation Committee (vol. VI, p. 13).

34 *Ibid.* V, 64–5, appendices, no. VII (paper submitted by Smuts to the War Cabinet, 6 September 1917).

35 *Ibid.* VI, 39–41.

36 Vol. 16, no. 227.

37 On the evolution of the war economy up to 1918 see *British War Economy*, by W. K. Hancock and M. M. Gowing (London, 1949), ch. I.

38 'Britain's Changing Strategic Position', by Noble Frankland, in *International Affairs*, vol. XXXIII, no. 44.

39 *The World Crisis*, by Winston S. Churchill (revised single-volume edition, London, 1931), p. 308.

40 Vol. 100, nos. 7 and 12; Lloyd George, *War Memoirs*, III, 1530–6.

41 *War Memoirs*, IV, ch. LXIII.

42 *Ibid.* p. 2184.

43 No. 5 of Box *H* is a typical speech of the earlier mood.

44 Box *H*, nos. 14, 15. Report by R. Wherry Anderson.

45 Mrs Gillett to the writer, 1 June 1959.

46 Lloyd George, *War Memoirs*, III, 1374.

47 Vol. 100, no. 77.

48 Vol. 18, no. 332.

49 In later years Amery wrote some good letters to Smuts about his holistic philosophy and sketched the philosophical approach which he proposed to adopt in a book of his own.

50 See *My Political Life*, II, 102–4.

51 *Ibid.* p. 105.

52 See preface by Smuts to *Not Without Honour. The Life and Writings of Olive Schreiner*, by Vera Buchanan-Gould.

53 Vol. 16, nos. 200, 201, 204, 205, 224, 228. In all she wrote him forty-eight letters from March to December 1917.

54 Vol. 20, no. 234 (11 June 1918).

55 Vol. 99, no. 193.

56 Vol. 18, no. 272.
57 Vol. 18, nos. 228, 263.
58 See *Peace Without Victory. Woodrow Wilson and the British Liberals,* by Laurence W. Martin (New Haven, 1958), *passim.*
59 Vol. 17, no. 74; vol. 18, no. 307.
60 Lloyd George, *War Memoirs,* v, 2462.
61 Vol. 18, no. 332.

CHAPTER 20

1 Vol. 20, no. 219.
2 Vol. 20, no. 217 (to Mrs Gillett, 2 January 1918).
3 Vol. 20, nos. 170, 172, 174.
4 Vol. 98, no. 27.
5 Vol. 20, no. 233.
6 An ironical footnote to the controversy which arose from the government's decisions on the allocation of manpower will be found in ch. VIII of *Men and Power,* by Lord Beaverbrook (London, 1958).
7 Lane compiled a lively chronicle of this mission.
8 Vol. 19, no. 12.
9 Lloyd George, *War Memoirs,* v, 2499 ff.
10 Vol. 20, no. 225.
11 Vol. 20, no. 184.
12 Vol. 20, no. 233.
13 Vol. 20, no. 231 (to Mrs Gillett). The quotation is from 'The Burial of Moses', by Mrs Cecil Frances Alexander.
14 Vol. 98, no. 35.
15 Vol. 100, no. 101.
16 *Loc. cit.*
17 Lord Lansdowne's letter was dated 30 July 1918 and appeared in the *Daily Chronicle* of 1 August 1918.
18 Cf. *The Globe,* 1 August 1918: article headed 'Ministers and Defeatists'.
19 Vol. 20, no. 17.
20 Box *H,* no. 22. No record has been found of this statement having been published.
21 Vol. 100, no. 113.
22 Smuts's letter of 8 June was published in *Tempestuous Journey* by Frank Owen (Hutchinson, 1954), pp. 476–7.
23 Nearly 22,800 Anzacs (17,386 Australians and 4408 New Zealanders) landed on Gallipoli in the week beginning 25 April 1915. See *The Story of Anzac* (Australian Official History, 1921), by C. E. W. Bean, p. 28.
24 Lloyd George, *War Memoirs,* VI, 3090.
25 Extracts from the diary of Mrs Gillett.
26 Lloyd George, *War Memoirs,* VI, 3122–3.
27 *Ibid.* p. 3240.
28 Vol. 20, nos. 201, 202.
29 Lloyd George, *War Memoirs,* VI, 3284.

30 *Ibid.* p. 3300.

31 Vol. 20, no. 253.

32 Vol. 20, no. 254.

33 Winston Churchill, *op. cit.*, p. 847.

34 Vol. 22, no. 141.

35 The original title of the paper was 'League of Nations. A Programme for the Peace Conference.' Later, when Smuts published it as a pamphlet, he changed the title to 'The League of Nations. A Practical Suggestion.' Under this title it is printed by David Hunter Miller in *The Drafting of the Covenant* (London, 1928), vol. II, document 5.

36 *Ibid.* p. 25.

37 *Ibid.* pp. 37–8.

38 *The Truth about the Peace Treaties*, by David Lloyd George (London, 1938), I, 620. Cf. Miller, *The Drafting of the Covenant*, I, 34. Miller made some very critical comments upon the memorandum when he first saw it but in retrospect he recognised its 'profound influence' upon President Wilson.

39 Vol. 20, no. 257.

40 Box *H*, no. 27.

41 See *British Opinion and the Last Peace*, by R. B. McCallum (London, 1944): a thoughtful study.

CHAPTER 21

1 *Peacemaking 1919*, by Harold Nicolson (2nd ed., London, 1945), p. 4.

2 Vol. 22, no. 9, and Nicolson, *Peacemaking 1919* (1st ed.), p. 107. Satow expressed himself on this on the eve of the Conference, Headlam-Morley after it had been in session four months, Nicolson in distant retrospect (1933).

3 Vol. 22, no. 195.

4 Vol. 22, no. 193; vol. 98, no. 64. Cf. 'Woodrow Wilson, Jan Smuts and the Versailles Settlement', by George Curry, in *American Historical Review*, July 1961, pp. 963–86.

5 Vol. 22, no. 75; vol. 98, no. 59. See also Curry, *op. cit.* p. 978, Miller, *The Drafting of the Covenant*, I, ch. IX and *Historical Studies: Australia and New Zealand*, vol. IX, no. 33, p. 105 (a review article by Sir John Latham showing that it was he, then Captain Latham, who drafted the form of words establishing the 'C' mandates).

6 Vol. 98, no. 59 and vol. 22, no. 206.

7 Vol. 22, no. 203. The hotly argued question of food deliveries (which was mixed up with questions concerning the German merchant fleet and means of payment) was not resolved until the Brussels Agreement of 16 March. The blockade was not completely lifted until 12 July, following German ratification of the Treaty.

8 Vol. 98, nos. 59 and 64. A draft had been presented to the Conference on 14 February. The final draft of the covenant was agreed on 11 April.

9 Vol. 22, no. 239.

10 Vol. 22, nos. 210, 212; vol. 98, no. 61.

11 Vol. 22, no. 213.

12 Vol. 101, no. 73.

13 See Lloyd George, *The Truth about the Peace Treaties*, I, 417, 427.

14 I am indebted to Sir Llewellyn Woodward for these reflections upon *apaisement* as used by Briand.

15 Vol. 22, nos. 214, 215.

16 *Field Marshal Sir Henry Wilson. His Life and Diaries*, by Major-General Sir C. E. Calwell (London, 1927), II, 175.

17 Vol. 101, no. 72.

18 *The Truth about the Peace Treaties*, I, p. 403. Sir Henry Wilson (*op. cit.* p. 175) mentions the presence of Edwin Montagu, but not that of Smuts, at the Fontainebleau party.

19 Vol. 98, no. 71.

20 Vol. 101, no. 78.

21 Vol. 22, no. 217.

22 Neither did Count Karolyi (*Memoirs*, London, 1956, p. 158), whose only regret was that the allies had not sent Smuts to Hungary when a decent and sensible social-democratic government was still in power.

23 Vol. 22, nos. 150, 222. In the very workmanlike report on his journey which Smuts submitted on 9 April he laid particular stress on the need for economic collaboration and was able to report that this need was appreciated in Buda Pesth, Vienna and Prague.

24 Vol. 101, no. 83.

25 Vol. 98, nos. 68, 73.

26 Vol. 22, nos. 224, 228.

27 Vol. 22, nos. 223, 229; vol. 98, nos. 73, 77.

28 Vol. 101, no. 85.

29 Lloyd George, *The Truth about the Peace Treaties*, I, 676.

30 Vol. 98, no. 79.

31 Vol. 22, no. 234.

32 Vol. 101, nos. 86, 90.

33 Vol. 101, no. 88. A pencilled note on the retained copy of the letter to Lloyd George records that he and President Wilson were not informed that each was receiving an (almost) identical letter. No copy was kept of the letter to Wilson; presumably it substituted the United States for the British Empire in line 9 of this quotation.

34 Vol. 22, no. 299 (16 May 1919).

35 Vol. 22, no. 239; no. 83. For a later defence of Wilson see his article, 'Woodrow Wilson's Place in History', in *New York Times*, 3 March 1921.

36 Vol. 22, no. 237.

37 Vol. 98, no. 83.

38 Vol. 22, no. 153.

39 Vol. 22, no. 154.

40 Vol. 101, no. 92.

41 Vol. 101, no. 96.

42 Vol. 22, no. 246.

43 Vol. 98, no. 86 (30 May 1919).

44 Vol. 101, no. 97.

45 Vol. 22, no. 300. The correspondence was reopened in 1921 when Smuts sent the President a copy of his article, 'Woodrow Wilson's Place in History'.

46 *The Truth about the Peace Treaties*, 1, 688–720. Lloyd George got the dates wrong. He says that the first two meetings were held on Sunday, 1 June, and the third on Monday; whereas the first meeting was held on Friday, 30 May, and the next two on Sunday, 1 June. There was no meeting on Monday.

47 Vol. 101, no. 98. Enclosed with the letter was a slightly shorter and more impersonal version of the same statement, entitled 'Revision of the Peace Treaty (Memo. by General Smuts)'.

48 Vol. 22, no. 239.

49 The correspondence, inwards as well as outwards, will be published extensively towards the end of four volumes of selections from the Smuts Archive, 1887–1919, which are now in the press.

50 Vol. 22, no. 251.

51 Vol. 22, no. 159.

52 Vol. 22, no. 158.

53 Vol. 22, no. 253.

54 *Loc. cit.*

55 Vol. 98, no. 90.

56 Vol. 22, no. 255.

57 Vol. 22, no. 161.

58 Vol. 22, no 259; vol. 98, no. 92.

59 Vol. 22, nos. 260, 263.

60 Vol. 22, no. 255.

61 Vol. 22, nos. 259, 260.

62 *Peacemaking 1919* (2nd ed.), p. 35.

63 *The Development of Modern France*, by D. W. Brogan (London, 1940), p. 547.

64 Vol. 22, no. 263.

65 Vol. 101, no. 99.

66 The document is most easily accessible in *Reparation at the Paris Peace Conference*, by Phillip Mason Burnett (Columbia Univ. Press), 1, 773–5. It was first published in full by Bernard Baruch in *The Making of the Reparation and Economic Sections of the Treaty* (New York, 1921).

67 The evidence is to be found in the relevant pages of Burnett, *op. cit.*, and in *Les Délibérations du Conseil des Quatre. Notes de l'officier Interprète*, by Paul Mantoux (Paris, 1955). I am indebted to my pupil, Mr Bruce Kent, for guiding me through the evidence; but an attempt to summarise it here would result in a note some pages in length. I can only say, first, that the evidence seems to me very strong; secondly, that it requires meticulous examination, the proper place for which is a specialist monograph.

68 Vol. 24, no. 276 (3 January 1921) and *Cape Times*, 7 February 1923.

69 Vol. 98, no. 298 (22 October 1920).

70 Vol. 98, no. 299 (7 February 1923).

71 Vol. 101, no. 100 (4 June 1919). Lloyd George's concern was to get a fair share of reparation for 'his people' and in March he had envisaged two alternative methods of doing so: *either* by fixing a ratio of apportionment among the allies *or* by including war pensions and reparation allowances among the reparation categories. At the end of March he had come down in favour of the second alternative, because of the immense political difficulties inherent in the first: public opinion in all the allied countries was almost as opposed to fixing inter-allied ratios as it was to fixing any rational total for German reparation.

72 Miller, *The Drafting of the Covenant*, I, 109.

73 Vol. 101, no. 100.

74 Vol. 22, no. 236.

75 Vol. 101, no. 100.

76 Vol. 98, no. 93.

77 Vol. 55, no. 174 (to Mrs Gillett, 10 April 1937).

78 Vol. 22, no. 251.

79 Students of British political pathology might find the *Globe*—its ownership, editorship, staffing and circulation—a rewarding study.

80 Box *G*, no. 6.

81 Vol. 98, no. 295 (17 July 1919).

CHAPTER 22

1 Vol. 15, no. 65 (5 March 1917).

2 See *Round Table*, August 1917, pp. 821 ff. The development of Nationalist propaganda for independence, culminating in the deputation to the Peace Conference, can most conveniently be followed in articles of the *Round Table* from 1917 to 1920.

3 Vol. 19, no. 28.

4 Vol. 15, no. 109 and enclosures; vol. 18, no. 345.

5 Vol. 19, no. 25.

6 Vol. 19, no. 28.

7 Vol. 19, nos. 50, 53; vol. 20, no. 126.

8 Vol. 19, no. 53.

9 Vol. 20, no. 208.

10 'Wie reken jy is die grootste figuur hier op die Konferensie?' 'Ons eie Oubaas Louis—daar is geeneen van hierdie mense wat by hom kan kers vashou nie.' I am particularly in debt to Major-General F. H. Theron, C.B., C.B.E., for his recollections of Botha at Paris, conveyed to me both in conversation and in writing. Theron at that time was a staff captain attached to the South African delegation at Paris. During the war, with intervals of military service in South-West Africa and France, he had served first Smuts, then Botha and then Smuts again in the capacity of a private secretary.

11 Vol. 98, no. 98 (to Alice Clark, 30 July 1919).

12 Vol. 22, no. 271.

13 Vol. 98, no. 99 (to Alice Clark).

14 Vol. 22, no. 272.

15 *Ibid.*

16 Vol. 21, no. 35.

17 See the *Round Table*, June 1917.

18 These typical phrases have been taken from articles in the *Westminster Gazette, New Statesman, Manchester Guardian, The Star* (Johannesburg), *Daily Express, The Times, Cape Times.*

19 Vol. 22, no. 273.

20 Vol. 21, no. 52.

21 Vol. 23, no. 28.

22 Vol. 22, nos. 274, 277.

23 Vol. 98, no. 104 (to Alice Clark, 26 November 1919).

24 Vol. 21, no. 16.

INDEX

Index

Index

Index

Smuts, J. C. (5) (*cont.*)
his religious Odyssey, 216
interest in Society of Friends, 489
and see holism
Smuts, J. C. (6): letters
to his wife, as Sybella Krige (10 December 1887), 17–18
to his wife after marriage: on eve of Bloemfontein Conference (1889), 94–5; from Standerton (2 June 1901), 130–1; during peace negotiations (12 May 1902), 155–6; (26 May 1902), 160; on end of war (1 June 1902), 164; from Stellenbosch (26 June 1902; first letter in Afrikaans), 164–5, 572 (10.2); from Pretoria, putting home to rights, 165; from Las Palmas (January 1906), 211; about move to Doornkloof (10 July 1909), 279; from Pretoria (10 October 1914), 385; from East Africa (1916), 420, 421, 423; on separations (11 January 1917), 424; from England (1917), 425, 426, 437, 438; on death of Wolstenholme, 457; on war prospects, 468, 473–4; on South African representation at Peace Conference, 497; on objections to peace treaty (20 May 1919), 524–5; (10 June 1919), 533; about Botha (December 1918), 553; about new responsibilities (3 September 1919), 557
to Botha: telegram raising procedural questions consequent upon his decision not to sign Treaty of Versailles, 534
to Hermanus Bredell (28 June 1904), 189
to Alice Clark: (New Year 1918), 470; on Peace Treaty (May 1919), 523; (June 1919), 532, 544; (30 July 1919), on voyage home, 555, 592 (22.13); 593 (22.23)
to Margaret Clark: (1 February 1906), 213; on preparations for Union Convention (24 August 1908), 259; *see also* letters to Arthur and Margaret Gillett
to de la Rey: on strategy (25 December 1900), 125; on command for invasion of Cape Colony (16 and 17 February 1901), 126, 127; on republican forces in Cape Colony (January 1902), 142
to Abraham Fischer covering his open letter to W. T. Stead (January 1902), 149
to Gandhi, 345–6
to Arthur and Margaret Gillett, 287–8; on outbreak of 1914–18 war, 377; in

1915, 399, 406; on conscientious objection (1917), 461; 10 November 1918, 495; on plight of Central Europe (April 1919), 517; (May 1919), 524; (June 1919), 532; on question of signing Peace Treaty (24, 28 June 1919), 534, 538; on problems of peace terms (14 May 1919), 544; (3 June 1919), 546; about Botha (September 1917), 551; on homecoming (August 1919), 555–6; on taking over from Botha (6 September 1919), 557, 560; (10 April 1936), 592 (21.77)
to T. L. Graham on United South Africa, 199
to J. Hayman (30 October 1898), 566 (5.1)
to Emily Hobhouse: (21 February 1904), 179, 182–5; prophesying Liberal ascendancy (March 1904), 187; on 'representative' government (April 1904), 188; on death of Kruger (July 1904), 189–90; on peace terms (1918), 481–2
to J. A. Hobson on Native franchise (13 July 1908), 255
to Hofmeyr: on *Brown* v. *Leyds*, 71; on war threat (10 May 1899), 91–2; telegrams (10, 12 June 1899) appealing for Afrikander solidarity, 97; letter (13 June 1899), same, 97–8; telegrams on franchise negotiations (19 June 1899 and 15, 16, 18 July 1899), 99
to J. M. Keynes: on Peace Treaty (10 June 1919), 532–3; on 'opportunities to help the world', 547
to Kruger, urging his return (1903), 188
to Leyds on failure of conciliation (30 April 1899), 87–8, 90
to Lloyd George: on anxiety about Italian front, 456; on Irish problems, 475; offering to lead Americans into battle (8 June 1918), 482–3; on peace terms (26 March 1919), 510–12; on reparations (11 April 1919), 518; objections to draft treaty (5 May 1919), 520; (14 May 1919), 522; (22 May 1919), 525; declining to serve on Commission on Austrian reparations (26, 27 May 1919), 526, 527; on British Empire Delegation and peace terms (2 June 1919), 530–1, calling for magnanimous peace (26 March 1919), 539; on 'friendly and sympathetic' spirit (3 June 1919), 544

Index

Smuts, J. C. (9) (*cont.*)

and terms for rebel generals, 388–90

anonymous abuse, 393, 406

and campaign in German South-West Africa, 394–400

and election of 1915, 403

command of forces in East Africa, 408–23, 437

attends Imperial War Conference and Cabinet (1917), 423, 424–9, (1918) 489

P.C., C.H. and other honours, 425

views on constitutional relations of Empire, 429–32, 522

and Irish problems, 432, 475

declines Palestine command, 433–5, 485

Middle East mission, 435, 472

joins British War Cabinet, 435–6

decision not to enter British politics, 436, 444, 504, 531, 535

and League of Nations, 438, 454, 457, 460, 463, 467, 500–2, 506–8, 536

as war organiser, 438

creation of Royal Air Force, 438–42

air-raid defence measures, 439, 441–2

War Priorities Committee, 442

his relations with Lloyd George, 444, 531

plan for Chiefs of Staff Committee, 445–6

visits France (April 1917), 448

member of War Policy Committee, 452–3

attitude to Flanders offensive, 453–4

addresses Welsh miners, 455–6

attends Rapallo Conference, 457

talks with Count Mensdorff, 466

and public opinion, 475

concern over American inactivity, 475, 482–6

prophetic vision, 476

speech in Glasgow (17 May 1918), 477–80

enumerates heads of Preliminaries of Peace, 494

Chairman of Demobilisation Committee, 495–6

prepares British brief for Peace Conference, 495–6

and South African security, 498, 543

and German East Africa, 498, 543

and mandatory system, 500, 507

resigns from War Cabinet, 504

represents South Africa at Peace Conference, 504, 505–48, 554; first phase, optimism, 507–8; second phase, foreboding, 510; third phase, prophetic, 521; fourth phase, revolt, 527–47; signs, 534, 544

opinion on Germany's reparations, 515, 540–1

mission to Hungary, 515–17

warns against intervention in Russia, 516

isolation, 523, 532, 534

declines to serve on Commission for Austrian reparations, 526

and expulsion of Germany from East and South-West Africa, 542–4

returns to South Africa (August 1919), 554

welcomed home, 555

succeeds Botha as Prime Minister, Minister of Defence and Minister of Native Affairs, 557–8

see also balance of power; Cape franchise; Coloured question; Commonwealth; education policy; franchise, imperial connection; language question; law; League of Nations; magnanimity; military capacity; pacifist connections; peace; peace brief; peace by negotiation; politics; reconciliation; republicanism; strategy; unconditional surrender; victory; war aims

Smuts, J. C. (10): friendships (*see also* under letters)

at Cambridge, 42–4

at Pretoria, 168

importance of, 282

with L. S. Amery, 458–60

with Louis Botha, 168, 191, 199, 270, 277, 282, 396, 397, 434, 532, 535, 549–57 *passim*, 561; political association, 230–45, 259, 273, 276, 349, 362, 535

with Ethel Brown, 41–2

with Alice Clark, 213, 217, 443, 509, 560

with Margaret Clark, 197, 204, 211–14, 216, 217; as Mrs Arthur Gillett, 287–8, 372, 377

with Lady Courtney, 212, 372, 426

with Arthur and Margaret Gillett (*see also* Clark, Margaret), 287, 377, 426, 461–2, 486–9, 503, 509

with Emily Hobhouse, 179–88, 197, 278, 282–7, 343, 363, 377, 406, 425–6, 442, 460, 481

with Hobson, J. A., 43, 213, 255–6, 462

with J. M. Keynes, 426, 532

with President Kruger, 68–9, 188, 277, 373

with F. S. Malan, 43, 99, 249, 270

with J. I. Marais, 20, 35–8, 40, 62, 63

with John X. Merriman, 99, 191, 270, 276–7, 278; difference over Rand labour trouble, 367–8, 372